CASES AND MATERIALS

LAW OF TRUSTS

CASES AND MATERIALS

LAW OF TRUSTS

Second Edition

Gary Watt MA (Oxon), Solicitor
Senior Lecturer in Law, Nottingham Law School

BLACKSTONE PRESS LIMITED

First published in Great Britain 1996 by Blackstone Press Limited,
Aldine Place, London W12 8AA.   Telephone 0181–740 2277

© Nottingham Law School, Nottingham Trent University, 1996

First edition 1996
Second edition 1999

ISBN: 1 85431 824 1

British Library Cataloguing in Publication Data
A CIP catalogue record for this book is available from the British Library.

Typeset by Style Photosetting Limited, Mayfield, East Sussex
Printed by Livesey Limited, Shrewsbury, Shropshire

All rights reserved. No part of this book may be reproduced or transmitted in any form
or by any means, electronic or mechanical, including photocopying, recording, or an
information storage or retrieval system without prior permission from the publisher.

FOREWORD

The books in the LLB series have been written for students studying law at undergraduate level. There are two books for each subject. The first is the *Learning Text* which is designed to teach you about the particular subject in question. However, it does much more than that. By means of Activities, Self Assessment, and End of Chapter Questions, the *Learning Text* allows you to test your knowledge and understanding as you work. Each chapter starts with 'Objectives' which indicate what you should be able to do by the end of it. You should use these Objectives in your learning — check them frequently and ask yourself whether you have attained them.

The second book is a volume of *Cases and Materials*. This is cross-referenced from the *Learning Text*. It contains the primary sources of law such as statutes and cases plus subsidiary sources such as extracts from journals, law reform papers and textbooks. This is your portable library. Although each volume can stand alone, they are designed to be complementary.

The two-volume combination aims to support your learning by challenging you to demonstrate your mastery of the principles and application of the law. They are appropriate whatever your mode of study — full-time or part-time.

CONTENTS

PREFACE

This volume is to be your portable library of source materials in the law of equity and trusts. Included are summaries of the salient facts and decisions in the major cases and extracts from those cases. The extracts are designed to be of sufficient length to encourage independent reflection and learning. Also included are extracts from statutory legislation, law reform proposals, academic articles and established scholarly texts. The aim has been to assemble an extensive and stimulating resource which will assist students of any trusts law degree course to approach the subject with the confidence which comes from the use of primary source materials.

Students should be aware that there are two essential ingredients to every successful learning experience: content and context. What makes a good lecture or tutorial? What makes a good textbook? Accurate legal content is only half the answer. Equally important is the context in which the factual information is presented. The aim of this portable library, and its companion volume, *Blackstone's LLB: Law of Trusts*, is to bridge the gulf between the traditional textbook and the tutorial experience. Through reflective exercises and self-assessment questions and answers, it is hoped that the student will more readily grasp and more deeply retain the essence of the law of equity and trusts.

Gary Watt
December 1998

ACKNOWLEDGEMENTS

Nottingham Law School and the publishers would like to thank the following for permission to reproduce copyright material:

Blackwell Publishers: extracts from G. H. Jones 'Delegation by Trustees: a reappraisal' (1995) MLR 381.

Butterworths & Co. (Publishers) Ltd for extracts from the *All England Law Reports* and *Company Law Cases*.

Her Majesty's Stationery Office: extracts from the Goodman Report (1976) and various statutory materials and Parliamentary papers.

Incorporated Council of Law Reporting for England and Wales: extracts from the Chancery Appeals and Division Reports, Appeal Cases and the Weekly Law Reports.

Jordan & Sons Ltd: extracts from *Family Court Reporter* and *Family Law Reports*.

Sweet & Maxwell Ltd: extracts from *The English Reports, Planning & Compensation Reports* and *Law Quarterly Review*.

Tolley Publishing Company: extracts from *Trusts Law International* (1988).

Times Newspapers Ltd: extract from *Goodchild v Goodchild* (1997).

The Daily Telegraph: 'RSPCA drops animal rights after threats to charity status' (1998).

TABLE OF CASES

Cases reported in full are shown in heavy type. The page at which the report is printed is shown in heavy type.

TABLE OF STATUTES

Statutes, and sections thereof, which are set out in full or in part are shown in heavy type. The page at which the statute or section is printed is shown in heavy type.

CHAPTER ONE

INTRODUCTION TO EQUITY AND TRUSTS

1.1 Historical Development of Equity and Trusts

1.1.1 THE HISTORICAL DEVELOPMENT OF EQUITY

Sir Peter Millett, 'Equity — the road ahead' (1995) 9(2) TLI 35

. . . It can no longer be doubted that equity has moved out of the family home and the settled estate and into the marketplace. Even in relation to express trusts, which are peculiarly the province of equity, the court has found itself most often called on to deal with the problems of pension schemes, which are features of the commercial world. Equitable doctrines have penetrated that world. The intervention of equity in commercial transactions, long resisted by common lawyers, can no longer be withstood. This development should be welcomed, for there is a clear need to subject those who take part in commercial transactions to the high standards which equity demands. In an age of professionalism, there are professionals, particularly in the field of public relations, who make their living by exploiting the willingness of fiduciaries to betray their trust.

It is of the first importance, of course, not to impose fiduciary obligations upon parties to a purely commercial relationship who deal with each other at arms's length. But fiduciary relationships arise whenever one party undertakes to act in the interest of another, and such relationships often arise in a commercial context. . . .

The common law provides redress for breach of contract, and in order to do justice it may imply terms into existing contracts and even imply the existence of a contract; but equity's approach is different. It is called into play, not by a breach of contract express or implied, but by unconscionable conduct, and the duties which it enforces are those which it considers to be inherent in the relationship of the parties. But the relationships which call for the intervention of equity today frequently arise in a commercial context.

The opinion that the Judicature Acts had the effect of fusing law and equity to the extent that they have become a single body of law rather than two separate systems of law administered together is, I believe, now widely discredited both in England and Australia. But Sir Anthony Mason, Chief Justice of Australia, writing recently in the *Law Quarterly Review*, was surely right to warn against the danger that concentration on the effect of the Judicature Acts to the exclusion of other considerations is likely to result in overemphasis on the state of equitable doctrine as it existed in 1873. The Judicature Acts did not fuse law and equity, but they did not freeze them in their then state of development either. The true nature of their relationship was well expressed by Somers J in *Elders Pastoral Ltd* v *Bank of New Zealand* [1989] 2 NZLR 180 in a passage expressly endorsed by Sir Anthony Mason in the article to which I have referred:

> Neither law nor equity is now stifled by its origin and the fact that both are administered by one Court has inevitably meant that each has borrowed from the other in furthering the harmonious development of the law as a whole. . . .

There is one important branch of the law in which there would be a major gain if, to borrow Lord Simon of Glaisdale's well-known metaphor, the waters of the two confluent streams of law and equity would become thoroughly intermixed. I refer to the law of restitution. This is a fast-developing area of the law. It is not exclusively, or even obviously, within the province of equity. The victim of a fraud, for example, who wishes to trace and recover his money would expect to have a simple cause of action. As he was a full legal and beneficial owner before the fraud took place he would expect to sue at common law; he should not need to invoke the jurisdiction of a court of equity unless he sought a proprietary remedy. But he is provided with a multiplicity of causes of action. He can bring a common law action for money had and received; but if there are any difficulties in tracing what has happened to his money this will not avail him. He will have to come to equity, which offers no fewer than three potential causes of action: the personal claims usually called knowing receipt and knowing assistance and the proprietary claim usually though misleadingly described as the tracing claim.

Harmonisation and rationalisation are long overdue. We need a unified restitutionary system, neither common law nor equitable, which provides personal and proprietary remedies where appropriate. Equity has a vital part to play in the creation of a unified system for several reasons:

(i)   only equity provides proprietary remedies;

(ii)   its action for knowing assistance is more effective and extensive than the common law action for conspiracy;
and

(iii)   its tracing rules are more effective in allowing the plaintiff to follow his money through the complex financial transactions involved in money laundering.

But the road ahead is strewn with boulders. The unsatisfactory and confused state into which the law in this area has fallen is little short of a disgrace. There has been a failure to analyse the priciples on which liability is based, compounded by a weakness of factual analysis and a consequential application of authorities on one ground of liability to another to which they are inapplicable. Even our terminology is confused. Equity ostensibly bases its intervention on the existence of a constructive trust, but there is no unanimity on the meaning or relevance of this concept. There are powerful arguments for dispensing with the concept itself as having no relevance in this context; but at least we should try to agree what we mean by the expression. At present the language of constructive trust has become such a fertile source of confusion that it would be better if it were abandoned. . . .

I have a firm belief in the inherent flexibility of equity and in its capacity to adjust to new situations by reference to the principles of just conduct and good conscience which have informed the exercise of the equitable jurisdiction for centuries. As the equity judges here and overseas travel the road ahead, I am confident that together they will ensure that equity will fulfil its traditional role and will continue to be, in the words of Kitto J, 'the saving supplement and complement of the common law'.

1.1.2   THE HISTORICAL DEVELOPMENT OF THE TRUST

A. W. B. Simpson, *An Introduction to the History of the Land Law,*
Oxford University Press, pp. 187–88

. . . from 1645 onwards the only free tenure of any importance which remained was socage, and the preservation of the feudal revenues had ceased to be of any importance. The economic purpose of the Statute of Uses had disappeared. This was bound to have an effect upon its treatment by the courts. Very probably it accelerated the rise of the passive trust, which is the most notable of all the evasions of that ill-used Statute. By about 1700 it had become possible to create trusts which apparently differed only in name from uses, but which were not executed by the Statute. Such trusts were enforced in Chancery just as uses had been before 1535, so that the separation of legal and equitable ownership was again possible. Such trusts were created by a conveyance to 'A, unto and to the use of A, in trust for B', and by adopting this simple variant on the formula 'to A to the use of B' a conveyancer was allowed to create equitable estates just as he had been before the Statute.

The history of the steps by which trusts came to be recognised forms an intriguing but somewhat obscure chapter of legal history. As we have seen, not all uses were executed by the Statute. Uses declared on a term of years were not, and were well known in the sixteenth century, but some Chancellors were not prepared to enforce them; they regarded them as fraudulent evasions of the Statute of Uses, since such uses were created to deprive the Crown of revenue. With the disappearance of the feudal revenues it was natural that such uses came to be enforceable in Chancery, and they came to be known as 'trusts'. No doubt the existence of such trusts, created by a conveyance of a term of years 'to A to the use of B', or 'in trust for B' had something to do with the revival of trusts of freehold, but no very direct connection has ever been shown. It must, however, have occurred to lawyers that there was no very sensible distinction between allowing A to convey a term of 1000 years to B, to be held on a passive trust for C, and allowing A to do the same with a fee simple, whatever the technical distinctions between the two situations may be; the one instutution may well have pointed the way to the other. Certainly it is only such trusts created on terms of years which can be said to have anything like a continuous history from the time of the Statute of Uses: after 1660 they became a common feature of conveyancing . . .

1.1.3   EQUITY AND TRUSTS IN MODERN COMMERCIAL CONTEXTS

J. H. Baker, *An Introduction to English Legal History*, **3rd edn, 1990, Butterworths, pp. 119–21**

EARLY CHANCERY PROCEDURE

The early history of the Chancery is difficult to uncover for want of full documentation; the procedure was informal, and for the first century little has survived beyond the files of bills. It seems probable that the English jurisdiction was established in its distinct form during the reign of Richard II, since already by 1393 there were complaints of its abuse. It was perhaps firmly settled while John of Waltham was master of the rolls (1381–86), a period when Canon lawyers dominated the staff. The procedure clearly owed something to the inquisitorial procedure of the canonists, and may have been modelled on the canonical *denunciatio evangelica*, though the Chancery never became a court of Canon law and its practitioners were always members of the inns of court.

No original writ was necessary, and all actions were commenced by informal complaint, either by bill or by word of mouth. Process in most actions was begun by writ of subpoena, a simple summons to appear in Chancery or else forfeit a penalty, in practice the penalty was not enforced, but a disobedient defendant was subject to proceedings for contempt. Pleading was in English and relatively informal. Evidence was taken by interrogation or written deposition. There was no jury; the court assembled a dossier of information until it saw fit to take action. The Chancery was always open; it was not tied to the terms and return-days, though for convenience it observed them as far as possible. It could sit anywhere, even in the chancellor's private house; and causes could be tried out of court by commission of *dedimus potestatem* to country gentlemen. These advantages enabled medieval chancellors to provide swift and inexpensive justice, especially to the poor and oppressed. Sheriffs and juries could be bypassed where undue pressure was feared; corruption could not prevent a fair hearing. The chancellor's eyes were not covered by the blinkers of due process, and he could go into all the facts to the extent that the available evidence permitted. He could order bonds and other writings to be cancelled where they would only serve unjust ends; and, conversely, he could order the discovery of documents which were needed to enforce legal rights. He could order parol contracts to be performed, and fiduciary obligations discharged. He could ensure that unfair advantage was not taken of the weak and foolish. And defendants could not easily evade this new and powerful justice; for contumacy they could be imprisoned, or their property sequestered.

By exercising this jurisdiction in conscience, the chancellor was nevertheless not causing any of the 'inconvenience' which the law eschewed. In Chancery each case turned on its own facts, and the chancellor did not interfere with the general rules observed in courts of law. The decrees operated *in personam*; they were binding on the parties in the cause, but were not judgments of record binding anyone else.

BUSINESS OF THE CHANCERY 1400–1600

The difficulty of measuring business in the early Chancery accounts for inconsistencies between writers on the subject. Its seems nevertheless to be generally agreed that business was steadily increasing towards the end of the fifteenth century, and that it increased dramatically during the sixteenth, until the court became so flooded with suits that it could scarcely cope. This expansion turned the Chancery into the third major court in Westminster Hall, but it was accompanied by a change in the general run of its business. At the beginning of the fifteenth century, the typical petition complained of weakness or poverty, or the abuse of position by an opponent. Throughout that century tort and commercial cases feature as prominently as property disputes, and there was also a substantial appellate jurisdiction over inferior urban courts. Frequently the relief sought related to an action at law: a plaintiff at law might need discovery, a defendant at law might need the action stopped. When the tide of business swelled, however, the greater part of it was in the sphere of real property. Some of this was attributable to the growing practice of creating uses or trusts of land; but there were many other ways of getting property cases into Chancery, and the work was by no means dominated by uses. Although the Chancery could not in theory interfere with the legal title, it could decree possession and could ensure that a successful party was put in possession; the procedure as settled in Tudor times was to issue a writ of execution, and if that was disobeyed a writ of attachment, an injunction to deliver possession, and a writ of assistance to the sheriff. It could also make decrees to 'quiet' possession, either to protect the party in possession or to restore possession wrested by force until the merits were tried. As the property jurisdiction waxed, the other aspects waned. The tort jurisdiction was largely given up. In the sphere of contract, the most important business came to be ordering the completion of conveyances, and relief from mortgages and penal bonds. A reason for this change we have already seen. The popularity of the Chancery in the later fifteenth century had been perceived as a challenge to the courts of law to change their ways, and was one of the spurs which goaded the King's Bench into extensive reforms in the law of contract and tort through actions on the case, and into adopting a bill procedure. Moreover, much of the business with which it had started had gone elsewhere. The kind of unusual violence or abuse of power which the regular system was powerless to redress needed attention at the highest level; complaints of this nature were increasingly diverted to the full council and became the foundation of the Star Chamber jurisdiction. The council also found new ways of dealing with poor men's causes. By Elizabethan times the Chancery was too busy to concern itself with petty matters, and in 1579 sent away a plaintiff who claimed a right of entry to hang washing in his neighbour's yard. The Chancery had ceased in reality to be an extraordinary court. Although it retained procedures which were extraordinary in the sense that they were outside the common law, and was beginning to develop principles of its own, it had become a court of constant resort.

1.2   Equity and the Common Law

Sir Anthony Mason, 'The Place of Equity and Equitable Remedies in the Contemporary Common Law World' (1994) 110 LQR 238

Viscount Simonds, it is said, cavilled at the description of equity as an appendix to the common law. His objection was that the description did not do justice to the important corpus of substantive law which the Court of Chancery brought into existence. Had his Lordship survived to witness the developments in equitable doctrine that have taken place since he voiced the objection almost 50 years ago, he would have regarded the description as an utterly misleading statement of equity's place in the scheme of things today, accurate though it may be as an historical explanation of equity before the Judicature Acts. By 'Equity' I mean the distinctive concepts, doctrines, principles and remedies which were developed and applied by the old Court of Chancery, as they have been refined and elaborated since.

Equitable doctrines and relief have extended beyond old boundaries into new territory where no Lord Chancellor's foot has previously left its imprint. In the field of public law, equitable relief in the form of the declaration and the injunction have played a critical part in shaping modern administrative law which, from its earliest days, has mirrored the way in which equity has regulated the exercise of fiduciary powers. Equitable doctrine and relief have penetrated the citadels of business and commerce, long thought, at least by common lawyers, to be immune from the intrusion of such alien principles. Equity, by its intervention in commerce, has subjected the participants in commercial transactions, where appropriate, to the higher standards of conduct for which it is noted and has exposed the participants to the advantages and detriments of relief *in rem*.

A similar effect has been achieved by resurrecting and expanding the traditional concept of unconscionable conduct as a basis for relief and recognising that the constructive trust is both an institution and a remedy. The concept of unconscionable conduct, along with the recognition of unjust enrichment which is partly a derivative of unconscionable conduct, has been the source of the recent rejuvenation of equity. Moreover, in the reshaping of branches of the law which straddle both common law and equity which has resulted in greater unity of principle, we have discovered that equity and the common law share much in common. The notion of unconscionability underlies some common law doctrines as well as equity. Estoppel and restitution are examples which come to mind. Here the interaction between common law and equity has resulted in dynamic development of legal principle, resulting in greater symmetry. Equity and common law now import from each other, just as they can and do import from other systems of law and learning. . . .

Equity has yielded to the common law some ground that conceivably it might have claimed for itself. The boundless expansion of the tort of negligence, based on the existence of a duty of care to one's neighbour has, in all probability, stultified the development of equitable compensation for breach of fiduciary and other equitable obligations. Equitable compensation, of which I shall have more to say, is now coming to the fore but its long sleep since 1875 or, more accurately, 1914 (when *Nocton v Lord Ashburton* [1914] AC 932 was decided) may be attributed to the rise of negligence and the extended notion of the duty of care.

What are the reasons for the onward march of equity after the physicians had pronounced it incapable of childbirth? They are, I think, many and varied, some of them not being of general application. Two can readily be identified. First, there were the Judicature Act 1873 (UK) and its counterparts in other jurisdictions ('the Judicature Acts'). By providing for the administration of the two systems of law by the one system of courts and by prescribing the paramountcy of equity, the Judicature Acts freed equity from its position on the coat-tails of the common law and positioned it for advances beyond its old frontiers. Secondly, the ecclesiastical natural law foundations of equity, its concern with standards of conscience, fairness, equality and its protection of relationships of trust and confidence, as well as its discretionary approach to the grant of relief, stand in marked contrast to the more rigid formulae applied by the common law and equip it better to meet the needs of the type of liberal democratic society which has evolved in the twentieth century.

It is remarkable that the common law has remained for so long impervious to the beguiling charms of equity. More than 100 years elapsed after the introduction of the original Judicature Act before lawyers became receptive to the notion, still regarded as heretical by some Australian commentators, that equity and common law are capable of constituting together a single body of law rather than two separate bodies of law administered together. The belated recognition of this truth by the House of Lords in *United Scientific Holdings Ltd v Burnley Borough Council* [1978] AC 904, particularly Lord Diplock's extreme statement that the waters of the two streams 'have surely mingled now,' has excited exasperation. There is perhaps more merit in Lord Simon of Glaisdale's prediction:

It may take time before the waters of two confluent streams are thoroughly intermixed; but a period has to come when the period has to come when the process is complete.

. . .

Conclusion

Equity and common law are converging and will continue to converge so that the differences in origin of particular principles should become of decreasing importance. It is inevitable that equitable relief in some of its forms will become available for the protection and enforcement of common law rights to a greater extent than was formerly the case. Likewise, compensatory damages may be granted in appropriate cases for breach of equitable duties and obligations but obviously this will not occur on the footing that there is an automatic entitlement to a common law remedy for a breach of equitable duty or obligation or vice versa. It will happen in the course of the law's evolution as it becomes established that, in given circumstances, it is appropriate to grant a particular remedy.

The underlying values of equity centred on good conscience will almost certainly continue to be a driving force in the shaping of the law unless the underlying values and expectations of society undergo a fairly radical alteration. If the present trend continues, the element of uncertainty which iss associated with the greater emphasis on good conscience will be dissipated by an increase in the number of decisions on a wide range of fact situations. Because the concepts employed are not susceptible of sharp definition, there is the risk of some erosion in the apparent distinctions which have been maintained hitherto between equitable concepts such as 'unconscionable' and 'inequitable' and common law concepts such as 'unfair' and 'unreasonable.' But it is important that we continue to adhere to the traditional concept of unconscionability as denoting conduct which involves one person unconscientiously taking advantage of another's special vulnerability or disadvantage in a way that is both unreasonable and oppressive. The recent decade might be regarded as a period of legal transition in which we have been moving from an era of strict law to one which gives greater emphasis to equity and natural law. As Roscoe Pound said in *The Spirit of the Common Law*, the endeavour to make morals and law coincide will be an important future goal.

1.3 End of Chapter Assessment Question

Common law and equity are working in different ways towards the same ends, and it is therefore as wrong to assert the independence of one from the other as it is to assert that there is no difference between them.

Critically discuss the above statement.

1.4 End of Chapter Assessment Outline Answer

Many students are wary of answering essay questions because, compared to a problem-type question, there can appear to be relatively little guidance in the question itself as to the sort of issues the assessor is wishing the students to address. In fact, an essay gives far more scope for students to express their own ideas than does a problem-type question. The trick is very early on to decide upon whatever legitimate interpretation of the question gives you the greatest opportunity to discuss those aspects of the subject with which you are most familiar. Having said that, whatever answer you give must adhere to the specific question asked. As you write your answer make express reference to the essay title every now and then, and be sure to finish the essay with a conclusion that really does tie together your thoughts.

While not intended to be a full answer to the present question, the following is a guide to the sort of issues a good answer might address, and a guide also to the way in which those issues might be presented.

Introduction

What immediately strikes one about the quote is that there are two distinct parts to it. The first asserts that, despite a shared aim, the common law and equity work in different ways, which is to say that they are methodologically distinct. With particular reference to equity, we will question whether or not it is strictly accurate to distinguish its aims from the means it uses to achieve those aims. It may be that this inquiry will lead us to conclude that the common law and equity are not trying to achieve the same things at all. The second part of the question asserts that the shared aims of common law and equity necessitate mutual dependence. Let us consider these two key assertions in turn.

Part One: Common law and equity are working in different ways towards the same ends

The first thing to ask is whether common law and equity are, indeed, 'working in different ways'. In other words, are they methodologically distinct. The first thing to reply is that the Judicature Acts 1873–5 did not entirely do away with the historical distinction between law and equity. Professor J.H. Baker (*An Introduction to English Legal History*) observed that:

> If, for reasons of history, equity had become the law peculiar to the Court of Chancery, nevertheless in broad theory equity was an approach to justice which give more weight than did the law to particular circumstances and hard cases.

What Professor Baker is saying here is that equity is a distinctive type of legal methodology, a particular form of legal reasoning and practice. This is true. It is typified by an attention to justice in individual 'hard' cases or *in personam* justice, based on the desire to ensure that legal powers and rights available to society at large are exercised in good conscience in individual cases. This does not mean that equity is a form of morality, but it does mean that whereas the common law seeks to establish a form of law common to all citizens, by way of rights that are enforceable against all-comers, equity seeks to restrain the unconscionable exercise of those rights.

A classic illustration is equity's concern for substance over form. Thus, whereas the common law requires that all transfers of legal title to land must be made by a formal deed (Law of Property Act 1925, s. 52), equity does not always require formal documentation before it will acknowledge that an equitable interest has been created in land. Thus where a legal freeholder invites a stranger to enter and build upon his land, and the stranger does so at his own expense in the reasonable expectation encouraged by the freeholder that he will thereby acquire a right in the land itself. Equity (by virtue of the doctrine or proprietory *estop*pel) stops the freeholder from asserting his 100 per cent legal ownership against the stranger. In short, the legal owner will not be allowed to evict the stranger as he might a common trespasser. This example illustrates equity's concern to ensure the conscionable use of legal rights, and to achieve *in personam* justice even though the political interest in ensuring certainty through legal formalities might thereby be sacrificed to some extent.

This example also illustrates another distinct feature of equitable methodology, namely recourse to maxims ('equity looks to substance not form') to dispose of hard cases. The common law does not appear to use maxims in quite the same way.

The second question is whether the common law and equity are working towards the same ends. As the discussion so-far suggests, the short-term, immediate aims of equity are quite different to the short-term immediate aims of the common law. We have seen that equity acts in competition with, or as a check upon, the operation of the common law. However, leaving aside this first-level distinction, it is clear that the common law and equity share the same ultimate aim. Namely, to establish a legal system that balances the need for certainty in the law, and hence a just scheme for regulating relations between members of society at large, with the need for justice in individual cases.

Part Two: It is wrong to assert the independence of the common law from equity and vice-versa

According to the way in which we have just outlined the methodology and function of equity, it is clear that equity has no existence or utility apart from the law. As the equitable maxim puts it: *equity follows the law*. It is therefore by its very nature dependent upon the law. Although, it must be admitted that not every jurist would agree with this dependent conception of equity. In fact, Sir Anthony Mason has recently commented extra-judicially that: 'by providing for the administration of the two systems of law by the one system of courts and by prescribing the paramountcy of equity, the Judicature Acts freed equity from its position on the coat-tails of the common law and positioned it for advances beyond its old frontiers' ('The Place of Equity and Equitable Remedies in the Contemporary Common Law World' (1994) 110 LQR 238, 239).

Conclusion

Whilst the common law and equity do work in diffferent ways, and have quite different immediate aims, they certainly agree upon their ultimate aim of setting in place a system of law that achieves the correct balance between certainty and justice. To this end it is obvious that the common law and equity are dependent upon one another, but this is really only because the English system has tended largely to equate the common law with certainty, and to equate equity with justice in individual cases (*in personam* justice). To the extent that this equation is a proper one, the quotation is accurate. But if it is accurate, it is also something of a truism, for it ends up saying, in effect, that in order to achieve a legal system that comprises both law and equity, it necessarily follows that equity and law must be dependent upon one another.

CHAPTER TWO

UNDERSTANDING TRUSTS

2.1 Trusts: To Define or Describe?

RECOGNITION OF TRUSTS ACT 1987

1. Applicable law and recognition of trusts

(1) The provisions of the Convention set out in the Schedule to this Act shall have the force of law in the United Kingdom.

Section 1   SCHEDULE
CONVENTION ON THE LAW APPLICABLE TO TRUSTS AND ON
THEIR RECOGNITION

CHAPTER 1—SCOPE

Article 1

This Convention specifies the law applicable to trusts and governs their recognition.

Article 2

For the purposes of this Convention, the term 'trust' refers to the legal relationship created—inter vivos or on death—by a person, the settlor, when assets have been placed under the control of a trustee for the benefit of a beneficiary or for a specified purpose.

A trust has the following characteristics—

(a) the assets constitute a separate fund and are not a part of the trustee's own estate;

(b) title to the trust assets stands in the name of the trustee or in the name of another person on behalf of the trustee;

(c) the trustee has the power and the duty, in respect of which he is accountable, to manage, employ or dispose of the assets in accordance with the terms of the trust and the special duties imposed upon him by law.

The reservation by the settlor of certain rights and powers, and the fact that the trustee may himself have rights as a beneficiary, are not necessarily inconsistent with the existence of a trust. . . .

TRUSTEE ACT 1925

68. . . .

(17) 'Trust' does not include the duties incident to an estate conveyed by way of mortgage, but with this exception the expressions 'trust' and 'trustee' extend to implied and constructive trusts, and to cases where the trustee has a beneficial interest in the trust property, and to the duties incident to the office of a personal representative, and 'trustee' where the context admits, includes a personal representative, and 'new trustee' includes an additional trustee; . . .

2.1.1   TRUSTS COMPARED WITH CONTRACTS

BESWICK v BESWICK [1968] AC 58, HL

FACTS: By an agreement in writing made in March, 1962, P. B., then aged over 70 and in poor health, agreed with his nephew, the defendant, that he would transfer to the nephew the goodwill and trade utensils of his coal round business. The nephew agreed to pay to P. B.'s wife after his death an annuity charged on the business at the rate of £5 per week for life. P. B.'s wife was not a party to the agreement. The nephew took over the business and in November, 1963, P. B. died. The nephew paid one sum of £5 to the widow, then aged 74 and in poor health, but refused to pay any further sum. The widow, having taken out letters of administration to her late husband's estate, brought an action against his nephew in her capacity as administratrix and also in her personal capacity asking (inter alia) for specific performance of the agreement.

HELD: That the widow, as administratrix of a party to the contract was entitled to an order for specific performance of the promise made by the nephew and was not limited to recovering merely nominal damages on the basis of the loss to the estate.

Further, that the widow was not entitled to enforce the obligation in her personal capacity.

LORD REID: . . . It so happens that the respondent is administratrix of the estate of her deceased husband and she sues both in that capacity and in her personal capacity. So it is necessary to consider her rights in each capacity.

For clarity I think it best to begin by considering a simple case where, in consideration of a sale by A to B, B agrees to pay the price of £1,000 to a third party X. Then the first question appears to me to be whether the parties intended that X should receive the money simply as A's nominee so that he would hold the money for behoof of A and be accountable to him for it, or whether the parties intended that X should receive the money for his own behoof and be entitled to keep it. That appears to me to be a question of construction of the agreement read in light of all the circumstances which were known to the parties. . . .

Reverting to my simple example the next question appears to me to be: Where the intention was that X should keep the £1,000 as his own, what is the nature of B's obligation and who is entitled to enforce it? It was not argued that the law of England regards B's obligation as a nullity, and I have not observed in any of the authorities any suggestion that it would be a nullity. There may have been a time when the existence of a right depended on whether there was any means of enforcing it, but today the law would be sadly deficient if one found that, although there is a right, the law provides no means for enforcing it. So this obligation of B must be enforceable either by X or by A. . . .

Lord Denning's view, expressed in this case not for the first time, is that X could enforce this obligation. But the view more commonly held in recent times has been that such a contract confers no right on X and that X could not sue for the £1,000. Leading counsel for the respondent based his case on other grounds, and as I agree that the respondent succeeds on other grounds, this would not be an appropriate case in which to solve this question. It is true that a strong Law Revision Committee recommended so long ago as 1937 (Cmd. 5449):

> That where a contract by its express terms purports to confer a benefit directly on a third party it shall be enforceable by the third party in his own name . . . (p. 31)

And, if one had to contemplate a further long period of Parliamentary procrastination, this House might find it necessary to deal with this matter. But if legislation is probable at any early date I would not deal with it in a case where that is not essential. So for the purposes of this case I shall proceed on the footing that the commonly accepted view is right.

What then is A's position? I assume that A has not made himself a trustee for X, because it was not argued in this appeal that any trust had been created. So, if X has no right, A can at any time grant a discharge to B or make some new contract with B. If there were a trust the position would be different. X would have an equitable right and

A would be entitled and, indeed, bound to recover the money and account for it to X. And A would have no right to grant a discharge to B. If there is no trust and A wishes to enforce the obligation, how does he set about it? He cannot sue B for the £1,000 because under the contract the money is not payable to him, and, if the contract were performed according to its terms, he would never have any right to get the money. So he must seek to make B pay X.

The argument for the appellant is that A's only remedy is to sue B for damages for B's breach of contract in failing to pay the £1,000 to X. Then the appellant says that A can only recover nominal damages of 40s. because the fact that X has not received the money will generally cause no loss to A: he admits that there may be cases where A would suffer damage if X did not receive the money but says that the present is not such a case.

Applying what I have said to the circumstances of the present case, the respondent in her personal capacity has no right to sue, but she has a right as administratrix of her husband's estate to require the appellant to perform his obligation under the agreement. He has refused to do so and he maintains that the respondent's only right is to sue him for damages for breach of his contract. If that were so, I shall assume that he is right in maintaining that the administratrix could then only recover nominal damages because his breach of contract has caused no loss to the estate of her deceased husband.

If that were the only remedy available the result would be grossly unjust. It would mean that the appellant keeps the business which he bought and for which he has only paid a small part of the price which he agreed to pay. He would avoid paying the rest of the price, the annuity to the respondent, by paying a mere 40s. damages. . . .

The respondent's . . . argument is that she is entitled in her capacity of administratrix of her deceased husband's estate to enforce the provision of the agreement for the benefit of herself in her personal capacity, and that a proper way of enforcing that provision is to order specific performance. That would produce a just result, and, unless there is some technical objection, I am of opinion that specific performance ought to be ordered. For the reasons given by your Lordships I would reject the arguments submitted for the appellant that specific performance is not a possible remedy in this case. I am therefore of opinion that the Court of Appeal reached a correct decision and that this appeal should be dismissed.

HARMER v *ARMSTRONG* [1934] 1 Ch 65, CA

FACTS: The defendant, A, agreed to purchase the copyright to certain publications off V Co. The plaintiff, H, asserted *inter alia* that A had entered this agreement as trustee for H, which A denied. V Co., with notice of the plaintiffs' claim, purported to rescind the contract with A. H brought an action for a declaration that A held the benefit of the agreement as trustee for H. H also sought an order for specific performance of the agreement, which is a form of order which would oblige V Co. to complete the sale to A, for the benefit of H (see **19.1**).

HELD: A had acted in the capacity of trustee for H. Therefore specific performance of the contract was ordered, with the result that A would hold the benefit of the contract on trust for H. Under contract law H would be unable to claim the benefit of the contract because he had not been privy to it, but because H was the beneficiary of a trust of which A was the trustee, H would be able to claim the benefit of the contract made between A and V Co.

LAWRENCE LJ: . . . It is well settled and not disputed by the plaintiffs that at common law no one can sue on a contract under seal except the contracting parties. If the contract be one not under seal, besides the actual contracting parties those from whom and between whom consideration proceeds can also sue. The rule is stated plainly by Lord Haldane in *Dunlop Pneumatic Tyre Co.* v *Selfridge & Co.* [1915] AC 847, as follows: 'My Lords, in the law of England certain principles are fundamental. One is that only a person who is a party to a contract can sue on it. Our law knows nothing of a jus quaesitum tertio arising by way of contract. Such a right may be conferred by way of property, as, for example, under a trust, but it cannot be conferred on a stranger to a contract as a right to enforce the contract in personam.' Lord Wright in *Vandepitte* v *Preferred Accident Insurance Corporation of New York* [1933] AC 70, after quoting the above extract from Lord Haldane's speech, states: 'In that case, as in *Tweddle* v *Atkinson* (1861) 1 B & S 393, only questions of direct contractual rights in law were in issue, but Lord Haldane states the equitable principle which qualifies the legal rule, and which has received effect in many cases'—then he cites certain cases as examples—

> that a party to a contract can constitute himself a trustee for a third party of a right under the contract and thus confer such rights enforceable in equity on the third party. The trustee then can take steps to enforce performance to the beneficiary by the other contracting party as in the case of other equitable rights. The action should be in the name of the trustee; if, however, he refuses to sue, the beneficiary can sue, joining the trustee as a defendant.

The rule that where a party to a contract is trustee for a third party and the trustee refuses to sue the beneficiary can sue, joining the trustee as a party, in my judgment, in no way depends upon whether the contract which the trustee has entered into is under seal or not. . . .

Whenever a party under a contract, at the date when he enters into it is (or thereafter constitutes himself) a trustee for a third party that party has a right conferred upon him by way of property to sue on the contract whether the contract be under seal or not and can, according to well settled principles, enforce that right in equity, joining the trustee as a defendant to the action. The right of a beneficiary in such a case as the present, however, is to enforce the agreement according to its tenor, that is to say in favour of the defendant Armstrong, and not in favour of the plaintiff beneficiaries. It was suggested by Sir Herbert Cunliffe that the rule I have stated applies in the case of contracts under seal only where the trust is disclosed on the face of the contract. I know of no such limitation to the rule and, in my judgment, such a limitation cannot be justified in principle. I can conceive that there may be cases in which the Court would hesitate, at the instance of one or more out of a number of beneficiaries, to enforce the performance of a contract made by the trustee with a third party, by reason of the complications which might arise if there were a genuine dispute as to whether it was for the benefit of the trust as a whole to enforce the contract at all. In such a case the Court has the power to decline to enforce the contract until the question whether it is for the benefit of the trust that the contract should be enforced has been determined in an application in the matter of the trust for leave to use the name of the trustee. In the present case, however, there is no such complication. The learned judge, having heard the evidence, has come to the clear conclusion that there was a trust and that the trustee had committed a breach of trust in not enforcing the contract. In these circumstances, I think that the present case is plainly one in which the Court ought to act on the equitable rule and decree specific performance of the contract. . . .

2.1.2   TRUSTS COMPARED WITH POWERS

METTOY PENSION TRUSTEES v *EVANS* [1991] 2 All ER 513, ChD

FACTS: See **11.3.1.1.**

WARNER J: The question then arises, if the discretion is a fiduciary power which cannot be exercised either by the receivers or by the liquidator, who is to exercise it? I heard submissions on that point. The discretion cannot be exercised by the directors of the company, because on the appointment of the liquidator all the powers of the directors ceased. I was referred to a number of authorities on the circumstances in which the court may interfere with or give directions as to the exercise of discretions vested in trustees, namely *Gisborne* v *Gisborne* (1877) 2 App Cas 300, *Re Hodges, Dovey* v *Ward* (1878) 7 Ch D 754, *Tabor* v *Brooks* (1878) 10 Ch D 273, *Klug* v *Klug* [1918] 2 Ch 67, *Re Allen-Meyrick's Will Trusts, Mangnall* v *Allen-Meyrick* [1966] 1 All ER 740, [1966] 1 WLR 499, *McPhail* v *Doulton* [1970] 2 All ER 228, [1971] AC 424, *Re Manisty's Settlement* [1973] 2 All ER 1203 at 1209–1211, [1974] Ch 17 at 25–26 and *Re Locker's Settlement Trusts, Meachem* v *Sachs* [1978] 1 All ER 216, [1977] 1 WLR 1323. None of those cases deals directly with a situation in which a fiduciary power is left with no one to exercise it. They point however to the conclusion that in that situation the court must step in. Mr Inglis-Jones and Mr Walker urge me to say that in this case the court should step in by giving directions to the trustees as to the distribution of the surplus in the pension fund. They relied in particular on this passage in the speech of Lord Wilberforce in *McPhail* v *Doulton* [1970] 2 All ER 228 at 247, [1971] AC 424 at 456–457:

> As to powers, I agree with my noble and learned friend Lord Upjohn in *Re Gulbenkian's Settlement* [1968] 3 All ER 785, [1970] AC 508 that although the trustees may, and normally will, be under a fiduciary duty to consider whether or in what way they should exercise their power, the court will not normally compel its exercise: It will intervene if the trustees exceed their power, and possibly if they are proved to have exercised it capriciously. But in the case of a trust power, if the trustees do not exercise it, the court will; I respectfully adopt as to this the statement in Lord Upjohn's opinion (see [1968] 3 All ER 785 at 793, [1970] AC 508 at 525). I would venture to amplify this by saying that the court, if called upon to execute the trust power, will do so in the manner best calculated to give effect to the settlor's or testator's intentions. It may do so by appointing new trustees, or by authorising or directing representative persons of the classes of beneficiaries to prepare a scheme of distribution, or even, should the proper basis for distribution appear, by itself directing the trustees so to distribute. The books give many instances where this has been done and I see no reason in principle why they should not do so in the modern field of discretionary trusts . . .

. . . In that latter part [of the passage] Lord Wilberforce was indicating how the court might give effect to a discretionary trust when called upon to execute it. It seems to me however that the methods he indicated could be equally appropriate in a case where the court was called upon to intervene in the exercise of a [fiduciary power]. In saying that I do not overlook that in *Re Manisty's Settlement* [1973] 2 All ER 1203 at 1210, [1974] Ch 17 at 25 Templeman J expressed the view that the only right and the only remedy of an object of the power who was aggrieved by the trustees' conduct would be to apply to the court to remove the trustees and appoint others in their place. However, the earlier authorities to which I was referred, such as *Re Hodges* and *Klug* v *Klug* had not been cited to Templeman J. I conclude that, in a situation such as this, it is open to the court to adopt whichever of the methods indicated by Lord Wilberforce appears most appropriate in the circumstances.

RE HAY'S SETTLEMENT TRUSTS [1981] 3 All ER 786, ChD

FACTS: Trustees of a settlement made in 1958 held the trust fund subject to a power to allocate it for the benefit of 'such persons or purposes' as they should in their discretion appoint. If they made no such appointment the trust fund would pass to the settlor's nieces and nephews. Only the settlor, her husband and the trustees could not be appointed to benefit from the fund. Questions arose as to how the court should supervise the exercise of such a wide discretionary power and how such a power differed from a trustees duties under a trust.

HELD: Whereas a trustee is bound to carry out the obligations of a trust, and if the trustee fails to do so the court will intervene to ensure that the trust is fulfilled, a mere power is very different. A trustee does not have to exercise a mere power, and will not be compelled to do so by the court, but the trustee must periodically consider whether or not to exercise the power. If the power is actually exercised the trustee must ensure that he or she acts in accordance with the terms of the power, and must consider both the range of potential beneficiaries and whether each individual appointment is appropriate.

SIR ROBERT MEGARRY VC: . . . The essential point is whether a power for trustees to appoint to anyone in the world except a handful of specified persons is valid. Such a power will be perfectly valid if given to a person who is not in a fiduciary position: the difficulty arises when it is given to trustees, for they are under certain fiduciary duties in relation to the power, and to a limited degree they are subject to the control of the courts. . . .

I propose to approach the matter by stages. First, it is plain that if a power of appointment is given to a person who is not in a fiduciary position, there is nothing in the width of the power which invalidates it per se. The power may be a special power with a large class of persons as objects; the power may be what is called a 'hybrid' power, or an 'intermediate' power, authorising appointment to anyone save a specified number or class of persons; or the power may be a general power. Whichever it is, there is nothing in the number of persons to whom an appointment may be made which will invalidate it. The difficulty comes when the power is given to trustees as such, in that the number of objects may interact with the fiduciary duties of the trustees and their control by the court. The argument of counsel for the defendants carried him to the extent of asserting that no valid intermediate or general power could be vested in trustees.

That brings me to the second point, namely, the extent of the fiduciary obligations of trustees who have a mere power vested in them, and how far the court exercises control over them in relation to that power. In the case of a trust, of course, the trustee is bound to execute it, and if he does not, the court will see to its execution. A mere power is very different. Normally the trustee is not bound to exercise it, and the court will not compel him to do so. That, however, does not mean that he can simply fold his hands and ignore it, for normally he must from time to time consider whether or not to exercise the power, and the court may direct him to do this.

When he does exercise the power, he must, of course (as in the case of all trusts and powers) confine himself to what is authorised, and not go beyond it. But that is not the only restriction. Whereas a person who is not in a fiduciary position is free to exercise the power in any way that he wishes, unhampered by any fiduciary duties, a trustee to whom, as such, a power is given is bound by the duties of his office in exercising that power to do so in a responsible manner according to its purpose. It is not enough for him to refrain from acting capriciously; he must do more. He must 'make such a survey of the range of objects or possible beneficiaries' as will enable him to carry out his fiduciary duty. He must find out 'the permissible area of selection and then consider responsibly, in individual cases, whether a contemplated beneficiary was within the power and whether, in relation to the possible claimants, a particular grant was appropriate': per Lord Wilberforce in *Re Baden (No. 1)* [1970] 2 All ER 228 at 240, 247, [1971] AC 424 at 449, 457.

I pause there. The summary of the law that I have set out above is taken from a variety of sources, principally *Re Gestetner (deceased)* [1953] 1 All ER 1150, [1953] Ch 672, *Re Gulbenkian's Settlement* [1968] 3 All ER 785 at 787, [1970] AC 508 at 518, 524–525 and *Re Baden (No. 1)* [1970] 2 All ER 228 at 246, [1971] AC 424 at 456. The last proposition, relating to the survey and consideration, at first sight gives rise to some difficulty. It is now well settled that no mere power is invalidated by it being impossible to ascertain every object of the power; provided the language is clear enough to make it possible to say whether any given individual is an object of the power, it need not be possible to compile a complete list of every object: see *Re Gestetner (deceased)* [1953] 1 All ER 1150 at 1155, [1953] Ch 672 at 688; *Re Gulbenkian's Settlement* [1968] 3 All ER 785, [1970] AC 508; *Re Baden (No. 1)* [1970] 2 All ER 228, [1971] AC 424. As Harman J said in *Re Gestetner (deceased)* [1953] 1 All ER 1150 at 1056, [1953] Ch 672 at 688, the trustees need not 'worry their heads to survey the world from China to Peru, when there are perfectly good objects of the class in England'.

That brings me to the third point. How is the duty of making a responsible survey and selection to be carried out in the absence of any complete list of objects? This question was considered by the Court of Appeal in *Re Baden (No. 2)*. That case was concerned with what, after some divergences of judicial opinion, was held to be a discretionary trust and not a mere power; but plainly the requirements for a mere power cannot be more stringent than those for a discretionary trust. The duty, I think, may be expressed along the following lines: I venture a modest degree of amplification and exegesis of what was said in *Re Baden (No. 2)* [1972] 2 All ER 1304 at 1310, 1315, [1973] Ch 9 at 20, 27. The trustee must not simply proceed to exercise the power in favour of such of the objects as happen to be at hand or claim his attention. He must first consider what persons or classes of persons are objects of the power within the definition in the settlement or will. In doing this, there is no need to compile a complete list of the objects, or even to make an accurate assessment of the number of them: what is needed is an appreciation of the width of the field, and thus whether a selection is to be made merely from a dozen or, instead, from thousands or millions. . . . Only when the trustee has applied his mind to 'the size of the problem' should he then consider in individual cases whether, in relation to other possible claimants, a particular grant is appropriate. In doing this, no doubt he should not prefer the undeserving to the deserving; but he is not required to make an exact calculation whether, as between deserving claimants, A is more deserving than B: see *Re Gestetner (deceased)* [1953] 1 All ER 1150 at 1155, [1953] Ch 672 at 688, approved in *Re Baden (No. 1)* [1970] 2 All ER 228 at 243–244, [1971] AC 424 at 453.

If I am right in these views, the duties of a trustee which are specific to a mere power seem to be threefold. Apart from the obvious duty of obeying the trust instrument, and in particular of making no appointment that is not authorised by it, the trustee must, first, consider periodically whether or not he should exercise the power; second, consider the range of objects of the power; and third, consider the appropriateness of individual appointments. I do not assert that this list is exhaustive; but as the authorities stand it seems to me to include the essentials, so far as relevant to the case before me. . . .

2.2 Special Categories of Trusts and Trustees

2.2.1 PROTECTIVE TRUSTS

TRUSTEE ACT 1925

33. Protective trusts

(1) Where any income, including an annuity or other periodical income payment, is directed to be held on protective trusts for the benefit of any person (in this section called 'the principal beneficiary') for the period of his life or for any less period, then, during that period (in this section called the 'trust period') the said income shall, without prejudice to any prior interest, be held on the following trusts, namely:—

(i) Upon trust for the principal beneficiary during the trust period or until he, whether before or after the termination of any prior interest, does or attempts to do or suffers any act or thing, or until any event happens, other than an advance under any statutory or express power, whereby, if the said income were payable during the trust period to the principal beneficiary absolutely during that period, he would be deprived of the right to receive the same or any part thereof, in any of which cases, as well as on the termination of the trust period, whichever first happens, this trust of the said income shall fail or determine;

(ii) If the trust aforesaid fails or determines during the subsistence of the trust period, then, during the residue of that period, the said income shall be held upon trust for the application thereof for the maintenance or support, or otherwise for the benefit, of all or any one or more exclusively of the other or others of the following persons (that is to say)—

(a) the principal beneficiary and his or her wife or husband, if any, and his or her children or more remote issue, if any; or

(b) if there is no wife or husband or issue of the principal beneficiary in existence, the principal beneficiary and the persons who would, if he were actually dead, be entitled to the trust property or the income thereof or to the annuity fund, if any, or arrears of the annuity, as the case may be;

as the trustees in their absolute discretion, without being liable to account for the exercise of such discretion, think fit. . . .

GIBBON v *MITCHELL AND OTHERS* [1990] 3 All ER 338, ChD

FACTS: The plaintiff had a protected life interest under a protective trust. On the mistaken advice of his accountants and solicitors, he executed a deed purporting to surrender his life interest in favour of his children. In fact, the surrender amounted to a forfeiture of his life interest under the protective trust, accordingly the trust fund became subject to a discretionary trust in favour of certain other beneficiaries. The plaintiff should have sought a variation under the Variation of Trusts Act 1958. When the true effect of his surrender became apparent he applied to court to have the deed of surrender set aside.

HELD: The application was granted and the deed of surrender set aside.

MILLETT J: . . . It is manifest from the very terms of the deed itself, let alone from the advice tendered by the solicitors which preceded it, that Mr Gibbon's object was to vest the entire capital and income of Henry's fund immediately in David and Jane to the exclusion of all other persons including himself. The deed did not, however, have that effect, because Mr Gibbon's life interest was subject to protective trusts. Accordingly, its purported surrender occasioned a forfeiture and brought into operation the discretionary trusts set out in s. 33 of the Trustee Act 1925. Furthermore, the release of Mr Gibbon's power of appointment in favour of children and remoter issue, far from vesting the reversionary interest in capital in Jane and David exclusively, vested it in all Mr Gibbon's children including after-born children.

The consequence of these two errors is that so long as the deed stands there is an interest in possession in favour of a class of discretionary objects which will continue during the remainder of Mr Gibbon's life, and on his death the capital will vest in David and Jane together with any future children born to Mr Gibbon. Far from carrying out Mr Gibbon's intention to vest the capital immediately and indefeasibly in David and Jane, it has a totally different effect and one which will preclude effect being given to his intention. In those circumstances, Mr Gibbon applies to the court to have the deed set aside.

It is not, in my view, a case for rectification, but rather for setting aside for mistake. Mr Gibbon's intention could not be carried into effect by this deed or any other deed executed by him. What was required was an application to the court under the Variation of Trusts Act 1958. The equitable remedy of rectification, however, is only one aspect of a much wider equitable jurisdiction to relieve from the consequences of mistake.

My attention has been drawn to a number of authorities on the circumstances in which a voluntary disposition can be rectified, reformed or set aside where it has been entered into under a mistake, contrary to the intentions of the disponor, or in excess of his instructions. . . .

In my judgment, these cases show that, wherever there is a voluntary transaction by which one party intends to confer a bounty on another, the deed will be set aside if the court is satisfied that the disponor did not intend the transaction to have the effect which it did. It will be set aside for mistake whether the mistake is a mistake of law or of fact, so long as the mistake is as to the effect of the transaction itself and not merely as to its consequences or the advantages to be gained by entering into it. The proposition that equity will never relieve against mistakes of law is clearly too widely stated (see *Stone* v *Godfrey* (1854) 5 De GM & G 76 and *Whiteside* v *Whiteside* [1949] 2 All ER 913 at 916).

I am satisfied on the internal evidence of the deed itself, as well as on the evidence provided by the contemporaneous correspondence, that Mr Gibbon executed the deed in the clear belief that it vested the entire beneficial interest in both capital and income in Jane and David immediately and indefeasibly to the exclusion of himself and everyone else. It did not; instead it brought into being a trust of income in favour of the discretionary objects mentioned in s. 33 of the Trustee Act 1925 during the remainder of his life, and a trust for capital for all his children, including future born children. That was contrary to his instructions and intentions. It is true that if he were asked the narrow question whether he intended to release his protected life interest or the power of appointment in favour of his children, he must have answered 'Yes', for he was expressly advised by his solicitors that both those steps were necessary in order to achieve his object. But he did not intend to surrender his protected life interest or to release the power of appointment save for the purpose and with the effect that the beneficial interest in the capital of the fund should forthwith vest indefeasibly in Jane and David. He did not have the intention of releasing his protected life interest or the power of appointment in vacuo or for its own sake, but solely to achieve the purposes I have stated.

Mr Gibbon did not merely execute the deed under a mistake of law as to the legal consequences of his doing so. He executed it under a mistake as to its legal effect. The deed itself shows that to be the case. Since its effect was not that which he intended, he is entitled to have it set aside. Equity acts on the conscience. The parties whose interest it would be to oppose the setting aside of the deed are the unborn future children of Mr Gibbon and the objects of the discretionary trust to arise on forfeiture, that is to say his grandchildren, nephews and nieces. They are all volunteers. In my judgment they could not conscionably insist on their legal rights under the deed once they had become aware of the circumstances in which they had acquired them.

I therefore relieve Mr Gibbon from the consequences of his mistake and set aside the deed. I also accede to the consequential application under the Variation of Trusts Act 1958 to delete the protective nature of the protected life interest. I am quite satisfied this is a proper case where I can exercise my discretion under the Act to do so.

2.2.2 PENSION FUND TRUSTS

2.2.2.1 Are pension funds different to other trusts?

G. Moffat, 'Pension Funds: A Fragmentation of Trust Law?' (1993) 56(4) MLR 471

. . . Has a distinctive common law of pension trusts been established? On the one hand, we can point to dicta suggestive of a duty on trustees to negotiate with employers (*Re Courage Group's Pension Schemes* [1987] 1 All ER 528), to the acceptance that beneficiaries in pension schemes are not mere volunteers (*Mettoy Pension Trustees Ltd v Evans* [1991] 2 All ER 513), to the recognition of a more proactive role for the courts in controlling the exercise of fiduciary powers (*Mettoy*), to the infusion of the contractual term of 'good faith' into an employer's exercise of a non-fiduciary power in a trust deed (*Imperial*) and to the implication that trustees cannot hide behind a shield of refusing to give reasons for decisions. In short, it is suggested that in the realm of pension trusts the courts are coming to recognise a distinctive set of trustees' powers and duties with attendant implications for the entitlement of the members of pension schemes. On the other hand, it can be claimed that existing conceptual structures contain sufficient flexibility to accommodate all of these developments. Even where the fit is a little uncomfortable, and the decision by the court in *Mettoy* to exercise the discretion might be so viewed, this can be interpreted as representing merely the cutting-edge of developments in an organic common law of trusts. Moreover, none of the developments just outlined diverge fundamentally from a common core of trust law to be found in the notion of fiduciary ownership supported by appropriate remedies, and enforceable at the behest of beneficiaries.

Is this, therefore, a rather trivial and irrelevant debate about labelling? The danger in seeing it as such is that change may be inhibited unnecessarily. Whether we say there is now a distinctive law of pension trusts, or merely that there are new developments in the existing law of trusts, is material if opting for one formulation rather than the other were to affect our subsequent understanding and interpretation of the law of trusts, be it in relation to pensions or other types of trust.

In respect of pension trusts, it would be unfortunate if the path towards legal development, opened up by the subversive potential of recent conceptual innovations, were obstructed by an overly mechanical process of analogising from the paradigm of the family trust; in short, by legal tradition. Conversely, the outcome of pension litigation leaves us with intriguing questions about the family trust. These are most aptly examined by inverting Sir Robert Megarry's proposition from *Cowan v Scargill*: is there any good reason why the 'rules' regulating pension trusts should apply in all their force to other trusts?

The tenor of this article has been to reject any necessary symbiosis between the two. But assimilation should not be rejected automatically either. For instance, the conundrum posed by pension fund surpluses has brought back into the spotlight the important question of how far the exercise of discretion by trustees should be controlled by the courts. In the last quarter of a century, courts have facilitated the practice in family trusts of conferring, often for fiscal or investment reasons, ever wider dispositive and administrative discretions on trustees. To cling to a non-interventionist approach to the subsequent control of trustees is in effect to tilt the balance of power still further away from beneficiaries and the court in favour of trustee autonomy. Reasons can be advanced for sustaining this approach. On a practical level, perhaps trustees do need to be protected in a family context from insistent questioning about their decisions, and the courts from having to adjudicate on family disputes. Perhaps trustees would raise fees to compensate for any increased administration costs associated with greater accountability. Moreover, a non-interventionist approach can be interpreted as simultaneously respecting the primacy of the settlor's intention and reinforcing a strong notion of trusting.

This article is not the place to explore these issues in any depth, but the idea of a strong notion of trusting serves to alert us to an inherent paradox in trust law. An oriental proverb has it that 'a little thing is a little thing but trust in a little thing is a big thing.' The paradox is that reliance can be placed in 'trusting' because the dimension of mistrust is incorporated into the legal form through those rules which circumscribe trustee freedom. If, however, a 'strong notion of trusting' or 'trust in a big thing' is to thrive and be relied upon, might it not need to be protected by a greater degree of mistrust? To achieve this would require modification of existing rules, one might even say reversal of existing principles. Here, though, advocates of change may find that they are pushing at an open door. After all, it can certainly be claimed that recent developments in trust law generally have been inspired more by pragmatism than by strict conceptualism.

Whatever the fates may have in store for trust law as a legal basis for pension schemes, the recent spate of litigation leaves an intriguing legacy. Might trust lawyers come to remember the furore over pension fund surpluses principally as a catalyst that prompted the completion of the restructuring of the conceptual framework of trust law, a process set in train by the decision to validate fiduciary special powers in *Re Gestetner Settlement* almost half a century ago?

2.2.2.2 The destination of pension fund surpluses

BRITISH COAL CORP v BRITISH COAL STAFF SUPERANNUATION SCHEME TRUSTEES LTD [1995] 1 All ER 912, ChD

FACTS: In 1947 the plaintiff national coalmining corporation established a superannuation scheme for its employees. In 1983, when the workforce was rapidly reducing, the plaintiff agreed with the government that the cost of providing enhanced benefits for those taking voluntary redundancy would be paid by instalments with interest over a ten-year period. As at 5 April 1993 the total outstanding instalments of capital due to the scheme in respect of redundancies up to 5 April 1992 was about £100m and the question which arose was whether that sum could be set off against an actuarial surplus of £989m revealed in the triennial actuarial valuation for the period to 5 April 1992. The plaintiff therefore applied to the court to determine whether it had the power to amend the scheme to achieve the desired set-off.

HELD: Per curiam. Although under trust law no one should be asked to exercise a discretion as to the application of a fund amongst a class of which he is a member, the analogy does not apply in the context of pension funds in relation to a fund which has not been wound up. In such a case, the employer, if he has the power to amend the pension scheme, is entitled to exercise it in any way which would further the purposes of the scheme and ensure that the legitimate expectations of the members are met without imposing any undue burden on the employer or building up an unnecessarily large surplus. It cannot be said therefore that any exercise of the power of amendment must be invalid if and in so far as the amendment might benefit the employer directly or indirectly *Imperial Group Pension Trust Ltd* v *Imperial Tobacco Ltd* [1991] 2 All ER 597 considered.

VINELOTT J: . . . I find the idea that a person who has a power to distribute a fund amongst a class which includes himself should be able to apply the fund or any part of it for his own benefit . . . outrageous. This does not rest on any technical rule of trust law; common sense dictates that no man should be asked to exercise a discretion as to the application of a fund amongst a class of which he is a member. He cannot be expected fairly to weigh his own merits against the merits of others.

Mr Inglis-Jones relied on [this principle] as applicable equally to a power to amend a scheme while it is still in operation. I think this argument is fallacious. It is dangerous to import concepts which have been developed in the field of private trusts created by the bounty of a settlor or testator and apply them uncritically in the field of pension funds. In the field of private trusts the court is concerned to ascertain the extent of the rights conferred on the beneficiaries by the trust and the extent of powers so conferred whether on trustees or on an individual, as the donee of the power. The beneficiaries are volunteers. A pension trust by contrast is constituted in order to provide benefits for employees who in most cases will have contributed to the pension fund and who, whether they have contributed or not, will have served the employer in the expectation that discretions as to the application of any surplus in the fund will be honestly and fairly exercised with proper regard being paid to their contributions and service. In the context where a pension fund is being wound up and where the employer is itself a company which is being wound up, or is one that has otherwise ceased to carry on business, and where the question is as to how far a power to distribute a surplus in the fund should be exercised in favour of the members and pensioners, the analogy with a fiduciary power in the full sense is a useful and close one. The power cannot be released. The employer, if he is entitled to so much of the fund as is not distributed amongst members and pensioners, cannot properly decide that he will have regard only to his own interest and that he will not distribute any part of the fund to the members or pensioners. He must give full and proper consideration to their claims. So also, if the company is in insolvent liquidation, the liquidator cannot exercise the power because of the conflict of duty that would otherwise arise. Even there the analogy, though close, is not perfect because it is not easy to conceive of a private trust which contains a precisely analogous power. In the context of a private trust if A is given power to distribute a fund amongst a class and is himself entitled to the fund in default of the exercise of power, the almost inevitable inference would be that the settlor or testator intended he should be free to consult his own interests and to exercise or refrain from exercising the power as he might wish, at least in a case where he was named in the trust instrument or will as the donee of the power and as the person taking the fund in default of the exercise of it.

However this may be, the position is quite different when the question relates to the exercise of a power of amendment of a pension fund which has not been wound up. The employer, if he has a power of amendment, is entitled to exercise it in any way which will further the purposes of the pension scheme to ensure that the legitimate expectations of the members and pensioners are met without, so far as possible, imposing any undue burden on the employer or building up an unnecessarily large surplus. The employer himself has an interest in maintaining a pension fund which is satisfactory to existing and attractive to future employees, and he has an interest in ensuring that it is effectively managed, for example in seeing that the powers of investment are confined within proper limits, if necessary by amendment, and that they are properly exercised. If the assets of the scheme are so large that all legitimate expectations of the members and pensioners can be met without continued contribution by him at the rate originally provided, he can by amendment reduce or suspend contributions for a period. What he cannot do is to set limits to the benefits provided for members or pensioners for a collateral purpose without regard to their legitimate expectations.

RE COURAGE GROUP'S PENSION SCHEMES [1987] 1 All ER 528, ChD

MILLETT J: . . . Hanson's proposals, which I have disallowed, were designed to remove for its own benefit, or for the benefit of employees in other companies in the Hanson Group, all but £10m of the surplus in the schemes. Its proposals would have had the effect of reducing or extinguishing the present expectation of employees of the Courage Group of companies of a continued suspension of their contributions. They thus raise the wider and controversial issue whether such surpluses should be regarded as available to the employer or as belonging wholly or partly to the members. If I have not addressed that issue, it is not because I have overlooked it, but because it does not arise directly for decision. It is right, however, that I should explain why I have not based my decision on the ground that Hanson's proposals would deprive the employees of an accrued legal entitlement.

Such surpluses arise from what, with hindsight, can be recognised as past overfunding. Prima facie, if returnable and not used to increase benefits, they ought to be returned to those who contributed to them. In a contributory scheme, this might be thought to mean the employer and the employees in proportion to their respective contributions. That, however, is not necessarily, or even usually, the case. In the case of most pension schemes, and certainly in the case of these schemes, the position is different. Employees are obliged to contribute a fixed proportion of their salaries or such lesser sum as the employer may from time to time determine. They cannot be required to pay more, even if the fund is in deficit; and they cannot demand a reduction or suspension of their own contributions if it is in surplus. The employer, by way of contrast, is obliged only to make such contributions if any as may be required to meet the liabilities of the scheme. If the fund is in deficit, the employer is bound to make it good; if it is in surplus, the employer has no obligation to pay anything. Employees have no right to complain if, while the fund is in surplus, the employer should require them to continue their contributions while itself contributing nothing. If the employer chooses to reduce or suspend their contributions, it does so ex gratia and in the interests of maintaining good industrial relations.

From this, two consequences follow. First, employees have no legal right to 'a contributions holiday'. Second, any surplus arises from past overfunding not by the employer and the employees pro rata to their respective contributions but by the employer alone to the full extent of its past contributions and only subject thereto by the employees.

It will, however, only be in rare cases that the employer will have any legal right to repayment of any part of the surplus. Regulations shortly to be made under s. 64 of the Social Security Act 1973, as amended by para 3 of Sch 10 to the Social Security Act 1986, are expected to confer power on the Occupational Pensions Board to authorise modifications to pension schemes in order to allow repayment to employers. Repayment will, however, still normally require amendment to the scheme, and thus co-operation between the employer and the trustees or committee of management. Where the employer seeks repayment, the trustees or committee can be expected to press for generous treatment of employees and pensioners, and the employer to be influenced by a desire to maintain good industrial relations with its workforce.

It is, therefore, precisely in relation to a surplus that the relationship between 'the company' as the employer and the members as its present or past employees can be seen to be an essential feature of a pension scheme. In the present case, the members of these schemes object to being compulsorily transferred to a new scheme of which they know nothing except that it has a relatively small surplus. While they have no legal right to participate in the surpluses in the existing schemes, they are entitled to have them dealt with by consultation and negotiation between their employers with a continuing responsibility towards them and the committee of management with a discretion to exercise on their behalf, and not to be irrevocably parted from these surpluses by the unilateral decisions of a take-over raider with only transitory interest in the share capital of the companies which employ them.

2.2.3   ASSET PROTECTION TRUSTS

2.2.3.1   *Barclays Bank* v *Quistclose*

BARCLAYS BANK LTD v *QUISTCLOSE INVESTMENTS LTD* [1970] AC 567, HL

FACTS: R. Ltd, who were in serious financial difficulties, having an overdraft with their bank, the appellants, of some £484,000 against a permitted limit of £250,000, commenced negotiations with X, a financier, with a view to obtaining a loan of £1,000,000, and it was suggested that such a loan might be made on condition that R. Ltd found a sum of £209,719 8s. 6d. which was needed to meet an ordinary share dividend which R. Ltd had declared on July 2, 1964. R. Ltd succeeded in obtaining a loan of that sum from the respondents. The loan was made on the agreed condition that it would be used to pay the dividend. The respondents' cheque was paid into a separate account opened specially for the purpose with the appellants, who knew that the money was borrowed and who agreed with R. Ltd that the account would only be used for the purpose of paying the dividend. Before the dividend had been paid, however, R. Ltd went into voluntary liquidation. The respondents brought an action against R. Ltd and the appellants claiming that the money had been held by R. Ltd on trust to pay the dividend; that, that trust having failed, it was held on a resulting trust for the respondents, and that the appellants had had notice of the trusts and were, accordingly, constructive trustees of the money for the respondents.

HELD: (1)   That arrangements of this character for the payment of a person's creditors by a third person gave rise to a relationship of a fiduciary character or trust in favour, as a primary trust, of the creditors, and, secondly, if the primary trust failed, of the third person.

(2)   That the fact that the transaction was one of loan giving rise to a legal action of debt did not exclude the implication of a trust enforceable in equity.

(3)   That the appellants had, on the facts, accepted the money with knowledge of the circumstances which made it, in law, trust money, and could not retain it against the respondents.

LORD WILBERFORCE: . . . Two questions arise, both of which must be answered favourably to the respondents if they are to recover the money from the bank. The first is whether as between the respondents and Rolls Razor Ltd the terms upon which the loan was made were such as to impress upon the sum of £209,719 8s. 6d. a trust in their favour in the event of the dividend not being paid. The second is whether, in that event, the bank had such notice the trust or of the circumstances giving rise to it as to make the trust binding upon them.

It is not difficult to establish precisely upon what terms the money was advanced by the respondents to Rolls Razor Ltd. There is on doubt that the loan was made specifically in order to enable Rolls Razor Ltd to pay the dividend. There is equally, in my opinion, no doubt that the loan was made only so as to enable Rolls Razor Ltd to pay the dividend and for no other purpose. This follows quite clearly from the terms of the letter of Rolls Razor Ltd to the bank of July 15, 1964, which letter, before transmission to the bank, was sent to the respondents under open cover in order that the cheque might be (as it was) enclosed in it. The mutual intention of the respondents and of Rolls Razor Ltd, and the essence of the bargain, was that the sum advanced should not become part of the assets of Rolls Razor Ltd, but should be used exclusively for payment of a particular class of its creditors, namely, those entitled to the dividend. A necessary consequence from this, by process simply of interpretation, must be that if, for any reason, the dividend could not be paid, the money was to be returned to the respondents: the word 'only' or 'exclusively' can have no other meaning or effect.

That arrangements of this character for the payment of a person's creditors by a third person, give rise to a relationship of a fiduciary character or trust, in favour, as a primary trust, of the creditors, and secondarily, if the primary trust fails, of the third person, has been recognised in a series of cases over some 150 years. . . .

. . . The transaction, it was said, between the respondents and Rolls Razor Ltd, was one of loan, giving rise to a legal action of debt. This necessarily excluded the implication of any trusts enforceable in equity, in the respondents' favour: a transaction may attract one action or the other, it could not admit of both.

My Lords, I must say that I find this argument unattractive. Let us see what it involves. It means that the law does not permit an arrangement to be made by which one person agrees to advance money to another, on terms that the money is to be used exclusively to pay debts of the latter, and if, and so far as not so used, rather than becoming a general asset of the latter available to his creditors at large, is to be returned to the lender. The lender is obliged, in such a case, because he is a lender, to accept, whatever the mutual wishes of lender and borrower may be, that the money he was willing to make available for one purpose only shall be freely available for others of the borrower's creditors for whom he has not the slightest desire to provide.

I should be surprised if an argument of this kind—so conceptualist in character—had ever been accepted. In trust it has plainly been rejected by the eminent judges who from 1819 onwards have permitted arrangements of this type to be enforced, and have approved them as being for the benefit of creditors and all concerned. There is surely no difficulty in recognising the co-existence in one transaction of legal and equitable rights and remedies: when the money is advanced, the lender acquires an equitable right to see that it is applied for the primary designated purpose (see *In re Rogers*, 8 Morr. 243 where both Lindley LJ and Kay LJ recognised this): when the purpose has been carried out (i.e. the debt paid) the lender has his remedy against the borrower in debt: if the primary purpose cannot be carried out, the question arises if a secondary purpose (i.e. repayment to the lender) has been agreed, expressly or by implication: if it has, the remedies of equity may be invoked to give effect to it, if it has not (and the money is intended to fall within the general fund of the debtor's assets) then there is the appropriate remedy for recovery of a loan. I can appreciate no reason why the flexible interplay of law and equity cannot let in these practical arrangements, and other variations if desired: it would be to the discredit of both systems if they could not. In the present case the intention to create a secondary trust for the benefit of the lender, to arise if the primary trust, to pay the dividend, could not be carried out, is clear and I can find no reason why the law should not give effect to it. . . .

Sir Peter Millett, 'The Quistclose Trust: Who can Enforce it?' (1985) 101 LQR 269

A lends a sum of money to B for the specific purpose of enabling him to pay his (B's) creditors or a particular class of them, and for no other purpose. Can the creditors or any of them (C) compel B to apply the money in payment of the debts owing to them? Or can A change his mind, release B from the obligation to apply the money only for the specified purpose, and either demand repayment or allow B to spend the money as he chooses for his own purposes? And where, pending its application by B, is the beneficial interest in the money? . . .

The solution of the problem raised at the beginning of this article is not difficult if basic principles are observed. Two questions are involved, (i) is the so-called 'primary trust' truly a trust or is it merely a power, so that B cannot be compelled to exercise it? (ii) if it is a trust, who are the beneficiaries? As in the case of any trust, the answers to both questions depend upon the manifestation of the intentions of the settlor, i.e. A. In the case of an ordinary express trust the answers depend on the construction of the trust instrument. The *Quistclose* trust, however, arises only partly from the language used. In most cases it arises largely, and in some cases wholly, by implication of law. It is a presumed or implied trust, and the answers to questions such as those raised above have to be inferred from the language and conduct of the parties and the circumstances of the case.

The answer to the first question, it is submitted is to be found in each case by considering whether A has an interest separate and distinct from that of B, in seeing that the primary trust is carried out. If the cases down to and including the *Quistclose* case are examined, it will be found that in none of them did A have any such separate interest of his own.

In *Toovey* v *Milne* (1819) 2 B & Ald 683, for example, A had no interest, separate and distinct from any interest of B, in seeing that B's debts were paid. He was B's brother-in-law; his object was to save B from bankruptcy. But this was not something which he could insist on against B's will. His intention, therefore, must be taken to have been to save B from bankruptcy by providing him with the funds with which, *if he chose*, he might pay C, but which otherwise he must return to A. Similarly, in the *Quistclose* case, A had no interest, separate and distinct from any interest of B, in seeing that the dividend was paid. A's object was to prevent the collapse of B which would inevitably follow if the dividend were not paid. Again, A's intention must be taken to have been to benefit B by providing it with funds with which, *if it chose*, it might pay the dividend, but which otherwise it must return to A.

In all the cases down to and including the *Quistclose* case, it is submitted, the purpose of the arrangements would be fulfilled if they were treated as leaving the beneficial interest in the fund in A throughout, but subject to a power in B, revocable by A at any time, to apply the fund for the stated purpose.

In the two more recent cases, however, this would not have been sufficient for A's purpose. In the *Northern Developments* case (unreported, 6 October 1978), as has already been pointed out, the banks had their own interest, separate and distinct from any interest of B or Kelly, in seeing that Kelly's creditors were paid. In the *Carreras Rothmans* case [see **2.2.3.2**], this was even more obviously true. A was not seeking to enable B to avoid liquidation, but to protect itself from the consequences of B's liquidation. In neither case would A have been content to confer on B a mere power which B should be free to exercise or not as it pleased. In each case, therefore, A must be taken to have intended to subject B to an enforceable obligation to apply the fund for the stated purpose.

It does not follow, however, that the obligation is owed to, or enforceable by, C. Whether this is the case must again depend upon the manifestation of A's intentions, collected from the language used, the conduct of the parties, and the circumstances of the case. If indeed it was his intention to benefit C, there is no difficulty in giving effect to that intention by treating the arrangements as constituting B a trustee of the fund for C. C will have a beneficial interest in the fund, and the trust will in the ordinary way be irrevocable by A, and enforceable by C (but not by A).

If, on the other hand, it was A's intention, not to benefit C except incidentally, but either to benefit B (though without conferring any beneficial interest upon him) or to advance his own commercial interests, then it is submitted the proper way to give effect to that intention is to treat the arrangements as leaving the beneficial interest in the fund in A throughout, subject to an obligation on the part of B, enforceable by A, to apply the fund for the stated purpose. In short, it should make no difference whether B is authorised or required to apply the fund for the stated purpose. In either case he holds the fund as trustee for A alone with, in the one case a power, and in the other a duty, to comply with A's directions Pending the actual application of the fund by B, A's directions would normally be revocable by him.

If the cases are examined, it will be found that in every case this analysis is the only one which fits the facts. In *Toovey v Milne*, for example, A had no conceivable reason to be generous to C. His object was to save B from bankruptcy; and benefit which might accrue to C was incidental. He could have achieved his object by paying C himself. Instead, he chose to provide B with the necessary funds. Thus he was simply authorising B to use his (A's) money to pay off his own debts to C. Similarly, in the *Quistclose* case, A had no conceivable reason for being generous to B's shareholders. Its object was to save B from the collapse which would follow a failure to pay the dividend, and any benefit which might accrue to the shareholders from the payment of the dividend was incidental. It was not practicable for A to pay the dividend direct; indeed, this would have given the game away. It had to appear as if the dividend was being paid by B in the normal way. Accordingly, A simply provided B with the necessary funds, and authorised it to use its (A's) money to pay the dividend to C. In the *Northern Developments* case, the banks had no reason to be generous to B, or Kelly, or Kelly's unsecured creditors (who included the Revenue). They were acting exclusively in their own commercial interests in the hope of averting the collapse of the group; any benefit which might accrue to B, or Kelly, or Kelly's creditors was incidental. They simply provided B with the necessary funds, and directed it to use their money to pay Kelly's unsecured creditors.

In the *Carreras Rothmans* case the situation was, if anything, even clearer. A had no reason to be generous to C, but had its own commercial reasons for wanting their debts paid. The natural way for A to achieve this was to renegotiate the terms of trade with B so that instead of paying the money to B for onward payment to C, A should pay the money directly to C. This, however, was not commercially practicable, first because B was entitled to trade discounts from C which were not available to A, and secondly (and more importantly) because such an arrangement would have alerted C to B's parlous financial position, and almost certainly have precipitated its collapse. The arrangements which were concluded were designed to achieve essentially the same result; they enabled B to pay C with A's money.

Only in one respect did the *Carreras Rothmans* case differ from earlier cases; for A clearly could not revoke the arrangements without B's consent. A's directions were thus not only mandatory, but irrevocable. This feature led Peter Gibson J. to conclude that the arrangements vested an enforceable beneficial interest in C. 'I do not comprehend,' he said, 'how a trust, which on no footing could [A] revoke unilaterally, and which was still capable of performance, could nevertheless leave the beneficial interest in [A.]' But why not? It is not the trust for A which is (normally) revocable, but the directions given by him. There is no conceptual difficulty in constituting B a trustee of a fund for A with an obligation to apply the money in accordance with A's directions, such directions to be irrevocable by A without B's consent. Indeed, it is difficult to see any logical reason why a trust to apply money in accordance with A's directions is a trust for A if his directions are revocable by A alone, but a trust for C if revocable by A only with B's consent. The only thing which might give C an enforceable right, surely, would be an agreement by A not to revoke his directions without C's consent.

The foregoing analysis is not only in accordance with ordinary trust principles, but solves the two main riddles deriving from the *Quistclose* case which have puzzled commentators. One is the fact, well-established by the authorities, that the primary trust is enforceable by A. But on what basis can A enforce it? It if it is taken to be a positive right to see that the money is applied for the stated purpose, then as has been pointed out, A's right is not the right of a beneficiary under the resulting trust, for if the primary purpose is fulfilled there is no resulting trust and A becomes a simple creditor. . . .

If Megarry V-Cs analysis is accepted, the only remaining character possessed by A is that of lender; and it may be suggested that A's right to enforce execution of the primary trust is, in reality, a right to specific performance of a condition of the contract of loan. There are several objections to this. In the first place, Lord Wilberforce's remarks in the *Quistclose* case were wide enough to embrace cases where the money was provided by A by way of gift or on a non-contractual basis, and there is no reason to confine them to cases of loan; in the second place, it is subversive of the whole basis of Lord Wilberforce's approach, which rests B's obligation firmly on an equitable and not a contractual footing. There is, in fact, only one explanation of A's undoubted right to enforce the primary trust which can be reconciled with basic principles. A can enforce the primary trust *because he is the beneficiary*.

The other puzzle is the basis on which the primary trust is said to have failed in several of the cases, particularly *Toovey* v *Milne* and the *Quistclose* case. It has already been suggested that this can only be on the basis that the purpose for which A lent the money was taken to be, not to pay C, but to save B from bankruptcy or collapse. But in itself this is not enough. A trust does not fail merely because the settlor's purpose in creating it has been frustrated; the trust must become illegal or impossible to perform. The settlor's motives must not be confused with the purposes of the trust; the frustration of the former does not by itself cause the failure of the latter. But if the true nature of the trust is that it is a trust to carry out A's recoverable directions, and A's purpose in giving those directions is frustrated, revocation is easily inferred. The true reason, it is submitted, why the primary trust to pay the dividend failed in the *Quistclose* case is that A's purpose in directing B to use the money to pay the dividend was to save B from collapse, and when B collapsed anyway A revoked the direction by demanding repayment.

If the foregoing analysis of the *Quistclose* trust is correct, then it is simply an example of what is sometimes called an 'illusory trust.' The best known example of such a trust is a disposition of property by a debtor to trustees for the benefit of his creditors. This is sometimes said to be an exception to the general rule that a voluntary settlement cannot be revoked by the settlor after it has been fully constituted. But the true view is that the apparent beneficiaries take no beneficial interest at all, the trustees holding the property transferred to them in trust for the debtor exclusively. . . .

2.2.3.2   Cases after *Quistclose*

RE EVTR LTD, GILBERT AND ANOTHER v BARBER [1987] BCLC 647, CA

FACTS: The company was in financial difficulties and Barber, who had won a fortune on premium bonds, agreed to assist it financially to enable it to acquire equipment to carry on business and to this end he deposited £60,000 with the company's solicitors who held it to the appellant's order. The company contracted with Q Ltd for the supply of new equipment to be delivered within seven months and in the meantime to supply the company with temporary equipment. The company also entered into a contract with C Ltd whereby C Ltd agreed to take over the company's obligations under the contract with Q Ltd by buying the new equipment and then leasing it to the company. B gave the company's solicitors written authority to release the £60,000 'for the sole purpose of buying new equipment' and the terms of this authority were known to the company. The money was released to the company of which £21,000 was paid to C Ltd and £39,000 was paid to Q Ltd. The company's bankers appointed receivers. Q Ltd refunded £29,000 to the company which represented the £39,000 less damages for breach of contract and C Ltd refunded approximately £19,000 to the company which represented the £21,000 less a sum owed by the company to C Ltd.

HELD: Appeal allowed. As the money had been paid to the company for a specific purpose, namely the purchase of the equipment, and as there would have been a resulting trust in favour of B had that purpose not been carried out it followed that when the moneys were repaid to the company on the failure of the purpose the company held the moneys on the basis of the original trust for B.

DILLON LJ: . . . On *Quistclose* principles, a resulting trust in favour of the provider of the money arises when money is provided for a particular purpose only, and that purpose fails. In the present case, the purpose for which the £60,000 was provided by the appellant to the company was, as appears from the authority to Knapp-Fishers, the purpose of [the company] buying new equipment. But in any realistic sense of the words that purpose has failed in that the company has never acquired any new equipment, whether the Encore System which was then in mind or anything else. True it is that the £60,000 was paid out by the company with a view to the acquisition of new equipment, but that was only at half-time, and I do not see why the final whistle should be blown at half-time. The proposed acquisition proved abortive and a large part of the £60,000 has therefore been repaid by the payees. The repayments were made because of, or on account of, the payments which made up the £60,000 and those were payments of trust moneys. It is a long-established principle of equity that, if a person who is a trustee receives money or property because of, or in respect of, trust property, he will hold what he receives as a constructive trustee on the trusts of the original trust property. An early application of this principle is the well-known case of *Keech v Sandford* (1726) Sel Cas Ch 61, 25 ER 223, but the instances in the books are legion. See also *Chelsea Estates Investment Trust Co. Ltd v Marche* [1955] 1 All ER 195, [1955] Ch 328 where somewhat similar reasoning applied to a mortgagee. It follows, in my judgment, that the repayments made to the receivers are subject to the same trusts as the original £60,000 in the hands of the company. There is now, of course, no question of the £48,536 being applied in the purchase of new equipment for the company, and accordingly, in my judgment, it is now held on a resulting trust for the appellant. . . .

CARRERAS ROTHMANS LTD v FREEMAN MATHEWS TREASURE LTD AND ANOTHER [1985] 1 Ch 207

FACTS: The plaintiff manufactured cigarettes which it advertised extensively. For many years, the defendant, a company carrying on the business of an advertising agency, had undertaken services for the plaintiff. In 1979 the defendant undertook all the plaintiff's placement work, namely, producing from the artwork all that was needed for the advertisements to be printed and buying space in publications and on bill boards. In doing that work the defendant negotiated favourable discounts for advertising space and incurred debts as a principal to third parties for the space bought and for certain technical services. The plaintiff paid the defendant an annual fee in monthly instalments for the placement work and each month the plaintiff would pay the defendant a sum equivalent to the amount of the invoices received by the defendant from third parties for liabilities incurred the previous month. The plaintiff paid the money in time for the defendant to pay the third parties when the debts became due for payment, which was usually at the end of the month. The defendant was in financial difficulties and, at the suggestion of the plaintiff, it agreed in July 1983 that a special account should be opened into which the plaintiff would pay a sum equivalent to the moneys due to third parties.

On 3 August the defendant went into a creditors' voluntary liquidation and its liquidation arranged for the special account to be frozen before the cheques were cleared.

The plaintiff brought an action against the defendant and its liquidator for a declaration that the moneys in the special account were held on trust for the sole purpose of paying the third party creditors and for an order for those moneys to be repaid to the plaintiff.

HELD: Under the terms of the July agreement the moneys paid by the plaintiff into the special account to meet the June debts owed by the defendant to third parties were never held by the defendant beneficially; that since the moneys had been placed in a special account for a specific purpose, equity required that the moneys were used only for that purpose; that, accordingly, the July agreement did create a trust and the plaintiff had a right to enforce the payment over of moneys in the special account to the third parties and the third parties had an interest in the orderly administration of those trust funds.

PETER GIBSON J: . . . It is of course true that there are factual differences between the *Quistclose* case and the present case. The transaction there was one of loan with no contractual obligation on the part of the lender to make payment prior to the agreement for the loan. In the present case there is no loan but there is an antecedent debt owed by the plaintiff. I doubt if it is helpful to analyse the *Quistclose* type of case in terms of the constituent parts of a conventional settlement, though it may of course be crucial to ascertain in whose favour the secondary trust operates (as in the *Quistclose* case itself) and who has an enforceable right. In my judgment the principle in all these cases is that equity fastens on the conscience of the person who receives from another property transferred for a specific purpose only and not therefore for the recipient's own purposes, so that such person will not be permitted to treat the property as his own or to use it for other than the stated purpose. Most of the cases in this line are cases where there has been an agreement for consideration so that in one sense each party has contributed to providing the property. But if the common intention is that property is transferred for a specific purpose and not so as to become the property of the transferee, the transferee cannot keep the property if for any reason that purpose cannot be fulfilled. I am left in no doubt that the provider of the moneys in the present case was the plaintiff. True it is that its own witnesses said that if the defendant had not agreed to the terms of the contract letter, the plaintiff would not have broken its contract but would have paid its debt to the defendant, but the fact remains that the plaintiff made its payment on the terms of that letter and the defendant received the moneys only for the stipulated purpose. That purpose was expressed to relate only to the moneys in the account. In my judgment therefore the plaintiff can be equated with the lender in *Quistclose* as having an enforceable right to compel the carrying out of the primary trust.

Mr Potts also submitted that the third party creditors had no enforceable rights and that where the beneficiaries under the primary trust have no enforceable rights, no trust is created. Mr Millett and Mr Higham also submitted that the third party creditors had no enforceable rights, though that submission was made primarily with an eye to an argument relevant to the section 95 point that the beneficial interest in the moneys paid into the special account always remained in the plaintiffs. In none of the many reported cases in the *Quistclose* line of cases, so far as I am aware, has any consideration been given to the question whether the person intended to benefit from the carrying out of the specific purpose which created the trust had enforceable rights. Thus the existence of enforceable rights in such persons has not been treated as crucial to the existence of a trust. Further in the one case in which so far as I am aware the question who, in addition to the provider of the property, had enforceable rights was determined by the court, it was held that the persons intended to benefit from the carrying out of the primary trust did have enforceable rights. That case is the decision of Sir Robert Megarry V-C in *In re Northern Developments (Holdings) Ltd* (unreported), 6 October 1978. In that case the eponymous company ('Northern') was the parent company of a group of companies including one ('Kelly') which was in financial straits. Seventeen banks agreed to put up a fund in excess of half a million pounds in an attempt to rescue Kelly. The banks already had other companies in the group as customers. They paid the moneys into an account in Northern's name for the express purpose of providing moneys for Kelly's unsecured creditors and for no other purpose, the amounts advanced being treated as advances to the banks' other customers in the group. The fund was used to sustain Kelly for a time, but then Kelly was put into receivership at a time when a little over half the fund remained unexpended. One of the questions for the court was who was entitled to that balance. Sir Robert Megarry V-C held that there was a *Quistclose* type of trust attaching to the fund, that trust was a purpose trust but enforceable by identifiable individuals, namely the banks as lenders, Kelly, for whose immediate benefit the fund was established, and Kelly's creditors. The reason given by Sir Robert Megarry V-C for holding that Kelly's creditors had enforceable rights were the words of Lord Wilberforce in the *Quistclose* case at p. 580 which I have already cited, describing the *Quistclose* type of trust as giving rise to a relationship of a fiduciary character or trust in favour of the creditors. However, Sir Robert Megarry V-C went on to describe the interests of the creditors in this way:

> The fund was established not with the object of vesting the beneficial interest in them, but in order to confer a benefit on Kelly (and so, consequentially, on the rest of the group and the bankers) by ensuring that Kelly's creditors would be paid in an orderly manner. There is perhaps some parallel in the position of a beneficiary entitled to a share of residue under a will. What he has is not a beneficial interest in any asset forming part of residue, but a right to compel the executor to administer the assets of the deceased properly. It seems to me that it is that sort of right which the creditors of Kelly had.

The interest of the banks was held to be under the secondary trust if the primary trust failed. In the light of that authority I cannot accept the joint submission that the third party creditors for the payment of whose debts the plaintiff had paid the moneys into the special account had no enforceable rights. In any event I do not comprehend how a trust, which on no footing could the plaintiff revoke, unilaterally, and which was expressed as a trust to pay third parties and was still capable of performance, could nevertheless leave the beneficial interest in the plaintiff which had parted with the moneys. On Sir Robert Megarry V-C's analysis the beneficial interest is in suspense until the payment is made.

I can dispose of Mr Potts' remaining arguments under this head more briefly. In my judgment the doctrine of illusory trusts has no application to the facts of the present case. That doctrine applies where a debtor for his own convenience settles property in favour of his creditors, the court treating the trust as a revocable one. In the present case, although the defendant agreed to the discharge of an asset, its book debt, by payment by its debtor, the plaintiff, in such a way that the moneys paid would be held on trust to pay its creditors, the defendant did not enter into the arrangement for its convenience but for good commercial reasons on the insistence of the plaintiff and the trust was not for its creditors generally but for a particular class of creditor. It cannot be said in the circumstances that the July agreement was intended to be revocable by the defendant alone. Nor can I accept Mr Potts' argument on specific performance. He submitted that where, as here, the beneficial interest in the moneys in the account has not yet become vested in the third party creditors, the court should not order payment. His argument was based on a suggested analogy with cases like *In re Wiltshire Iron Co.* (1868) LR 3 Ch App 440 and *In re Oriental Bank Corporation* (1884) 28 ChD 634 in which the court refused to allow the completion of contracts after the commencement of a winding up where the property, the subject of the contracts, remained in the company's ownership at the commencement of the winding up. In the present case the plaintiff seeks an order not for specific performance but for the carrying out of the primary trust in respect of moneys which not only are not the property of the defendant but never have been. At the commencement of the liquidation its previous asset, the book debt, had been discharged. I see no reason why the court should not so order.

In my judgment therefore a trust was created by the July agreement, the trust was completely constituted by the payment of moneys into the special account and the plaintiff as the provider of the moneys has an equitable right to an order for the carrying out by the defendant of the trust.

2.3   End of Chapter Assessment Question

If we were asked what is the greatest and most distinctive achievement performed by Englishmen in the field of jurisprudence I cannot think that we should have any better answer to give than this, namely the development from century to century of the trust idea.

What is so great and distinctive about trusts?

2.4   End of Chapter Assessment Outline Answer

In answering this essay question, did you take advantage of the lessons learned from attempting the essay question at the end of **Chapter 1**? Again, the key to a sound answer is planning, structure and content.

Introduction

In this brief specimen essay it is intended to support Maitland's famous assertion that the trust idea is the greatest and most distinctive achievement of English law in the field of jurisprudence. First, to give just a flavour of the distinctiveness of the trust concept, we will consider what distinguishes it from the concept of contract. It is sometimes suggested that whatever has been achieved by the trust concept could equally have been achieved through the law of contract — we will see that that claim is ill-founded. Secondly, we will seek to illustrate the greatness of the trust idea, not in terms of its abstract conceptual appeal, but in terms of the advantages of the trust concept as seen in its practical application to real problems.

Trusts compared to contracts

A contract is a private relationship between the parties under which their rights and obligations are generally enforceable only against each other (*Beswick* v *Beswick* [1968] AC 58). It is of the essence of a trust that a settlor can give property to a trustee on trust for a third party, and thereby grant the third party (the beneficiary) rights against the trustee to see that the trust is properly discharged. A contract, even if for the benefit of a third party, does not create a right in that third party against the contracting parties. The English law of contract recognises no *jus quaesitum tertio*. It is clear that the contract idea is constrained by its privity rule and other rules such as the need for consideration. The trust, it is submitted, is a more flexible concept. Thus, it is by means of the trust that benefits may be conferred on persons who are not competent to contract, such as those under a legal disability, and those as yet unborn.

The practical advantages of the trust concept

The ability of the trust to attach to assets has led to a number of practical applications. It can be used: to provide for property to be held for the benefit of persons subject to legal disability (minors are not permitted to hold the legal estate in land, but are permitted to be the beneficiary under a trust of land); to provide for property to be held for persons in succession, e.g. 'to A for life, to A's children in remainder'; to provide for property to be held by a number of owners concurrently, e.g. co-ownership of land; to protect family property from the bankruptcy or extravagance of particular beneficiaries; to take into account the possible changes in the future circumstances of beneficiaries in making a gift, instead of making outright gift; to apply property for purposes, rather than persons; to make collective investment e.g. pension funds (see below); to enable clubs (unincorporated non-profit associations) to receive and hold property; to minimise tax liability, by restructuring property ownership; to protect assets from creditors in the event of insolvency (see below); to concentrate managerial power (in relation to, for example, pension funds, trade unions and clubs); to achieve privacy in dealings with property (hiding true beneficial ownership behind legal ownership), e.g. by means of a secret trust.

Let us focus on just one of these practical applications of the trust idea.

Pension fund trusts

The use of *trusts* for holding pension funds yields a number of advantages over other instrumentalities, such as the corporation. Trusts are a useful vehicle for pension provision because they allow the managerial control of large funds to be concentrated in the hands of a few trustees. But the great advantages of the use of a trust over most other devices is the fact that the beneficiaries under a trust have a proprietary interest in the fund. This gives them security in the event of the insolvency of the employer corporation, and allows them to leave their entitlement to others in the event of their death. The use of a trust also brings with it the added advantage of subjecting the pension fund manager to strict equitable obligations.

However, it must be admitted that the use of trusts in pension provision is not always advantageous. The main problems in relation to occupational pension schemes stem from the potential for fraudulent use of the (often vast) funds involved. The potential for abuse stems in turn from the fact that in the usual case at least half the scheme trustees will be representatives of the employer company, and the employer very often has the power to appoint new trustees. If the employee's representatives are not astute to spot a fraud on the fund (and fraud, by its very nature, is often hard to detect) the trust fund can be wrongfully employed for the employer's personal purposes. This sort of fraudulent activity lay at the root of the Maxwell scandal in the late 1980s, and prompted the *Report of the Pension Law Review Committee* chaired by Professor Roy Goode (and known as 'The Goode Report'), published in September 1993, which in turn prompted the enactment of the Pensions Act 1995.

Conclusion

It is hoped that this brief essay has shown that the trust concept is both conceptually distinct and practically advantageous. It is well worthy of Maitland's accolade.

CHAPTER THREE

CAPACITY AND FORMALITY REQUIREMENTS

3.1 Capacity

3.1.1 MENTAL INCAPACITY

SIMPSON v SIMPSON [1992] 1 FLR 601, ChD

FACTS: The testator's mental well-being had become increasingly impaired after an operation to remove a tumour from his brain. After the operation he transferred 70 per cent of his estate into the joint names of himself and his wife, and sent a letter to his solicitor expressing his intention to sell his cottage in due course and make a gift to his wife of half the proceeds. After the testator's death his children by an earlier marriage sued his widow. They questioned, *inter alia*, whether the testator had possessed sufficient capacity to transfer his beneficial interests into his and his wife's joint names, and whether the letter to his solicitor could have amounted to a declaration of trust in favour of his wife.
HELD: On the basis of the evidence, including that of medical experts, it was clear that a patient with the testator's medical complaint would deteriorate to a point where a lack of mental capacity must be presumed. In the absence of evidence to rebut the presumption, the purported dispositions to the testator's wife were ineffective to transfer his beneficial interests in the various properties. In particular, he had not had capacity to declare a trust by the letter to his solicitor. In any event the letter had not shown an intention to make an *immediate* gift to his wife and consequently could not take effect as a declaration of trust.

MORRITT J: . . . It was common ground between the parties that the test to be applied is that laid down in *Re Beaney dec'd*; *Beaney* v *Beaney* [1978] 1 WLR 770, namely:

> The degree or extent of understanding required in respect of any instrument is relative to the particular transaction which it is to effect. In the case of a will the degree required is always high. In the case of a contract a deed made for consideration or a gift inter vivos, whether by deed or otherwise, the degree required varies with the circumstances of the transaction. Thus at one extreme, if the subject matter and value of the gift are trivial in relation to the donor's other assets a low degree of understanding will suffice. But at the other extreme, if its effect is to dispose of the donor's only asset of value and thus, for practical purposes, to pre-empt the devolution of his estate under his will or on his intestacy then the degree of understanding required is as high as that required for a will, and the donor must understand the claims of all potential donees and the extent of the property to be disposed of.

3.1.2 MINORITY (INFANCY)

FAMILY LAW REFORM ACT 1969

1. Reduction of age of majority from 21 to 18

(1) As from the date on which this section comes into force a person shall attain full age on attaining the age of eighteen instead of on attaining the age of twenty-one; and a

person shall attain full age on that date if he has then already attained the age of eighteen but not the age of twenty-one.

(2)   The foregoing subsection applies for the purposes of any rule of law, and, in the absence of a definition or of any indication of a contrary intention, for the construction of 'full age', 'infant', 'infancy', 'minor', 'minority' and similar expressions in—

(a)   any statutory provision, whether passed or made before, on or after the date on which this section comes into force; and

(b)   any deed, will or other instrument of whatever nature (not being a statutory provision) made on or after that date.

(3)   In the statutory provisions specified in Schedule 1 to this Act for any reference to the age of twenty-one years there shall be substituted a reference to the age of eighteen years; . . .

EDWARDS v CARTER [1893] AC 360, HL

FACTS: A husband agreed, one month before attaining his majority, that he would vest his future inheritance, upon his father's death, in a trust set up by his father. The trust was expressed in terms to benefit the husband, his wife and their future issue. The husband's father died four years later, and a further year later the husband purported to repudiate the settlement. The Court of Appeal held that he was bound by the settlement he had entered into as a minor. Certain of his creditors appealed to the House of Lords, the respondents were the trustees of the settlement.

HELD: The decision of the Court of Appeal was affirmed. The husband's settlement was not void. It was voidable, on account of his infancy at the time that the settlement was made, but he had failed to repudiate the settlement within a reasonable time and it would therefore stand.

LORD HERSCHELL LC: . . . My Lords, I did not understand the learned counsel for the appellants really to dispute the proposition that the repudiation in order that the obligations may be got rid of must be within a reasonable time after the minor ceases to be a minor. The controversy has been as to what elements may be taken into account in determining whether more than a reasonable time has elapsed. In the present case, as I have shewn your Lordships, there was no repudiation at all during the lifetime of the father. Down to the death of the father nothing had been done by the son; and it is impossible not to see that if the son had repudiated in the lifetime of the father it is in the highest degree probable that the disposition made by the father would have been different from what it was, as it is certain that the position of those taking, or at all events of one of those taking, under the will of the father was altered for the worse by reason of this repudiation if the repudiation was effective.

Now, my Lords, the first question is whether the infant was entitled to wait until an actual sum of money came to him to which this covenant could apply before he made the repudiation. I think that is a proposition which it is absolutely impossible to regard with seriousness—that this covenant being binding unless he repudiates it within a reasonable time, he is entitled to wait to see how in respect of any particular sum of money the covenant will operate, and when he has made up his mind whether with regard to that sum of money it will be beneficial to him or not, he can then, and not till then, be said to have his proper opportunity of making the determination!

Then it is said that in considering whether a reasonable time has elapsed you must take into account the fact that he did not know what were the terms of the settlement, and that it contained this particular covenant. He knew that he had executed a deed—he must be taken to have known that that deed though binding upon him could be repudiated when he came of age. And, my Lords, it seems to me that in measuring a reasonable time, whether in point of fact he had or had not acquainted himself with the nature of the obligations which he had undertaken is wholly immaterial. The time must be measured in precisely the same way whether he had so made himself acquainted or not. I do not say that he was under any obligation to make himself acquainted with the nature of the deed which, having executed as an infant, he might or might not at his pleasure repudiate when he came of age. All I say is this, that he cannot maintain that the reasonable time when measured must be a longer time because he has chosen not to make himself acquainted with the nature of the deed which he has executed.

My Lords, having put aside those two contentions, the only question comes to be, Has a reasonable time been exceeded? The learned judges in the court below expressed their opinion that the period which elapsed, a period of between four and five years, was more than a reasonable time. It is not at all necessary for your Lordships to lay down what would have been a reasonable time in this case. It is enough to say that in my opinion it is impossible to hold that the learned judges in the court below have in any way erred in saying that more than a reasonable time had elapsed.

I therefore move your Lordships that this appeal be dismissed with costs.

3.2 Formalities

3.2.1 *INTER VIVOS* TRANSACTIONS

LAW OF PROPERTY ACT 1925

1. Legal estates and equitable interests
. . .
(6) A legal estate is not capable of subsisting or of being created in an undivided share in land or of being held by an infant.

52. Conveyances to be by deed
(1) All conveyances of land or of any interest therein are void for the purpose of conveying or creating a legal estate unless made by deed.
(2) This section does not apply to—
(a) assents by a personal representative;
(b) disclaimers made in accordance with [sections 178 to 180 or sections 315 to 319 of the Insolvency Act 1986], or not required to be evidenced in writing;
(c) surrenders by operation of law, including surrenders which may, by law, be effected without writing;
(d) leases or tenancies or other assurances not required by law to be made in writing;
(e) receipts not required by law to be under seal;
(f) vesting orders of the court or other competent authority;
(g) conveyances taking effect by operation of law.

53. Instruments required to be in writing
(1) Subject to the provisions hereinafter contained with respect to the creation of interests in land by parol—
(a) no interest in land can be created or disposed of except by writing signed by the person creating or conveying the same, or by his agent thereunto lawfully authorised in writing, or by will, or by operation of law;
(b) a declaration of trust respecting any land or any interest therein must be manifested and proved by some writing signed by some person who is able to declare such trust or by his will;
(c) a disposition of an equitable interest or trust subsisting at the time of the disposition, must be in writing signed by the person disposing of the same, or by his agent thereunto lawfully authorised in writing or by will.
(2) This section does not affect the creation or operation of resulting, implied or constructive trusts.

GREY v INLAND REVENUE COMMISSIONERS [1960] AC 1, HL

FACTS: Between 1949 and 1950 H executed six settlements in favour of his grandchildren. Grey was one of the trustees of those settlements. On 1 February 1955 H transferred 18,000 £1 shares to the trustees. On 18 February H orally and irrevocably directed that the shares should be held on the trusts of the six settlements, 3,000 shares to each settlement. On 25 March the trustees made written declarations of trust in accordance with H's directions. The instruments declaring the trusts were assessed to *ad valorem* stamp duty (a tax charged 'according to the value' of an instrument) as voluntary dispositions in accordance with the Finance Act 1910. The trustees appealed against the assessment.

HELD: H's oral direction would have constituted a 'disposition' of his equitable interest in the shares, but was ineffective for failing to satisfy the requirement of writing within s. 53(1)(c) of the Law of Property Act 1925. Accordingly, only the later formal declarations by the trustees were effective to transfer H's equitable interest in the shares. Those formal declarations constituted 'instruments' for the purposes of the Stamp Act 1891 and had been rightly assessed to *ad valorem* stamp duty.

LORD RADCLIFFE: My Lords, if there is nothing more in this appeal than the short question whether the oral direction that Mr Hunter gave to his trustees on 18 February 1955, amounted in any ordinary sense of the words to a 'disposition of an equitable interest or trust subsisting at the time of the disposition', I do not feel any doubt as to my answer. I think that it did. Whether we describe what happened in technical or in more general terms, the full equitable interest in the eighteen thousand shares concerned, which at that time was his, was (subject to any statutory invalidity) diverted by his direction from his ownership into the beneficial ownership of the various equitable owners, present and future, entitled under his six existing settlements.

But that is not the question which has led to difference of opinion in the courts below. Where opinions have differed is on the point whether his direction was a 'disposition' within the meaning of s. 53(1)(c) of the Law of Property Act 1925, the argument for giving it a more restricted meaning in that context being that s. 53 is to be construed as no more than a consolidation of three sections of the Statute of Frauds, s. 3, s. 7 and s. 9. So treated 'disposition', as it is said, is merely the equivalent of the former words of s. 9, 'grants and assignments', except that testamentary disposition has to be covered as well, and a direction to a trustee by the equitable owner of the property prescribing new trusts on which it is to be held is a declaration of trust but not a grant or assignment. The argument concludes, therefore, that neither before 1 January 1926, nor since did such a direction require to be in writing signed by the disponor or his agent in order to be effective.

In my opinion, it is a very nice question whether a parol declaration of trust of this kind was or was not within the mischief of s. 9 of the Statute of Frauds. The point has never, I believe, been decided and perhaps it never will be. Certainly it was long established as law that, while a declaration of trust respecting land or any interest therein required writing to be effective, a declaration of trust respecting personalty did not. Moreover, there is warrant for saying that a direction to his trustee by the equitable owner of trust property prescribing new trusts of that property was a declaration of trust. But it does not necessarily follow from that that such a direction, if the effect of it was to determine completely or pro tanto the subsisting equitable interest of the maker of the direction, was not also a grant or assignment for the purposes of s. 9 and, therefore, required writing for its validity. Something had to happen to that equitable interest in order to displace it in favour of the new interests created by the direction; and it would be at any rate logical to treat the direction as being an assignment of the subsisting interest to the new beneficiary or beneficiaries or, in other cases, a release or surrender of it to the trustee.

I do not think, however, that that question has to be answered for the purposes of this appeal. It can only be relevant if s. 53(1) of the Law of Property Act 1925 is treated as a true consolidation of the three sections of the Statute of Frauds concerned and as governed, therefore, by the general principle, with which I am entirely in agreement, that a consolidating Act is not to be read as effecting changes in the existing law unless the words it employs are too clear in their effect to admit of any other construction. If there is anything in the judgments of the majority of the Court of Appeal which is inconsistent with this principle I must express my disagreement with them. But, in my opinion, it is impossible to regard s. 53 of the Law of Property Act 1925 as a consolidating enactment in this sense. It is here that the premises on which Upjohn J and the Master of the Rolls (Lord Evershed) founded their conclusions are, I believe, unsound.

The Law of Property Act 1925 itself was, no doubt, strictly a consolidating statute. But what it consolidated was not merely the Law of Property Act 1922, a statute which had itself effected massive changes in the law relating to real property and conveyancing, but also the later Law of Property (Amendment) Act 1924. The Statute of Frauds sections had not been touched by the Act of 1922; but they were, in effect, repealed and re-enacted in altered form by the operation of s. 3 of the Act of 1924 and the provisions of sch. 3 to that Act. The schedule is divided into two Parts, the contents of Part 1 being described simply as 'Amendments' and the contents of Part 2 being headed by the description 'Provisions for facilitating the consolidation . . .' I suppose that the authors of the Act of 1924 understood what was the significance of the division of sch. 3 into these two Parts under their different headings. I cannot say that I do. Each Part, when examined, is seen to contain numerous amendments of various previous statutes relating to real property and conveyancing, apart from the Act of 1922 itself, and in this sort of matter I cannot see how one can satisfactorily measure the degrees of substance involved in the various changes. The point is that they were avowedly changes. It is para. 15 of Part 2 of sch. 3 which deals with the Statute of Frauds; and though the introductory words do seem to suggest that the sections concerned are only being re-enacted in different words, it is apparent, when they are read through, that this is not so, and that alterations of more or less moment are in fact being made. This new wording is what is carried into s. 53 of the Act of 1925.

For these reasons, I think that there is no direct link between s. 53(1)(c) of the Act of 1925 and s. 9 of the Statute of Frauds. The link was broken by the changes introduced by the amending Act of 1924, and it was those changes, not the original statute, that s. 53 must be taken as consolidating. If so, it is inadmissible to allow the construction of the word 'disposition' in the new Act to be limited or controlled by any meaning attributed to the words 'grant' or 'assignment' in s. 9 of the old Act.

I agree that the appeal should be dismissed.

OUGHTRED v INLAND REVENUE COMMISSIONERS [1960] AC 206, HL

FACTS: 200,000 shares in WJ & Son were held upon trust for Mrs O for life, thereafter to her son, P, absolutely. Mrs O also owned 72,700 shares absolutely. By an oral agreement, and in order to avoid estate duty payable on the shares in the event of Mrs O's death, the parties determined to exchange their interests. Mrs O promised to transfer the 72,200 shares to P, and P promised to transfer his remainder interest in the 200,000 shares to Mrs O. Written documents of transfer were later executed in accordance with the terms of the oral agreement. The Inland Revenue brought the present action claiming *ad valorem* stamp duty on the document which recorded the transfer of the equitable interest in the 200,000 shares. Mrs O argued that no value had passed by virtue of the later documents, the equitable interest having been transferred by the earlier oral agreement, and accordingly there was no basis on which to charge *ad valorem* stamp duty on the later document.
HELD: (Viscount Radcliffe and Lord Cohen dissenting): Mrs O did not have a beneficial interest in the 200,000 shares until the execution of the later documents. It followed, therefore, that the later document was an instrument transferring value, and that it should be subject to *ad valorem* stamp duty at £663. Mrs O had argued that in as much as the oral agreement was an agreement of sale and purchase it gave rise in equity to a constructive trust of the remainder interest in her favour, subject only to Mrs O performing her side of the agreement to transfer the 72,700 shares to P. She argued, in other words, that the oral agreement had transferred the equitable ownership of the 200,000 shares to her, and that P had thereafter held those shares as constructive trustee for her. The formality requirements laid down in s. 53(1)(c) did not enter into the case, she argued, because of the provision in s. 53(2) that constructive trusts were not subject to any formality requirements. The majority of their Lordships rejected this submission. By analogy with this 'simple case of a contract for sale of land' they pointed out that the deed which comes after the contract and completes the sale has never been regarded as 'not stampable *ad valorem*'. It followed, on this reasoning, that the later instrument of transfer to Mrs O had transferred real value and was stampable *ad valorem* as the Inland Revenue had contended. Dissenting, Viscount Radcliffe, observed that Mrs O need never have called for the subsequent written instrument of transfer, and that she could have simply called upon the trustees of the settlement of the 200,000 shares to transfer the bare

legal title to her. For Viscount Radcliffe the subsequent written transfer by P was nothing more than a transfer of the bare legal title to Mrs O, it did not transfer any equitable interest at all and should not have been assessed to *ad valorem* stamp duty.

LORD RADCLIFFE: . . . The reasoning of the whole matter, as I see it, is as follows. On 18 June 1956, the son owned an equitable reversionary interest in the settled shares; by his oral agreement of that date he created in his mother an equitable interest in his reversion, since the subject-matter of the agreement was property of which specific performance would normally be decreed by the court. He thus became a trustee for her of that interest sub modo; having regard to subs. (2) of s. 53 of the Law of Property Act 1925, subs. (1) of that section did not operate to prevent that trusteeship arising by operation of law. On 26 June the appellant transferred to her son the shares which were the consideration for her acquisition of his equitable interest; on this transfer he became in a full sense and without more the trustee of his interest for her. She was the effective owner of all outstanding equitable interests. It was thus correct to recite in the deed of release to the trustees of the settlement, which was to wind up their trust, that the trust fund was by then held on trust for her absolutely. There was, in fact, no equity to the shares that could be asserted against her, and it was open to her, if she so wished, to let the matter rest without calling for a written assignment from her son. Given that the trustees were apprised of the making of the oral agreement and of the appellant's satisfaction of the consideration to be given by her, the trustees had no more to do than to transfer their legal title to her or as she might direct. This and no more is what they did.

It follows that, in my view, this transfer cannot be treated as a conveyance of the son's equitable reversion at all. The trustees had not got it; he never transferred or released it to them; how, then, could they convey it? With all respect to those who think otherwise, it is incorrect to say that the trustees' transfer was made either with his authority or at his direction. If the recital as to the appellant's rights was correct, as I think that it was, he had no remaining authority to give or direction to issue. A release is, after all, the normal instrument for winding-up a trust when all the equitable rights are vested and the legal estate is called for from the trustees who hold it. What the release gave the trustees from him was acquittance for the trust administration and accounts to date, and the fact that he gave it in consideration of the legal interest in the shares being vested in his mother adds nothing on this point. Nor does it, with respect, advance the matter to say, correctly, that, at the end of the day, the appellant was the absolute owner of the shares, legal and equitable. I think that she was; but that is description, not analysis. The question that is relevant for the purpose of this appeal is how she came to occupy that position; a position which, under English law, could be reached by more than one road.

Lastly, I ought, perhaps, to say that I do not myself see any analogy between the operations embraced by the oral agreement and documents and the common case of a sale of shares by an owner for whom they are held by a nominee or bare trustee. What is sold there is the shares themselves, not the owner's equitable interest. What is passed by the transfer executed by his nominee is the shares, according to the contract, without any incumbrance on the title, equitable or legal. It is, I think, a misunderstanding of the law to speak of the nominee as transferring his beneficiary's previous equitable interest to the purchaser.

For the reasons which I have given, I am in favour of allowing the appeal.

LORD JENKINS . . . It is said further that, in the present case, the disputed transfer transferred nothing beyond a bare legal estate, because, in accordance with the well-settled principle applicable to contracts of sale between contract and completion, the appellant became under the oral agreement beneficially entitled in equity to the settled shares, subject to the due satisfaction by her of the purchase consideration, and, accordingly, the entire beneficial interest in the settled shares had already passed to her at the time of the execution of the disputed transfer, and there was nothing left on which the disputed transfer could operate except the bare legal estate.

The Commissioners of Inland Revenue seek to meet this argument by reference to s. 53(1)(c) of the Law of Property Act 1925. They contend that, as the agreement of 18 June 1956, was an oral agreement, it could not, in view of s. 53(1)(c), effect a disposition of a subsisting equitable interest or trust, and, accordingly, that Peter's subsisting equitable interest under the trusts of the settlement, in the shape of his reversionary interest, remained vested in him until the execution of the disputed transfer, which, in these circumstances, operated as a transfer on sale to the appellant of Peter's reversionary interest and additionally as a transfer not on sale to the appellant of the legal interest in the settled shares. It was by this process of reasoning that the commissioners arrived at the opinion expressed in the Case Stated that the disputed transfer attracted both the ad valorem duty exigible on a transfer on sale of the reversionary interest and also the fixed duty of 10s. This argument is attacked on the appellant's side by reference to s. 53(2) of the Act of 1925, which excludes the creation or operation of resulting, implied or constructive trusts from the provisions of s. 53(1). It is said that, inasmuch as the oral agreement was an agreement of sale and purchase, it gave rise, on the principle to which I have already adverted, to a constructive trust of the reversionary interest in favour of the appellant subject to performance by her of her obligation to transfer to Peter the free shares forming the consideration for the sale. It is said that this trust, being constructive, was untouched by s. 53(1)(c) in view of the exemption afforded by s. 53(2), and that the appellant's primary argument still holds good.

I find it unnecessary to decide whether s. 53(2) has the effect of excluding the present transaction from the operation of s. 53(1)(c), for, assuming in the appellant's favour that the oral contract did have the effect in equity of raising a constructive trust of the settled shares for her untouched by s. 53(1)(c), I am unable to accept the conclusion that the disputed transfer was prevented from being a transfer of the shares to the appellant on sale because the entire beneficial interest in the settled shares was already vested in the appellant under the constructive trust, and there was, accordingly, nothing left for the disputed transfer to pass to the appellant except the bare legal estate. The constructive trust in favour of a purchaser which arises on the conclusion of a contract for sale is founded on the purchaser's right to enforce the contract in proceedings for specific performance. In other words, he is treated in equity as entitled by virtue of the contract to the property which the vendor is bound under the contract to convey to him. This interest under the contract is, no doubt, a proprietary interest of a sort, which arises, so to speak, in anticipation of the execution of the transfer for which the purchaser is entitled to call. But its existence has never (so far as I know) been held to prevent a subsequent transfer, in performance of the contract, of the property contracted to be sold from constituting for stamp duty purposes a transfer on sale of the property in question. Take the simple case of a contract for the sale of land. In such a case, a constructive trust in favour of the purchaser arises on the conclusion of the contract for sale, but (so far as I know) it has never been held on this account that a conveyance subsequently executed in performance of the contract is not stampable ad valorem as a transfer on sale. Similarly, in a case like the present one, but uncomplicated by the existence of successive interests, a transfer to a purchaser of the investments comprised in a trust fund could not, in my judgment, be prevented from constituting a transfer on sale for the purposes of stamp duty by reason of the fact that the actual transfer had been preceded by an oral agreement for sale.

In truth, the title secured by a purchaser by means of an actual transfer is different in kind from, and may well be far superior to, the special form of proprietary interest which equity confers on a purchaser in anticipation of such transfer. This difference is of particular importance in the case of property such as shares in a limited company. Under the contract, the purchaser is, no doubt, entitled in equity as between himself and the vendor to the beneficial interest in the shares, and (subject to due payment of the purchase consideration) to call for a transfer of them from the vendor as trustee for him. But it is only on the execution of the actual transfer that he becomes entitled to be registered as a member, to attend and vote at meetings, to effect transfers on the register, or to receive dividends otherwise than through the vendor as his trustee.

The parties to a transaction of sale and purchase may, no doubt, choose to let the matter rest in contract. But if the subject-matter of a sale is such that the full title to it can only be transferred by an instrument, then any instrument they execute by way of transfer of the property sold ranks for stamp duty purposes as a conveyance on sale, notwithstanding the constructive trust in favour of the purchaser which arose on the conclusion of the contract. . . .

NEVILLE v *WILSON* [1996] 3 WLR 460, HL

FACTS: Until his death in 1958, N carried on a business through his family company, N Ltd. Shortly before N's death N Ltd acquired all the issued share capital of U Ltd. As a result of subsequent arrangements 120 shares in U Ltd were held by nominees for N Ltd, and N Ltd became the registered holder of the remaining shares in U Ltd. In 1969 the shareholders in N Ltd orally agreed the informal liquidation of N Ltd and its liabilities were discharged and the balance of its assets distributed to its shareholders. After 1969 N Ltd was struck off the register and dissolved. The business of U Ltd thereafter continued on a profitable basis. In 1985 the shareholders fell out and by 1989 U Ltd's business assets had been sold leaving it with only cash assets. The plaintiffs, two of N's children who had been shareholders in N Ltd, commenced proceedings against the defendants, all of whom had been shareholders in N Ltd, to determine, inter alia, the beneficial ownership of the 120 shares in U Ltd held by nominees. The judge held that the beneficial ownership of those shares had vested in the Crown as bona vacantia on the dissolution of N Ltd. The plaintiffs appealed.

HELD: Allowing the appeal, that the 1969 agreement had involved the division of N Ltd's equitable interest in the 120 shares among the shareholders in N Ltd in proportion to their existing shareholdings in N Ltd; that the effect of each shareholder's agreement to the liquidation was to constitute him an implied or constructive trustee for the other shareholders, so that s. 53(2) of the Law of Property Act 1925 applied to dispense with the requirement of s. 53 (1)(c) of that Act that a disposition of an equitable interest should be in writing signed by the person making the disposal; and that, accordingly, the 1969 agreement was effective, with the result that N Ltd's equitable interest in the 120 shares in U Ltd had not vested in the Crown as bona vacantia when N Ltd had been struck off the register and the cash representing those shares was to be divided proportionately between the plaintiffs and the defendants.

NOURSE LJ: . . . The substantial questions now in issue are whether there was an agreement for the informal liquidation of the company and, if so, whether it had the effect of disposing of the company's equitable interest in the shares of another company. The latter question involves a consideration of s. 53(1)(c) and (2) of the Law of Property Act 1925 and a point left open by the House of Lords in *Oughtred* v *Inland Revenue Commissioners* [1960] AC 206. . . .

[Having considered the facts Nourse LJ proceeded on the basis that in about April 1969 the shareholders of N Ltd agreed to the informal liquidation of N Ltd and the division of N Ltd's equitable interest in the 120 ordinary shares in U Ltd amongst themselves in proportions corresponding to their existing shareholdings.]

The effect of the agreement, more closely analysed, was that each shareholder agreed to assign his interest in the other shares of N Ltd's equitable interest in exchange for the assignment by the other shareholders of their interests in his own aliquot share. Each individual agreement having been a disposition of a subsisting equitable interest not made in writing, there then arises the question whether it was rendered ineffectual by s. 53 of the Law of Property Act 1925 . . .

> (1)   Subject to the provisions hereinafter contained with respect to the creation of interests in land by parol . . . (c) a disposition of an equitable interest or trust subsisting at the time of the disposition, must be in writing signed by the person disposing of the same, or by his agent thereunto lawfully authorised in writing or by will. (2) This section does not affect the creation or operation of resulting, implied or constructive trusts.

Those provisions have been considered in a number of authoritative decisions starting with *Grey* v *Inland Revenue Commissioners* [1960] AC 1 and *Oughtred* v *Inland Revenue Commissioners* [1960] AC 206. Mr Jacob relied on *In re Vandervell's Trusts (No. 2)* [1974] Ch 269; *Oughtred* v *Inland Revenue Commissioners* [1960] AC 206 and *Vandervell* v *Inland Revenue Commissioners* [1967] 2 AC 291. In the *Vandervell* cases the facts were materially different and neither is of assistance here. The question depends on the correct view of a point left open in *Oughred* v *Inland Revenue Commissioners* [1960] AC 206. . . .

The views of their Lordships [in *Oughtred*] as to the effect of s. 53 can be summarised as follows. Lord Radcliffe, agreeing with Upjohn J, thought that subsection (2) applied. He gave reasons for that view. Lord Cohen and Lord Denning thought that it did not. Although neither of them gave reasons, they may be taken to have accepted the submissions of Mr Wilberforce at pp. 220–222. Lord Keith and Lord Jenkins expressed no view either way. We should add that when the case was in this court Lord Evershed MR, in delivering the judgment of himself, Morris and Ormerod LJJ, said [1958] Ch 678, 687:

> In this court the case for the Crown has, we think, been somewhat differently presented, and in the end of all, the question under section 53 of the Law of Property Act 1925, does not, in our judgment, strictly call for a decision. We are not, however, with all respect to the judge, prepared to accept, as we understand it, his conclusion upon the effect of s. 53 of the Law of Property Act 1925.

The basis of this court's decision was the same as that adopted by the majority of the House of Lords. . . .

So far as it is material to the present case, what subsection (2) says is that subsection (1)(c) does not affect the creation or operation of implied or constructive trusts. Just as in *Oughtred* v *Inland Revenue Commissioners* [1969] AC 206 the son's oral agreement created a constructive trust in favour of the mother, so here each shareholder's oral or implied agreement created an implied or constructive trust in favour of the other shareholders. Why then should subsection (2) not apply? No convincing reason was suggested in argument and none has occurred to us since. Moreover, to deny its application in this case would be to restrict the effect of general words when no restriction is called for, and to lay the ground for fine distinctions in the future. With all the respect which is due to those who have thought to the contrary, we hold that subsection (2) applies to an agreement such as we have in this case.

For these reasons we have come to the conclusion that the agreement entered into by the shareholders of [N Ltd] in about April 1969 was not rendered ineffectual by s. 53 of the Act of 1925. The plaintiffs' alternative claim succeeds and they are entitled to relief accordingly. That means that [N Ltd's] equitable interest in the 120 shares did not vest in the Crown as bona vacantia in 1970. Taking into account the dispositions of the testator's will, we calculate the result to be that the cash now representing the 120 shares will be divided in the global proportions 77.33 to the plaintiffs and 42.66 to the defendants. In that connection we should record that the defendants resisted the appeal because, as we understand it, they preferred their chances of persuading the Crown to disclaim its interest in their favour to the certainty of obtaining a smaller but nevertheless substantial interest if the appeal succeeded. As to the wisdom of that course, we express no view.

On grounds not argued before Morritt J, the appeal is allowed.

3.2.2 TESTAMENTARY TRUSTS

GOODCHILD v *GOODCHILD*, The Times, 12 May 1997, CA

FACTS: A husband and wife executed their wills simultaneously and in identical form in favour of the survivor of them and thereafter to their son. The wife died in 1991, and in accordance with their wills, the husband received her estate. The husband remarried in 1992 and executed a new will leaving everything to his new wife. The husband died in 1993. The son and his wife claimed financial provision from the estate.
HELD: The doctrine of mutual wills required a clear contract between the two testators that the wills would not be revoked and would remain unaltered. There was no reason to import into that doctrine the lesser requirements applicable to the creation of secret and constructive trusts.

Where the evidence showed a failure to make a clear agreement for mutual wills, but the first testator's understanding of the effect of her will was such as to impose on the second testator, free as he was of any legal obligation, a moral obligation to give effect to what the first testator believed they mutually intended, namely to leave their estates to their son, the court could award financial provision for the son's maintenance under the Inheritance (Provision for Family and Dependants) Act 1975.

LEGGATT LJ: said that the judge had held that the identical wills of Joan and Dennis were not mutual wills as there was no clear agreement that they were to be mutually binding.

He had nevertheless allowed a claim by their son, Gary, on Dennis's estate under section 2 of the 1975 Act on the basis that Joan's mistaken belief that the terms of the wills were mutually binding imposed a moral obligation on Dennis which was a special circumstance exceptional enough to justify the claim.

The plaintiffs' case was that it was sufficient to show a common understanding between the testators at the time the wills were executed: Mr Gordon drew an analogy with secret trusts where equity would not permit property transferred to another on the faith of such understanding to be dealt with differently from that understanding: see *In re Cleaver, dec'd* [1981] 1 WLR 939, 947 and *Ottaway v Norman* [1972] Ch 698, 711.

Furthermore, the taking of benefit on the strength of binding agreement sufficed to create a constructive trust: see *In re Dale, dec'd* [1994] Ch 31 and the cases cited there.

His Lordship said that those submissions foundered at the same point; as was put in argument by Lord Justice Morritt, the reason why if mutual wills were to take effect an agreement was necessary, was that without it the property of the second testator was not bound, whereas a secret trust concerned only the property of a person in the position of the first testator.

For the doctrine to apply there had to be a contract at law: see *Dale* (at p. 38) and the cases cited there. In *Cleaver* there was specific evidence as to the testators' mutual intentions at the time the wills were made, not so in the present case.

Even if a binding agreement were not required, it would still be necessary to prove that both testators intended not merely that Gary should be the ultimate beneficiary but that the survivor should not prevent that happening if he or she thought fit.

There was no presumption that a present plan would be immutable in future. A key feature of the concept of mutual wills was the irrevocability of the mutual intentions.

Not only had they to be binding when made, but the testators had to have undertaken, and so had to be bound, not to change their intentions after the death of the first testator.

Although when Dennis and Joan executed their wills they wanted Gary to inherit the combined estates, there was no express agreement not to revoke the wills; nor could any such agreement be implied from the fact the survivor was in a position to leave both estates to Gary.

What was required was a mutual intention that both wills should remain unaltered and that the survivor should be bound to leave the combined estates to the son.

The judge was entitled from the evidence to decline to infer any agreement between Dennis and Joan that would prevent the survivor of them from interfering with the succession.

As regards the claim under the 1975 Act, Mr Sunnucks contended, inter alia, no provision should have been made for Gary as he was capable of earning his own living; that there was no special circumstances in the case to justify any moral claim and that the judge below showed confusion between the principles of family provisions and those relating to mutual wills. He replied on *In re Coventry, dec'd* [1980] Ch 46.

His Lordship disagreed. The principles by which the court proceeded were clear. There was in the present case the plainest possible basis for concluding that, whereas Dennis and Joan had not made a clear agreement for mutual wills, none the less Joan's understanding of the effect of her will was such as to impose on Dennis a moral obligation, once Gary's need for reasonable financial provision was established.

The judge concluded Gary was barely able to meet his financial requirements. The appraisal of all the circumstances was for the judge.

He had properly directed himself and was not shown to have erred in principle or even to have reached a conclusion that was surprising or untoward. The judgment was not only sensible: it was unimpeachable.

RE DALE [1994] Ch 31, ChD

FACTS: In 1988 a husband and wife each executed identical wills in favour of the testators' daughter and son, in equal shares or the survivor of them.

On the issue whether for the doctrine of mutual wills to apply it was necessary for the second testator to die to have obtained a personal financial benefit under the will of the first testator to die.

HELD: That the application of the doctrine of mutual wills required the parties to have entered into a legally binding contract to make and not to revoke mutual wills and that the first testator to die had performed his part of the agreement; that, since the aim of the principle underlying the doctrine was to prevent fraud on the first testator to die, it was not confined to cases in which the surviving testator had benefited under the will of the first testator to die but extended also to cases where the two testators had left their property to beneficiaries other than themselves; and that, accordingly, the preliminary issue would be answered in the negative.

MORRITT J: . . . For the defendant it is submitted that it is essential that the will of each testator should bequeath to the other a direct personal and financial benefit either absolutely or for life. The defendant contends that this submission is right in principle because the agreement between the testators must amount to a contract at law and without such a benefit there would be no consideration sufficient to support a contract. The submission is further justified, it is argued, on the ground that even if there is sufficient consideration to support a contract at law the implied or constructive trust in respect of the second testator's own property can only arise if the agreement is specifically enforceable at the suit of the personal representatives of the first testator. It is submitted that mutual benefit is essential for that purpose too because otherwise the contract lacks mutuality and sufficient consideration. It is contended that in all the reported cases in which the doctrine has been applied there has been such mutual benefit. Finally, it is submitted, the ratio decidendi of *Dufour* v *Pereira* (1769) 1 Dick 419, both as expressed in that case and as applied in subsequent reported cases, requires that such mutual benefit should exist.

For the plaintiff it is submitted that it is not necessary for there to be a contract at law, but if it is there is sufficient consideration and case for specific performance at the suit of the personal representatives of the first testator even in the absence of mutual benefit. It is contended that this submission is supported by authority, both affirmatively and negatively in that there is no reported case which states that such mutual benefit is not only a sufficient but a necessary condition for the doctrine to apply.

I propose to deal with the submissions for the defendant in the order in which I have described them. There is no doubt that for the doctrine to apply there must be a contract at law. It is apparent from all the cases to which I shall refer later, but in particular from *Gray* v *Perpetual Trustee Co. Ltd* [1928] AC 391, that it is necessary to establish an agreement to make and not revoke mutual wills, some understanding or arrangement being insuffient—'without such a definite agreement there can no more be a trust in equity than a right to damages at law:' see *per* Viscount Haldane, at p. 400. Thus, as the defendant submitted, it is necessary to find consideration sufficient to support a contract at law. The defendant accepted that such consideration may be executory if the promise when performed would confer a benefit on the promisee or constitute a detriment to the promisor. But, it was submitted, the promise to make and not revoke a mutual will could not constitute a detriment to the first testator because he would be leaving his property in the way that he wished and because he would be able, on giving notice to the second testator, to revoke his will and make another if he changed his mind. Accordingly, it was argued, consideration for the contract had to take the form of a benefit to the second testator.

I do not accept this submission. It is to be assumed that the first testator and the second testator had agreed to make and not to revoke the mutual wills in question. The performance of that promise by the execution of the will by the first testator is in my judgment sufficient consideration by itself. But, in addition, to determine whether a promise can constitute consideration it is necessary to consider whether its performance would have been so regarded: cf. *Chitty on Contracts*, 26th ed. (1989), vol. 1, p. 160, para. 161. Thus it is to be assumed that the first testator did not revoke the mutual will notwithstanding his legal right to do so. In my judgment, this too is sufficient detriment to the first testator to constitute consideration. Thus mutual benefit is not necessary for the purpose of the requisite contract. What is necessary to obtain a decree of specific performance of a contract in favour of a third party is not, in my judgment, a relevant question when considering the doctrine of mutual wills. A will is by its very nature revocable: cf. *In the Estate of Heys, decd; Walker* v *Gaskill* [1914] P 192. It seems to me to be inconceivable that the court would order the second testator to execute a will in accordance with the agreement at the suit of the personal representatives of the first testator or to grant an injunction restraining the second testator from revoking it. The principles on which the court acts in imposing the trust to give effect to the agreement to make and not revoke mutual wills must be found in the cases dealing with that topic, not with those dealing with the availability of the remedy of specific performance. . . .

3.2.3 SECRET TRUSTS

3.2.3.1 Fully secret trusts

RE BOYES (1884) 26 ChD 531, ChD

FACTS: B made an absolute gift to his executor by his will. The executor accepted that he was to hold the gift on trust for other persons, but the names of those persons were not communicated to the executor during B's lifetime. Only after B's death were informal letters found which detailed the intended objects of the gift.
HELD: This was not a valid fully secret trust. To be valid the precise objects of the trust must have been communicated, and the trust accepted, during the testator's lifetime. However, if B had placed a sealed envelope of detailed instructions into the executor's hands before B's death, this would have constituted constructive notice of the trusts to the executor, and the executor would have been deemed to have accepted the trusts as detailed in the letter.

KAY J: . . . There is another well-known class of cases where no trust appears on the face of the will, but the testator has been induced to make the will, or, having made it, has been induced not to revoke it by a promise on the part of the devisee or legatee to deal with the property, or some part of it in a specified manner. In these cases the Court has compelled discovery and performance of the promise, treating it as a trust binding the conscience of the donee, on the ground that otherwise a fraud would be committed, because it is to be presumed that if it had not been for such promise the testator would not have made or would have revoked the gift [but] no case has ever yet decided that a testator can by imposing a trust upon his devisee or legatee, the objects of which he does not communicate to him, enable himself to evade the *Statute of Wills* by declaring those objects in an unattested paper found after his death. . . .

I cannot help regretting that the testator's intention of bounty should fail by reason of an informality of this kind, but in my opinion it would be a serious innovation upon the law relating to testamentary instruments if this were to be established as a trust in her favour. . . .

RE KEEN [1937] 1 Ch 236

FACTS: K, the testator left £10,000 in his will to his friends, H and E, 'to be held upon trust and disposed of by them among such person, persons or charities as may be notified by me to them' . . . 'during my lifetime'. In advance of the execution of his will K handed a sealed envelope to E. The envelope contained the name of a lady to whom K had not been married. E was aware of the contents of the envelope but did not actually open it until after K's death.
HELD: This was not a valid half-secret trust. The communication via the envelope had preceded the execution of the will and was inconsistent with the terms of the will, the will would therefore take effect as read and the legacy would fall into residue. Further, the clause in K's will purported to reserve to K the power to make future testamentary dispositions by simply notifying the trustees during his lifetime of his intentions. The intended effect of the clause, therefore, was to exclude the requirement of the Wills Act that a duly executed codicil be used to amend a will. The clause would not be permitted to have that effect and must fail.

LORD WRIGHT MR: . . . The summons came before Farwell J, who decided adversely to the claims of the lady on the short ground that she could not prove that she was a person notified to the trustees by the testator during his lifetime within the words of clause 5. His opinion seems to be that the clause required the name and identity of the lady to be expressly disclosed to the trustees during the testator's lifetime so that it was not sufficient to place these particulars in the physical possession of the trustees or one of them in the form of a memorandum which they were not to read till the testator's death.

I am unable to accept this conclusion, which appears to me to put too narrow a construction on the word 'notified' as used in clause 5 in all the circumstances of the case. To take a parallel, a ship which sails under sealed orders, is sailing under orders though the exact terms are not ascertained by the captain till later. I note that the case of a trust put into writing which is placed in the trustees' hands in a sealed envelope, was hypothetically treated by Kay J as possibly constituting a communication in a case of this nature: *In re Boyes* (1884) 26 ChD 531. This, so far as it goes, seems to support my conclusion. The trustees had the means of knowledge available whenever it became necessary and proper to open the envelope. I think Mr Evershed was right in understanding that the giving of the sealed envelope was a notification within clause 5.

This makes it necessary to examine the matter on a wider basis, and to consider the principles of law which were argued both before Farwell J and this Court, but which the judge found it merely necessary to mention.

. . . The principles of law or equity relevant in a question of this nature have now been authoritatively settled or discussed.

OTTAWAY v NORMAN [1972] Ch 698

FACTS: By his will H left his bungalow to his housekeeper together with a legacy of £1,500 and half the residue of his estate. On her death the housekeeper left her property to strangers. O sued her executor, N, alleging that the housekeeper had orally agreed with H to leave the various assets to O in her will.

HELD: There had been an arrangement between H and the housekeeper under which the latter had agreed to pass on the bungalow, furnishings and fixtures to O. It followed that N now held the bungalow under a constructive trust for the benefit of O. The essential elements which had to be proved were (1) the intention of H to subject the housekeeper to an obligation in favour of O; (2) communication of that intention to the housekeeper; and (3) the acceptance of that obligation by her either expressly or by acquiescence. It was immaterial whether the informal agreement had come before or after the execution of the will. Nor was it necessary to show that the housekeeper had committed a deliberate and conscious wrong. However, Brightman J did hold that clear evidence would be needed before the court would assume that the testator had not meant what he said in his will and that the standard of proof was analogous to that required before a court would rectify a written instrument.

BRIGHTMAN J: . . . I will deal first with the main principles of law before I seek to assess the value of the evidence. The general principle can, for present purposes, be sufficiently explained by reference to two cases. In *Re Gardner, Huey v Cunnington* [1920] 2 Ch 523, a testatrix had given all her estate to her husband for his use and benefit during his life 'knowing that he will carry out my wishes'. Four days later she signed a memorandum expressing the wish that what she described as 'the money I leave to my husband' should on his death be equally divided among certain named beneficiaries. She died in 1919 possessed of personal estate only, and her husband died four days later. After his death his wife's will and the memorandum were found in his safe, and there was parol evidence that shortly after the execution of the will the testatrix had said in his presence that her property after his death was to be equally divided between the named beneficiaries, and that he assented thereto. It was held—

that the husband, who took jure mariti the corpus of his wife's estate for his own benefit, could not properly refuse to carry into effect her wishes as to the disposition of the property after his death, expressed to him by her before her death, and assented to by him. He therefore held the corpus, subject to his life interest, as a trustee for the beneficiaries named in the memorandum.

It will be observed from the terms of the will that the testatrix gave her husband an express life interest leaving the reversion expectant thereon undisposed of.

Lord Sterndale MR said:

> The obligation upon the husband and his next of kin seems to me to arise from this, that he takes the property in accordance with and upon an undertaking to abide by the wishes of the testatrix, and if he were to dispose of it in any other way he would be committing a breach of trust, or as it has been called in some of the cases a fraud. I do not think it matters which you call it. The breach of trust or the fraud would arise when he attempted to deal with the money contrary to the terms on which he took it.

Warrington LJ said:

> The question is really this: Can the husband, who, as a result of the particular form in which the testamentary disposition of the wife is made, takes at law for his own benefit the corpus of her personal estate, properly refuse to carry into effect a wish as to the disposition of that property expressed to him by the wife before her death and assented to and accepted by him? The principle upon which the jurisdiction of the court is based is stated, in extremely clear language, by Lord Davey in *French* v *French*. 'The basis of the jurisdiction'—that is the jurisdiction to which I have referred—'is of course that the testator has died, leaving the property by his will in a particular manner on the faith and in reliance upon an express or implied promise by the legatee to fulfil his wishes, and your Lordships will at once see that it makes no difference whatever whether the will be made before the communication to the legatee or afterwards, because, as was said, I think, by Vice-Chancellor Turner in one of the cases which were cited, the presumption is that the testator would have revoked his will and made another disposition if he had not relied upon the promise, express or implied, made by the legatee to fulfil his wishes'.

The second case is *Blackwell* v *Blackwell* [see **3.2.3.2**] . . .

> It will be convenient to call the person on whom such a trust is imposed the 'primary donee' and the beneficiary under that trust the 'secondary donee'. The essential elements which must be proved to exist are: (i) the intention of the testator to subject the primary donee to an obligation in favour of the secondary donee; (ii) communication of that intention to the primary donee; and (iii) the acceptance of that obligation by the primary donee either expressly or by acquiescence. It is immaterial whether these elements precede or succeed the will of the donor. I am informed that there is no recent reported case where the obligation imposed on the primary donee is an obligation to make a will in favour of the secondary donee as distinct from some form of inter vivos transfer. But it does not seem to me that that can really be a distinction which can validly be drawn on behalf of the defendant in the present case. The basis of the doctrine of a secret trust is the obligation imposed on the conscience of the primary donee and it does not seem to me that there is any materiality in the machinery by which the donee intends that that obligation shall be carried out. . . .

RE SNOWDEN [1979] 1 Ch 528

FACTS: By her will dated 10 January 1974, she gave the residue of her estate to her two executors and trustees to hold for her brother absolutely. The brother died six days after the testatrix, on 22 January 1974, having by his will made his son, the first defendant, his executor and sole residuary beneficiary:

The will of the testatrix was made in the following circumstances. First, an attendance note of 30 August 1973, by S, her solicitor and executor, recorded that she was not clear how best to deal with things but thought the easiest way was to leave legacies to nephews and nieces 'leaving it to [her brother] to split up the remainder as he thought best'. Second, on the morning of 10 January 1974, her brother, after speaking to the testatrix, gave S instructions over the telephone which appeared to have been carried out in the will as drafted. The brother further said that as S knew 'she wants me [her brother] to deal with the final division for her'. Third, on the afternoon of 10 January 1974, the will was executed in the presence of two witnesses. S was unable to be present.

She was asked whether she wanted the bulk of her estate to go to her brother instead of to a niece and she said 'yes'. The statement by S of February 1974 recorded that she had wanted 'to be fair to everyone', dwelling on what her brother had done for her and wanting the residue to be left to her brother to 'look after the division for her'.

On a summons by S to determine whether the estate of the testatrix was held on trust for the brother's son absolutely the question arose whether the gift of residue to the brother was subject to a secret trust.

HELD: (1) That in order to establish a secret trust where no question of fraud arose the standard of proof was no more than the ordinary civil standard of proof required for the establishment of an ordinary trust.

(2) That there was insufficient evidence to show that the testatrix intended to bind her brother by any legally enforceable trust as to the disposition of residue, and that there was no more than a moral obligation imposed on him to distribute it as she herself might have done; accordingly he, and through him the first defendant, took the residue free from any secret trust.

SIR ROBERT MEGARRY V-C: This originating summons raises a question of the standard of evidence that is required to establish a secret trust; and this is a subject which has its difficulties. . . .

Now it seems perfectly clear that the will was executed by the testatrix on the basis of some arrangement that was made between her and her brother regarding the gift of residue to him. The question is what that arrangement was. In particular, did it impose a trust, or did it amount to a mere moral or family obligation? If it was a trust, what were the terms of that trust? Although these questions are distinct, they are obviously interrelated to some degree. The more uncertain the terms of the obligation, the more likely it is to be a moral obligation rather than a trust: many a moral obligation is far too indefinite to be enforceable as a trust. As Sir Arthur Hobhouse said in a somewhat different case, *Mussoorie Bank Ltd* v *Raynore* (1882) 7 App. Cas 321, 331, uncertainty in the subject of the gift 'has a reflex action upon the previous words', throwing doubt on the testator's intention, and seeming to show that he could not have intended his words to be imperative words.

I cannot say that there is no evidence from which it could be inferred that a secret trust was created. At the same time, that evidence is far from being overwhelming. One question that arises is thus whether the standard of proof required to establish a secret trust is merely the ordinary civil standard of proof, or whether it is a higher and more cogent standard. If it is the latter, I feel no doubt that the claim that there is a secret trust must fail. On this question, *Ottaway* v *Norman* [1972] Ch 698 was cited; it was, indeed, the only authority that was put before me. According to the headnote, the standard of proof 'was not an exceptionally high one but was analogous to that required before the court would rectify a written instrument.' When one turns to the judgment, one finds that what Brightman J said, at p. 712, was that Lord Westbury's words in *McCormick* v *Grogan* (1869) LR 4 HL, 82, 97, a case on secret trusts, did not mean that an exceptionally high standard of proof was needed, but meant no more than that:

> if a will contains a gift which is in terms absolute, clear evidence is needed before the court will assume that the testator did not mean what he said. It is perhaps analogous to the standard of proof which this court requires before it will rectify a written instrument, for there again a party is saying that neither meant what they have written.

On this, I would make four comments. First, the headnote seems to me to be liable to mislead, since it omits the judge's precautionary word 'perhaps' which preceded 'analogous', and so gives a firmness to the proposition which the judge avoided. Second, the standard for rectification is indeed high, and certainly higher than the ordinary standards. Lord Thurlow's requirement of 'strong irrefragable evidence' (*Countess of Shelburne* v *Earl of Inchiquin* (1784) 1 Bro CC 338, 341) no longer holds the field, to the relief of those who find in the second word problems both of pronunciation and of meaning. But there is high authority for saying that there must be evidence 'of the clearest and most satisfactory description' (*Fowler* v *Fowler* (1859) 4 De G & J 250, 264, *per* Lord Chelmsford LC which will establish the mistake with a 'high degree of conviction'

(*Crane* v *Hegeman-Harris Co. Inc.* [1939] 4 All ER 68, 71, *per* Sir Wilfrid Greene MR) and will 'leave no fair and reasonable doubt upon the mind that the deed does not embody the final intention of the parties', (*Fowler* v *Fowler* 4 De G & J 250, 265, *per* Lord Chelmsford LC). What is required is 'convincing proof' (*Joscelyne* v *Nissen* [1970] 2 QB 86, 98, *per* Russell LJ in delivering the judgment of the Court of Appeal). I feel some uncertainty about the difference between these terms and the 'exceptionally high standard of evidence' which Brightman J rejected; perhaps it lies in the word 'exceptionally'.

Third, I feel some doubt about how far rectification is a fair analogy to secret trusts in this respect. Many cases of rectification do of course involve a party in saying that neither meant what they have written, and requiring that what they have written should be altered. On the other hand, the whole basis of secret trusts, as I understand it, is that they operate outside the will, changing nothing that is written in it, and allowing it to operate according to its tenor, but then fastening a trust on to the property in the hands of the recipient. It is at least possible that very different standards of proof may be appropriate for cases where the words of a formal document have to be altered and for cases where there is no such alteration but merely a question whether, when the document has been given effect to, there will be some trust of the property with which it dealt. Fourth, I am not sure that it is right to assume that there is a single, uniform standard of proof for all secret trusts. The proposition of Lord Westbury in *McCormick* v *Grogan* LR 4 HL 82, 97 with which Brightman J was pressed in *Ottaway* v *Norman* [1972] Ch 698 was that the jurisdiction in cases of secret trust was

> founded altogether on personal fraud. It is a jurisdiction by which a Court of Equity, proceeding on the ground of fraud, converts the party who has committed it into a trustee for the party who is injured by that fraud. Now, being a jurisdiction founded on personal fraud, it is incumbent on the court to see that a fraud, a malus animus, is proved by the clearest and most indisputable evidence.

Of that, it is right to say that the law on the subject has not stood still since 1869, and that it is now clear that secret trusts may be established in cases where there is no possibility of fraud. *McCormick* v *Grogan* LR 4 HL 82 has to be read in the light both of earlier cases that were not cited, and also of subsequent cases, in particular *Blackwell* v *Blackwell* [1929] AC 318. It seems to me that fraud comes into the matter in two ways. First, it provides an historical explanation of the doctrine of secret trusts: the doctrine was evolved as a means of preventing fraud. That, however, does not mean that fraud is an essential ingredient for the application of the doctrine: the reason for the rule is not part of the rule itself. Second, there are some cases within the doctrine where fraud is indeed involved. There are cases where for the legatee to assert that he is a beneficial owner, free from any trust, would be a fraud on his part.

It is to this latter aspect of fraud that it seems to me that Lord Westbury's words are applicable. If a secret trust can be held to exist in a particular case only by holding the legatee guilty of fraud, then no secret trust should be found unless the standard of proof suffices for fraud. On the other hand, if there is no question of fraud, why should so high a standard apply? In such a case, I find it difficult to see why the mere fact that the historical origin of the doctrine lay in the prevention of fraud should impose the high standard of proof for fraud in a case in which no issue of fraud arises. In accordance with the general rule of evidence, the standard of proof should vary with the nature of the issue and its gravity: see *Hornal* v *Neuberger Products Ltd* [1957] 1 QB 247. . . .

3.2.3.2 Half-secret trusts

BLACKWELL v *BLACKWELL* [1929] AC 318, HL

FACTS: The testator, B, left a legacy of £12,000 to five persons by a codicil to his will, and directed them to apply the income 'for the purposes indicated by me to them', with power to apply two-thirds of the capital 'to such person or persons indicated by me to them'. The beneficiaries of the trusts (a mistress and her illegitimate son) were communicated orally by B to the intended trustees, with detailed instructions being given to one of the intended trustees. The intended trustees accepted the trusts before the intended trustees. The intended trustees accepted the trusts before the execution of the codicil. B's widow challenged the validity of the half-secret trust and claimed the £12,000 for herself.

HELD: The evidence of the oral arrangement was admissible and proved a valid half-secret trust in favour of B's mistress and illegitimate son. Viscount Sumner saw no relevant distinction between fully secret and half-secret trusts. 'In both cases', he observed, 'the testator's wishes are incompletely expressed in his will. Why should equity, over a mere matter of words, give effect to them in one case and frustrate them in the other?' For his lordship the 'fraud' to be prevented was the same in both cases.

VISCOUNT SUMNER: . . . In the authorities it has been common to classify these cases according as the terms of the will make the gift in question absolute or fiduciary. If it is by force of the words of the will that the residuary legatee takes what is given in trust without any specification of the trust, then parol evidence to show what that trust is would contradict the written will. Accordingly the crucial point is whether or not it is the will itself that gives this fund to the residuary legatee in such a case. Now s. 9 of the Wills Act prescribes the form, in which any disposition in a will must be testified, if it is to be valid, but it does not deal with the construction of wills, or the application of the general law of trusts to interests created by wills. It is one thing to say that in itself the trust cannot be given effect to, not being expressed in the will, but it is quite another to say that, when for this reason the trust fails, the will gives the fund to the legatee in trust for the residuary legatee, as if the document, signed and witnessed, had said so in words. The question appears to be whether the resulting trust in favour of the named residuary legatee in such a case arises as part of the will or only as the result of the application of equitable doctrines to a portion of the testator's estate, which in the circumstances of the will has not been consistently disposed of. . . .

I think the conclusion is confirmed, which the frame of s. 9 of the Wills Act seems to me to carry on its face, that the legislation did not purport to interfere with the exercise of a general equitable jurisdiction, even in connection with secret dispositions of a testator, except in so far as reinforcement of the formalities required for a valid will might indirectly limit it. The effect, therefore, of a bequest being made in terms on trust, without any statement in the will to show what the trust is, remains to be decided by the law as laid down by the courts before and since the Act and does not depend on the Act itself.

The limits, beyond which the rules as to unspecified trusts must not be carried, have often been discussed. A testator cannot reserve to himself a power of making future unwitnessed dispositions by merely naming a trustee and leaving the purposes of the trust to be supplied afterwards, nor can a legatee give testamentary validity to an unexecuted codicil by accepting an indefinite trust, never communicated to him in the testator's lifetime: *In re Boyes*. To hold otherwise would indeed be to enable the testator to 'give the go-by' to the requirements of the Wills Act, because he did not choose to comply with them. It is communication of the purpose to the legatee, coupled with acquiescence or promise on his part, that removes the matter from the provision of the Wills Act and brings it within the law of trusts, as applied in this instance to trustees, who happen also to be legatees. If I am right in thinking that there is no contradiction of the Wills Act in applying the same rule, whether the trustee is or is not so described in the will, and the whole topic is detached from the enforcement of the Wills Act itself, then, whether the decisions in equity are or are not open to doubt in themselves, I think that, in view of the subject-matter of these decisions and the length of time during which they have been acquiesced in, your Lordships may well in accordance with precedent refuse to overrule them lest titles should be rendered insecure and settlements, entered into in reliance on their authority, should now be distributed. It is to be remembered that the rule as to trusts not expressed in a will is not limited to relations such as the testator in this case was concerned to provide for, but may have been applied in many other connections. I pretend to no means of knowledge of my own, but it seems to me probable that effect has been given to these cases to a substantial extent and therefore that, to avoid possible injustice, your Lordships should refuse to interfere with them now.

3.3 End of Chapter Assessment Question

Explain, with reasons, what formalities (if any) must be complied with in order to make the following actions valid and enforceable in a court of law?

(a)   Bill, the freehold owner of Whitehouse, declares that he henceforth holds the legal title to Whitehouse on trust for his son, Charlton.

(b)   Tony, the sole life beneficiary under a trust set up by his father, gives notice to the trustees that he disclaims his interest in favour of his son, to whom the trustees should henceforth pay all the income from the trust.

(c)   Rob, who died recently, left property to Patrick by his will, having previously informed Patrick that he should secretly hold the property as trustee for the benefit of Rob's mistress.

(d)   Berty is the sole beneficial owner of a number of shares held in trust for him by a trust company wholly owned and controlled by him for the last 20 years. He now decides to instruct the company to transfer the shares to his wife.

3.4 End of Chapter Assessment Outline Answer

(a)   Bill has declared himself to be trustee of freehold land for the benefit of his son. The declaration of the trust of land may be made orally, but it will not be enforceable in court unless it is 'mainfested and proved' in writing signed by Bill (or by his will (s. 53(1)(b), Law of Property Act 1925).

(b)   In contrast with (a) what we have here is not the creation of a new trust, but an *inter vivos* (life-time) dealing with an existing trust. The only relevant statutory formality requirement is s. 53(1)(c), Law of Property Act 1925 which provides that: 'a disposition of an equitable interest or trust subsisting at the time of the disposition, must be in writing'. This writing must be signed by Tony, or by an agent authorised by him in writing. In contrast with (a), where the declaration was valid, but unenforceable until manifested in writing, the disposition here is not valid at all unless *made in* writing. The reason for this formality requirement is to prevent hidden oral transactions with equitable interests under trusts.

Lord Radcliffe in *Grey* v *Inland Revenue Commissioners* [1960] AC 1 did suggest that 'there is warrant for saying that a direction to his trustee by the equitable owner of trust property prescribing new trusts of that property was a declaration of trust', but even if that were the case, his Lordship observed that the direction might nevertheless be a disposition falling within s. 53(1)(c) (and thus in need of written form) if 'the effect of it was to determine completely or *pro tanto* the subsisting equitable interest of the maker of the direction'.

(c)   Secret trusts are a means by which a testator is able to by-pass the formality requirements laid down in the Wills Act. As Dankwerts J put it in *Re Young*, 'the whole theory of the formation of a secret trust is that the Wills Act has nothing to do with the matter'. The secret trust in the instant case is said to be a fully secret trust. This is where X formally leaves property by his will to Y in circumstances where Y is informally made aware by X during X's lifetime (and Y expressly or impliedly accepts) that Y is to hold the property as trustee for the benefit of Z. On the face of the will Y will appear to be the beneficial owner of the property.

Although fully secret trusts have certain testamentary characteristics they are valid, despite lack of testamentary formalities, because the trustee accepts the trust during the settlor's lifetime. They are essentially *inter vivos* express trusts and therefore operate independently of the Wills Act 1837. Generally, the declaration of an express trust does not need to comply with any formality. However, even if the property comprised land, the secret trustee could not rely upon the lack of formality to defeat the trust. The jurisdiction to enforce a secret trust is aimed at preventing equitable fraud on the part of the alleged trustee. His conscience would bind him to carry out the trust, he would, despite the settlor's *expressed* intention to create a trust, become a *constructive* trustee. The creation and operation of constructive trusts need not comply with any formality (s. 53(2), Law of Property Act 1925).

(d)   This is a case of a bare trust, where the beneficiary has given a direction to his trustee to transfer the legal estate to some other person, the intention being that the equitable interest should pass simultaneously. This type of transaction was one of the many matters considered by the House of Lords in *Vandervell* v *IRC* [1967] 1 All ER 1.

In 1958, Mr Vandervell, the immensely wealthy controlling director and shareholder of VP Ltd, decided to give 100,000 of his shares in the company to the Royal College of Surgeons (RCS) to found a chair in pharmacology. The shares were currently held by his bank under a bare trust for him. Accordingly, V directed the bank to transfer 100,000 shares to the RCS. It was intended that the RCS should keep the shares for a limited period only, and should relinquish them after receiving £150,000 income on the shares by way of dividends.

As to whether the direction to the bank had been void for lack of written formality, the House of Lords held that s. 53(1)(c) only applied to cases where the equitable interest in property had been disposed of independently of the legal interest in that property. The object of s. 53(1)(c) was to prevent hidden oral transactions in equitable interests which might defraud other parties (such as the Inland Revenue).

In cases, such as the present, where the equitable owner had directed his bare trustee to deal with the legal and equitable estates simultaneously, s. 53(1)(c) had no application.

CHAPTER FOUR

CERTAINTY REQUIREMENTS

4.1 Introduction

KNIGHT v *KNIGHT* (1840) 3 Beav 148

LORD LANGDALE MR: . . . The principal question is, whether a trust in favour of the male descendants of Richard Knight is created by the will of the testator Richard Payne Knight.

That the testator wished that his estates, or at least, that some estates should be preserved in the male line of his grandfather, and had a reliance, or in the popular sense, a trust that the person to whom he gave his property, and those who should succeed to it, would act upon and realise that wish, admits of no doubt. He has expressed his wish and his reliance in terms which are, to that extent, sufficiently clear.

But it is not every wish or expectation which a testator may express, nor every act which he may wish his successors to do, that can or ought to be executed or enforced as a trust in this Court; and in the infinite variety of expressions which are employed, and of cases which thereupon arise, there is often the greatest difficulty in determining, whether the act desired or recommended is an act which the testator intended to be executed as a trust, or which this Court ought to deem fit to be, or capable of being enforced as such. In the construction and execution of wills, it is undoubtedly the duty of this Court to give effect to the intention of the testator whenever it can be ascertained: but in cases of this nature, and in the examination of the authorities which are to be consulted in relation to them, it is, unfortunately, necessary to make some distinction between the intention of the testator and that which the Court has deemed it to be its duty to perform; for of late years it has frequently been admitted by Judges of great eminence that, by interfering in such cases, the Court has sometimes rather made a will for the testator, than executed the testator's will according to his intention; and the observation shews the necessity of being extremely cautious in admitting any, the least, extension of the principle to be extracted from a long series of authorities, in respect of which such admissions have been made.

As a general rule, it has been laid down, that when property is given absolutely to any person, and the same person is, by the giver who has power to command, recommended, or entreated, or wished, to dispose of that property in favour of another, the recommendation, entreaty, or wish shall be held to create a trust.

First, if the words are so used, that upon the whole, they ought to be construed as imperative.

Secondly, if the subject of the recommendation or wish be certain; and,

Thirdly, if the objects or persons intended to have the benefit of the recommendation or wish be also certain.

In simple cases there is no difficuty in the application of the rule thus stated. . . .

4.2   A Question of Construction

4.2.1   THE EFFECTS OF PRECEDENT ON CONSTRUCTION

RE STEELE'S WILL TRUSTS [1948] 1 Ch 603, ChD

FACTS: S, the testatrix, left a diamond necklace to her son, to be held by him for his eldest son and so on 'as far as the rules of law and equity will permit', adding 'I request my said son to do all in his power by his will or otherwise to give effect to this my wish'. The phrasing of the gift exactly reproduced the wording of a similar gift in a previous reported case. In that case the gift had been held to be effective.

HELD: In choosing to adopt the precise wording used in a previous reported case the testatrix had made clear her intention to achieve the result which was achieved in that previous case, namely a trust binding on the son. Accordingly the wording of the present gift would take effect as a valid trust of the necklace.

WYNN-PARRY J: . . . The manner in which the modern view has evolved is, I think, simply this, that the courts have indicated that there is established in the older authorities no binding or overriding rule of construction which would disentitle one to look at each will and to extract from that will what was the true intention of the particular testator or testatrix. Indeed, in *In re Hamilton* [1895] 2 Ch 370. Lindley LJ quoted with approval the words of Cotton LJ in the case of *In re Adams and the Kensington Vestry* (1884) 27 ChD 394, 410:

> I have no hesitation in saying myself, that I think some of the older authorities went a great deal too far in holding that some particular words appearing in a will were sufficient to create a trust. Undoubtedly confidence, if the rest of the context shows that a trust is intended, may make a trust, but what we have to look at is the whole of the will which we have to construe, and if the confidence is that she will do what is right as regards the disposal of the property. I cannot say that that is, on the true construction of the will, a trust imposed upon her. Having regard to the later decisions, we must not extend the old cases in any way, or rely upon the mere use of any particular words, but, considering all the words which are used, we have to see what is their true effect, and what was the intention of the testator as expressed in his will.

. . .

The case of *Shelley* v *Shelley* (1868) LR 6 Eq 540 has stood for eighty years and I have before me a will which, as I have already observed, is, as regards the relevant passage, couched in exactly the same language mutatis mutandis as that which was considered by Wood V-C in *Shelley* v *Shelley*. That appears to me to afford the strongest indication that the testatrix in this case, by her will, which appears clearly upon the face of it to have been a will prepared with professional aid, indicated that the diamond necklace in question should devolve in the same manner as the jewellery was directed to devolve by the order in *Shelley* v *Shelley*. Having regard to that strong indication of intention, and having regard to the fact that I cannot see any good reason why, notwithstanding the admitted trend of modern decisions, I should treat *Shelley* v *Shelley* as wrongly decided and therefore a case which I ought not to follow, I come to the conclusion that I must declare that upon the true construction of the will of the testatrix the diamond necklace should have been held upon trust for Charles Steele for his life and after his death for the second plaintiff Charles Ronald Steele for his life and after his death for David Steele, the third plaintiff, for his life and after the death of the survivor of them upon trust for the eldest son or grandson of the third plaintiff David Steele and otherwise in the manner decided in *Shelley* v *Shelley* including the ultimate trust in default of any male issue of David Steele (who takes an absolutely vested interest) in favour of Charles Steele absolutely and that the order in this case will follow mutatis mutandis the minutes which appear in the case of *Shelley* v *Shelley*.

4.2.2   A PRAGMATIC APPROACH TO CONSTRUCTION

RE ANDREW'S TRUST [1905] 2 Ch 48, ChD

FACTS: The Bishop of Jerusalem had died and a fund was set up to finance the education of his children. When all the children had grown up and their education had been completed, there remained a surplus of monies in the fund.

HELD: The surplus should be divided equally between the Bishop's children. It should not be held on resulting trust for the subscribers to the fund. The donations were treated as a gift to the children, albeit for the primary purpose of their education.

KEKEWICH J: . . . The Court is asked to determine how these shares and dividends ought to be dealt with, all the children being still alive and of full age. The summons is framed on the footing that the children are entitled to be recouped out of this fund the moneys spent on their maintenance and education out of what came to them under their father's will. They were entitled to some fortune under that will, and apparently it was in part applied in their maintenance and education. If the proposed plan were adopted each child would take, not an equal share of the fund, but such a share as would represent the amount expended on his or her education out of the father's estate. If they are masters of the fund it can, of course, be done by agreement; but the Court is asked to decide whether that is right or not, and it is necessary that the point should be decided. . . .

I have been referred by counsel for the applicants to *In re Trusts of the Abbott Fund* [1900] 2 Ch 326, but it is absolutely different from the case now before the Court. There a fund had been raised for the maintenance and support of two distressed ladies, and on the death of the survivor there was still money in the hands of the trustees. Stirling J held that there was a resulting trust of this balance for the subscribers. He did not think that the ladies ever became absolute owners of the fund, and probably no one reading the case is likely to differ from that conclusion. Here I am dealing with different facts, including the fact that the children are still alive, and I do not think myself much guided, and certainly not in the slightest degree bound, by the authority of that case.

It seems to me that the guiding principle is to be found in several authorities examined by Wood V-C in . . . *re Sanderson's Trust* 3 K & J 497—and the judgment of the Vice-Chancellor in that case. One passage may be usefully cited:

> There are two classes of cases between which the general distinction is sufficiently clear, although the precise line of demarcation is occasionally somewhat difficult to ascertain. If a gross sum be given, or if the whole income of the property be given, and a special purpose be assigned for that gift, this Court always regards the gift as absolute, and the purpose merely as the motive of the gift, and therefore holds that the gift takes effect as to the whole sum or the whole income, as the case may be.

Here the only specified object was the education of the children. But I deem myself entitled to construe 'education' in the broadest possible sense, and not to consider the purpose exhausted because the children have attained such ages that education in the vulgar sense is no longer necessary. Even if it be construed in the narrower sense it is, in Wood V-C's language, merely the motive of the gift, and the intention must be taken to have been to provide for the children in the manner (they all being then infants) most useful. . . .

Therefore, I am prepared to hold that the shares and accumulated dividends belong to the children.

PAUL v CONSTANCE [1977] 1 All ER 195, CA

FACTS: Mrs P and Mr C lived together as man and wife. C received £950 in settlement of an action for personal injuries, which they decided to deposit in a bank account. The account was opened in C's sole name so as to avoid any embarrassment in view of the fact that C and P were unmarried. C frequently assured P that the money in the account was as much hers as his and that she could make withdrawals with C's written authority. In fact only one withdrawal was ever made from the account, the sum withdrawn being then divided equally between C and P. On the other hand, further monies were paid into the account, notably their joint winnings from playing 'bingo'. C eventually died intestate and his executors closed the bank account, the balance being then roughly equivalent to the original deposit of £950. P claimed that the money in the account had been held by C in trust for P and C.

HELD: The words frequently used by C to assure P of her joint entitlement to the monies in the account were sufficient to constitute a declaration of trust. The absence of the word 'trust' was not fatal to the finding of an express declaration of trust, taking into account the 'unsophisticated character of the deceased and his relationship with the plaintiff'. The Court of Appeal acknowledged that this was a 'borderline' case, but found a trust on the facts. The plaintiff's claim succeeded.

SCARMAN LJ: . . . A number of issues were canvassed at the trial, but the only point taken by the defendant on her appeal to this court goes to the question whether or not there was, in the circumstances of this case, an express declaration of trust. It is conceded that if there was the trust would be enforceable. The one question is whether there was an express declaration of trust.

The case has been argued with great skill and ability by counsel on both sides, and I should like to express my appreciation for the way in which counsel for the defendant opened the appeal and the way in which the counsel for the plaintiff, very shortly and vigorously, put his contentions.

Counsel for the defendant drew the attention of the court to the so-called three certainties that have to be established before the court can infer the creation of a trust. He referred us to Snell's Principles of Equity in which the three certainties are set out. We are concerned only with one of the three certainties, and it is this:

> The words [that is the words of the declaration relied on] must be so used that on the whole they ought to be construed as imperative. [A little later on the learned author says:] No particular form of expression is necessary for the creation of a trust, if on the whole it can be gathered that a trust was intended. 'A trust may well be created, although there may be an absence of any expression in terms imposing confidence.' A trust may thus be created without using the word 'trust', for what the court regards is the substance and effect of the words used.

Counsel for the defendant has taken the court through the detailed evidence and submits that one cannot find anywhere in the history of events a declaration of trust in the sense of finding the deceased man, Mr Constance, saying: 'I am now disposing of my interest in this fund so that you, Mrs Paul, now have a beneficial interest in it.' Of course, the words which I have just used are stilted lawyers' language, and counsel for the plaintiff was right to remind the court that we are dealing with simple people, unaware of the subtleties of equity, but understanding very well indeed their own domestic situation. It is right that one should consider the various things that were said and done by the plaintiff and Mr Constance during their time together against their own background and in their own circumstances.

Counsel for the defendant drew our attention to two cases, both of them well enough known (at any rate in Lincoln's Inn, since they have been in the law reports for over 100 years), and he relies on them as showing that, though a man may say in clear and unmistakable terms that he intends to make a gift to some other person, for instance his child or some other member of his family, yet that does not necessarily disclose a declaration of trust; and, indeed, in the two cases to which we have been referred the court held that, though there was a plain intention to make a gift, it was not right to infer any intention to create a trust. [His Lordship then referred to the cases of *Jones* v *Lock* (see **4.3.2**) and *Richards* v *Delbridge* (1874) LR 18 Eq 11.

There is no suggestion of a gift by transfer in this case. The facts of those cases do not, therefore, very much help the submission of counsel for the defendant, but he was able to extract from them this principle: that there must be a clear declaration of trust, and that means there must be clear evidence from what is said or done of an intention to create a trust or, as counsel for the defendant put it, 'an intention to dispose of a property or a fund so that somebody else to the exclusion of the disponent acquires the beneficial interest in it'. He submitted that there was no such evidence.

When one looks to the detailed evidence to see whether it goes as far as that—and I think that the evidence does have to go as far as that—one finds that from the time that Mr Constance received his damages right up to his death he was saying, on occasions, that the money was as much the plaintiff's as his. When they discussed the account, he would say to her: 'The money is as much yours as mine.' The judge, rightly treating the basic problem in the case as a question of fact, reached this conclusion. He said, 'I have read through my notes, and I am quite satisfied that it was the intention of [the plaintiff] and Mr Constance to create a trust in which both of them were interested'.

In this court the issue becomes: was there sufficient evidence to justify the judge reaching that conclusion of fact? In submitting that there was, counsel for the plaintiff draws attention first and foremost to the words used. When one bears in mind the unsophisticated character of Mr Constance and his relationship with the plaintiff during the last few years of his life, counsel for the plaintiff submits that the words that he did use on more than one occasion namely 'This money is as much yours as mine', convey clearly a present declaration that the existing fund was as much the plaintiff's as his own. The judge accepted that conclusion. I think he was well justified in doing so and, indeed, I think he was right to do so. There are, as counsel for the plaintiff reminded us, other features in the history of the relationship between the plaintiff and Mr Constance which support the interpretation of those words as an express declaration of trust. I have already described the interview with the bank manager when the account was opened. I have mentioned also the putting of the 'bingo' winnings into the account, and the one withdrawal for the benefit of both of them.

It might, however, be thought that this was a borderline case, since it is not easy to pinpoint a specific moment of declaration, and one must exclude from one's mind any case built on the existence of an implied or constructive trust; for this case was put forward at the trial and is now argued by the plaintiff as one of express declaration of trust. It was so pleaded, and it is only as such that it may be considered in this court. The question, therefore, is whether in all the circumstances the use of those words on numerous occasions as between Mr Constance and the plaintiff constituted an express declaration of trust. The judge found that they did. For myself, I think he was right so to find. I therefore would dismiss the appeal.

RE OSOBA [1979] 2 All ER 393, CA

FACTS: A testator, O, made a bequest to his wife of the rents from certain leasehold properties for her maintenance and for the training of his daughter 'up to University grade'. O's wife died and shortly thereafter his daughter completed her university education. O's son claimed a share of the residue which had not been used for the daughter's education.

HELD: The gift of residue was an absolute gift to the wife and daughter in equal shares, the expression of the purposes for which the gift was to be used being merely an indication of O's motive for making the gift. Further, as there had been no words of severance of the gift as between the wife and her daughter, they were deemed to hold the residue as joint tenants. Accordingly, ever since her mother's death, the daughter had held the whole of the fund absolutely for her own benefit.

BUCKLEY LJ: . . . If a testator has given the whole fund, whether of capital or income, to a beneficiary, whether directly or through the medium of a trustee, he is regarded, in the absence of any contra-indication, as having manifested an intention to benefit that person to the full extent of the subject matter, notwithstanding that he may have expressly stated that the gift is made for a particular purpose, which may prove to be impossible of performance or which may not exhaust the subject matter. This is because the testator has given the whole fund; he has not given so much of the fund as will suffice or be required to achieve the purpose, nor so much of the fund as a trustee or anyone else should determine, but the whole fund. This must be reconciled with the testator's having specified the purpose for which the gift is made. This reconciliation is achieved by treating the reference to the purpose as merely a statement of the testator's motive in making the gift. Any other interpretation of the gift would frustrate the testator's expressed intention that the whole subject-matter shall be applied for the benefit of the beneficiary. These considerations have, I think, added force where the subject-matter is the testator's residue, so that any failure of the gift would result in intestacy. The specified purpose is regarded as of less significance than the dispositive act of the testator, which sets the measure of the extent to which the testator intends to benefit the beneficiary. . . .

4.3   Certainty of Intention

4.3.1   FORMAL DISPOSITIONS

Formal dispositions are usually (though not exclusively) contained within wills. What
has to be done in each case is, quite literally, to construe the *will* of the testator. As Goff
LJ stated in *Re Osoba* [1979] 2 All ER 393: the court should 'endeavor to ascertain his
intention from the words he has used . . . in the light of such knowledge of relevant facts
as we know he must have had'.

4.3.2   INFORMAL DEALINGS

JONES v *LOCK* (1865) Ch App 25, CA

FACTS: J, an ironmonger, returned home from conducting some business in Birmingham.
When criticised by his family for failing to bring a present for his nine month old son, he
produced a cheque in the sum of £900 made payable to himself, said, 'I give this to baby
for himself' and placed the cheque in the baby's hand. He then took the cheque and said,
'I am going to put it away for him'. Six days afterwards J died, and the cheque was found
among his possessions. At issue was whether the baby was entitled to the cheque.
HELD: There had been no gift or valid declaration of trust. Accordingly, the baby was
not entitled to the cheque. The Lord Chancellor refused to find an intention to declare a
trust in 'loose conversations of this sort'. He observed that, had the father not died, he
would have been very surprised to discover that he was not able to use the £900, but
was bound to hold it in trust for his baby son.

LORD CRANWORTH LC: This is a special case, in which I regret to say that I cannot
bring myself to think that, either on principle or on authority, there has been any gift or
any valid declaration of trust. No doubt a gift may be made by any person sui juris and
compos mentis, by conveyance of a real estate or by delivery of a chattel; and there is no
doubt also that, by some decisions, unfortunate I must think them, a parol declaration
of trust of personalty may be perfectly valid even when voluntary. If I give any chattel
that, of course, passes by delivery, and if I say, expressly or impliedly, that I constitute
myself a trustee of personalty, that is a trust executed, and capable of being enforced
without consideration. I do not think it necessary to go into any of the authorities cited
before me; they all turn upon the question, whether what has been said was a declaration
of trust or an imperfect gfft. In the latter case the parties would receive no aid from a
court of equity if they claimed as volunteers. But when there has been a declaration of
trust, then it will be enforced, whether there has been consideration or not. Therefore the
question in each case is one of fact; has there been a gift or not, or has there been a
declaration of trust or not? I should have every inclination to sustain this gift, but
unfortunately I am unable to do so; the case turns on the very short question whether
Jones intended to make a declaration that he held the property in trust for the child; and
I cannot come to any other conclusion than that he did not. I think it would be of very
dangerous example if loose conversations of this sort, in important transactions of this
kind, should have the effect of declarations of trust. . . .

It was all quite natural, but the testator would have been very much surprised if he had
been told that he had parted with the £900, and could no longer dispose of it. It all turns
upon the facts, which do not lead me to the conclusion that the testator meant to deprive
himself of all property in the note, or to declare himself a trustee of the money for the child.
I extremely regret this result, because it is obvious that, by the act of God, this unfortunate
child has been deprived of a provision which his father meant to make for him.

4.3.3   ESTABLISHING EXPRESS TRUSTS IN COMMERCIAL CONTEXTS

RE KAYFORD LTD [1975] 1 All ER 604

FACTS: The company carried on a mail-order business. Customers either paid the full
purchase price or a deposit when ordering goods. By November 1972 the company was

in financial difficulties. Being concerned for the customers of the company who had sent and were sending money for goods, the company took advice on how the customers might be protected in the event of the company becoming insolvent. They were advised by accountants to open a separate bank account to be called 'Customers' Trust Deposit Account' into which all further sums sent by customers for goods not yet delivered should be paid, so that, should the company be forced into liquidation, those sums could be refunded to the customers who had sent them. The company accepted that advice and on 27 November 1972 its managing director gave instructions by telephone to the company's bank. Instead of opening a new account, however, he agreed to use a dormant deposit account in the company's name for that purpose. The account had a credit balance of £47·80. On 8 December discussions were held about putting the company into liquidation. On 11 December the accountants were told of the oral account arrangements with the bank and realised that their advice had not been precisely carried out. They advised that the oral arrangements be confirmed in writing. On the same day the company resolved to go into liquidation. The letter to the bank was sent on the following day, and the words 'Customer Trust Deposit Account' were then added to the name of the account. In the liquidation proceedings the question arose whether the sums of money paid into the bank account were held on trust for those who had sent them or whether they formed part of the general assets of the company.

HELD: In the circumstances a trust had been created. All the requisites of a valid trust of personalty were present and the company had manifested a clear intention to create a trust since, from the outset, the whole purpose of what had been done had been to ensure that the moneys sent remained in the beneficial ownership of those who had sent them. Although payment into a separate banking account was a useful (though by no means conclusive) indication of an intention to create a trust, there was nothing to prevent the company from binding itself by a trust even if there were no effective banking arrangements. Accordingly the moneys were held in trust for those who had sent them. . . .

MEGARRY J: . . . The question for me is whether the money in the bank account (apart from the dormant amount of £47·80 and interest on it), is held on trust for those who paid it, or whether it forms part of the general assets of the company. Counsel for the joint liquidators, one of whom is in fact Mr Wainwright, has contended that there is no trust, so that the money forms part of the general assets of the company and so will be available for the creditors generally. On the other hand, there is a Mr Joels, who on 12 December paid the company £32·20 for goods which have not been delivered; and counsel for him seeks a representation order on behalf of all others whose moneys have been paid into the bank account, some 700 or 800 in number. I make that order. Counsel for the representative beneficiary, of course, argued for the existence of an effective trust. I may say at the outset that on the facts of the case counsel for the joint liquidators was unable to contend that any question of a fraudulent preference arose. If one leaves on one side any case in which an insolvent company seeks to declare a trust in favour of creditors, one is concerned here with the question not of preferring creditors but of preventing those who pay money from becoming creditors, by making them beneficiaries under a trust. I should add that I had some initial doubts about whether Mr Joels was the most suitable representative beneficiary, in view of the date when he paid his money, and whether counsel for the joint liquidators, in representing Mr Wainwright (as well as the other joint liquidator), was not to some degree committed to arguing against the efficacy of the course that Mr Wainwright had advised; but discussion has allayed these doubts.

Now there are clearly some loose ends in the case. Mr Kay, advised to establish a 'Customers' Trust Deposit Account', seems to have thought that it did not matter what the account was called so long as there was a separate account; and so the dormant deposit account suggested by the bank manager was used. The bank statement for this account is before me, and on the first page, for which the title is simply 'Deposit account Kayford Limited', nearly £26,000 is credited. The second and third pages have the words 'Customer Trust Deposit Account' added after the previous title of the account; and Mr Joels's payment was made after these words had been added. Mr Kay also left matters resting on a telephone conversation with the bank manager until he wrote his letter of

12 December to the bank. That letter reads: 'We confirm our instructions regarding the opening of the Deposit Account for customer deposits for new orders'; and he then makes some mention of other accounts with the bank. The letter goes on: 'Please ensure the Re-opened Deposit account is titled "Customer Trust Deposit account".' Then he gives the reference number and asks for confirmation that this has been done. Nevertheless, despite the loose ends, when I take as a whole the affidavits of Mr Wainwright, Mr Kay and Mr Hall (the bank manager) I feel no doubt that the intention was that there should be a trust. There are no formal difficulties. The property concerned is pure personalty, and so writing, though desirable, is not an essential. There is no doubt about the so-called 'three certainties' of a trust. The subject-matter to be held on trust is clear, and so are the beneficial interests therein, as well as the beneficiaries. As for the requisite certainty of words, it is well settled that a trust can be created without using the words 'trust' or 'confidence' or the like: the question is whether in substance a sufficient intention to create a trust has been manifested.

In *Re Nanwa Gold Mines Ltd* [1955] 1 WLR 1080 the money was sent on the faith of a promise to keep it in a separate account, but there is nothing in that case or in any other authority that I know of to suggest that this is essential. I feel no doubt that here a trust was created. From the outset the advice (which was accepted) was to establish a trust account at the bank. The whole purpose of what was done was to ensure that the moneys remained in the beneficial ownership of those who sent them, and a trust is the obvious means of achieving this. No doubt the general rule is that if you send money to a company for goods which are not delivered, you are merely a creditor of the company unless a trust has been created. The sender may create a trust by using appropriate words when he sends the money (though I wonder how many do this, even if they are equity lawyers), or the company may do it by taking suitable steps on or before receiving the money. If either is done, the obligations in respect of the money are transformed from contract to property, from debt to trust. Payment into a separate bank account is a useful (though by no means conclusive) indication of an intention to create a trust, but of course there is nothing to prevent the company from binding itself by a trust even if there are no effective banking arrangements.

Accordingly, of the alternative declarations sought by the summons, the second, to the effect that the money is held in trust for those who paid it, is in my judgment the declaration that should be made. I understand that questions may be raised as to resorting to the interest on the moneys as a means of discharging the costs of the summons; on that I will, of course, hear argument. I should, however, add one thing. Different considerations may perhaps arise in relation to trade creditors; but here I am concerned only with members of the public, some of whom can ill afford to exchange their money for a claim to a dividend in the liquidation, and all of whom are likely to be anxious to avoid this. In cases concerning the public, it seems to me that where money in advance is being paid to a company in return for the future supply of goods or services, it is an entirely proper and honourable thing for a company to do what this company did, on skilled advice, namely, to start to pay the money into a trust account as soon as there begin to be doubts as to the company's ability to fulfil its obligations to deliver the goods or provide the services. I wish that, sitting in this court, I had heard of this occurring more frequently; and I can only hope that I shall hear more of it in the future.

RE MULTI GUARANTEE CO. LTD [1957] BCLC 257, CA

FACTS: Multi Guarantee Ltd (MG) was incorporated to market warranties for domestic appliances which provided insuance after the manufacturer's guarantee expired. Vallance Ltd (V) owned a chain of shops and it operated the MG scheme. V collected premiums from its customers and then paid them over to MG. V became concerned that MG had not obtained proper insuance coverage for the scheme and it entered into negotiations with MG in order to protect the interests of its customers. At the time the negotiations were commenced the premium moneys paid by the customers to MG were held in a designatcd account, the IBA account. Eventually the moneys in the IBA account were transferred into a joint deposit account which could only be drawn on under the joint signatures of MG's and V's solicitors. There were no detailed terms as to the basis on which withdrawals could be made from the account. It was eventually agreed that the moneys in the account should be released to V but before this could be done MG went into a creditors' voluntary winding up. In the present proceedings V appealed against the judgment of the trial judge rejecting their claim that when MG paid the insurance premiums into the joint account it constituted itself a trustee of them.

HELD: Appeal dismissed. On the facts MG never manifested a sufficient intention to create a trust as the requisite certainty of words was not present and accordingly the premium moneys formed part of the general assets of MG. In addition, there was no basis for holding that the liquidator in claiming that MG had not divested itself of the beneficial interest in the premium moneys was acting in a dishonest or shabby way so as not to be entitled to uphold the interests of the general body of MG's creditors and claim that the moneys formed part of the general assets of the company.

NOURSE LJ: This is a case where it is claimed that a company now in liquidation constituted itself a trustee of one of its assets for the benefit of a particular creditor, so as to remove that asset from those which are now available to satisfy the claims of the general body of creditors. . . .

In the circumstances, in order to succeed on this appeal Vallances must show, on the totality of the evidence, that when Multi Guarantee transferred the moneys into the joint account it constituted itself a trustee of them or, in other words, that it effectively divested itself of all beneficial interest therein. As to that, counsel for the liquidator (Mr Chadwick QC) objects that, although there was certainty as to the subject matter of the alleged trust, there was no certainty either of words or as to beneficiaries. I will deal with those objections in turn.

In *Re Kayford Ltd* [1975] 1 All ER 604 at 607, [1975] 1 WLR 279 at 282, where the same question arose in the same sort of context, Megarry J dealt with the requisite certainty of words in this way:

As for the requisite certainty of words, it is well settled that a trust can be created without using the words 'trust' or 'confidence' or the like: the question is whether in substance a sufficient intention to create a trust has been manifested.

Accordingly, the question in the present case is whether in substance a sufficient intention to create a trust was manifested by Multi Guarantee. And it is agreed that that in turn means: Was it manifested by Mr Ronald Meddes?

I hope and believe that I have referred to all the material extracts from the contemporaneous documents which must, in the nature of things, be the best guide to whether the requisite intention was manifested at the time. Although those documents may well disclose that an intention that the account should be a trust account in the full sense existed in the minds of Mr Vallance and Mr Denney, I can find no evidence that it ever existed in the mind of Mr Meddes. In order to see what was in his mind it is necessary to consider both how the matter was put to him on behalf of Vallances and also whether he thought, or was advised, that Multi Guarantee would have no further need of the moneys once they had been put into the joint account.

As to the first of these matters, I have already indicated my view that there is no evidence that it was ever suggested to Mr Meddes that the £251,000, as opposed to the £67,000, should be put into a trust account. As to the second, it is, I think, clear from the documents that it was at the time considered possible that Multi Guarantee would need the money either to arrange alternative cover itself or, perhaps more important, for the purpose of meeting claims which might be made against it by Vallances' customers direct. At all events, it is not, to my mind, made clear that Mr Meddes was content to release the moneys at that time, bearing in mind particularly that the question of an indemnity by Vallances to Multi Guarantee was clearly on the table. I do not see how a sensible businessman could have been expected to release moneys entirely out of the control of his company until at least he knew against what it was that his company had to be indemnified and what were to be the terms of the indemnity. . . .

Having considered all the points which have been urged on us by counsel for Vallances, I for my part am satisfied, for the reasons given by Harman J and for the additional reasons which I have stated, that the conclusion at which the judge arrived was entirely correct and cannot be faulted. In my judgment, Mr Meddes never did manifest a sufficient intention to create a trust and the requisite certainty of words was simply not there. The facts of this case come nowhere near those which were considered by this court in *Re Chelsea Cloisters Ltd (in liq)* (1980) 41 P & CR 98, the authority most favourable to the submissions of counsel for Vallances on this part of the appeal. . . .

4.4   Certainty of Subject Matter

4.4.1   UNCERTAIN PROPERTY

4.4.1.1   Traditional trusts

The leading case is *Palmer* v *Simmonds* (1854) 2 Drew 221. In that case a testatrix left her residuary estate to Thomas Harrison 'for his own use and benefit', and expressing her 'confidence' (or trust) in him that he would leave the bulk of her residuary estate to certain named persons if he should die without issue. Kindersley V-C asked himself 'What is the meaning then of bulk?' His conclusion was that 'what is meant is not the whole but the greater part . . . When, therefore, the testatrix uses that term, can I say that she has used a term expessing a definite, clear, certain part of her estate, or the whole of her estate? I am bound to say that she has not designated the subject as to which she express her confidence; and I am therefore of the opinion that there is no trust'.

4.4.1.2   Commercial trusts

RE LONDON WINE CO. (SHIPPERS) LTD [1986] PCC 121, ChD

FACTS: LW Ltd was a wine merchant which ran its business on the basis that wine ordered by customers was held on trust by the company from the date of each customer's order and until delivery to the customers. However, the bottles representing each order were not physically separated from the company's stocks until delivery. So, in the present case, where the customer ordered 20 bottles of Lafite 1970 out of the company's 80 bottle holding, the question arose whether the subject matter was sufficiently certain for the company to be treated as trustee of the customer's order.
HELD: There was no trust of the 20 bottles. An express trust had certainly been intended by the company but the subject matter had not been removed from the company's general stock and there was therefore insufficient certainty of subject matter. To have achieved certainty of the trust of 20 bottles the company could have declared itself trustee of 'one quarter' of the general stock of 80 bottles.

OLIVER J: . . . As regards the creation of a trust, this is put in this way. On the assumption that no property passed in the goods at law . . . there was, it is submitted, clearly an intention that the property should pass so far as the company had it in its power to make it do so. One has only to look at the terms of its circulars with their references to '*your* wines', to the purchaser being 'the beneficial owner' and to the company having a lien. This is reinforced when one looks at the terms of the letters of confirmation which list the quantities and types of wine and confirm that the purchaser is 'the sole beneficial owner of these wines', . . . By issuing these documents, the acknowledged purpose of which was to enable the purchasers to deal with their wines by sale or charge, the company, it is said, evinced the clearest possible intention to declare itself a trustee and once you find such intention, it matters not that the instrument expressing it fails to do so in unequivocal terms or, indeed, that there is no instrument at all. Reliance is placed upon the recent case of *In re Kayford Ltd* where Megarry, J said: '. . . [I]t is well settled that a trust can be created without using the words 'trust' or 'confidence' or the like: the question is whether in substance a sufficient intention to create a trust has been manifested'.

   That, of course, is a proposition with which it is impossible to quarrel but I do not find that case, where the evidence of intention to create a trust was exceptionally clear and where the trust property was from the outset specifically set aside and identified, one which assists me very much in ascertaining whether, in the very different circumstances of the instant case, a trust has been effectively declared. Mr Wright, in his reply, put it rather differently. A trust he said, may be constituted not merely by direct and express declaration but also by the consequences flowing from the acts of the persons themselves to which consequences the law attaches the label 'trust'. A trust, to put it another way, is the technical description of a legal situation; and where you find (i) an intention to create a beneficial interest in someone else, (ii) an acknowledgement of that intention and (iii) property in the ownership of the person making the acknowledgement which answers the description in the acknowledgement, then there is, at the date of the acknowledgement, an effective and completed trust of all the property of the acknowledger answering to that description. This is, I think, in essence the same submission as that made by Mr Stamler—he submits that where one is dealing with a homogeneous mass there is no problem about certainty. So long as the mass can be identified and there is no uncertainty about the quantitative interest of the beneficiary the court will find no difficulty in administering the trust if it once finds the necessary intention to create an equitable interest in property of the type comprised in the mass. I think, indeed, that if the case is to be made out at all, it must be put in this way, for the submission itself is based on the premise that there are no specific or ascertained goods in which the beneficiary is interested. Were it otherwise there would be no need to invoke the concept of trust for the title would have passed under the Sale of Goods Act (as, indeed Mr Wright submits in categories 1 and 2, it did). If trust there be, then it must be a trust of the homogeneous *whole* and the terms of the trust must be that the trustee is to hold that whole upon trust to give effect thereout to the proportionate interest of the beneficiary. Thus if we postulate the case of the company having in warehouse 1,000 cases of a particular wine and selling 100 cases to X the circumstances of this case indicate, it is submitted, that the company created an equitable tenancy in common between itself and X in the whole 1,000 cases in the proportions of 9/10ths and 1/10th.

It is with regret that I feel compelled to reject these submissions, for I feel great sympathy with those who paid for their wine and received an assurance that they had title to it. But I find it impossible to spell either out of the acknowledgements signed by the company or out of the circumstances any such trust as is now sought to be set up. Granted that the references to 'beneficial interest' are appropriate words for the creation of a trust; granted, even (although this I think is very difficult to spell out) that that was the company's intention, it seems to me that any such trust must fail on the ground of uncertainty of subject-matter. I appreciate the point taken that the subject-matter is part of a homogeneous mass so that specific identity is of as little importance as it is, for instance, in the case of money. Nevertheless, as it seems to me, to create a trust it must be possible to ascertain with certainty not only what the interest of the beneficiary is to be but to what property it is to attach.

I cannot see how, for instance, a farmer who declares himself to be a trustee of two sheep (without identifying them) can be said to have created a perfect and complete trust whatever rights he may confer by such declaration as a matter of contract. And it would seem to me to be immaterial at the time he has a flock of sheep out of which he could satisfy the interest. Of course, he could by appropriate words, declare himself to be a trustee of a specified proportion of his whole flock and thus create an equitable tenancy in common between himself and the named beneficiary, so that a proprietary interest would arise in the beneficiary in an undivided share of all the flock and its produce. But the *mere* declaration that a given number of animals would be held upon trust could not, I should have thought, without very clear words pointing to such an intention, result in the creation of an interest in common in the proportion which that number bears to the number of the whole at the time of the declaration. And where the mass from which the numerical interest is to take effect is not itself ascertainable at the date of the declaration such a conclusion becomes impossible.

In the instant case, even if I were satisfied on the evidence that the mass was itself identifiable at the date of the various letters of confirmation I should find the very greatest difficulty in construing the assertion that 'you are the *sole* and beneficial owner of' 10 cases of such and such a wine as meaning or being intended to mean 'you are the owner of such proportion of the total stock of such and such a wine now held by me as 10 bears to the total number of cases comprised in such stock.' All other things apart, such construction would be a total negation of the assertion 'you are the sole owner.' . . .

. . . *In re Wait* [1927] 1 Ch 606 shows that no lien arises from the mere payment of the purchase price. As Lord Atkin pointed out, it is not the law that whenever there is a contract of which equity will decree specific performance a beneficial interest in the subject-matter of the contract passes as a necessary corollary. Even if, therefore, specific performance could be decreed of the purchasers' contracts in the instant case, the decree could not affect any specific goods in the company's possession, for under the contracts the goods were never ascertained, and leaving aside any question of notice, I do not see how the possibility of a decree against the company for the delivery *in specie* of so many cases of wine could affect the bank merely because it happened to have a charge over wine of that description which the company had acquired but never appropriated to the contract. . . .

HUNTER v MOSS [1994] 3 All ER 215, CA

FACTS: The defendant was the registered owner of 95 per cent of the issued share capital of a limited company. The trial judge held that the defendant had orally declared a valid trust of 50 of his shares (being 5 per cent of the total issued share capital of the company). The defendant applied by motion to have the judgment set aside, on the ground, *inter alia*, that there could not have been a valid declaration of trust because the subject matter of the trust was uncertain. The deputy judge dismissed the motion whereupon the defendant appealed.

HELD: The appeal was dismissed. All the shares in the company were identical in nature, it was therefore quite valid to declare a trust of 50 shares without specifying which 50 shares were intended to form the subject matter of the trust. *Re London Wine Co. (Shippers) Ltd* was distinguished.

DILLON LJ: . . . I pass then to the second point of uncertainty. It is well established that for the creation of a trust there must be the three certainties referred to by Lord Langdale in his judgment in *Knight v Knight* (1840) 3 Beav 148, 49 ER 68. One of those is, of course, that there must be certainty of subject matter. All these shares were identical in one class: 5% was 50 shares and Mr Moss held personally more than 50 shares. It is well known that a trust of personalty can be created orally. . . .

In the present case there was no question of an imperfect transfer. What is relied on is an oral declaration of trust. Again, it would not be good enough for a settlor to say. 'I declare that I hold fifty of my shares on trust for B', without indicating the company he had in mind of the various companies in which he held shares. There would be no sufficient certainty as to the subject matter of the trust. But here the discussion is solely about the shares of one class in the one company.

It is plain that a bequest by Mr Moss to Mr Hunter of 50 of his ordinary shares in MEL would be a valid bequest on Mr Moss's death which his executors or administrators would be bound to carry into effect. Mr Hartman sought to dispute that and to say that if, for instance, a shareholder had 200 ordinary shares in ICI and he wanted to give them to A, B, C and D equally he could do it by giving 200 shares to A, B, C and D as tenants in common, but he could not validly do it by giving 50 shares to A, 50 shares to B, 50 shares to C and 50 shares to D because he has not indicated which of the identical shares A is to have and which B is to have. I do not accept that. That such a testamentary bequest is valid, appears sufficiently from the cases of *Re Clifford, Mallam v McFie* [1912] 1 Ch 29 and *Re Cheadle, Bishop v Holt* [1900] 2 Ch 620. It seems to me, again, that if a person holds, say, 200 ordinary shares in ICI and he executes a transfer of 50 ordinary shares in ICI either to an individual donee or to trustees, and hands over the certificate for his 200 shares and the transfer to the transferees or to brokers to give effect to the transfer, there is a valid gift to the individual or trustees/transferees of the 50 shares without any further indentification of their numbers. It would be a completed gift without waiting for registration of the transfer. (See *Re Rose (decd), Rose v IRC* [1952] 1 All ER 1217, [1952] Ch 499.) In the ordinary way a new certificate would be issued for the 50 shares to the transferee and the transferor would receive a balance certificate in respect of the rest of his holding. I see no uncertainty at all in those circumstances.

Mr Hartman, however, relied on two authorities in particular. One is a decision of Oliver J in the case of *Re London Wine Co. (Shippers) Ltd* [1986] PCC 121 which was decided in 1975.

. . . It seems to me that that case is a long way from the present. It is concerned with the appropriation of chattels and when the property in chattels passes. We are concerned with a declaration of trust, accepting that the legal title remained in Mr Moss and was not intended, at the time the trust was declared, to pass immediately to Mr Hunter. Mr Moss was to retain the shares as trustee for Mr Hunter.

Mr Hartman also referred to *Mac-Jordan Construction Ltd* v *Brookmount Erostin Ltd* [1992] BCLC 350. . . .

In reliance on that case Mr Hartman submits that no fiduciary relationship can attach to an unappropriated portion of a mixed fund. The only remedy is that of a floating charge. He refers to a passage in the judgment of Lord Greene MR in *Re Diplock's Estate, Diplock* v *Wintle* [1948] 2 All ER 318 at 346, [1948] Ch 465 at 519 where he said:

> The narrowness of the limits within which the common law operated may be linked with the limited nature of the remedies available to it . . . In particular, the device of a declaration of charge was unknown to the common law and it was availability of that device which enabled equity to give effect to its wider conception of equitable rights.

So Mr Hartman submits that the most that Mr Hunter could claim is to have an equitable charge on a blended fund. He mentions the decision of Chitty J in *Re Earl of Lucan* (1890) 45 Ch 470 which points out that, where there was merely an equitable charge which did not grant perfect and complete rights to the chargee and it was given by way of gift to a volunteer, there could be no specific performance in favour of the volunteer who would have no priority over the creditors of the grantor. As I see it, however, we are not concerned in this case with a mere equitable charge over a mixed fund. Just as a person can give, by will, a specified number of his shares of a certain class in a certain company, so equally, in my judgment, he can declare himself trustee of 50 of his ordinary shares in MEL, or whatever the company may be, and that is effective to give a beneficial proprietary interest to the beneficiary under the trust. No question of a blended fund thereafter arises and we are not in the field of equitable charge.

Therefore, I agree with the deputy judge on the conclusion of the uncertainty point which he dealt with in his November judgment.

4.4.2 UNCERTAIN BENEFICIAL INTERESTS

RE GOLAY [1965] 2 All ER 660

FACTS: The testator directed his executors 'to let Tossy . . . enjoy one of my flats during her lifetime and to receive a reasonable income from my other properties . . . ' The issue was whether the direction to allow a 'reasonable' income was void for uncertainty.

HELD: The words 'reasonable income' invited an objective determinaion by the court, which the court was quite capable of carrying out. As the judge said, 'the court is constantly involved in making such objective assessments of what is reasonable'.

UNGOED-THOMAS J: Another question that arises is whether this gift of reasonable income fails for uncertainty. There are two classes of case with which I am concerned in interpreting this particular provision in the will: the first is where a discretion is given to specified persons to quantify the amount; the other class of case is where no such discretion is expressly conferred on any specified person. It is common ground that in this case the trustees are not given that discretion, so that, if 'reasonable income' does not fail for uncertainty, then it would be open to a beneficiary to go to court to ascertain whether any amount quantified by the trustees was a 'reasonable' amount in accordance with the provisions of the will.

Does this gift of a 'reasonable income' without specifying any person to quantify it fail for uncertainty? The principal case referred to on this question was *Jackson* v *Hamilton* (1846) 3 J & Lat 702, an Irish case where the testator:

> did devise and by his will request that his said trustees should from time to time retain in their hands any reasonable sum or sums of money which should be sufficient to

remunerate them for the trouble they should have in carrying the trusts of his will into execution.

It seems from the report, that no objection against the quantum was taken on the ground of uncertainty. It was also argued before me that a discretion was in the first place given to the trustees to decide what the amount should be and that the master quantified the amount, so that the court would have been merely exercising the discretion which the will had given to the trustees and had been surrendered to the court. The master, however, when the matter came before him, had no difficulty in quantifying what was 'reasonable' remuneration and Lord Sugden LC confirmed the course which the master had taken. Indeed, it is conceded in this case—and I think rightly conceded—that the court would have no difficulty in quantifying 'reasonable income'.

It is, however, submitted that what the court is concerned with in the interpretation of this will is not to ascertain what is 'reasonable income' in the opinion of the court but to ascertain the testator's intention in using the words 'reasonable income'. The question therefore comes to this: whether the testator by the words 'reasonable income' has given a sufficient indication of his intention to provide an effective determinant of what he intends so that the court in applying that determinant can give effect to the testator's intention.

Whether the yardstick of 'reasonable income' were applied by trustees under a discretion given to them by a testator or applied by a court in course of interpreting and applying the words 'reasonable income' in a will, the yardstick sought to be applied by the trustees in the one case and the court in the other case would be identical. The trustees might be other than the original trustees named by the testator and the trustees could even surrender their discretion to the court. It would seem to me to be drawing too fine a distinction to conclude that an objective yardstick which different persons sought to apply would be too uncertain, not because of uncertainty in the yardstick but as between those who seek to apply it.

In this case, however, the yardstick indicated by the testator is not what he or any other specified person subjectively considers to be reasonable but what he identifies objectively as 'reasonable income'. The court is constantly involved in making such objective assessments of what is reasonable and it is not to be deterred from doing so because subjective influences can never be wholly excluded. In my view the testator intended by 'reasonable income' the yardstick which the court could and would apply in quantifying the amount so that the direction in the will is not in my view defeated by uncertainty.

4.5 Certainty of Object

4.5.1 FIXED TRUSTS

4.5.1.1 The class ascertainability test

See the discussion of *IRC* v *Broadway Cottages* [1955] 1 Ch 20 in *McPhail* v *Doulton* [1971] AC 424 (**4.5.2.1**).

4.5.2 DISCRETIONARY TRUSTS

4.5.2.1 Adoption of the individual ascertainability test

McPHAIL v *DOULTON (RE BADEN'S DEED TRUSTS (No. 1))* [1971] AC 424, HL

FACTS: Mr B settled a trust for the benefit of certain persons connected with a company controlled by him. The deed granted the trustees an absolute discretion to apply the net income 'to or for the benefit of any officers and employees or ex-officers or ex-employees of the company or to any relatives or dependants of any such persons in such amounts at such times and on such conditions (if any) as they think fit . . .'. The first question was whether the deed had (1) granted the trustees a power of appointment among the class, or (2) had subjected them to a discretionary trust. The second question, which flowed from the first, was 'is the gift void for uncertainty'? If the gift was in the form of a power, the trustees would have been able to appoint (distribute part of the fund to) any applicant of whom it could be said with certainty that they were or were not within the class of 'staff, relatives or dependants'. If, on the other hand, the gift was in the nature of a trust, the trustees would only have been able to appoint beneficiaries if every member of the class had been identified.

HELD: The deed created a trust, not a power. However, the trust would not fail for uncertainty of object, even though it would not be possible to draw up a complete fixed list of every potential beneficiary within the class. Lord Wilberforce rejected what he considered to be a narrow and artificial distinction between discretionary trusts and powers of appointment in the context of gifts of this sort.

LORD WILBERFORCE: . . . In this House, the appellants contended, and this is the first question for consideration, that the provisions of cl. 9(a) constitute a trust and not a power. If that is held to be the correct result, both sides agree that the case must return to the Chancery Division for consideration, on this footing, whether this trust is valid. But here comes a complication. In the present state of authority, the decision as to validity would turn on the question whether a complete list (or on another view a list complete for practical purposes) can be drawn up of all possible beneficiaries. This follows from the Court of Appeal's decision in *Inland Revenue Comrs* v *Broadway Cottages Trust* [1995] 1 Ch 20 as applied in later cases by which, unless this House decides otherwise, the Court of Chancery would be bound. The respondents invite your Lordships to review this decision and challenge its correctness. So the second issue which arises, if cl. 9(a) amounts to a trust, is whether the existing test for its validity is right in law and if not, what the test ought to be.

Before dealing with these two questions some general observations, or reflections, may be permissible. It is striking how narrow and in a sense artificial is the distinction, in cases such as the present, between trusts or as the particular type of trust is called, trust powers, and powers. It is only necessary to read the learned judgments in the Court of Appeal to see that what to one mind may appear as a power of distribution coupled with a trust to dispose of the undistributed surplus, by accumulation or otherwise, may to another appear as a trust for distribution coupled with a power to withhold a portion and accumulate or otherwise dispose of it. A layman and, I suppose, also a logician, would find it hard to understand what difference there is.

It does not seem satisfactory that the entire validity of a disposition should depend on such delicate shading. And if one considers how in practice reasonable and competent trustees would act, and ought to act, in the two cases, surely a matter very relevant to the question of validity, the distinction appears even less significant. To say that there is no obligation to exercise a mere power and that no court will intervene to compel it, whereas a trust is mandatory and its execution may be compelled, may be legally correct enough, but the proposition does not contain an exhaustive comparison of the duties of persons who are trustees in the two cases. A trustee of an employees' benefit fund, whether given a power or a trust power, is still a trustee and he would surely consider in either case that he has a fiduciary duty; he is most likely to have been selected as a suitable person to administer it from his knowledge and experience, and would consider he has a responsibility to do so according to its purpose. It would be a complete misdescription of his position to say that, if what he has is a power unaccompanied by an imperative trust to distribute, he cannot be controlled by the court if he exercised it capriciously, or outside the field permitted by the trust (cf *Farwell on Powers*). Any trustee would surely make it his duty to know what is the permissible area of selection and then consider responsibly, in individual cases, whether a contemplated beneficiary was within the power and whether, in relation to other possible claimants, a particular grant was appropriate.

Correspondingly a trustee with a duty to distribute, particularly among a potentially very large class, would surely never require the preparation of a complete list of names, which anyhow would tell him little that he needs to know. He would examine the field, by class and category; might indeed make diligent and careful enquiries, depending on how much money he had to give away and the means at his disposal, as to the composition and needs of particular categories and of individuals within them; decide on certain priorities or proportions, and then select individuals according to their needs or qualifications. If he acts in this manner, can it really be said that he is not carrying out the trust?

Differences there certainly are between trusts (trust powers) and powers, but as regards validity should they be so great as that in one case complete, or practically complete ascertainment is needed, but not in the other? Such distinction as there is would seem to lie in the extent of the survey which the trustee is required to carry out; if he has to distribute the whole of a fund's income, he must necessarily make a wider and more systematic survey than if his duty is expressed in terms of a power to make grants. But just as, in the case of a power, it is possible to underestimate the fiduciary obligation of the trustee to whom it is given, so, in the case of a trust (trust power), the danger lies in overstating what the trustee requires to know or to enquire into before he can properly execute his trust. The difference may be one of degree rather than of principle; in the well-known words of Sir George Farwell (*Farwell on Powers*) trusts and powers are often blended, and the mixture may vary in its ingredients. . . .

This makes it necessary to consider whether, in so doing, the court should proceed on the basis that the relevant test is that laid down in the *Broadway Cottages* case or some other test. That decision gave the authority of the Court of Appeal to the distinction between cases where trustees are given a *power* of selection and those where they are bound by a *trust* for selection. In the former case the position, as decided by this House, is that the power is valid if it can be said with certainty whether any given individual is or is not a member of the class and does not fail simply because it is impossible to ascertain every member of the class. (The *Gulbenkian* case [1968] All ER 785.) But in the latter case it is said to be necessary, for the trust to be valid, that the whole range of objects (I use the language of the Court of Appeal) should be ascertained or capable of ascertainment.

The respondents invited your Lordships to assimilate the validity test for trusts to that which applies to powers. Alternatively, they contended that in any event the test laid down in the *Broadway Cottages* case was too rigid, and that a trust should be upheld if there is sufficient practical certainty in its definition for it to be carried out, if necessary with the administrative assistance of the court, according to the expressed intention of the settlor. I would agree with this, but this does not dispense from examination of the wider argument. The basis for the *Broadway Cottages* case principle is stated to be that a trust cannot be valid unless, if need be, it can be executed by the court, and (though it is not quite clear from the judgment where argument ends and decision begins) that the court can only execute it by ordering an equal distribution in which every beneficiary shares. So it is necessary to examine the authority and reason for this supposed rule as to the execution of trusts by the court.

Assuming, as I am prepared to do for present purposes, that the test of validity is whether the trust can be executed by the court, it does not follow that execution is impossible unless there can be equal division. As a matter of reason, to hold that a principle of equal division applies to trusts such as the present is certainly paradoxical. Equal division is surely the last thing the settlor ever intended; equal division among all may, probably would, produce a result beneficial to none. Why suppose that the court would lend itself to a whimsical execution? And as regards authority, I do not find that the nature of the trust, and of the court's powers over trusts, calls for any such rigid rule. Equal division may be sensible and has been decreed, in cases of family trusts for a limited class, here there is life in the maxim 'equality is equity', but the cases provide numerous examples where this has not been so, and a different type of execution has been ordered, appropriate to the circumstances. . . .

The conclusion which I would reach, implicit in the previous discussion, is that the wide distinction between the validity test for powers and that for trust powers, is unfortunate and wrong, that the rule recently fastened on the courts by the *Broadway Cottages* case ought to be discarded, and that the test for the validity of trust powers ought to be similar to that accepted by this House in *Re Gulbenkian's Settlement Trusts* for powers, namely that the trust is valid if it can be said with certainty that any given individual is or is not a member of the class.

Assimilation of the validity test does not involve the complete assimilation of trust powers with powers. As to powers, I agree with my noble and learned friend Lord Upjohn in *Re Gulbenkian's Settlement* that although the trustees may, and normally will, be under a fiduciary duty to consider whether or in what way they should exercise their power, the court will not normally compel its exercise. It will intervene if the trustees exceed their powers, and possibly if they are proved to have exercised it capriciously. But in the case of a trust power, if the trustees do not exercise it, the court will; I respectfully adopt as to this the statement in Lord Upjohn's opinion. I would venture to amplify this by saying that the court, if called on to execute the trust power, will do so in the manner best calculated to give effect to the settlor's or testator's intentions. It may do so by appointing new trustees, or by authorising or directing representative persons of the classes of beneficiaries to prepare a scheme of distribution, or even, should the proper basis for distribution appear, by itself directing the trustees so to distribute. The books give many instances where this has been done and I see no reason in principle why they should not do so in the modern field of discretionary trusts (see *Brunsden* v *Woolredge* (1765) Amb 507, *Supple* v *Lowson* (1842) 1 Hare 580, *Liley* v *Hey* (1773) 2 Amb 728 and *Lewin on Trusts*). Then, as to the trustees' duty of enquiry or ascertainment, in each case the trustees ought to make such a survey of the range of objects or possible beneficiaries as will enable them to carry out their further fiduciary duty (cf *Liley* v *Hey*). A wider and more comprehensive range of enquiry is called for in the case of trust powers than in the case of powers.

Two final points: first, as to the question of certainty, I desire to emphasise the distinction clearly made and explained by Lord Upjohn, between linguistic or semantic uncertainty which, if unresolved by the court, renders the gift void, and the difficulty of ascertaining the existence or whereabouts of members of the class, a matter with which the court can appropriately deal on an application for directions. There may be a third case where the meaning of the words used is clear but the definition of beneficiaries is so hopelessly wide as not to form 'anything like a class' so that the trust is administratively unworkable or in Lord Eldon LC's words one that cannot be executed (*Morice* v *Bishop of Durham*). I hesitate to give examples for they may prejudice future cases, but perhaps 'all the residents of Greater London' will serve. I do not think that a discretionary trust for 'relatives' even of a living person falls within this category.

4.5.2.2 Application of the individual ascertainability test

RE BADEN'S DEED TRUSTS (No. 2) [1972] 2 All ER 1304, CA

FACTS: Having considered the Baden's Deed Trusts in *McPhail* v *Doulton* (see above) the House of Lords remitted the case to the High Court to apply the individual ascertainability test to the deed, to determine, *inter alia*, whether the class 'relatives' was sufficiently certain. The judgment of the High Court was appealed
HELD: The term 'relatives' was conceptually certain and the trust was therefore valid. However, their Lordships did differ in their conception of 'relatives'. Sachs LJ took 'relatives' to mean any persons who could 'trace legal descent from a common ancestor', whereas Stamp LJ took it mean 'legal next-of-kin' of the employees.

SACHS LJ: . . . The test to be applied to each of these words is: 'can it be said with certainty that any given individual is or is not a member of the class?' (*per* Lord Wilberforce), words which reflect those of Lord Reid and Lord Upjohn in *Re Gulbenkian's Settlement Trusts*. Being in general agreement, as already indicated, with everything that Brightman J has said as regards the two relevant words, it is sufficient first to make some observations as to the approach to be adopted to the questions raised before us and then in the light of those observations to deal comparatively compactly with the effect of the use of the two relevant words.

It is first to be noted that the deed must be looked at through the eyes of a businessman seeking to advance the welfare of the employees of his firm and of those so connected with the employees that a benevolent employer would wish to help them. He would not necessarily be looking at the words he uses with the same eyes as those of a man making a will. Accordingly, whether a court is considering the concept implicit in relevant words, or whether it is exercising the function of a court of construction, it should adopt that same practical and common sense approach which was enjoined by Upjohn J in *Re Sayer Trust* and by Lord Wilberforce in the present case and which would be used by an employer setting up such a fund.

The next point as regards approach that requires consideration is the contention, strongly pressed by counsel for the defendant executors, that the court must always be able to say whether any given postulant is *not* within the relevant class as well as being able to say whether he is within it. In construing the words already cited from the speech of Lord Wilberforce in the present case (as well as those of Lord Reid and Lord Upjohn in the *Gulbenkian* case), it is essential to bear in mind the difference between conceptual uncertainty and evidential difficulties. That distinction is explicitly referred to by Lord Wilberforce when he said:

> . . . as to the question of certainty, I desire to emphasise the distinction clearly made and explained by Lord Upjohn, between linguistic or semantic uncertainty which, if unresolved by the court, renders the gift void, and the difficulty of ascertaining the existence or whereabouts of members of the class, a matter with which the court can appropriately deal on an application for directions.

As counsel for the defendant executors himself rightly observed, 'the court is never defeated by evidential uncertainty', and it is in my judgment clear that it is conceptual certainty to which reference was made when the 'is or is not a member of the class' test was enunciated. (Conceptual uncertainty was in the course of argument conveniently exemplified, rightly or wrongly matters not, by the phrase 'someone under a moral obligation' and contrasted with the certainty of the words 'first cousins.) Once the class of persons to be benefited is conceptually certain it then becomes a question of fact to be determined on evidence whether any postulant has on enquiry been proved to be within it; if he is not so proved then he is not in it. That position remains the same whether the class to be benefited happens to be small (such as 'first cousins') or large (such as 'members of the X Trade Union' or 'those who have served in the Royal Navy'). The suggestion that such trusts could be invalid because it might be impossible to prove of a given individual that he was *not* in the relevant class is wholly fallacious—and only the persuasiveness of counsel for the defendant executors has prevented me from saying that the contention is almost unarguable. . . .

As regards the suggested uncertain numerative range of that concept of the word 'relative' (a matter which strictly would only be relevant to the abandoned 'administratively unworkable' point) and also when considering the practical side of the functions of the trustees, it is germane to note that in *Re Scarisbrick's Will Trusts* Sir Raymond Evershed MR observed with regard to a class of 'relations': 'That class is, in theory, capable of almost infinite expansion, but proof of relationship soon becomes extremely difficult in fact.' That factor automatically narrows the field within which the trustees select. Further, a settlor using the word 'relatives' in the context of this deed (which is not the same context as that of a will) would assume that the trustees would in the exercise of their discretion make their selection in a sensible way from the field, however wide. Thus in practice they woud presumably select those whom a reasonable and honest employee or ex-employee would introduce a 'relative', rather than as a 'kinsman' or as a 'distant relative'. Indeed, on a construction summons some such definition might emerge for the word 'relative'—but that is not relevant to the present appeal as the widest meaning that has been suggested for that word does not in my judgment produce uncertainty.

As a footnote to this conclusion it is interesting to observe that no case was cited to us in which a court has actually decided that a trust was invalid on account of the use of that word, whatever may have been said obiter. If this is due to a tendency to construe deeds and wills so as to give effect to them rather than to invalidate trusts, that is an approach which is certainly in accord with modern thought. . . .

MEGAW LJ: . . . The main argument of counsel for the defendant executors was founded on a strict and literal interpretation of the words in which the decision of the House of Lords in *Re Gulbenkian's Settlement Trusts* was expressed. That decision laid down the test for the validity of powers of selection. It is relevant for the present case, because in the previous excursion of this case to the House of Lords it was held that there is no relevant difference in the test of validity, whether the trustees are given a power of selection or, as was held by their Lordships to be the case in the trust deed, a trust for selection. The test in either case is what may be called the *Gulbenkian* test. The *Gulbenkian* test, as expressed by Lord Wilberforce (and again in almost identical words in a later passage) is this:

> . . . the power is valid if it can be said with certainty whether any given individual is or is not a member of the class and does not fail simply because it is impossible to ascertain every member of the class.

The executors' argument concentrates on the words 'or is not' in the first of the two limbs of the sentence quoted above: 'if it can be said with certainty whether any given individual is *or is not* a member of the class'. It is said that those words have been used deliberately, and have only one possible meaning; and that, however startling or drastic or unsatisfactory the result may be—and counsel for the defendant executors does not shrink from saying that the consequence is drastic—this court is bound to give effect to the words used in the House of Lords' definition of the test. It would be quite impracticable for the trustees to ascertain in many cases whether a particular person was *not* a relative of an employee. The most that could be said is: 'There is no proof that he is a relative'. But there would still be no 'certainty' that such a person was not a relative. Hence, so it is said, the test laid down by the House of Lords is not satisfied, and the trust is void. For it cannot be said with certainty, in relation to any individual, that he is not a relative.

I do not think it was contemplated that the words 'or is not' would produce that result. It would, as I see it, involve an inconsistency with the latter part of the same sentence: 'does not fail simply because it is impossible to ascertain every member of the class'. The executors' contention, in substance and reality, is that it *does* fail 'simply because it is impossible to ascertain every member of the class'.

The same verbal difficulty, as I see it, emerges also when one considers the words of the suggested test which the House of Lords expressly rejected. That is set out by Lord Wilberforce in a passage immediately following the sentence which I have already quoted. The rejected test was in these terms: '. . . it is said to be necessary . . . that the whole range of objects . . . shall be ascertained or capable of ascertainment'. Since that test was rejected, the resulting affirmative proposition, which by implication must have been accepted by their Lordships, is this: a trust for selection will not fail simply because the whole range of objects cannot be ascertained. In the present case, the trustees could ascertain, by investigation and evidence, many of the objects; as to many other theoretically possible claimants, they could not be certain. Is it to be said that the trust fails because it cannot be said with certainty that such persons are not members of the class? If so, is that not the application of the rejected test; the trust failing because 'the whole range of objects cannot be ascertained?'

In my judgment, much too great emphasis is placed in the executors' argument on the words 'or is not'. To my mind, the test is satisfied if, as regards at least a substantial number of objects, it can be said with certainty that they fall within the trust; even though, as regards a substantial number of other persons, if they ever for some fanciful reason fell to be considered, the answer would have to be, not 'they are outside the trust', but 'it is not proven whether they are in or out'. What is a 'substantial number' may well be a question of common sense and of degree in relation to the particular trust: particularly where, as here, it would be fantasy, to use a mild word, to suggest that any practical difficulty would arise in the fair, proper and sensible administration of this trust in respect of relatives and dependants.

I do not think that this involves, as counsel for the defendant executors suggested, a return by this court to its former view which was rejected by the House of Lords in the *Gulbenkian* case. If I did so think, I should, however reluctantly, accept his argument and its consequences. But as I read it, the criticism in the House of Lords of the decision of this court in that case related to this court's acceptance of the view that it would be sufficient if it could be shown that *one single person* fell within the scope of the power or trust. The essence of the decision of the House of Lords in the *Gulbenkian* case, as I see it, is *not* that it must be possible to show with certainty that any given person is *or is not* within the trust; but that it is not, or may not be, sufficient to be able to show that one individual person is within it. If it does not mean that, I do not know where the line is supposed to be drawn, having regard to the clarity and emphasis with which the House of Lords has laid down that the trust does not fail because the whole range of objects cannot be ascertained. . . .

STAMP LJ: . . . Counsel for the defendant executors, fastening on those words, 'if it can be said with certainty that any given individual is or is not a member of the class', submitted in this court that a trust for distribution among officers and employees or ex-officers or ex-employees or any of their relatives or dependants does not satisfy the test. You may say with certainty that any given individual is or is not an officer, employee, ex-officer or ex-employee. You may say with certainty that a very large number of given individuals are relatives of one of them; but, so the argument runs, you will never be able to say with certainty of many given individuals that they are not. I am bound to say that I had thought at one stage of counsel's able argument that this was no more than an exercise in semantics and that the phrase on which he relies indicated no more than that the trust was valid if there was such certainty in the definition of membership of the class that you could say with certainty that some individuals were members of it; that it was sufficient that you should be satisfied that a given individual presenting himself has or has not passed the test and that it matters not that having failed to establish his membership—here his relationship—you may, perhaps wrongly, reject him. There are, however, in my judgment serious difficulties in the way of a rejection of counsel's submission.

The first difficulty, as I see it, is that the rejection of counsel's submission involves holding that the trust is good if there are individuals—or even one—of whom you can say with certainty that he is a member of the class. That was the test adopted by and the decision of the Court of Appeal in the *Gulbenkian* case where what was under consideration was a power of distribution among a class conferred on trustees as distinct from a trust for distribution: but when the *Gulbenkian* case came before the House of Lords that test was decisively rejected and the more stringent test on which counsel for the defendant executors insists was adopted. Clearly Lord Wilberforce in expressing the view that the test of validity of a discretionary trust ought to be similar to that accepted by the House of Lords in the *Gulbenkian* case did not take the view that it was sufficient that you could find individuals who were clearly members of the class; for he himself remarked, towards the end of his speech as to the trustees' duty of enquiring or ascertaining, that in each case the trustees ought to make such a survey of the range of objects or possible beneficiaries as will enable them to carry out their fiduciary duty. It is not enough that trustees should do nothing but distribute the fund among those objects of the trust who happen to be at hand or present themselves. Lord Wilberforce, after citing that passage which I have already quoted from the speech of Lord Upjohn in the *Gulbenkian* case, put it more succinctly by remarking that what this did say (and he agreed) was that the trustees must select from the class, but that passage did not mean (as had been contended) that they must be able to get a complete list of all possible objects. I have already called attention to Lord Wilberforce's opinion that the trustees ought to make such a survey of the range of objects or possible beneficiaries as will enable them to carry out their fiduciary duty, and I ought perhaps to add that he indicated that a wider and more comprehensive range of enquiry is called for in the case of what I have called discretionary trusts than in the case of fiduciary powers. But, as I understand it, having made the appropriate survey, it matters not that it is not complete or fails to yield a result enabling you to lay out a list or particulars of every single beneficiary. Having done the best they can, the trustees may proceed on the basis similar to that adopted by the court where all the beneficiaries cannot be ascertained and distribute on the footing that they have been: see, for example, *Re Benjamin* [1902] 1 Ch 723. What was referred to as 'the complete ascertainment test' laid down by this court in the *Broadway Cottages* case is rejected. So also is the test laid down by this court in the *Gulbenkian* case. Validity or invalidity is to depend on whether you can say of any individual—and the accent must be on that word 'any', for it is not simply the individual whose claim you are considering who is spoken of—that he 'is or is not a member of the class', for only thus can you make a survey of the range of objects or possible beneficiaries.

If the matter rested there, it would in my judgment follow that, treating the word 'relatives' as meaning descendants from a common ancestor, a trust for distribution such as is here in question would not be valid. Any 'survey of the range of the objects or possible beneficiaries' would certainly be incomplete, and I am able to discern no principle on which such a survey could be conducted or where it should start or finish. The most you could do, so far as regards relatives, would be to find individuals who are clearly members of the class—the test which was accepted in the Court of Appeal, but rejected in the House of Lords, in the *Gulbenkian* case.

The matter does not, however, rest there, and I must return to examine more closely Lord Wilberforce's reasons for rejecting the *Broadway Cottages* test. . . . He cited cases where prior to the time of Sir Richard Arden MR a discretionary trust had been executed otherwise than by equal division. *Harding* v *Glyn* (1739) 1 Atk 469, he said, was an early case where the court executed a discretionary trust for 'relations'—and it is a discretionary trust for relations that I am considering—by distributing to the next-of-kin in equal shares. . . .

Harding v *Glyn* accordingly cannot be regarded simply as a case where in default of appointment a gift to the next-of-kin is to be implied as a matter of construction, but as authority endorsed by the decision of the House of Lords that a discretionary trust for 'relations' was a valid trust to be executed by the court by distribution to the next-of-kin. The class of beneficiaries thus becomes a clearly defined class and there is no difficulty in determining whether a given individual is within it or without it.

Does it then make any difference that here the discretionary trust for relations was a reference not to the relations of a deceased person but of one who was living? I think not. The next-of-kin of a living person are as readily ascertainable at any given time as the next-of-kin of one who is dead. A trust for the next-of-kin of a person, without more, was not a trust for the next-of-kin according to the statutes which would regulate the distribution of the personal property of a deceased person had he died intestate, but a trust for his nearest blood relations: see *Re Gray's Settlement*. To execute a discretionary trust for the relations or relatives of a living person by distribution among his nearest blood relations appears to me a satisfactory method of so doing; and, if it were necessary to give a construction to the word 'relatives' in relating to a living person in an inter vivos settlement, to construe it as a reference to his nearest blood relations would be far more likely to give effect to the intention than a construction which embraced all who were descended from one of his ancestors. Putting aside the doctrine ut res magis valeat quam pereat, which would *if necessary* have persuaded me that the word 'relatives' in this settlement should be construed to mean nearest blood relations, nothing could be more improbable than that Mr Baden should have intended the trustees to be at liberty to make grants to a relative of an employee of whose very existence that employee might be ignorant. 'Nearest blood relations or dependants' makes more sense. . . .

In coming to these conclusions I remain haunted by a remark towards the end of Lord Wilberforce's speech when, in considering the possible unworkability of a trust, he speaks of 'relations' as if it were a very wide class; for I confess that I find a difficulty in treating a discretionary trust as one which may be executed by the trustees among a wider class than would be contemplated if the court were required to execute it. . . .

The only other challenge to the validity of the trust is directed against the use of the word 'dependants' which it is said introduces a linguistic or semantic uncertainty. That in the context the word connotes financial dependence I do not doubt, and although in a given case there may be a doubt whether there be a sufficient degree of dependence to satisfy the qualification of being a 'dependant', that is a question which can be determined by the court and does not introduce linguistic uncertainty.

4.5.3 GIFTS SUBJECT TO CONDITIONS

4.5.3.1 Gifts subject to conditions precedent

RE BARLOW'S WILL TRUSTS [1979] 1 All ER 296

FACTS: A testatrix died leaving a collection of paintings in her will. Having made some specific bequests she gave the remainder of the paintings to her executor on a trust for sale but subject to a direction that 'any members of my family and any friends of mine who may wish to do so' should be allowed to purchase any of the paintings at far below their market values. The executor took out a summons for a declaration as to whether the gift to the 'friends' was void for uncertainty. He also sought a direction as to the proper meaning of 'family' in the context of this gift.

HELD: The direction did not fail for uncertainty. If it could be said with certainty that a particular claimant qualified as a 'friend' a sale of paintings to that person would be valid under the terms of the will. This was because uncertainty as to whether other persons may or may not be 'friends' could have no effect on the quantum of the gift to those persons who clearly qualified as 'friends'. In the same way that it was unnecessary to establish a precise definition of 'friend' for the gift to be effective, it was also unnecessary to restrict the meaning of family to 'statutory next-of-kin'. For the purposes of the present gift it was sufficient to define family as 'blood relations'.

BROWNE-WILKINSON J: . . . Counsel for the fourth defendant, who argued in favour of the validity of the gift, contended that the tests laid down in the *Gulbenkian* case and *McPhail* v *Doulton* were not applicable to this case. The test, he says, is that laid down by the Court of Appeal in *Re Allen* [1953] Ch 810 as appropriate in cases where the validity of a condition precedent or description is in issue, namely that the gift is valid if it is possible to say of one or more persons that he or they undoubtedly qualify even though it may be difficult to say of others whether or not they qualify.

The distinction between the *Gulbenkian* test and the *Re Allen* test is, in my judgment, well exemplified by the word 'friends'. The word has a great range of meanings; indeed, its exact meaning probably varies slightly from person to person. Some would include only those with whom they had been on intimate terms over a long period; others would include acquaintances whom they liked. Some would include people with whom their relationship was primarily one of business; others would not. Indeed, many people, if asked to draw up a complete list of their friends, would probably have some difficulty in deciding whether certain of the people they knew were really 'friends' as opposed to 'acqaintances'. Therefore, if the nature of the gift was such that it was legally necessary to draw up a complete list of 'friends' of the testatrix, or to be able to say of any person that 'he is not a friend', the whole gift would probably fail even as to those who, by any conceivable test, were friends. But in the case of a gift of a kind which does not require one to establish all the members of the class (e.g. 'a gift of £10 to each of my friends'), it may be possible to say of some people that, on any test, they qualify. Thus in *Re Allen* Evershed MR took the example of a gift to X 'if he is a tall man'; a man 6 feet 6 inches tall could be said on any reasonable basis to satisfy the test, although it might be impossible to say whether a man, say 5 feet 10 inches high satisfied the requirement.

So in this case, in my judgment, there are acquaintances of a kind so close that, on any reasonable basis, anyone would treat them as being 'friends'. Therefore, by allowing the disposition to take effect in their favour, one would certainly be giving effect to part of the testatrix's intention even though as to others it is impossible to say whether or not they satisfy the test.

In my judgment, it is clear that Lord Upjohn in *Re Gulbenkian* was considering only cases where it was necessary to establish all the members of the class. He made it clear that the reason for the rule is that in a gift which requires one to establish all the members of the class (e.g. 'a gift to my friends in equal shares') you cannot hold the gift good in part, since the quantum of each friend's share depends on how many friends there are. So all persons intended to benefit by the donor must be ascertained if any effect is to be given to the gift. In my judgment, the adoption of Lord Upjohn's test by the House of Lords in *McPhail* v *Doulton* is based on the same reasoning, even though in that case the House of Lords held that it was only necessary to be able to survey the class of objects of a power of appointment and not to establish who all the members were. But such reasoning has no application to a case where there is a condition or description attached to one or more individual gifts; in such cases, uncertainty as to some other persons who may have been intended to take does not in any way affect the quantum of the gift to persons who undoubtedly possess the qualification. Hence, in my judgment, the different test laid down in *Re Allen*. The recent decision of the Court of Appeal in *Re Tuck's Settlement Trust* [1978] Ch 49 establishes that the test in *Re Allen* is still the appropriate test in considering such gifts, notwithstanding the *Gulbenkian* and *McPhail* v *Doulton* decisions: see *per* Lord Russell of Killowen.

Accordingly, in my judgment, the proper result in this case depends on whether the disposition in cl. 5(a) is properly to be regarded as a series of individual gifts to persons answering the description 'friend' (in which case it will be valid), or a gift which requires the whole class of friends to be established (in which case it will probably fail).

The effect of cl. 5(a) is to confer on friends of the testatrix a series of options to purchase. Although it is obviously desirable as a practical matter that steps should be taken to inform those entitled to the options of their rights, it is common ground that there is no legal necessity to do so. Therefore, each person coming forward to exercise the option has to prove that he is a friend; it is legally necessary, in my judgment, to discover who all the friends are. In order to decide whether an individual is entitled to purchase, all that is required is that the executors should be able to say of that individual whether he has proved that he is a friend. The word 'friend', therefore, is a description or qualification of the option holder. . . .

I therefore hold that the disposition does not fail for uncertainty, but that anyone who can prove that by any reasonable test he or she must have been a friend of the testatrix is entitled to exercise the option. Without seeking to lay down any exhaustive definition of such test, it may be helpful if I indicate certain minimum requirements: (a) the relationship must have been a long-standing one; (b) the relationship must have been a social relationship as opposed to a business or professional relationship; (c) although there may have been long periods when circumstances prevented the testatrix and the applicant from meeting, when circumstances did permit they must have met frequently. If in any case the executors entertain any real doubt whether an applicant qualifies, they can apply to the court to decide the issue.

4.6　End of Chapter Assessment Question

Vincent, a renowned artist, died in 1997. His will contains the following provisions:

(a)　'To my favourite artist, Theodore van Damme, I devise my country studio and gardens on the Isle of Mull absolutely in full confidence that he will make such use of them as I should have made myself and that at his death he will leave them to the Royal Academy and in default of any disposition by him thereof by his will or testament I hereby direct that all my estate and property acquired by him under this my will shall at his death be given to the Royal Academy absolutely'.

(b)　'To my executors, my personal estate (excluding my art collection) to hold upon trust for such artists as they shall select having regard to their knowledge of my personal taste in art.'

(c)　To my executors, the greater part of my art collection to be held by them on trust for my favourite model, Lucille Gachet, subject to any pictures which my friends may choose.'

Consider the validity of each provision, and the consequences, where relevant, of invalidity.

4.7　End of Chapter Assessment Outline Answer

This question is designed to test your ability to apply the 'three certainties' requirement for an express trust to three dispositions in a will. Each of the three dispositions happens to take one of the three certainties as its focus, you should therefore be warned that real life (as well as real examination) examples may not separate the three certainties so neatly. You should always bear in mind that uncertain subject matter or uncertain object may indicate an uncertain intention.

(a)　The primary issue here is whether or not this disposition evinces certainty of intention to create a trust. Certainty of intention is also referred to as certainty of 'words'. The question to be determined is whether the words used in making the disposition are imperative, so as to fix the donee with trust obligations in relation to the realty. There is no magic formula for determining in every case whether or not a trust has been created.

Each disposition must be construed as a whole in order to glean the testator's true intentions. The general rule is that precedent should not be conclusive of the question of construction (*Re Hamilton* (1895) 2 Ch 370). However, if the disposition is made in terms which reproduce exactly the peculiar wording of the disposition in a previous reported case, the court may infer that the person making the disposition intended to achieve the same result as that achieved in the previous reported case (*Re Steele's Will Trusts* [1948] Ch 603). That appears to have been the testator's intention here.

His disposition repeats almost verbatim the form of the disposition in the House of Lords case of *Comiskey* v *Bowring-Hanbury* [1905] AC 84. The testator left to his wife 'the whole of my real and personal estate and property absolutely in full confidence that she will make such use of it as I should have made myself and that at her death she will devise it to such one or more of my nieces as she may think fit and in default of any disposition by her thereof by her will or testament I hereby direct that all my estate and property acquired by her under this my will shall at her death be equally divided among the surviving said nieces'.

In that case it was held that, upon a true construction of the words of the will, the disposition took effect as a trust, under which the wife had a life interest, the superadded direction that the nieces should acquire an interest *in any event* showed that the wife was not intended to acquire an absolute interest in the estate.

It would appear, therefore, that the testator has constituted Theodore a trustee for himself for life and for the Royal Academy in remainder.

(b)   This disposition is certainly intended to be in the nature of a trust. The use of the word 'trust' is nearly always conclusive, and the word 'shall' emphasises that there is an imperative obligation to distribute the testator's personal estate.

The object of any trust must be certain before a court will acknowledge that a valid trust has been created. The main reason for the requirement of certainty of object is to ensure that the trustees can identify the persons in whose favour they are required to distribute the fund. Where the trustees have a discretion as to which beneficiaries within a class will take a benefit, it is not necessary to be able to list every member in the class. It *is* necessary, however, for the trustees to be able to say of any individual claimant whether they do or do not fall within the class of possible beneficiaries. This 'individual ascertainability' test was laid down in relation to discretionary trusts by a bare majority of the House of Lords in the case of *McPhail v Doulton*. Lord Wilberforce, who delivered the leading speech, held that the trustees of a discretionary trust must survey the class of potential beneficiaries in order to form some idea of the number of persons within it. In order to carry out this survey, and in order to exercise a fair discretion in the distribution of the fund amongst the class of potential beneficiaries, the class must be capable of reasonably precise definition. Lord Wilberforce referred to this as the requirement of 'linguistic or semantic' certainty, now more usually referred to as the requirement of conceptual certainty (see, in particular, the judgments of the Court of Appeal in *Re Baden's Deed Trusts (No. 2)*).

The discretionary trust in the instant case will only be valid if the trustees (and ultimately the court) could say for certain of any claimant whether they are or are not an 'artist'. The difficulty with the term 'artist' is that an artist is merely a person who produces 'art', and it is difficult to find any two people who can agree upon what 'art' is. Art and artist are conceptually uncertain words. Nevertheless, in accordance with the maxim *certum est quod certum reddi potest*, the courts will treat as certain that which can be made certain. So, is there any way in which the term 'artist' can be rendered certain?

One possibility is to define the concept along lines approved by the testator (the testator in the instant case actually urges this approach upon his trustees). It may be that the testator had written books or letters in which he attempted to define the term. If a usable definition can be found the court may see fit to direct the trustees to take the testator's own definition of the term 'artist' as a way of remedying the uncertainty of the concept. However, although the court approved an approach similar to this in *Re Tepper's Will* [1987] 1 All ER 970 in relation to an *individual* gift subject to a condition subsequent (the gift was made on condition that the donee remained 'within the Jewish faith and shall not marry outside the Jewish faith', the judge admitting evidence of the testator's own practice in order to render certain the meaning of the term 'Jewish'), it is doubtful that it would be applied to a gift, such as the present, which is held on trust to be *divided* amongst a class.

On balance, it is very doubtful that the court would remedy the uncertainty inherent in the description 'artist' and the discretionary trust will therefore fail for uncertainty of object. The consequence of the invalidity of the trust is that the trustees will hold the fund on trust for the residuary beneficiaries under the testator's will.

(c)   This trust will fail for uncertainty of subject matter. The trustee cannot possibly know what is meant by the 'greater part' of the art collection. It could mean the greater part by value, or the greater part in terms of the number of pieces, or even the greater part in terms of physical bulk. In *Palmer v Simmonds* (1854) 2 Drew 221 a trust of 'the bulk of my estate' failed for uncertainty of subject matter. The usual consequence of invalidity due to unascertainable subject matter is that the trust fails absolutely and the person in possession of the property takes it absolutely (this is what happened in *Palmer v Simmonds* itself). However, where the persons in possession of the property are executors (i.e. already trustees by status) the property will be held by them on resulting trust for the residuary beneficiaries under the testator's will.

Finally, there is the issue of the individual gifts of paintings to the testator's friends. These gifts are absolute gifts subject only to a condition precedent, namely that each claimant must prove that he or she is the testator's 'friend'. It is the nature of such gifts that the donee takes the whole of the subject matter (i.e. the painting or paintings), this can be contrasted with a discretionary trust where the beneficiaries *share* the fund. Because there is no need to share a fund between a class of persons the test of certainty of object is less stringent in relation to a gift subject to a condition precedent. Such a gift will be valid in relation to any person who can prove that they are a friend, even though persons may exist of whom it cannot be said whether or not they are a friend (*Re Barlow's Will Trusts* [1979] 1 All ER 296). In the instant case, however, the individual gifts subject to a condition precedent were intended to operate as a charge upon the larger trust of the 'greater part' of the art collection. As the larger trust has failed it is most doubtful that the court would enforce the charge (the individual gifts) against the art collection in the hands of the executors or the residuary beneficiaries.

CHAPTER FIVE

THE CONSTITUTION OF TRUSTS

5.1 Constitution by Transfer of Legal Title to Trustees

5.1.1 WHERE THE TRUST PROPERTY CONSISTS OF SHARES

MILROY v LORD (1862) 2 DE G F & J 264

FACTS: A settlor owned shares in a bank which he purported to transfer to L by deed, to be held by L on trust for M. The settlor later passed the share certificates to L. L was the settlor's attorney and was therefore authorised to transfer the shares to M, but ultimately there could only be valid transfer of the shares by registration, at the bank, of M as owner of the shares. This registration was never carried out. The issue was whether M could claim the shares under a trust created by the settlor.

HELD: On the facts no valid trust had been created, M had not provided consideration for the shares, he was therefore a mere 'volunteer'. Applying the maxim that 'equity does not assist a volunteer', it followed that the settlement would not be binding on the settlor (even if he had wished it to be so) unless the settlor had 'done everything which, according to the nature of the property comprised in the settlement, was necessary to be done in order to transfer the property'. The settlor could have transferred the property to M by way of gift, or transferred the property to L upon trust for M, but neither method of constituting the settlement had been effective on the facts of the present case, because there could be no valid transfer of the shares without registration. Further, if the settlement was intended to take place by transfer the court would not give effect to it by finding a valid declaration of trust. The court will, on a proper reading of the facts, construe every settlement as either an attempted outright gift, an attempted trust by transfer to trustees or an attempted declaration of trust constituting the settlor trustee. If the settlor's chosen mode of constitution fails the court will not perfect the settlement by allowing it to take effect by another of the modes.

TURNER LJ: Under the circumstances of this case, it would be difficult not to feel a strong disposition to give effect to this settlement to the fullest extent, and certainly I spared no pains to find the means of doing so, consistently with what I apprehend to be the law of the court; but, after full and anxious consideration, I find myself unable to do so. I take the law of this court to be well settled, that, in order to render a voluntary settlement valid and effectual; the settlor must have done everything which, according to the nature of the property comprised in the settlement, was necessary to be done in order to transfer the property and render the settlement binding upon him. He may of course do this by actually transferring the property to the persons for whom he intends to provide, and the provision will then be effectual, and it will be equally effectual if he transfers the property to a trustee for the purposes of the settlement, or declares that he himself holds it in trust for those purposes; and if the property be personal, the trust may, as I apprehend, be declared either in writing or by parol; but, in order to render the settlement binding, one or other of these modes must, as I understand the law of this court, be resorted to, for there is no equity in this court to perfect an imperfect gift. The cases I think go further to this extent, that if the settlement is intended to be effectuated by one of the modes to which I have referred, the court will not give effect to it by applying another of those modes. If it is intended to take effect by transfer, the court will not hold the intended transfer to operate as a declaration of trust, for then every imperfect instrument would be made effectual by being converted into a perfect trust. These are the principles by which, as I conceive, this case must be tried.

Applying, then, these principles to the case, there is not here any transfer either of the one class of shares or of the other to the objects of the settlement, and the question therefore must be, whether a valid and effectual trust in favour of those objects was created in the defendant Samuel Lord or in the settlor himself as to all or any of these shares. Now it is plain that it was not the purpose of this settlement, or the intention of the settlor, to constitute himself a trustee of the bank shares. The intention was that the trust should be vested in the defendant Samuel Lord, and I think therefore that we should not be justified in holding that by the settlement, or by an parol declaration made by the settlor, he himself became a trustee of these shares for the purposes of the settlement. By doing so we should be converting the settlement or the parol declaration to a purpose wholly different from that which was intended to be effected by it, and, as I have said, creating a perfect trust out of an imperfect transaction. . . .

The more difficult question is, whether the defendant Samuel Lord did not become a trustee of these shares? Upon this question I have felt considerable doubt; but in the result, I have come to the conclusion that no perfect trust was ever created in him. The shares, it is clear, were never legally vested in him; and the only ground on which he can be held to have become a trustee of them is, that he held a power of attorney under which he might have transferred them into his own name; but he held that power of attorney as the agent of the settlor; and if he had been sued by the plaintiffs as trustee of the settlement for an account under the trust, and to compel him to transfer the shares into his own name as trustee, I think he might well have said—These shares are not vested in me; I have no power over them except as the agent of the settlor, and without his express directions I cannot be justified in making the proposed transfer, in converting an intended into an actual settlement. A court of equity could not, I think, decree the agent of the settlor to make the transfer, unless it could decree the settlor himself to do so, and it is plain that no such decree could have been made against the settlor. In my opinion, therefore, this decree cannot be maintained as to the fifty Louisiana Bank shares.

RE ROSE [1952] 1 All ER 1217, CA

FACTS: In March 1943 R transferred 10,000 shares in an unlimited company to his wife and on the same day transferred a further 10,000 shares in the same company to trustees to hold upon the terms of a settlement. The transfers were in an authorised form. In the event the transfers were not registered by the company until June 1943. R died in 1947 after which, in accordance with certain tax regulations, the Inland Revenue claimed estate duty on the shares because the gift had not been completed before April 1943.
HELD: R had done everything in his power to transfer his legal and equitable interest in the shares on the date of the transfer in March 1943. The factors which delayed the registration of the legal title until after April 1943 were beyond R's control. Counsel for the Inland Revenue had argued that the purported transfer must have been entirely ineffective according to *Milroy* v *Lord*, but the court held that *Milroy* v *Lord* would not invalidate a transfer in a case such as the present where the donor, after the purported transfer, would not be permitted to assert any beneficial ownership in the shares at all. R had divested himself entirely of his equitable interest in the shares and accordingly his estate would not be liable to pay tax thereon. This result was not effected by the fact that, between March 1943 and the date when the legal title was registered with the company, R continued to hold the legal title as a nominal trustee.

SIR RAYMOND EVERSHED MR: [Having purported to distinguish *Milroy* v *Lord* on its facts, his Lordship continued:] . . . a man purporting to transfer property executes documents which are not apt to effect that purpose, the court cannot then extract from those documents some quite different transaction and say that they were intended merely to operate as a declaration of trust which ex facie they are not, but if a document is apt and proper to transfer the property—is, in truth, the appropriate way in which the property must be transferred—it does not seem to me to follow from the earlier statement that, as a result, either during some limited period or otherwise, there may not arise, for the purpose of giving effect to the transfer, some trust. The simplest case will, perhaps, provide an illustration. If a man executes a document transferring all his equitable interest, say, in shares, that document, operating, and intended to operate, as a transfer, will give rise to and take effect as a trust, for the assignor will then be a trustee of the legal estate in the shares for the person in whose favour he has made an assignment of his beneficial interest. For my part, I do not think that *Milroy* v *Lord* is an authority which compels this court to hold that in this case, where, in the terms of the judgment of Turner LJ, the settlor did everything which, according to the nature of the property comprised in the settlement, was necessary to be done by him in order to transfer the property, the result necessarily negatives the conclusion that, pending registration, the settlor was a trustee of the legal interest for the transferee.

The view of the limitations of *Milroy* v *Lord* which I have tried to express was much better expressed by Jenkins J in the recent case which also bears the name of *Re Rose* (though that is a coincidence). It is true that the main point, the essential question to be determined, was whether there had been a transfer eo nomine of certain shares within the meaning of a will. The testator in that case, Rose, by his will had given a number of shares to one Hook, but the gift was subject to this qualification, 'if such . . . shares have not been transferred to him previously to my death'. The question was: Had the shares been transferred to him in the circumstances? He had executed (as had Mr Rose in the present case) a transfer in appropriate form, and handed the transfer and the certificate to Hook, but, at the time of his death, the transfer had not been registered. It was said, therefore, that there had been no transfer, and (following the argument of counsel for the Crown) there had been no passing to Hook of any interest, legal or beneficial, whatever, by the time the testator died. If that view were right, then, of course, Hook would be entitled to the shares under the will. But Jenkins J went a little more closely into the matter because it was obvious that on one view of it, if it were held that there was a 'transfer' within the terms of the will, though the transfer was inoperative in the eye of the law and not capable of being completed after the death, then Mr Hook suffered the misfortune of getting the shares neither by gift inter vivos nor by testamentary benefaction. Therefore, Jenkins J considered *Milroy* v *Lord* and in regard to it he used this language ([1948] 2 All ER 978):

> I was referred to *Milroy* v *Lord*, and also to *Re Fry* [1946] Ch 312. Those cases, as I understand them, turn on the fact that the deceased donor had not done all in his power, according to the nature of the property given, to vest the legal interest in the property in the donee. In such circumstances it is well settled that there is no equity to complete the imperfect gift. If any act remains to be done by the donor to complete the gift at the date of the donor's death, the court will not compel his personal representatives to do that act and the gift remains incomplete and fails. In *Milroy* v *Lord* the imperfection was due to the fact that the wrong form of transfer was used for the purpose of transferring certain bank shares. The document was not the appropriate document to pass any interest in the property at all.

Then he refers to *Re Fry*, which is another illustration. Jenkins J continued (ibid):

> In this case, as I understand it, the testator had done everything in his power to divest himself of the shares in question in favour of Mr Hook. He had executed a transfer. It is not suggested that the transfer was not in accordance with the company's regulations. He had handed that transfer together with the certificates to Mr Hook. There was nothing else the testator could do.

I venture respectfully to adopt the whole of the passage I have read which, in my judgment, is a correct statement of the law. If that be so, then it seems to me that it cannot be asserted on the authority of *Milroy* v *Lord*, and I venture to think it also cannot be asserted as a matter of logic and good sense or principle, that because, by the regulations of the company, there had to be a gap before Mrs Rose could, as between herself and the company, claim the rights which the shares gave her vis-à-vis the company, Mr Rose was not in the meantime a trustee for her of all his rights and benefits under the shares. That he intended to pass all those rights, as I have said, seems to me too plain for argument. I think the matter be put, perhaps, in a somewhat different fashion though it reaches the same end. Whatever might be the position during the period between the execution of this document and the registration of the shares, the transfers were on 30 June 1943, registered. After registration, the title of Mrs Rose was beyond doubt complete in every respect, and if Mr Rose had received a dividend between execution and registration and Mrs Rose had claimed to have that dividend handed to her, what would Mr Rose's answer have been? It could no longer be that the purported gift was imperfect; it had been made perfect. I am not suggesting that the perfection was retroactive, but what could he say? How could he, in the face of his own statement under his seal, deny the proposition that he had, on 30 March 1943 transferred the shares to his wife? By the phrase 'transfer the shares' surely must be meant transfer to her 'the shares and all my rights, title and interest thereunder'. Nothing else could sensibly have been meant. Nor can he, I think, make much of the fact that this was a voluntary settlement on his part. Being a case of an unlimited company, as I have said, Mrs Rose had herself to undertake by covenant to accept the shares subject to their burdens—in other words, to relieve her husband of his liability as a corporator. I find it unnecessary to pursue the question of consideration, but it is, I think, another feature which would make exceedingly difficult and, I think sensibly impossible, the assertion on Mr Rose's part of any right to retain the dividend I have mentioned. Nor is the Crown's argument made any easier by the circumstances that another emanation of the Crown has adjudicated that stamp duty ad valorem under s. 74 of the Act of 1910 was payable on this transfer as a disposition of the subject-matter transferred.

. . . I do not think that *Milroy* v *Lord* covers the case and I agree with Roxburgh J in his conclusion to that effect. I also think that on principle the statement which counsel for the Crown has made the foundation of his argument, if it covers this case, is too widely stated. If, as I have said, the phrase 'transfer the shares' is taken to be and to be and to mean a transfer of all rights and interests in them, then I can see nothing contrary to the law in a man saying that so long as, pending registration, the legal estate remains in the donor, he was, by the necessary effect of his own deed, a trustee of that legal estate. Nor do I think that that is an unjustifiable addition to or gloss on the words used in the transfer. I find it, indeed, for my part, a less difficult matter in the way of interpretation than to say that this was, on its terms, merely a conditional gift, merely a transfer as a gift to Mrs Rose of a particular right, viz, the right to get herself registered and thenceforward, but not before, to enjoy the benefits which the donor previously had in these shares. That, I think, is nothing like what the deed sets out to do. I have said that I reject the proposition that the distinction between a case such as this and a case such as *Milroy* v *Lord* is, as counsel for the Crown urged, indefensible. I think it is sensible and real, and for these reasons I would dismiss the appeals.

5.1.2   WHERE TRUST PROPERTY COMPRISES LAND

LAW OF PROPERTY ACT 1925

52.   Conveyances to be by deed

  (1)   All conveyances of land or of any interest therein are void for the purpose of conveying or creating a legal estate unless made by deed.

  (2)   This section does not apply to—

  (a)   assents by a personal representative;

  (b)   disclaimers made in accordance with [sections 178 to 180 or sections 315 to 319 of the Insolvency Act 1986] or not required to be evidenced in writing;

  (c)   surrenders by operation of law, including surrenders which may, by law, be effected without writing;

  (d)   leases or tenancies or other assurances not required by law to be made in writing;

  (e)   receipts [other than those falling within section 115 below];

  (f)   vesting orders of the court or other competent authority;

  (g)   conveyances taking effect by operation of law.

5.1.2.1 Registered land

LAND REGISTRATION ACT 1925

19. Registration of disposition of freeholds

(1) The transfer of the registered estate in the land or part thereof shall be completed by the registrar entering on the register the transferee as the proprietor of the estate transferred, but until such entry is made the transferor shall be deemed to remain proprietor of the registered estate; and, where part only of the land is transferred, notice thereof shall also be noted on the register.

5.2 Constitution by Transfer where the Subject of the Gift or Trust is an Equitable Interest

RE McARDLE [1951] 1 Ch 669, CA

FACTS: The testator, M, left his residuary estate upon trust for his widow for life remainder to his five children in equal shares. During the lifetime of M's widow, one of the children, MM, carried out improvements to a property forming part of the testator's residuary estate. The testator's other children signed a document in these terms: 'To MM . . . In consideration of your carrying out certain alterations and improvements to the property' . . . 'at present occupied by you, we the beneficiaries under the will of M hereby agree that the executor's . . . shall repay to you from the said estate when so distributed the sum of £488 in settlement of the amount spent on such improvements'. Accordingly, when the widow died MM claimed the £488. However, the other children of M objected to the claim. The questions which arose for consideration were, first, whether the signed document could take effect as a binding contract, and secondly, in the alternative, if it failed as a contract could the document constitute an effective assignment of an equitable interest to MM.

HELD: The document did not constitute an enforceable contract, because the works of improvement had been completed before the execution of the document and therefore the consideration for the agreement was wholly past. Nor could the document constitute a perfect gift of the equitable interest. The document had been expressed in the form of a contract for valuable consideration and it would therefore be artificial to construe it as being a valid equitable assignment. Accordingly MM had no entitlement in law or equity to receive the £488. To remedy this the beneficiaries would have had to have authorised the executors to pay the £488, until this had been done the beneficiaries had not done all within their power to dispose of their interest in the £488.

EVERSHED MR: The real question and it is by no means easy—is whether this document of 1945 was an effective equitable assignment which passed to Mrs Marjorie McArdle an indefensible interest in a proportionate part of the residuary estate; for, if it is not, then I think it is clear, owing to the well-established doctrine of consideration, that is must fail to give her a claim which she can litigate since there was and is no consideration passing from her to support her claim.

The judge came to the conclusion that there was here an equitable assignment, and that it was unnecessary, on the authorities, for such an equitable assignment, in a case in which the subject-matter is existing property, to be supported by valuable consideration. The problem is vexed and difficult. I think it is accurately stated in Snell's *Principles of Equity* (22nd ed.), pp. 57 and 58, as follows:

> Whether value is necessary for an equitable assignment is not clearly settled. It has been held that value is not necessary for an assignment of a legal thing in action which complies with the statutory provisions . . . and it would seem to be unnecessary also for an assignment of an equitable thing in action, such as a legacy or an interest in trust funds, provided that the assignment is complete and perfect; there is no reason

why a man should not be able to give away an equitable interest as freely as he can give away a legal interest. But value appears to be necessary for an equitable assignment of a legal thing in action; . . . such an assignment being inoperative at law, the assistance of equity is needed to make it effective, and equity will not assist to make perfect an imperfect gift. Value is certainly necessary for the assignment of rights of property not yet in existence

—for the reason that where the property is not in existence something else has to be done by the giver to give effect to the gift. It can operate only in contract, if there is no subject-matter then capable of being given.

The sentence in that passage, 'provided that the assignment is complete and perfect', is important; also the further sentence, 'there is no reason why a man should not be able to give away an equitable interest'. What the writer is saying there, and I accept it, is this: if what is done amounts to a gift, complete and perfect, of a subject-matter which is an equitable chose in action, then there is no reason in principle or in authority why the donee should not take the benefit just as much as he will if the giver gives him a pound note and puts it in his hand. Since the transaction is thus perfect, the question of consideration becomes irrelevant, for consideration is only necessary to support the assertion of a right to have made perfect something which is not yet perfect—for example, a contractual right.

Therefore I am prepared to accept, for the purposes of this judgment, the view that if what was done on 30 April 1945, was to assign, to make over, something completely and perfectly to Mrs Marjorie McArdle, she is entitled to succeed notwithstanding the absence of consideration. But it seems to me equally clear that whether the transaction had that effect is a matter of the intention to be derived from the transaction itself and the evidence of it. '"The mode" (I quote from White and Tudor's *Leading Cases in Equity* (9th ed.), p. 105) "or form of assignment is absolutely immaterial provided the intention of the parties is clear"' . . .

. . . It seems to me plain from the form that this document took (and it was Monty McArdle's document) that the transaction was neither complete nor perfect, which it is essential that a voluntary equitable assignment should be. In other words, I do not think that it was a gift. The whole tenor of the document (not forgetting the stamp upon it) is quite contrary to the form which would have been appropriate to a gift. I quite agree with Mr Astell Burt that there are cases showing clearly that, if a person entitled to a share, either immediately ascertained or to be later ascertained, in the residue of an estate, directs and authorises the trustee to hand over that share or a part of it to another, that may well, and I will assume prima facie will, be treated by the court as operating as an equitable assignment—that is, as a voluntary gift of the share or the proportionate part as the case may be. But it does so because (and this is indeed Mr Astell Burt's own test) the alleged donor has done everything that it lies in his power to do to make it complete and perfect. If this document had taken that form or had that effect, or if the intention that it should have that effect were clear (I refer to the passage I quoted from White and Tudor's *Leading Cases in Equity* (9th ed.), p. 105), then it would have operated as an equitable assignment. I regret that it has not that effect. I am for myself sorry that the other parties have been able, as I think they have, to evade the obligation which they imposed on themselves in 1945. But that is a matter for their conscience and not for this court. . . .

5.3   Assistance from the Common Law

5.3.1   CLAIMS OF PERSONS WITHIN THE MARRIAGE CONSIDERATION

PULLAN v KOE [1913] 1 Ch 9

FACTS: By a marriage settlement of 1859 a husband and wife covenanted to settle the wife's after-acquired property upon trusts for the benefit of the husband, the wife and their future children. In 1879 the wife's mother made a gift to her of £285 which the wife paid into her husband's bank account. A portion of this money was later invested in two bearer bonds which remained at the bank (gathering interest) until the husband's death in 1909. The trustees of the marriage settlement brought the present action against the husband's estate claiming that the bonds should be held for the benefit of the beneficiaries of the marriage settlement.

HELD: Under the Statute of Limitations the trustees were far too late to sue at common law for damages on the covenant. However, the husband had received the bonds with notice of the trusts of the marriage settlement and had given no valuable consideration for the bonds. Being, therefore, a mere volunteer, he took the bonds subject to the trusts of the marriage settlement. Accordingly, even though their legal action had been time-barred, the trustees were able to claim the bonds in equity on behalf of the beneficiaries. A person can contract (whether or not for value and whether or not by deed) to assign property which is to come into existence in the future, and when it comes into existence, equity treats as done that which ought to be done and will insist upon the specific performance of the contract. While it is true that the court will not assist a volunteer, here the plaintiffs (the trustees) were parties to the contract, and were acting on behalf of persons within the marriage consideration.

SWINFEN EADY J: . . . In my opinion as soon as the 285l. was paid to the wife it became in equity bound by and subject to the trusts of the settlement. The trustees could have claimed that particular sum, could have obtained at once the appointment of a receiver of it, if they could have shewn a case of jeopardy, and, if it had been invested and the investment could be traced, could have followed the money and claimed the investment.

This point was dealt with by Jessel MR, in *Smith v Lucas* 18 Ch D 531 where he said:

> What is the effect of such a covenant in equity? It has been said that the effect in equity of the covenant of the wife, as far as she is concerned, is that it does not affect her personally, but that it binds the property: that is to say, it binds the property under the doctrine of equity that that is to be considered as done which ought to be done. That is in the nature of specific performance of the contract no doubt. If, therefore, this is a covenant to settle the future-acquired property of the wife, and nothing more is done by her, the covenant will bind the property.

Again in *Collyer v Isaacs* 19 ChD 842 Jessel MR said:

> A man can contract to assign property which is to come into existence in the future, and when it has come into existence, equity, treating as done that which ought to be done, fastens upon that property, and the contract to assign thus becomes a complete assignment. If a person contract for value, e.g., in his marriage settlement, to settle all such real estate as his father shall leave him by will, or purports actually to convey by the deed all such real estate, the effect is the same. It is a contract for value which will bind the property if the father leaves any property to his son.

The property being thus bound, these bonds became trust property, and can be followed by the trustees and claimed from a volunteer.

Again the trustees are entitled to come into a Court of Equity to enforce a contract to create a trust, contained in a marriage settlement, for the benefit of the wife and the issue of the marriage, all of whom are within the marriage consideration. The husband covenanted that he and his heirs, executors, and administrators should, as soon as circumstances would admit, convey, assign, and surrender to the trustees the real or personal property to which his wife should become beneficially entitled. The trustees are entitled to have that covenant specifically enforced by a Court of Equity. In *In re D'Angibau* 15 Ch D 228 and in *In re Plumptre's Marriage Settlement* [1910] 1 Ch 609 it was held that the Court would not interfere in favour of volunteers, not within the marriage consideration, but here the plaintiffs are the contracting parties and the object of the proceeding is to benefit the wife and issue of the marriage. In *In re D'Angibau* Cotton LJ said:

> As a rule the Court will not enforce a contract as distinguished from a trust at the instance of persons not parties to the contract: *Colyear v Countess of Mulgrave* (1886) 2

Keen 81. The Court would probably enforce a contract in a marriage settlement at the instance of the children of the marriage, but this is an exception from the general rule in favour of those who are specially the objects of the settlement.

. . .

RE KAY'S SETTLEMENT [1939] 1 All ER 245

FACTS: In 1907 Mary Winifred Kay, a spinster, executed a voluntary conveyance in favour of herself for life and after her death for her issue, containing a covenant to settle after-acquired property. She married and had three children and became entitled to other property. She refused a request by the trustees of the settlement to bring in the property on the ground that, as the settlement was purely voluntary, they ought not to take steps to enforce the covenant or to recover damages.
HELD: Trustees directed not to take any such steps.

SIMONDS J; The trustees have issued this summons, making as parties to if, first, the settlor herself, and, secondly, her infant children, who are beneficiaries under the settlement. But, be it observed, though beneficiaries, her children are, for the purpose of this settlement, to be regarded as volunteers, there being no marriage consideration, which would have entitled them to sue, though they are parties to this application. The trustees ask whether, in the event which has happened of the settlor having become entitled to certain property, they should take proceedings against her to compel performance of the covenant or to recover damages on her failure to implement it . . . The settlor has appeared by Mr Evershed and has contended, as she was entitled to contend, that the only question before the court was whether the trustees ought to be directed to take such proceedings; that is to say, she contended that the only question before the court was precisely that question which Eve J had to deal with in *Re Pryce* [1917] 1 Ch 234. She has said that the question before me is not primarily whether, if she were sued, such an action would succeed (as to which she might have a defence, I know not what), but whether, in the circumstances as they are stated to the court, the trustees ought to be directed to take proceedings against her.

As to that, the argument before me has been, on behalf of the children of the marriage, beneficiaries under the settlement, that, although it is conceded that the trustees could not successfully take proceedings for specific performance of the agreements contained in the settlement, yet they could successfully, and ought to be directed to, take proceedings at law to recover damages for the non-observance of the agreements contained in the settlement. . . . In the circumstances I must say that I felt considerable sympathy for the argument which was put before me by Mr Winterbotham on behalf of the children, that there was, at any rate, on the evidence before the court today, no reason why the trustees should not be directed to take proceedings to recover what damages might be recoverable at law for breach of the agreements entered into by the settlor in her settlement. But on a consideration of *Re Pryce* it seemed to me that so far as this court was concerned the matter was concluded and that I ought not to give any directions to the trustees to take the suggested proceedings.

In *Re Pryce* the circumstances appear to me to have been in no wise different from those which obtain in the case which I have to consider. In that case there was a marriage settlement made in 1887. It contained a covenant to settle the wife's after-acquired property. . . . The husband died in 1907, and there was no issue of the marriage. Subject to his widow's life interest in both funds, the ultimate residue of the wife's fund was held in trust for her statutory next of kin, and the husband's fund was held in trust for him absolutely. The widow was also tenant for life under her husband's will. The trustees of the marriage settlement in that case took out a summons 'to have it determined whether these interests and funds were caught by the provisions of the settlement, and, if so, whether they should take proceedings to enforce them'. . . .

Eve J, in a considered judgment, held that although the interests to which I have referred were caught by the covenant of the wife and the agreement by the husband respectively, yet the trustees ought not to take any steps to recover any of them. In the case of the wife's fund he said that her next of kin were volunteers, who could neither maintain an action to enforce the covenant nor for damages for breach of it, and that the court would not give them by indirect means what they could not obtain by direct procedure; therefore he declined to direct the trustees to take proceedings either to have the covenant specifically enforced or to recover damages at law. The learned judge, as I have said, took time to consider his judgment. Many of the cases which have been cited to me, though not all of them apparently, were cited to him, and after deciding that no steps should be taken to enforce specific performance of the covenant he used these words [1917] 1 Ch at 214:

> The position of the wife's fund is somewhat different, in that her next of kin would be entitled to it on her death; but they are volunteers, and although the court would probably compel fulfilment of the contract to settle at the instance of any persons within the marriage consideration—see *per* Cotton LJ in *Re D'Angibau* (1880) 15 ChD 228 at 242—and in their favour will treat the outstanding property as subjected to an enforceable trust—*Pullan* v *Koe* [1913] 1 Ch 9—volunteers have no right whatever to obtain specific performance of a mere covenant which has remained as a covenant and has never been performed; see *per* James LJ in *Re D'Angibau* at 246. Nor could damages be awarded either in this court, or, I apprehend, at law, where, since the Judicature Act 1873, the same defences would be available to the defendant as would be raised in an action brought in this court for specific performance or damages.

That is the exact point which has been urged on me with great insistence by Mr Winterbotham. Whatever sympathy I might feel for his argument, I am not justified in departing in any way from this decision, which is now twenty-one years old. The learned judge went on:

> In these circumstances, seeing that the next of kin could neither maintain an action to enforce the covenant nor for damages for breach of it, and that the settlement is not a declaration of trust constituting the relationship of trustee and cestui que trust between the defendant and the next of kin, in which case effect could be given to the trusts even in favour of volunteers, but is a mere voluntary contract to create a trust, ought the court now for the sole benefit of these volunteers to direct the trustees to take proceedings to enforce the defendant's covenant? I think it ought not; to do so would be to give the next of kin by indirect means relief they cannot obtain by any direct procedure, and would in effect be enforcing the settlement as against the defendant's legal right to payment and transfer from the trustees of the parents' marriage settlement.

It is true that in those last words the learned judge does not specifically refer to an action for damages, but it is clear that he has in his mind directions both with regard to an action for specific performance and an action to recover damages at law—or, now, in this court.

In those circumstances it appears to me that I must follow the learned judge's decision and I must direct the trustees not to take any steps either to compel performance of the covenant or to recover damages through her failure to implement it.

5.3.2 CLAIMS OF PERSONS WHO ARE PARTIES TO THE COVENANT TO SETTLE

CANNON v *HARTLEY* [1949] 1 Ch 213, ChD

FACTS: H and his wife, their marriage having broken down, executed a deed of separation. Their daughter, C, was also a party to the settlement. By the terms of the deed H covenanted to settle after-acquired property in the following terms: 'If and whenever during the lifetime of the wife of [C] [H] shall become entitled . . . under the will . . . of either of his parents to any money exceeding in net amount or value £1,000 he will forthwith . . . settle one half of such money or property upon trust for himself for life and for the wife for life after his death and subject thereto in trust for the daughter absolutely'. In due course H became entitled to a valuable share of his mother's estate. Shortly thereafter H's wife died. H refused to execute a settlement in accordance with his covenant to settle. C brought this action claiming damages for breach of the covenant. HELD: Because C had been a party to the deed and a direct covenantee of the covenant to settle she was entitled to a significant award of compensatory damages at common law. Although equity will not assist a mere volunteer, in the present case C did not require the assistance of equity, she was entitled, as a party to the covenant, to enforce directly her common law right to the benefits of that covenant. When a person executes a deed any covenants within the deed are deemed, at common law, to have been made for legal consideration. Accordingly, as valid consideration had been given at common law the problems associated with C being a mere volunteer in equity did not arise.

ROMER J: The question with which I have now to deal follows on my finding that the reversionary interest to which the defendant became entitled under his father's will was caught by cl. 7 of the deed of separation. It has been argued on behalf of the defendant that the plaintiff, not having given any consideration for this covenant by her father, is not only unable to apply to a court of equity for the enforcement of the covenant by way of specific performance, but that she is also disqualified from suing at common law for damages for breach of the covenant.

. . . the defendant relies (and this appears to be the foundation of his defence) upon some observations made by Eve J in *In re Pryce* [1917] 1 Ch 234. and on the subsequent decisin of Simonds J in *In re Kay's Settlement* [1939] Ch 329. I think the point of the observations of Eve J in *In re Pryce* [1939] Ch 329 appear sufficiently in *In re Kay's Settlement*.

[His Lordship referred to the Facts of the decision in *Re Kay's Settlement* [1939] Ch 329.]

Now it appears to me that neither *In re Pryce* [1917] 1 Ch 234 nor *In re Kay's Settlement* [1939] Ch 329 is any authority for the proposition which has been submitted to me on behalf of the defendant. In neither case were the claimants parties to the settlement in question, nor were they within the consideration of the deed. When volunteers were referred to in *In re Pryce* it seems to me that what Eve J intended to say was that they were not within the class of non-parties, if I may use that expression, to whom Cotton LJ recognised in *In re D'Angibau* 15 ChD 228 that the court would afford assistance. In the present case the plaintiff, although a volunteer, is not only a party to the deed of separation but is also a direct covenantee under the very covenant upon which she is suing. She does not require the assistance of the court to enforce the covenant for she has a legal right herself to enforce it. She is not asking for equitable relief but for damages at common law for breach of covenant.

For my part, I am quite unable to regard *In re Pryce* which was a different case dealing with totally different circumstances, or anything which Eve J said therein, as amounting to an authority negativing the plaintiff's right to sue in the present case. I think that what Eve J was pointing out in *In re Pryce* was that the next of kin who were seeking to get an indirect benefit had no right to come to a court of equity because they were not parties to the deed and were not within the consideration of the deed and, similarly, they would have no right to proceed at common law by an action for damages, as the court of common law would not entertain a suit at the instance of volunteers who were not parties to the deed which was sought to be enforced, any more than the court of equity would entertain such a suit.

It was suggested to me in argument that in such a case as the present, where the covenant is to bring in after-acquired property, an action for damages for breach of that covenant is in effect the same as a suit for specific performance of a covenant to settle. I myself think that the short answer to that is that the two things are not the same at all. The plaintiff here is invoking no equitable relief; she is merely asking for monetary compensation for a breach of covenant. . . .

I shall accordingly direct an inquiry as to the damages sustained by the plaintiff for breach by the defendant of the covenant with the plaintiff contained in cl. 7 of the deed of separation and the plaintiff will have her costs of the action, the costs of the inquiry to be reserved.

5.3.3   THE RULE IN *STRONG* v *BIRD*

RE STEWART [1908] 2 Ch 251

FACTS: The testator, S, by a codicil to his will, left all the monies in a certain bank account to his widow. The will appointed the widow to be one of his executors. A few days before S's death he purchased, through agents, some valuable 'bearer bonds'. In the event the bonds were not delivered until after his death, at which time they were delivered to S's executors. S's widow brought this action against the other executors to determine whether she was entitled to the bonds in addition to the monies in the bank account.

HELD: The rule in *Strong* v *Bird* was not restricted to the release of a debt and it was irrelevant that the intended donee might not be the sole executor, but one of many. The widow was entitled to claim the bonds under the rule because S had expressed an *inter vivos* intention to make a gift to his widow of his personal estate and that intention had continued until his death.

NEVILLE J: . . . *Strong* v *Bird* LR 18 Eq 315 . . . purports to lay down a principle of general application, and I think I am bound to apply that principle to the present case. The decision is, as I understand it, to the following effect: that where a testator has expressed the intention of making a gift of personal estate belonging to him to one who upon his death becomes his executor, the intention continuing unchanged, the executor is entitled to hold the property for his own benefit. The reasoning by which the conclusion is reached is of a double character—first, that the vesting of the property in the executor at the testator's death completes the imperfect gift made in the life-time, and, secondly, that the intention of the testator to give the beneficial interest to the executor is sufficient to countervail the equity of beneficiaries under the will, the testator having vested the legal estate in the executor. The whole of the property in the personal estate in the eyes of the law vesting in each executor, it seems to me immaterial whether the donee is the only executor or one of several; nor do I think the rule is confined to cases of the release of a debt owing by the donee. The intention to give, however, must not be an intention of testamentary benefaction, although the intended donee is the executor, for in that case the rule cannot apply, the prescribed formalities for testamentary disposition not having been observed: see *Selwin* v *Brown* (1735) 3 Bro PC 607; *In re Hyslop* [1894] 3 Ch 522

5.3.3.1   Extension of the rule to administrators?

RE JAMES [1935] 1 Ch 449, ChD

FACTS: J senior, the deceased, died intestate in 1924. His son, J junior died intestate in 1933. Mrs J had been employed by J senior as a housekeeper. She had received no payment for her services, but had been regularly assured by J senior that his house and furniture would be hers upon his death. After the death of J senior, J junior had left the house taking only a few small articles with him. He left Mrs J in occupation of the house and left the deeds to the house in her possession. After the death of J junior letters of administration were granted to Mrs J, constituting her administratrix of the estate of J junior. The question arose whether the rule in *Strong* v *Bird* should be extended to perfect an otherwise imperfect gift to a donee who had not been appointed by the testator to be his executor, but had only fortuitously been appointed his administratrix by the court.

HELD: The otherwise imperfect gift to the housekeeper was perfected by her appointment as administratrix to the estate of J junior. She had thereby acquired the legal estate to the property, while the equitable estate was hers by virtue of J junior's intention to give the property to her, which intention continued up until his death.

FARWELL J: I am completely satisfied on the evidence before me that there was a continuing intention in the donor up to the time of his death to give the property to the defendant.

At the time of his death the position was that the defendant was in possession both of the property and the title deeds as donee from the intestate; but the legal estate in the property was still in the donor. The case was argued on behalf of the defendant on the footing that the position was the same as in a case of an imperfect gift of personalty and I do not therefore propose to consider whether possession of the title deeds and the property gave the defendant an equitable interest in the land which she could have successfully asserted. I will deal with it as though it were an imperfect gift of personalty. It is now well settled that in such a case equity will not aid the donee, but on the other hand if the donee gets the legal title to the property vested in him he no longer wants the assistance of equity and is entitled to rely on his legal title as against the donor or persons claiming through him : see *Strong* v *Bird*. In my judgment these principles apply here. The defendant by her appointment as one of the administratrices has got the legal estate vested in her and she needs no assistance from equity to complete her title. Under these circumstances she cannot be compelled at the suit of persons claiming through the donor to surrender her property. It follows that in my judgment the plaintiff here must recognise the title of the defendant to the property and no steps should be taken to recover it from her.

RE GONIN [1977] 2 All ER 720

FACTS: The plaintiff returned home to look after her parents. It was the plaintiff's understanding that, in consideration of her going to live with them and looking after them for the rest of their lives, they would make a gift of the house in which they lived and its contents to her. The freehold of the property comprising the house and adjoining land was owned by the mother. Unknown to the plaintiff, her mother signed a cheque in the plaintiff's favour for £33,000 which the plaintiff was to have on the mother's death, which the plaintiff claimed to be proof of her intention that the plaintiff should have the house at her death. Over the years the mother made gifts of specific items of furniture to the plaintiff. In 1963 the mother sold part of the house for £7,000, and placed the proceeds of the sale in her bank account. Some time later, she sold three building plots which formed part of the property for £12,000. She offered that money to the plaintiff as a gift but the plaintiff did not take up the offer. The mother died intestate in November 1968. In September 1970 the plaintiff obtained letters of administration to the mother's estate. It was the plaintiff's case (*inter alia*) that there had been a continuing intention on the part of the mother to give her the property and its contents and that, since the legal title to the property had vested in her as administratrix, the intended gift had thereupon been perfected under the rule in *Strong* v *Bird*.
HELD: The plaintiff's claim in respect of the freehold property failed. On the assumption that the doctrine that the legal title to a gift was perfected when the intended donee had been appointed executor of and proved the intending donor's will, applied to administrators as well as executors, what the plaintiff had to show, for the rule in *Strong* v *Bird* to apply, was a continuing intention on the part of the mother that the plaintiff had to immediately take both the land and the furniture. So far as the land was concerned, no such intention could be found. The manner in which the mother had dealt with the sale of the portions of the land pointed clearly against her having any such intention by 1963. Furthermore by drawing the cheque in favour of the plaintiff she had indicated that it was her intention that the plaintiff should inherit the cheque on her death, not that there was to be an immediate gift of land.

WALTON J: . . . I now turn to the second way in which Miss Gonin's case is put, namely reliance on the doctrine in *Strong* v *Bird*. It was accepted by both counsel before me, following the decision of Farwell J in *Re James, James* v *James* that the doctrine applied to administrators as well as to executors. I shall accordingly proceed on that agreed view of the law but I feel that before I do so I must express my own difficulties in accepting this position, leaving it to a higher court to determine what, if any, validity they have.

I start from the simple proposition that if the defendant in *Strong* v *Bird* itself had been an administrator instead of an executor the case would have been decided the other way, since it distinctly proceeded on the basis that at law the appointment of the person as an executor effected a release of any debt due from the executor to the testator, a doctrine which was never applied to an administrator. . . .

One can see why this should be so: by appointing the executor, the testator has by his own act made it impossible for the debtor to sue himself. And, indeed, so far has the rule been taken that although it will no longer apply if the person appointed executor has renounced probate, yet it will still apply if power to prove has been reserved to him.

. . .

The appointment of an administrator, on the other hand, is not the act of the deceased but of the law. It is often a matter of pure chance which of many persons equally entitled to a grant of letters of administration finally takes them out. Why, then, should any special tenderness be shown to a person so selected by law and not the will of the testator, and often indifferently selected among many with an equal claim? It would seem an astonishing doctrine of equity that if the person who wishes to take the benefit of the rule in *Strong* v *Bird* manages to be the person to obtain a grant then he will be able to do so, but if a person equally entitled manages to obtain a prior grant, then he will not be able to do so. This appears to me to treat what ought to be a simple rule of equity, namely that if the legal title to a gift is perfected by the appointment by the intending donor of the intended donee as his executor, and the latter proves his will, then the coincidence of the donor's having intended the gift and having vested the legal estate in the intended donee should coalesce into absolute ownership, as something in the nature of a lottery. I cannot think that equity is so undiscriminating. I am of course aware that *Re James, James* v *James* was cited with no dissent by Buckley J (as he then was) in *Re Ralli's Will Trusts, Calvocoressi* v *Rodocanachi*, though I think the matters there in issue were fundamentally different from those which arose under the rule in *Strong* v *Bird*, and as I read his judgment, *Re James* was only used as an illustration. However, in spite of these doubts I shall follow, as I have said, *Re James*, leaving it for another court to consider at some appropriate time whether there is or is not any solid foundation for these misgivings.

In order for the rule in *Strong* v *Bird* to apply at all I have to find a continuing intention on the part of the deceased that Miss Gonin should immediately take both the land and the furniture. In my judgment, so far as the land is concerned no such continuing intention can be found.

5.3.4   THE 'ACCIDENTAL' CONSTITUTION OF A TRUST

RE RALLI'S WILL TRUSTS [1963] 3 All ER 940

FACTS: At all material times H was the legatee under her father's will of one half of his residuary estate subject to her mother's life interest. Her mother died on 19 January 1961. By cl. 7 of H's marriage settlement, dated 31 January 1924, she covenanted with the trustees that she would assign after-acquired property to the trustees to be held on the trusts therein declared which, as events happened, were after H's death, for the benefit of children of her sister. This clause extended to H's reversionary interest in one half of the testator's residuary estate but did not operate as an assignment of it. Clause 8 provided, among other things, that all the property comprised within the terms of the covenant should be subject in equity to the settlement, but that the trustees should not be bound to take steps to enforce the covenant. H never executed any assignment of her share in the testator's residue to the trustees of the settlement, nor was any notice of the settlement ever given to the trustees of the testator's will. In 1946 the plaintiff was appointed a trustee of the testator's will and he became the sole surviving trustee both of the will and of the settlement. On 6 September 1956, H died childless and a widow. The plaintiff sought to maintain that H's vested reversion in half of the testator's residue was held on the trusts of the settlement. The defendants, who were H's legal personal representatives, contended that the covenant to settle the property was executory and unenforceable for the benefit of the children of H's sister, they being volunteers outside the marriage consideration.

HELD: (1) Clause 8, on its true construction, was distinct from cl. 7 and constituted an independent declaration of trust by H of any property falling within the ambit of the covenant in cl. 7, which declaration operated while cl. 7 remained unperformed; and accordingly pending transfer to the trustees of the settlement of H's equitable interest in one half of the testator's residue that interest of hers was subject in equity to the trusts of the settlement by virtue of her declaration of trust contained in cl. 8.

(2) The plaintiff, by virtue of having been appointed trustee of the will, was at law the owner of the investments constituting the one half of the testator's residue, and the capacity in which he became possessed of the investments was irrelevant in considering whether an imperfect gift was completed (*Strong* v *Bird* (1874) LR 18 Eq 315, and *Re James* [1935] All ER Rep 235, applied); in the present case, as the plaintiff was the trustee both of the will and of the settlement, he did not need to invoke the help of a court of equity in order to perfect the alleged trusts, and the legal personal representatives of H could not successfully assert in equity a claim disentitling him to stand on his legal rights, because they were in no better position than that in which H would have been, and she could not have asserted such a claim as she had covenanted to assign the investments to be held on the trusts of the settlement. . . .

BUCKLEY J: . . . Clause 7 declares the trusts to which property within the covenant is to become subject as soon as the covenant is honoured. Clause 8, on the other hand, must relate to the period when property is within the covenant but the covenant has not yet been honoured. If during that period the property is to be subject in equity to the settlement, this can only be because the settlor intended that she would during that period, pending the transfer of the property to the trustees, herself hold the property on the trusts of the settlement. This, in my judgment, was the intention which, on the true construction of cl. 8, the settlor expressly stated in that clause. There was no reason why at the date of the settlement she should not in this way declare herself a trustee of any property then vested in her to which the covenant applied. There is nothing in the language of cl. 8 to suggest that in respect of property then belonging to the settlor it was intended to have an executory operation, or, indeed, anything other than an immediate binding effect. There appears to me to be no repugnancy between the intention so expressed and the covenant to settle.

For these reasons I think that the plaintiff's submission in this respect is right and that Helen held, and since her death the defendants have held and now hold, her equitable interest in her share of the testator's residue on the trusts of the settlement. If this is so, the rule that equity will not assist a volunteer to enforce an executory contract to make a settlement has no application to this case, for the relevant trust has been completely declared by the defendants' predecessor in title and such declaration is binding on them and is enforceable by and for the benefit of the beneficiaries under the settlement, whether they are volunteers or not.

If this view is right, this disposes of the case, but I think I should go on to state what would be my view, if I were mistaken in the view I have expressed. The investments representing the share of residue in question stand in the name of the plaintiff. This is because he is now the sole surviving trustee of the testator's will. Therefore, say the defendants, he holds these investments primarily on the trusts of the will, that is to say, in trust for them as part of Helen's estate. The plaintiff is, however, also the sole surviving covenantee under cl. 7 of the settlement, as well as the sole surviving trustee of that settlement. This, however, affords him no answer, say the defendants, to their claim under the will unless the plaintiff, having transferred the property to them in pursuance of the trusts of the will, could compel them to return it in pursuance of their obligation under the covenant, and this, they say, he could not do. In support of this last contention they rely on *Re Plumptre's Marriage Settlement, Underhill* v *Plumptre* [1910] 1 Ch 609; *Re Pryce, Neville* v *Pryce* [1917] 1 Ch 234; and *Re Kay's Settlement, Broadbent* v *Macnab* [1939] Ch 329.

The plaintiff, on the other hand, contends that, as he already holds the investments, no question of his having to enforce the covenant arises. The fund having come without impropriety into his hands is now, he says, impressed in his hands with the trusts on which he ought to hold it under the settlement; and because of the covenant it does not lie in the mouth of the defendants to say that he should hold it in trust for Helen's estate. . . .

Counsel for the plaintiff says that the capacity in which the trustee has become possessed of the fund is irrelevant. Thus in *Strong* v *Bird*, an imperfect gift was held to be completed by the donee obtaining probate of the donor's will of which he was executor, notwithstanding that the donor died intestate as to her residue and that the donee was not a person entitled as on her intestacy. Similarly in *Re James, James* v *James* [see **5.3.3.1**], a grant of administration to two administrators was held to perfect an imperfect gift by the intestate to one of them, who had no beneficial interest in the intestate's estate.

In my judgment the circumstance that the plaintiff holds the fund because he was appointed a trustee of the will is irrelevant. He is at law the owner of the fund and the means by which he became so have no effect on the quality of his legal ownership. The question is: for whom, if anyone, does he hold the fund in equity? In other words, who can successfully assert in equity against him disentitling him to stand on his legal right? It seems to me to be indisputable that Helen, if she were alive, could not do so, for she has solemnly covenanted under seal to assign the fund to the plaintiff and the defendants can stand in no better position. It is, of course, true that the object of the covenant was not that the plaintiff should retain the property for his own benefit, but that he should hold it on the trusts of the settlement. It is also true that, if it were necessary to enforce performance of the covenant, equity would not assist the beneficiaries under the settlement, because they are mere volunteers; and that for the same reason the plaintiff, as trustee of the settlement, would not be bound to enforce the covenant and would not be constrained by the court to do so, and indeed, it seems, might be constrained by the court not to do so. As matters stand, however, there is no occasion to invoke the assistance of equity to enforce the performance of the covenant. It is for the defendants to invoke the assistance of equity to make good their claim to the fund. To do so successfully they must show that the plaintiff cannot conscientiously withhold it from them. When they seek to do this, he can point to the covenant which, in my judgment, relieves him from any fiduciary obligation that he would otherwise owe to the defendants as Helen's representatives. In so doing the plaintiff is not seeking to enforce an equitable remedy against the defendants on behalf of persons who could not enforce such a remedy themselves; he is relying on the combined effect of his legal ownership of the fund and his legal right to enforce the covenant. That an action on the covenant might be statute-barred is irrelevant, for there is no occasion for such an action. . . .

5.4   Assistance from Roman Law

5.4.1   THE ENGLISH LAW FORMULATION OF THE DOCTRINE *DONATIO MORTIS CAUSA*

SEN v HEADLEY [1991] 2 All ER 636, CA

FACTS: Mrs S had lived with a man for several years. On his death bed he gave her the keys to a box containing the deeds to his house and told her that the house was hers. HELD: This was a valid *donatio mortis causa*. The court rejected the orthodox assumption that *donatio mortis causa* could not apply to gifts of land.

NOURSE LJ: . . . There have been several judicial statements of what, in general terms, is necessary to constitute a *donatio mortis causa*: see *Cain v Moon* [1896] 2 QB 283 at 285 (Lord Russell of Killowen CJ), *Re Craven's Estate, Lloyds Bank Ltd v Cockburn* [1937] 3 All ER 33 (Farwell J) and *Delgoffe v Fader* [1939] 3 All ER 682 at 685 (Luxmoore LJ). Regard must also be had to what was said by this court in *Birch v Treasury Solicitor* [1950] 2 All ER 1198 the most authoritative of the modern decisions. If the question whether the subject matter is capable of passing by way of *donatio mortis causa* is put on one side, the three general requirements for such a gift may be stated very much as they are stated in *Snell's Equity* (29th edn, 1990) pp. 380–383. First, the gift must be made in contemplation, although not necessarily in expectation, of impending death. Secondly, the gift must be made upon the condition that it is to be absolute and perfected only on the donor's death, being revocable until that event occurs and ineffective if it does not. Thirdly, there must be a delivery of the subject matter of the gift, or the essential *indicia* of title thereto, which amounts to a parting with dominion and not mere physical possession over the subject matter of the gift. . . .

We have traced the need for there to be a parting with dominion over the subject-matter of the gift, i.e. with the ability to control it, to the judgment of Lord Kenyon CJ in *Hawkings v Blewitt* (1798) 2 Esp 662 at 663, where he said:

In the case of a donatio mortis causa possession must be immediately given. That has been done here; a delivery has taken place; but it is also necessary that by parting with the possession, the deceased should also part with the dominion over it. That has not been done here.

A similar view was taken in *Reddel* v *Dobree* (1839) 10 Sim 244 and *Re Johnson* (1905) 92 LT 357. In each of those three cases the alleged donor delivered a locked box to the alleged donee and either retained or took back the key to it; in *Reddel* v *Dobree* he also reserved and exercised a right to take back the box. In each of them it was held that the alleged donor had retained dominion over the box and that there had been no *donatio mortis causa*.

It appears therefore that the need for there to be a parting with dominion was first identified in cases where the subject matter of the gift was a locked box and its contents. In *Birch* v *Treasury Solicitor*, as we have seen, a similar need was recognised where the subject matter of the gift was a chose in action. Without in any way questioning that need, we think it appropriate to observe that a parting with dominion over an intangible thing such as a chose in action is necessarily different from a parting with dominion over a tangible thing such as a locked box and its contents. We think that in the former case a parting with dominion over the essential *indicia* of title will *ex hypothesi* usually be enough. . . .

We do not suggest that there might never be a state of facts where there was a parting with dominion over the essential *indicia* of title to a chose in action but nevertheless a retention of dominion over the chose itself. And it is just possible to conceive of someone, who, in contemplation of impending death, had parted with dominion over the title deeds of his house to an alleged donee, nevertheless granting a tenancy of it to a third party; for which purpose proof of the title to the freehold by production of the deeds is not usually necessary. On facts such as those there might be a case for saying that the alleged donor had not parted with dominion over the house. But nothing comparable happened here. It is true that in the eyes of the law Mr Hewett, by keeping his own set of keys to the house, retained possession of it. But the benefits which thereby accrued to him were wholly theoretical. He uttered the words of gift, without reservation, two days after his readmission to hospital, when he knew that he did not have long to live and when there could have been no practical possibility of his ever returning home. He had parted with dominion over the title deeds. Mrs Sen had her own set of keys to the house and was in effective control of it. In all the circumstances of the case, we do not believe that the law requires us to hold that Mr Hewett did not part with dominion over the house. We hold that he did.

Having now decided that the third of the general requirements for a *donatio mortis causa* was satisfied in this case, we come to the more general question whether land is capable of passing by way of such a gift. . . .

Let it be agreed that the doctrine is anomalous, anomalies do not justify anomalous exceptions. If due account is taken of the present state of the law in regard to mortgages and choses in action, it is apparent that to make a distinction in the case of land would be to make just such an exception. A *donatio mortis causa* of land is neither more nor less anomalous than any other. Every such gift is a circumvention of the Wills Act 1837. Why should the additional statutory formalities for the creation and transmission of interests in land be regarded as some larger obstacle? The only step which has to be taken is to extend the application of the implied or constructive trust arising on the donor's death from the conditional to the absolute estate. Admittedly that is a step which the House of Lords would not have taken in *Duffield* v *Elwes* and, if the point had been a subject of decision, we would have loyally followed it in this court. But we cannot decide a case in 1991 as the House of Lords would have decided it, but did not decide it, in 1827. We must decide it according to the law as it stands today. . . .

5.5   End of Chapter Assessment Question

Herbert Chance, wishing to make future provision for his adult son, entered into the following covenant in a deed to which his friends Allan Smith and Clifford Overy were the only other parties.

> I promise to settle the sum of £100,000 in cash, or assets of equivalent value, for the benefit of my son for his life, to his issue in remainder. This bounty to be held on trust by Allan Smith and Clifford Overy in accordance with the terms of the settlement annexed hereto.

Some years later Herbert had fallen grievously ill. As he lay on his death bed, his friend, Mr Overy reminded Herbert of the covenant he had made. The next day, when Mr Overy came to visit, Herbert passed to him a sealed envelope. 'In there', he said 'are the share certificates for £100,000 of my shares in the family company. I want my son to have them in accordance with the terms of the settlement annexed to the covenant'. Herbert died minutes later.

Advise the son whether or not he will be able to claim any benefit under the settlement.

5.6   End of Chapter Assessment Outline Answer

The son has given no money or money's worth in consideration of his father's promise to settle the £100,000, nor can the son claim to have been within marriage consideration, for his father's promise had not been made in consideration of any marriage. Nor had the son been a party to the deed containing the covenant. Accordingly, the son cannot show any common law entitlement to have the covenant performed. The son is therefore a mere volunteer.

A volunteer (a person claiming the benefit of a voluntary promise to create a trust) cannot enforce the promise by action in court, and must therefore show that the promise has already been performed, i.e. that the trust has already been validly constituted. In other words, the volunteer must show that there has been a valid declaration by the settlor that he is to henceforth hold the property as trustee, or that there has been a valid transfer of the property to trustees to hold on trust (*Milroy* v *Lord* (1862) 2 De GF & J 264). On the present set of facts it is clear that Herbert did not intend to declare himself to be a trustee. The courts will not spell out a valid declaration of trust from a failed attempt to create a trust by transfer to trustees, therefore the son's only hope is to show that there had been a valid transfer to the trustees.

The difficulty with proving a valid transfer to the trustees is that Herbert had not done everything within his power that was necessary to be done in order to effect a transfer of the shares. To transfer the legal title in shares it is necessary not only to hand over the share certificates, but also to complete stock transfer forms and have the new owner registered at the company. It appears, therefore, that the trust has not been completely constituted.

The son is in difficulty. He cannot prove that he is entitled as a beneficiary under a validly constituted trust, and he cannot enforce the promise to create the trust because he has given no consideration for the promise. The son is a mere volunteer, and equity will not assist a volunteer.

Nor will he be able to rely upon the 'Roman law' doctrine of *donatio mortis causa*, for not only will the court refuse to spell out an absolute gift from a failed trust (*Jones* v *Lock* (1865) LR 1 Ch App 25), but, further the gift does not appear to have been made in contemplation of death, nor intended to revert to Herbert in the event of his recovery from illness. What is more, it has even been doubted that there can be a valid *donatio mortis causa* of shares (*Re Weston* [1902] 1 Ch 680). (Having said that, there seems to be no logical reason for disallowing a *donatio* of shares, and there is support for the view that delivery of share certificates is enough to hand over 'the essential indicia or evidence of title' in order to effect a valid *donatio* (*Staniland* v *Willott* [1852] 3 Mac & G 664).

The son, may, however, have one final argument up his sleeve: Mr Smith and Mr Overy were parties to the deed in which the covenant to settle is contained. They therefore have a common law right to enforce the covenant against Herbert's estate. If the trust has not been completely constituted (as appears to be the case) they could sue for damages for breach of covenant at a level calculated to compensate for the loss of the son's anticipated life interest in the £100,000 (see *Re Cavendish-Browne's Settlement Trusts* [1916] WN 341 — although there is a counter-argument that the trustees should only receive nominal damages because they themselves have not lost out as a result of the breach of covenant!). As trustees, they could not, of course, hold the damages for their own benefit. They would be obliged to hold them on trust for Herbert's son. It appears, then, that if the trustees choose to take proceedings against Herbert's estate in order to enforce the covenant, Herbert's son will at last receive the benefit of his life interest in the £100,000.

However, will this indirect claim, using the trustees as intermediaries, be allowed? According to *Re Pryce* [1917] 1 Ch 234 and *Re Kay's Settlement* [1939] Ch 329 it will not. In those cases the court directed the trustees not to take steps to enforce the covenant for the benefit of volunteers. As the volunteers could not enforce the covenant by direct means the court refused to allow them to acquire the benefit of it by indirect means. However, the trustees in both those cases had sought the court's directions as to the proper course to take. Does it necessarily follow that the trustees in the instant case would be acting in breach of trust were they to take it upon themselves to enforce the covenant against Herbert's estate, without ever having sought the court's directions on the issue? It would, at the very least, be difficult to argue that the trustees had breached a trust which had not yet been constituted.

If this final line of argument fails, and it is hard to imagine a court looking sympathetically upon it, it is doubtful that Herbert's son has any real prospects of success in an action to enforce the trust, for he has no common law right of action and equity will not assist him.

CHAPTER SIX

PERPETUITIES AND PUBLIC POLICY LIMITATIONS ON THE FORMATION OF TRUSTS

6.1 The Rule Against Remoteness of Vesting

The Rules Against Perpetuities and Excessive Accumulations, Consultation Paper No. 133 (1993)

Part IV Criticisms of the Present Law

A. *The rule against perpetuities*

4.2 Whilst the 1964 Act has undoubtedly been successful in curing many of the problems of the common law rule against perpetuities, there nevertheless remains a range of grounds on which the present law may be criticised. We welcome views on the extent to which the points made below are justified. Each of these criticisms will be looked at in detail, under the following headings:

    (a) complexity;

    (b) uncertainty;

    (c) inconsistency;

    (d) interference with commercial transactions;

    (e) harshness;

    (f) lack of adaptability;

    (g) expenses.

  (a) Complexity . . .

4.3 The principal reasons for the complexity of the rule against perpetuities are as follows:

    (i)   the interaction of the common law and the 1964 Act;

    (ii) the existence of three perpetuity periods;

    (iii) the 1964 Act and other statutes relating to the rule.

(i) Interaction of common law and the 1964 Act

4.4 A working knowledge of both the common law rule and the 1964 Act is needed in applying the rule against perpetuities to dispositions, whether they were made before or after the 1964 Act came into force. In the case of pre-1964 Act dispositions, the common law rule continues to apply since, subject to one exception, the 1964 Act was not retrospective. The number of such dispositions in effect, although diminishing, still remains significant, and perpetuity problems may arise in relation to a contingent interest many years after its creation. In most cases the common law rule alone will apply, but the 1964 Act applies where the disposition has been varied by a deed or court order since that Act came into force. The 1964 Act similarly applies where a general power of appointment has been exercised on or after 16th July 1964 even if the power was created before that date; however, the common law rule applies to a special power in those circumstances. As regards post-1964 Act dispositions, knowledge of the common law is still needed to determine the validity of an interest notwithstanding the introduction of the simple s. 1(1) period, since 'wait and see' can only be invoked once it has been established that an interest is void for perpetuity at common law. In addition, since the 1964 Act operates largely by way of amending the common law rule, familiarity with the common law is essential in order fully to understand the Act. . . .

(ii)   The existence of three perpetuity periods

4.6   The rule would no doubt be simpler to apply if the three perpetuity periods were replaced by one. However, the periods in sections 1(1) and 9(2) of the 1964 Act are relatively simple. Furthermore, problems which have been suggested regarding the identification of lives in being may be more theoretical than practical. Where there is a royal lives clause it is necessary to maintain a record of lives in being, but this task is assisted by reference books. We have been told of problems arising in recent years in relation to clauses in dispositions made before the First World War which refer to the lineal descendants of Queen Victoria. King Olav V of Norway was one such descendant and, prior to his death in 1991, it was known that any such dispositions made since his birth in 1903 remained valid; now, however, the remaining descendants born in the early years of the twentieth century are somewhat obscure German princelings, making it difficult for practitioners to keep aware of whether any descendants remain alive. However, it seems likely that dispositions with such clauses are no longer commonly found, since from several years before the 1964 Act came into force the standard form of royal lives clause referred to the descendants of George V. In any event most modern settlements are designed to come to an end before the end of the specified period, so that it is rarely necessary to know the exact date upon which the 21 years from the death of the last royal survivor occurs. . . .

(iii)   The 1964 Act and other statutory provisions

4.8   The 1964 Act is complex in itself. While we appreciate the pragmatic grounds which required the Act to operate by way of amending the common law, the result in some cases is that the amendments perpetuate and increase complexities of the common law. For example, the age reduction rules in s. 4 increase complexity since they do not reduce the age at which an interest is stipulated to vest to 21 for all purposes, and further complications arise where a disposition is contingent on more than one child attaining an age exceeding 21. Difficulties also arise with other statutory provisions which impinge upon the rule against perpetuities. For example, the Social Security Act 1973, s. 69, as amended, exempts certain pension schemes from the rule against perpetuities, but invoking this section is made complex by the wide range of conditions to be satisfied. . . .

Law Commission Report 251: The Law of Trusts: The Rules Against Perpetuities and Excessive Accumulations, 11 February 1998

Part XI   Summary of Recommendations

11.1   The rule against perpetuities should not apply except as provided by statute. (Draft Bill, Cl 1(1).

11.2   The rule against perpetuities should only apply—

(1)   to successive estates and interests in property held in trust, including an estate or interest which—

(a)   is subject to a condition precedent; or

(b)   arises under either a right of reverter on the determination of a determinable fee simple, or under a resulting trust on the determination of a determinable interest;

(2)   where property is held on trust for an estate or interest subject to a condition subsequent, a right of re-entry (or the equivalent right in property other than land) that is exercisable on breach of that condition;

(3)   to powers of appointment; and

(4)   where a will limits chattels in such a way as to create successive *legal* interests in them under the doctrine of executory bequests, to those interests. (Draft Bill, Cl 1(2)–(6).)

11.3 Interests created by instruments which either nominate benefits under a pension scheme or by the exercise of a power of advancement under such a scheme should be subject to the rule against perpetuities. (Draft Bill. Cl 2(5).)

11.4 We recommend that the rule against perpetuities should not apply to an interest or right arising under—

(1) an occupational pension scheme;

(2) a personal pension scheme;

(3) a public service pension scheme; or

(4) a self-employed pension arrangement. (Draft Bill, Cls 2(4); 20(5).)

11.5 The Lord Chancellor should have power to specify further exceptions to the rule against perpetuities by statutory instrument. (Draft Bill, Cl. 3.)

11.6 The restrictions on the scope of the rule against perpetuities that we recommend in paragraphs 11.2–11.4 above, should only apply to instruments taking effect on or after the date on which any legislation is brought into force. (Draft Bill, Cl 15(1), (3), (22.)

11.7 There should be one fixed perpetuity period of 125 years. (Draft Bill, Cl 5(1).)

11.8 The 125-year period should be overriding and should apply whatever the instrument creating the estate or interest may provide. (Draft Bill, Cl 5(2).)

11.9 The perpetuity period should commence when the instrument creating the estate, interest, right or power to which the rule applies takes effect. (Draft Bill, Cl 6(1).)

11.10 In relation to any estate, interest or right created by the exercise of a special power of appointment, the perpetuity period should commence when the instrument creating the power takes effect. (Draft Bill, Cl 6(2).)

11.11 In respect of interests created where a nomination or advancement is made under a pension scheme, the perpetuity period shall be taken to start on the date on which the person making the nomination became a member of the scheme. (Draft Bill, Cl 6(3).)

11.12 Subject to two exceptions set out in the following paragraphs, the 125-year perpetuity period—

(1) should only apply prospectively to instruments taking effect on or after the date on which any legislation is brought into force; (Draft Bill, Cl 15(1).) but

(2) should not apply to wills that were executed before that date, but where the testator died afterwards. (Draft Bill, Cls 15(1), 16.)

11.13 The first exception is that trustees of a trust that was in existence at the time when the legislation was brought into force should have a power to elect by means of an irrevocable deed that the trust should be subject to—

(1) the statutory 125-year perpetuity period; and

(2) those other provisions of the legislation in Clauses 6–11 of the Draft Bill that relate to the operation of the rule against perpetuities.

11.14 This power should be exercisable only if—

(1) the trust contained an express perpetuity period of lives in being plus 21 years; and

(2) the trustees believe that it is difficult or impracticable to ascertain the existence or whereabouts of the measuring lives in being so that they could not determine the date at which the perpetuity period would come to an end. (Draft Bill, Cl 12.)

11.15 The second exception is that where a disposition is made under a special power of appointment, then whether or not that special power was created before or after the commencement of any legislation, the perpetuity period applicable to the disposition should be 125 years commencing on the effective date of the instrument which created the special power of appointment. (Draft Bill. Cl 6(2).)

11.16 For the purposes of the recommendation in paragraph 11.15, a nomination of benefits made under a pension scheme should be treated in a similar way to a special power. (Draft Bill, Cl 6(3).)

11.17 In relation to the 125-year perpetuity period, the principle of 'wait and see' should apply to those estates, interests, rights and powers which are subject to the rule against perpetuities, in the same way as it does under the 1964 Act. (Draft Bill, Cl 7.)

11.18 The legislation should not affect the rule of law which limits the duration of non-charitable purpose trusts. (Draft Bill, Cl 18.)

11.19 Subject to the exception explained below, in paragraph 11.21, the statutory restrictions on accumulations should be repealed. (Draft Bill, Cls 13 and 21.)

11.20   The rule would cease to apply only in relation to instruments taking effect after the date on which any legislation was brought into force, including any special power of appointment created before but exercised after that date. (Draft Bill, Cl 15(1).)

11.21   Where an instrument confers a power or duty to accumulate on trustees of property that is held in trust for charitable purposes, the direction to accumulate should cease to have effect 21 years after the first day on which the income must or may be accumulated. (Draft Bill, Cl 14(1)–(3).)

11.22   This limitation should apply whether the settlor was an individual or a corporation, but it would be applicable only to instruments taking effect after the legislation was brought into force. (Draft Bill, Cls 14(1), 15(1).)

11.23   Where the power or duty came to an end, the income should be applied for the persons or purposes for whom or which it would have been applicable had there been no power or duty to accumulate. (Draft Bill, Cl 14(4).)

6.1.1   THE COMMON LAW RULE

RE WILMER'S TRUSTS [1903] 2 Ch 411, CA

FACTS: W, a testatrix, devised her residuary real estate on trustees upon trust to pay the income therefrom to M for life and thereafter to M's sons successively in tail male (which means that the land must pass from male heir to male heir). W died in October 1880 at which time M had not given birth to any sons who could qualify as beneficiaries under the trust. She was, however, pregnant with a son, S, who was born in February 1881. The question was whether S could take the property absolutely, or whether he merely held a life interest in accordance with the limitations specified in the trust.

HELD: The limitations coming into effect after S's life estate did not infringe the rule against remoteness of vesting. A child *en ventre sa mere* (in its mother's womb) at the effective date of the gift, who is subsequently born, must be treated as having been a life in being at the effective date of the gift. Accordingly, S, who had been alive at the testatrix's death, was a life in being. Because the tail male limitations would certainly have been satisfied within 21 years of S's death (in fact they would have come into effect immediately upon S's death) those limitations fell within the perpetuity period and did not infringe the rule against remoteness of vesting.

VAUGHAN WILLIAMS LJ: . . . When the testatrix died there was in existence a foetus, which turned out, when the birth resulted, to be a male child. That was a living thing at the date when the testatrix died. The limitation is perfectly good if that living thing is to be taken to have been at the date of her death that which it turned out to be. With that I entirely agree. I do not think . . . for every purpose of the law, a child, during the period of gestation and before it is actually born, is to be treated as living. In many cases that is not so. Take a case which is very remote from this, but which illustrates what I mean. A child in the womb of its mother cannot be murdered. Of course it is a living child for some purposes, but it must have a separate existence before it can be made the subject of a charge of murder. In *Blackstone's Commentaries*, 4th ed. vol. i. 129, 130, it is stated that in contemplation of law life begins as soon as an infant is able to stir in the mother's womb:

> For if a woman is quick with child, and by a potion, or otherwise, killeth it in her womb; or if any one beat her, whereby the child dieth in her body, and she is delivered of a dead child; this, though not murder, was by the antient law homicide or manslaughter.

Then the learned author goes on:

> An infant in ventre sa mère, or in the mother's womb, is supposed in law to be born for many purposes. It is capable of having a legacy, or a surrender of a copyhold estate made to it. It may have a guardian assigned to it; and it is enabled to have an estate limited to it's use, and to take afterwards by such limitation, as if it were then actually born.

And the rule as to a posthumous child being capable of taking in remainder is stated in the same work, vol. ii. 169. I merely mention this because part of Mr Buckmaster's argument seems to have proceeded upon the assumption that although, according to Buckley J's judgment, there was a rule that a child during the period of gestation was to be treated as 'a life in being', that was a rule of law applicable in some cases only. In my opinion, upon the authorities, that rule is applicable when you have to deal with the rule against perpetuities. For *that* purpose it is plain that, as soon as the child is born, that satisfies the limitation, and you retrospectively treat the life of that child as 'a life in being' at the death of the testator. When you arrive at that conclusion, it seems to me impossible to raise the point that Mr Sargant raised, though he was quite right in his general statement of the law. That general statement of the law, as I have already pointed out, Buckley J recognised to the full in his judgment; but you cannot, in applying the law as to remoteness, look at the event which has actually happened, but at the event which might have happened. 'If', says the learned judge, 'the limitations are such that events might have so turned out that the rules as to remoteness would have been infringed, then the limitations fail, although in the events which actually did happen the legal period was not exceeded'. But it appears to me that, upon a proper application of the rule I have referred to as regards a child in ventre matris, the moment the child has been born so as to satisfy the limitations, you must treat that event, as it has so turned out, for all purposes with reference to the rule against perpetuities, as having become a fact prior to the death of the testatrix. If so, then Mr Sargant's argument fails. Mr Sargant indeed recognised that himself, because his complaint against Buckley J's judgment was this. He assented to the proposition that you must refer back to the state of facts as though they had turned out at the earlier date, but he says that, although you are to do that, you are not entitled to say that at the moment of death it was known that those events would happen which ultimately did happen. I confess I cannot follow that. It appears to me that when you talk of the relation back of a thing—of a thing being retrospectively recognised—you really are saying that, for the purposes you have to deal with, those facts must be taken as the exact facts at the death of the testator—that is to say, here we must treat it as the actual fact that there was a third son in existence prior to the death of the testatrix. Upon these grounds I am of opinion that the judgment of Buckley J must be affirmed, and the appeal dismissed with costs. . . .

RE KELLY [1932] IR 255

MEREDITH J: . . . If the lives of dogs or other animals could be taken into account in reckoning the maximum period of 'lives in being and twenty-one years afterwards' any contingent or executory interest might be properly limited, so as only to vest within the lives of specified carp, or tortoises, or other animals that might live for over a hundred years, and for twenty-one years afterwards, which, of course, is absurd. 'Lives' means human lives. It was suggested that the last of the dogs could in fact not outlive the testator by more than twenty-one years. I know nothing of that. The court does not enter into the question of a dog's expectation of life. In point of fact neighbours' dogs and cats are unpleasantly long-lived; but I have no knowledge of their precise expectation of life. Anyway the maximum period is exceeded by the lives of specified butterflies and twenty-one years afterwards. And even, according to my decision—and, I confess, it displays this weakness on being pressed to a logical conclusion—the expiration of the life of a single butterfly, even without the twenty-one years, would be too remote, despite all the world of poetry that may be thereby destroyed . . . there can be no doubt that 'lives' means lives of human beings, not of animals or trees in California.

6.1.1.1 The lack of common sense in the common law rule

RE GAITE'S WILL TRUSTS [1949] 1 All ER 459, ChD

FACTS: A testatrix, G, gave £5,000 to trustees upon trust to pay the income to HG for her life, and thereafter to pay the income and capital to such of HG's grandchildren as should be living at G's death or within five years of it, provided that such grandchildren reached 21 or (in the case of females) married earlier. At the death of the testatrix, HG was 67 and had two children and one grandchild. On the question whether the gift to HG's grandchildren infringed the rule against remoteness of vesting because of the possibility that HG might produce children more than 21 years after G's death.

HELD: Quite apart from any question of physical impossibility it would be a legal impossibility for HG to produce a child who could produce legal issue after the end of the perpetuity period. This is because the Marriage Act 1929 provided that a child under the age of 16 could not lawfully marry. Accordingly the gifts to the grandchildren were valid.

ROXBURGH J: . . . I must assume that Mrs Hagar Gaite, who was alive at the date of the death of the testatrix, might have had a child within five years after the death of the testatrix. What is impossible is that that child of Mrs Hagar Gaite, ex hypothesi born after the death of the testatrix, could itself have had a child within that period of five years, and that is essential to qualify for membership of the class. I do not base my judgment on physical impossibility. I leave all questions of that sort open for consideration when they arise because the matter is, in my judgment, concluded—and counsel for the second defendant admitted it was concluded—by the Age of Marriage Act 1929, s. 1(1), which provides: A marriage between persons either of whom is under the age of sixteen shall be void. Ex hypothesi, the child of Mrs Hagar Gaite born after the death of the testatrix must be under the age of 16 years at the expiration of five years from the death of the testatrix, and, therefore that child could not lawfully be married and have lawful children. In construing the rule, I must have regard to the statute law of England, and, therefore, I hold that the rule is not infringed.

(NOTE: In 1949 the law did not recognise illegitimate children and so the gift in *Re Gaite* could not have been said to infringe the *common law* rule against perpetuities. Ever since 1969 the law has drawn no distinction between legitimate and illegitimate children (Family Law Reform Act 1969, s. 1).)

THE COMMON LAW RULE OF REMOTENESS OF VESTING

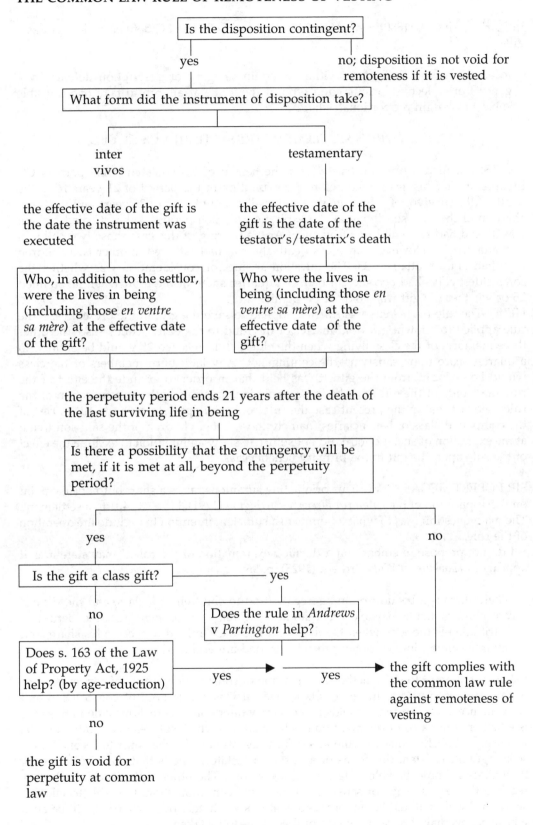

6.1.2 CLASS GIFTS

In *Pearks* v *Moseley* (1880) 5 App Cas 714, 723 Lord Selborne LC defined a class gift as a gift—

> to all those who shall come within a certain category or description defined by a general or collective formula, and who, if they take at all, are to take one divisible subject in certain proportionate shares. . . .

RE CLIFFORD'S SETTLEMENT TRUSTS [1981] 1 Ch 63, ChD

FACTS: C settled a fund on trustees for the benefit of his son's children 'born in C's lifetime or after his death who before the expiration of the period of 21 years from the death of the survivor of C and the said son shall attain the age of 25 years and the other children of the said son living at the expiration of such period'. When C died his son was 32 and had two children of his own. At the hearing of this case those two children had attained 25. However, since C's death the son had fathered another two children who had not yet attained 25. The question arising for consideration was whether the son's eldest child had become entitled to a quarter share of the fund when he attained 25 or whether the gift was void for perpetuity.

HELD: The rule in *Andrews* v *Partington* applied to save the gift. In the present case, the rule applied to allow a gift of a quarter of the fund to the eldest child. Also, the other three members of the class living when the eldest child reached 25 would be entitled to a quarter share upon satisfying the contingency. Any later born members of the class would be excluded from the gift. It was held that in order to exclude the effect of the rule the words of the gift must be inescapably incompatible with the application of the rule. The fact that in the present case the rule could not apply to save the gift to *part* of the compound class of beneficiaries (namely those 'other children of the said son living at the expiration of such period') did not suffice to show an intention to exclude the effect of the rule upon the gift to the primary beneficiaries.

SIR ROBERT MEGARRY VC: This originating summons raises a short but not easy point on the application of the rule in *Andrews* v *Partington* (1791) 3 Bro CC 401 to a settlement. The main question is as to what amounts to a sufficient intention to exclude the operation of the rule. . . .

I do not propose to embark on a detailed examination of the rule. I may state it as it appears in *Hawkins on Wills*, 3rd ed. (1925), p. 96:

> Where there is a bequest of an aggregate fund to children as a class, and the *share of each* child is made payable on attaining a given age, or marriage, the period of distribution is the time when the *first* child becomes entitled to receive his share, and children coming into existence after that period are excluded.

I shall not attempt to say whether this is a rule of construction, a rule of convenience or even a rule of law. Whichever it is, and even if it is a rule both of construction and convenience, it is clear that it yields to a contrary intention. The real question in this case is whether or not a contrary intention has been shown which suffices to exclude the rule. It is well established that the rule arises from the attempt by the court to reconcile two seemingly inconsistent directions of a settlor or testator. One is that the whole class of the children should be able to take, whenever born. The other is that a child who has reached the requisite age or satisfied the requisite condition should be able to take his share forthwith, without being forced to wait to see whether other children will be born whose claims may diminish the size of the shares to be taken.

From time to time the courts have had to consider whether a sufficient intention to exclude the rule has appeared in the will or settlement. Mere words of comprehensiveness, such as 'all or any' or 'all and every' the children of X, will normally not suffice, nor will words of futurity, such as 'all children whether now living or hereafter to be born': see generally *In re Wernher's Settlement Trusts* [1961] 1 WLR 136, approved (and not 'affirmed,' as the headnote states) in *In re Chapman's Settlement Trusts* [1977] 1 WLR 1163.

On the other hand, if the gift is to children 'whenever born,' the phrase will exclude the rule (*In re Edmondson's Will Trusts* [1972] 1 WLR 183); for the phrase is sufficiently specific and emphatic to be inconsistent with the closing of a class as long as it is still possible for any more children to be born. One way of putting the distinction is to say that phrases such as 'all and every' or 'hereafter to be born' are in no way necessarily inconsistent with the class closing as soon as one member of the class has become absolutely entitled: 'all and every' the children born before then can take, and so can children 'hereafter to be born' before then. In each case, meaning and content are given to the phrases, even though the point of time by which 'all and every' the children, or the children 'hereafter be born,' are to be ascertained is not the indefinite future but a future made finite by reference to the date when the first member of the class becomes absolutely entitled. 'Whenever born,' on the other hand, is an expression which cannot easily be qualified by a phrase such as 'before then.' It is an expression which is essentially inconsistent with the application of the rule. . .

I return to Mr Knox's first proposition, to the effect that if the rule is incapable of applying to one limb of a compound class, it cannot apply to the class at all. I do not see why that should be so. It is in the nature of the rule that it should be brought into operation by one member of the class attaining the requisite age, even though the attainment of that age by other members of the class can then do nothing to bring the rule into operation. I know of no requirement that every member of the class must be capable of being the one who pulls the trigger, as it were. I can see no impossibility of making the gift to the compound class march in step with the application of the rule, nor anything to make it clear that the rule is not to apply to something to which it is capable of applying. The mere fact that the rule cannot apply to part of a compound class does not appear to me to demonstrate any incompatibility of the rule with the other part, or with the gift as a whole. Inapplicability is one thing, contradiction another. Furthermore, the inconvenience which the rule is intended to obviate is just as much present for those defined by the words of gift in respect of which the rule can operate as it would be if those were the only words of gift. In the present case, exclude the rule, and the eldest child, who became 25 years old over two and-a-half years ago, must wait until the son dies before discovering the minimum size of her share, and, perhaps another 21 years before knowing its exact size. I would be slow to treat the settlement as imposing this inconvenience, in the interests of possible future children to be born to the son later in life, especially as two children of the son were alive when the settlement was made, and the right of a child to take a share absolutely at 25 appears in the foreground of the gift. I accept, of course, that this is difficult terrain in uncharted territory; but doing the best that I can, I would reject this first proposition. . . . .

In the result, my conclusion is that it is not sufficiently clear from the language of this settlement that the rule in *Andrews v Partington* is to be excluded, and so that rule applies to the settlement. Accordingly, the answer to question (1) in the originating summons, asking whether the eldest child became absolutely and indefeasibly entitled to a quarter share of capital under the trusts of the settlement on attaining the age of 25 years, is 'Yes'.

6.1.3   AGE REDUCING PROVISIONS

Applicable to gifts taking effect on or before 15 July 1964.

LAW OF PROPERTY ACT 1925

163.   Validation of certain gifts void for remoteness

(1)   Where in a will, settlement or other instrument the absolute vesting either of capital or income of property, or the ascertainment of a beneficiary or class of beneficiaries, is made to depend on the attainment by the beneficiary or members of the class of an age exceeding twenty-one years, and thereby the gift to that beneficiary or class or any member thereof, or any gift over, remainder, executory limitation, or trust arising on the total of partial failure of the original gift, is, or but for this section would be, rendered void for remoteness, the will, settlement, or other instrument shall take effect for the purposes of such gift, gift over, remainder, executory limitation, or trust as if the absolute

vesting or ascertainment aforesaid had been made to depend on the beneficiary or member of the class attaining the age of twenty-one years, and that age shall be substituted for the age stated in the will, settlement, or other instrument.

(2)   This section applies to any instrument executed after the commencement of this Act and to any testamentary appointment (whether made in exercise of a general or special power), devise, or bequest contained in the will of a person dying after such commencement, whether the will is made before or after such commencement.

(3)   This section applies without prejudice to any provision whereby the absolute vesting or ascertainment is also made to depend on the marriage of any person, or any other event which may occur before the age stated in the will, settlement, or other instrument attained.

6.1.4   PERPETUITIES AND ACCUMULATIONS ACT 1964

6.1.4.1   Express perpetuity period

PERPETUITIES AND ACCUMULATIONS ACT 1964

1.   Power to specify perpetuity period
(1)   Subject to section 9(2) of this Act and subsection (2) below, where the instrument by which any disposition is made so provides, the perpetuity period applicable to the disposition under the rule against perpetuities, instead of being of any other duration, shall be of a duration equal to such number of years not exceeding eighty as is specified in that behalf in the instrument.

(2)   Subsection (1) above shall not have effect where the disposition is made in exercise of a special power of appointment, but where a period is specified under that subsection in the instrument creating such a power the period shall apply in relation to any disposition under the power as it applies in relation to the power itself.

6.1.4.2   Fertility presumptions

PERPETUITIES AND ACCUMULATIONS ACT 1964

2.   Presumptions and evidence as to future parenthood
(1)   Where in any proceedings there arises on the rule against perpetuities a question which turns on the ability of a person to have a child at some future time, then—
(a)   subject to paragraph (b) below, it shall be presumed that a male can have a child at the age of fourteen years or over, but not under that age, and that a female can have a child at the age of twelve years or over, but not under that age or over the age of fifty-five years; but
(b)   in the case of a living person evidence may be given to show that he or she will or will not be able to have a child at the time in question.

(2)   Where any such question is decided by treating a person as unable to have a child at a particular time, and he or she does so, the High Court may make such order as it thinks fit for placing the persons interested in the property comprised in the disposition, so far as may be just, in the position they would have held if the question had not been so decided.

(3)   Subject to subsection (2) above, where any such question is decided in relation to a disposition by treating a person as able or unable to have a child at a particular time, then he or she shall be so treated for the purpose of any question which may arise on the rule against perpetuities in relation to the same disposition in any subsequent proceedings.

(4)   In the foregoing provisions of this section references to having a child are references to begetting or giving birth to a child, but those provisions (except subsection (1)(b)) shall apply in relation to the possibility that a person will at any time have a child by adoption, legitimation or other means as they apply to his or her ability at that time to beget or give birth to a child.

6.1.4.3   The 'wait and see' principle

PERPETUITIES AND ACCUMULATIONS ACT 1964

3.   Uncertain as to remoteness

(1)   Where, apart from the provisions of this section and sections 4 and 5 of this Act, a disposition would be void on the ground that the interest disposed of might not become vested until too remote a time, the disposition shall be treated, until such time (if any) as it becomes established that the vesting must occur, if at all, after the end of the perpetuity period, as if the disposition were not subject to the rule against perpetuities; and its becoming so established shall not effect the validity of anything previously done in relation to the interest disposed of by way of advancement, application of intermediate income or otherwise.

(2)   Where, apart from the said provisions, a disposition consisting of the conferring of a general power of appointment would be void on the ground that the power might not become exercisable until too remote a time, the disposition shall be treated, until such time (if any) as it becomes established that the power will not be exercisable within the perpetuity period, as if the disposition were not subject to the rule against perpetuities.

(3)   Where, apart from the said provisions, a disposition consisting of the conferring of any power, option or other right would be void on the ground that the right might be exercised at too remote a time, the disposition shall be treated as regards any exercise of the right within the perpetuity period as if it were not subject to the rule against perpetuities and, subject to the said provisions, shall be treated as void for remoteness only if, and so far as, the right is not fully exercised within that period.

(4)   Where this section applies to a disposition and the duration of the perpetuity period is not determined by virtue of section 1 or 9(2) of this Act, it shall be determined as follows—

(a)   where any persons falling within subsection (5) below are individuals in being and ascertainable at the commencement of the perpetuity period the duration of the period shall be determined by reference to their lives and no others, but so that the lives of any description of persons falling within paragraph (b) or (c) of that subsection shall be disregarded if the number of persons of that description is such as to render it impracticable to ascertain the date of death of the survivor;

(b)   where there are no lives under paragraph (a) above the period shall be twenty-one years.

(5)   The said persons are as follows—

(a)   the person by whom the disposition was made;

(b)   a person to whom or in whose favour the disposition was made, that is to say—

(i)   in the case of a disposition to a class of persons, any member or potential member of the class;

(ii)   in the case of an individual disposition to a person taking only on certain conditions being satisfied, any person as to whom some of the conditions are satisfied and the remainder may in time be satisfied;

(iii)   in the case of a special power of appointment exercisable in favour of members of a class, any member or potential member of the class;

(iv)   in the case of a special power of appointment exercisable in favour of one person only, that person or, where the object of the power is ascertainable only on certain conditions being satisfied, any person as to whom some of the conditions are satisfied and the remainder may in time be satisfied;

(v)   in the case of any power, option or other right, the person on whom the right is conferred;

(c)   a person having a child or grandchild within sub-paragraphs (i) to (iv) of paragraph (b) above, or any of those children or grandchildren, if subsequently born, would by virtue of his or her descent fall within those sub-paragraphs;

(d)   any person on the failure or determination of whose prior interest the disposition is limited to take effect.

6.1.4.4   The class closing provisions

PERPETUITIES AND ACCUMULATIONS ACT 1964

4.   Exclusion of class members to avoid remoteness

. . .

(3)   Where the inclusion of any persons, being potential members of a class of unborn persons who at birth would become members or potential members of the class, prevents the foregoing provisions of this section from operating to save a disposition from being void for remoteness, those persons shall thenceforth be deemed for all the purposes of the disposition to be excluded from the class, and the said provisions shall thereupon have effect accordingly.

(4)   Where, in the case of a disposition to which subsection (3) above does not apply, it is apparent at the time the disposition is made or becomes apparent at a subsequent time that, apart from this subsection, the inclusion of any persons, being potential members of a class or unborn persons who at birth would become members or potential members of the class, would cause the disposition to be treated as void for remoteness, those persons shall, unless their exclusion would exhaust the class, thenceforth be deemed for all the purposes of the disposition to be excluded from the class.

(5)   Where this section has effect in relation to a disposition to which section 3 above applies, the operation of this section shall not affect the validity of anything previously done in relation to the interest disposed of by way of advancement, application or intermediate income or otherwise.

(6)   . . .

(7)   For the avoidance of doubt it is hereby declared that a question arising under section 3 of this Act or subsection (1)(a) above of whether a disposition would be void apart from this section is to be determined as if subsection (6) above had been a separate section of this Act.

6.1.4.5   The age reducing provisions

PERPETUITIES AND ACCUMULATIONS ACT 1964

4.   Reduction of age . . . to avoid remoteness

(1)   Where a disposition is limited by reference to the attainment by any person or persons of a specified age exceeding twenty-one years, and it is apparent at the time the disposition is made or becomes apparent at a subsequent time—

(a)   that the disposition would, apart from this section, be void for remoteness, but

(b)   that it would not be so void if the specified age had been twenty-one years, the disposition shall be treated for all purposes as if, instead of being limited by reference to the age in fact specified, it had been limited by reference to the age nearest to that age which would, if specified instead, have prevented the disposition from being so void.

(2)   Where in the case of any disposition different ages exceeding twenty-one years are specified in relation to different persons—

(a)   the reference in paragraph (b) of subsection (1) above to the specified age shall be construed as a reference to all the specified ages, and

(b)   that subsection shall operate to reduce each such age so far as is necessary to save the disposition from being void for remoteness.

6.1.4.6   The problem of the unascertained spouse

PERPETUITIES AND ACCUMULATIONS ACT 1964

5.   Condition relating to death of surviving spouse

Where a disposition is limited by reference to the time of death of the survivor of a person in being at the commencement of the perpetuity period and any spouse of that person, and that time has not arrived at the end of the perpetuity period, the disposition shall be treated for all purposes, where to do so would save it from being void for remoteness, as if it had been limited by reference to the time immediately before the end of that period.

6.1.4.7 Miscellaneous provisions

PERPETUITIES AND ACCUMULATIONS ACT 1964

6. Saving and acceleration of expectant interests

A disposition shall not be treated as void for remoteness by reason only that the interest disposed of is ulterior to and dependent upon an interest under a disposition which is so void, and the vesting of an interest shall not be prevented from being accelerated on the failure of a prior interest by reason only that the failure arises because of remoteness.

7. Powers of appointment

For the purposes of the rule against perpetuities, a power of appointment shall be treated as a special power unless—

(a) in the instrument creating the power it is expressed to be exercisable by one person only, and

(b) it could, at all times during its currency when that person is of full age and capacity, be exercised by him so as immediately to transfer to himself the whole of the interest governed by the power without the consent of any other person or compliance with any other condition, not being a formal condition relating only to the mode of exercise of the power:

Provided that for the purpose of determining whether a disposition made under a power of appointment exercisable by will only is void for remoteness, the power shall be treated as a general power where it would have fallen to be so treated if exercisable by deed.

6.2 The Rule Against Excessive Accumulation of Income

6.2.1 THE MODERN RULE

LAW OF PROPERTY ACT 1925

164. General restrictions on accumulation of income

(1) No person may . . . settle or dispose of any property in such manner that the income thereof shall . . . be . . . accumulated for any longer period than one of the following, namely:—

(a) the life of the grantor or settlor; or

(b) a term of twenty-one years from the death of the grantor, settlor or testator; or

(c) the duration of the minority or respective minorities of any person or persons living or en ventre sa mere at the death of the grantor, settlor or testator; or

(d) the duration of the minority or respective minorities only of any person or persons who under the limitations of the instrument directing the accumulations would, for the time being, if of full age, be entitled to the income directed to be accumulated.

(e) the period of 21 years from the date of making the disposition;

(f) the duration of the minority or minorities of any person in being at the date of making an inter vivos disposition.

In every case where any accumulation is directed otherwise than as aforesaid, the direction shall (save as hereinafter mentioned) be void; and the income of the property directed to be accumulated shall . . . go to and be received by the person or persons who would have been entitled thereto if such accumulation had not been directed.

(Note: Paragraphs (e) and (f) were added by the Perpetuities and Accumulations Act 1964. They apply therefore only to gifts taking effect after 15 July 1964.)

6.2.2 AN EXCEPTION TO THE MODERN RULE ON ACCUMULATIONS

LAW OF PROPERTY ACT 1925

165. Qualification of restrictions on accumulation

Where accumulations of surplus income are made during a minority under any statutory power or under the general law, the period for which such accumulations are made is not . . . to be taken into account in determining the periods for which accumulations are permitted to be made by [s. 164], and accordingly an express trust for accumulation for any other permitted period shall not be deemed to have been invalidated or become invalid, by reason of accumulations also having been made as aforesaid during such minority.

6.3   The Rule Against Inalienability of Capital

See purpose trusts at **Chapter 7**.

6.4   The Rules Against Perpetuity and Charities

RE TYLER [1891] 3 Ch 252, CA

FACTS: A testator gave a fund to the trustees of a certain charity and as a condition of the gift he directed them to keep his family vault at Highgate Cemetery 'in good repair, and name legible, and to rebuild when it shall require'. If the trustees failed to comply with his request the monies were directed to pass to another charity.

HELD: The condition for the maintenance and repair of the vault was valid and binding on the first charity. Further, that the gift over to the second charity on failure to comply with the condition was good. The rule against perpetuities has no application to a transfer, on a certain event, of property from one charity to another.

LINDLEY LJ: . . . Mr Justice Stirling has decided that the condition on which the gift over is to take effect is valid, and the appeal to us is against so much of his order as decares that the condition of repairing and rebuilding the family vault is a valid condition and binding on the defendants, the London Missionary Society; the defendants asking that that may be reversed.

There is no doubt whatever that this condition, in one sense, tends to a perpetuity. The tomb or value is to be kept in repair, and in repair for ever. There is also no doubt, and I think it is settled, that a gift of that kind cannot be supported as a charitable gift. But, then, this case is said to fall within an exception to the general rule relating to perpetuities. It is common knowledge that the rule as to perpetuities does not apply to property given to charities; and there are reasons why it should not. It is an exception to the general rule; and we are guided in the application of that doctrine by the case which has been referred to of *Christ's Hospital v Grainger* 1 Mac & G 460. It is sufficient for me to refer to the head-note for the facts. The bequest there was 'to the corporation of Reading, on certain trusts for the benefit of the poor of the town of Reading, with a proviso that, if the corporation of Reading should, for one whole year, neglect to observe the directions of the will, the gift should be utterly void, and the property be transferred to the corporation of London, in trust for a hospital in the town of London.' It was argued that that gift over was invalid, and Lord Cottingham disposes of the argument in this way:

> It was then argued that it was void, as contrary to the rules against perpetuities. These rules are to prevent, in the cases to which they apply; property from being inalienable beyond certain periods. Is this effect produced, and are these rules invaded by the transfer, in a certain event, of property from one charity to another? If the corporation of Reading might hold the property for certain charities in Reading, why may not the corporation of London hold it for the charity of Christ's Hospital in London? The property is neither more nor less alienable on that account.

Guided by that decision, and acting on that principle, Mr Justice Stirling held that this condition was a valid condition; and it appears to me that he was right. What is this gift when you come to look at it? It is a gift of £42,000 Russian 5 per Cent. Stock to the

London Missionary Society. What for? It is for their charitable purposes. It is a gift to them for the purposes for which they exist. Then there is a gift over to another charity in a given event—that is to say, the non-repair of the testator's vault. It seems to me to fall precisely within the principle on which *Christ's Hospital* v *Grainger* was decided. A gift to a charity for charitable purposes, with a gift over on an event which may be beyond the ordinary limit of perpetuities to another charity—I cannot see that there is anything illegal in this. Mr Buckley has put it in the strongest way he can. He says that, if you give effect to this condition, you will be enabling people to evade the law relating to perpetuities. I take it this decision will not go the length—certainly I do not intend it should, so far as I am concerned—that you can get out of the law against perpetuities by making a charity a trustee. That would be absurd; but that is not this case. This property is given to the London Missionary Society for their charitable purposes. Then, there is a condition that, if the tomb is not kept in order, the fund shall go over to another charity. That appears to me, both on principle and authority, to be valid; and I do not think it is a sufficient answer to say that such a conclusion is an inducement to do that which contravenes the law against perpetuities. There is nothing illegal in keeping up a tomb; on the contrary, it is a very laudable thing to do. It is a rule of law that you shall not tie up property in such a way as to infringe what we know as the law against perpetuities; but there is nothing illegal in what the testator has done here. The appeal must be dismissed with costs.

FRY LJ: I am of the same opinion . . . Keeping the tomb in repair is not an illegal object. If it were, the condition tending to bring about an illegal act would itself be illegal; but to repair the tomb is a perfectly lawful thing. All that can be said is that it is not lawful to tie up property for that purpose. But the rule of law against perpetuities applies to property, not motives; and I know of no rule which says that you may not try to enforce a condition creating a perpetual inducement to do a thing which is lawful. That is this case.

6.5 Other Public Policy Restrictions

6.5.1 TRUSTS CREATED TO PREJUDICE THE SETTLOR'S CREDITOR ARE VOID

RE BUTTERWORTH (1882) 19 ChD 588, CA

FACTS: A trader, B, before embarking upon a new business, made a voluntary settlement (that is, without receiving consideration) for the benefit of his wife and children. His business eventually became insolvent, his liabilities far exceeding his assets.
HELD: (*Obiter*): Irrespective of whether or not B had been solvent at the date of the settlement, the settlement was void as against the trustee in the liquidation. The settlement had clearly been executed with the intention of putting the settlor's property out of the reach of his creditors. A person is not entitled to go into a hazardous business, and immediately before doing so settle all his property voluntarily, the object being this: 'If I succeed in business, I make a fortune for myself. If I fail, I leave my creditors unpaid. They will bear the loss.' Accordingly, the settlement was void for public policy reasons as an attempt to defraud creditors.

SIR GEORGE JESSEL MR: . . . The principle of *Mackay* v *Douglas* LR 14 Eq 106, and that line of cases, is this, that a man is not entitled to go into a hazardous business, and immediately before doing so settle all his property voluntarily, the object being this: 'If I succeed in business, I make a fortune for myself. If I fail, I leave my creditors unpaid. They will bear the loss.' That is the very thing which the statute of Elizabeth was meant to prevent. The object of the settlor was to put his property out of the reach of his future creditors. He contemplated engaging in this new trade and he wanted to preserve his property from his future creditors. That cannot be done by a voluntary settlement. That is, to my mind, a clear and satisfactory principle.

Now, as I understand the evidence in this case, the baker did very well as a baker, and probably he may not have recollected the old proverb *ne sutor ultra crepidam*. When he went into business as a grocer he was going into a business which it appears he did not understand, and it is obvious that the object was—(I am taking that as a fair inference)—to save his property for his wife and children in case the new business did not succeed. Well, that actually happened. The new business did not succeed; he lost money by it, and it probably brought him to bankruptcy.

His object was, as I have said, to make himself safe against that eventuality, and, if that was his object, then I think the principle of *Mackay* v *Douglas* applies, and that the deed was void also under the statute of Elizabeth. But, as I have said before, it is not really necessary to decide this point, because I am clearly of opinion that the deed is void under the 91st section of the Bankruptcy Act. . . .

INSOLVENCY ACT 1986

423. Transactions defrauding creditors

(1) This section relates to transactions entered into at an undervalue, and a person enters into such a transaction with another person if—

(a) he makes a gift to the other person or he otherwise enters into a transaction with the other on terms that provide for him to receive no consideration;

(b) he enters into a transaction with the other in consideration of marriage; or

(c) he enters into a transaction with the other for a consideration the value of which, in money or money's worth, is significantly less than the value, in money or money's worth, of the consideration provided by himself.

(2) Where a person has entered into such a transaction, the court may, if satisfied under the next subsection, make such order as it thinks fit for—

(a) restoring the position to what it would have been if the transaction had not been entered into, and

(b) protecting the interests of persons who are victims of the transaction.

(3) In the case of a person entering into such a transaction, an order shall only be made if the court is satisfied that it was entered into by him for the purpose—

(a) of putting assets beyond the reach of a person who is making, or may at some time make, a claim against him, or

(b) of otherwise prejudicing the interests of such a person in relation to the claim which he is making or may make.

(4) In this section 'the court' means the High Court or—

(a) if the person entering into the transaction is an individual, any other court which would have jurisdiction in relation to a bankruptcy petition relating to him;

(b) if that person is a body capable of being wound up . . . any other court having jurisdiction to wind it up.

(5) In relation to a transaction at an undervalue, references here and below to a victim of the transaction are to a person who is, or is capable of being, prejudiced by it; and in the following two sections the person entering into the transaction is referred to as 'the debtor'.

6.6 End of Chapter Assessment Question

Consider the validity of the following clauses in the will of X:

Clause One: 'I bequeath my stocks and shares to my trustees on trust for such of my grandchildren as shall attain the age of 30.'

Clause Two: 'To my son, Leonard, a life interest in the income earned from my country properties, to determine if ever the income of the fund becomes payable to another person. In the event of determination of the interest the income from the properties shall be held by my trustees on trust for such of my children and in such shares as my trustees shall in their absolute discretion think fit.'

Clause Three: 'In the event of any of the beneficiaries under this will converting or marrying into Islam, the estate hereby limited to him or her shall cease and determine and be utterly void.'

Evidence has been produced to show that the testatrix was survived by a daughter aged 60, a son (Leonard) aged 50, a granddaughter aged 30 and two grandsons aged 25 and 23 respectively. The eldest granddaugher wishes to convert to Islam in order to marry her Muslim boyfriend.

6.7 End of Chapter Assessment Outline Answer

Clause One

According to the common law rule against remoteness of vesting, the gift to the grandchildren is clearly void because it cannot be said that all the grandchildren of the testatrix will attain the age of 30, if they attain that age at all, within 21 years of the death of the last surviving life in being. This is because the testatrix's son might father another child, and all the lives in being might die immediately after that child's birth. (The *daughter* of the testatrix, on the other hand, will be presumed to be past the age of childbearing — Perpetuities and Accumulations Act 1964, s. 2.) This is clearly an especially harsh result from the point of view of the granddaughter who has already satisfied the contingency, and the two living grandsons who will shortly satisfy the contingency themselves. To lessen the hardship of the common law rule, the rule in *Andrews* v *Partington* will apply at common law to close the class immediately upon the testatrix's death (because one grandchild has already satisfied the contingency at that time) to include all grandchildren then living, i.e. the grandaughter aged 30 and the two grandsons aged 25 and 23 respectively.

The rule in *Andrews* v *Partington* does not, however, go far enough from the point of view of grandchildren who might be born after the date of the class closing. The gift to them will be void for remoteness at common law, even after the application of the rule in *Andrews* v *Partington*. Because the gift to them is void at common law it is permissible to turn to the 1964 Act. Under the Act the trustees are permitted to wait until the end of the perpetuity period to see how many grandchildren attain the age of 30. Statutory class closing and age reducing provisions also come into play. Thus if grandchildren born after the class has closed (for the purposes of the rule in *Andrews* v *Partington*) have only reached the age of, say, 28 by the end of the perpetuity period, the 1964 Act permits the class to be closed at the end of the perpetuity period to include all grandchildren then living who are aged 21 or over (Perpetuities and Accumulations Act 1964, s. 4). However, if at the end of the perpetuity period there are grandchildren alive who are under the age of 21, the class will be closed to exclude them from taking an interest.

Clause Two

Although a trust set up to defraud the settlor's creditors will generally be invalid, a trust set up to protect another person from their creditors will be valid if it takes the form of a 'protective trust' (see Trustee Act 1925, s. 33). Protective trusts will often defeat the interests of the spendthrift's creditors, but that to some extent is also the purpose of the insolvency legislation itself. The statutory scheme for distribution of the insolvent person's estate is designed to satisfy the creditors as far as is reasonably possible, but the statutory insolvency scheme is designed also to discharge the liabilities of the insolvent person and to allow them, eventually, to have a fresh start (Insolvency Act 1986).

Clause Three

In *Blathwayt* v *Baron Cawley* [1975] 3 All ER 625 Lord Wilberforce opined that: 'Discrimination is not the same thing as choice: it operates over a larger and less personal area, and neither by express provision nor by implication has private selection yet become a matter of public policy.' In relation to religious discrimination, specifically, Lord Cross had this to say:

> . . . it is true that it is widely thought nowadays that it is wrong for a government to treat some of its citizens less favourably than others because of differences in their religious beliefs; but it does not follow from that that it is against public policy for an adherent of one religion to distinguish in disposing of his property between adherents of his faith and those of another. So to hold would amount to saying that although it is in order for a man to have a mild preference for one religion as opposed to another it is disreputable for him to be convinced of the importance of holding true religious beliefs and of the fact that his religious beliefs are the true ones.

In *Blathwayt* a clause of a testator's will provided that, in the event that one of the beneficiaries under his will should 'be or become a Roman Catholic . . . the estate hereby limited to him shall cease and determine and be utterly void'. It later transpired that a life tenant had indeed become a Roman Catholic. The judge at first instance held that his estate should be forfeit, a judgment which was ultimately upheld in the House of Lords. It follows that clause three of the present will is valid and that the granddaughter's interest will be forfeit if she marries into Islam. As to the element of restricting freedom to marry. Whereas a general condition in restraint of marriage will be void for public policy (*Long* v *Dennis* (1767) 4 Burr 2052 at 2059), a specific restriction on marriage to particular individuals or classes of person will not be void (*Duggan* v *Kelly* (1848) 10 I Eq R 47).

The impact of the Human Rights Act 1998 (which received the Royal Assent on 9 November 1998) on this area of the law has yet to be established.

CHAPTER SEVEN

PURPOSE TRUSTS

7.1 Trusts Purely for Private Purposes

RE ASTOR [1952] Ch 534

FACTS: Non-charitable trusts were declared of substantially all the issued shares shares of 'The Observer Limited' for purposes including the 'maintenance . . . of good understanding . . . between nations'' and 'the preservation of the independence and integrity of newspapers'.

HELD: The trusts were invalid because they were not for the benefit of individuals, but for a number of non-charitable purposes which no one could enforce. The trusts would, in any event, have been void for uncertainty.

ROXBURGH J: . . . The question on which I am giving this reserved judgment is whether the non-charitable trusts . . . are void. Counsel for the trustees of the 1951 settlement and for the Attorney-General have submitted that they are void on two grounds: (i) that they are not trusts for the benefit of individuals; (ii) that they are void for uncertainty. Lord Parker of Waddington dealt with the first of these two questions in his speech in *Bowman* v *Secular Society Ltd*, and I will cite two important passages. The first ([1917] AC 437) is:

> The question whether a trust be legal or illegal or be in accordance with or contrary to the policy of the law only arises when it has been determined that a trust has been created, and is then only part of the larger question whether the trust is enforceable. For, as will presently appear, trusts may be unenforceable and therefore void, not only because they are illegal or contrary to the policy of the law, but for other reasons.

The second (ibid, 441) is:

> A trust to be valid must be for the benefit of individuals, which this is certainly not, or must be in that class of gifts for the benefit of the public which the courts in this country recognise as charitable in the legal as opposed to the popular sense of that term.

Commenting on those passages, counsel for the trustees of the 1945 settlement observed that *Bowman* v *Secular Society Ltd* arose out of a will and he asked me to hold that Lord Parker intended them to be confined to cases arising under a will. But they were, I think, intended to be quite general in character.

. . . if the purposes are not charitable, great difficulties . . . arise both in theory and in practice. In theory, because, having regard to the historical origins of equity, it is difficult to visualise the growth of equitable obligations which nobody can enforce, and in practice, because it is not possible to contemplate with equanimity the creation of large funds devoted to non-charitable purposes which no court and no department of State can control, or, in the case of maladministration, reform. Therefore, Lord Parker's second proposition would prima facie appear to be well founded. . . . no officer has ever been constituted to take, in the case of non-charitable purposes, the position held by the Attorney-General in connection with charitable purposes, and no case has been found in the reports in which the court has ever directly enforced a non-charitable purpose against a trustee. Indeed, where, as in the present case, the only beneficiaries are purposes and an at present unascertainable person, it is difficult to see who could inititate such proceedings. If the purposes are valid trusts, the settlors have retained no beneficial interest and could not initiate them. It was suggested that the trustees might proceed ex parte to enforce the trusts against themselves. I doubt that, but at any rate nobody could enforce the trusts against them. . . .

In *Re Dean* a testator devised his freehold estates, subject to and charged with an annuity of £750 and to a term of fifty years granted to his trustees, to the use of the plaintiff for life, with remainders over, and he gave to his trustees his horses, ponies and hounds. And he charged his said freehold estates with the payment to his trustees, for the term of fifty years, if any of the said horses and hounds should so long live, of an annual sum of £750. And he declared that his trustees should apply the said annual sum in the maintenance of the horses and hounds for the time being living, and in maintaining the stables, kennels and buildings inhabited by the said animals in such condition of repair as his trustees might deem fit, and, in consideration of the mainten-ance of his horses, ponies, and hounds being a charge on his said estate as aforesaid, he gave all his personal estate not otherwise disposed of to the plaintiff absolutely. North J said (41 ChD 556):

> Then it is said, that there is no cestui que trust who can enforce the trust, and that the court will not recognise a trust unless it is capable of being enforced by someone. I do not assent to that view. There is not the least doubt that a man may if he pleases, give a legacy to trustees, upon trust to apply it in erecting a monument to himself, either in a church or in a churchyard, or even in unconsecrated ground, and I am not aware that such a trust is in any way invalid, although it is difficult to say who would be the cestui que trust of the monument. In the same way I know of nothing to prevent a gift of a sum of money to trustees, upon trust to apply it for the repair of such a monument. In my opinion such a trust would be good, although the testator must be careful to limit the time for which it is to last, because, as it is not a charitable trust, unless it is to come to an end within the limits fixed by the rule against perpetuities, it would be illegal. But a trust to lay out a certain sum in building a monument, and the gift of another sum in trust to apply the same to keeping that monument in repair, say, for ten years, is, in my opinion, a perfectly good trust, although I do not see who could ask the court to enforce it. If persons beneficially interested in the estate could do so, then the present plaintiff can do so; but, if such persons could not enforce the trust, still it cannot be said that the trust must fail because there is no one who can actively enforce it.

This is the best case . . . from the point of view of counsel for the trustees of the 1945 settlement, because North J did, undoubtedly, uphold the particular directions, whether or not they could be 'actively enforced'. But, putting it at its highest, he merely held that there were certainly classes of trusts, of which this was one, in which that objection was not fatal. He did not suggest that it was not generally fatal outside the realm of charity.

In *Pirbright v Salway* [1896] WN 86 a testator, after expressing his wish to be buried in the inclosure in which his child lay in a certain churchyard, bequeathed to the rector and churchwardens of the parish church £800 consols, the interest and dividends to be derived therefrom to be applied, so long as the law for the time being permitted, in keeping up the inclosure and decorating the same with flowers. It was held by Stirling J that the gift was valid for at least a period of twenty-one years from the testator's death, and, semble, that it was not charitable. In *Re Hooper* a testator bequeathed to his executors and trustees money out of the income of which to provide, so far as they legally could do so, for the care and upkeep of certain graves, a vault and certain monuments. Maugham J said ([1932] 1 Ch 39):

> This point is one to my mind of doubt, and I should have felt some difficulty in deciding it if it were not for *Pirbright v Salway* . . . That was a decision arrived at by

Stirling J after argument by very eminent counsel. The case does not appear to have attracted much attention in text-books, but it does not appear to have been commented upon adversely, and I shall follow it.

In *Re Hooper* and probably also in *Pirbright* v *Salway* there was a residuary legatee to bring before the court any failure to comply with the directions. But I think that Maugham J regarded both cases as exceptions from the general principle.

Last in this group is *Re Thompson*. . . . The testator bequeathed a legacy of £1,000 to a friend to be applied by him in such manner as he should think fit towards the promotion and furthering of fox-hunting and devised and bequeathed his residuary estate to Trinity Hall in the university of Cambridge. An originating summons was taken out by the executors to determine whether the legacy was valid or failed for want of a definite object or for uncertainty or on other grounds. During the course of the argument, counsel for the friend observed:

> True, there is no cestui que trust who can enforce the application of the legacy, but that is immaterial: *Re Dean* (1889) 41 ChD 552. The object to which the legacy is to be applied is sufficiently defined to be enforced.

But Clauson J interposed ([1934] Ch 343):

> The college, as residuary legatees, seem to have an interest in the legacy, as, but for the trust for its application, they would be entitled to it. The procedure adopted by Knight Bruce V-C in *Pettingall* v *Pettingall*, cited in Jarman on Wills, 7th edn, vol. 2, p. 877, might be followed in this case.

And in his judgment he said (ibid, 344):

> In my judgment the object of the gift has been defined with sufficient clearness and is of a nature to which effect can be given. The proper way for me to deal with the matter will be, not to make, as it is asked by the summons, a general declaration, but, following the example of Knight Bruce V-C in *Pettingall* v *Pettingall*, to order that, upon the defendant Mr Lloyd [the friend] giving an undertaking (which I understand he is willing to give) to apply the legacy when received by him towards the object expressed in the testator's will, the plaintiffs do pay to the defendant Mr Lloyd the legacy of £1,000; and that, in case the legacy should be applied by him otherwise than towards the promotion and furthering of fox-hunting, the residuary legatees are to be at liberty to apply.   .

I understand Clauson J to have held, in effect, that there was somebody who could enforce the purpose indicated because the college, as residuary legatees, would be entitled to the legacy but for the trust for its application, and they could apply to the court to prevent any misapplication or breach of the undertaking given by Mr Lloyd. I infer from what the learned judge said that he would not have upheld the validity of this non-charitable purpose if there had been no residuary legatee, and no possibility of making such an order as was made in *Pettingall* v *Pettingall*. . . .

Let me, then, sum up the position so far. On the one side, there are Lord Parker's two propositions with which I began. These were not new, but merely re-echoed what Sir William Grant MR had said (9 Ves 405) in *Morice* v *Bishop of Durham* as long ago as 1804: 'There must be somebody, in whose favour the court can decree performance'. The position was recently re-stated by Harman J in *Re Wood*, where he said ([1949] 1 All ER 1101): 'a gift on trust must have a cestui que trust', and this seems to be in accord with principle. On the other side is a group of cases relating to horses and dogs, graves and monuments—matters arising under wills and intimately connected with the deceased—in which the courts have found means of escape from these general propositions. . . . The rest may, I think, properly be regarded as anomalous and exceptional and in no way destructive of the proposition which traces descent from or through Sir William Grant MR, through Lord Parker of Waddington, to Harman J. Perhaps the late Sir Arthur Underhill was right in suggesting that they may be concessions to human weakness or sentiment: see Underhill's Law of Trusts and Trustees, 8th edn, p. 79 [10th edn, p. 97]. They cannot, in my judgment, of themselves (and no other justification has been suggested to me) justify the conclusion that a court of equity will recognise as an equitable obligation affecting the income of large funds in the hands of trustees a direction to apply it in furtherance of enumerated non-charitable purposes in a manner which no court or department can control or enforce. I hold that the trusts here in question are void on the first of the grounds submitted by counsel for the trustees of the settlement of 1951 and counsel for the Attorney-General.

The second ground on which the relevant trusts are challenged is uncertainty. . . . The purposes must be so defined that, if the trustees surrendered their discretion, the court could carry out the purposes declared, not a selection of them arrived at by eliminating those which are too uncertain to be carried out. If, for example, I were to eliminate all the purposes except those declared in para. 4, and to decree that those declared in para. 4 ought to be performed, should I be executing the trusts of the settlement? But how, in any case, could I decree in what manner the trusts applicable to income were to be performed? The settlement gives no guidance at all. Counsel for the trustees of the 1945 settlement suggested that the trustees might apply to the court ex parte for a scheme. It is not, I think, a mere coincidence that no case has been found outside the realm of charity in which the court has yet devised a scheme of ways and means for attaining enumerated trust purposes. If it were to assume this (as I think) novel jurisdiction over public, but not charitable, trusts, it would, I believe, necessarily require the assistance of a custodian of the public interest analogous to the Attorney-General in charity cases who would not only help to formulate schemes but could be charged with the duty of enforcing them and preventing maladministration. There is no such person. Accordingly, in my judgment, the trusts for the application of income during 'the specified period' are void also for uncertainty. But while I have reached my decision on two separate grounds, both, I think, have their origin in a single principle, namely, that a court of equity does not recognise as valid a trust which it cannot both enforce and control. This seems to me to be good equity and good sense.

7.2   Trusts of Imperfect Obligation

RE HOOPER [1932] 1 Ch 38

FACTS: A testator made a bequest and declared that the income therefrom should be used for the care and upkeep of certain graves, a vault, certain monuments, a tablet and a window.

HELD: The upkeep of the tablet and window was valid as a charitable purpose. The trust for the upkeep of the graves, vault and monument in the churchyard would take effect as a trust of imperfect obligation and income could be applied for this purpose for 21 years.

MAUGHAM J: . . . The trustees here have the sum of 1000l. which they have to hold upon trust to 'invest the same and to the intent that so far as they legally can do so and in any manner that they may in their discretion arrange they will out of the annual income thereof' do substantially four things: first, provide for the care and upkeep of the grave and monument in the Torquay cemetery; secondly, for the care and upkeep of a vault and monument there in which lie the remains of the testator's wife and daughter; thirdly, for the care and upkeep of a grave and monument in Shotley churchyard near Ipswich, where the testator's son lies buried; and, fourthly, for the care and upkeep of the tablet in Saint Matthias' Church at Ilsham to the memories of the testator's wife and children and the window in the same church to the memory of his late father. All those four things have to be done expressly according to an arrangement made in the discretion of the trustees and so far as they legally can do so. I do not think that is distinguishable from the phrase 'so long as the law for the time being permits,' and the conclusion at which I arrive, following the decision I have mentioned, is that this trust is valid for a period of twenty-one years from the testator's death so far as regards the three matters which involve the upkeep of graves or vaults or monuments in the churchyard or in the cemetery. As regards the tablet in St. Matthias' Church and the window in the same church there is no question but that that is a good charitable gift, and, therefore, the rule against perpetuities does not apply.

7.3 Devices for Avoiding the Rule against Trusts purely for Private Purposes

RE CHARDON [1928] 1 Ch 464, ChD

FACTS: A clause of C's will was in the following terms:

> I give unto my trustees the sum of £200 free of duty upon trust to invest the same upon any of the investments hereinafter authorised and pay the income thereof to the South Metropolitan Cemetery Company West Norwood during such period as they shall continue to maintain and keep the graves of my great grandfather and the said Priscilla Navone in the said Cemetery in good order and condition with flowers and plants thereon as the same have hitherto been kept by me.

HELD: The gift was valid. One of the principles underlying the rule against the validity of pure purpose trusts is that purposes are often perpetual and thus funds applied for such purposes might be rendered inalienable. In the present case, however, the fund given to the company was not inalienable, but could be disposed of by the company at any time that a purchaser or donee could be found. Nor did the gift offend the rule against remoteness of vesting, here the gift had vested absolutely in the company (at law a person theoretically distinct from its members) within the perpetuity period.

ROMER J: This is a very interesting, and, I think, very difficult case to determine, but as I have formed a definite opinion as to the right answer to be given to the question I do not think there would be any advantage in my considering the matter further.

The gift with which I have to deal is in these terms:

> I give unto my trustees the sum of two hundred pounds free of duty upon trust to invest the same upon any of the investments hereinafter authorised and pay the income thereof to the South Metropolitan Cemetery Company West Norwood during such period as they shall continue to maintain and keep the graves of my great grandfather and the said Priscilla Navone in the said Cemetery in good order and condition with flowers and plants thereon as the same have hitherto been kept by me.

It is argued that that is a void gift, and on reading it the mind is naturally directed to the cases in which it has been established over and over again that a trust to keep in repair a tomb not in a church is invalid, either because it offends the rule against perpetuities, the beneficial interest not necessarily vesting in a life in being and twenty-one years; or because the beneficial interest never vests in any one at all. One is therefore inclined at first sight to come, I think too hastily, to the conclusion that any trust not being a charitable trust which may go on, as this one may go on, indefinitely beyond lives in being and twenty-one years is invalid. But then when the matter is considered a little more closely this question presents itself: If this be a bad gift it must be because there is some principle of law or equity that makes it bad. Now there is a rule to the effect that vested interests in property cannot be rendered inalienable. But the interest of the cemetery company under the gift in question is certainly not inalienable; they could dispose of it, if they could find a purchaser, to-morrow. There is also the well known rule against perpetuities which is quite a different rule from that against inalienability, and that rule is that the vesting of property real or personal (and it also applies to interests legal or equitable) cannot be postponed beyond lives in being and twenty-one years. This gift does not appear to offend against that rule. The interest of the cemetery company, such as it is, vests at once. It has been pointed out on more than one occasion, perhaps it was last pointed out in the case to which my attention was called of *Wainwright v Miller* [1897] 2 Ch 255, that the rule against perpetuities is not dealing with the duration of interests but with their commencement, and so long as the interest vests within lives in being and twenty-one years it does not matter how long that interest lasts. This is pointed out by Mr Gray in his book, and if it were not the case, the limitation of a fee simple would offend the rule against perpetuities. It is well known that in many settlements the limitations continue long beyond the lives in being and twenty-one years. I cannot see therefore that this gift offends against the rule against perpetuities, as I understand that rule. . . .

7.4 Purpose Trusts with Indirect Human Beneficiaries

RE DENLEY'S TRUST DEED [1968] 3 All ER 65

FACTS: Land was settled on trustees for use as a sports ground 'primarily' for the benefit of the employees of a company, and 'secondarily' for the benefit of such other persons (if any) as the trustees may allow to use the same. The gift was limited to take effect within 21 years of the death of certain named persons.

HELD: Because of the private nexus between the potential beneficiaries of the trust and a particular company the trust was not sufficiently 'public' to be charitable. *Prima facie*, then, it would be void as a non-charitable purpose trust. However, where the trust, though expressed to be for a purpose, is directly or indirectly for the benefit of an individual or individuals, it falls outside the mischief of the beneficiary principle. The rule against enforcing non-charitable purpose trusts should be confined to those which are abstract or impersonal. In the present case there were clearly indirect human beneficiaries and the trust would therefore be valid. Goff J was satisfied that, in contrast with the case of a pure purpose trust, there were persons here who would bring the matter to court if the trustees failed to meet their obligations. (Note: being for present and future indirect beneficiaries the trust would have failed the rule against inalienability of capital had it not been for the express limitation to the perpetuity period.)

GOFF J: . . . I think that there may be a purpose or object trust, the carrying out of which would benefit an individual or individuals, where that benefit is so indirect or intangible or which is otherwise so framed as not to give those persons any locus standi to apply to the court to enforce the trust, in which case the beneficiary principle would, as it seems to me, apply to invalidate the trust, quite apart from any question of uncertainty or perpetuity. Such cases can be considered if and when they arise. The present is not, in my judgment, of that character, and it will be seen that cl. 2(d) of the trust deed expressly states that, subject to any rules and regulations made by the trustees, the employees of the company shall be entitled to the use and enjoyment of the land.

Apart from this possible exception, in my judgment the beneficiary principle of *Re Astor*, which was approved in *Re Endacott (decd)* [1959] 3 All ER 562; see particularly by Harman LJ, is confined to purpose or object trusts which are abstract or impersonal. The objection is not that the trust is for a purpose or object per se, but that there is no beneficiary or cestui que trust. The rule is so expressed in *Lewin on Trusts* (16th edn) p.17, and in my judgment, with the possible exception which I have mentioned, rightly so. In *Re Wood, Barton v Chilcott* [1949] Ch 498, Harman J said:

> There has been an interesting argument on the question of perpetuity, but it seems to me, with all respect to that argument, that there is an earlier obstacle which is fatal to the validity of this bequest, namely, that a gift on trust must have a cestui que trust, and there being here no cestui que trust the gift must fail.

Again, in *Leahy v A-G of New South Wales* [1959] AC 457, Viscount Simonds, delivering the judgment of the Privy Council, said:

> A gift can be made to persons (including a corporation) but it cannot be made to a purpose or to an object: so, also [and these are the important words] a trust may be

created for the benefit of persons as cestuis que trust but not for a purpose or object unless the purpose or object be charitable. For a purpose or object cannot sue, but, if it be charitable, the Attorney-General can sue to enforce it.

Where, then, the trust, though expressed as a purpose, is directly for the benefit of an individual or individuals, it seems to me that it is in general outside the mischief of the beneficiary principle.

. . . The trust in the present case is limited in point of time so as to avoid any infringement of the rule against perpetuities and, for the reasons which I have given, it does not offend against the beneficiary principle; and unless, therefore, it be void for uncertainty, it is a valid trust.

As it is a private trust and not a charitable one, it is clear that, however it be regarded, the individuals for whose benefit it is designed must be ascertained or capable of ascertainment at any given time: see *Inland Revenue Comrs* v *Broadway Cottages Trust, Inland Revenue Comrs* v *Sunnylands Trust* [1955] Ch 20.

It is conceded that 'the employees of the company', which must mean for the time being, are so ascertained or ascertainable, but counsel for the first defendant submits that the inclusion in the class of such other person or persons (if any) as the trustees may allow is fatal, and that the qualification 'secondarily' in relation to such persons does not help. In my judgment, however, this is not so. I accept counsel for the second defendant's submission that the provision as to other persons is not a trust but a power operating in partial defeasance of the trust in favour of the employees which it does not therefore make uncertain. Moreover, as it is a power, it is not necessary that the trustees should know all possible objects in whose favour it is exercisable: see *Re Gulbenkian's Settlement Trusts, Hacobian* v *Maun*. Therefore, in my judgment, it is a valid power. If this were a will, a question might arise whether this provision might be open to attack as a delegation of the testamentary power. I do not say that would be so, but in any case it cannot be said of a settlement inter vivos.

Another question, perhaps of difficulty, might arise if the trustees purported to admit not a given individual or individuals but a class which they failed to specify with certainty, whether in such a case this would import uncertainty into and invalidate the whole trust or would be merely an invalid exercise of the power; but, as that has not in fact occurred, I need not consider it.

There is, however, one other aspect of uncertainty which has caused me some concern; that is, whether this is in its nature a trust which the court can control, for as Lord Eldon LC said in *Morice* v *Bishop of Durham*:

> As it is a maxim that the execution of a trust shall be under the control of the court, it must be of such a nature that it can be under that control; so that the administration of it can be reviewed by the court; or, if the trustee dies, the court itself can execute the trust: a trust, therefore, which, in case of mal-administration could be reformed; and a due administration directed; and then, unless the subject and the objects can be ascertained upon principles familiar in other cases, it must be decided that the court can neither reform mal-administration nor direct a due administration.

The difficulty which I have felt is that there may well be times when some of the employees wish to use the sports club for one purpose while others desire to use it at the same time for some other purpose of such nature that the two cannot be carried on together. The trustees could, of course, control this by making rules and regulations under cl. 2(d) of the trust deed, but they might not. In any case, the employees would probably agree amongst themselves, but I cannot assume that they would. If there were an impasse, the court could not resolve it, because it clearly could not either exercise the trustees' power to make rules or settle a scheme, this being a non-charitable trust: see *Re Astor*.

In my judgment, however, it would not be right to hold the trust void on this ground. The court can, as it seems to me, execute the trust both negatively by restraining any improper disposition or use of the land, and positively by ordering the trustees to allow the employees and such other persons (if any) as they may admit to use the land for the purpose of a recreation or sports ground. Any difficulty there might be in practice in the beneficial enjoyment of the land by those entitled to use it is, I think, really beside the point. The same kind of problem is equally capable of arising in the case of a trust to permit a number of persons—for example, all the unmarried children of a testator or settlor—to use or occupy a house or to have the use of certain chattels; nor can I assume that in such cases agreement between the parties concerned would be more likely, even if that be a sufficient distinction, yet no one would suggest, I fancy, that such a trust would be void.

In my judgment, therefore, the provisions of cl. 2(c) are valid.

7.5   Gifts to Unincorporated Non-profit Associations

7.5.1   ABSOLUTE GIFTS TO MEMBERS SUBJECT TO THE CONTRACTUAL RULES OF THE CLUB

RE RECHER'S WILL TRUST [1971] 3 All ER 401

FACTS: R, a testatrix, left a share of her residuary estate to 'The Anti-Vivisection Society'. HELD: The gift should not be construed as a gift in trust for the purposes of the society. Rather, the gift should be construed as a legacy to the present members of the society as an accretion to the funds which constituted the subject matter of the contract by which the members had bound themselves *inter se*. There would be no breach of the rule against inalienability of capital because if all the members agreed, they could decide to wind up the society and divide the net assets amongst themselves beneficially. The only reason the gift failed in the present case was because the society had ceased to exist by the time of R's death.

BRIGHTMAN J: . . . Having reached the conclusion that the gift in question is not a gift to the members of the London and Provincial Society at the date of death, as joint tenants or tenants in common so as to entitle a member as of right to a distributive share, nor an attempted gift to present and future members beneficially, and is not a gift in trust for the purposes of the society, I must now consider how otherwise, if at all, it is capable of taking effect.

As I have already mentioned, the rules of the London and Provincial Society do not purport to create any trusts except insofar as the honorary trustees are not beneficial owners of the assets of the society, but are trustees on trust to deal with such assets according to the directions of the committee.

A trust for non-charitable purposes, as distinct from a trust for individuals, is clearly void because there is no beneficiary. It does not, however, follow that persons cannot band themselves together as an association or society, pay subscriptions and validly devote their funds in pursuit of some lawful non-charitable purpose. An obvious example is a members' social club. But it is not essential that the members should only intend to secure direct personal advantages to themselves. The association may be one in which personal advantages to the members are combined with the pursuit of some outside purpose. Or the association may be one which offers no personal benefit at all to the members, the funds of the association being applied exclusively to the pursuit of some outside purpose. Such an association of persons is bound, I would think, to have some sort of constitution; i.e. the rights and liabilities of the members of the association will inevitably depend on some form of contract inter se, usually evidenced by a set of rules. In the present case it appears to me clear that the life members, the ordinary members and the associate members of the London Provincial Society were bound together by a contract inter se. Any such member was entitled to the rights and subject to the liabilities defined by the rules. If the committee acted contrary to the rules, an individual member would be entitled to take proceedings in the courts to compel observance of the rules or to recover damages for any loss he had suffered as a result of the breach of contract. As and when a member paid his subscription to the association, he would be subjecting his money to the disposition and expenditure thereof laid down by the rules. That is to say, the member would be bound to permit, and entitled to require, the honorary trustees and other members of the society to deal with that subscription in accordance with the lawful directions of the committee. Those directions would include the expenditure of that subscription, as part of the general funds of the association, in furthering the objects of the association. The resultant situation, on analysis, is that the London Provincial Society represented an organisation of individuals bound together by a contract under which their subscriptions became, as it were, mandated towards a certain type of expenditure as adumbrated in r. 1. Just as the two parties to a bipartite bargain can vary or terminate their contract by mutual assent, so it must follow that the life members, ordinary members and associate members of the London and Provincial Society could, at any moment of time, by unanimous agreement (or by majority vote if the rules so prescribe), vary or terminate their multi-partite contract. There would be no limit to the type of variation or termination to which all might agree. There is no private trust or trust for charitable purposes or other trust to hinder the process. It follows that if all members agreed, they could decide to wind up the London and Provincial Society and divide the net assets among themselves benefi- cially. No one would have any locus standi to stop them so doing. The contract is the same as any other contract and concerns only those who are parties to it, that is to say, the members of the society.

The funds of such as association may, of course, be derived not only from the subscriptions of the contracting parties but also from donations from non-contracting parties and legacies from persons who have died. In the case of a donation which is not accompanied by any words which purport to impose a trust, it seems to me that the gift takes effect in favour of the existing members of the association as an accretion to the funds which are the subject-matter of the contract which such members have made inter se, and falls to be dealt with in precisely the same way as the funds which the members themselves have subscribed. So, in the case of a legacy, in the absence of words which purport to impose a trust, the legacy is a gift to the members beneficially, not as joint tenants or as tenants in common so as to entitle each member to an immediate distributive share, but as an accretion to the funds which are the subject-matter of the contract which the members have made inter se. . . .

RE GRANT'S WT [1979] 3 All ER 359

FACTS: G, the testator, had been financial secretary of the Chertsey Constituency Labour Party, which had since become the Chertsey and Walton Constituency Labour Party. The new constituency party was subject to rules laid down by the National Executive Committee of the Labour Party and the national annual party conference. By his will, G devised all his real and personal estate (for the benefit of the Chertsey headquarters of the new constituency party) to the committee in charge of property at the headquarters. HELD: The gift could not take effect as a gift to the current members of the new constituency party subject to their contractual rights and duties *inter se* because the members were not free, under the rules of their association, to dispose of the property in any way they thought fit. On the contrary, the rules made it plain that the decisions of the members of the local party were subject to the control of the national Labour Party. The gift must therefore fail as infringing the rule against inalienability of capital.

VINELOTT J: . . . Brightman J observed in *Re Recher's Will Trusts* that: 'It would astonish a layman to be told there was a difficulty in his giving a legacy to an unincorporated non-charitable society which he had or could have supported without trouble during his lifetime.' The answer to this apparent paradox is, it seems to me, that subscriptions by members of the Chertsey and Walton CLP must be taken as made on terms that they will be applied by the general committee in accordance with the rules for the time being, including any modifications imposed by the annual party conference or the NEC. In the event of the dissolution of the Chertsey and Walton CLP any remaining fund represen- ting subscriptions would (as the rules now stand) be held on a resulting trust for the original subscribers. Thus although the members of the CLP may not be able themselves to alter the purposes for which a fund representing subscriptions is to be used or to alter the rules so as to make such a fund divisible amongst themselves the ultimate proprietary right of the original subscribers remains. There is, therefore, no perpetuity and no non-charitable purpose trust. But if that analysis of the terms on which subscriptions are held is correct, it is fatal to the argument that the gift in the testator's will should be construed as a gift to the members of the Chertsey and Walton CLP at the testator's death, subject to a direction not amounting to a trust that it be used for headquarters' purposes. Equally it is in my judgment impossible, in particular having regard to the gift over to the national Labour Party, to read the gift as a gift to the members of the national Labour Party at the testator's death, with a direction not amounting to a trust, that the national party permit it to be used by the Chertsey and Walton CLP for headquarters' purposes.

The first ground is of itself conclusive, but there is another ground which reinforces this conclusion. The gift is not in terms a gift to the Chertsey and Walton CLP, but to the Labour Party Property Committee, who are to hold the property for the benefit of, that is in trust for, the Chertsey headquarters of the Chertsey and Walton CLP. The fact that a gift is a gift to trustees and not in terms to an unincorporated association militates against construing it as a gift to the members of the association at the date when the gift takes effect, and against construing the words indicating the purposes for which the property is to be used as expressing the testator's intention or motive in making the gift and not as imposing any trust. This was, indeed, one of the considerations which led the Privy Council in *Leahy's* case to hold that the gift '. . . upon trust for such Order of Nuns of the Catholic Church or the Christian Brothers as my Executors and Trustees should select' would, apart from the Australian equivalent of the Charitable Trusts (Validation) Act 1954, have been invalid.

I am, therefore, compelled to the conclusion that the gift of the testator's estate fails. . . .

7.5.2 SUMMATIVE EXERCISE

Note how the following case draws together consideration of the various modes of construing gifts to unincorporated associations.

RE LIPINKSI [1976] 1 Ch 235, ChD

FACTS: The testator, L, left one half of his residuary estate to the trustees of an association for Jewish Youth. The gift was expressly made in memory of his late wife to be used 'solely' in the work of constructing new buildings for the association. The trust was not charitable because it produced insufficient benefit to the general public. The question was whether it was void as a pure purpose trust.

HELD: The trust was valid for any one of three reasons. First, applying *Re Denley*, because there were indirect human beneficiaries; secondly, because, applying *Re Recher* [1971] 3 All ER 40, the gift should be construed as an outright gift to the members of the association, subject to the rules of the association; or thirdly, applying *Re Turkington*, because the members of the association were both the trustees and the beneficiaries and thus able to vest the capital in themselves according to the rule in *Saunders* v *Vautier*.

OLIVER J: This is a summons raising two points of construction of a residuary bequest under the will of a testator, Harry Lipinski, who died on May 30, 1969. The testator had been a widower for some years at his death. He was of the Jewish faith and had taken an active part in various Jewish organisations in Hull. His last will, which I have to construe, is dated December 21 1967, but he had made two previous wills, in March 1966 and October 1966, in each of which the residuary legatees named were the same as in his last will. In the will of March 1966 he directed his residuary estate to be held as to one half for the Hull Judeans (Maccabi) Association in memory of his late wife, as to one quarter for the Hull Hebrew School (Talmud Torah), and as to one quarter for the Hull Hebrew Board of Guardians.

If he had reproduced this in the later document, this summons would have been unnecessary; but, unfortunately, in his will dated December 21, 1967, he added to the bequests to the Hull Judeans (Maccabi) Association and the Hull Hebrew Board of Guardians the words which have made this summons necessary. The will, which reproduces in all material respects the provisions of the will of October 1966, is, in the relevant provisions, in these terms:

> I give and devise the rest residue and remainder of my estate real and personal whatsoever and wheresoever unto my trustees upon trust to sell call in and convert into money the same with power to postpone such sale calling in and conversion and to hold the net proceeds of sale thereof and my ready money after payment there out of my just debts and my funeral and testamentary expenses upon trust:—(a) as to one half thereof for the Hull Judeans (Maccabi) Association in memory of my late wife to be used solely in the work of constructing the new buildings for the association and/or improvements to the said buildings; (b) as to one quarter thereof for the Hull Hebrew School (Talmud Torah); (C) as to the remaining one quarter for the Hull Hebrew Board of Guardians to be used solely in the work of constructing the new buildings for the association and/or improvements to the said building.

That was clause 4 of the will. The testator made a codicil of December 31, 1967, confirming his will, but adding, inter alia, the following provision:

> I declare that the receipt of the chairman or treasurer or other proper officer for the time being of any association or institution referred to in my will or any codicil thereto shall in each case be sufficient discharge to my trustees.

His will and codicil were duly proved on September 8, 1969, and this summons was issued by the executors on July 21, 1972. It raises the questions whether, in broad terms, each of the bequests in clause 4(a) and (c) of the will is a valid bequest or is void for impracticability or otherwise. . . .

Up to January 7, 1973, when an extraordinary general meeting of the association adopted the present constitution, as a result of which the association is now a registered charity, it never appears formally to have adopted a constitution, but it is the evidence of its president, Mr Wienberg, that a document which he produces and which is headed 'Proposed Constitution of Hull Judeans Maccabi Association' was always treated as the constitution and referred to when any question arose. It is by reference to that document that the status of the association at the testator's death, in my judgment, falls to be determined. Now, that document starts with clause 1:

> Name. The name of the association shall be the Hull Judeans Maccabi Association. It shall be a branch of the Union of Maccabi Associations of Great Britain & Ireland, and shall accept all provisions relating to branches, laid down in the constitution of the union from time to time.

. . .

Then, under clause 2, which is headed 'Aims and Objects':

> (a) To promote the interest, and the active participation of Anglo-Jewish youth of both sexes, in amateur sports, in all forms of cultural, and in non-political, communal activities. (b) To inculcate within its ranks a team spirit, a conception of fair play, good citizenship and self discipline. (c) To provide members of the association with facilities for training and friendly competition in all its activities. (d) To promote and foster the interest to cultivate a knowledge of Jewish history, of the Hebrew language and national traditions. (e) To provide for the advancement of the Jewish religious education and to develop within Jewish youth the principles of the spirit of the Jewish faith. (f) Generally to encourage the development in Jewish youth of the mind, spirit and body, in the traditions of the Maccabeans. (g) To foster better understanding between Jews and non Jews, by means of sporting, cultural and social intercourse. (h) To co-operate with any organisation, association or club, whose aims and objects are similar to those of the association. . . .

The principles applicable to this type of case were stated by Cross J in *Neville Estates Ltd* v *Madden* [1962] Ch 832, 849, and they are conveniently summarised in *Tudor, Charities*, 6th ed. (1967), p. 150, where it is said:

In *Neville Estates Ltd* v *Madden* Cross J expressed the opinion (which is respectfully accepted as correct) that every such gift might, according to the actual words used, be construed in one of three quite different ways: (a) As a gift to the members of the association at the date of the gift as joint tenants so that any member could sever his share and claim it whether or not he continued to be a member. (b) As a gift to the members of the association at the date of the gift not as joint tenants, but subject to their contractual rights and liabilities towards one another as members of the association. In such a case a member cannot sever his share. It will accrue to the other members on his death or resignation, even though such members include persons who become members after the gift took effect. If this is the effect of the gift, it will not be open to objection on the score of perpetuity or uncertainty unless there is something in its terms or circumstances or in the rules of the association which precludes the members at any given time from dividing the subject of the gift between them on the footing that they are solely entitled to it in equity. (c) The terms or circumstances of the gift or the rules of the association may show that the property in question—i.e., the subject of the gift—is not to be at the disposal of the members for the time being but is to be held in trust for or applied for the purposes of the association as a quasi-corporate entity. In this case the gift will fail unless the association is a charitable body.

That summary may require, I think, a certain amount of qualification in the light of subsequent authority, but for present purposes I can adopt it as a working guide. Mr Blackburne, for the next-of-kin, argues that the gift in the present case clearly does not fall within the first category, and that the addition of the specific direction as to its employment by the association prevents it from falling into the second category. This is, therefore, he says, a purpose trust and fails both for that reason and because the purpose is perpetuitous. He relies upon this passage from the judgment of the Board in *Leahy* v *Attorney-General for New South Wales* [1959] AC 457, 458:

If the words 'for the general purposes of the association' were held to import a trust, the question would have to be asked, what is the trust and who are the beneficiaries? A gift can be made to persons (including a corporation) but it cannot be made to a purpose or to an object: so also, a trust may be created for the benefit of persons as cestuis que trust but not for a purpose or object unless the purpose or object be charitable. For a purpose or object cannot sue but, if it be charitable, the Attorney-General can sue to enforce it.

Mr Blackburne points out, first, that the gift is in memory of the testator's late wife (which, he says, suggests an intention to create a permanent memorial or endowment); secondly, that the gift is *solely* for a particular purpose (which would militate strongly against any suggestion that the donees could wind up and pocket the money themselves, even though their constitution may enable them to do so); and, thirdly, that the gift contemplates expenditure on 'improvements,' which connotes a degree of continuity or permanence. All this, he says, shows that what the testator had in mind was a permanent endowment in memory of his late wife.

For my part, I think that very little turns upon the testator's having expressed the gift as being in memory of his late wife. I see nothing in this expression which suggests any intention to create a permanent endowment. It indicates merely, I think, a tribute which the testator wished to pay, and it is not without significance that this self-same tribute appeared in the earlier will in which he made an absolute and outright gift to the association. The evidential value of this in the context of a construction summons may be open to doubt, and I place no reliance upon it. It does, however, seem to me that nothing is to be derived from these words beyond the fact that the testator wished the association to know that his bounty was a tribute to his late wife.

I accept, however, Mr Blackburne's submission that the designation of the sole purpose of the gift makes it impossible to construe the gift as one falling into the first of Cross J's categories, even if that were otherwise possible. But I am not impressed by the argument that the gift shows an intention of continuity. Mr Blackburne prays in aid *In re Macaulay's Estate* [1943] Ch 435 which is reported as a note to *In re Price* [1943] Ch 422, where the gift was for the 'maintenance and improvement of the Theosophical Lodge at Folke-stone.' The House of Lords held that it failed for perpetuity, the donee being a non-charitable body. But it is clear from the speeches of both Lord Buckmaster and Lord Tomlin that their Lordships derived the intention of continuity from the reference to 'maintenance.' Here it is quite evident that the association was to be free to spend the capital of the legacy. As Lord Buckmaster said in *In re Macaulay's Estate*, at p. 436:

> In the first place it is clear that the mere fact that the beneficiary is an unincorporated society in no way affects the validity of the gift. . . . The real question is what is the actual purpose for which the gift is made. There is no perpetuity if the gift were for the individual members for their own benefit, but that, I think, is clearly not the meaning of this gift. Nor again is there a perpetuity if the society is at liberty in accordance with the terms of the gift, to spend both capital and income as they think fit.

In re Price itself is authority for the proposition that a gift to an unincorporated non-charitable association for objects upon which the association is at liberty to spend both capital and income will not fail for perpetuity, although the actual conclusion in that case has been criticised—the point that the trust there (the carrying on of the teachings of Rudolf Steiner) was a 'purpose trust' and thus unenforceable on that ground was not argued. It does not seem to me, therefore, that in the present case there is a valid ground for saying that the gift fails for perpetuity.

But that is not the end of the matter. If the gift were to the association simpliciter, it would, I think, clearly fall within the second category of Cross J's categories. At first sight, however, there appears to be a difficulty in arguing that the gift is to members of the association subject to their contractual rights inter se when there is a specific direction or limitation sought to be imposed upon those contractual rights as to the manner in which the subject matter of the gift is to be dealt with. This, says Mr Blackburne, is a pure 'purpose trust' and is invalid on that ground, quite apart from any question of perpetuity. I am not sure, however, that it is sufficient merely to demonstrate that a trust is a 'purpose' trust. With the greatest deference, I wonder whether the dichotomy postulated in the passage which I have referred to in the judgment of the Board in *Leahy's* case [1959] AC 457, 478 is not an over-simplification. Indeed, I am not convinced that it was intended as an exhaustive statement or to do more than indicate the broad division of trusts into those where there are ascertainable beneficiaries (whether for particular purposes or not) and trusts where there are none. Indeed, that this is the case, as it seems to me, is to be derived from a later passage on p. 484 of the report, which is in these terms:

> At the risk of repetition their Lordships would point out that, if a gift is made to individuals, whether under their own names or in the name of their society, and the conclusion is reached that they are not intended to take beneficially, then they take as trustees. If so, it must be ascertained who are the beneficiaries. If at the death of the testator the class of beneficiaries is fixed and ascertained or ascertainable within the limit of the rule against perpetuities, all is well. If it is not so fixed and not so ascertainable the trust must fail. Of such a trust no better example could be found than a gift to an Order for the benefit of a community of nuns, once it is established that the community is not confined to living and ascertained persons. A wider question is opened if it appears that the trust is not for persons but for a non-charitable purpose. As has been pointed out no one can enforce such a trust. What follows? Ex hypothesi the trustees are not themselves the beneficiaries yet the trust fund is in their hands, and they may or may not think fit to carry out their testator's wishes. If so, it would seem that the testator has imperfectly exercised his testamentary power; he has delegated it, for the disposal of his property lies with them, not with him. Accordingly, the subject matter of the gift will be undisposed of or fall into the residuary estate as the case may be.

There would seem to me to be, as a matter of common sense, a clear distinction between the case where a purpose is prescribed which is clearly intended for the benefit of ascertained or ascertainable beneficiaries, particularly where those beneficiaries have the power to make the capital their own, and the case where no beneficiary at all is intended (for instance, a memorial to a favourite pet) or where the beneficiaries are unascertainable: as in the case, for instance, of *In re Price* [1943] Ch 422. If a valid gift may be made to an unincorporated body as a simple accretion to the funds which are the subject matter of the contract which the members have made inter se—and *Neville Estates Ltd* v *Madden* [1962] Ch 832 and *In re Recher's Will Trusts* [1972] Ch 526 show that it may—I do not really see why such a gift, which specifies a purpose which is within the powers of the association and of which the members of the association are the beneficiaries, should fail. Why are not the beneficiaries able to enforce the trust or, indeed, in the exercise of their contractual rights, to terminate the trust for their own benefit? Where the donee association is itself the beneficiary of the prescribed purpose, there seems to me to be the strongest argument in common sense for saying that the gift should be construed as an absolute one within the second category—the more so where, if the purpose is carried out, the members can by appropriate action vest the resulting property in themselves, for here the trustees and the beneficiaries are the same persons.

Is such a distinction as I have suggested borne out by the authorities? The answer is, I think, 'not in terms,' until recently. But the cases appear to me to be at least consistent with this. For instance, *In re Clarke* [1901] 2 Ch 110 (the case of the Corps of Commissionaires); *In re Drummond* [1914] 2 Ch 90 (the case of the Old Bradfordians) and *In re Taylor* [1940] Ch 481 (the case of the Midland Bank Staff Association), in all of which the testator had prescribed purposes for which the gifts were to be used, and in all of which the gifts were upheld, were all cases where there were ascertainable beneficiaries; whereas in *In re Wood* [1949] Ch 498 and *Leahy's* case (where the gifts failed) there were none. *In re Price* is perhaps out of line, because there was no ascertained beneficiary and yet Cohen J was prepared to uphold the gift even on the supposition that (contrary to his own conclusion) the purpose was non-charitable. But, as I have mentioned, the point about the trust being a purpose trust was not argued before him.

A striking case which seems to be not far from the present is *In re Turkington* [1937] 4 All ER 501, where the gift was to a masonic lodge 'as a fund to build a suitable temple in Stafford.' The members of the lodge being both the trustees and the beneficiaries of the temple, Luxmoore J construed the gift as an absolute one to the members of the lodge for the time being.

Directly in point is the more recent decision of Goff J in *In re Denley's Trust Deed* [1969] 1 Ch 373 where the question arose as to the validity of a deed under which land was held by trustees as a sports ground: primary for the benefit of employees of [a particular company] and secondarily for the benefit of such other person or persons . . . as the trustees may allow to use the same . . .'. The latter provision was construed by Goff J as a power and not a trust. The same deed conferred on the employees a right to use and enjoy the land subject to regulations made by the trustees. Goff J held that the rule against enforceability of non-charitable 'purpose or object' trusts was confined to those which were abstract or impersonal in nature where there was no beneficiary or cestui que trust. A trust which, though expressed as a purpose, was directly or indirectly for the benefit of an individual or individuals was valid provided that those individuals were ascertainable at any one time and the trust was not otherwise void for uncertainty.
. . .

I respectfully adopt this, as it seems to me to accord both with authority and with common sense.

If this is the right principle, then on which side of the line does the present case fall? Mr Morritt has submitted in the course of his argument in favour of charity that the testator's express purpose 'solely in the work of constructing the new buildings for the association' referred and could only refer to the youth centre project, which was the only project for the erection of buildings which was under consideration at the material time. If this is right, then the trust must, I think, fail, for it is quite clear that that project as ultimately conceived embraced not only the members of the association, but the whole Jewish community in Hull, and it would be difficult to argue that there was any ascertainable beneficiary. I do not, however, so construe the testator's intention. The evidence is that the testator knew the association's position and that he took a keen interest in it. I infer that he was kept informed of its current plans. The one thing that is quite clear from the minutes is that from 1965 right up to the testator's death there was great uncertainty about what was going to be done. There was a specific project for the purchase of a house in 1965. By early 1966 the youth centre was back in favour. By October 1966 it was being suggested that the association should stay where they were in their rented premises. The meeting of March 21 is, I think, very significant because it shows that they were again thinking in terms of their own exclusive building and that the patrons (of whom the testator was one) would donate the money when it was needed. At the date of the will, the association had rejected the youth centre plans and were contemplating again the purchase of premises of their own; and thereafter interest shifted to the community centre. I am unable to conclude that the testator had any specific building in mind; and, in my judgment, the reference to 'the' buildings for the association means no more than whatever buildings the association may have or may choose to erect or acquire. The reference to improvements reflects, I think, the testator's contemplation that the association might purchase or might, at his death, already have purchased an existing structure which might require improvement or conversion, or even that they might, as had at one time been suggested, expend money in improving the premises which they rented from the Jewish Institute. The association was to have the legacy to spend in this way for the benefit of its members.

I have already said that, in my judgment, no question of perpetuity arises here, and accordingly the case appears to me to be one of the specification of a particular purpose for the benefit of ascertained beneficiaries, the members of the association for the time being. There is an additional factor. This is a case in which, under the constitution of the association, the members could, by the appropriate majority, alter their constitution so as to provide, if they wished, for the division of the association's assets among themselves. This has, I think, a significance. I have considered whether anything turns in this case upon the testator's direction that the legacy shall be used 'solely' for one or other of the specified purposes. Mr Rossdale has referred me to a number of cases where legacies have been bequeathed for particular purposes and in which the beneficiaries have been held entitled to override the purpose, even though expressed in mandatory terms.

Perhaps the most striking in the present context is *In re Bowes* [1896] 1 Ch 507, where money was directed to be laid out in the planting of trees on a settled estate. That was a 'purpose' trust, but there were ascertainable beneficiaries, the owners for the time being of the estate; and North J held that the persons entitled to the settled estate were entitled to have the money whether or not it was laid out as directed by the testator. . . .

I can see no reason why the same reasoning should not apply in the present case, simply because the beneficiary is an unincorporated non-charitable association. I do not think the fact that the testator has directed the application 'solely' for the specified purpose adds any legal force to the direction. The beneficiaries, the members of the association for the time being, are the persons who could enforce the purpose and they must, as it seems to me, be entitled not to enforce it or, indeed, to vary it.

Thus, it seems to me that whether one treats the gift as a 'purpose' trust or as an absolute gift with a superadded direction or, on the analogy of *In re Turkington* [1937] 4 All ER, 501 as a gift where the trustees and the beneficiaries are the same persons, all roads lead to the same conclusion.

In my judgment, the gift is a valid gift . . .

7.5.3 MANDATE TO OFFICERS OF THE ASSOCIATION

CONSERVATIVE AND UNIONIST CENTRAL OFFICE v BURRELL
[1980] 3 All ER 42, ChD

FACTS: *Re Grant's WT* (7.5.1 above) concerned a gift to a local Labour Party association. The present case considered gifts to the central office of the Conservative Party. The central office had been assessed to corporation tax on the ground that it was a 'company' within the meaning of s. 526(5) of the Income and Corporation Taxes Act 1970. Included within the definition of 'company' were unincorporated associations of two or more persons bound together for common purposes (not being business purposes) by mutual undertakings and rules governing the holding and control of property. Appealing against the tax assessment the central office contended that it was not an unincorporated association within this definition.

HELD: Funds held by the central office were not held on behalf of an unincorporated association within the 1970 Act definition. It became necessary to consider, therefore, upon what basis donations were received by the central office. It was held *per curiam* (for the sake of clarity) that when a contributor makes a donation to the treasurer, or other officer, of the central office the officer receives the donation as an agent and subject to a mandate that it be used for the political purposes for which it was given. The law of agency, not of trusts, is applicable. Once the donation has been mixed with the general funds under the officer's control the mandate becomes irrevocable. In other words, it is then too late for the contributor to reclaim the donation. However, the contributor has a remedy against the officials to restrain or make good a misapplication of the mixed fund except where the contributors donation can be shown, on normal accounting principles, to have been legitimately expended before the misapplication of the mixed fund.

VINELOTT J: . . . suppose that an explorer were to invite subscriptions to a fund to finance an expedition to explore some unexplored area of the world. That would clearly not be a charitable purpose and there is no unincorporated association which can be conjured up as the owner of the subscribed fund. Counsel's submission for the Crown, if well founded, would lead to the conclusion that either the subscribers would remain the beneficial owners of the moneys subscribed, the explorer having no more than a revocable mandate to use them for the stated purpose, or alternatively the subscribed fund would belong beneficially to the explorer who would be free to abandon the exploration and spend the moneys on himself. Counsel for the Crown frankly accepted that this consequence follows from his argument and said that the latter alternative is the correct one. The law would be in a very sorry state if it were so, but I do not think it is. It appears to me that if someone invites subscriptions on the representation that he will use the fund subscribed for a particular purpose, he undertakes to use the fund for that purpose and for no other and to keep the subscribed fund and any accretions to it (including any income earned by investing the fund pending its application in pursuance of the stated purpose) separate from his own moneys. I can see no reason why if the purpose is sufficiently well defined, and if the order would not necessitate constant and possible ineffective supervision by the court, the court should not make an order directing him to apply the subscribed fund and any accretions to it for the stated purpose. The example I have given would probably not meet these criteria, but is it is not difficult to imagine a case where a fund was subscribed for a purpose which would meet these criteria, for instance, a fund raised by subscription for immediate distribution to a class of persons who were not objects of charity, the subscriptions being invited on terms which did not give rise to any private trust. There appears to me to be a clear analogy between an invitation to subscribe to a fund on a representation that it will be used for a particular purpose and a third party contract of the kind considered in *Beswick* v *Beswick* [1967] 2 All ER 1197. However, apart from the possible remedy of specific performance I can see no reason why the court should not restrain the recipient of such a fund from applying it (or any accretions to it such as income of investments made with it) otherwise that in pursuance of the stated purpose. If that is so, then it appears to me that the recipient of the fund is clearly not the beneficial owner of it and that the income of it is not part of his total income for tax purposes. Equally, whilst the purpose remains unperformed and capable of performance the subscribers are clearly not the beneficial owners of the fund or of the income (if any) derived from it. If the state purpose proves impossible to achieve or if there is any surplus remaining after it has been accomplished there will be an implied obligation to return the fund and any accretions thereto to the subscribers in proportion to their original contributions, save that a proportion of the fund representing subscriptions made anonymously or in circumstances in which the subscribers receive some benefit (for instance, by subscription to a whist drive or raffle) might then devolve as bona vacantia.

The answer of counsel for the Crown to the solution I have endeavoured to formulate was that it confused property and contract. He said that the subscriptions are moneys given, not consideration for any contractual undertaking. I do not see why the fact that subscriptions are made for a stated purpose should not found an obligation binding on the recipient to use the moneys subscribed for that purpose, to keep them separate from his own moneys and to return them if this purpose is frustrated or if the funds subscribed are more than is needed to accomplish it. The reply of counsel for the Crown reflects the argument of counsel for the appellant in *Barclays Bank Ltd* v *Quistclose Investments Ltd* [1968] 3 All ER 651 and invites the answer given by Lord Wilberforce who said ([1968] 3 All ER 651 at 655): 'I can appreciate no reason why the flexible interplay of law and equity cannot let in these practical arrangements, and other variations if desired: it would be to the discredit of both systems if they could not.'

Counsel for the Crown also relied on a passage in the judgment of Brightman J in *Re Recher's Will Trusts* [1971] 3 All ER 401 at 405 where he said: 'It would astonish a layman to be told that there was a difficulty in his giving a legacy to an unincorporated non-charitable society which he had or could have supported without trouble during his lifetime.' In the present case, said counsel for the Crown, a testamentary bequest to the Conservative Party would be void unless it could be construed as a gift to the members of an unincorporated association who could (by resolution if the rules so provide or acting unanimously if they do not) revoke or amend the rules and either distribute the moneys amongst themselves or apply them in any other way they might wish. Similarly, it is said, unless moneys given to the Conservative Party inter vivos can be taken as given to an unincorporated association the gift will either fail or alternatively take effect as a gift to the party treasurers or the party leader. This argument to my mind places too much stress on a single sentence in the judgment of Brightman J. A testamentary gift to a named society which is not an incorporated body must fail unless it can be construed as a gift to the members of an unincorporated association either as joint tenants or as an accretion to the funds of the association to be applied in accordance with its rules (commonly with a view to the furtherance of its objects). But in the case of a testamentary gift there is no room for the implication of any contract between the testator and the persons who are to receive the bequest. In the case of an inter vivos subscription the intention of the subscriber can be given effect by the implication of contractual under-takings of the kind I have described. On further consideration that seems to me to be the proper explanation of the status of the subscriptions made by members of the Chertsey and Walton Constituency Labour Party on which I made some observations in *Re Grant's Will Trusts* [1979] 3 All ER 359. The right of subscribers to the return of their subscriptions so far as not used for the purposes for which they were subscribed rests on an implied contractual term and not on a resulting trust. The facts in *Re Thackrah* [1939] 2 All ER 4 may provide another analogy. There, a testamentary gift to the secretary of the Oxford Group was held invalid on the ground that the evidence did not establish the existence of 'an association of individuals banded together under the name of the Oxford Group', Bennett J observed ([1939] 2 All ER 4 at 6): 'Before one can find an association, there must be some rules, either written or oral, by which those who are supposed to be members of it are tied together. I think that they would probably be written rules. There must be some constitution.' But the Oxford Group was the name given to the religious movement and I can see no reason why a donation inter vivos to the secretary of a movement so named to be used for the purposes of the group should not have been contractually enforceable (at least to the extent of preventing the secretary from misapplying it or mixing it with his own moneys) and the facts stated in the report of *Re Thackrah* [1939] 2 All ER 4 suggest that some donations had been so given in order to provide for the maintenance of the offices and staff which the Oxford Group apparently had.

In my judgment, therefore, this appeal succeeds.

7.6 Distribution of Surplus Donations

7.6.1 *BONA VACANTIA*

CUNNACK v *EDWARDS* [1896] 2 Ch 679, CA

FACTS: A society had been established to raise a fund by members' subscriptions to provide annuities for the widows of deceased members. The last member died in 1879 and the last widow died in 1892, the society having then a surplus or unexpended fund of £1,250.

HELD: The widows, and not the members, were the beneficiaries of the society's funds, accordingly there would be no resulting trust of the surplus in favour of the estates of the members of the society. As Smith LJ stated 'as the member paid his money to the society, so he divested himself of all interest in this money for ever, with this one reservation, that if the member left a widow she was to be provided for during her widowhood'. The fund would pass to the Crown as *bona vacantia*.

LORD HALSBURY LC: In the year 1810 a certain number of persons associated themselves together for the purpose of providing for their widows. They were not incorporated, and though they obtained some of the advantages which are involved in incorporation—inasmuch as they came under the protection of the Friendly Societies Acts—I do not think, for the purpose of this inquiry, those facts are important. The question which the Court has to determine would, I think, have remained the same if they had been simply an associate body of persons for the purpose which I have described. The society has lasted to a very recent period, but is now extinct. All the members are dead, but a remnant of the common fund, amounting to something over 1200*l.*, now remains.

Chitty J has held that there is a resulting trust in favour of the personal representatives of those who contributed to the fund. I think we are all of opinion that that view cannot be maintained. The entire beneficial interest has been exhausted in respect of each contributor. It was, as I shall have to repeat in another view of the case, a perfectly businesslike arrangement: each man contributed a certain sum of money to a common fund upon the bargain that his widow was to receive, upon terms definitely settled, a certain annuity proportionate to the time during which the husband had contributed to the common fund. There never was and never could be any interest remaining in the contributor other than the right that his wife, if she survived him, should become entitled to a widow's portion thus provided. This was the final and exhaustive destination of all the sums contributed to the common fund. Under these circumstances, I am at a loss to see what room there is for the contention that there is any resulting trust.

. . . this was not a charitable institution. The only other alternative remaining is that which I adopt, namely, that these funds are bona vacantia, and belong to the Crown in that character.

7.6.2 CONTRACT

RE WEST SUSSEX CONSTABULARY'S BENEVOLENT FUND TRUSTS
[1970] 1 All ER 54

FACTS: The fund existed to provide for widows and orphans of deceased members. When the West Sussex Constabulary amalgamated with other forces in 1968 the question arose as to how the funds should be distributed. Sources of the fund were (1) members subscriptions; (2) receipts from entertainments, raffles and sweepstakes; (3) collecting boxes; and (4) donations and legacies.

HELD: Surplus of sources 1, 2 and 3 would pass to the Crown as *bona vacantia*. Surplus of source 4 would be held on resulting trusts for the donors. Equity would 'cut the gordion knot' of accounting difficulties by dividing the surplus in proportion to the sources from which it had arisen. Surplus of source 1 could not be the subject of a resulting trust because the members had received consideration for the payment of their subscriptions in the form of the benefits of membership. Surplus of source 2 could not be the subject of a resulting trust because, first, such payments had been made for consideration; and, secondly, they were not direct donations to the fund, but merely donations of net profits after payment out of prizes etc. Surplus of source 3 would not be deemed subject to a resulting trust because donors to collecting boxes are presumed to have intended to part with their monies out and out.

GOFF J: . . . it was argued that there is a resulting trust, with several possible consequences. If this be the right view there must be a primary division into three parts, one representing contributions from former members, another contributions from the surviving members, and the third moneys raised from outside sources. The surviving members then take the second, and possibly by virtue of r. 10 the first also. Rule 10 is as follows:

> Any member who voluntarily terminates his membership shall forfeit all claim against the Fund except in the case of a member transferring to a similar Fund of another force in which instance the contributions paid by the member to the West Sussex Constabulary's Widows, Children and Benevolent (1930) Fund may be paid into the Fund of the force to which the member transfers.

Alternatively, the first may belong to the past members on the footing that r. 10 is operative so long as the fund is a going concern, or may be *bona vacantia*. The third is distributable in whole or in part between those who provided the money, or again is *bona vacantia*.

In my judgment the doctrine of resulting trust is clearly inapplicable to the contributions of both classes. Those persons who remained members until their deaths are in any event excluded because they have had all they contracted for, either because their widows and dependants have received or are in receipt of the prescribed benefits, or because they did not have a widow or dependants. In my view that is inherent in all the speeches in the Court of Appeal in *Cunnack* v *Edwards* [1895] 1 Ch 489. Further, whatever the effect of r. 10 may be on the contribution of those members who left prematurely, they and the surviving members alike are also unable to claim under a resulting trust, because they put up their money on a contractual basis and not one of trust: see per Harman J, in *Re Gillingham Bus Disaster Fund, Bowman* v *Official Solicitor* [1958] Ch 300.

The only case which has given me difficulty on this aspect of the matter is *Re Hobourn Aero Components Ltd's Air-Raid Distress Fund, Ryan* v *Forrest*, where in somewhat similar circumstances it was held there was a resulting trust. The argument postulated, I think, the distinction between contract and trust but in another connection, namely whether the fund was charitable. There was in that case a resolution to wind up but that was not, at all events as expressed, the ratio decidendi (see *per* Cohen J) but as his Lordship observed there was no argument for bona vacantia. Moreover no rules or regulations were ever made and although in fact £1 per month was paid or saved for each member serving with the forces, there were no prescribed contractual benefits. In my judgment that case is therefore distinguishable.

Accordingly, in my judgment all the contributions of both classes are bona vacantia, but I must make a reservation with respect to possible contractual rights. In *Cunnack* v *Edwards* and *Braithwaite* v *A-G* [1909] 1 Ch 510, all the members had received or provision had been made for all the contractual benefits. Here the matter has been cut short. . . .

I must now turn to the moneys raised from outside sources. Counsel for the Attorney-General made an overriding general submission that there could not be a resulting trust of any of the outside moneys because in the circumstances it is impossible to identify the trust property. No doubt something could be achieved by complicated accounting, but this, he submitted, would not be identification but notional reconstruction. I cannot accept that argument. In my judgment in a case like this the present equity will cut the gordian knot by simply dividing the ultimate surplus in proportion to the sources from which it has arisen. Chitty J in *Cunnack* v *Edwards* at first instance, was prepared to order an inquiry notwithstanding the difficulty that it involved going back over many years and despite the fact that the early records were not available, but that was a difficulty of ascertaining the original contributions, not of working out surpluses or interest calculations year by year. . . .

There may be cases of tolerable simplicity where the court will be more refined, but in general where a fund has been raised from mixed sources interest has been earned over the years and income and possibly capital expenditure has been made indiscriminately out of the fund as an entirety, and when the venture comes to an end prematurely or otherwise, the court will not find itself baffled but will cut the gordian knot as I have said.

Then counsel divided the outside moneys into three categories: first, the proceeds of entertainments, raffles and sweepstakes; secondly, the proceeds of collecting boxes; and thirdly, donations including legacies, if any, and he took particular objections to each. I agree that there cannot be any resulting trust with respect to the first category. I am not certain whether Harman J meant to decide otherwise in the *Gillingham Bus Disaster* case. The statement of facts refers to 'street collections and so forth'. There is mention of whist drives and concerts in the argument, but the judge himself did not speak of anything other than gifts. If he did, however, I must respectfully decline to follow his judgment in that regard, for whatever may be the true position with regard to collection boxes, it appears to me to be impossible to apply the doctrine of resulting trust to the proceeds of entertainments and sweepstakes and such-like money raising operations for two reasons. First, the relationship is one of contract and not of trust. The purchaser of a ticket may have the motive of aiding the cause or he may not. He may purchase a ticket merely because he wishes to attend the particular entertainment or to try for the prize, but whichever it be he pays his money as the price of what is offered and what he receives. Secondly, there is in such cases no direct contribution to the fund at all. It is only the profit, if any, which is ultimately received, and there may even be none. In any event the first category cannot be any more susceptible to the doctrine than the second to which I now turn.

Here one starts with the well-known dictum of PO Lawrence J in *Re Welsh Hospital (Netley) Fund Thomas v A-G* [1921] 1 Ch 655:

> So far as regards the contributions to entertainments, street collections, etc., I have no hesitation in holding that they must be taken to have parted with their money out and out. It is inconceivable that any person paying for a concert ticket or placing a coin in a collecting box presented to him in the street should have intended that any part of the money so contributed should be returned to him when the immediate object for which the concert was given or the collection made had come to an end. To draw such an inference would be absurd on the face of it.

. . . This was approved by Denning LJ in *Re Hillier* [1953] 2 All ER 1547 in the Court of Appeal, although it is true that he went on to say that the law makes a presumption of charity:

> Let me first state the law as I understand it in regard to money collected for a specific charity by means of a church collection, a flag day, a whist drive, a dance, or some such activity. When a man gives money on such an occasion, he gives it, I think, beyond recall. He parts with his money out and out. . . .

In *Re Ulverston & District New Hospital Building Fund, Birkett v Barrow and Furness Hospital Management Committee* [1956] Ch 622, Jenkins LJ threw out a suggestion that there might be a distinction in the case of a person who could prove that he put a specified sum in a collecting box, and in the *Gillingham* case Harman J, after noting this, decided that there was a resulting trust with respect to the proceeds of collections. He said:

> In my judgment the Crown has failed to show that this case should not follow the ordinary rule merely because there was a number of donors who, I will assume, are unascertainable. I see no reason myself to suppose that the small giver who is anonymous has any wider intention than the large giver who can be named. They all give for the one object. If they can be found by inquiry the resulting trust can be executed in their favour. If they cannot I do not see how the money could then, with all respect to Jenkins LJ, change its destination and become bona vacantia. It will be merely money held on a trust for which no beneficiary can be found. Such cases are common, and where it is known that there are beneficiaries, the fact that they cannot be ascertained does not entitle the Treasury Solicitor to come in and claim. The trustees must pay the money into court like any other trustee who cannot find his beneficiary. I conclude, therefore, that there must be an inquiry for the subscribers to this fund.

It will be observed that Harman J considered that the *Welsh Hospital (Netley)* case, *Re Hillier* and *Re Ulverston* did not help him greatly because they were charity cases. It is true that they were and, as will presently appear, in my view that is very significant in relation to the third category, but I do not think it was a valid objection with respect to the second, . . . I agree that all who put their money into collecting boxes should be taken to have the same intention, but why should they not all be regarded as intending to part with their money out and out, absolutely, in all circumstances? I observe that PO Lawrence J used very strong words. He said any other view was inconceivable and absurd on the face of it. That commends itself to my humble judgment . . .

This does not appear to me to transgress the principle which Harman J laid down in the *Gillingham* case, where he said:

> This doctrine does not rest, in my judgment, on any evidence of the state of mind of the settlor, for in the vast majority of cases no doubt he does not expect to see his money back; he has created a trust which, so far as he can see, will absorb the whole of it. The resulting trust arises where that expectation is, for some unforeseen reason, cheated of fruition, and is an inference of law based on after-knowledge of the event.

I accept that fully but I also accept the submission of counsel for the Attorney-General that equity will not impute an intention which it considers would be absurd on the face of it.

That brings me to the third category. Here counsel says that *Re Hillier* and *Re Ulverston* show that there is a distinction to be drawn between initial failure, where apart from expenses the fund is intact, and subsequent failure or surplus to requirements when identity is lost, and I agree they do. Then he says that in the latter type of case at least the court must or should attribute to specific donors the same intention of parting with their money irrevocably as it imputes to those who place their money in collecting boxes. He found himself in particular on a passage in the judgment of Sir Raymond Evershed MR in *Re Hillier*, which is as follows:

> In my judgment, there is no good answer to the summary of his argument which counsel for the Attorney-General put before us, which was to this effect: It is sought to find a common intention, limited to a single and specific object, among all givers of a particular category; the particular category put forward is that of donors who, in response to the brochure, made use of document 1 to specify the Slough hospital; but whatever might be the interpretation properly put on these documents, as it were, in vacuo, the fact is that the category selected not only included persons who subscribed after the passing of the Act, but also consisted of persons who must be taken to have been aware of the pre-brochure contributions, and aware also of the fact that their gifts would be intermingled with those of others who would not in any circumstances expect, or be entitled to claim a return of their money; and, therefore, no such intention can be found common to donors of a particular category differentiating them from the rest of the contributors on whose part no claim for any return could be substantiated. More briefly, but, in my judgment, no less correctly, the matter was thus put by junior counsel for the Attorney-General in reply when he said that where there are many sources of contribution to a charitable fund, then all contributors should, in the absence of special circumstances, be taken to contribute on terms common to all, and the only such terms possible in the present case deny any right to a return of their money to all contributors.

On this part of his case, however, the argument appears to me to break down because those were charity cases, and the question was whether the gifts were made for a particular purpose or with a general charitable intention, which, of course, does not arise where the purpose is not charitable. Moreover, and this in my judgment is crucial, the actual purpose was equivocal and it was made abundantly clear that the fact that the gifts were going to be combined with the proceeds of collecting boxes and entertainments was material only because of that very fact. Had the purpose of the donation been unambiguous it could not have been affected by such mixture. The passage on which counsel relied and which I have cited from *Re Hillier* must be read in the light of what Sir Raymond Evershed MR had already said, and in any case one has his own explanation in *Re Ulverston*, where Lord Evershed MR said:

The language which I used, and which Jenkins LJ has quoted in his judgment (and particularly my acceptance of the arguments of counsel for the Attorney-General), should be read in the context of the supposition which I was making, that is, that the language of the brochure being equivocal, it was legitimate to assist its construction and effect by the inference to be drawn from the stated circumstances that contributions were being sought at the same time both from persons responding to the brochure appeal by using the form supplied and from persons whom Jenkins LJ has called anonymous donors. I did not intend to lay it down (and I do not think it would be right so to do) that the fact of anonymous donations being made and sought contemporaneously would control in favour of a general charitable intention gifts made by name in response to an appeal which, according to its natural and proper interpretation, was an appeal for a single and particular purpose. . . .

Therefore where as in the present case, the object was neither equivocal nor charitable, I can see no justification for infecting the third category with the weaknesses of the first and second, and I cannot distinguish this part of the case from *Re Abbott Fund Trusts, Smith v Abbott* [1900] 2 Ch 326.

I will hear counsel on the form of order and in any case will direct a minute to be signed and circulated, but in general I direct two inquiries. (1) What donations of specific amounts other than through collecting boxes but including legacies were at any time given to the fund and by whom, and whether any living donors have since died and, if so, who are their personal representatives and who are the personal representatives of any testators by whom such legacies were bequeathed. (2) What is the total amount of: (a) the contributions made by the members since the inception of the fund; (b) the proceeds of entertainments, sweepstakes, collections and any similar money raising activities; and (c) such donations including legacies. I then direct the total net assets after payment of costs to be divided between these three portions pro rata.

And I make the following declarations: first, that the portion attributable to donations and legacies is held on a resulting trust for the donors or their estates and the estates of the respective testators; and secondly, that the remainder of the fund is bona vacantia. These declarations are, however, without prejudice to: (1) any claim which may be made in contract by any person or the personal representatives of any person who was at any time a member; and (2) any right of claim of the trustees to be indemnified against any such claim out of the whole fund including the portion attributable to donations and legacies.

RE BUCK'S CONSTABULARY WIDOWS' AND ORPHANS' FUND FRIENDLY SOCIETY (No. 2) [1979] 1 All ER 623

FACTS: The Society had been established to make provision for widows and orphans of deceased members of the Bucks Constabulary. In 1968 the Bucks Constabulary was amalgamated with other constabularies to form the Thames Valley Constabulary. The trustee of the society applied to court to determine (1) whether the surplus assets should be distributed among the persons who were members of the society at the date of its dissolution or whether they should pass to the Crown as *bona vacantia*, and (2) if the assets were to be distributed among the members whether they should be distributed in equal shares or *pro rata* the members' payment of subscriptions. Members voluntary subscriptions had made up the majority of the fund.

HELD: (1) As there had been members in existence at the time of the dissolution, the surplus would be held upon resulting trusts for those members to the total exclusion of any claim on behalf of the Crown. The *Re West Sussex* case was distinguished on the basis that it involved a simple unincorporated association, whereas the present case involved a friendly society.

(2) Claims of members of a friendly society *inter se* on surplus funds held on trust for their benefit were governed by the contract between them, and where the contract, as here, provided no other method of distribution such funds were *prima facie* to be distributed in equal shares.

WALTON J: . . . There can be no doubt, therefore, that in the present case the whole of the property of the society is vested in the trustees for the use and benefit of the society and the members thereof and of all persons claiming through the members according to the rules of the society. I do not think I need go through the rules in detail. They are precisely what one would expect in the case of an association whose main purpose in life was to enable members to make provision for widows and orphans. Members paid a contribution in exchange for which in the event of their deaths their widows and children would receive various benefits. There is a minimal benefit for which provision is made in the case of a member suffering very severe illness indeed, but, as counsel for the Treasury Solicitor was able to demonstrate from an analysis of the accounts, virtually the entire expenditure of the association was, as indeed one would expect, on the provision of widows' and orphans' benefits. But, of course, there is no trust whatsoever declared in their favour. I am not called on, I think, to decide whether they are, within the meaning of s. 49(1), persons claiming through the members according to the rules of the society or whether they are simply the beneficiaries of stipulations by the members for the benefit of third parties. All parties are agreed that accrued rights of such persons must be given full effect. There is indeed no rule which says what is to happen to surplus assets of the society on a dissolution. But in view of s. 49(1) there is no need. The assets must continue to be held, the society having been dissolved, and the widows and orphans being out of the way, simply for the use and benefit of the members of the society, albeit they will all now be former members.

This indeed appears so obvious that in a work of great authority on all matters connected with friendly societies, Baden Fuller, the learned author says this:

> If the rules provide for the termination of the society they usually also provide for the distribution of the funds in that event, but if on the termination of a society no provision has been made by the rules for the distribution of its funds, such funds are divisible among the existing members at the time of the termination or dissolution in proportion to the amount contributed by each member for entrance fees and subscriptions, but irrespective of fines or payments made to members in accordance with the rules.

In my judgment this accurately represents the law, at any rate so far as the beneficiaries of the trust on dissolution are concerned, although not necessarily so far as the quantum of their respective interests is concerned; a matter which still remains to be argued. The effective point is that the claims of the Treasury Solicitor to the funds as bona vacantia are unsustainable in the present case. I say 'in the present case' because there are undoubtedly cases where the assets of an unincorporated association do become bona vacantia. To quote Baden Fuller again:

> A society may sometimes become defunct or moribund by its members either all dying or becoming so reduced in numbers that it is impossible either to continue the society or to dissolve it by instrument; in such cases the surplus funds, after all existing claims (if any) under the rules have been satisfied or provided for, are not divisible among the surviving members . . . or the last survivor . . . or the representative of the last survivor . . . nor is there any resulting trust in favour of the personal representatives of the members of the society . . . not even in favour of honorary members in respect of donations by them . . . but a society which, though moribund, had at a testator's death one member and three annuitant beneficiaries, was held to be existing so as to prevent the lapse of a legacy bequeathed to it by the testator . . . In these circumstances two cases seem to occur: if the purposes of the society are charitable, the surplus will be applicable *cy-près* . . . but if the society is not a charity, the surplus belongs to the Crown as *bona vacantia*.

Before I turn to a consideration of the authorities, it is I think pertinent to observe that all unincorporated societies rest in contract to this extent, that there is an implied contract between all of the members inter se governed by the rules of the society. In default of any rule to the contrary, and it will seldom if ever be that there is such a rule, when a member ceases to be a member of the association he ipso facto ceases to have any interest in its funds. Once again, so far as friendly societies are concerned, this is made very clear by s. 49(1), that it is the members, the present members, who, alone, have any rights in the assets. As membership always ceases on death, past members or the estates of deceased members therefore have no interest in the assets. Further, unless expressly so provided by the rules, unincorporated societies are not really tontine societies, intended to provide benefits for the longest liver of the members. Therefore, although it is difficult to say in any given case precisely when a society becomes moribund, it is clear that if a society is reduced to a single member neither he, still less his personal representatives on his behalf, can say he is or was the society and therefore entitled solely to its fund. It may be that it will be sufficient for the society's continued existence if there are two members, but if there is only one the society as such must cease to exist. There is no association, since one can hardly associate with oneself or enjoy one's own society. And so indeed the assets have become ownerless. . . .

Finally, although there is at any rate one later case, for the purpose of this review there comes a case which gives me great concern, *Re West Sussex Constabulary's Widows, Children and Benevolent (1930) Fund Trusts*. The case is indeed easily distinguishable from the present case in that what was there under consideration was a simple unincorporated association and not a friendly society, so that the provisions of s. 49(1) of the 1896 Act do not apply. Otherwise the facts in that case present remarkable parallels to the facts in the present case. Goff J decided that the surplus funds had become bona vacantia . . .

[His Lordship read the judgment of Goff J (see above).]

It will be observed that the first reason given by the judge for his decision is that he could not accept the principle of the members' clubs as applicable. This is a very interesting reason, because it is flatly contrary to the successful argument of Mr Ingle Joyce who appeared for the Attorney-General in the case Goff J purported to follow, *Cunnack* v *Edwards*. His argument was as follows:

> This society was nothing more than a club, in which the members had no transmissible interest: *In re St James Club*. Whatever the members, or even the surviving member, might have done while alive, when they died their interest in the assets of the club died with them.

and in the Court of Appeal he used the arguments he had used below. If all that Goff J meant was that the purposes of the fund before him were totally different from those of a members' club then of course one must agree, but if he meant to imply that there was some totally different principle of law applicable one must ask why that should be. His second reason is that in all the cases where the surviving members had taken, the organisation existed for the benefit of the members for the time being exclusively. This may be so, so far as actual decisions go, but what is the principle? Why are the members not in control, complete control, save as to any existing contractual rights of the assets belonging to their organisation? One could understand the position being different if valid trusts had been declared of the assets in favour of third parties, for example charities, but that this was emphatically not the case was demonstrated by the fact that Goff J recognised that the members could have altered the rules prior to dissolution and put the assets into their own pockets. If there was no obstacle to their doing this, it shows in my judgment quite clearly that the money was theirs all the time. Finally he purports to follow *Cunnack* v *Edwards* and it will be seen from the analysis which I have already made of that case that it was extremely special in its facts, resting on a curious provision of the 1829 Act which is no longer applicable. As I have already indicated, in the light of s. 49(1) of the 1896 Act the case before Goff J is really distinguishable, but I regret that, quite apart from that, I am wholly unable to square it with the relevant principles of law applicable.

The conclusion therefore is that, as on dissolution there were members of the society here in question in existence, its assets are held on trust for such members to the total exclusion of any claim on behalf of the Crown.

7.7   End of Chapter Assessment Question

The Whitestone Sportsclub is a largely autonomous body run by a committee elected by its members (who are employees of Whitestone Ltd). It manages a sports centre on land leased to trustees of the Club for a period of 21 years and is financed by subscriptions from members. The decisions of the committee are subject to veto by the board of directors of the company but the board has only rejected one decision, a proposal last year to charge a higher subscription to senior staff. The constitution of the Club provides that on its dissolution its assets shall belong to Whitestone Ltd. By his will, Mr White (a former director of Whitestone Ltd) left £100,000 to the Club to provide a cricket ground and modest pavilion for employees. The committee have voted to use the money, not for a cricket ground, but for a football pitch.

Mr White's widow, his residuary legatee, claims the legacy. Advise her.

7.8   End of Chapter Assessment Outline Answer

Mrs White should be advised that her husband's testamentary gift to the sportsclub will only be valid if it can be construed to be either (1) a gift to the members of the association as joint tenants; (2) a gift to the existing members subject to their respective contractual rights and liabilities towards one another as members of the association; (3) a trust for the benefit of the present members of the association; *or* (4) a trust (limited to the perpetuity period) for the benefit of the present and future members of the association. Because the gift was testamentary, it is *not possible* to construe the gift to be (5) a donation to the officers of the sportsclub subject to a mandate or agency (*Conservative and Unionist Central Office* v *Burrell* [1982] 1 WLR 522).

In other words, Mrs White should be advised that the legacy, whether given on trust or for the members beneficially, will fall into residue (for her benefit) if she can show that it infringes the rule against inalienability of capital.

What is more, if she can show that the legacy was made on trust to achieve purposes of a purely private, non-charitable and impersonal nature, the gift will also fail for lack of a beneficiary (*Re Shaw* [1957] 1 WLR 729). However, the fact that the employees of Whitestone Ltd are intended to benefit from the cricket ground, suggests that the legacy will not be construed in this way.

Let us take each of the possible constructions in turn.

(1)   Absolute gift to the members as joint tenants

If a gift is made to a club only very rarely will a sensible construction allow it to be divided among the present members in individual shares. Whether this construction will be admitted will depend in large part upon the subject matter of the gift. Thus, where a gift of land is made for the purposes of establishing a cricket ground it is most unlikely that the donor intended the individual members to divide the land up physically and for each member to take allotments in it.

(2)   Absolute gifts to members subject to the contractual rules of the club

This construction was accepted *(obiter)* by Cross J in *Neville Estates Ltd* v *Madden* [1962] Ch 382 and followed by Brightman J in *Re Recher's WT* [1972] 3 All ER 401. In the latter case, a testatrix left a share of her residuary estate to 'The London and Provincial Anti-Vivisection Society'. Brightman J held that the society's existing funds already formed the subject matter of a contract in accordance with which the members had bound themselves *inter se*, and that the testatrix's legacy should be construed as a gift to the *present* members of the society beneficially, as an accretion to the society's general funds. In short, this legacy was a gift to existing persons, not a trust for purposes. As such it did not breach the rule against inalienability of capital because if all the members agreed, they could decide to wind up the society and divide the net assets amongst themselves beneficially.

The construction approved in *Re Recher's* was applied to the facts of *Re Grant's WT* [1979] 3 All ER 359, but failed to save the gift in that case. Vinelott J held that the gift could not take effect as a gift to the current members of the association (the local labour party) subject to their contractual rights and duties *inter se* because the members were not free, under the rules of their association, to dispose of the property in any way they thought fit. On the contrary, the rules made it plain that the decisions of the members of the local party were subject to the control of the national Labour Party.

Applying this to the instant case, where we are told that 'the decisions of the committee are subject to veto by the board of directors' and that on its dissolution the club's assets 'shall belong to Whitestone Ltd', it seems to be fairly clear that the *Re Recher's* construction will fail to apply in this case as it did in *Re Grant's*.

(3) Gifts on trust for the present members of the association or club

If a disposition can be construed to be a trust of this sort it will clearly comply with the rule against inalienability of capital, but only where the beneficiaries will certainly be able to appropriate the capital to their use and benefit within the perpetuity period (*Re Turkington* [1937] 4 All ER 501). However, there seems no reason to suppose that the gift in the instant case was intended to benefit present members only. The very nature of a cricket ground suggests that future members of the club are intended to benefit just as much as present members.

(4) Gifts on trust for the present and future members of the association or club

It is not necessary that the words 'on trust' be used in order for the disposition to be construed as a trust. As Viscount Simonds stated in the Privy Council in *Re Leahy* [1959] AC 457 at 484:

> if a gift is made to individuals, whether under their own names or in the name of their society, and the conclusion is reached that they are not intended to take beneficially, then they take as trustees. If so, it must be ascertained who are the beneficiaries. If at the death of the testator the class of beneficiaries is fixed and ascertained or ascertainable within the limit of the rule against perpetuities, all is well. If it is not so fixed and not so ascertainable the trust must fail.

Perhaps the best reported examples of dispositions which were construed as gifts on trust for the present and future members of the association or club are those in *Re Leahy* itself (a gift on trust for certain religious orders) and *Re Denley's Trust Deed* [1969] 1 Ch 373 (a gift on trust for the employees of a company).

The trust in *Denley* succeeded because the trust had been expressly limited to take effect within 21 years. The trust in *Leahy* had not been limited in this way and would have failed had it not been saved by a particular New South Wales statute which validated the trust as charitable.

Applying these cases, it appears that the gift in the instant case could be construed as a trust of the *Denley* type. However, the fact that the land is leased to the trustees of the Club for a period of 21 years only, should not mislead us into thinking that the legacy is valid on the basis that it is bound to take place within the perpetuity period or not at all. In fact, a lease can be renewed or otherwise extended well beyond the perpetuity period.

Conclusion

It appears that not one of the currently accepted modes of construing valid gifts to unincorporated, non-profit, non-charitable associations falls on all fours with the legacy in the instant case. It is therefore by no means certain that the legacy will be applied to the specified ends, or be otherwise applied, within the perpetuity period. Consequently, the legacy to the sportsclub breaches the rule against inalienability of capital, fails and falls into the residue of Mr White's estate. As a result, Mrs White, the residuary beneficiary of that estate, should be delighted with your advice!

CHAPTER EIGHT

CHARITABLE TRUSTS

8.1 Charities Law in Context

Report of the Goodman Committee: Charity Law and Voluntary Organisations (1976)

Importance of charitable status

16.   One of the questions to which we have given a great deal of attention is whether there is a better way of defining the scope and ambit of charity but before we can come to that we have to consider whether the result of the cases is satisfactory; whether there should be amendments in detail; or whether the whole concept is wrong and charity should either be narrowed or expanded in some more fundamental way. . . .

17.   On the one hand, we had evidence suggesting that the scope of charities should be restricted to what is said to be its meaning as generally understood in its ordinary sense. In short, that it should be restricted to the relief of the poor and of people suffering from deprivation of one sort or another. On the other hand, we have had evidence suggesting that the benefits accorded to charities should be extended to other voluntary bodies which have not so far been considered to come at all within the ambit of charities. Such bodies include pressure groups and, in fact, any voluntary organisation, political or otherwise. We do not agree with either of these views and we feel that at the outset we should make clear our reasons.

21.   There are many fields where the control which tends to go with state assistance can be unwelcome and this applies especially to the arts and provision for cultural and recreational facilities. Charity is increasingly moving into these fields and this is a development which in our opinion is to be welcomed.

Should the concept of charity be expanded?

22.   But then comes the question where is it to stop? Parallel to the pressure to restrict the ambit of charity, there is also the desire to extend it and to afford to all 'non-profit distributing organisations' (NPDOs) the privileges afforded to charities. There would have to be stringent provisions to avoid abuse but otherwise the objects and activities of the NPDO would be irrelevant. Thus professional bodies, political parties and pressure groups of all sorts could be accorded the privileges now confined to charities. . . . While, therefore, we believe that the ambit of charity should remain flexible and capable of growth (and as a corollary that some objects may with time cease to be charitable), we think that the existing concept should remain despite the difficulties of definition.

Criteria for charitable status

26.   We have now reached the position that the scope of charity should not be restricted (except perhaps in so far as objects which once were accepted as charitable may have in the course of time ceased to have the relevant characteristics of charity); that it should continue its natural process of development, but that it should not include all voluntary activities. How then can we distinguish charitable objects from other objects? Is it possible to frame the definition which will neatly include every object which ought to be regarded as charitable and as neatly exclude everything which ought not to be so

regarded, or can we at least point to the general criteria which should govern the decision whether an object is charitable or not and leave it to the Charity Commissioners and the courts to develop the concept as they have done in the past, or is there any other way?

Benefit to the community

27.   It is clear that there must be a desire to benefit the community but many things which are far removed from charity may benefit the community. For instance, a highly successful commercial venture, generating exports and providing massive employment is of immense benefit to the community but it is not charitable. Conversely, the importance of the tax factors to charities has led some to suggest that one should first consider what purposes or activities should be subsidised and to define charity to conform to the answer so found. To argue thus turns the argument upside down. If the field open for tax benefits is undefined, it follows that any purpose which some may consider deserving of subsidy would qualify to be regarded as charitable. But the government may choose to subsidise certain types of industry and lame ducks and public utilities which cannot be run at a profit and although these might in 1601, when they were provided, if at all, by private enterprise have been regarded as charitable, they cannot now be so regarded. It would seem therefore that the concept of charity must be confined to an object to benefit the community in certain particular ways, such as relief of distress, or deprivation, and, in its more modern manifestations, the improvement of the quality of life in relation to the arts, recreation, amenities and our national heritage.

Altruism

28.   Although altruism is not definable in legal terms it is nevertheless an important element in our social thinking which makes for a better quality of life. Generally speaking, it may be said that charity and the private profit of the donor are mutually exclusive and it is for this reason that at a later part in this report we have suggested that gifts to relatives or to employees of the donor even for the relief of poverty should no longer be regarded as charitable. . . .

Definition of charity

29.   Given these two criteria of benefit to the community and altruism, the decision in particular cases is at present left to the Charity Commissioners and the court, who refer to the preamble to the Act of 1601 as summarised by Lord Macnaghten in the *Pemsel* case and to as many of the hundreds of decided cases as they may feel to be relevant to the case before them. There has never been a definition of charity and many people believe that the time has come to formulate one. Others point out that to define is to confine believing the very flexibility of the law in relation to charities is, and should continue to be, its strength. They emphasise the difficulty of finding a definition in sufficiently wide terms to encompass all that is now considered charitable, or may in the future be so considered and nothing else. There has been much concern too that if any new definition were adopted, the entire body of case law established over the centuries would cease to be relevant. On the other hand, it is said that the cases have established law which is unsatisfactory in that it is out of tune with modern modes of thought and social needs and that it is inflexible. . . . We do not believe that it is possible to formulate a definition of this sort, and we are comforted by the fact that the same conclusion was reached in the debates leading to the passing of the 1960 Act. For instance, in relation to the element of public benefit, there are a large number of cases which consider the degree of public benefit required and the nature of that public benefit whether direct or indirect. We do not think that all these cases should be swept aside, nor would it be possible without a complete codification to incorporate them in a statute. What we have done in the succeeding chapters is to consider some of the fields in which the existing case law is the subject of criticism and to suggest a number of amendments of a specific nature which could be made.

Categories of charity

32.   We have also given particular consideration to the question whether a greater degree of certainty can be introduced in relation to the categories of objects which should qualify as charitable. The preamble to the Act of 1601 is written in language inappropriate to contemporary concepts and it has led, and will lead, to mental gymnastics if it is to encompass within its terms the many forms of human endeavour now or hereafter

deserving to fall within the scope of charity, while excluding those which should lie outside. What we suggest therefore would be beneficial would be to produce an updated version of the preamble to the Act of 1601 and we have therefore produced a list, in general terms, of objects deemed to be charitable. It is based upon the *Pemsel* classification extended by references in relation to the fourth head to objects which are now considered to be within the scope of charity. It is, we hope, formulated in modern and simple language. We place particular emphasis on ensuring the continued flexibility of the law in this respect and propose that the formulation should be such as not to close the categories of charity and thus crystallise and prevent the future development of the scope of charity. As it would be made clear that this new classification is an updated version of the old classification, we do not think that the existing case law would become irrelevant.

JOSEPH ROWNTREE MEMORIAL TRUST HOUSING ASSOCIATION v *ATTORNEY GENERAL* [1983] 2 WLR 284, ChD

FACTS: The plaintiff was a charitable housing association which desired to build individual dwellings for sale to elderly people on long leases in consideration of a capital payment. On the tenant's death the lease would be assigned to the tenant's spouse or a family member, provided that person was also elderly. Failing such an assignment the lease would revert to the association who would pay to the tenant's estate 70% of the then current market value of the lease. The Charity Commissioners objected to the scheme on the grounds *inter alia* that it operated by way of contract, benefitted private individuals rather than a charitable class and could produce a financial profit for those individuals.

HELD: The scheme was a valid charitable scheme for the relief of the aged notwithstanding the objections of the Charity Commissioners.

PETER GIBSON J: . . . The plaintiffs have identified a particular need for special housing to be provided for the elderly in the ways proposed and it seems to me that on any view of the matter that is a charitable purpose, unless the fundamental objections of the Charity Commissioners to which I have referred are correct. To these I now turn.

The first objection is, as I have stated, that the scheme makes provision for the aged on a contractual basis as a bargain rather than by way of bounty. This objection is sometimes expressed in the form that relief is charitable only where it is given by way of bounty and not by way of bargain: see *Halsbury's Laws of England*, 4th ed., vol. 5 (1974), para. 516. But as the editors recognise this does not mean that a gift cannot be charitable if it provides for the beneficiaries to contribute to the cost of the benefits they receive. There are numerous cases where beneficiaries only receive benefits from a charity by way of bargain. *In re Cottam* [1955] 1 WLR, 1299 and *In re Resch's Will Trusts* [1969] 1 AC 514 provide examples. Another class of cases relates to fee-paying schools: see for example *Abbey Malvern Wells Ltd* v *Ministry of Local Government and Planning* [1951] Ch 728. Another example relates to a gift for the provision of homes of rest for lady teachers at a rent: *In re Estlin* (1903) 89 LT 88. It is of course crucial in all these cases that the services provided by the gift are not provided for the private profit of the individuals providing the services. . . .

The second objection was that the schemes do not satisfy the requirement that the benefits they provide must be capable of being withdrawn at any time if the beneficiary ceases to qualify. . . . But it does not seem to me to be an essential part of the charitable purpose to secure that this should always be so. . . .

The third objection was that the schemes were for the benefit of private individuals and not for a charitable class. I cannot accept that. The schemes are for the benefit of a charitable class, that is to say the aged having certain needs requiring relief therefrom. The fact that, once the association and the trust have selected individuals to benefit from the housing, those individuals are identified private individuals does not seem to me to make the purpose in providing the housing a non-charitable one . . .

The fourth objection was that the schemes were a commercial enterprise capable of producing a profit for the beneficiary. I have already discussed the cases which show that the charging of an economic consideration for a charitable service that is provided does not make the purpose in providing the service non-charitable, provided of course that no profits accrue to the provider of the service. It is true that a tenant under the schemes may recover more than he or she has put in, but that is at most incidental to the charitable purpose. It is not a primary objective. The profit—if it be right to call the increased value of the equity a profit as distinct from a mere increase avoiding the effects of inflation, as was intended—is not a profit at the expense of the charity, and indeed it might be thought improper, if there be a profit, that it should accrue to the charity which has provided no capital and not to the tenant which has provided most if not all the capital. Again, I cannot see that this objection defeats the charitable character of the schemes. . . .

8.1.1 THE MANAGEMENT OF CHARITIES

CHARITIES ACT 1993

41. Duty to keep accounting records
   (1) The charity trustees of a charity shall ensure that accounting records are kept in respect of the charity which are sufficient to show and explain all the charity's transactions, and which are such as to—
   (a) disclose at any time, with reasonable accuracy, the financial position of the charity at that time, and
   (b) enable the trustees to ensure that, where any statements of accounts are prepared by them under section 42(1) below, those statements of accounts comply with the requirements of regulations under that provision.

42. Annual statements of accounts
   (1) The charity trustees of a charity shall (subject to subsection (3) below) prepare in respect of each financial year of the charity a statement of accounts complying with such requirements as to its form and contents as may be prescribed by regulations made by the Secretary of State. . . .

45. Annual reports
   (1) The charity trustees of a charity shall prepare in respect of each financial year of the charity an annual report containing—
   (a) such a report by the trustees on the activities of the charity during that year, and
   (b) such other information relating to the charity or to its trustees or officers, as may be prescribed by regulations made by the Secretary of State. . . .

47. Public inspection of annual reports etc.
   (1) Any annual report or other document kept by the Commissioners in pursuance of section 45(6) above shall be open to public inspection at all reasonable times—
   (a) during the period for which it is so kept; or
   (b) if the Commissioners so determine, during such lesser period as they may specify.

48. Annual returns by registered charities
   (1) Every registered charity shall prepare in respect of each of its financial years an annual return in such form, and containing such information, as may be prescribed by regulations made by the Commissioners.

8.2 The Legal Definition of Charity

8.2.1 STATUTORY DEFINITION

Statute of Charitable Uses 1601

Preamble
Whereas Lands, Tenements, Rents, Annuities, Profits, Hereditaments, Goods, Chattels, Money and Stocks of Money, have been heretofore given, limited, appointed and

assigned, as well as by the Queen's most excellent Majesty, and her most noble Progenitors, as by sundry other well disposed persons; some for Relief of aged, impotent and poor People, some for the Maintenance of sick and maimed Soldiers and Mariners, Schools of Learning, Free Schools, and Scholars in Universities, some for the Repair of Bridges, Ports, Havens, Causeways, Churches, Sea-Banks and Highways, some for the Education and Preferment of Orphans, some for or towards Relief, Stock or Maintenance for Houses of Correction, some for the Marriages of Poor Maids, some for Supportation, Aid and Help of young Tradesmen, Handicraftsmen and Persons decayed, and others for the Relief or Redemption of Prisoners or Captives, and for Aid or Ease of any poor Inhabitants concerning Payments of Fifteens [a tax on moveable property], setting out of Soldiers and other Taxes; which Lands, Tenements, Rents, Annuities, Profits, Hereditaments, Goods, Chattels, Money and Stocks of Money, nevertheless have not been employed according to charitable Intent of the givers and Founders thereof, by reason of Frauds, Breaches of Trust, and Negligence in those that should pay, deliver and employ the same: For Redress and Remedy whereof, Be it enacted. . . .

MORICE v BISHOP OF DURHAM [1803–13] All ER Rep 451, CA

FACTS: A bequest was made to the Bishop upon trust for 'such objects of benevolence and liberality as the Bishop of Durham in his own discretion shall most approve'.
HELD: This was not a charitable trust, as it failed the requirement that such a trust be exclusively charitable. The bequest was not a gift to the bishop personally, it was a gift to be held by him on trust for an uncertain and unspecified purpose. Every non-charitable trust must have a definite object: 'There must be somebody, in whose favour the court can decree performance'. In the present case the human object of the trust was uncertain and so the benefit of the trust resulted to the testator's estate.

SIR WILLIAM GRANT MR: . . . Is this a trust for charity? Do purposes of liberality and benevolence mean the same as objects of charity? That word in its widest sense denotes all the good affections men ought to have towards each other; in its most restricted and common sense relief of the poor. In neither of these senses is it employed in this court. Here its signification is derived chiefly from the statute 43 Eliz., c. 4 [relating to charitable gifts]. Those purposes are considered charitable which that statute enumerates or which by analogies are deemed within its spirit and intendment, and to some such purpose every bequest to charity generally shall be applied. But, it is clear, liberality and benevolence can find numberless objects not included in that statute in the largest construction of it. The use of the word 'charitable' seems to have been purposely avoided in this will in order to leave the bishop the most unrestrained discretion. Supporting the uncertainty of the trust no objection to its validity, could it be contended to be an abuse of the trust to employ this fund upon objects which all mankind would allow to be objects of liberality and benevolence though not to be said, in the language of this court, to be objects also of charity? But what rule of construction could it be said that all objects of liberality and benevolence are excluded which do not fall within the statute of Elizabeth? The question is not whether he may not apply it upon purposes strictly charitable, but whether he is bound so to apply it? I am not aware of any case in which the bequest has been held charitable where the testator has not either used that word to denote his general purpose or specified some particular purpose, which this court has determined to be charitable in its nature.

8.2.2 THE FOUR HEADS OF CHARITY

COMMISSIONERS FOR SPECIAL PURPOSES OF THE INCOME TAX v PEMSEL [1891] AC 531, HL

FACTS: The question was whether a trust 'for the general purposes of maintaining, supporting and advancing the missionary establishment among heathen nations of the Protestant Episcopal Church, commonly known as the Moravian Church' was for charitable purposes.

HELD: This trust was not charitable. According to Lord Macnaghten: 'charity' in its legal sense comes under four principal heads: trusts for the relief of poverty; trusts for the advancement of education; trusts for the advancement of religion; and trusts for other purposes beneficial to the community, not falling under any of the preceding heads.

LORD MACNAGHTEN: . . . That according to the law of England a technical meaning is attached to the word 'charity,' and to the word 'charitable' in such expressions as 'charitable trusts,' or 'charitable purposes,' cannot, I think, be denied. The Court of Chancery has always regarded with peculiar favour those trusts of a public nature which, according to the doctrine of the Court derived from the piety of early times, are considered to be charitable. Charitable uses or trusts form a distinct head of equity. Their distinctive position is made the more conspicuous by the circumstance that owing to their nature they are not obnoxious to the rule against perpetuities, while a gift in perpetuity not being a charity is void. Whatever may have been the foundation of the jurisdiction of the Court over this class of trusts, and whatever may have been the origin of the title by which these trusts are still known, no one I think who takes the trouble to investigate the question can doubt that the title was recognised and the jurisdiction established before the Act of 43 Eliz. and quite independently of that Act. The object of that statute was merely to provide new machinery for the reformation of abuses in regard to charities. But by a singular construction it was held to authorise certain gifts to charity which otherwise would have been void. And it contained in the preamble a list of charities so varied and comprehensive that it became the practice of the Court to refer to it as a sort of index or chart. At the same time it has never been forgotten that the 'objects there enumerated,' as Lord Chancellor Cranworth observes (1), 'are not to be taken as the only objects of charity but are given as instances.' Courts of Law, of course, had nothing to do with the administration of trusts. Originally, therefore, they were not concerned with charities at all. But after the passing of the Act 9 Geo. 2, commonly known as the Statute of Mortmain, which avoided in certain cases gifts to 'uses called charitable uses,' alienations and dispositions to charitable uses sometimes came under the cognizance of Courts of Law, and those Courts, as they were bound to do, construed the words 'charitable uses' in the sense recognised in the Court of Chancery, and in the Statute of Elizabeth, as their proper meaning. I have dwelt for a moment on this point, because it seems to me that there is a disposition to treat the technical meaning of the term 'charity' rather as the idiom of a particular Court than as the language of the law of England. And yet of all words in the English language bearing a popular as well as a legal signification I am not sure that there is one which more unmistakeably has a technical meaning in the strictest sense of the term, that is a meaning clear and distinct, peculiar to the law as understood and administered in this country, and not depending upon or coterminous with the popular or vulgar use of the word. . . .

No doubt the popular meaning of the words 'charity' and 'charitable' does not coincide with their legal meaning; and no doubt it is easy enough to collect from the books a few decisions which seem to push the doctrine of the Court to the extreme, and to present a contrast between the two meanings in an aspect almost ludicrous. But still it is difficult to fix the point of divergence, and no one as yet has succeeded in defining the popular meaning of the word 'charity.' The learned counsel for the Crown did not attempt the task. Even the paraphrase of the Master of the Rolls is not quite satisfactory. It would extend to every gift which the donor, with or without reason, might happen to think beneficial for the recipient; and to which he might be moved by the consideration that it was beyond the means of the object of his bounty to procure it for himself. That seems to me much too wide. If I may say so without offence, under conceivable circumstances, it might cover a trip to the Continent, or a box at the Opera. But how does it save Moravian missions? The Moravians are peculiarly zealous in missionary work. It is one of their distinguishing tenets. I think they would be surprised to learn that the substantial cause of their missionary zeal was an intention to assist the poverty of heathen tribes. How far then, it may be asked, does the popular meaning of the word 'charity' correspond with its legal meaning? 'Charity' in its legal sense comprises four principal divisions: trusts for the relief of poverty; trusts for the advancement of education; trusts for the advancement of religion; and trusts for other purposes beneficial to the community, not falling under any of the preceding heads. The trusts last referred to are not the less charitable in the eye of the law, because incidentally they benefit the rich as well as the poor, as indeed, every charity that deserves the name must do either directly or indirectly. It seems to me that a person of education, at any rate, if he were speaking as the Act is speaking with reference to endowed charities, would include in the category educational and religious charities, as well as charities for the relief of the poor. Roughly speaking, I think he would exclude the fourth division. Even there it is difficult to draw the line. A layman would probably be amused if he were told that a gift to the Chancellor of the Exchequer for the benefit of the nation was a charity. Many people, I think, would consider a gift for the support of a lifeboat a charitable gift, though its object is not the advancement of religion, or the advancement of education, or the relief of the poor. And even a layman might take the same favourable view of a gratuitous supply of pure water for the benefit of a crowded neighbourhood. But after all, this is rather an academical discussion. If a gentleman of education, without legal training, were asked what is the meaning of 'a trust for charitable purposes,' I think he would most probably reply, 'That sounds like a legal phrase. You had better ask a lawyer.' . . .

SCOTTISH BURIAL REFORM AND CREMATION SOCIETY LTD v GLASGOW CORPORATION [1968] AC 138, HL

FACTS: The appellant was a non-profit making company incorporated in order to promote cremation, which service it had carried out in Glasgow for many years. It provided opportunities for religious observance but had not been incorporated on any religious basis. On the question whether it was a charity and entitled to relief from rates. HELD: The objects of the company were for the benefit of the community and fell within the fourth of Lord Macnaghten's heads of charity. It was noted, however, that the 'four heads' were a classification of convenience and not necessarily a comprehensive set of charitable classes, that Lord Macnaghten's words should not be given the force of statute and that the law of charity is a continually evolving subject. The fundamental question was whether the objects of a gift fell, in the light of current social needs, within the 'spirit and intendment' of the preamble to the Act of 1601.

LORD UPJOHN: . . . Before your Lordships, as in the courts below, the matter has been argued upon the basis, first: does the provision of a crematorium fall within the fourth class of Lord Macnaghten's famous classification in *Income Tax Special Purposes Commissioners v Pemsel*, that is, 'trusts for other purposes beneficial to the community, not falling under any of the preceding heads'? But it is familiar law that not every such purpose is charitable so. secondly, the appellant company must establish that it falls within the spirit and intendment of the preamble to the Statute of Elizabeth I: see *In re Macduff* [1896] 2 Ch 451 *per* Lindley LJ and *Williams' Trustees v Inland Revenue Commissioners* [1947] AC 447 *per* Lord Simonds.

Upon the first point it must be remembered that Lord Macnaghten's classification was taken from Sir Samuel Romilly's argument in *Morice v Bishop of Durham* (1805) 10 Ves 522 162 years ago when the great majority of the inhabitants of the country were living in conditions which to-day would be regarded as of the utmost squalor. The concept of purposes beneficial to the community might then appear to have the qualities of a class and so perhaps, to a lesser extent, in 1891. This so-called fourth class is incapable of further definition and can to-day hardly be regarded as more than a portmanteau to receive those objects which enlightened opinion would regard as qualifying for consideration under the second heading.

My Lords, I agree with the majority . . . that the objects of the appellant company fall well within this fourth division.

The disposal of the dead is, and always has been, not merely a purpose beneficial to the community but a matter of public necessity. . . .

My Lords, I conclude by saying that the authorities show that the 'spirit and intendment' of the preamble to the Statute of Elizabeth have been stretched almost to breaking point. In the nineteenth and early twentieth centuries this was often due to a desire on the part of the courts to save the intentions of the settlor or testator from failure from some technical rule of law. Now that it is used so frequently to avoid the common man's liability to rates or taxes, this generous trend of the law may one day require reconsideration.

My Lords, for the reasons I have given I would allow this appeal.

LORD WILBERFORCE: . . . Lord Macnaghten's grouping of the heads of recognised charity in *Pemsel's* case is one that has proved to be of value and there are many problems which it solves. But three things may be said about it, which its author would surely not have denied: first that, since it is a classification of convenience, there may well be purposes which do not fit neatly into one or other of the headings; secondly, that the words used must not be given the force of a statute to be construed; and thirdly, that the law of charity is a moving subject which may well have evolved even since 1891. . . .

It was argued for the respondents that the company's purposes were neither for the benefit of the community nor, in any event. within the intendment of the preamble to the Statute of Elizabeth I. One or other of these arguments was accepted by the Lord Ordinary and by three members of the Inner House. As to the first of these, there was some suggestion that the necessary basis of fact had not been shown, and that the appellants should have averred, and if necessary proved, that their services were more inexpensive and more sanitary than normal methods of burial. In my opinion, the appellants rightly made no such averment, for no such comparison was called for. All they had to do was to show that the provision of inexpensive and sanitary methods, and of cremation in particular, was for the benefit of the community. As to this, the facts speak for themselves. . . .

One other point requires mention. The company makes charges for its services to enable it, in the words of the joint agreed minute, to fulfil effectively the objects for which it was formed. These charges, though apparently modest, are not shown to be higher or lower than those levied for other burial services. In my opinion, the fact that cremation is provided for a fee rather than gratuitously does not affect the charitable character of the company's activity, for that does not consist in the fact of providing financial relief but in the provision of services. That the charging for services for the achievement of a purpose which is in itself shown to be charitable does not destroy the charitable element was clearly, and, in my opinion, rightly, decided in *Inland Revenue Commissioners* v *Falkirk Temperance Café Trust* (1927) SC 261 as well as in English authorities.

I am therefore of opinion that the appellant makes good its claim to rating relief and I would allow the appeal.

8.2.3   THE FIRST HEAD: RELIEF OF POVERTY

8.2.3.1   The public benefit requirement under the first head

RE SCARISBRICK [1951] Ch 622, CA

FACTS: The testatrix, S, left one half of her residuary estate upon ultimate trusts for such of the relations of her son and daughters as the survivor of her son and daughters shall deem to be 'in needy circumstances'. The judge at first instance held that the trust for relations was not a valid charitable trust because the beneficiaries did not constitute a section of the poor, but merely individual poor persons.

HELD: The disposition was a valid charitable trust for the relief of poverty. Gifts or trusts for the relief of poverty were an exception to the rule, which applied to every other form of charitable disposition, that an element of general public benefit must be shown. The true question in a case of this sort was whether the gift was for the relief of poverty amongst a class of persons, in which case it would be valid, or whether it was a gift to individuals motivated by a desire to relieve their poverty, in which case it would not be a valid charitable trust. In the present case the gift was for a class of poor persons. The fact that the survivor of the son and daughters had the power to elect beneficiaries did not alter this conclusion, that power having been included merely to avoid disputes.

LORD EVERSHED MR: It has been most forcibly pointed out by the Attorney-General's opponents that, if the words are intended (as he says) to be a disposition in relief of poverty, then the persons selected must qualify as 'poor' when the disposition in their favour takes effect, and the disposition ought to be confined also to the relief of their poverty. If these were the purposes to be achieved, then the method selected of appointment by the deed or will of a person who was entitled to a prior life interest in the entire fund, and the unlimited terms of the discretion conferred by the power itself, could hardly (it was said) be less appropriate. An appointment by deed, without conditions which might be exceedingly difficult in this case effectively to frame, confers an immediate reversionary interest on the appointee, and he or she would, therefore, be entitled to take though he or she did not survive the life tenant, and however much in the meantime his or her circumstances might have changed. And an appointment by will (unless made very shortly indeed before the appointor's death) would hardly get over better the difficulty of possible change of circumstances. Thus (according to the argument) the machinery devised by the testatrix could only be really effective in the special case of an appointment by deed accompanied by a surrender pro tanto of the appointor's life interest. Then, further, the persons to be benefited are not those judged 'poor' by some objective standard, but such as shall, in the opinion of the appointor, be 'in needy circumstances,' a qualification capable without extravagance or caprice of covering a far wider class than the poor. In spite, however, of these difficulties I have on the whole come to the conclusion that the primary intention of the testatrix was the relief of poverty properly so called, and that the choice of bad or unworkable machinery is not, alone or in conjunction with the other elements in the case, sufficient to cause the alternative view of the construction to prevail. The phrase 'in needy circumstances' is, to my mind, merely periphrastic for 'poor,' . . . The 'poor relations' cases may be justified on the basis that the relief of poverty is of so altruistic a character, that the public element may necessarily be inferred thereby; or they may be accepted as a hallowed, if illogical, exception. In any case the exception is in favour of trusts for 'poor relations' and not of trusts of a particular type for poor relations. If the latter were the true view, then only those cases would be treated as exceptions to the general rule which, on their facts, were in substance identical with the 'poor relations' cases in the books. Such a conclusion would lead inevitably to fine and irrational distinctions. The exception, in my view, is of 'poor relations' cases generally, that is, of cases in which relief of poverty is to be exercised within a class of persons identified by reference to relationship with particular individuals, and not within a class constituting, in strictness, a section of the community . . .

DINGLE v TURNER [1972] 1 All ER 878, HL

FACTS: The testator, D, gave his residuary estate to trustees upon trust for his wife for her life and thereafter to place £10,000 with trustees upon trust 'to apply the income thereof in paying pensions to poor employees of E Dingle & Co. Ltd' who were old or disabled.

HELD: The terms of the will created a valid charitable trust for the relief of poverty, despite the nexus between the beneficiaries and the named company. (The *Oppenheim* case was distinguished on the basis that the trust there had not been for the relief of poverty.) In the case of trusts for the relief of 'poverty' the distinction between a public charitable trust and a private non-charitable trust depended upon whether, on a true construction of the gift, it was for the relief of poverty amongst a particular description of poor people or was merely a gift to particular poor persons (approving *Re Scarisbrick*, above).

LORD CROSS: . . . The status of some of the 'poor relations' trusts as valid charitable trusts was recognised more than 200 years ago and a few of those then recognised are still being administered as charities today. In *Re Compton* Lord Greene MR said that it was 'quite impossible' for the Court of Appeal to overrule such old decisions and in the *Oppenheim* case Lord Simonds in speaking of them remarked on the unwisdom of—'. . . [casting] doubt on decisions of respectable antiquity in order to introduce a greater harmony into the law of charity as a whole'. Indeed counsel for the appellant hardly ventured to suggest that we should overrule the 'poor relations' cases. His submission was that which was accepted by the Court of Appeal in Ontario in *Re Cox (decd)* [1951] OR 205—namely that while the 'poor relations' cases might have to be left as long standing anomalies there was no good reason for sparing the 'poor employees' cases which only date from *Re Gosling* (1900) 48 WR 300 decided in 1900 and which have been under suspicion ever since the decision in *Re Compton* in 1945. But the 'poor members' and the 'poor employees' decisions were a natural development of the 'poor relations' decisions and to draw a distinction between different sorts of 'poverty' trusts would be quite illogical and could certainly not be said to be introducing 'greater harmony' into the law of charity. Moreover, although not as old as the 'poor relations' trusts, 'poor employees' trusts have been recognised as charities for many years; there are now a large number of such trusts in existence; and assuming, as one must, that they are properly administered in the sense that benefits under them are only given to people who can fairly be said to be, according to current standards, 'poor persons' to treat such trusts as charities is not open to any practical objection. So as it seems to me it must be accepted that wherever else it may hold sway the *Compton* rule has no application in the field of trusts for the relief of poverty and that there the dividing line between a charitable trust and a private trust lies where the Court of Appeal drew it in *Re Scarisbrick*.

The *Oppenheim* case was a case of an educational trust and although the majority evidently agreed with the view expressed by the Court of Appeal in the *Hobourn Aero* case, that the *Compton* rule was of universal application outside the field of poverty, it would no doubt be open to this House without overruling *Oppenheim* to hold that the scope of the rule was more limited. If ever I should be called on to pronounce on this question—which does not arise in this appeal—I would as at present advised be inclined to draw a distinction between the practical merits of the *Compton* rule and the reasoning by which Lord Greene MR sought to justify it. That reasoning—based on the distinction between personal and impersonal relationships—has never seemed to me very satisfactory and I have always—if I may say so—felt the force of the criticism to which my noble and learned friend Lord MacDermott subjected it in his dissenting speech in the *Oppenheim* case. For my part I would prefer to approach the problem on far broader lines. The phrase a 'section of the public' is in truth a vague phrase which may mean different things to different people. In the law of charity judges have sought to elucidate its meaning by contrasting it with another phrase 'a fluctuating body of private individuals'. But I get little help from the supposed contrast for as I see it one and the same aggregate of persons may well be describable both as a section of the public and as a fluctuating body of private individuals. The ratepayers in the Royal Borough of Kensington and Chelsea, for example, certainly constitute a section of the public; but would it be a misuse of language to describe them as a 'fluctuating body of private individuals'? After all, every part of the public is composed of individuals and being susceptible of increase or decrease is fluctuating. So at the end of the day one is left where one started with the bare contrast between 'public' and 'private'. No doubt some classes are more naturally describable as sections of the public than as private classes while other classes are more naturally describable as private classes than as sections of the public. The blind, for example, can naturally be described as a section of the public; but what they have in common—their blindness—does not join them together in such a way that they could be called a private class. On the other hand, the descendants of Mr Gladstone might more reasonably be described as a 'private class' than as a section of the public, and in the field of common employment the same might well be said of the employees in some fairly small firm. But if one turns to large companies employing many thousands of men and women most of whom are quite unknown to one another and to the directors the answer is by no means so clear. One might say that in such a case the distinction between a section of the public and a private class is not applicable at all or even that the employees in such concerns as ICI or GEC are just as much 'sections of the public' as the residents in some geographical area. In truth the question whether or not the potential beneficiaries of a trust can fairly be said to constitute a section of the public is a question of degree and cannot be by itself decisive of the question whether the trust is a charity. Much must depend on the purpose of the trust. It may well be that, on the one hand, a trust to promote some purpose, prima facie charitable, will constitute a charity even though the class of potential beneficiaries might fairly be called a private class and that, on the other hand, a trust to promote another purpose, also prima facie charitable, will not constitute a charity even though the class of potential beneficiaries might seem to some people fairly describable as a section of the public.

In answering the question whether any given trust is a charitable trust the courts—as I see it—cannot avoid having regard to the fiscal privileges accorded to charities. As counsel for the Attorney-General remarked in the course of the argument the law of charity is bedevilled by the fact that charitable trusts enjoy two quite different sorts of privilege. On the one hand, they enjoy immunity from the rules against perpetuity and uncertainty and although individual potential beneficiaries cannot sue to enforce them the public interest arising under them is protected by the Attorney-General. If this was all there would be no reason for the courts not to look favourably on the claim of any 'purpose' trust to be considered as a charity if it seemed calculated to confer some real benefit on those intended to benefit by it whoever they might be and if it would fail if not held to be a charity. But that is not all. Charities automatically enjoy fiscal privileges which the increased burden of taxation have become more and more important and in deciding that such and such a trust is a charitable trust the court is endowing it with a substantial annual subsidy at the expense of the taxpayer. Indeed, claims of trusts to rank as charities are just as often challenged by the Revenue as by those who would take the fund if the trust was invalid. It is, of course, unfortunate that the recognition of any trust as a valid charitable trust should automatically attract fiscal privileges, for the question whether a trust to further some purpose is so little likely to benefit the public that it ought to be declared invalid and the question whether it is likely to confer such great benefits on the public that it should enjoy fiscal immunity are really two quite different questions. The logical solution would be to separate them and to say—as the Radcliffe Commission proposed—that only some charities should enjoy fiscal privileges. But as things are, validity and fiscal immunity march hand in hand and the decisions in the *Compton* and *Oppenheim* cases were pretty obviously influenced by the consideration that if such trusts as were there in question were held valid they would enjoy an undeserved fiscal immunity. To establish a trust for the education of the children of employees in a company in which you are interested is no doubt a meritorious act; but however numerous the employees may be the purpose which you are seeking to achieve is not a public purpose. It is a company purpose and there is no reason why your fellow taxpayers should contribute to a scheme which by providing 'fringe benefits' for your employees will benefit the company by making their conditions of employment more attractive.

8.2.4   THE SECOND HEAD: THE ADVANCEMENT OF EDUCATION

8.2.4.1   Educative value of art

RE PINION [1964] 1 All ER 890, CA

FACTS: The testator, P, left his freehold studio, together with his paintings and some antique furniture, silver, china etc. to be offered to the National Trust to be kept together as a collection. The income from his residue was left to be used for the maintenance of the collection. If the National Trust declined the gift P's executors were directed to keep the collection as a museum. In fact evidence was produced to show that the collection was of low quality and that P's own pictures were 'atrociously bad' and that the National Trust had turned down the gift. On the question whether this was a valid trust for the advancement of education.
HELD: It was not. Expert evidence was admissible to assist the court in determining the educative value of a trust. In the present case the experts concluded that the collection had no value as a means of education. The judge took the view that P's aim had been, not to educate, but to enhance his own reputation and that of his family.

HARMAN LJ: . . . For myself a reading of the will leads me rather to the view that the testator's object was not to educate anyone, . . . there is a strong body of evidence here that as a means of education this collection is worthless. The testator's own paintings, of which there are over fifty, are said by competent persons to be in an academic style and 'atrociously bad' and the other pictures without exception to be worthless. . . . Indeed one of the experts expresses his surprise that so voracious a collector should not by hazard have picked up even one meritorious object. The most that a skilful cross-examination extracted from the expert witnesses was that there were a dozen chairs which might perhaps be acceptable to a minor provincial museum and perhaps another dozen not altogether worthless, but two dozen chairs do not make a museum and they must, to accord with the will, be exhibited stifled by a large number of absolutely worthless pictures and objects.

It was said that this is a matter of taste, and de gustibus non est disputandum, but here I agree with the judge that there is an accepted canon of taste on which the court must rely, for it has itself no judicial knowledge of such matters, and the unanimous verdict of the experts is as I have stated. The learned judge with great hesitation concluded that there was that scintilla of merit which was sufficient to save the rest. I find myself on the other side of the line. I can conceive of no useful object to be served in foisting on the public this mass of junk. It has neither public utility nor educative value. I would hold that the testator's project ought not to be carried into effect and that his next-of-kin is entitled to the residue of his estate.

8.2.4.2 Educative value of sport

RE DUPREE'S TRUSTS [1944] 2 All ER 443, ChD

FACTS: At issue was the charitable nature of a gift of £5,000 for the promotion of an annual chess tournament for boys and young men under 21 resident in the City of Portsmouth. Two of the trustees were the chairman of the Portsmouth Education Committee and the headmaster of Portsmouth Grammar School.
HELD: Chess is something more than a game, it is an historic institution which encourages foresight, concentration, memory and ingenuity. The trust was therefore a valid charitable trust for the advancement of education, although the judge acknowledged that the case 'may be a little near the line,' and could put the courts on a 'slippery slope'. The identities of the trustees assisted the judge in reaching his conclusion in the present case.

VAISEY J: . . . I think this case may be a little near the line, and I decide it without attempting to lay down any general propositions. One feels, perhaps, that one is on rather a slippery slope. If chess, why not draughts: if draughts, why not bezique, and so on, through to bridge, whist, and, by another route, stamp collecting and the acquisition of birds' eggs? When those particular pursuits come up for consideration in connection with the problem whether or no there is in existence a charitable trust, the problem will have to be faced and dealt with. I say nothing about that. Nor do I say that, if this trust had been without a geographical limitation, if it had been for the promotion of chess playing *in vacuo* or at large, the area of what is regarded as charitable might not have been over-stepped. But, having regard to the evidence before me, and having regard to what is known about the game of chess by everybody, and, in particular, to the fact that the encouragement of chess playing here is for the benefit of a well-defined area, and, also, the fact that it is of the essence of the constitution of the trusteeship that two of the trustees should be closely connected with educational activities in the borough, I think I am bound, in the present case, to hold that there is a good charitable trust, and answer the question by declaring that the trusts constituted by the deed of June 30, 1932, are valid charitable trusts. . . .

INLAND REVENUE COMMISSIONERS v McMULLEN [1981] AC 1, HL

FACTS: The Football Association created the FA Youth Trust in 1972. The objects of the trust were 'to organise or provide or assist in the organisation and provision of facilities which will enable and encourage pupils of schools and universities in any part of the United Kingdom to play Association Football or other games or sports and thereby to assist in ensuring that due attention is given to the physical education and development of such pupils as well as to the development and occupation of their minds'. The Charity Commissioners agreed to register the trust as a charity. The Crown appealed against the registration.

HELD: On the proper construction of the objects of the trust the word 'thereby' showed that the purpose of the trust was not merely to organise the playing of sport, but to promote physical education. Regard being had to the need for a balanced education and the fact that the benefits were limited to students, this was a valid charitable trust for the advancement of education. A majority of their Lordships held that a benign construction should be given to ambiguity in the wording of a purportedly charitable trust. The possibility that the trust might be charitable under the Recreational Charities Act 1958 was left open.

LORD HAILSHAM OF ST. MARYLEBONE . . . The mere playing of games or enjoyment of amusement of competition is not per se charitable, nor necessarily educational, though they may (or may not) have an educational or beneficial effect if diligently practised. Neither am I deciding in the present case even that a gift for physical education per se and not associated with persons of school age or just above would necessarily be a good charitable gift. That is a question which the courts may have to face at some time in the future. But in deciding what is or is not an educational purpose for the young in 1980 it is not irrelevant to point out what Parliament considered to be educational for the young in 1944 when, by the Education Act of that year, in ss. 7 and 53 (which are still on the statute book), Parliament attempted to lay down what was then intended to be the statutory system of education organised by the state, and the duties of the local education authorities and the minister in establishing and maintaining the system. Those sections are so germane to the present issue that I cannot forbear to quote them both. Section 7 provides (in each of the sections the emphasis being mine):

> The statutory system of public education shall be organised in three progressive stages to be known as primary education, secondary education, and further education; and it shall be the duty of the local education authority for every area, so far as their powers extend, to contribute towards *the spiritual, moral, mental, and physical development of the community by securing that efficient education throughout those stages shall be available to meet the needs of the population of their area,*

and in s. 53(1) and (2) of the same Act it is said:

> (1) It shall be the duty of every local education authority to secure that the facilities for primary secondary and further education provided for their area include adequate facilities for recreation and *social and physical training,* and for that purpose a local education authority, with the approval of the minister, may establish maintain and manage, or assist the establishment, maintenance and management of *camps, holiday classes, playing fields, play centres, and other places (including playgrounds, gymnasiums, and swimming baths not appropriated to any school or college), at which facilities for recreation and for such training as aforesaid are available for persons for whom primary secondary or further education is provided by the authority, and may organise games, expeditions and other activities for such persons, and may defray or contribute towards the expenses thereof.* (2) A local education authority, in making arrangements for the provision of facilities or the organisation of activities under the powers conferred on them by the last foregoing subsection shall, *in particular, have regard to the expediency of co-operating with any voluntary societies or bodies whose objects include the provision of facilities or the organisation of activities of a similar character.*

There is no trace in these sections of an idea of education limited to the development of mental, vocational or practical skills, to grounds or facilities the special perquisite of particular schools, or of any schools or colleges, or term-time, or particular localities, and there is express recognition of the contribution which extra-curricular activities and voluntary societies or bodies can make even in the promotion of the purely statutory system envisaged by the Act. In the light of s. 7 in particular I would be very reluctant to confine the meaning of education to formal instruction in the classroom or even the playground, and I consider it sufficiently wide to cover all the activities envisaged by the settlor in the present case.

8.2.4.3 The public benefit requirement in educational trusts

OPPENHEIM v TOBACCO SECURITIES TRUST CO. LTD [1951] AC 297, HL

FACTS: A settlement directed trustees to apply the income from the trust fund 'in providing for . . . the education of children of employees or former employees of the British-American Tobacco Co. Ltd . . . or any of its subsidiary or allied companies in such manner . . . as the acting trustees shall in their absolute discretion . . . think fit'. The employees referred to numbered over 110,000. The issue was whether the class of potential beneficiaries constituted a sufficient section of the general public.
HELD: (Lord MacDermott dissenting): Despite the huge number of potential benefici-aries, they were identified by the personal nexus between them and the employer company. Accordingly, the trust did not satisfy the requirement that it produce a benefit to a sufficient section of the community. The words 'section of the' community have no special meaning, but they indicate, first, that the possible beneficiaries must not be numerically negligible, and secondly, that they must not be distinguishable from other members of the public by reason of a relationship to a particular individual.

LORD SIMONDS: . . . In the case of trusts for educational purposes the condition of public benefit must be satisfied. The difficulty lies in determining what is sufficient to satisfy the test, and there is little to help your Lordships to solve it. If I may begin at the bottom of the scale, a trust established by a father for the education of his son is not a charity. The public element, as I will call it, is not supplied by the fact that from that son's education all may benefit. At the other end of the scale the establishment of a college or university is beyond doubt a charity. 'Schools of learning, free schools, and scholars in universities' are the very words of the preamble to the Charitable Uses Act 1601 (43 Eliz. c. 4). So also the endowment of a college, university or school by the creation of scholarships or bursaries is a charity, and none the less because competition may be limited to a particular class of persons. It is on this ground, as Lord Greene MR pointed out in *Re Compton* [1945] 1 All ER 206 that the so-called 'founder's kin' cases can be rested. The difficulty arises where the trust is not for the benefit of any institution either then existing or by the terms of the trust to be brought into existence, but for the benefit of a class of persons at large. Then the question is whether that class of persons can be regarded as such a 'section of the community' as to satisfy the test of public benefit. These words 'section of the community' have no special sanctity, but they conveniently indicate (i) that the possible (I emphasise the word 'possible') beneficiaries must not be numerically negligible, and (ii) that the quality which distinguishes them from other members of the community, so that they form by themselves a section of it, must be a quality which does not depend on their relationship to a particular individual. It is for this reason that a trust for the education of members of a family or, as in *Re Compton* of a number of families cannot be regarded as charitable. A group of persons may be numerous, but, if the *nexus* between them is their personal relationship to a single propositus or to several propositi, they are neither the community nor a section of the community for charitable purposes.

I come then, to the present case where the class of beneficiaries is numerous, but the difficulty arises in regard to their common and distinguishing quality. That quality is being children of employees of one or other of a group of companies. I can make no distinction between children of employees and the employees themselves. In both cases the common quality is found in employment by particular employers. The latter of the two cases to which I first referred, the *Re Hobourn Aero Components Ltd* [1946] Ch 194 case, is a direct authority for saying that such a common quality does not constitute its possessors a section of the public for charitable purposes. In the former case, *Re Compton*, Lord Greene MR had by way of illustration placed members of a family and employees of a particular employer on the same footing, finding neither in common kinship nor in common employment the sort of *nexus* which is sufficient. My Lords, I am so fully in agreement with what was said by Lord Greene in both cases and by my noble and learned friend, then Morton LJ, in the *Hobourn* case, that I am in danger of repeating its purport without improving on their words. No one who has been versed for many years in this difficult and very artificial branch of the law can be unaware of its illogicalities, but I join with my noble and learned friend in echoing the observations which he cited from the judgment of Russell LJ in *Re Grove Grady* [1929] 1 Ch 582, and I agree with him that the decision in *Re Drummond* [1914] 2 Ch 90 ' . . . imposed a very healthy check upon the extension of the legal definition of "charity" . . .' It appears to me that it would be an extension, for which there is no justification in principle or authority, to regard common employment as a quality which constitutes those employed a section of the community. It must not, I think, be forgotten that charitable institutions enjoy rare and increasing privileges, and that the claim to come within that privileged class should be clearly established. With the single exception of *Re Rayner*, which I must regard as of doubtful authority, no case has been brought to the notice of the House in which such a claim as this has been made, where there is no element of poverty in the beneficiaries, but just this and no more, that they are the children of those in a common employment. Learned counsel for the appellant sought to fortify his case by pointing to the anomalies that would ensue from the rejection of his argument. For, he said, admittedly those who follow a profession or calling—clergymen, lawyers, colliers, tobacco-workers and so on—are a section of the public, and how strange then it would be if, as in the case of railwaymen, those who follow a particular calling are all employed by one employer. Would a trust for the education of railwaymen be charitable, but a trust for the education of men employed on the railways by the Transport Board not be charitable? And what of service of the Crown, whether in the civil service or the armed forces? Is there a difference between soldiers and soldiers of the King? My Lords, I am not impressed by this sort of argument and will consider on its merits, if the occasion should arise, the case where the description of the occupation and the employment is in effect the same, where in a word, if you know what a man does, you know who employs him to do it. It is to me a far more cogent argument, as it was to my noble and learned friend in the *Hobourn* case, that, if a section of the public is constituted by the personal relation of employment, it is impossible to say that it is not constituted by a thousand as by 100,000 employees, and, if by a thousand, then by a hundred, and, if by a hundred, then by ten. I do not mean merely that there is a difficulty in drawing the line, though that, too, is significant. I have it also in mind that, though the actual number of employees at any one moment might be small, it might increase to any extent, just as, being large, it might decrease to any extent. If the number of employees is the test of validity, must the court take into account potential increase or decrease, and, if so, as at what date?

I would end, my Lords, where I began—by saying that I concur in the reasoning of the Court of Appeal in the *Hobourn* case, but there are certain points in the argument for the appellants about which I should say a few words. It was urged by counsel for the Attorney-General, who was allowed to address the House, that there was here a valid charitable trust created, since there was no private person who could sue to enforce the trust. I am not persuaded that this would be so, if the trust were otherwise enforceable, but, in any case, the test is not a valid one. If this trust is charitable, the Attorney-General can sue to enforce it. It does not follow that it is charitable because no one else can sue to enforce it.

I would also, as I have previously indicated, say a word about the so-called 'poor relations' cases. I do so only because they have once more been brought forward as an argument in favour of a more generous view of what may be charitable. It would not be right for me to affirm or to denounce or to justify these decisions. I am concerned only to say that the law of charity, so far as it relates to 'the relief of aged, impotent and poor people' (I quote from the Charitable Uses Act 1601) and to poverty in general, has followed its own line, and that it is not useful to try to harmonise decisions on that branch of the law with the broad proposition on which the determination of this case must rest. . . .

8.2.4.4 Preferences

INLAND REVENUE COMMISSIONERS v *EDUCATIONAL GRANTS ASSOCIATION LTD* [1967] 1 Ch 123

FACTS: The taxpayer company (hereinafter called 'the association') was established for the advancement of education in general terms by making grants towards the cost of education of individuals. It was promoted by a director of MB Ltd. The council of management were all connected with MB Ltd and met at MB Ltd's premises. The income of the association consisted primarily of money paid under a deed of covenant by MB Ltd and a letter was circulated to senior employees of MB Ltd inviting applications for grants. Between 76 and 85 per cent of the income in the relevant years was applied for the children of persons connected with MB Ltd but MB Ltd were nowhere mentioned in the memorandum of association of the taxpayer association. The association claimed exemption from income tax. . . . There was no dispute over the income applied to the educational establishments and individuals not connected with MB Ltd but the Inland Revenue Commissioners rejected the other claims and the association appealed to the special commissioners, who allowed the appeal.

HELD: (1) that to come within the exemption of s. 447(1)(b), a company had not only to be established for charitable purposes only, that was, either expressly or impliedly for the public benefit, as this association admittedly was, but it had to be shown that the income was applied in fact for those charitable purposes and for those purposes by way of public benefit; that in the present case, although the objects expressed in the memorandum were the advancement of education without any preference for a private class within that of the general public, there had been a preferential application of income to persons connected with MB Ltd, and that while that application was clearly within the expressed object of advancement of education, it was not for the public benefit; and that, accordingly, the application was not within the section and the claim for exemption failed.

(Note: The judgment of Pennycuick J was later confirmed on Appeal: [1967] 1 Ch 993.)

PENNYCUICK J: . . . The first step is to construe the constituent instrument of the corporation, normally its memorandum of association. If one finds that all its expressed objects (leaving aside merely ancillary objects) are exclusively for charitable purposes, the first requirement is satisfied. In this connection, however, it is of the first importance to bear in mind that, with one or two qualifications not now in point, an object is not charitable unless it is directed to the public benefit: see, as regards education, *Oppenheim v Tobacco Securities Trust Co. Ltd* [1951] AC 297 and in particular the speech of Lord Simonds. I will read only one sentence: 'It is a clearly established principle of the law of charity that a trust is not charitable unless it is directed to the public benefit.' So a charitable object is, by definition, an object for the public benefit. Where the objects are expressed in general terms—for example. 'the advancement of education'—it is unnecessary and would be unusual to add specifically the words 'for the public benefit'; but the object can only be regarded as charitable if those words are implied. The advancement of education for private benefit, or in part for public benefit and in part for private benefit, is not an exclusively charitable purpose.

The second step is to consider how the income has in fact been applied. The words 'to charitable purposes only' are repeated in the second requirement, but on analysis it seems clear that where the first requirement is satisfied, then, so long as the income is expended at all (in contradistinction to being accumulated), the second requirement must equally be satisfied if the application is within the powers of the corporation. If the purposes of the corporation are exclusively charitable, any application within those purposes must necessarily be charitable, too. Nevertheless, the repetition of the words 'to charitable purposes only' in the second requirement is striking.

Here again, the element of public benefit is of the first importance. The objects of the corporation, in order that they may be exclusively charitable, must be confined to objects for the public benefit. Equally, the application of the income, if it is to be within those objects, must be for the public benefit. Conversely, the application of income otherwise than for the public benefit must be outside the objects and ultra vires. For example, under an object for the advancement of education, once that is accepted as an exclusively charitable object, the income must be applied for the advancement of education by way of public benefit. An application of income for the advancement of education by way of private benefit would be ultra vires, and nonetheless so by reason that, in the nature of things, the members of a private class are included in the public as a whole. . . .

Mr Goulding, for the Inland Revenue Commissioners . . . devoted much of his argument to repelling the application of the *Koettgen* case [1954] 1 Ch 252 to the present one. The headnote to the Koettgen case is as follows: 'A testatrix bequeathed her residuary estate on trust "for the promotion and furtherance of commercial education ..." [of certain beneficiaries]'.

She further directed that in selecting the beneficiaries 'it is my wish that the ... trustees shall give a preference to any employees of JB & Co. (London) Ltd or any members of the families of such employees; failing a sufficient number of beneficiaries under such description then the persons eligible shall be any persons of British birth as the ... trustees may select Provided that the total income to be available for benefiting the preferred beneficiaries shall not in any one year be more than 75 per cent of the total available income for that year.'

In the event of the failure of those trusts there was a gift over to a named charity. It was admitted that the trust was for the advancement of education, but it was contended for the charity that having regard to the direction to prefer a limited class of persons the trusts were not of a sufficiently public nature to constitute valid charitable trusts.

HELD: That the gift to the primary class from whom the trustees could select beneficiaries contained the necessary element of benefit to the public, and that it was when that class was ascertained that the validity of the trust had to be determined; so that the subsequent direction to prefer, as to 75 per cent of the income, a limited class did not affect the validity of the trust, which was accordingly a valid and effective charitable trust.

That headnote, I think, accurately represents the effect of what the judge decided.

... The other case considered by the special commissioners was *Caffoor* v *Income Tax Commissioner, Colombo* [1961] AC 584, in the Privy Council. The headnote, so far as now relevant, is as follows:

> By the terms of a trust deed executed in Ceylon in 1942 the trust income after the death of the grantor was to be applied by the board of trustees, the appellants, in their absolute discretion for all or any of a number of purposes which included '(2) ... (b) the education instruction or training in England or elsewhere abroad of deserving youths of the Islamic Faith' in any department of human activity. 'The recipients of the benefits . . . shall be selected by the board from the following classes of persons and in the following order:— (i) male descendants along either the male or female line of the grantor or of any of his brothers or sisters failing whom' youths of the Islamic faith born of Moslem parents of the Ceylon Moorish community permanently resident in Colombo or elsewhere in Ceylon. . . .
> HELD: . . . (2) that in view of what was in effect the absolute priority to the benefit of the trust income which was conferred on the grantor's own family by clause (2)(b)(i) of the trust deed this was a family trust and not a trust of a public character solely for charitable purposes, and the income thereof was accordingly not entitled to the exemption claimed. . . .

In his speech, Lord Radcliffe, giving the decision of the Privy Council, made the following comments on the *Koettgen* case:

> It was argued with plausibility for the appellants that what this trust amounted to was a trust whose general purpose was the education of deserving young people of the Islamic faith, and that its required public character was not destroyed by the circumstances that a preference in the selection of deserving recipients was directed to be given to members of the grantor's own family. Their Lordships go with the argument so far as to say that they do not think that a trust which provides for the education of a section of the public necessarily loses its charitable status or its public character merely because members of the founder's family are mentioned explicitly as qualified to share in the educational benefits or even, possibly, are given some kind of preference in the selection. They part with the argument, however, because they do not consider that the trust which is now before them comes within the range of any such qualified exception.

He went on to say that, there, the grantor's own family has, in effect, absolute priority. . . .

I think it right, however, to add that for myself I find considerable difficulty in the *Koettgen* decision. I should have thought that a trust for the public with preference for a private class comprised in the public might be regarded as a trust for the application of income at the discretion of the trustees between charitable and non-charitable objects. However, I am not concerned here to dispute the validity of the *Koettgen* decision. I only mention the difficulty I feel as affording some additional reason for not applying the *Koettgen* decision by analogy in connection with the second requirement of the subsection.

I return now to the present case. The association has claimed that the purposes of the association are exclusively charitable, which imports that the purposes must be for the public benefit. The revenue have admitted that claim. I have then to consider whether the association has applied its income within its expressed objects and by way of public benefit. There is no doubt that the application has been within its expressed objects, but has it been by way of public benefit? In order to answer this question, I must, I think, look at the individuals and institutions for whose benefit the income has been applied, and seek to discern whether these individuals and institutions possess any, and. if so, what, relevant characteristics by virtue of which the income has been applied for their benefit. One may for this purpose look at the minutes of the council, circular letters and so forth. Mr. Goulding at one time appeared to suggest that one might look at the actual intention of the members of the council. I do not think that is so.

When one makes this inquiry, one finds that between 75 per cent and 85 per cent of the income of the association has been expended upon the education of children connected with Metal Box. The association is intimately connected with Metal Box in the many respects found in the case stated. It derives most of its income from Metal Box. The council of management, as the special commissioners found, has followed a policy of seeking applications for grants from employees and ex-employees of Metal Box, though these applications are not, of course, always successful. The inference is inescapable that this part of the association's income—i.e., 75 per cent to 85 per cent—has been expended for the benefit of these children by virtue of a private characteristic; i.e., their connection with Metal Box. Such an application is not by way of public benefit. It is on all fours with an application of 75 per cent. to 85 per cent. of the income of a trust fund upon the education of a settlor's children. It follows, in my judgment, that, as regards the income which has been applied for the education of children connected with Metal Box, . . . the claim for relief fails.

8.2.5   THE THIRD HEAD: THE ADVANCEMENT OF RELIGION

8.2.5.1   What is religion?

THORNTON v HOWE (1862) Beav 14

FACTS: A gift of land was made to assist in the promotion and publication of the 'sacred writings of the late Joanna Southcote', whom the then Master of the Rolls described as 'a foolish ignorant woman'. She had claimed that she was with child by the Holy Spirit and would give birth to a Second Messiah.
HELD: The gift was held to be a charitable gift for the advancement of religion. The court would not make any distinction between one sect and another provided, as here, that there was nothing in its preachings which would make persons immoral or irreligious. The decision, however, must be read in the context of its consequences. Being a charitable gift of land the gift failed under the Statute of Mortmain (now repealed) and passed to the donor's heir.

SIR JOHN ROMILLY MR: . . . In the first place, it is said that this, if a lawful and legitimate purpose, is a charity and therefore void, so far as the real estate is concerned, by reason of the Statute of Mortmain; and, secondly, it is also said that this is wholly void, both as to realty and personalty, by reason of the immorality and irreligious tendency of the writings of Joanna Southcote, which, by this disposition of her property, the testatrix intended to circulate and make more extensively known.

On the latter point, being unacquainted with the writings of Joanna Southcote, it became my duty to look into them, for the purpose of satisfying myself on this point, and the result of my investigation is, that there is nothing to be found in them which, in my opinion, is likely to corrupt the morals of her followers, or make her readers irreligious.

She was, in my opinion, a foolish, ignorant woman, of an enthusiastic turn of mind, who had long wished to become an instrument in the hands of God to promote some great good on earth. By constantly thinking of this, it became in her mind an engrossing and immovable idea, till at last she came to believe that her wish was accomplished, and that she had been selected by the Almighty for this purpose. Of course she had, during her life, many followers, and probably has some now, as every person will have who has attained to such a pitch of self-confidence as sincerely to believe himself to be the organ of communication with man-kind specially selected for that purpose by the Divine Author of his being.

Into the history of her life, her personal disputations and conversations with the devil, her prophecies and her inter-communings with the spiritual world, I have found much that, in my opinion, is very foolish, but nothing which is likely to make persons who read them either immoral or irreligious. I cannot, therefore, say that this devise of the testatrix is invalid by reason of the tendency of the writings of Joanna Southcote.

On the other hand, the contention raised that this is a gift to promote objects which are within the meaning of what this Court, for shortness, terms 'charitable objects,' and that, consequently, it is within the provisions of the Statute of Mortmain, presents a more serious objection to this devise.

The 43 Eliz. c. 4, is usually referred to for the purpose of testing the enumeration of the various subject-matters which are there considered to be charitable uses, and what testamentary dispositions come within the Statute of Mortmain. The preamble of this statute clearly points out an object within which this would fall. I am of opinion, that if a bequest of money be made for the purpose of printing and circulating works of a religious tendency, or for the purpose of extending the knowledge of the Christian religion, that this is a charitable bequest, and this Court will, upon a proper application being made to it, sanction and settle a scheme for this purpose, and, in truth, it is but lately that I have had in Chambers to settle and approve of a scheme of this description. In this respect, I am of opinion that the Court of Chancery makes no distinction between one sort of religion and another. . . .

Neither does the Court, in this respect, make any distinction between one sect and another. It may be that the tenets of a particular sect inculcate doctrines adverse to the very foundation of all religion, and that they are subversive of all morality. In such a case, if it should arise, the Court will not assist the execution of the bequest, but will declare it to be void; but the character of the bequest, so far as regards the Statute of Mortmain, would not be altered by this circumstance. The general immoral tendency of the bequest would make it void, whether it was to be paid out of pure personalty or out of real estate. But if the tendency were not immoral, and although this Court might consider the opinions sought to be propagated foolish or even devoid of foundation, it would not, on that account, declare it void, or take it out of the class of legacies which are included in the general terms charitable bequests.

The words of the bequest here are, 'to propagate the sacred writings of Joanna Southcote.' The testatrix, it is clear, as a disciple or believer in Joanna Southcote, who, from her writings, it is clear, was a very sincere Christian; but she laboured under the delusion that she was to be made the medium of the miraculous birth of a child at an advanced period of her life, and that thereby the advancement of the Christian religion on earth would be occasioned. But her works, as far as I have looked at them, contain but little upon this subject, and nothing which could shake the faith of any sincere Christian. In truth, though her works are in a great measure incoherent and confused, they are written obviously with a view to extend the influence of Christianity. . . .

8.2.5.2   The public benefit requirement in trusts for the advancement of religion

GILMOUR v *COATS* [1949] AC 426, HL

FACTS: The sum of £500 was settled upon trust to pay the income therefrom for the purposes of a community of strictly cloistered nuns. The nuns devoted themselves to

prayer, meditation, fasting, penance and self-sanctification. They conducted private religious services, but were not engaged in any good works outside of the convent.
HELD: The trust for the purposes of the cloistered community did not satisfy the public benefit. Accordingly this was not a valid charitable trust for the advancement of religion. The potential for religious edification of others through the example set by the nuns was said to be too vague. Nor did their Lordships accept the argument, made by analogy to educational trusts, that the public benefit requirement had been met through the fact that membership of the community was potentially open to any woman in the whole world. Lord Simonds made the following general observation on the law of charities and the four heads of charity: 'the law of charity . . . has been built up not logically but empirically . . . To argue by a method of syllogism or analogy from the category of education to that of religion ignores the historical processes of law'.

LORD SIMONDS: . . . My Lords, I would speak with all respect and reverence of those who spend their lives in cloistered piety, and in this House of Lords Spiritual and Temporal, which daily commences its proceedings with intercessory prayers, how can I deny that the Divine Being may in His wisdom think fit to answer them? But, my Lords, whether I affirm or deny, whether I believe or disbelieve, what has that to do with the proof which the court demands that a particular purpose satisfies the test of benefit to the community? Here is something which is manifestly not susceptible of proof. But, then it is said, this is a matter not of proof but of belief, for the value of intercessory prayer is a tenet of the Catholic faith, therefore, and, in such prayer there is benefit to the community. But it is just at this 'therefore' that I must pause. It is, no doubt, true that the advancement of religion is, generally speaking, one of the heads of charity, but it does not follow from this that the court must accept as proved whatever a particular church believes. The faithful must embrace their faith believing where they cannot prove: the court can act only on proof. A gift to two or ten or a hundred cloistered nuns in the belief that their prayers will benefit the world at large does not from that belief alone derive validity any more than does the belief of any other donor for any other purpose. The importance of this case leads me to state my opinion in my own words but, having read again the judgment of Lord Greene MR, I will add that I am in full agreement with what he says on this part of the case.

I turn to the second of the alleged elements of public benefit, edification by example, and I think that this argument can be dealt with very shortly. It is, in my opinion, sufficient to say that this is something too vague and intangible to satisfy the prescribed test. The test of public benefit has, I think, been developed in the last two centuries. Today it is beyond doubt that that element must be present. No court would be rash enough to attempt to define precisely or exhaustively what its content must be. But it would assume a burden which it could not discharge if now for the first time it admitted into the category of public benefit something so indirect, remote, imponderable and, I would add, controversial as the benefit which may be derived by others from the example of pious lives.

NEVILLE ESTATES LTD v MADDEN [1961] 3 All ER 769, ChD

FACTS: NE Ltd claimed specific performance of a contract for the sale of land owned by a synagogue. The trustees of the synagogue claimed that the synagogue existed for charitable purposes and that the consent of the Charity Commissioners would be required before sale could proceed.
HELD: The synagogue's purposes were charitable. *Gilmour* v *Coats* being distinguished on the basis that the members of the synagogue 'spend their lives in the world, whereas the members of the Carmelite Priory live secluded from the world'. Cross J held that the court was entitled to assume 'that some benefit accrues to the public from the attendance at places of worship of persons who live in the world and mix with their fellow citizens. As between different religions the law stands neutral, but it assumes that any religion is at least likely to be better than none'.

CROSS J: . . . the trust with which I am concerned resembles that in *Gilmour* v *Coats* [1949] AC 426 in this, that the persons immediately benefited by it are not a section of the public but the members of a private body. All persons of the Jewish faith living in or about Catford might well constitute a section of the public, but the members for the time being of the Catford Synagogue are no more a section of the public than the members for the time being of a Carmelite priory. The two cases, however, differ from one another in that the members of the Catford Synagogue spend their lives in the world, whereas the members of a Carmelite priory live secluded from the world. If once one refuses to pay any regard—as the courts refused to pay any regard—to the influence which these nuns living in seclusion might have on the outside world, then it must follow that no public benefit is involved in a trust to support a Carmelite priory. As Lord Greene MR, said in the Court of Appeal: 'Having regard to the way in which the lives of the members were spent, the benefit was a purely private one'. But the court is, I think, entitled to assume that some benefit accrues to the public from the attendance at places of worship of persons who live in this world and mix with their fellow citizens. As between different religions the law stands neutral, but it assumes that any religion is at least likely to be better than none.

But then it is said—and it is this part of the argument that has caused me the greatest difficulty: But this is a case of self help. Suppose that a body of persons, being dissatisfied with the facilities for the education of small children provided in their district, form an association for the education of the children of members. A committee is formed; each member pays a subscription; the funds of the society are employed in hiring premises and paying a teacher; and the rules provide that the association cannot be dissolved by the members at any given moment but is to continue for the benefit of the members existing from time to time. No doubt the public benefits by the fact that the children of the members receive an education. But could it possibly be argued that the association was a charity and was entitled to the great fiscal advantages which a charity enjoys? Or would it make any difference if the committee allowed the children of non-members to attend the classes free of charge if there was room for them, in the same way as members of the public, though having no right to enter the synagogue, are not in practice refused admission?

I feel the force of this analogy; but, as Lord Simonds pointed out in *Gilmour v Coats*, it is dangerous to reason by analogy from one head of charity to another. . . .

RE HETHERINGTON [1990] 1 Ch 1, ChD

FACTS: The testatrix, H, left a legacy to 'the Roman Catholic Church Bishop of Westminster for the repose of the souls of my husband and my parents and my sisters and also myself when I die', and left the residue of her estate 'to the Roman Catholic Church St Edwards Golders Green for Masses for my soul'.
HELD: The gifts were for charitable purposes. However, to be valid the gift must be construed as a gift for the purpose of saying masses in public. The celebration of a religious rite in private would not contain the necessary element of public benefit.

SIR NICHOLAS BROWNE-WILKINSON V-C: . . . In my judgment the cases establish the following propositions.

(1) A trust for the advancement of education, the relief of poverty or the advancement of religion is prima facie charitable and assumed to be for the public benefit. *National Anti-Vivisection Society v Inland Revenue Commissioners* [1948] AC 31, 42 and 65. This asumption of public benefit can be rebutted by showing that in fact the particular trust in question cannot operate so as to confer a legally recognised benefit on the public, as in *Gilmour v Coats* [1949] AC 426.

(2) The celebration of a religious rite in public does confer a sufficient public benefit because of the edifying and improving effect of such celebration on the members of the public who attend. As Lord Reid said in *Gilmour v Coats* [1949] AC 426, 459:

> A religion can be regarded as beneficial without it being necessary to assume that all its beliefs are true, and a religious service can be regarded as beneficial to all those who attend it without it being necessary to determine the spiritual efficacy of that service or to accept any particular belief about it.

(3) The celebration of a religious rite in private does not contain the necessary element of public benefit since any benefit by prayer or example is incapable of proof in the legal sense, and any element of edification is limited to a private, not public, class of those present at the celebration: see *Gilmour v Coats*; *Yeap Cheah Neo v Ong Cheng Neo* (1875) LR 6 PC 381 and *Hoare v Hoare* (1886) 56 LT 147.

Where there is a gift for a religious purpose which could be carried out in a way which is beneficial to the public (i.e. by public Masses) but could also be carried out in a way which would not have sufficient element of public benefit (i.e. by private Masses) the gift is to be construed as a gift to be carried out only by the methods that are charitable, all non-charitable methods being excluded: see *In re White* [1893] 2 Ch 41, 52–53; and *In re Banfield* [1968] 1 WLR 846.

Applying those principles to the present case, a gift for the saying of Masses is prima facie charitable, being for a religious purpose. In practice, those Masses will be celebrated in public which povides a sufficient element of public benefit. The provision of stipends for priests saying the Masses, by relieving the Roman Catholic Church pro tanto of the liability to provide such stipends, is a further benefit. The gift is to be construed as a gift for public Masses only on the principle of *In re White*, private Masses not being permissible since it would not be a charitable application of the fund for a religious purpose. . . .

8.2.6   THE FOURTH HEAD: OTHER PURPOSES BENEFICIAL TO THE COMMUNITY

8.2.6.1   Trusts for animals

RE GROVE-GRADY [1929] 1 Ch 557, CA

FACTS: The testatrix left her residuary estate to her trustees upon trust to found an institution called 'The Beaumont Animals Benevolent Society', provided that all officials of the society should be declared anti-vivisectionists and opponents of all blood-sports, including angling. The objects of the society included the acquisition of land 'for the purpose of providing a refuge or refuges for the preservation of all animals birds or other creatures not human . . . and so that all such animals birds or other creatures not human shall there be safe from molestation or destruction by man'.
HELD: At first instance Romer J held that the gift was a valid charitable trust for purposes beneficial to the community. His decision was reversed by the majority of the Court of Appeal. The present gift lacked the required element of public benefit. It did not seek to diminish the cruel treatment of animal life generally, but only those within the society's compound. The public does not come into the matter at all.

ROMER J: . . . Does a trust for the benefit of the lower animals tend to promote public morality? In my opinion that question must be answered in the affirmative. It has the very same tendency as Swinfen Eady LJ said was possessed by a gift for the benefit and protection of animals. Its tendency is to stimulate humane and generous sentiments in man towards the lower animals, and by these means promote feelings of humanity and morality generally, repress brutality, and thus elevate the human race. It is, however, urged in opposition to this contention that whatever may be said in its favour with respect to a trust for animals beneficial to mankind, it ought not to prevail in the case of a trust that includes within its scope animals that are positively harmful to the human race; and this, it is said, is a trust of that kind. If it be a relevant consideration that under this trust the residuary estate may be employed for the purpose of protecting rats in England or rabbits in Australia, it might perhaps be suggested that the human race is quite as likely to obtain moral elevation by acquiring habits of kindness towards its enemies as by acquiring those habits towards its friends.

LORD HANWORTH MR: . . . In this proposed refuge all creatures are to find freedom and safety from molestation or destruction by man. Whatever animals, birds or other creatures, ferae naturae, may be living therein or obtain access thereto, are to find sanctuary. The fox and the rabbit, birds of all sorts with the stoat and the weasel and rats as neighbours, and hawks and crows as spectators, are to live and enjoy themselves after their kind. The struggle for existence is to be given free play—that weapon wherewith nature maintains its balance against over fertility: see Darwin's Origin of Species, ch. iii. It is not a sanctuary for any animals of a timid nature whose species is in danger of dying out: nor is it a sanctuary for birds which have almost entirely left our shores and may be attracted once more by a safe seclusion to nest and rear their young. No such purpose is indicated, nor indeed possible. The one characteristic of the refuge is that it is free from the molestation of man, while all the fauna within it are to be free to molest and harry one another.

Such a purpose does not, in my opinion, afford any advantage to animals that are useful to mankind in particular, or any protection from cruelty to animals generally. It does not denote any elevating lesson to mankind. . . .

H. Muir, 'RSPCA drops animal rights after threat to charity status', *The Daily Telegraph*, 7 February 1998

The RSPCA has withdrawn a key policy statement declaring support for 'animal rights' following warnings from the Charity Commissioners that it risked breaching its charitable status.

Copies of the society's latest policy pamphlet have been circulated without the Declaration on Animal Rights, which has been a prominent feature for the past 20 years.

The disclosure will hearten country sports enthusiasts as they redouble efforts to weaken the 'animal rights' element within the RSPCA.

It is the first time the document, which was revised last year, has appeared without the declaration since it was agreed at a meeting in 1977.

In 1996, the Society withdrew two other documents which detailed the philosophies that underpin the concept of 'animal rights'.

The move came after pressure from the commission which believed that some of the positions taken by the RSPCA placed greater emphasis on the fate of animals than humans.

This conflicted with the group's charitable status which requires the society to seek the improvement of mankind through the prevention of cruelty to animals.

Dr Richard Ryder, a member of the society's ruling council and a former chairman, said last night: 'The commission seems to be acting as an official Government censor in suppressing the expression of religious and ethical opinion.

That this censorship should come at a time when the RSPCA is being infiltrated by foxhunters is very unfortunate. I am not suggesting that the commissioners are pro deer or foxhunting, but if they were they could hardly be doing more to help those infiltrating the society.'.

The declaration stated: 'Inasmuch as there is ample evidence that many animal species are capable of feeling, we condemn totally the infliction of suffering upon our fellow creatures and the curtailment of their behavioural and other needs save where this is necessary for their own individual benefit.

'We do not accept that a difference in species alone [any more than a difference in race] can justify wanton exploitation or oppression in the name of science or sport, or for use as food, for commercial profit or for other human gain.'

By contrast, the new policy document explains the limits now placed upon the RSPCA: 'Readers should be aware of the constraints placed by current charity law on all animal welfare charities. They cannot pursue policies which, while benefiting animals, would have a detrimental effect on humankind. Further, they cannot oppose uses of animals for which there are no alternatives but which may cause pain, suffering or distress and where there is an overriding benefit to humans. All policy statements which follow should be read in that context.'

Last year, the British Field Sports Society estimated that about 3,000 country sports enthusiasts responded to an appeal to join the RSPCA and seek policy changes. A Charity Commission spokesman was unavailable for comment.

8.2.6.2 Trusts for private hospitals

RE RESCH'S WILL TRUSTS [1969] 1 AC 514, PC

FACTS: The testator left his residuary estate (then valued around $8M) to trustees upon trust to pay two-thirds of the income 'to the Sisters of Charity for a period of 200 years so long as they shall conduct the St Vincent's Private Hospital'. The hospital did not seek to make a commercial profit, but its charges for treatment, while not necessarily excluding the poor, were not low. On the question whether this was a valid charitable trust.

HELD: It was a valid charitable trust for purposes beneficial to the community. The requisite public benefit had been satisfied because evidence showed that the public needed accommodation and treatment of the type provided by the hospital. A gift for the purposes of a hospital is prima facie a good charitable gift, but the presumption could be rebutted if evidence showed that the hospital was carried on commercially for the benefit of private individuals.

LORD WILBERFORCE: . . . A gift for the purposes of a hospital is prima facie a good charitable gift. This is now clearly established both in Australia and in England, not merely because of the use of the word 'impotent' in the preamble to 43 Eliz. c. 4, though the process of referring to the preamble is one often used for reassurance, but because the provision of medical care for the sick is, in modern times, accepted as a public benefit suitable to attract the privileges given to charitable institutions. This has been recognised in the High Court in Australia in *Taylor* v *Taylor* (1910) 10 CLR 218 and *Kytherian Association of Queensland* v *Sklavos* (1958) 101 CLR 56: in England in *In re Smith, decd* [1962] 1 WLR 763.

In spite of this general proposition, there may be certain hospitals, or categories of hospitals, which are not charitable institutions (see *In re Smith, decd*). Disqualifying indicia may be either that the hospital is carried on commercially, i.e., with a view to making profits for private individuals, or that the benefits it provides are not for the public, or a sufficiently large class of the public to satisfy the necessary tests of public character. Each class of objection is taken in the present case. As regards the first, it is accepted that the private hospital is not run for the profit, in any ordinary sense, of individuals. Moreover, if the purposes of the hospital are otherwise charitable, they do not lose this character merely because charges are made to the recipients of benefits—see *Inland Revenue Commissioners* v *Falkirk Temperance Café Trust* (1927) SC 261. *Salvation Army (Victoria) Property Trust* v *Fern Tree Gully Corporation* (1951) 85 CLR 159. But what is said is that surpluses are made and are used for the general purposes of the Sisters of Charity. This association, while in a broad sense philanthropic, has objects which may not be charitable in the legal sense. Furthermore its purposes, though stated in its 'constitutions' are not limited by law, other than the canon law of the Roman Catholic Church, and under this, they are empowered, and may be obliged, to alter their purposes so as to include other objects which may not be strictly charitable.

Their Lordships do not consider it necessary to enter upon these latter considerations . . . . The share of income given by the will must be devoted entirely to the purposes of the private hospital. The character, charitable or otherwise, of the general activities of the Sisters, is not therefore a material consideration. . . .

8.2.7   RECREATIONAL TRUSTS

INLAND REVENUE COMMISSIONERS v *BADDELEY* [1955] AC 572, HL

FACTS: Land including a mission church, lecture room and store was given to trustees on trust to permit the leaders of the mission to promote thereon 'the religious, social and physical well-being of persons resident in the county boroughs of West Ham and Leyton . . . by the provision of facilities for religious services and instruction and for the social and physical training and recreation of such aforementioned persons who for the time being are in the opinion [of the leaders of the mission] members of or likely to become members of the Methodist Church'.

HELD: The trust was not for the relief of poverty, for 'relief' implied the meeting of a need or quasi-necessity, such as the provision of a dwelling. Nor could the trust be charitable as being for a purpose beneficial to the community. The trust did not benefit a sufficient section of the public because the beneficiaries had been selected not only by reference to a particular geographical area, but by the further condition that they share a particular creed. Further, promotion of 'religious, social and physical well-being' was too wide a statement of the trust's objects, and accordingly the trust would be void for potentially including non-charitable purposes.

VISCOUNT SIMONDS: . . . It is, in my opinion, particularly important in cases falling within the fourth category to keep firmly in mind the necessity of the element of general public utility, and I would not relax this rule. For here is a slippery slope. In the case under appeal the intended beneficiaries are a class within a class; they are those of the inhabitants of a particular area who are members of a particular church: the area is comparatively large and populous and the members may be numerous. But, if this trust is charitable for them, does it cease to be charitable as the area narrows down and the numbers diminish? Suppose the area is confined to a single street and the beneficiaries to those whose creed commands few adherents: or suppose the class is one that is determined not by religious belief but by membership of a particular profession or by pursuit of a particular trade. These were considerations which influenced the House in the recent case of *Oppenheim* [1951] AC 297. That was a case of an educational trust, but I think that they have even greater weight in the case of trusts which by their nominal classification depend for their validity upon general public utility.

RECREATIONAL CHARITIES ACT 1958

1. General provision as to recreational and similar trusts, etc.
  (1) Subject to the provisions of this Act, it shall be and be deemed always to have been charitable to provide, or assist in the provision of, facilities for recreation or other leisure-time occupation, if the facilities are provided in the interests of social welfare:
  Provided that nothing in this section shall be taken to derogate from the principle that a trust or institution to be charitable must be for the public benefit.
  (2) The requirement of the foregoing subsection that the facilities are provided in the interests of social welfare shall not be treated as satisfied unless—
     (a) the facilities are provided with the object of improving the conditions of life for the persons for whom the facilities are primarily intended; and
     (b) either—
        (i) those persons have need of such facilities as aforesaid by reason of their youth, age, infirmity or disablement, poverty or social and economic circumstances; or
        (ii) the facilities are to be available to the members or female members of the public at large.
  (3) Subject to the said requirement, subsection (1) of this section applies in particular to the provision of facilities at village halls, community centres and women's institutes, and to the provision and maintenance of grounds and buildings to be used for purposes of recreation or leisure-time occupation, and extends to the provision of facilities for those purposes by the organising of any activity.

RE GUILD [1992] 2 AC 310, HL

FACTS: The testator, G, left the residue of his estate 'to the town council of North Berwick for the use in connection with the sports centre in North Berwick or some similar purpose in connection with sport'. The IRC claimed that the transfer of value was liable to capital transfer tax. The executor appealed, claiming that the gift was for charitable purposes and therefore exempt from the tax.
HELD: On a proper construction of s. 1(2)(a) of the Recreational Charities Act 1958 a gift for the provision of recreational facilities could be charitable notwithstanding the fact that the intended beneficiaries were not in a position of social disadvantage and did not suffer from any particular deprivation. Accordingly, the gift in the present case was a charitable one, the facilities having been provided in the interests of social welfare. In construing the second part of the gift, 'or some similar purpose in connection with sport', it should be presumed that G had intended those other purposes to share the aspects of social welfare provision and public benefit which had been present in the first part of the gift. Such a benignant construction should be applied to deeds whose wording was ambiguous and susceptible to two constructions, one which would render the trust void, the other which would render it a valid charitable trust.

LORD KEITH OF KINKEL: . . . Section 1(2) of the 1958 Act does not exactly contain a definition but . . . it does state the essential elements which must be present if the requirement that the facilities should be provided in the interests of social welfare is to be met. It is difficult to envisage a case where, although these essential elements are present, yet the facilities are not provided in the interests of social welfare. Nor do I consider that the reference to social welfare in subsection (1) can properly be held to colour subsection (2)(a) to the effect that the persons for whom the facilities are primarily intended must be confined to those persons who suffer from some form of social deprivation. That this is not so seems to me to follow from the alternative conditions expressed in subsection (2)(b). If it suffices that the facilities are to be available to the members of the public at large, as sub-paragraph (ii) provides, it must necessarily be inferred that the persons for whom the facilities are primarily intended are not to be confined to those who have need of them by reason of one of the forms of social deprivation mentioned in sub-paragraph (i).

The fact is that persons in all walks of life and all kinds of social circumstances may have their conditions of life improved by the provision of recreational facilities of suitable character. The proviso requiring public benefit excludes facilities of an undesirable nature . . . I would therefore reject the argument that the facilities are not provided in the interests of social welfare unless they are provided with the object of improving the conditions of life for persons who suffer from some form of social disadvantage. It suffices if they are provided with the object of improving the conditions of life for members of the community generally. The Lord President, whose opinion contains a description of the facilities available at the sports centre which it is unnecessary to repeat, took the view that they were so provided. I respectfully agree, and indeed the contrary was not seriously maintained.

. . . The leading characteristics of the sports centre lie in the nature of the facilities which are provided there and the fact that those facilities are available to the public at large. These are the characteristics which enable it to satisfy section 1 of the Act of 1958.

8.2.8   TRUSTS FOR POLITICAL PURPOSES

NATIONAL ANTI-VIVISECTION SOCIETY v INLAND REVENUE COMMISSIONERS [1947] 2 All ER 217, HL

FACTS: The society claimed to be exempt from income tax as being 'a body of persons established for charitable purposes only'.

HELD: The overriding test of charitable status was whether the purposes of the organisation existed for the public benefit. The society failed that test as, on balance, the object of the society was detrimental to the public benefit (Lord Porter dissenting). Further, a prime object of the society was political, namely, to secure the repeal of the Cruelty to Animals Act 1876 and to see it replaced by an enactment absolutely prohibiting vivisection. The court could not award charitable status to a trust for a political purpose. Lord Simonds stated *obiter* that the concept of what is charitable may change from age to age, and that a trust which was once held to be charitable might one day cease to be so, in which case the trust fund should be applied by *cy près*.

LORD SIMONDS: . . . One of the tests, and a crucial test, whether a trust is charitable, lies in the competence of the court to control and reform it. I would remind your Lordships that it is the King as parens patriae who is the guardian of charity and that it is the right and duty of his Attorney-General to intervene and inform the court, if the trustees of a charitable trust fall short of their duty. So too it is his duty to assist the court, if need be, in the formulation of a scheme for the execution of a charitable trust. But, my Lords, is it for a moment to be supposed that it is the function of the Attorney-General on behalf of the Crown to intervene and demand that a trust shall be established and administered by the court, the object of which is to alter the law in a manner highly prejudicial, as he and His Majesty's Government may think, to the welfare of the state? This very case would serve as an example, if upon the footing that it was a charitable trust it became the duty of the Attorney-General on account of its maladministration to intervene. . . . I conclude upon this part of the case that a main object of the society is political and for that reason the society is not established for charitable purposes only. . . .

McGOVERN AND OTHERS v ATTORNEY GENERAL AND ANOTHER
[1981] 3 All ER 493

FACTS: The Amnesty International organisation set up a trust to administer those of its purposes which were considered to be charitable. Its aims included the release of and humane treatment of prisoners of conscience, research into the observance of human rights and the dissemination of the results of such research. It applied to the Charity Commissioners for registration of the trust as a charity under s. 4 of the Charities Act 1960. Registration was refused.

HELD: On appeal to the High Court the Commissioners decision was confirmed, the trust was not a trust for exclusively charitable purposes. The major part of the trust purposes was of a political, and therefore non-charitable, nature. The court did state, however, that had the provisions as to research stood alone they would have been charitable. The subject matter of the research was 'capable of adding usefully to the store of human knowledge'. The judge noted that human rights has become an accepted academic discipline. He also stated that it should be benignly presumed that the trustees would not implement the research in a political manner.

SLADE J: As a broad proposition, I would thus accept that a trust for the relief of human suffering and distress would prima facie be capable of being of a charitable nature, within the spirit and intendment of the preamble to the Statute of Elizabeth, as being what counsel for the plaintiffs termed a 'charity of compassion'. It does not, however, follow that a trust established for good compassionate purposes will necessarily qualify as a charity according to English law, any more than it necessarily follows that such a qualification will attach to a trust for the relief of poverty or for the advancement of education or for the advancement of religion. There are other requirements which it must still satisfy if it is to enjoy charitable status. I now turn to the requirement of public benefit.

The requirement of public benefit

Save in the case of gifts to classes of poor persons, a trust must always be shown to promote a public benefit of a nature recognised by the courts as being such, if it is to qualify as being charitable. The question whether a purpose will or may operate for the public benefit is to be answered by the court forming an opinion on the evidence before it; see *National Anti-Vivisection Society* v *Inland Revenue Comrs* [1947] 2 All ER 217 at 221 *per* Lord Wright. No doubt in some cases a purpose may be so manifestly beneficial to the public that it would be absurd to call evidence on this point. In many other instances, however, the element of public benefit may be much more debatable. Indeed, in some cases the court will regard this element as being incapable of proof one way or the other and thus will inevitably decline to recognise the trust as being of a charitable nature.

Trusts to promote changes in the law of England are generally regarded as falling into the latter category and as being non-charitable for this reason. . . .

Thus far, the only types of political trust to which I have directed specific attention have been those of which a main object is to procure a change in the law of this country. The principles established by *Bowman's* case and the *National Anti-Vivisection Society* case will render such trusts non-charitable, whether or not they are of a party political nature. Conversely, however, several cases cited to me illustrate that trusts of which a main object is to promote the interests of a particular political party in this country fail to achieve charitable status, even though they are not directed towards any particular change in English law: see, for example, *Bonar Law Memorial Trust* v *Inland Revenue Comrs* (1933) 17 Tax Cases 508 and *Re Hopkinson (deceased), Lloyds Bank Ltd* v *Baker* [1949] 1 All ER 346. In my judgment any such trusts are plainly 'political trusts' within the spirit, if not the letter, of Lord Parker's pronouncement, and the same reasons for the court's refusing to enforce them would apply, but a fortiori. Since their nature would ex hypothesi be very controversial, the court could be faced with even greater difficulties in determining whether the objects of the trust would be for the public benefit; correspondingly, it would be at even greater risk of encroaching on the function of the legislature and prejudicing its reputation for political impartiality, if it were to promote such objects by enforcing the trust.

I now turn to consider the status of a trust of which a main object is to secure the alteration of the laws of a *foreign* country. The mere fact that the trust was intended to be carried out abroad would not by itself necessarily deprive it of charitable status. A number of trusts to be executed outside this country have been upheld as charities, though the judgment of Evershed MR in *Camille and Henry Dreyfus Foundation Inc* v *Inland Revenue Comrs* [1954] 2 All ER 466 at 471–472 illustrates that certain types of trust, for example trusts for the setting out of soldiers or the repair of bridges or causeways, might be acceptable as charities only if they were to be executed in the United Kingdom. The point with which I am at present concerned is whether a trust of which a direct and main object is to secure a change in the laws of a foreign country can *ever* be regarded as charitable under English law. Though I do not think that any authority cited to me precisely covers the point, I have come to the clear conclusion that it cannot.

I accept that the dangers of the court encroaching on the functions of the legislature or of subjecting its political impartiality to question would not be nearly so great as when similar trusts are to be executed in this country. I also accept that on occasions the court will examine and express an opinion on the quality of a foreign law. Thus, for example, it has declined to enforce or recognise rights conferred or duties imposed by a foreign law, in certain cases where it has considered that, on the particular facts, enforcement or recognition would be contrary to justice or morality. I therefore accept that the particular point made by Mr Tyssen (about the law stultifying itself) has no application in this context. There is no obligation on the court to decide on the principle that any foreign law is ex hypothesi right as it stands; it is not obliged for all purposes to blind itself to what it may regard as the injustice of a particular foreign law.

In my judgment, however, there remain overwhelming reasons why such a trust still cannot be regarded as charitable. All the reasoning of Lord Parker in *Bowman* v *Secular Society Ltd* [1917] AC 406 seems to me to apply a fortiori in such a case. A fortiori the court will have no adequate means of judging whether a proposed change in the law of a foreign country will or will not be for the public benefit. Evershed MR in *Camille and Henry Dreyfus Foundation Inc* v *Inland Revenue Comrs* [1954] 2 All ER 466 at 471 expressed the prima facie view that the community which has to be considered in this context, even in the case of a trust to be executed abroad, is the community of the United Kingdom. Assuming that this is the right test, the court in applying it would still be bound to take account of the probable effects of attempts to procure the proposed legislation, or of its actual enactment, on the inhabitants of the country concerned, which would doubtless have a history and social structure quite different from that of the United Kingdom. Whatever might be its view as to the content of the relevant law from the standpoint of an English lawyer, it would, I think, have no satisfactory means of judging such probable effects on the local community.

Furthermore, before ascribing charitable status to an English trust of which a main object was to secure the alteration of a foreign law, the court would also, I conceive, be bound to consider the consequences for this country as a matter of public policy. In a number of such cases there would arise a substantial prima facie risk that such a trust, if enforced, could prejudice the relations of this country with the foreign country concerned (cf *Habershon* v *Vardon* (1851) 4 De G & Sm 467, 64 ER 916). The court would have no satisfactory means of assessing the extent of such risk, which would not be capable of being readily dealt with by evidence and would be a matter more for political than for legal judgment. For all these reasons, I conclude that a trust of which a main purpose is to procure a change in the laws of a foreign country is a trust for the attainment of political objects within the spirit of Lord Parker's pronouncement and, as such, is non-charitable.

8.3   Exclusivity Requirement

RE COXEN [1948] 1 Ch 747, ChD

FACTS: The testator gave the residue of his estate, some £200,000, to the Court of Aldermen of the City of London upon trust to (1) spend £100 towards an annual dinner for the aldermen upon their meeting together upon the business of his trust; (2) to pay one guinea to each alderman who attended the whole of a committee meeting in connection with the trust; (3) to apply the remainder for the benefit of certain medical charities. On the question whether the trust was valid.

HELD: All the trusts were valid charitable trusts. The provisions in favour of the aldermen personally were made to ensure the better administration of the main charitable trusts. In any event, even if those provisions had not themselves been charitable, the sums involved were so insignificant in comparison to that part of the fund devoted to the medical charities that the provisions for the benefit of the aldermen personally could be seen as merely ancillary to the principal trust and would take effect on that basis. In cases where the non-charitable allocation was so significant as not to be 'ancillary' the whole trust must fail, unless the non-charitable part could be precisely quantified in which case only that part would fail.

JENKINS J: . . . It remains to consider whether the trusts in question are indeed invalid. In my judgment they are not. It is no doubt perfectly true that a trust simply to provide an annual dinner for the Court of Aldermen of the City of London is not charitable, any more than the trust to provide dinners for the Painters Stainers' Company in *In re Barnett* 24 TLR 788 was charitable. It is also no doubt perfectly true that a trust simply to pay periodical guineas to selected aldermen of the City of London is not charitable. But the trusts here in question are of a different character. The annual dinner is to be provided for the Court of Aldermen as trustees of the charitable trust when they meet on the business of the trust, and the guineas are payable only to aldermen who are members of the committee administering the charity when they meet for that purpose, and subject to the express condition that a member in order to qualify for his guinea must be present during the whole of the given committee meeting. The annual dinner and the guinea attendance fees can therefore fairly be regarded as in the nature of remuneration in kind or in cash to the trustees and committee of management for their services in administering the affairs of the trust, and as I have already said the testator no doubt thought that these concrete expressions of his appreciation of the time and trouble involved would be conducive, in the ways mentioned above, to the attainment of its charitable purpose. In other words, his motive and object providing for the annual dinner and the guinea attendance fees was I think clearly to benefit the charity and not the members for the time being of the Court of Aldermen or the members for the time being of the committee appointed by them. It cannot be said that these particular modes of furthering his charitable purpose are in fact incapable of furthering it. On the contrary I think there is every reason to suppose that it will be furthered thereby, and, of this I think the testator was the best possible judge. Himself a former alderman, sheriff and Lord Mayor, no one could know the Court of Aldermen better than he did, or be more capable than he was of devising the most effective method of enlisting their interest in, and sympathy and support for, a charitable project which, after all, has no particular connection with the City of London. . . .

CHARITABLE TRUSTS (VALIDATION) ACT 1954

1. Validation and modification of imperfect trust instruments

(1) In this Act, 'imperfect trust provision' means any provision declaring objects for which property is to be held or applied, and so describing those objects that, consistently with the terms of the provision, the property could be used exclusively for charitable purposes, but could nevertheless be used for purposes which are not charitable.

(2) Subject to the following provisions of this Act, any imperfect trust provision contained in an instrument taking effect before the sixteenth day of December, nineteen hundred and fifty-two, shall have, and be deemed to have had, effect in relation to any disposition or covenant to which this Act applies—

(a) as respects the period before the commencement of this Act, as if the whole of the declared objects were charitable; and

(b) as respects the period after that commencement as if the provision had required the property to be held or applied for the declared objects in so far only as they authorise use for charitable purposes.

(3)   A document inviting gifts of property to be held or applied for objects declared by the document shall be treated for the purposes of this section as an instrument taking effect when it is first issued.

(4)   . . .

CHICHESTER DIOCESAN FUND AND BOARD OF FINANCE (INCORPORATED) v SIMPSON [1944] AC 341, HL

FACTS: The testator, CD, left the residue of his estate on trust 'for such charitable institution or institutions or other charitable or benevolent object or objects as his executors might in their absolute discretion select'. The residue was distributed amongst several charities. After the distribution the testator's statutory next-of-kin claimed that the residuary gift was not a valid charitable bequest because the words 'charitable or benevolent' had rendered the gift uncertain.

HELD: Upon a true construction of the clause the word 'or' indicated that 'benevolent' was intended to be an alternative to 'charitable'. Accordingly, the gift was void for uncertainty. (This decision meant, of course, that the statutory, next-of-kin had to try and recover the misapplied property — see *Re Diplock* (**18.2**).

VISCOUNT SIMON LC: My Lords, the will with which we are concerned in this appeal is one in which a public-spirited testator has directed his executors to apply the very substantial residue of his property 'for such charitable institution or institutions or other charitable or benevolent object or objects in England' as they should select. The Court of Appeal (Lord Greene MR, Clauson and Goddard LJJ), overruling Farwell J, has decided that this is not a valid testamentary disposition. After studying the powerful judgment of the Master of the Rolls and weighing the arguments which have been presented to the House, I cannot doubt that a gift expressed in the terms which I have quoted, in the absence of context to vary its prima facie meaning, is void for uncertainty.

The fundamental principle is that the testator must by the terms of his will himself dispose of the property with which the will proposes to deal. With one single exception, he cannot by his will direct executors or trustees to do the business for him. That exception arises when the testator is minded to make gifts for charitable purposes, and where he directs his executors or trustees, within such limitations as he chooses to lay down, to make the selection of charities to be benefited. This exception from the general principle that the testator has to decide in his will the specific destination of his property is allowed because of the special favour which the English law shows to charities, and the conception of what is charitable for such purposes has been elaborately worked out so that the courts are able to determine whetber a particular gift is charitable or not, but when, as here, the expression is 'charitable or benevolent,' it is impossible to attribute to the word 'benevolent' an equal precision or to regard the courts as able to decide with accuracy the ambit of that expression. It is not disputed that the two words 'charitable' and 'benevolent' do not ordinarily mean the same thing. They overlap in the sense that each of them, as a matter of legal interpretation, covers some common ground, but also something which is not covered by the other. It appears to me that it inevitably follows that the phrase 'charitable or benevolent' occurring in a will must, in its ordinary context, be regarded as too vague to give the certainty necessary before such a provision can be supported or enforced.

Is there, then, any special context in this will which would justify a different interpretation? I have listened with much sympathy to the efforts to find one, but it does not seem to me, notwithstanding the late Farwell J's opinion, that there is any context which might give to the impeached phrase a special meaning. The conjunction 'or' may be sometimes used to join two words the meaning of which is the same, but, as the conjunction appears in this will, it seems to me to indicate a variation rather than an identity between the coupled conceptions. Its use is analogous in the present instance to its use in a phrase like 'the House of Lords or the House of Commons,' rather than to its use in a phrase like 'the House of Lords or the Upper Chamber'. I regret that we have to arrive at such a conclusion, but we have no right to set at nought an established principle such as this in the construction of wills, and I, therefore, move the House to dismiss the appeal.

8.4 *Cy Près*

8.4.1 INITIAL FAILURE

IN RE RYMER [1895] 1 Ch 19

FACTS: A testator bequeathed a legacy of £5000 'to the rector for the time being of St. Thomas' Seminary for the education of priests in the diocese of Westminster for the purpose of such seminary'. At the date of the will St. Thomas' Seminary was carried on at Hammersmith; but shortly before the testator's death the seminary ceased to exist, and the students who were being educated there were removed to another seminary near Birmingham.

HELD: (affirming the decision of Chitty J), that the bequest was for the benefit of the particular institution, and, that institution having ceased to exist in the testator's lifetime, the legacy could not be applied *cy-près*, but lapsed and fell into the residue.

LORD HERSCHELL LC: . . . The contention on behalf of the appellant is that from the gift now in question is to be inferred an intention on the part of the testator to benefit priests by educating them quite apart from their education taking place or in connection with this particular seminary; that it is quite immaterial that he has designated that particular seminary; and that the gift can be regarded as a charitable one that must take effect even though that seminary should have ceased to exist at the time of the death of the testator. I am unable so to construe this bequest. I think in all these cases (and they may all be looked at for the purpose of throwing light on this bequest) the testator had in view particular institutions, and although their objects may be the same, he graduates his bounty towards them, shewing, for instance, that it was the education of the orphans at this or that institution which he had in his mind, and not merely the education of orphans, if I may say so, at large. In the first place I observe that he says: 'I give the following charitable legacies to the following institutions and persons'—the persons are named in connection with the institutions. There is no person named except in connection with an institution, and therefore he indicates at the outset that the legacy is to be a legacy to the institution, although he names the officer of the institution who is to take it. It seems to me, therefore, that we start with that indication. Then he mentions St. Thomas' Seminary, it is true, in conjunction with the words 'for the education of priests in the diocese of Westminster.' It is said that those are his words and not part of the title of the institution; but it would be obviously a piece of prudence to insert those words in order to make sure that the bequest should go to the St Thomas' Seminary which he had in view, not to any St. Thomas' Seminary which might possibly have existed not having that object and being a different institution. But the gift is to be for the purposes of such seminary, and then it is to be observed that, although he does not make it a condition of the gift, he does couple it with the request that a yearly mass for the repose of his soul may be said at the said seminary. The whole is localised and connected with that institution as distinctly, as it seems to me, as a bequest could be. That is the construction which I put upon the language which the testator has used. . . . I do not think it would be in accordance with sound principle to hold or that any prior decisions necessitate our holding, where the conclusion is once arrived at that the main object of the testator or testatrix was to benefit a particular institution, that that was not of the essence of the bequest and that if that institution has ceased to exist the charitable legacy ought still to be held as effectual, and the money to be applied by the court on the *cy-près* principle.

For these reasons, I think the appeal should be dismissed with costs.

RE HARWOOD [1935] All ER 918

FACTS: A testatrix, by her will, gave £200 to the W Peace Society, Cambridge, £300 to the Peace Society of Belfast, and £300 to the Peace Society of Dublin. The W Peace Society had ceased to exist before the death of the testatrix. There was no evidence that there ever had been a Peace Society of Belfast. The Peace Society of Dublin had never existed, but there had been in existence the Dublin Peace Society, which, however, had ceased to exist before the death of the testatrix.

HELD: (i) where a testator shows in the will itself some care to identify the particular charitable society he wishes to benefit, the difficulty of showing any general charitable intent if the society once existed, but has ceased to exist before the death of the testator, is very great; (ii) the testatrix had so identified the W Peace Society, and, therefore, it was not open to the court to hold that there was any such general charitable intent as to allow the application of the *cy-près* doctrine, and the gift to the W Peace Society accordingly failed; (iii) as there was a clear intention to benefit by the legacy to the Peace Society of Belfast any society whose object was the promotion of peace and which was connected with Belfast, there was a general charitable intent, and the *cy-près* doctrine applied; (iv) the testatrix's ideas as to the particular society she wished to benefit by the gift to the non-existent Peace Society of Dublin were extremely vague, but there was an intention to benefit any society whose object was the promotion of peace and which was connected with Dublin, the *cy-près* doctrine therefore applied.

FARWELL J: . . . The first question that I have to determine is whether a gift of £200 'to the Wisbech Peace Society, Cambridge', fails. The evidence is that this particular society ceased to exist in the testatrix's lifetime. It is said that it is being still carried on as part of the work of the Peace Committee of the Society of Friends. The onus is upon them to show that they are the persons entitled to take. The evidence in this case is so unsatisfactory that I cannot say that that onus has been discharged.

That leaves the question whether there is any general charitable intent, so as to admit of the application of the *cy-près* doctrine. In the will there is a long list of various charitable societies, including charities whose work is devoted to peace. It is said that as this is one of a long list of charitable legacies there is a general charitable intent. On the other hand, it is said that where there is a gift to a particular society, which once existed but ceased to exist before the death of the testator or testatrix, the gift lapses and there is no room for the *cy-près* doctrine. I have been referred to *Re Davis* [1902] 1 Ch 876. In that case the learned judge was able to come to the conclusion that as to one particular gift there was a general charitable intent; but in that case no such society as that named in the will had ever existed. It was not a case of a society which had been in existence and had ceased to exist. I do not decide that it can never be possible for the court to hold that there is a general charitable intent in a case where the charity named in the will once existed but ceased to exist before the death. Without deciding that, it is enough for me to say that, where the testator selects as the object of his bounty a particular charity and shows in the will itself some care to identify the particular society which he desires to benefit, the difficulty of finding any general charitable intent in such case if the named society once existed, but ceased to exist before the death of the testator, is very great. Here the testatrix has gone out of her way to identify the object of her bounty. In this particular case she has identified it as being 'the Wisbech Peace Society, Cambridge (which is a branch of the London Peace Society)'. Under those circumstances, I do not think it is open to me to hold that there is in this case any such general charitable intent as to allow the application of the *cy-près* doctrine.

Accordingly, in my judgment, the legacy of £200 fails and is undisposed of.

Then there is the gift to the 'Peace Society of Belfast'.

The claimant for this legacy is the Belfast Branch of the League of Nations Union. I am quite unable on the evidence to say that that was the society which this lady intended to benefit, and I doubt whether the lady herself knew exactly what society she did mean to benefit. I think she had a desire to benefit any society which was formed for the purpose of promoting peace and was connected with Belfast. Beyond that, I do not think that she had any very clear idea in her mind. That is rather indicated by the pencil note which was found after her death. At any rate, I cannot say that by the description, 'the Peace Society of Belfast', the lady meant the Belfast Branch of the League of Nations Union; but there is enough in this case to enable me to say that, although there is no gift to any existing society, the gift does not fail. It is a good charitable gift and must be applied *cy-près*. The evidence suggests that at some time or other, possibly before the late war, there may have been a society called the Peace Society of Belfast. It is all hearsay evidence; there is nothing in the least definite about it, and it does not satisfy me that there ever was any society in existence which exactly fits the description in this case, and, there being a clear intention on the part of the lady, as expressed in her will, to benefit societies whose object was the promotion of peace and there being no such society as that named in her will, in this case there is a general charitable intent, and, accordingly, the doctrine of *cy-près* applies.

The next legacy is 'to the Peace Society of Dublin the sum of £300'. The claimant to that legacy is a society known as the League of Nations Society of Ireland. The way in which the claim is put is not the same as in the case of the Belfast Society. It is said that there was a society known as the Dublin Peace Society, the name of which was afterwards changed to the Irish Peace Society; that it ceased to exist many years ago, and that what was left of its funds was handed over to this new society, when it came into existence, and the old society is now being carried on by the existing society. The evidence does not satisfy me that that is so, and I am unable to say that the League of Nations Society of Ireland is entitled to the legacy. Then it is said that since there was at one time a society which answers the description in the will, and has now ceased to exist, there is a lapse and the legacy fails. I think that it is very probable that, if there was now a society in existence known as the Dublin Peace Society, having regard to the evidence here, such a society would have had little difficulty in establishing that it was the society which the lady intended to benefit; but the evidence shows that there never was a society which answered the exact description in the will, 'the Peace Society of Dublin'. It is also clear from the memorandum which the lady left, which was found after her death, that her ideas as to any particular society which she desired to benefit by this gift were extremely vague; her one idea seems to have been to benefit any society whose object was the promotion of peace which was connected with Dublin. Under those circumstances, there never having been any society which exactly answers the description in the will, this again is a case where the doctrine of *cy-près* applies.

8.4.2 THE MODERN LAW OF *CY PRÈS*

CHARITIES ACT 1993

PART IV APPLICATION OF PROPERTY CY-PRÈS AND ASSISTANCE AND SUPERVISION OF CHARITIES BY COURT AND COMMISSIONERS

Extended powers of court and variation of charters

13. Occasions for applying property cy-près
(1) Subject to subsection (2) below, the circumstances in which the original purposes of a charitable gift can be altered to allow the property given or part of it to be applied cy-près shall be as follows—
(a) where the original purposes, in whole or in part—
(i) have been as far as may be fulfilled; or
(ii) cannot be carried out, or not according to the directions and to the spirit of the gift; or
(b) where the original purposes provide a use for part only of the property available by virtue of the gift; or
(c) where the property available by virtue of the gift and other property applicable for similar purposes can be more effectively used in conjunction, and to that end can suitably, regard being had to the spirit of the gift, be made applicable to common purposes; or
(d) where the original purposes were laid down by reference to an area which then was but has since ceased to be a unit for some other purpose, or by reference to a class of persons or to an area which has for any reason since ceased to be suitable, regard being had to the spirit of the gift, or to be practical in administering the gift; or
(e) where the original purposes, in whole or in part, have, since they were laid down,—
(i) been adequately provided for by other means; or

(ii)   ceased, as being useless or harmful to the community or for other reasons, to be in law charitable; or

(iii)   ceased in any other way to provide a suitable and effective method of using the property available by virtue of the gift, regard being had to the spirit of the gift.

(2)   Subsection (1) above shall not affect the conditions which must be satisfied in order that property given for charitable purposes may be applied cy-près except in so far as those conditions require a failure of the original purposes.

(3)   References in the foregoing subsections to the original purposes of a gift shall be construed, where the application of the property given has been altered or regulated by a scheme or otherwise, as referring to the purposes for which the property is for the time being applicable.

(4)   Without prejudice to the power to make schemes in circumstances falling within subsection (1) above, the court may by a scheme made under the court's jurisdiction with respect to charities, in any case where the purposes for which the property is held are laid down by reference to any such area as is mentioned in the first column in Schedule 3 to this Act, provide for enlarging the area to any such area as is mentioned in the second column in the same entry in that Schedule.

(5)   It is hereby declared that a trust for charitable purposes places a trustee under a duty, where the case permits and requires the property or some part of it to be applied cy-près, to secure its effective use for charity by taking steps to enable it to be so applied.

8.4.3   THE DISPOSAL OF SURPLUS DONATIONS

CHARITIES ACT 1993

14.   Application cy-près of gifts of donors unknown or disclaiming

(1)   Property given for specific charitable purposes which fail shall be applicable cy-près as if given for charitable purposes generally, where it belongs—

(a)   to a donor who after—

(i)   the prescribed advertisements and inquiries have been published and made, and

(ii)   the prescribed period beginning with the publication of those advertisements has expired,

cannot be identified or cannot be found; or

(b)   to a donor who has executed a disclaimer in the prescribed form of his right to have the property returned.

(2)   Where the prescribed advertisements and inquiries have been published and made by or on behalf of trustees with respect to any such property, the trustees shall not be liable to any person in respect of the property if no claim by him to be interested in it is received by them before the expiry of the period mentioned in subsection (1)(a)(ii) above.

(3)   For the purposes of this section property shall be conclusively presumed (without any advertisement or inquiry) to belong to donors who cannot be identified, in so far as it consists—

(a)   of the proceeds of cash collections made by means of collecting boxes or by other means not adapted for distinguishing one gift from another; or

(b)   of the proceeds of any lottery, competition, entertainment, sale or similar money-raising activity, after allowing for property given to provide prizes or articles for sale or otherwise to enable the activity to be undertaken.

(4)   The court may by order direct that property not falling within subsection (3) above shall for the purposes of this section be treated (without any advertisement or inquiry) as belonging to donors who cannot be identified where it appears to the court either—

(a)   that it would be unreasonable, having regard to the amounts likely to be returned to the donors, to incur expense with a view to returning the property; or

(b)   that it would be unreasonable, having regard to the nature, circumstances and amounts of the gifts, and to the lapse of time since the gifts were made, for the donors to expect the property to be returned.

(5)   Where property is applied cy-près by virtue of this section, the donor shall be deemed to have parted with all his interest at the time when the gift was made; but where property is so applied as belonging to donors who cannot be identified or cannot be found, and is not so applied by virtue of subsection (3) or (4) above—

(a)   the scheme shall specify the total amount of that property; and

(b)   the donor of any part of that amount shall be entitled, if he makes a claim not later than six months after the date on which the scheme is made, to recover from the charity for which the property is applied a sum equal to that part, less any expenses properly incurred by the charity trustees after that date in connection with claims relating to his gift; and

(c)   the scheme may include directions as to the provision to be made for meeting any such claim.

(6)   Where—

(a)   any sum is, in accordance with any such directions, set aside for meeting any such claims, but

(b)   the aggregate amount of any such claims actually made exceeds the relevant amount,

then, if the Commissioners so direct, each of the donors in question shall be entitled only to such proportion of the relevant amount as the amount of his claim bears to the aggregate amount referred to in paragraph (b) above; and for this purpose 'the relevant amount' means the amount of the sum so set aside after deduction of any expenses properly incurred by the charity trustees in connection with claims relating to the donors' gifts.

(7)   For the purposes of this section, charitable purposes shall be deemed to 'fail' where any difficulty in applying property to those purposes makes that property or the part not applicable cy-près available to be returned to the donors.

(8)   In this section 'prescribed' means prescribed by regulations made by the Commissioners, and such regulations may, as respects the advertisements which are to be published for the purposes of subsection (1)(a) above, make provision as to the form and content of such advertisements as well as the manner in which they are to be published.

(9)   Any regulations made by the Commissioners under this section shall be published by the Commissioners in such manner as they think fit.

(10)   In this section, except in so far as the context otherwise requires, references to a donor include persons claiming through or under the original donor, and references to property given include the property for the time being representing the property originally given or property derived from it.

(11)   This section shall apply to property given for charitable purposes, notwithstanding that it was so given before the commencement of this Act.

8.5   End of Chapter Assessment Question

Reginald died recently. Consider which of the following provisions in his will might be a valid charitable legacy.

(a)   £100,000 to my trustees on trust to provide temporary shelter for Old Etonians who have fallen on hard times. Preference to be given to my old class mates.

(b)   £10,000 to my trustees to support research into the likely consequences for political and public life of a legal ban on the Society of Free and Accepted Masons.

(c)   £5,000 to my trustees to promote the playing of card games by deprived youth as an alternative to watching television.

(d)   £5,000 to my psychotherapist, Doctor F. Sreud, to buy a new couch for the greater comfort of his many grateful patients.

8.6   End of Chapter Assessment Outline Answer

Your answer should commence with a brief introduction to the way in which charity is defined at law. You should explain the relationship between the preamble to the Statute of Elizabeth I 1601, and the four heads of charity suggested by Lord Macnaghten in *Commissioners for Special Purpose of the Income Tax* v *Pemsel* [1891] AC 531. You should then take each part of the question in turn and attempt to identify whether or not the provision falls within the legal definition of charity and yields the necessary public benefit in order to be charitable.

(a)   This provision might be charitable under the first head of charity: the relief of poverty. It is somewhat reminiscent of the gift in *Re Niyazi's Will Trusts* [1978] 1 WLR 910. There a testator provided that his residuary estate should be held by his trustees upon trust to pay the capital and income to a local authority in a needy part of Cyprus 'on condition that the same shall be used for the purposes only of the construction of or as a contribution towards the cost of the construction of a working men's hostel'. Megarry V-C held that this was a valid charitable trust for the relief of poverty. The word 'hostel' suggested a poor inhabitant. The judge also took into account the fact that the relatively modest size of the fund made it unlikely that a 'grandiose building' would be erected.

The word 'shelter' as used in the present legacy also suggests a poor inhabitant. The fact that the beneficiaries are Old Etonians will not disqualify them from benefiting from a charitable trust. In *Re Gardom* [1914] 1 Ch 662 a trust for 'ladies of limited means' was held to be charitable, as was a trust for 'distressed gentlefolk' in *Re Young* [1951] Ch 344. The courts have never been slow to allow the charitable relief of the impoverished upper classes. The inclusion of a preference does not invalidate educational trusts (*Re Koettgen* [1954] 1 All ER 581), and is even less likely to invalidate a trust for the relief of poverty. As long as the potential benefiting class is sufficiently large there should be no problem (*Re Segelman* [1995] 2 All ER 676). However, there may be a problem if too narrow a class of beneficiaries is actually preferred, if that class, as here, is defined by some personal connection to the testator or to each other, thereby excluding benefits to society at large. Thus, in *IRC* v *Educational Grants Association Ltd* [1967] 2 All ER 893, evidence showed that 76 per cent to 85 per cent of the association's income had been applied to educate the children of persons connected with an associated commercial company. Despite this, the association had claimed a tax refund from the Inland Revenue. The Inland Revenue refused the refund, claiming that the association had failed to apply its funds to exclusively charitable ends. The court held for the IRC.

(b)   Trusts for research may be charitable if they are for the advancement of education, thus falling within the second of Lord Macnaghten's heads of charity.

In *Re Shaw* [1957] 1 WLR 729 George Bernard Shaw left his residuary estate on trust to research into a new English alphabet. This failed as a charitable trust for the advancement of education. The judge held that 'if the object be merely the increase of knowledge, that is not in itself a charitable object unless it be combined with teaching or education'. Accordingly, the clause is Reginald's will is more likely to be recognised to be a valid charitable trust for education were it to include express provision for dissemination of the research outcomes. There has, however, been limited recognition that the educational benefits of research might still be charitable if confined to the researchers themselves, provided that the subject matter of the research is a worthy object of study (*Re Hopkins* [1965] Ch 669).

The political aspect of the research is a bit of a red-herring. Although a trust established for political purposes will not be recognised to be charitable, research into political matters can be charitable (*McGovern* v *Attorney-General* [1981] 3 All ER 493), provided it is not undertaken to support a political campaign.

(c)   The courts have in general been reluctant to acknowledge sport to be a charitable object in itself, but have been willing to support it where it is being pursued in an educational context (*Re Dupree's Trusts* [1944] 2 All ER 443). The playing of card games, as an alternative to television, might be thought to be educational. However, the educational value of television might be expected to be higher than that afforded by most card games. Without more detail as to the nature of the card games and the professions of the trustees, the court is unlikely to approve this gift as charitable. However, subject to proof of a sufficient public benefit, this trust could be a charitable trust for the advancement of education, or even a charitable trust within the Recreational Charities Act 1958.

(d)   It is acknowledged that trusts for private hospitals can be charitable within the fourth head of charity: other purposes beneficial to the community (*Re Resch's Will Trusts* [1969] 1 AC 514). The legacy of £5,000 to the psychotherapist might be analogous to the case of a private hospital.

However, the fact that the psychotherapist benefits personally from the gift militates against the recognition of charity in this case. In fact, in *Re Incorporated Council of Law Reporting for England and Wales* [1972] 1 Ch 73 the members of the Court of Appeal expressly doubted that the provision of 'tools of a trade' would be charitable.

CHAPTER NINE

VARIATION OF TRUSTS

9.1 Modes of Varying Trusts

9.1.1 THE RULE IN *SAUNDERS* v *VAUTIER*

According to the rule in *Saunders* v *Vautier* (1841) 10 LJ Ch 354 an adult beneficiary who is solely and absolutely entitled to the trust property may bring the trust to an end. The trustee will hold the trust property on what is called a 'bare trust' for the sole beneficiary. Beyond this, and perhaps more remarkable, is the aspect of the rule which applies where there are several beneficiaries. If they are all *sui juris* (adult and of sound mind) and together absolutely entitled to the trust property, they may unanimously agree to terminate the trust and may demand that the trust property be handed over to them. The rule does not apply where the beneficiaries' interests are *contingent*.

9.1.2 TRUSTEE ACT 1925, s. 57

TRUSTEE ACT 1925

57. Power of court to authorise dealings with trust property

(1) Where in the management or administration of any property vested in trustees, any sale, lease, mortgage, surrender, release, or other disposition, or any purchase, investment, acquisition, expenditure, or other transaction, is in the opinion of the court expedient, but the same cannot be effected by reason of the absence of any power for that purpose vested in the trustees by the trust instrument, if any, or by law, the court may by order confer upon the trustees, either generally or in any particular instance, the necessary power for the purpose, on such terms, and subject to such provisions and conditions, if any, as the court may think fit and may direct in what manner any money authorised to be expended, and the costs of any transaction, are to be paid or borne as between capital and income.

(2) The court may, from time to time, rescind or vary any order made under this section, or may make any new or further order.

(3) An application to the court under this section may be made by the trustees, or by any of them, or by any person beneficially interested under the trust.

(4) This section does not apply to trustees of a settlement for the purposes of the Settled Land Act 1925.

ANKER-PETERSEN v *ANKER-PETERSEN* (1991) 16 LS GAZ 32, ChD

FACTS: The plaintiff, tenant for life of a fund held on the trusts of his father's will, applied to the court under s. 57 of the Trustee Act 1925, alternatively s. 1 of the Variation of Trusts Act 1958, for approval of an extension of the trustees' powers of investment. Under the will, moneys were to be invested as from time to time sanctioned by law for the investment of trust moneys; they were thus governed by the Trustee Investments Act 1961. The proposed extensions would give the trustees power (1) to invest in assets of any kind as if they were beneficial owners; (2) to delegate to investment managers; (3) to hold investments through nominees; and (4) to borrow money for any purpose. Beneficial interests under the will were not affected and the proposals were supported by all the defendants.

HELD: The proposals were approved. The judge stated that where the beneficial interests under the trusts would remain unaltered by the variation, it was preferable for such applications to be brought under s. 57 of the Trustee Act 1925 than under the Variation of Trusts Act 1958. The *Law Society Gazette* report summarised the findings of Judge Paul Baker QC in the following terms:

JUDGE PAUL BAKER QC: There seemed no reason to adopt a restrictive construction of s. 57, its manifest object being to enlarge the inherent administrative jurisdiction of the court—hitherto confined to cases of emergency—and there was a power 'either generally or in any particular instance' to effect a wide range of transactions, including investment. Despite the general terms of s. 1 of the Act of 1958, they did not seem to enlarge the scope of the powers which the court could authorise. If no alterations of beneficial interests were contemplated it was more convenient to use s. 57 of the Act of 1925, because the trustees were the natural persons who make the applications, the consent of every adult beneficiary was not essential and the court was not required to give consent on behalf of every category of beneficiary separately but—more realistically—would consider the interests collectively in income and in capital. Those factors led to a less costly application without imperilling the legitimate interests of the beneficiaries.

9.1.3   TRUSTEE ACT 1925, s. 53

TRUSTEE ACT 1925

53.   Vesting orders in relation to infant's beneficial interests
Where an infant is beneficially entitled to any property the courts may, with a view to the application of the capital or income thereof for the maintenance, education, or benefit of the infant, make an order—
  (a)   appointing a person to convey such property; or
  (b)   in the case of stock, or a thing in action, vesting in any person the right to transfer or call for a transfer of such stock, or to receive the dividends or income thereof, or to sue for and recover such thing in action, upon such terms as the court may think fit.

RE MEUX'S WT [1957] 2 All ER 630, ChD

FACTS: G was the life tenant of a will trust; G's sons would take in remainder. When his eldest son was still an infant G applied to court for an order varying the trust. The application was made under s. 53 of the Trustee Act 1925, requesting that a person be appointed to convey the infant's interest to G at a fair price. G would then re-settle the sale proceeds on terms similar to the original trust, except G would no longer have an interest under the trust and D would have a contingent interest rather than a vested interest.
HELD: The court could approve of the variation under s. 53 Trustee Act 1925 as an 'application . . . for . . . the benefit of the infant'.

WYNN-PARRY J: . . . There is, first, a sale, and that is a transaction, or part of the transaction; and, secondly, there is the application of the proceeds of sale by the proposed settlement. Counsel for the defendant trustees submitted that it was the sale of the reversion alone which would produce the benefit to the infant, namely, freedom from liability to what otherwise would be heavy estate duty, and that the application of moneys by settlement was something which was not of 'benefit' to the infant; and he further submitted that it was the application which must be beneficial and which alone could justify the sale.
    I agree with counsel that, if the proper way of looking at s. 53 and at the proposed transaction is to say that two separate transactions are involved, or, alternatively, that there is a transaction in which two steps are to be taken, it appears that I have no

jurisdiction. If, on the other hand, the proposed transaction can be regarded as a single transaction, the component parts of which ought not to be regarded separately for the purpose of seeing what is the impact thereon of the opening language of s. 53 of the Trustee Act 1925, then it appears to me that I should be justified in saying that, there being admittedly an application, this is a case in which the words 'with a view to the application of the capital or income thereof for the maintenance, education, or benefit of the infant' in s. 53 are satisfied.

I entirely accept that in this case the proposed settlement is not introduced in any way as a colourable transaction. It is an absolutely essential part of the transaction looked at as a whole, for no court would consider, in view of the limitations of the testator's will, that it would be fair to those whose interests come after that of the first defendant, merely to bar the entail and sell the property without making provision for their interests. That consideration leads me inevitably to the conclusion that what I am dealing with in this case is one single transaction which I am not entitled to cut up in separate pieces, as suggested by counsel for the defendant trustees. When looked at as one transaction, there can be no doubt whatsoever that the transaction is one of which it may be postulated that it is overwhelmingly in favour of the first defendant, and, indeed, of the other infant defendants. I come, therefore, to the conclusion that, for the reasons which I have given, this case is distinguishable from *Re Heyworth's Settlements* [1956] 2 All ER 21, and that the court has jurisdiction to approve a transaction on the lines indicated in the question and involving a settlement on the lines of the exhibit to which I have referred. The details of the settlement will have to be dealt with in chambers.

9.1.4 VARIATION OF TRUSTS ACT 1958

See **9.2** below.

9.1.5 VARIATION UNDER THE COURT'S INHERENT JURISDICTION

RE NEW [1901] 2 Ch 534, ChD

FACTS: The trustees wished to approve a proposal to reorganise a limited company in which the trust owned shares, but they had no power to do so. The beneficiaries could not approve the reorganisation because they were not all *sui juris,* but the reorganisation would certainly have been to their benefit. Accordingly the trustees applied to the court for a variation under the court's inherent jurisdiction.
HELD: The court could approve the variation under its inherent jurisdiction to alter the administration of a trust in cases of 'emergency', where circumstances have arisen which the settlor of the trust had not foreseen and had not made provision for. Such variations would be approved only where the variation was desirable in the best interests of the beneficiaries.

ROMER LJ: As a rule, the Court has no jurisdiction to give, and will not give, its sanction to the performance by trustees of acts with reference to the trust estate which are not, on the face of the instrument creating the trust, authorised by its terms. The cases of *In re Crawshay* WN (1888) 246, decided by North J, and *In re Morrison* [1901] 1 Ch 701, decided by Buckley J, are instances where the Court was asked to sanction steps to be taken by trustees which it thought unjustifiable, and which it declared it had no jurisdiction to authorise. But in the management of a trust estate, and especially where that estate consists of a business or shares in a mercantile company, it not infrequently happens that some peculiar state of circumstances arises for which provision is not expressly made by the trust instrument, and which renders it most desirable, and it may be even essential, for the benefit of the estate and in the interest of all the *cestuis que trust,* that certain acts should be done by the trustees which in ordinary circumstances they would have no power to do. In a case of this kind, which may reasonably be supposed to be one not foreseen or anticipated by the author of the trust, where the trustees are embarrassed by the emergency that has arisen and the duty cast upon them to do what is best for the estate, and the consent of all the beneficiaries cannot be obtained by reason of some of them not being sui juris or in existence, then it may be right for the Court, and the Court in a proper case would have jurisdiction, to sanction on behalf of all concerned such acts on behalf of the trustees as we have above referred to. By way merely of illustration, we may take the case where a testator has declared that some property of his shall be sold at a particular time after his death, and then, owing to unforeseen change of circumstances since the testator's death, when the time for sale arrives it is found that to sell at that precise time would be ruinous to the estate, and that it is necessary or right to postpone the sale for a short time in order to effect a proper sale: in such a case the Court would have jurisdiction to authorise, and would authorise, the trustees to postpone the sale for a reasonable time.

It is a matter of common knowledge that the jurisdiction we have been referring to, which is only part of the general administrative jurisdiction of the Court, has been constantly exercised, chiefly at chambers. Of course, the jurisdiction is one to be exercised with great caution, and the Court will take care not to strain its powers. It is impossible, and no attempt ought to be made, to state or define all the circumstances under which, or the extent to which, the Court will exercise the jurisdiction; but it need scarcely be said that the Court will not be justified in sanctioning every act desired by trustees and beneficiaries merely because it may appear beneficial to the estate; and certainly the Court will not be disposed to sanction transactions of a speculative or risky character. But each case brought before the Court must be considered and dealt with according to its special circumstances. As a rule, these circumstances are better investigated and dealt with in chambers. Very often they involve matters of a delicate and private nature, the publication of which is not requisite on any good ground and might cause great injury to the trust estate.

With these general observations we pass to the cases now before us. The circumstances and the evidence have been considered by us. We do not think it is necessary to refer to them in detail. We need only say that they relate to a prosperous limited company whose shares are fully paid up, and to a condition of affairs that has arisen which makes it desirable, in the interests of all the shareholders, that by their consent the company should be reconstituted by the company being wound up and a new company formed to take over its assets. The new company is to be like the old company, except that the capital is larger and that the new company will have power to issue debentures. The shares in the old company will be represented by fully paid-up shares and debentures in the new company. Every shareholder who is sui juris agrees to the scheme; but some shares are held by trustees who wish the sanction of the Court to their assenting on behalf of beneficiaries who are not sui juris or not in existence, the other beneficiaries agreeing. We understand that Cozens-Hardy J was himself satisfied that the course proposed to be adopted by the trustees was one which, if it could be, should be sanctioned by the Court. We think, under the circumstances of the case, that the Court has jurisdiction to sanction, and ought to sanction, the proposed acts of the trustees. But the evidence should be supplemented so as to make clearer the points urged in the course of the argument before us as to the importance of further capital being provided by the proposed reconstruction of the company, the issue of debentures by the new company, and the difficulties that will arise if the trustees are obliged to stand aloof and to take no part in any reconstruction. Then, in the cases where the trustees are not by the terms of the trust instrument authorised to invest in the shares or debentures of such a company as the proposed new company, they must undertake to apply to the Court for leave to further retain the shares and debentures they will obtain under the scheme of reconstruction, if they desire to retain them beyond one year from the time the reconstruction is carried out.

9.1.6 COMPROMISE OF DISPUTES—A DUBIOUS JURISDICTION TO 'VARY' TRUSTS

CHAPMAN v *CHAPMAN* [1954] AC 429, HL

FACTS: A variation was sought to achieve certain tax advantages for infant and unborn beneficiaries. The variation was sought under the court's inherent jurisdiction to compromise disputes.

HELD: The court could vary a trust under that inherent jurisdiction only in cases of genuine dispute; the jurisdiction could not be used to sanction a bargain made by the beneficiaries *inter se*. The general view of their Lordships was that a so-called 'variation' by compromising a dispute was not really a variation at all, because when a genuine dispute is resolved the compromised-solution ought to represent the proper original state of the trusts as the settlor/testator had intended them. (Lord Cohen disagreed on this point.)

LORD SIMONDS LC: . . . This brings me to the question which alone presents any difficulty in this case. It is whether this fourth category, which I may call the compromise category, should be extended to cover cases in which there is no real dispute as to rights and, therefore, no compromise, but it is sought by way of bargain between the beneficiaries to rearrange the beneficial interests under the trust instrument and to bind infants and unborn persons to the bargain by order of the court.

My Lords, I find myself faced at once with a difficulty which I do not see my way to overcome. For though I am not as a rule impressed by an argument about the difficulty of drawing the line since I remember the answer of a great judge that, though he knew not when day ended and night began, he knew that midday was day and midnight was night, yet in the present case it appears to me that to accept this extension in any degree is to concede exactly what has been denied. It is the function of the court to execute a trust, to see that the trustees do their duty and to protect them if they do it, to direct them if they are in doubt and, if they do wrong, to penalise them. It is not the function of the court to alter a trust because alteration is thought to be advantageous to an infant beneficiary. It was, I thought, significant that counsel was driven to the admission that since the benefit of the infant was the test, the court had the power, though in its discretion it might not use it, to override the wishes of a living and expostulating settlor, if it assumed to know better than he what was beneficial for the infant. This would appear to me a strange way for a court of conscience to execute a trust. If, then, the court has not, as I hold it has not, power to alter or rearrange the trusts of a trust instrument, except within the limits which I have defined, I am unable to see how that jurisdiction can be conferred by pleading that the alteration is but a little one. . . .

9.1.7 SETTLED LAND

SETTLED LAND ACT 1925

64. General power for the tenant for life to effect any transaction under an order of the court

(1) Any transaction affecting or concerning the settled land, or any part thereof, or any other land (not being a transaction otherwise authorised by this Act, or by the settlement) which in the opinion of the court would be for the benefit of the settled land, or any part thereof, or the persons interested under the settlement, may, under an order of the court, be effected by a tenant for life, if it is one which could have been validly effected by an absolute owner.

(2) In this section 'transaction' includes any sale [. . .] exchange, assurance, grant, lease, surrender, reconveyance, release, reservation, or other disposition, and any purchase or other acquisition, and any covenant, contract, or option, and any application of capital money [. . .] and any compromise or other dealing, or arrangement; [. . .] and 'effected' has the meaning appropriate to the particular transaction; and the references to land include references to restrictions and burdens affecting land.

9.2 Variation of Trusts Act 1958

VARIATION OF TRUSTS ACT 1958

1. Jurisdiction of courts to vary trusts

(a) Where property, whether real or personal, is held on trusts arising, whether before or after the passing of this Act, under any will, settlement or other disposition, the court may if it thinks fit by order approve on behalf of—

(a) any person having, directly or indirectly, an interest, whether vested or contingent, under the trusts who by reason of infancy or other incapacity is incapable of assenting, or

(b) any person (whether ascertained or not) who may become entitled, directly or indirectly, to an interest under the trusts as being at a future date or on the happening of a future event a person of any specified description or a member of any specified class of persons, so however that this paragraph shall not include any person who would be of that description, or a member of that class, as the case may be, if the said date had fallen or the said event had happened at the date of the application to the court, or

(c) any person unborn, or

(d) any person in respect of any discretionary interest of his under protective trusts where the interest of the principal beneficiary has not failed or determined,
any arrangement (by whomsoever proposed, and whether or not there is any other person beneficially interested who is capable of assenting thereto) varying or revoking all or any of the trusts, or enlarging the powers of the trustees of managing or administering any of the property subject to the trusts:

Provided that except by virtue of paragraph (d) of this subsection the court shall not approve an arrangement on behalf of any person unless the carrying out thereof would be for the benefit of that person.

(2) In the foregoing subsection 'protective trusts' means the trusts specified in paragraphs (i) and (ii) of subsection (1) of section thirty-three of the Trustee Act 1925, or any like trusts, 'the principal beneficiary' has the same meaning as in the said subsection (1) and 'discretionary interest' means an interest arising under the trust specified in paragraph (ii) of the said subsection (1) or any like trusts.

(3) . . . the jurisdiction conferred by subsection (1) of this section shall be exercisable by the High Court, except that the question whether the carrying out of any arrangement would be for the benefit of a person falling within paragraph (a) of the said subsection (1) shall be determined by order of the authority having jurisdiction under Part VII of the Mental Health Act 1983, if that person is a patient within the meaning of the said Part VII.

(4) . . .

(5) Nothing in the foregoing provisions of this section shall apply to trusts affecting property settled by Act of Parliament.

(6) Nothing in this section shall be taken to limit the powers conferred by section sixty-four of the Settled Land Act 1925, section fifty-seven of the Trustee Act 1925, or the powers of the authority having jurisdiction under Part VII of the Mental Health Act 1983.

9.2.1 HOW DOES THE VARIATION OCCUR?

RE HOLT'S SETTLEMENT [1968] 1 All ER 470, ChD

FACTS: The plaintiff, a life tenant under a trust, made an application to vary the trusts under which she held her interest. Under the proposed variation she would surrender half her income as life tenant, which income would be accumulated for her children. According to the original trusts her children were to take in remainder upon their attaining 21; under the proposed variation they would have to attain the age of 30 before their interests would vest in possession. Under the proposed scheme the variation would take place by resettling the income on new trusts with the new terms. It was argued that the Perpetuities and Accumulations Act would apply to the new trusts, as the Act applied to all 'instruments' taking effect after the commencement of the Act in 1964.
HELD: On the preliminary question, whether the variation was effected by the court order approving the arrangement or whether the variation was effected by the arrangement itself, it was held that the variation was effected by the arrangement, the court order being effective merely to provide the necessary consents of certain persons to the arrangement varying the trusts. In any event, the court order and the arrangement could together constitute an 'instrument' for the purposes of the Perpetuities and Accumulations Act 1964, thus validating certain provisions in the proposed new trusts which relied for their legitimacy upon the 1964 Act. It was further held that, although the arrangement

would involve the revocation of the original trusts and the resettlement of the income under new trusts, this process could properly be described as a 'variation' of the original trusts. As a final point, the court was asked to approve the arrangement on behalf of persons unborn who might become entitled under the trusts. It was held that, in deciding to consent to the proposal on their behalf, the court was entitled to take the sort of risks that an adult beneficiary would have been prepared to take on their own behalf when considering whether to approve the variation. On this latter point *Re Cohen's Will Trusts* was applied and *Re Cohen's Settlement Trusts* was distinguished.

MEGARRY J: . . . the basic issue is whether an order under the Act of 1958 by itself varies the terms of the trust. Put rather differently, the question is whether the Act of 1958 does no more than empower the court to supply on behalf of the infants, unborn persons and others mentioned in s. 1(1), that binding approval which they cannot give, leaving the other beneficiaries to provide their own approvals in some other document which will bind them. In the present case the arrangement was drafted on the assumption that the order of the court will ipso facto vary the terms of the trusts, for the 'operative date' is defined as being the date of the order approving this arrangement, and the perpetuity period and the accumulation period (which are made use of in the terms of the trusts) each commence on the operative date.

The only authority directly on the point which has been cited to me is the decision in *Re Viscount Hambleden's Will Trusts* [1960] 1 All ER 353. I do not think I need read the provisions of the trusts in that case. It was a summons under the Act of 1958 and the judgment of Wynn-Parry J, as reported, is very short. The report does however, include certain interlocutory observations. Wynn-Parry J, made it clear that his view was that the order of the court ipso facto varied the trusts. He had had cited to him the decision of Vaisey J, in *Re Joseph's Will Trusts* [1959] 3 All ER 474n where that learned judge had inserted words in the order of the court which authorised and directed the trustees to carry the arrangement into effect. Wynn-Parry J, said:

> I do not agree with that decision. I take the view that I have no jurisdiction to make an order including words directing the trustees to carry the arrangement into effect, and those words should be deleted from the draft minutes. Nothing is required except the approval of the court to the arrangement. If that approval is given, the trusts are ipso facto altered, and the trustees are bound thereafter to give effect to the arrangement.

. . . The argument against the doctrine of ipso facto variation as laid down in the *Hambleden* case (an argument for which counsel do not bear the sole responsibility) is somewhat as follows. It starts with the well-known mischief which the Act of 1958 was designed to meet, a mischief confirmed by the House of Lords decision in *Chapman* v *Chapman* [1954] AC 429. If under a trust every possible beneficiary was under no disability and concurred in the re-arrangement or termination of the trusts then under the doctrine of *Saunders* v *Vautier* (1841) 10 LJ Ch 354, those beneficiaries could dispose of the trust property as they thought fit; for in equity the property was theirs. Yet if any beneficiary was an infant, or an unborn or unascertained person, it was held that the court had no general inherent or other jurisdiction to concur in any such arrangement on behalf of that beneficiary. Accordingly, some while after the decision of the House of Lords to this effect the Act of 1958 conferred on the court the power contained in s. 1. But, proceeds the argument, that Act did no more than allow the court to provide the binding assent which the infant himself could not provide, and the wording of the Act of 1958, shows this to be so. The Act merely provides that '. . . the court may if it thinks fit by order approve on behalf of [the infants] any arrangement . . . varying or revoking all or any of the trusts . . . '; so that all Parliament has done is to empower the court to provide the binding approval of an arrangement which the infants themselves could not give. . . .

Counsel for the trustees boldly asserted that, when correctly read, the Act of 1958 indirectly did what *Re Viscount Hambleden's Will Trusts* said it did. He went back to the words of s. 1(1) and emphasised that the power of the court was a power exercisable 'by order' and that that power was a power to approve an arrangement 'varying or revoking' all or any of the trusts. In emphasising those phrases, he said that the right way to read the section was to say that the power of the court was merely a power to make an order approving an arrangement which in fact varied or revoked the trusts, and not an arrangement which failed to do any such thing. When the adults by their counsel assented to the arrangement and the court on behalf of the infants by order approved the arrangement, then there was an arrangement which varied or revoked the trusts. So the order of the court both conferred jurisdiction and exercised it. . . .

Rather than read into the Act of 1958 words that are not there, said counsel, one should construe the Act of 1958 as authorising an order which is efficacious to achieve its avowed object. He pointed to the long title of the Act of 1958 which reads: 'An Act to extend the jurisdiction of courts of law to vary trusts in the interests of beneficiaries and sanction dealings with trust property'. I hope that counsel for the trustees, too, will pardon me if I say that I did not find his argument compelling. Indeed, at times I think it tended to circularity. But I find it tempting; and I yield. It is not a construction which I think the most natural. But it is not an impossible construction; it accords with the long title; it accords with the practice which has been relied on for many years in some thousands of cases; and it accords with considerations of convenience. The point is technical, and I do not think that I am doing more than straining a little at the wording in the interests of legislative efficacy. . . .

Finally, before turning to the second main point, I should mention that in this case the arrangement carries out its purpose by revoking all the existing trusts and establishing a new set of trusts. That being so, it is said that some difficulty arises on the wording of s. 1(1) of the Act of 1958. This merely empowers the court to approve an arrangement 'varying or revoking all or any of the trusts', and so, it is said, the court cannot approve an arrangement which, instead of merely 'revoking' or merely 'varying', proceeds to revoke and then to set up new trusts, thereby producing an effect equivalent to the process of settlement and resettlement. The section, it is argued, says nothing of establishing new trusts for old. As a matter of principle, however, I do not really think that there is anything in this point, at all events in this case. Here the new trusts are in many respects similar to the old. In my judgment, the old trusts may fairly be said to have been varied by the arrangement whether the variation is effected directly by leaving some of the old words standing and altering others, or indirectly, by revoking all the old words and then setting up new trusts partly, though not wholly, in the likeness of the old. One must not confuse machinery with substance; and it is the substance that matters. Comparing the position before and after the arrangement takes effect, I am satisfied that the result is a variation of the old trusts, even though effected by the machinery of revocation and resettlement. . . .

. . . Under an arrangement approved by the court the trusts may be brought wholly to an end. On the other hand they may be varied, and there is no limit, other than the discretion of the court and the agreement of the parties, to the variation which may be made. Any variation owes its authority not to anything in the initial settlement but to the statute and the consent of the adults coming, as it were, *ab extra*. This certainly seems to be so in any case not within the Act where a variation or resettlement is made under the doctrine of *Saunders* v *Vautier* [1835–42] All ER Rep 58, by all the adults joining together, and I cannot see any real difference in principle in a case where the court exercises its jurisdiction on behalf of the infants under the Act of 1958. . . .

The point that at one stage troubled me concerns the unborn issue. Counsel for the trustees, as in duty bound, put before me a contention that it was possible to conceive of an unborn infant who would be so circumstanced that the proposed rearrangement would be entirely to his disadvantage. He postulated the case of a child born to Mrs Wilson next year, and of Mrs Wilson dying in childbirth, or shortly after the child's birth. In such a case, he said the benefit of the acceleration of interest resulting from Mrs Wilson surrendering the moiety of her life interest would be minimal, and there would be no saving of estate duty. All that would happen in regard to such an infant would be that the vesting of his interest would be postponed from age twenty-one to age thirty, and the only possible advantage in that would be the non-financial moral or social advantage to which I have just referred. In support of this contention he referred me to the decision of Stamp, J, in *Re Cohen's Settlement Trusts, Eliot-Cohen* v *Cohen* [1965] 3 All ER 139. There, the scheme originally proposed was not approved by the court because there was a possibility of there being a beneficiary who would get no advantage whatsoever from the proposed arrangement; it would merely be to his detriment.

Counsel for the plaintiff, however, points out that there is an essential distinction between that case and this; for there, whatever the surrounding circumstances, the unborn person contemplated could not benefit from the arrangement. In the present case, he says, all that counsel for the trustees has done is to put forward the case of an infant who might be born next year; and it would be a result of the surrounding circumstances, and not of the time of birth or the characteristics of the infant, that that infant might derive no benefit from the arrangement proposed. Counsel for the plaintiff referred me to *Re Cohen's Will Trusts, Re Cohen's Settlement Trusts* [1959] 1 WLR 865, where Danckwerts J, held that in exercising the jurisdiction under the Act of 1958 the court must, on behalf of those persons for whom it was approving the arrangement, take the sort of risk which an adult would be prepared to take. Accordingly, says counsel for the plaintiff, counsel for the trustees' special infant to be born next year was in the position that although there was the chance that its mother would die immediately afterwards, there was also the alternative chance that its mother would survive his birth for a substantial period of time. In the latter event, which was the more probable, the advantages of the arrangement would accrue to the infant. In short, he distinguished the decision of Stamp J, in *Re Cohen's Settlement Trusts* on the footing that that was the case of an unborn person whose prospects were hopeless, whatever the events, whereas in the present case the hypothetical unborn person has the normal prospects of events occurring which will either improve or not improve his position. Such an unborn person falls, he says, into the category of unborn persons on whose behalf the court should be prepared to take a risk if the arrangement appears on the whole to be for their benefit.

It seems to me that this is a proper distinction to make, and I accept it. Accordingly, I hold that the arrangement is for the benefit of the classes of persons specified in s. 1(1) of the Act of 1958, and I approve it.

9.2.2   CONSENTS GIVEN BY THE COURT

9.2.2.1   Persons under legal disability (s. 1(1)(a))

This class includes infants and any other persons who are incapable of assenting to the arrangement varying the trusts. Included in this categaory would be persons of unsound mind and certain persons suffering from severe physical disability.

9.2.2.2   Persons with mere expectations (s. 1(1)(b))

RE SUFFERT'S SETTLEMENT [1960] 3 All ER 561, ChD

FACTS: An application was made to vary a settlement. Under the original terms of the settlement, the applicant had a life interest in the fund under a protective trust and her children would take in the remainder upon their attaining 21. If she had no children she could exercise a general power of appointment over the remainder in favour of persons of her choice. In default of exercising the power of appointment the fund would pass to her statutory next-of-kin. At the date of the application her statutory next-of-kin were three adult cousins. One of these cousins had been joined as a respondent to the application and had given approval to the proposed arrangement varying the trusts. The applicant was, in fact, a childless spinster aged 61.

HELD: The court made an order approving the variation and gave consent on behalf of persons unborn and unascertained who might have become entitled under the terms of the original settlement. However, the judge stated that the order would not be effective to bind the applicant's two adult cousins who had not joined in the application. The court could not consent to the arrangement on their behalf as they fell within the proviso to s. 1(1)(b) of the Variation of Trusts Act 1958, and they must give their own consent before the arrangement could be binding on them. The two cousins came within the proviso because they would have been the applicant's 'next-of-kin' had the applicant died on the date of her application to court.

BUCKLEY J: . . . The arrangement is one which, I think, it is proper to approve on behalf of any persons who may become entitled under the trusts of the settlement at the death of the applicant, whose interests I am able to bind under the Variation of Trusts Act 1958.

The persons who would be her next of kin if she were to die today are the fourth respondent and two other cousins who are not parties but are sui juris; and the question which I have to decide is how s. 1 of the Act of 1958 is applicable to such case. Section 1(1) provides:

> Where property, whether real or personal, is held on trusts arising, whether before or after the passing of this Act, under any will, settlement or other disposition, the court may if it thinks fit by order approve on behalf of . . . (b) any person (whether ascertained or not) who may become entitled, directly or indirectly, to an interest under the trusts as being at a future date or on the happening of a future event a person of any specified description or a member of any specified class of persons . . .

Pausing there, the persons who would take in default of appointment under cl. 5 of the settlement, as being what I shall shortly call the statutory next of kin of the applicant are, I think, a specified class of persons. They are a specified class of persons who may become entitled to an interest under the trusts at a future date. It cannot be ascertained at present because, of course, it is not possible to ascertain anybody's statutory next of kin while that person is alive. Down to that point it seems to me that the terms of the section are appropriate to apply to them, subject to what I shall say about the argument of counsel for the applicant. Then the subsection goes on:

> so however that this paragraph shall not include any person who would be of that description, or a member of that class, as the case may be, if the said date had fallen or the said event had happened at the date of the application to the court.

The date of the application to the court must, I think, be the date on which the originating summons was issued. I should have thought at first glance, at any rate, that what the subsection required, in a case of this kind, was to treat the applicant as having died on the date of the issue of the summons, to find out who in that event would have been her statutory next of kin. Any persons (excluding infants, because they come under a different heading in the Act) who were within that class would be persons whose interests, so the section provides, the court cannot bind. Counsel for the applicant has submitted, however, that that interpretation of the subsection would give rise to difficulties; and he says that there is no such class of persons as the next of kin of a person who is still alive and that there is no future date or future event to which it is possible to relate the ascertaining of that class. I find it difficult to follow that argument. Of course it is impossible to say who are the statutory next of kin of somebody who is alive, but it is not impossible to say who are the persons who would fill that description on a hypothesis that the propositus is already dead. Here there is a class of persons who will take an interest on the death of the applicant as life tenant, and they are a class of persons who will be ascertained on the death, so that they will acquire their interest and be ascertained at one and the same date. I feel unable to conclude that they are not persons who may become entitled to an interest under the trusts as being at a future date (namely, the death of the applicant) persons falling within the class of her statutory next of kin. If that view is right then the section provides that I cannot bind the interest of anyone who is at present in existence who would be a member of that class if the applicant had died on the date of the issue of the summons.

The order that I am prepared to make in this case will not, in my judgment, bind either of the two absent potential next of kin; and the result of that will be that the trustees will not be free, except at their own risk, to treat the trusts as effectively varied until they have obtained the consent of those two persons who have got contingent interests in the fund. If the consents of these two persons are obtained by the trustees then they will be protected as regards those two persons. The trustees will be protected as regards the fourth respondent by his consent which he gives here today, and they will be protected by my order in relation to any other persons who may become entitled to participate who are not at the moment in existence.

Counsel for the applicant says that this interpretation of the section would give rise to peculiar difficulties in certain other circumstances; for instance, if there were a case where protective trusts were declared in favour of a woman and the protective life interest had already determined at the date of the application, so that discretionary trusts had come into operation. He says that there would be difficulties then regarding any man who might become a husband of the woman in the future. He also says that it is difficult to apply the section to a case, for instance, where there is a trust for the persons who would be the statutory next of kin of A if A were to die at some arbitrarily fixed date in the future, because it is impossible to begin to adapt that class by assuming death at some other date. I do not feel that it is open to me, by reference to instances of that kind, to constrain what I think is the natural interpretation of the section and its application to the case before me. Those are cases which will have to be considered if and when they arise. In the present case, my view is that my order will not bind the two ladies who are not parties but are potential statutory next of kin, but I am willing to make an order to bind anyone else who is unborn and unascertained who might become interested.

RE MONCRIEFF'S SETTLEMENT TRUSTS [1962] 3 All ER 838, ChD

FACTS: An application was made to vary a settlement. Under the original terms the applicant held a life interest in the fund. On her death the fund would be held on trust for any of her children that she might appoint under a general power of appointment. In default of appointment the fund would be held on trust for her children in equal shares. If she had no children the fund would be held on trust for purposes or persons appointed by her will. In default of such appointment the fund was to be held for her statutory next-of-kin, assuming she had no husband. The applicant's only child was an adopted son; he was joined as the first respondent to the application. Other respondents were four cousins and the trustees of the settlement.

HELD: Approval was given for the arrangement varying the trusts. The court was able to consent on behalf of the adopted son because he was an infant and the variation would be for his benefit (Variation of Trusts Act 1958, s. 1(1)(a)). The court was also able to consent on behalf of the cousins under s. 1(1)(b), as they were persons who might become entitled in the future as being the applicant's 'next-of-kin'. Crucially, they would not be entitled as next-of-kin had the applicant died at the date of the application to court, accordingly the cousins did not fall within the proviso to s. 1(1)(b) and their own consent would not be required before approving the proposed arrangement for the variation of the trusts.

BUCKLEY J: . . . By virtue of s. 16 of the Adoption Act 1958, the first respondent (the applicant's adopted son) would be entitled to participate in any property as to which she dies intestate as though he were her child born in lawful wedlock. Therefore, if the applicant were to die today, the first respondent, subject to any rights of the applicant's husband, would be the only person entitled to any interest in any of her estate as to which she died intestate. I am not concerned with the interest of the husband because the trust in cl. 5 of the settlement is for persons who would be interested if she died a widow and intestate. Section 1(1) of the Variation of Trusts Act 1958, enables me to approve the arrangement on behalf of

> . . . (b) any person (whether ascertained or not) who may become entitled, directly or indirectly, to an interest under the trusts as being at a future date or on the happening of a future event a person of any specified description or a member of any specified class of persons . . .

The first respondent would fall within that description, but the paragraph goes on:

> . . . so however that this paragraph shall not include any person who would be of that description, or a member of that class, as the case may be, if the said date had fallen or the said event had happened at the date of the application to the court . . .

The first respondent is excluded, therefore, from the persons on whose behalf I can sanction the arrangement under s. 1(1)(b), but none of the other persons who might become entitled to participate in the estate of the applicant, were she to survive the first respondent and then die intestate, is excluded; because none of them would be within the class of next of kin if she died today. Therefore, I am in a position to approve the arrangement on behalf of all persons, whether ascertained or not, who might become interested in the applicant's estate at a future date with the exception of the first respondent.

At the time when the summons was drafted, the effect of that was not appreciated and certain persons were joined who would, in certain events, be the persons who would be the applicant's next of kin. In my view, it was unneccessary for those persons to be joined. Their interests can be looked after by the trustees, and they are persons who may never fall within the class of beneficiaries because they may predecease the applicant or the first respondent may survive the applicant. The summons could have been framed with the settlor as applicant and the first respondent and the trustees as respondents. I am not criticising counsel for the way in which the summons was framed, because at the time it was settled it was not realised that it was not necessary to join all possible future next of kin.

[His Lordship considered the scheme and approved it on behalf of the infants and all other persons who might thereafter become interested in the trust fund.]

KNOCKER v YOULE [1986] 2 All ER 914, ChD

FACTS: An application was made to vary a settlement. The applicants were the settlor's son and daughter. Under the original terms of the settlement, income was directed to be paid to the daughter at 21, for her life. She had a general power to appoint those who would take after her. In default of appointment the fund would be held on trust for the settlor's son. In the event that the trusts should fail, the income on the fund was to be paid to the settlor's wife for her life or until re-marriage, thereafter to be held on trust for the settlor's four sisters in equal shares, and for the sisters' issue upon the death of any of the sisters. At the date of the application to court the settlor's wife and four sisters had long since died. The question arose for consideration whether the court could grant its approval to the settlement on behalf of the sisters' numerous issue ('the cousins'). They had not been made respondents to the application.

HELD: The court would not approve the arrangement varying the trusts at this time and the summons was adjourned. 'Issue' of the four sisters would not fall within any of the categories of person detailed in s. 1(1) of the Variation of Trusts Act 1958 on whose behalf the court could give consent. They must give their own consent to the arrangement. Although their interests were very remote and contingent, they nevertheless had more than a mere expectation that they would acquire an interest under the trusts; they had an interest directly conferred by the settlement.

WARNER J: What counsel invited me to do was in effect to interpret the word 'interest' in s. 1(1) loosely, as a layman might, so as not to include an interest that was remote. I was referred to two authorities: *Re Moncrieff's Settlement Trusts* [1962] 3 All ER 838 and the earlier case of *Re Suffert's Settlement, Suffert v Martyn-Linnington* [1960] 3 All ER 561. In both those cases, however, the class in question was a class of prospective next of kin, and, of course it is trite law that the prospective or presumptive next of kin of a living person do not have an interest. They have only a spes successionis, a hope of succeeding, and quite certainly they are the typical category of persons who fall within s. 1(1)(b). Another familiar example of a person falling within that provision is a potential future spouse. It seems to me, however, that a person who has an actual interest directly conferred on him or her by a settlement, albeit a remote interest, cannot properly be described as one who 'may become' entitled to an interest.

The second difficulty (if one could think of a way of overcoming the first) is that there are, as I indicated earlier, 17 cousins who, if the failure or determination of the earlier trusts declared by the settlement had occurred at the date of the application to the court, would have been members of the specified class, in that they were then living and over 21. Therefore, they are *prima facie* excluded from s. 1(1)(b) by what has been conveniently called the proviso to it, that is to say the part beginning 'so however that this paragraph shall not include . . .' They are in the same boat, if I may express it in that way, as the first cousins in *Re Suffert's Settlement* and the adopted son in *Re Moncrieff's Settlement Trusts*. The court cannot approve the arrangement on their behalf; only they themselves can do so.

Counsel for the plaintiffs suggested that I could distinguish *Re Suffert's Settlement* and *Re Moncrieff's Settlement Trusts* in that respect for two reasons.

First, he suggested that the proviso applied only if there was a single event on the happening of which one could ascertain the class. Here, he said, both Mr Knocker and Mrs Youle must die without exercising their general testamentary powers of appointment to the full before any of the cousins could take anything. But it seems to me that what the proviso is referring to is the event on which the class becomes ascertainable, and that that is a single event. It is, in this case, the death of the survivor of Mrs Youle and Mr Knocker, neither of them having exercised the power to the full; in the words of cl. 7 of the settlement, it is 'the failure or determination of the trusts hereinbefore declared concerning the trust fund'.

The second reason suggested by counsel for the plaintiffs why I should distinguish the earlier authorities was that the event hypothesised in the proviso was the death of the survivor of Mr Knocker and Mrs Youle on the date when the originating summonses were issued, that is to say on 6 January 1984. There is evidence that on that day there were in existence wills of both of them exercising their testamentary powers to the full. The difficulty about that is that the proviso does not say '. . . so however that this paragraph shall not include any person who would have become entitled if the said event had happened at the date of the application to the court'. It says:

> . . . so however that this paragraph shall not include any person who would be of that description, or a member of that class, as the case may be, if the said date had fallen or the said event had happened at the date of the application to the court.

So the proviso is designed to identify the presumptive members of the class at the date of the application to the court and does not advert to the question whether at that date they would or would not have become entitled.

I was reminded by counsel of the principle that one must construe Acts of Parliament having regard to their purpose, and it was suggested that the purpose here was to exclude the need to join as parties to applications under the Variation of Trusts Act 1958 people whose interests were remote. In my view, however, that principle does not enable me to take the sort of liberty with the language of this statute that I was invited to take. It is noteworthy that remoteness does not seem to be the test if one thinks in terms of presumptive statutory next of kin. The healthy issue of an elderly widow who is on her deathbed, and who has not made a will, have an expectation of succeeding to her estate; that could hardly be described as remote. Yet they are a category of persons on whose behalf the court could, subject of course to the proviso, approve an arrangement under this Act. On the other hand, people in the position of the cousins in this case have an interest that is extremely remote. None the less, it is an interest, and the distinction between an expectation and an interest is one which I do not think that I am entitled to blur. So, with regret, having regard to the particular circumstances of this case, I have to say that I do not think that I have jurisdiction to approve these arrangements on behalf of the cousins.

I will stand the summonses over generally with liberty to any party to restore.

9.2.2.3   The unborn (s. 1(1)(c))

See *Re Holt's Settlement* at **9.2.1**.

PRACTICE DIRECTION, 27 July 1976 [1976] 3 All ER 160, ChD

1.   Where any infants or unborn beneficiaries will be affected by an arrangement under the Variation of Trusts Act 1958, evidence must normally be before the court which shows that their guardians ad litem or the trustees support the arrangement as being in the interests of the infants or unborn beneficiaries, and exhibits a case to counsel and counsel's written opinion to this effect. In nearly every case such a written opinion is

helpful, and in complicated cases it is usually essential to the understanding of the *guardian ad litem* and the trustees, and to the consideration by the court of the merits and the fiscal consequences of the arrangement.

2.   Where the interests of two or more infants, or two or more of the infants and unborn beneficiaries, are similar, a single written case to counsel and opinion will suffice; and no case to counsel or written opinion is required in respect of those who fall within the proviso to s. 1(1) of the 1958 Act (discretionary interests under protective trusts). Further, in proper cases the requirement of a case to counsel and a written opinion may at any stage be dispensed with by the master or the judge.

3.   The effect of this practice direction is to extend to variations of trusts the long-established practice in the Chancery Division of requiring a case to counsel and counsel's opinion when proceedings in which an infant is interested are compromised: see the Supreme Court Practice.

By the direction of the Vice-Chancellor.

9.2.2.4 Protective trusts (s. 1(1)(d))

See Trustee Act 1925, s. 33 at **2.2.1**.

9.2.3 THE BENEFIT REQUIREMENT

9.2.3.1 Financial benefits

In the great majority of cases, the benefit provided by the Act is a tax-planning advantage, and so, ultimately, a financial one.

9.2.3.2 Social and moral benefits

RE WESTON'S SETTLEMENTS [1968] 3 All ER 338, CA

FACTS: the plaintiff had settled two trusts in favour of his children. He now sought a variation of those trusts which would permit the trust to be exported to Jersey; this would involve the appointment of Jersey trustees and the transfer of the trust property to them. The application was made for the purpose of avoiding capital gains tax and estate duty.

HELD: The application for a variation failed.

LORD DENNING MR: . . . Before the Variation of Trusts Act 1958, there was much discussion as to the power of the court to sanction the variation of trusts. If the beneficiaries were all sui juris, they could agree between themselves to revoke or vary the trusts. If there were infant beneficiaries or unborn persons, it needed the consent of the court. But the jurisdiction of the court so to consent was very limited. The court could not sanction it except in case of a compromise of disputed rights, see *Chapman v Chapman* [1954] AC 429. By the Variation of Trusts Act 1958, this limitation was removed. The court has power to approve a variation or revocation of the trust, if it thinks fit, on behalf of infants or unborn persons. The statute gives no guide as to the way in which this discretion should be exercised. It provides: 'The court may *if it thinks fit* by order approve.' Likewise with the appointment of new trustees, the Trustee Act 1925, gives no guide. It simply says the court may appoint new trustees 'whenever it is expedient'. There being no guidance in the statutes, it remains for the court to do the best it can.

Two propositions are clear:—(i) in exercising its discretion, the function of the court is to protect those who cannot protect themselves. It must do what is truly for their benefit; (ii) it can give its consent to a scheme to avoid death duties or other taxes. Nearly every variation that has come before the court has tax avoidance for its principal object; and no-one has ever suggested that this is undesirable or contrary to public policy.

I think it necessary, however, to add this third proposition: (iii) the court should not consider merely the financial benefit to the infants or unborn children, but also their educational and social benefit. There are many things in life more worthwhile than money. One of these things is to be brought up in this our England, which is still 'the envy of less happier lands'. I do not believe it is for the benefit of children to be uprooted from England and transported to another country simply to avoid tax. It was very different with the children of the Seale family, which Buckley J, considered. That family had emigrated to Canada many years before, with no thought of tax avoidance, and had brought up the children there as Canadians. It was very proper that the trusts should be transferred to Canada. But here the family had only been in Jersey three months when they presented this scheme to the court. The inference is irresistible: the underlying purpose was to go there in order to avoid tax. I do not think that this will be all to the good for the children. I should imagine that, even if they had stayed in this country, they would have had a very considerable fortune at their disposal, even after paying tax. The only thing that Jersey can do for them is to give them an even greater fortune. Many a child has been ruined by being given too much. The avoidance of tax may be lawful, but it is not yet a virtue. The Court of Chancery should not encourage or support it—it should not give its approval to it—if by so doing it would imperil the true welfare of the children already born or yet to be born.

There is one thing more. I cannot help wondering how long these young people will stay in Jersey. It may be to their financial interest at present to make their home there permanently, but will they remain there once the capital gains are safely in hand, clear of tax? They may well change their minds and come back to enjoy their untaxed gains. Is such a prospect really for the benefit of the children? Are they to be wanderers over the face of the earth, moving from this country to that, according to where they can best avoid tax? I cannot believe that to be right. Children are like trees: they grow stronger with firm roots.

The long and short of it is, as the judge said, that the exodus of this family to Jersey is done to avoid English taxation. Having made great wealth here, they want to quit without paying the taxes and duties which are imposed on those who stay. So be it. If it really be for the benefit of the children, let it be done. Let them go, taking their money with them, but, if it be not truly for their benefit, the court should not countenance it. It should not give the scheme its blessing. The judge refused his approval. So would I. I would dismiss this appeal.

9.2.3.3   Benefit by deferral

RE T'S SETTLEMENT TRUSTS [1963] 3 All ER 759, ChD

FACTS: The applicant had a life interest in half of the trust fund; one remaining quarter was held on trust for the applicant's daughter upon her attaining 21 and the final quarter would pass to the daughter upon the applicant's death. The applicant sought the court's approval for a variation which would place the daughter's interest under protective trusts for her life on account of the daughter's immature and irresponsible attitude towards money.
HELD: The court refused to approve the variation as requested, but approved an alternative proposal under which the vesting of the daughter's interest would be postponed until she attained 30. She would hold a protected life interest in the meantime.

WILBERFORCE J: . . . When the case was first opened it appeared to me to be very doubtful whether a proposal of this kind was such as the court had power to approve under the Variation of Trusts Act 1958, or, if the jurisdiction existed, whether it was such an arrangement as the court in its discretion should approve. It was obvious that it differed widely from the normal type of arrangement submitted under the Act of 1958 when one or more beneficiaries under a trust ask the court to approve on behalf of other beneficiaries, being under a disability, or not in existence, a recasting of their respective interests in such a way as to improve those beneficiaries' position. Here the application is made by the infant's mother who has no interest under the particular trusts which are sought to be varied (she has only a life interest in a part of the trust funds which is not sought to be affected) and the only beneficial interest which is sought to be changed is that of the infant, which is, under the settlement as it stands, the maximum interest which a person may have, namely an absolute interest.

It was submitted by the applicant that the terms of s. 1 of the Variation of Trusts Act 1958, are very wide. Any arrangement may be approved and 'arrangement' has an extensive meaning (see *Re Steed's Will Trusts, Sandford* v *Stevenson* [1960] 1 Ch 407). The words ' by whomsoever proposed' allow any person, not necessarily a beneficiary, to apply to the court. The jurisdiction may be exercised whenever benefit is shown, and 'benefit' is a word of wide meaning: it is not restricted to material benefit. On this basis I was urged to approve the arrangement.

This argument, based on the language of the Act of 1958, has much force, but it seems to me necessary to bear in mind the following considerations. The Court of Chancery has never claimed for itself a power to direct a settlement of an infant's property. Indeed it has more than once been stated authoritatively that it cannot do so (see, for example, *Re Leigh, Leigh* v *Leigh* (1888) 40 ChD 290). It acquired under the Infant Settlements Act 1855, a limited jurisdiction to settle an infant's property on marriage, but this has not been extended to other cases. There is no reason to suppose that the absence of the wider jurisdiction was part of the mischief which the Act of 1958 was intended to remedy, and, in view of the well-accepted limits on the court's jurisdiction laid down by statute and authority, it seems unlikely that it was. I am certainly reluctant to suppose that a whole new jurisdiction has been incidentally conferred by the use of general words. There are obvious difficulties in attributing so wide a meaning to the Act of 1958. For example, is the court to consult the wishes of the infant? That is, as has been found here, a matter of considerable difficulty, and where, as here, the infant is nearly twenty-one, it seems preferable, if her wishes can be taken into account, to leave the matter over until she can decide for herself. Or can the court impose a settlement against the infant's wishes? To do this would involve going much further than the court goes under the Act of 1855 and would place on the court a heavy responsibility (which it does not have generally in variation of trusts applications) of considering and estimating the views of other persons (often including parents and medical and psychological experts) as to what is for the infant's benefit. No doubt in one sense or in one view it may be a benefit for a young person not to become possessed of a large sum of money at twenty-one, but I think that it would be quite wrong for the court simply on such considerations to claim jurisdiction to settle the property. It is obviously not possible to define exactly the point at which the jurisdiction of the court under the Variation of Trusts Act 1958, stops or should not be exercised. Moreover, I have no desire to cut down the very useful jurisdiction which this Act has conferred on the court, but I am satisfied that the proposal as originally made to me falls outside it. Though presented as a variation it is in truth a complete new re-settlement. The former trust funds were to be got in from the former trustees and held on totally new trusts such as might be made by an absolute owner of the funds. I do not think that the court can approve this. Alternatively, if it can, I think that it should not do so, because to do so represents a departure from well and soundly established principles.

As to its substance, the proposal goes much too far, because it is not confined to dealing in a beneficial way with the special requirements of this infant but seeks authorisation for a complete re-settlement, which could only be justified if the court accepted (as, in my view, it should not) that such a re-settlement is a 'benefit' within the meaning of the Act.

I have, on previous hearings, indicated to the parties that this was the view I took, and they have now, with my encouragement, submitted an alternative proposal, that is, that the infant's right to capital should be deferred for a period, she being given a protected life interest meanwhile. This proposal can take effect by way of variation of the settlement simply by introducing after the previous provision conferring on the infant an interest at twenty-one or marriage a clause to the effect that her share shall not then vest absolutely but shall be retained by the trustees on protective trusts for her until she attains the specified age, on which, if no forfeiture has occurred, she becomes entitled to the capital: if a forfeiture has occurred, the protective trusts are to continue with power to the trustees to bring them to an end when they think fit. The trustees will also have powers to advance capital, and there will be a special provision enabling the infant out of the fund to buy and equip a house. An arrangement of this kind is one which I can, in the circumstances, approve.

On the evidence, which I have fully considered in chambers and to which I shall not refer in detail here, it appears to me to be a definite benefit for this infant for a period during which it is to be hoped that independence may bring her to maturity and responsibility to be protected against creditors (in fact to a greater extent than she would be protected if she were left to set up a similar trust herself at twenty-one) and this is the kind of benefit which seems to me to be within the spirit of the Act of 1958.

I desire to make it plain that it is only because a strong case on the facts is made out for protection of this nature that, even to this extent, I am willing, so close to this infant's majority, to interfere with the dispositions of the settlement. I approve on behalf of the infant the arrangement in the schedule.

9.2.3.4   The benefit of familial harmony

RE TINKER'S SETTLEMENT [1960] 3 All ER 85, ChD

FACTS: An application was made to vary a settlement. The applicant was the settlor, the respondents were his son and daughter, both of whom were beneficiaries under the settlement. The son would take an absolute interest in half the settled fund upon the settlor's death, or upon the son attaining 30, whichever first occurred. If the son died before that age his share would accrue to the daughter. The daughter would attain a life interest in the other half of the fund upon her attaining 30, whichever first occurred. If the son died before that age his share would accrue to the daughter. The daughter would attain a life interest in the other half of the fund upon her attaining 30, the remainder to pass to such of her children as she should appoint, and in default of appointment the remainder would pass to her children in equal shares upon their attaining 21 (or, for females, earlier marriage). In the event of none of the daughter's children attaining a vested interest, that half of the fund would accrue to the settlor's son. At the date of the application to vary the trusts the income on the settled fund was being accumulated pending the vesting in possession of the beneficiaries' interests. The settlor applied for the settlement to be varied because he had not appreciated that, according to the terms of the settlement, if his son died before the settlor, or before attaining the age of 30, any children of the son then living would take no interest under the settlement because of the accruer in favour of the sister. He also wished the direction as to the accumulation of income to be removed.
HELD: The accumulation provision would be removed, but the judge refused to approve a variation whereby the accruer clause in favour of the sister would be removed. Such a variation would not be for the benefit of the sister's infant children and unborn issue.

RUSSELL J: I am prepared to approve under s. 1 of the Variation of Trusts Act 1958, an arrangement by which the trusts of the settlement of April 4, 1951, are altered so as to put an end to the accumulation period, that is, to approve the arrangement of which approval is sought under para. (1) of the summons. The accumulation period must necessarily relate to the death of the settlor when the trusts might become extinct and give rise to a liability for estate duty., I have no doubt that in the case of the son's half it will mean that income which would probably have accumulated for the next four and a half years with additional benefit to capital will not now do so, and, in the case of the daughter's half, income which would probably have accumulated for the next nine years will not now do so. Nevertheless, weighing the risks one against the other, it must be for the benefit of the next generation, for whom I am now concerned, that the trust for accumulation should be ended.

I am, however, also asked under para. (2) of the summons to approve an arrangement to cover a defect in the settlement. The son is given by the settlement the capital of his half absolutely on attaining thirty, and it is provided that if he die under thirty his half goes over to his sister's half, which is settled on her for life with the remainder to her children; and the defect, it will be observed, is that if he has children himself in the next four and a half years (before he is thirty) and then dies under thirty no part of his half will go for the benefit of his children, but it will all go over to his sister's half, There is some evidence, in the form of an affidavit by the settlor, to suggest that there is a possible claim for rectification of the settlement, so as to procure that the son's half in the event shall go to his own children. I do not think that I need rehearse the details of it, but it is quite clear that, before I sanction this arrangement, which involves half of the son's share being given, in the event mentioned, to his children and not accruing to the daughter's half, I must be satisfied that the arrangement is beneficial to the unborn children of the daughter. It seems to me that it is one of the weakest claims for rectification that I have seen, perhaps only rivalled by that in *Constantinidi v Ralli* [1935] Ch 427 which was referred to in argument, and I cannot bring myself to think that I would be benefiting the daughter's children if I gave away half of that which will come to the daughter's share, if the son dies under thirty.

Counsel for the applicant has argued that this is a sensible and fair thing to do because somebody has blundered—somebody has forgotten about the son's children—and it would seem very hard that this half of this substantial settlement should go away from his children to his sister and her children. In a broad sense, so the argument runs, it would be beneficial to the sister's children as members of the family viewed as a whole that something which was reasonable and fair should be done. I cannot apply the jurisdiction under the Variation of Trusts Act 1958, in that broad way. Although it may very well be that one can throw that kind of consideration into the scale beside a financial benefit which has already been established, yet one cannot regard that sort of consideration as a benefit in itself. I would myself be only too pleased if I were able to approve this proposed arrangement, but, having regard to the type of claim for rectification which is adumbrated, I do not find myself able to approve such a compromise or arrangement or variation under the Act of 1958 as is sought under para. (2) of the summons.

RE REMNANT'S SETTLEMENT TRUSTS [1970] 1 Ch 560, ChD

FACTS: The testator of a will trust provided by clauses in his will that any of his grandchildren practising Roman Catholicism at the date of his daughter's death would thereby forfeit any entitlement to the fund. According to the testator's definition persons 'practise' Roman Catholicism if, *inter alia*, they have attended a Roman Catholic Church for worship at least once a year, or if they marry a Roman Catholic. An application was made to vary the trusts in several respects, including the removal of the forfeiture provision.
HELD: The court approved of the proposed arrangement for the variation of the trusts. Even though removal of the forfeiture provision carried the risk that certain family members, who would have taken in the event of forfeiture, might be financially worse off as a result of the variation, nevertheless the variation could properly be said to be for their benefit in the wider sense of that word, as tending towards familial harmony and marital choice.

PENNYCUICK J: The real difficulty arises as regards Mrs Hooper's children. Plainly since they are Protestants—and there is no reason to suppose that any of them will become a Roman Catholic—and since the Crosthwaite children may well all be Roman Catholics at the relevant time, the Hooper children have a real and substantial chance of taking under the forfeiture provisions the whole of the Merrial share. So, leaving other considerations apart, the deletion of the forfeiture provisions must be detrimental to them. However, that is by no means the end of the matter. In the first place they are being given an accelerated interest in £10,000. Then there are the non-financial considerations which seem to me to loom large in this matter.

The three considerations set out by Mrs Crosthwaite, and elaborated by counsel, are these: first, that the forfeiture provisions represent a deterrent to each of the Hooper children from adopting the Roman Catholic faith should she be minded to do so; secondly, that they operate as a deterrent to each of the Hooper children in the selection of a husband when the time comes; and thirdly, that the forfeiture provisions represent a source of possible family dissension. I am not sure that there is very much weight in the first of those considerations because there is no reason to suppose that any of these children has any particular concern with the Roman Catholic faith. On the other hand, I do think there is very real weight in the second and in the third considerations. Obviously a forfeiture provision of this kind might well cause very serious dissension between the families of the two sisters. On the best consideration I can give it I think that the deletion of the forfeiture provisions on the terms contained in the arrangement, including the provision for acceleration in £10,000, should be regarded as for the benefit of the three Hooper children.

I have not found this an easy point, but I think I am entitled to take a broad view of what is meant by 'benefit,' and so taking it, I think this arrangement can fairly be said to be for their benefit.

On that last point I was referred to *In re Weston's Settlements* [1969] 1 Ch 223, where Lord Denning MR said, at p. 245:

> But I think it necessary to add this third proposition: (iii) The court should not consider merely the financial benefit to the infants or unborn children, but also their educational and social benefit.

I do not think Lord Denning intended to use the words 'educational' and 'social' in any restrictive sense. I think the court is entitled and bound to consider not merely financial benefit but benefit of any other kind.

It remains to consider the children of Lord Remnant and Mrs Tyser. They are, of course, in an entirely different position because they can take nothing anyway, unless all the children of both the testator's daughters die young, or unless, alternatively, all the children of the testator's daughters incur a forfeiture. In their case I doubt whether the non-financial considerations, except perhaps the bar to family unity, are of any real significance. It must be very unlikely that any child of Lord Remnant would be influenced in his choice either of a religion or of a spouse by the possibility of receiving this extremely remote interest. It seems to me, however, that the small financial benefit which has been provided for these children is sufficient to represent a benefit to them in all the circumstances of the case. I need hardly say that the view which I have taken as regards benefit has been advanced by counsel for each class of infant concerned.

I conclude then that the carrying out of this arrangement will be for the benefit of all the persons born and unborn on whose behalf I am concerned to approve the arrangement.

It remains to consider whether the arrangement is a fair and proper one. As far as I can see, there is no reason for saying otherwise, except that the arrangement defeats this testator's intention. That is a serious but by no means conclusive consideration. I have reached the clear conclusion that these forfeiture provisions are undesirable in themselves in the circumstances of this case and that an arrangement involving their deletion is a fair and proper one. I propose accordingly to approve the arrangement with one or two modifications which are not material to this judgment.

I would only like to add this word of caution. The effect of any particular forfeiture provision must depend on the nature of the provision itself and upon the circumstances in which it is likely to operate. A forfeiture provision is by no means always intrinsically undesirable. Again, you may have the position that a forfeiture provision benefits exclusively one or the other party concerned, and in that case it might be very difficult to say that the deletion of the provision was for the benefit of that party, unless there was the fullest financial compensation. However, I am not concerned to go further into those matters. It is sufficient for me to say that on the facts of this particular case the deletion of the forfeiture provisions, upon the terms of the arrangement, is for the benefit of everyone concerned. . . .

9.2.3.5 Risks of detriment?

RE ROBINSON'S SETTLEMENT TRUSTS [1976] 3 All ER 61, ChD

FACTS: An application was made to vary the terms of a settlement. If approved the new arrangement would carry with it the risk that the beneficiaries might suffer a loss due to certain tax liabilities.
HELD: Approval would be given provided that some of the infant beneficiary's income entitlement was set aside to purchase insurance cover against the risk of a large capital transfer tax liability.

TEMPLEMAN J: This is an application under the Variation of Trusts Act 1958 which involves the division of a trust fund between life tenant and remaindermen. One of the remaindermen is an infant of about 17.

Under what might be termed the old-fashioned calculations for estate duty, such a division was comparatively simple. The rates of estate duty were such that the amount which a remainderman stood to inherit if nothing was done was usually very small. In most schemes it was possible to make a division whereby the remainderman took more in any event than he would otherwise take on the death of the life tenant.

. . . In the present instance figures have been produced which show, for example, that if nothing is done and capital transfer tax is paid on the death of the life tenant, the share of the infant will be somewhere between £58,000 and £60,000 if no alterations in the law are made in the meantime. Under the proposed arrangement, produced as a result of the independent advice of actuaries, the share which the remaindermen get is of a gross value of £58,000, and if capital transfer tax is payable—as to which there is a doubt in the present instance—the tax will reduce the share by something like £11,000 or £14,000. This entails a serious possibility of a loss accruing to the remaindermen. I was much pressed by all counsel, including counsel for the third defendant, with the observations of Stamp J in *Re Cohen's Settlement Trusts* [1965] 3 All ER 139 and of Danckwerts J in *Re Cohen's Will Trusts* [1959] 1 WLR 865 to the effect that a reasonable view of a bargain must be taken. It is not necessary to insist that in all possible circumstances the infant is bound to benefit. It is said that capital transfer tax may not be payable and, if it is, then even taking into account the possible shortfall of £14,000, there will be acceleration of the income of the share which the infant is to take, and her mother, the life tenant, is only about 55 years old, and so, in the normal course of events, acceleration will catch up with the shortfall.

Acceleration of income, at present rates of taxation on income, will take a good deal of catching up to compensate for a shortfall of £14,000. I cannot assume that the life tenant will live long enough to procure that the arrangement viewed as a whole will benefit the infant. I must be satisfied that the arrangement is beneficial.

I expressed doubts and sent the parties away to consider insurance. In the old days of estate duty insurance could be effected by the life tenant to make good any shortfall so far as the reversion was concerned. Capital transfer tax introduces a new complication in that an insurance policy effected and kept up by the life tenant may itself be liable to capital transfer tax with disastrous consequences.

Therefore, although it is slightly anomalous, if the infant is to be protected against the possibility of shortfall, that protection can only be, to some extent, at the expense of the infant in that a policy must be kept up out of income.

I am quite satisfied that it would not be sensible to leave matters entirely as they are. There are other people interested besides the infant, and to preserve the present trusts with present, and future, rates of income and capital taxation does not seem sensible. I am satisfied that the life tenant will only receive under the arrangement a reasonable and fair proportion having regard to the value of her life interest in her present situation.

In these circumstances I think I can accept the arrangement, provided that the infant's income is to a certain extent made available for insurance in order to protect the infant's own share against loss caused by the premature death of the life tenant. . . .

It seems to me if insurance of £8,000 with profits is effected, I can, relying on the observations of Stamp and Danckwerts JJ, approve this arrangement, although I still think it is a borderline case. Great powers of advocacy were used to persuade me that capital transfer tax has made such a change that the possible result of a death must be disregarded, the actuarial division accepted and a risk taken. I do not take that view. I start with the principle that all these schemes should, if possible, prove that an infant is not going to be materially worse off. There are difficulties with capital transfer tax, and borderline cases, and one may then have to take a broad view, but not a galloping, gambling view.

In my judgment, taking a reasonably prudent view, insurance of £8,000 in the present instance will be sufficient, and I am prepared to sanction the arrangement thus amended.

9.3   Resettlement or Variation?

See *Re Holt's Settlement* at **9.2.1**.

RE BALL'S SETTLEMENT [1968] 2 All ER 438, ChD

FACTS: An application was made to vary the terms of a settlement. Under the original terms the settlor had a life interest in the income of the fund, with a power to appoint his two sons (or their families) as beneficiaries in remainder. Neither family was to take more than half of the value of the fund under the power of appointment. Under the terms of the proposed new arrangement the two sons would be given life interests in half the fund each, then to their children in equal shares. The settlor's life interest and power of appointment would be removed.

HELD: The new arrangement would be approved as the changes were, in reality, likely to have effect merely upon the detail of the trust and would not change it in substance. The arrangement could properly be described as a 'variation'.

MEGARRY J: . . . On the summons as so amended the question is whether the arrangement can fairly be said to be covered by the word 'varying' so that the court has power to approve it.

There was some discussion of the ambit of this word in *Re Holt's Settlement, Wilson v Holt* [1968] 1 All ER 470. It was there held that if in substance the new trusts were recognisable as the former trusts, though with variations, the change was comprehended within the word 'varying', even if it had been achieved by a process of revocation and new declaration. In that case, the new trusts were plainly recognisable as the old trusts with variations. In the present case, the new trusts are very different from the old. The settlor's life interest vanishes: so does the power of appointment, though that will now be released. In place of the provision in default of appointment for absolute interests for the two sons if they survived the settlor, and if not, for their issue stirpitally, there is now a life interest for each son, and vested absolute interests for the children of the sons born before October 1, 1977. There is a clean sweep of the somewhat exiguous administrative provisions and an equally exiguous new set in their place. The arrangement also makes altogether new provisions for insurance policies, both those which provide for death duties and are to be added to the trust fund, and those which provide for the excluded persons and are to be held on separate trusts; but these portions of the arrangement, I should say, are not made part of the settlement as revised, but are to operate independently and outside its terms. All that remains of the old trusts are what I may call the general drift or purport, namely that a moiety of the trust fund is to be held on certain trusts for each son and certain of his issue. Is the word 'varying' wide enough to embrace so categorical a change? . . .

If an arrangement changes the whole substratum of the trust, then it may well be that it cannot be regarded merely as varying that trust. But if an arrangement, while leaving the substratum, effectuates the purpose of the original trust by other means, it may still be possible to regard that arrangement as merely varying the original trusts, even though the means employed are wholly different and even though the form is completely changed.

I am, of course, well aware that this view carries me a good deal farther than I went in *Re Holt*. I have felt some hesitation in the matter, but on the whole I consider that this is a proper step to take. The jurisdiction of the Act of 1958 is beneficial and, in my judgment, the court should construe it widely and not be astute to confine its beneficent operation. I must remember that in essence the court is merely contributing on behalf of infants and unborn and unascertained persons the binding assents to the arrangement which they, unlike an adult beneficiary, cannot give. So far as is proper, the power of the court to give that assent should be assimilated to the wide powers which the ascertained adults have.

In this case, it seems to me that the substratum of the original trusts remains. True, the settlor's life interest disappears; but the remaining trusts are still in essence trusts of half of the fund for each of the two named sons and their families, with defined interests for the sons and their children in place of the former provisions for a power of appointment among the sons and their children and grandchildren and for the sons to take absolutely in default of appointment. In the events which are likely to occur, the differences between the old provisions and the new may, I think, fairly be said to lie in detail rather than in substance. Accordingly, in my judgment, the arrangement here proposed, with the various revisions to it made in the course of argument, can properly be described as varying the trusts of the settlement. Subject to the summons being duly amended, I therefore approve the revised arrangement. I may add that since the hearing of this case I have considered the speeches of their lordships in *Re Holmden's Settlement Trusts, Inland*

Revenue Comrs. v *Holmden* [1968] 1 All ER 148, but although these suggest certain questions of interest and difficulty, I find in them nothing to make me resile from the views that I have expressed.

9.4   Exporting the Trust

RE SEALE'S MARRIAGE SETTLEMENT [1961] 3 WLR 262, ChD

FACTS: A married couple, beneficiaries under the settlement, were domiciled in England at the date of the settlement, but had since emigrated to Canada. They had three children, one of whom had recently attained 21 and would therefore be entitled to an interest in possession upon the death of both parents. The parents applied to the court for a variation of the trusts which would permit the English trustees to transfer the fund to Canadian trustees. Accordingly the applicants also asked the court to appoint a Canadian trust corporation in place of the English trustees.
HELD: The variation would be approved and the new trustees would be appointed.

BUCKLEY J: . . . Under section 1 of the Variation of Trusts Act 1958, the court has jurisdiction where property is held on trust under any will or settlement or other disposition to approve on behalf of the various classes of persons mentioned in the section any arrangement varying or revoking all or any of the trusts or enlarging the powers of the trustees of managing or administering any of the property subject to the trust. So far as I am aware this is the first case in which that jurisdiction is invoked for the purpose of converting an English trust into a trust governed by some other system of law. If it were merely a question of varying the trusts, it seems to me there might be difficulty in saying that this court could properly vary the trusts under the settlement by substituting trusts of a kind which would fall to be administered by some other law; but, having regard to the fact that the court can approve an arrangement which revokes all the trusts of the settlement, it seems to be clear that the court must have jurisdiction to approve an arrangement which, in effect, does revoke all the trusts of the English settlement in the event of the trust property becoming subject to the trusts of a settlement which would be recognised and enforced in some other jurisdiction. It seems to me I have jurisdiction to approve a scheme on the lines of the scheme I am asked to approve in the present case.

The evidence establishes to my satisfaction that the husband and the wife intend to continue to live in Canada, that their children who are living in Canada and have been brought up as Canadians are likely to continue to live in Canada, and that it will be for the general advantage of all the beneficiaries that the administrative difficulties and the difficulties of other kinds which result from the fact that it is an English settlement and the beneficiaries all reside in Canada should be brought to an end; and I am satisfied that the arrangement is sensible and advantageous for all concerned. . . .

See *Re Weston's Settlements* at **9.2.3.2.**

RE WINDEATT'S WT [1969] 2 All ER 324, ChD

FACTS: An application was made under section 1 of the Variation of Trusts Act 1958 for approval of an arrangement varying the will trusts. The applicant, the testator's daughter, had, at the date of the application, lived in Jersey for 19 years and her children had been born there. Her proposal was to appoint two trustees resident in Jersey in place of the sole surviving English trustee, and to transfer the trust fund to the newly appointed Jersey trustees to be held by them on trusts similar to the original will trust.
HELD: The court would approve of the arrangement. The applicant had satisfied the court that Jersey was the permanent family home.

PENNYCUICK J: . . . I think it is clear that I have jurisdiction to make the order. I was referred to *Re Seale's Marriage Settlement* [1961] 3 WLR 262 . . . This decision covers the matter of jurisdiction. I am told, also, that in at least two subsequent cases other judges have made comparable orders. The only difficulty results from *Re Weston's Settlement* [1969] 1 Ch 223, before Stamp J, and before the Court of Appeal. In that case, the judge on the particular facts of the case exercised his discretion under the Act to refuse to sanction an arrangement, and the Court of Appeal affirmed his decision. The judge in *Re Weston* referred to *Re Seale*, as did the Court of Appeal, without disapproval. *Re Weston* went on its own facts entirely, which were extremely striking. The settlor there, with his family, had moved to Jersey only a very short time before the application to the court was made. It might well be inferred that the whole object of moving to Jersey was to escape a particular fiscal liability, and it appeared that their stay in that country might well be transitory. . . .

It seems to me that *Re Weston's Settlements* was decided on its own particular facts, and on those facts it is a decision with which I am, if I may respectfully say so, in the most complete agreement. The facts of the case now before me are quite different. Here, the family has been in Jersey for 19 years and has made a genuine and permanent home in Jersey. The children were born there.

There is no other reason why it would not be right to exercise the jurisdiction in the present case. Accordingly I propose to make an order in the terms of the minutes proposed, subject to one small alteration in the proposed draft declaration of trust, which has been discussed, and a note of which will be endorsed on counsel for the plaintiff's brief.

9.5 The Settlor's Intentions

RE STEED'S WT [1960] 1 Ch 407, CA

FACTS: By the terms of the will trusts the testator left a farm to his housekeeper under a protective trust for her life. She had a power to appoint those who would take after her, and in default of appointment the farm would be held on trust for her next-of-kin. In the event she exercised the power of appointment in her own favour. Later, the trustees resolved to sell the farm under powers conferred by the will. Opposing the sale, the wife made an application to vary the trusts under the Variation of Trusts Act 1958, so that the trustees would thereafter hold the farm on trust for her absolutely. The trustees did not approve of the application.
HELD: The application was dismissed.

LORD EVERSHED MR: In the present case, the proposed variation (that is, the 'arrangement') which the plaintiff puts forward may be most briefly and accurately stated as involving this: in clause 9 of the will the words: 'upon protective trusts as defined by section 33 of the Trustee Act 1925,' should be omitted, and similarly in the next clause the word 'protective' should be omitted. If those words were omitted, the result would be that the plaintiff would become absolutely entitled to the property, because she would then be the life tenant, having appointed by irrevocable deed to herself the reversion; and that is what she seeks. . . .

The duty of the court, as I read the section on the facts of this case, is that they must approve it on behalf of the only person or persons who might have an interest under the discretionary trusts and whose presence under the trusts now prevents the plaintiff saying that she can put an end to the settlement.

Having regard to the plaintiff's age, no doubt it is true to say that she will not and cannot now have children, but she might marry, and marry more than once. She says, with some reason, that having lived for 53 years unmarried she does not feel in the least likely to marry now. That may well be right, though many have said that before and subsequent events have proved them wrong. That, however, is neither here nor there. There does exist a discretionary trust, and a future husband of the plaintiff's is a person interested under those trusts, on whose behalf the court must now approve the proposal.

Having regard to what has happened between the plaintiff and her brother, it is possible that, strictly speaking, there has been a forfeiture, and if so, the future husband or husbands would be within paragraph (b) of the subsection, but if not, he would be within paragraph (d). Again, I think that does not, for present purposes, matter.

I repeat that the duty of the court is now to consider whether in the exercise of its discretion, which is framed in the widest possible language, it should approve the arrangement on behalf of what has been described in argument as the spectral spouse of the plaintiff. In doing that, what must the court consider? Not, I conceive, merely the material benefit or detriment of such spouse. Certainly not if he is to be regarded as being a person under paragraph (d), though if he is to be regarded as falling under paragraph (b) it is expressly enjoined that the court shall not approve the arrangement unless it is for his benefit.

As I have said, I do not so read this Act as to mean that the court's duty in the exercise of this very wide and, indeed, revolutionary discretion is confined to saying: 'Would it really much harm this spectral spouse if we approve the proposal?' Bearing in mind, of course, the admitted possibility that the spouse might cease to be spectral and become a reality, I think what the court is bound to do is to see whether, looked at on behalf of the person indicated, it approves the arrangement. It is the arrangement which has to be approved, not just the limited interest of the person on whose behalf the court's duty is to consider it. . . .

Having so formulated the duty, I have, for my part, come to the conclusion that it would not be right for the court in the exercise of its discretion to approve this variation or arrangement. I am not uninfluenced in coming to that conclusion by any means by the circumstance that the judge obviously did not think it was a proposal which should be approved, though it is quite true that for reasons which I have indicated it may be said he was looking at it and basing his jurisdiction upon an interpretation of the section which I have not been altogether able to share, namely, it was his duty to approve it on behalf of the proposer, the plaintiff, and also that the scheme must be regarded as intended to be in some sense inter partes and, therefore, that he had to approve it on behalf of the trustees.

Disagreeing, if that is a fair view of his judgment, with that premise, nevertheless it is quite clear, I think, that the judge was by no means unsympathetic to the feelings and views of the plaintiff, but, on the other hand, was no less clear in his mind that the arrangement was one which so cut at the root of the testator's wishes and intentions that it was not one which the court should approve.

After all, if the court is asked to approve this proposal on behalf of a spectral spouse (if I may revert to that phrase), it must ask, I take it, why is the spectral spouse there at all under the trust? If one asks that question, nearly everything else, as it seems to me, follows. There is no doubt why the spectral spouse is there. It was part of the testator's scheme, made as I think manifest by the language which I have read from the clauses in the will, that it was the intention and the desire of the testator that this trust should be available for the plaintiff so that she would have proper provision made for her throughout her life, and would not be exposed to the risk that she might, if she had been handed the money, part with it in favour of another individual about whom the testator felt apprehension, which apprehension is plainly shared by the trustees.

For those reasons, therefore, I also conclude adversely to the plaintiff that we should not exercise jurisdiction under the Act of 1958 to approve the arrangement which has been put forward, and which I have tried to define. That is the end of the case. I only repeat the sympathy I have felt in a distressing matter of this kind, both with the plaintiff and with the trustees, whose difficulties in discharging their duty are obvious. I should like to express the hope that perhaps time, the healer, will do much to put an end to these troubles.

GOULDING AND ANOTHER v JAMES AND ANOTHER [1997] 2 All ER 239, CA

FACTS: In 1992 the testatrix made a will under the terms of which her residuary estate was to be divided into two equal parts to be given to her daughter, J, and the latter's husband. In 1994 the testatrix revoked the will and replaced it with a new will, which provided for the creation of will trusts under which J had a life interest in possession of the residuary estate subject to which the testatrix's grandson, M, was to take absolutely on surviving to the age of 40. However, if M failed to reach 40 or die before J, whether or not he had reached the age of 40, his children living at the date of his death were to take absolutely by substitution. The testatrix died in December 1994. J and M applied to the court for a variation of the will trusts under s. 1(1)(c) of the Variation of Trusts Act 1958. The new arrangement provided that the will would be varied and the residuary estate should be deemed to have devolved since the date of the testatrix's death as if the will had provided for the residuary estate to be held as to 45% for J absolutely, 45% for M absolutely and the remaining 10% held on the trusts of a grandchildren's trust fund. The trustees of the will accepted that the proposed variation would benefit the unborn great grandchildren of the testatrix. However, the judge dismissed the application, on the ground that to vary the trusts in the manner sought would be contrary to the testatrix's intentions and wishes as disclosed in the evidence that J should not be able to touch the capital of the estate at any time and that M's interest should be postponed until he reached the age of 40. J and M appealed.

HELD: Since J and M were sui juris and so legally entitled to do what they wanted with their beneficial interests contrary to any expressed intentions and wishes of the testatrix, those intentions and wishes had little, if any, relevance to the exercise of the court's jurisdiction on behalf of the testatrix's unborn great grandchildren. It followed that the judge had erred in the exercise of his direction by allowing extrinsic evidence of those subjective wishes to outweigh considerations of objective and substantial benefit to the unborn great grandchildren, the class on whose behalf the court was empowered to act. Accordingly, the appeal would be allowed and the arrangements approved.

MUMMERY LJ: . . . The 1958 Act was described by Lord Evershed MR in *Re Steed's Will Trusts, Sandford v Stevenson* [1960] 1 All ER 487 at 493 as conferring 'a revolutionary discretion'. Although the 1958 Act makes no mention of the settlor or testator, rules of court were made requiring the joinder of the settlor, if living, as a defendant to an application under the Act.

RSC Ord. 93, r. 6(2) provides.

> In addition to any other persons who are necessary and proper defendants to the originating summons by which an application under the said section 1 is made, the settlor and any other person who provided property for the purposes of the trusts to which the application relates must, if still alive and not the plaintiff, be made a defendant unless the Court for some special reason otherwise directs.

The authorities

For a jurisdiction invoked thousands of times over almost forty years there are remarkably few reported cases on its construction. An important point about the nature of the court's jurisdiction has been established by the highest authority. In *Re Holmden's Settlement Trusts, IRC v Holmden* [1968] 1 All ER 148 at 151, a revenue case not cited to the judge, Lord Reid said:

> Under the Variation of Trusts Act, 1958, the court does not itself amend or vary the trusts of the original settlement. The beneficiaries are not bound by variations because the court has made the variation. Each beneficiary is bound because he has consented to the variation. If he was not of full age when the arrangement was made he is bound because the court was authorised by the Act of 1958 to approve of it on his behalf and did so by making an order. If he was of full age and did not in fact consent he is not affected by the order of the court and he is not bound. So the arrangement must be regarded as an arrangement made by the beneficiaries themselves. The court merely acted on behalf of or as representing those beneficiaries who were not in a position to give their own consent and approval. So we have an alteration of the settlement which was not made by the settlor or by the court as being empowered to make it, but which was made by the beneficiaries quite independently of the settlor or of any power, express or implied, given or deemed to have been given by him.

. . . Mr Green [on behalf of the unborn great grandchildren of Mrs Froud] relied on passages to similar effect in three judgments of Megarry J: *Re Holt's Settlement, Wilson v Holt* [1968] 1 All ER 470 at 479, *Re Ball's Settlement Trusts* [1968] 2 All ER 438 at 442 and

Spens v IRC, Hunt v IRC [1970] 3 All ER 294 at 301. The effect of Megarry J's observation in those decisions is this. First, what varies the trust is not the court, but the agreement or consensus of the beneficiaries. Secondly, there is no real difference in principle in the rearrangement of the trusts between the case where the court is exercising its jurisdiction on behalf of the specified class under the 1958 Act and the case where the resettlement is made by virtue of the doctrine in *Saunders v Vautier* (1841) 4 Beav 115 and by all the adult beneficiaries joining together. Thirdly, the court is merely contributing on behalf of infants and unborn and unascertained persons the binding assents to the arrangement which they, unlike an adult beneficiary, cannot give. The 1958 Act has thus been viewed by the courts as a statutory extension of the consent principle embodied in the rule in *Saunders v Vautier*. The principle recognises the rights of beneficiaries, who are sui juris and together absolutely entitled to the trust property, to exercise their proprietary rights to overbear and defeat the intention of a testator or settlor to subject property to the continuing trusts, powers and limitations of a will or trust instrument.

The role of the court is not to stand in as, or for, a settlor in varying the trusts. As Mr Green emphasised, the court acts 'on behalf of' the specified class and, in appropriate cases, supplies consent for persons incapable of consenting. The court does not, in Mr Green's submission, simply approve an arrangement; it approves an arrangement 'on behalf of' a specified class. Mr Green accepted that, in so acting, the court has a discretion. The court *may*, if it thinks fit, by order, approve on behalf of the specified beneficiaries. He pointed, however, to the proviso in s. 1(1) of the 1958 Act, which highlights 'benefit' as a mandatory factor in the exercise of discretion. Except in para (d) cases, the court is directed not to approve an arrangement on behalf of any person, unless the carrying out thereof would be for the benefit of that person. Although Mr Green accepted that in some cases, such as *Re Steed's Will Trusts*, the intentions, wishes and motives of the settlor or testator may be relevant and weighty, in this case he contended that they are not relevant, because they do not relate to the class of persons for whom the court approves the arrangement. Alternatively, if they are relevant, it is not a proper exercise of the discretion in this case to allow extrinsic evidence of Mrs Froud's wishes to outweigh the undoubted benefit to be conferred on her great grandchildren, on whose behalf the court is empowered to act.

The submissions of the trustees
On behalf of the trustees, Mr Halpern, though not opposing the appeal, deployed the arguments that found favour with the judge. . . .

Conclusion
I have given Mr Halpern's submission careful consideration, but I would have no hesitation in allowing this appeal and approving the original arrangement, set out in the draft order proffered by Mr Green, on behalf of the unborn great grandchildren of Mrs Froud. In my judgment, the legal position is as follows. (1) The court has a discretion whether or not to approve a proposed arrangement. (2) That discretion is fettered by only one express restriction. The proviso to s. 1 prohibits the court from approving an arrangement which is not for the benefit of the classes referred to in (a), (b) or (c). The approval of this arrangement is not prevented by that proviso, since it is plainly the case that it is greatly for the benefit of the class specified in s. 1(1)(c). (3) It does not follow from the fact of benefit to unborns that the arrangement must be approved. In *Re Van Gruisen's Will Trusts, Bagger v Dean* [1964] 1 All ER 843 at 844 Ungoed-Thomas J said:

> It is shown that actuarially the provisions for the infants and unborn persons are more beneficial for them under the arrangement than under the present trusts of the will. That, however, does not conclude the case. The court is not merely concerned with this actuarial calculation, even assuming that it satisfies the statutory requirement that the arrangement must be for the benefit of the infants and unborn persons. The court is also concerned whether the arrangement as a whole, in all the circumstances, is such that it is proper to approve it. The court's concern involves, inter alia, a practical and business-like consideration of the arrangement, including the total amounts of the advantages which the various parties obtain, and their bargaining strength.

(4)   That overall discretion described by Ungoed-Thomas J is to be exercised with regard to all relevant factors properly considered in the statutory context. The context is that the court is empowered to approve an arrangement 'on behalf of' the members of a specified class. As Lord Denning MR said in *Re Weston's Settlements* [1968] 3 All ER 338 at 342, 'in exercising its discretion, the function of the court is to protect those who cannot protect themselves'.

In relation to the members of the specified class who cannot act for themselves, the court is almost in the position of a 'statutory attorney', a striking expression used by Mr E. I. Goulding QC in his illuminating submissions to the Court of Appeal in *Re Weston's Settlements* [1969] 1 Ch 223 at 236. The court is not in the position of a statutory attorney for the settlor or for the adult beneficiaries and the court is not, as was made clear in *Re Holmden's Settlement*, in the position of a statutory settlor. (5) Viewed in that context, an important factor in this case is that Mrs June Goulding and Mr Marcus Goulding are sui juris and Mrs Froud's intentions and wishes related to their beneficial interests under the testamentary trusts rather than to the contingent interests of her unborn great grandchildren whom the court is concerned to protect. Mr Halpern did not dispute that Mrs June Goulding and Mr Marcus Goulding are legally entitled to do what they want with their beneficial interests in the residuary estate. Mrs June Goulding, for example, is entitled, contrary to the firmest of intentions expressed by her late mother, to assign her life interest to her husband or to dispose of it for a capital sum and give that capital sum to her husband. Mrs Froud's contrary non-testamentary wishes could not inhibit Mrs June Goulding's proprietary rights, as a person beneficially entitled to the life interests in residue. (6) In these circumstances the critical question is what relevance, if any, can Mrs Froud's intentions and wishes with regard to the interests in residue taken under the will by her daughter and grandson and with regard to the exclusion of her son-in-law from direct or indirect benefit, have to the exercise of the court's jurisdiction on behalf of unborn great grandchildren of Mrs Froud?

On this crucial question the judge was impressed by Mr Halpern's submission that Mrs Froud's intentions and wishes are important and should be taken into account on the authority of the Court of Appeal decision in *Re Steed's Will Trusts*. I do not accept Mr Halpern's submission that the Court of Appeal in that case laid down any rule, principle or guideline of general application on the importance of the intentions and wishes of a settlor or testator to applications to approve arrangements under the 1958 Act. (7) . . .

The central fact in *Re Steed's Will Trusts* was that the testator had manifested in the terms of his will a particular purpose in creating a protective trust; that was to protect the life tenant from improvident dealings with property in favour of certain members of her family. The Court of Appeal was satisfied that the testator's purpose, evidenced in the will, was still justified at the time of the application to vary. That was a view also shared by the trustees, who opposed the application by the protected life tenant. In those circumstances there was an overwhelming reason for the continuation of the protective trusts and in the continuance of the interest of the para (d) class of person. That explained and justified the court's refusal of approval. The court in that case was not engaged in the exercise demanded in this case of deciding whether a mandatory benefit, bargained on behalf of a specified class, is outweighed by some other countervailing discretionary factor, such as the purpose of the trust or the intention of the testatrix in making it. (8) The fact that the rules of court require a living settlor to be joined as a party to proceedings under the 1958 Act does not mean that the court attaches any overbearing or special significance to the wishes of a settlor. Mr Halpern accepted that the nature of the jurisdiction under the 1958 Act is such that even the most carefully planned and meticulously drafted intentions of a settlor or testator are liable to be overridden by an arrangement agreed between sui juris beneficiaries and by the sanction of the court under the 1958 Act.

Mr Halpern also accepted that even the most determined settlor or testator cannot exclude the jurisdiction of the court under the 1958 Act. The court has a discretion to approve an arrangement under the Act, even though the settlement or will may make it crystal clear that the settlor or testator does not want any departure from any of the strict terms of the trust.

In *Re Remnant's Settlement Trusts, Hooper v Wenhasten* [1970] 2 All ER 554 at 559 Pennycuick J had to consider a forfeiture provision relating to a beneficiary being a practising Roman Catholic. The forfeiture provision plainly expressed a strongly held wish on the part of the testator as to who should not benefit under his will. The court nevertheless approved an arrangement deleting that forfeiture provision and thereby defeated the testator's clear intentions. The court did so because Pennycuick J was of the view it was for the benefit of all concerned to delete that provision; he was satisfied that the arrangement was a fair and proper one. . . .

To sum up. The flaw in the judge's refusal to approve the arrangement is that, in reliance on the supposed scope of the decision in *Re Steed's Will Trusts*, he allowed extrinsic evidence of the subjective wishes of Mrs Froud as regards her daughter, son-in-law and grandson to outweigh considerations of objective and substantial benefit to the class on whose behalf the court is empowered to act. If the judge had adopted the correct approach to the exercise of his discretion, he could only have come to the conclusion that the intentions and wishes of Mrs Froud, expressed externally to her will in relation to the adult beneficiaries and an adult non-beneficiary, had little, if any, relevance or weight to the issue of approval on behalf of the future unborn great grandchildren, whose interest in residue was multiplied five-fold under the proposed arrangement.

For all these reasons, I would allow this appeal. I would also approve the proposed arrangement set out in the draft minute of order.

9.6   End of Chapter Assessment Question

By his will Abdul provided that £500,000 should be held on trust for his wife, Fatima, for life, with remainder to such of their children as should attain the age of 21 absolutely. Abdul died in 1995 leaving two sons, Bashir and Dan, aged 7 and 5 respectively. The trustees of the fund are experienced businessmen, and due to their efforts the fund is now worth £700,000.

Fatima feels that the income from the fund is more than sufficient to meet her needs, and wishes to surrender her interest in one half of the income of the fund in favour of Bashir and Dan. Additionally, she is worried about the effect of inherited wealth on Bashir and Dan, and would like to postpone their interests until they are 35 years old. In the meantime she would like the income on their respective shares to be accumulated until they attain 30 or die.

Fatima wishes to settle in Guernsey where she has friends. Bashir and Dan attend Harrchester School in England and it is proposed that they should complete their education in England. Fatima believes that the trust could be administered more easily in Guernsey and wishes to export the administration of the trust to Guernsey.

The trustees have opposed Fatima's proposed variations of the trust.

Advise Fatima.

9.7   End of Chapter Assessment Outline Answer

Fatima is seeking to vary Abdul's Will Trust. In the first place she is seeking to vary the beneficial interests under the trusts by surrendering part of her interest and by postponing the vesting of her children's interests. In the second place she is seeking to export the administration of the trust to Guernsey.

First, the remoulding of the beneficial interests. In order to achieve this Fatima should apply for a variation under the Variation of Trusts Act 1958. Section 1 empowers the court to approve 'any arrangement . . . varying or revoking all or any of the trusts'. She should join the trustees of Abdul's Will Trust as defendants to the application and they should only consent to the proposed arrangement if they are satisfied that it would be for the benefit of Bashir and Dan. Bashir and Dan are too young to give their own consents to the arrangement and so the court may, if it thinks fit, consent on their behalf (s. 1(1)(a)). The court will only do so if satisfied that the proposed arrangement would be for their 'benefit'. The usual benefit of an arrangement is a financial one, but 'benefit' may extend to 'social or moral benefit' (per Megarry J in *Re Holt's Settlement* [1969] 1 Ch 100). There can be no doubt that Fatima's surrender of half her income entitlement will be for the financial benefit of the children, and so the crucial question is whether the proposed postponement of their interests until they reach 35 is also for their benefit. In *Re T's Settlement* [1963] 3 All ER 759, the court approved an arrangement whereby the vesting of an infant's interest was postponed from 21 to 30 and held upon protective trusts in the meantime. The perceived benefit of the variation was the protection of the infant from her own immaturity. It is unlikely, however, that similar reasoning could apply in the case of Bashir and Dan. They are surely too young for it to be said that a deferral will prove to be for their benefit. In any event, the postponement, as requested, is probably for too long. Fatima should be advised to apply for the proposed variation in about ten years time, when her children's personalities are more developed and when the court will be in a better position to judge whether the variation would be for their benefit. The court will even hear evidence from Bashir and Dan at that time, although their wishes will not, in themselves, determine the outcome of the hearing. Fatima should be further advised to reduce the postponed age to a more reasonable figure, perhaps 25. Fatima's health or age may be such that she cannot risk waiting, or does not wish to wait, for ten years before making the application. She should be advised, however, that the court will be unlikely to vary the trust today on the terms of the proposed arrangement.

In the past courts have come to the view that if the proposed arrangement would change the whole 'substratum' of the trust, to the extent that it cannot properly be called a variation at all, such an arrangement will not be approved (see *Re Ball's Settlement* [1968] 2 All ER 438). However, the modern Court of Appeal has emphasised that the prime consideration of the court when exercising its discretion under the 1958 Act, should be the benefit to the beneficiaries (*Goulding* v *James*). This is the only consideration laid down by the Act, and should not be subordinated to consideration of the settlor's intentions. It might follow that the 'substratum' test will fall from favour, particularly if the 'substratum' equates to the settlor's fundamental intentions. In the present case, although the form of the trust would change considerably, it cannot be said that it would be unrecognisable in its new form. The root purpose of providing for the children would remain.

We turn now to consider the proposed export of the trust to Guernsey. What is being proposed is a change in the jurisdiction governing the operation of the trust. This will not involve a variation so much as a 'revocation' of the English trusts and their replacement by Guernsey trusts on similar terms. Such an arrangement was approved by Buckley J in *Re Seale's Marriage Settlement* [1961] 3 WLR 262 because the Variation of Trusts Act 1958 expressly authorises the court to approve arrangements 'varying or revoking' the trusts. In that case, however, the infant beneficiaries of the English settlement, and their parents, had lived in Canada (the new jurisdiction) for a number of years. In the present case there is no evidence that Bashir and Dan will ever leave England, nor that their mother intends to live in Guernsey in the long term. Consequently, there is little evidence that the export of the trust will be for the children's benefit. Short-term savings in administration costs will not be a 'benefit' sufficient to persuade the court to approve the proposed arrangement. In the absence of any suggestion that the trust property or the infant beneficiaries are to be based in Guernsey, there appears to be nothing on the facts of the present case which would justify the export of the trust. Fatima should be advised that this proposed arrangement is unlikely to be approved.

CHAPTER TEN

TRUSTEE APPOINTMENTS

10.1 Appointment of the Trustee

Bell, C., 'Some reflections on choosing trustees', *Trust Law & Practice*, **January 1988**

The findings of a small research project dealing with several aspects of trusteeship and recently carried out by the author were an important source of material for this article. As part of the project, a survey was carried out among a group of solicitors in Lancashire and Cumbria who do trust work on a regular basis in an attempt to determine the attitude of practitioners in the field of trusts to a number of matters relating to the appointment of trustees.

Non-professional trustees
The solicitors' survey showed that despite the onerous nature of the office of trustee, getting suitable private individuals to agree to become trustees is not a major problem. Friendship for the settlor/testator or a sense of duty arising from the fact that the settlor/testator is a relative are the main reasons for private individuals agreeing to act as trustees. However, knowledge of the beneficiaries and a desire to help them was also highlighted in the solicitors' survey as a factor. It is interesting to note that private individuals who agree to act as trustees usually regard it as an honour and not a chore.

Clearly a non-professional trustee must be trustworthy. However, the solicitors' survey revealed that he ought also to have some or all of the following attributes: (i) a genuine interest in the objects of the trust; (ii) financial acumen and preferably with some business experience; (iii) sound judgment; (iv) common sense; and (v) strength of character to deal with difficult beneficiaries. The message from the survey was that it helps if a non-professional trustee is 'street wise'.

In the opinion of the solicitors questioned, very few private individuals who become trustees have a clear conception of the duties and responsibilities of trusteeship prior to their appointment. However, it seems that most of them do have some general appreciation of what is involved before becoming trustees.

Most trusts of any size are handled either solely by professional trustees or (more usually) by a mixture of professional and non-professional trustees. Although the latter combination generally works well in practice some problems clearly do arise. Sometimes non-professional trustees may have difficulty in understanding the niceties of trust law and fail to appreciate requirements, the reasons for which are obvious to professional trustees. Further in relation to the operation of discretionary powers, non-professional trustees may not infrequently try to 'bend' the rules for well-meaning reasons. Finally, there can be some disagreement between non-professional and professional trustees over investment/sale policies. Sometimes, non-professional trustees may be reluctant to follow a professional recommendation as to investment which the professional trustees are prepared to accept....

TRUSTEE ACT 1925

36. Power of appointing new or additional trustees
  (1) Where a trustee, either original or substituted, and whether appointed by a court or otherwise, is dead, or remains out of the United Kingdom for more than twelve

months, or desires to be discharged from all or any of the trusts or powers reposed in or conferred on him, or refuses or is unfit to act therein, or is incapable of acting therein, or is an infant, then, subject to the restrictions imposed by this Act on the number of trustees,—

(a)   the person or persons nominated for the purpose of appointing new trustees by the instrument, if any, creating the trust; or

(b)   if there is no such person, or no such person able and willing to act, then the surviving or continuing trustees for the time being, or the personal representatives of the last surviving or continuing trustee;

may, by writing, appoint one or more other persons (whether or not being the persons exercising the power) to be a trustee or trustees in the place of the trustee so deceased, remaining out of the United Kingdom, desiring to be discharged, refusing, or being unfit or being incapable, or being an infant, as aforesaid.

(2)   Where a trustee has been removed under a power contained in the instrument creating the trust, a new trustee or new trustees may be appointed in the place of the trustee who is removed, as if he were dead, or, in the case of a corporation, as if the corporation desired to be discharged from the trust, and the provisions of this section shall apply accordingly, but subject to the restrictions imposed by this Act on the number of trustees.

(3)   . . .

(4)   The power of appointment given by subsection (1) of this section or any similar previous enactment to the personal representatives of a last surviving or continuing trustee shall be and shall be deemed always to have been exercisable by the executors for the time being (whether original or by representation) of such surviving or continuing trustee who have proved the will of their testator or by the administrators for the time being of such trustee without the concurrence of any executor who has renounced or has not proved.

(5)   But a sole or last surviving executor intending to renounce, or all the executors where they all intend to renounce, shall have and shall be deemed always to have had power, at any time before renouncing probate, to exercise the power of appointment given by this section, or by any similar previous enactment, if willing to act for that purpose and without thereby accepting the office of executor.

(6)   Where a sole trustee, other than a trust corporation, is or has been originally appointed to act in a trust, or where, in the case of any trust, there are not more than three trustees (none of them being a trust corporation) either original or substituted and whether appointed by the court or otherwise, then and in any such case—

(a)   the person or persons nominated for the purpose of appointing new trustees by the instrument, if any, creating the trust; or

(b)   if there is no such person, or no such person able and willing to act, then the trustee or trustees for the time being;

may, by writing appoint another person or other persons to be an additional trustee or additional trustees, but it shall not be obligatory to appoint any additional trustee, unless the instrument, if any, creating the trust, or any statutory enactment provides to the contrary, nor shall the number of trustees be increased beyond four by virtue of any such appointment.

(7)   Every new trustee appointed under this section as well before as after all the trust property becomes by law, or by assurance, or otherwise, vested in him, shall have the same powers, authorities, and discretions, and may in all respects act as if he had been originally appointed a trustee by the instrument, if any, creating the trust.

(8)   The provisions of this section relating to a trustee who is dead include the case of a person nominated trustee in a will but dying before the testator, and those relative to a continuing trustee include a refusing or retiring trustee, if willing to act in the execution of the provisions of this section.

(9)   Where a trustee is incapable, by reason of mental disorder within the meaning of the Mental Health Act 1983, of exercising his functions as trustee and is also entitled in possession to some beneficial interest in the trust property, no appointment of a new trustee in his place shall be made by virtue of paragraph (b) of subsection (1) of this section unless leave to make the appointment has been given by the authority having jurisdiction under Part VII of the Mental Health Act 1983.

37. Supplemental provisions as to appointment of trustees

(2)   Nothing in this Act shall authorise the appointment of a sole trustee, not being a trust corporation, where the trustee, when appointed, would not be able to give valid receipts for all capital money arising under the trust.

40. Vesting of trust property in new or continuing trustees

(1)   Where by a deed a new trustee is appointed to perform any trust, then—

(a)   if the deed contains a declaration by the appointor to the effect that any estate or interest in any land subject to the trust, or in any chattel so subject, or the right to recover or receive any debt or other thing in action so subject, shall vest in the persons who by virtue of the deed become or are the trustees for performing the trust, the deed shall operate, without any conveyance or assignment, to vest in those persons as joint tenants and for the purposes of the trust the estate, interest or right to which the declaration relates; and

(b)   if the deed is made after the commencement of this Act and does not contain such a declaration, the deed shall, subject to any express provision to the contrary therein contained, operate as if it had contained such a declaration by the appointor extending to all the estates, interests and rights with respect to which a declaration could have been made.

(2)   Where by a deed a retiring trustee is discharged under the statutory power without a new trustee being appointed, then—

(a)   if the deed contains such a declaration as aforesaid by the retiring and continuing trustees, and by the other person, if any, empowered to appoint trustees, the deed shall, without any conveyance or assignment, operate to vest in the continuing trustees alone, as joint tenants, and for the purposes of the trust, the estate, interest or right to which the declaration relates; and

(b)   if the deed is made after the commencement of this Act and does not contain such a declaration, the deed shall, subject to any express provision to the contrary therein contained, operate as if it had contained such a declaration by such persons as aforesaid extending to all the estates interests and rights with respect to which a declaration could have been made.

(3)   An express vesting declaration, whether made before or after the commencement of this Act, shall, notwithstanding that the estate, interest or right to be vested is not expressly referred to, and provided that the other statutory requirements were or are complied with, operate and be deemed always to have operated (but without prejudice to any express provision to the contrary contained in the deed of appointment or discharge) to vest in the persons respectively referred to in subsections (1) and (2) of this section, as the case may require, such estates, interests and rights as are capable of being and ought to be vested in those persons.

(4)   This section does not extend—

(a)   to land conveyed by way of mortgage for securing money subject to the trust, except land conveyed on trust for securing debentures or debenture stock;

(b)   to land held under a lease which contains any covenant, condition or agreement against assignment or disposing of the land without licence or consent, unless, prior to the execution of the deed containing expressly or impliedly the vesting declaration, the requisite licence or consent has been obtained, or unless, by virtue of any statute or rule of law, the vesting declaration, express or implied, would not operate as a breach of covenant or give rise to a forfeiture;

(c)   to any share, stock, annuity or property which is only transferable in books kept by a company or other body, or in manner directed by or under an Act of Parliament.

41. Power of court to appoint new trustees

(1)   The court may, whenever it is expedient to appoint a new trustee or new trustees, and it is found inexpedient, difficult or impracticable so to do without the assistance of the court, make an order appointing a new trustee or new trustees either in substitution for or in addition to any existing trustee or trustees, or although there is no existing trustee. . . .

(4)   Nothing in this section gives power to appoint an executor or administrator.

43. Powers of new trustee appointed by the court
Every trustee appointed by a court of competent jurisdiction shall, as well before as after the trust property becomes by law, or by assurance, or otherwise, vested in him, have the same powers, authorities, and discretions, and may in all respects act as if he had been originally appointed a trustee by the instrument, if any, creating the trust.

IN RE SICHEL'S SETTLEMENTS (SICHEL v SICHEL) [1916] 1 Ch 358, ChD

FACTS: Life policies were assigned to trustees by deed to hold upon the terms of an existing settlement. That settlement contained a power to appoint new trustees in certain situations. The situations did not include the possibility of a trustee becoming unfit to act, which is one of the situations in which, according to s. 36(1) of the Trustee Act 1925 (and its predecessor, s. 10(1) of the Trustee Act 1893), a trustee could normally be appointed under such a power. The donee of the power appointed two trustees, having purportedly been the appointments made on the basis of the previous trustee's breaches of trust and consequent unfitness to act.
HELD: Following *In re Wheeler* [1896] 1 Ch 315, the donees of the power were restricted to making appointments in the situations expressly specified in the power. Accordingly, the appointment on the basis of the previous trustee's unfitness was invalid. The court appointed new trustees.

NEVILLE J: There is no question that both these trustees were unfit to act in the trusts, because the one who absconded had been guilty of the grossest defalcations previously; but it is said I am precluded from holding that the power given by sub-s. 1 of s. 10 can be exercised by the persons nominated in the deed to appoint new trustees unless the words contained in the deed indicating the occasions upon which the appointment can be exercised correspond precisely with those contained in sub-s. 1. What precludes me is a decision of Kekewich J in the year 1895 in the case of *In re Wheeler and De Rochow* [1896] 1 Ch 315, which I understand has been treated as an authority ever since, and which, therefore, I think I have no power to interfere with, in which he held that the words 'person or persons nominated for the purpose of appointing new trustees by the instrument creating the trust' in sub-s. 1 of s. 10 refer to the person or persons nominated for the purpose of appointing new trustees in the particular event which has happened. On reading Kekewich J's judgment it seems to me that the meaning of that is that the power of the person or persons nominated for the purpose of appointing new trustees in the instrument are not enlarged in any sense by s. 10, sub-s. 1, [now s. 36(1) of the Law of Property Act 1925], but you are still bound to see whether they are purporting to exercise the power given by the words contained in the instrument, and if the event there referred to has not happened, then the appointment is bad. . . . If I were free to exercise my own judgment in the matter, I should declare that the appointment was good; but I think I am bound to follow the decision of Kekewich J, although I cannot say that I concur in it, and the consequence is I hold that the appointment is bad. I will make an order appointing the defendants trustees of both settlements with the usual vesting order.

TRUSTS OF LAND AND APPOINTMENT OF TRUSTEES ACT 1996

19. Appointment and retirement of trustee at instance of beneficiaries
    (1)   This section applies in the case of a trust where—
    (a)   there is no person nominated for the purpose of appointing new trustees by the instrument, if any, creating the trust, and
    (b)   the beneficiaries under the trust are of full age and capacity and (taken together) are absolutely entitled to the property subject to the trust.
    (2)   The beneficiaries may give a direction or directions of either or both of the following descriptions—
    (a)   a written direction to a trustee or trustees to retire from the trust, and
    (b)   a written direction to the trustees or trustee for the time being (or, if there are none, to the personal representative of the last person who was a trustee) to appoint by writing to be a trustee or trustees the person or persons specified in the direction.

(3) Where—
    (a) a trustee has been given a direction under subsection (2)(a),
    (b) reasonable arrangements have been made for the protection of any rights of his in connection with the trust,
    (c) after he has retired there will be either a trust corporation or at least two persons to act as trustees to perform the trust, and
    (d) either another person is to be appointed to be a new trustee on his retirement (whether in compliance with a direction under subsection (2)(b) or otherwise) or the continuing trustees by deed consent to his retirement,
he shall make a deed declaring his retirement and shall be deemed to have retired and be discharged from the trust.

(4) Where a trustee retires under subsection (3) he and the continuing trustees (together with any new trustee) shall (subject to any arrangements for the protection of his rights) do anything necessary to vest the trust property in the continuing trustees (or the continuing and new trustees).

(5) This section has effect subject to the restrictions imposed by the Trustee Act 1925 on the number of trustees.

20. Appointment of substitute for incapable trustee

(1) This section applies where—
    (a) a trustee is incapable by reason of mental disorder of exercising his functions as trustee,
    (b) there is no person who is both entitled and willing and able to appoint a trustee in place of him under section 36(1) of the Trustee Act 1925, and
    (c) the beneficiaries under the trust are of full age and capacity and (taken together) are absolutely entitled to the property subject to the trust.

(2) The beneficiaries may give to—
    (a) a receiver of the trustee,
    (b) an attorney acting for him under the authority of a power of attorney created by an instrument which is registered under section 6 of the Enduring Powers of Attorney Act 1985, or
    (c) a person authorised for the purpose by the authority having jurisdiction under Part VII of the Mental Health Act 1983,
a written direction to appoint by writing the person or persons specified in the direction to be a trustee or trustees in place of the incapable trustee.

IN RE MAY'S WT [1941] 1 Ch 109, ChD

FACTS: A testator appointed three trustees in his will. One of the trustees, his widow, happened to have been in Belgium at the date of the German invasion. The other two trustees took out a summons to establish whether they were empowered to appoint a new trustee in her place.
HELD: The continuing trustees did not have the power to appoint new trustees, because there was nothing to suggest that the widow was 'incapable of acting' within the meaning of s. 36(1) of the Trustee Act 1925. The court would appoint a new trustee under s. 41(1) of the Trustee Act, it being otherwise inexpedient, difficult or impractical to make an appointment.

CROSSMAN: J: I feel that there is some danger in declaring that the plaintiffs, as continuing trustees, have power, pursuant to the Trustee Act 1925, to appoint a new trustee of the will in the place of the widow. Especially do I feel that there is danger in laying down any rule, as a rule may well be susceptible of misuse. I cannot come to any conclusion covering more than this particular case. I can find no evidence that the lady is really 'incapable of acting' within the meaning of s. 36, sub-s. 1.
    The case seems to be one in which the right course is for the Court to appoint a new trustee. The evidence is enough to justify the Court's doing so under s. 41, sub-s. 1. Therefore, subject to the production of the proper affidavit of fitness, I will appoint the person whom the summons asks may be appointed to be a trustee in the place of the widow, and will make the necessary vesting orders. I will dispense with service of this application on the widow.

IN RE TEMPEST [1860] 1 Ch App 485, CA

FACTS: The will of Sir C. R. Tempest, Bart. appointed Stonor and Fleming as trustees of certain real estates. A codicil to the will appointed Stonor, Fleming and Lord Camoys as trustees of certain charitable trusts. Stonor predeceased the testator. Fleming and one Arthur Tempest, the testator's uncle, were empowered by the will to appoint new trustees of the real estates, but they could not agree upon a replacement trustee. Most of the beneficiaries concurred with Arthur Tempest's choice, but Fleming opposed it on the ground that the proposed trustee was connected with a branch of the family with whom the testator had not been on friendly terms. The surviving trustees of the charitable trusts were, on the other hand, able to agree to a replacement trustee of those trusts.
HELD: The trustee proposed by Arthur Tempest should not be appointed to the trusts. Certain principles were laid down to guide appointments by the court.

SIR G. J. TURNER LJ: . . . the discretion which the Court has and exercises in making such appointments, is not, as I conceive, a mere arbitrary discretion, but a discretion in the exercise of which the Court is, and ought to be, guided by some general rules and principles, and, in my opinion, the difficulty which the Court has to encounter in these cases lies not so much in ascertaining the rules and principles by which it ought to be guided, as in applying those rules and principles to the varying circumstances of each particular case. The following rules and principles may, I think, safely be laid down as applying to all cases of appointments by the Court of new trustees.

First, the Court will have regard to the wishes of the persons by whom the trust has been created, if expressed in the instrument creating the trust, or clearly to be collected from it. I think this rule may be safely laid down, because if the author of the trust has in terms declared that a particular person, or a person filling a particular character, should not be a trustee of the instrument, there cannot, as I apprehend, be the least doubt that the Court would not appoint to the office a person whose appointment was so prohibited, and I do not think that upon a question of this description any distinction can be drawn between express declarations and demonstrated intention. The analogy of the course which the Court pursues in the appointment of guardians affords, I think, some support to this rule. The Court in those cases attends to the wishes of the parents, however informally they may be expressed.

Another rule which may, I think, safely be laid down is this—that the Court will not appoint a person to be trustee with a view to the interest of some of the persons interested under the trust, in opposition either to the wishes of the testator or to the interests of others of the *cestuis que trusts*. I think so for this reason, that it is of the essence of the duty of every trustee to hold an even hand between the parties interested under the trust. Every trustee is in duty bound to look to the interests of all, and not of any particular member or class of members of his *cestuis que trusts*.

A third rule which, I think, may safely be laid down, is,—that the Court in appointing a trustee will have regard to the question, whether his appointment will promote or impede the execution of the trust, for the very purpose of the appointment is that the trust may be better carried into execution. . . .

. . . but, on the other hand, if the continuing or surviving trustee refuses to act with a trustee who may be proposed to be appointed—and I make this observation with reference to what appears to have been said by Mr Fleming, as to Mr Petre having come forward in opposition to his wishes—I think it would be going too far to say that the Court ought, on that ground alone, to refuse to appoint the proposed trustee; for this would, as suggested in the argument, be to give the continuing or surviving trustee a veto upon the appointment of the new trustee. In such a case, I think it must be the duty of the Court to inquire and ascertain whether the objection of the surviving or continuing trustee is well founded or not, and to act or refuse to act upon it accordingly. If the surviving or continuing trustee has improperly refused to act with the proposed trustee, it might be a ground for removing him from the trust. Upon the facts of this case, however, it seems to me that the objections taken by Mr Fleming to the appointment of Mr Petre were and are well founded, and upon the whole case, therefore, my opinion is, that the order under appeal, so far as it appoints Mr Petre, ought to be discharged.

10.1.1   ACTIONS OF THE TRUSTEE UPON APPOINTMENT

RE BROGDEN (1888) 38 ChD 546, ChD

FACTS: In this case a trustee failed to get in certain monies due to the trust. Indeed, he waited so long before attempting to get the funds in, the trust suffered a loss of £17,250 (no small sum in 1888).

HELD: The trustee had breached his trust by failing to take action to get in the funds. He was obliged to sue for their recovery unless he had reasonable grounds for believing that an action would be fruitless. The burden rested on the trustee to show that such belief was reasonably held. The onus was on the trustee to show that the loss would have occurred despite his breach, and in the present case that defence had not successfully been made out.

FRY LJ: . . . It has been urged upon us that if a trustee does as much for his *cestui que trust* as he does for himself, he has performed his duty. I cannot accept for one moment that view of the duty of trustees. A trustee undoubtedly has a discretion as to the mode and manner, and very often as to the time in which and at which he shall carry his duty into effect. But his discretion is never an absolute one; it is always limited by the duty—the dominant duty, the guiding duty—of recovering, securing, and duly applying the trust fund. And no trustee can claim any right of discretion which does not agree with that paramount obligation. Mr Budgett appears not to have seen clearly the duty which he had assumed, and instead of endeavouring to perform the duty, he endeavoured to arrive at some settlement with Messrs. Brogden which would save them from the obligation to pay the money, and which I have no doubt Mr Budgett thought was a more desirable arrangement for Mrs Billing and her family than the actual receipt of the money and the investment in some security which would bring in a lower rate of interest than Messrs Brogden were willing to pay. . . .

But then it is said by Mr Budgett that no loss has accrued to the *cestuis que trust* by reason of his want of diligence:—he says that if he had been diligent, no greater good would have come to the Billing family than has come to them. In my judgment, the burden of sustaining any such argument as that rests distinctly upon the trustee who sets it up. When the *cestui que trust* has shewn that the trustee has made default in the performance of his duty, and when the money which was the subject of the trust is not forthcoming, the *cestui que trust* has made out, in my judgment, a *prima facie* case of liability upon the trustee, and if the trustee desire to repel that by saying that if he had done his duty no good would have flowed from it, the burden of sustaining that argument is plainly upon the trustee.

10.2   Disclaimer of the Trust

IN RE LORD AND FULLERTON'S CONTRACT [1896] 1 Ch 228, CA

FACTS: A testator having real and personal property in England and abroad left his residuary estate to trustees upon trust for sale. One of the trustees disclaimed the trusts of the will except as to the property abroad. The remaining trustees sold land of the testator in England.

HELD: That the disclaimer had no effect, and that the disclaiming trustee was a necessary party to the conveyance.

LINDLEY LJ: . . . Treating this, therefore, as a partial disclaimer—as a disclaimer of the offices of trustee and executor so far as the property in this country is concerned—the point is reduced to this: Will that enable the three trustees who are the vendors to make a good title? Now, although the point, so far as I know, is new in species, I think the purchaser is right—that is to say, that according to our law it is not competent for a trustee to execute or to rely on a partial disclaimer of the office either of executor or of trustee, or of the property devised to him. Let us consider what his position is in this case. It is to be observed that he is executor as well as trustee. What would be the position under this document if he remitted personal estate from America to this country? Would not he be responsible for it? Would this disclaimer by him affect him in any way? I should say, obviously not. He would be clearly responsible for the property in respect of his office if he accepts the office at all—in other words, from a purchaser's point of view, if he is not proved not to have accepted he must be deemed to have accepted the office of the trust; and then the ordinary principle applies, that it is not competent for a man to do that partially: he must either do it altogether or not at all. . . .

IN RE LYSAGHT, DECD. [1966] 1 Ch 191, ChD

FACTS: The testatrix settled the net residue of her estate on trustees to pay out of it £5,000 to the Royal College of Surgeons. This endowment was required to be held on certain trusts by the college. One of these trusts was to grant a studentship to the sons of medical practitioners, provided that the students were 'not of the Jewish or Roman Catholic faith'. The council of the college informed the trustees that they could only accept the trusts with the 'invidious' proviso removed.
HELD: The court allowed the college to carry the trust into effect without the element of religious discrimination. This was to give effect to the testatrix's paramount charitable intention, for the whole trust would fail if the discriminatory provision was allowed to remain.

BUCKLEY J: . . . I do not understand the college to assert that it would be legally incapable of accepting the trusts of the endowment and giving them effect with due regard to the provision for religious discrimination. It is not suggested that this would be ultra vires the college. What I understand from their solicitor's letter which is in evidence and from what counsel has stated in court is that on account of the character of the college and of the purposes which it exists to serve, the college would be unalterably opposed to accepting and administering a trust containing any provision for religious discrimination.

Obviously a trustee will not normally be permitted to modify the terms of his trust on the ground that his own opinions or convictions conflict with them. If his conscience will not allow him to carry out the trust faithfully in accordance with its terms, he must make way for a trustee who can and will do so. But how, if the identity of the trustee selected by the settlor is essential to his intention? If it is of the essence of a trust that the trustees selected by the settlor and no one else shall act as the trustees of it and those trustees cannot or will not undertake the office, the trust must fail . . . I have already reached the conclusion that it is an essential part of the testatrix's intention that the college should be the trustee of the endowment fund. The college is, as I have said, unalterably opposed to accepting the trust if any provision for religious discrimination is an effective part of it. That part or paragraph (D) which requires religious discrimination, if it is to be insisted upon, will consequently defeat the testatrix's intention entirely, for in that case the college must disclaim the trust with the result that it will fail.

The impracticability of giving effect to some inessential part of the testatrix's intention cannot, in my judgment, be allowed to defeat her paramount charitable intention.

10.3   Retirement and Discharge of the Trustee

10.3.1   MODES OF RETIREMENT

Trustees may retire whenever the trust instrument entitles them to do so and, as a last resort, whenever the court approves an application for retirement. Apart from these instances the Trustee Act 1925 details two modes of retirement.

10.3.1.1   Retirement under s. 36 Trustee Act 1925

You will recall that this section provides, *inter alia*, for the appointment of a new trustee, or trustees, 'in the place of' a trustee 'desiring to be discharged'. The crucial point to note is that a retirement purported to be carried out in pursuance of this section will only be valid to discharge the trustee if at least one new trustee has been appointed in their place.

10.3.1.2   Retirement under s. 39 Trustee Act 1925

The main difference between s. 39 and s. 36 is that s. 39 permits retirement of a trustee without the appointment of a replacement trustee. There are however, other important distinctions between the two sections, as a reading of them makes plain.

TRUSTEE ACT 1925

39.   Retirement of trustee without a new appointment

(1)   Where a trustee is desirous of being discharged from the trust, and after his discharge there will be either a trust corporation or at least two individuals to act as trustees to perform the trust, then, if such trustee as aforesaid by deed declares that he is desirous of being discharged from the trust, and if his co-trustees and such other person, if any, as is empowered to appoint trustees, by deed consent to the discharge of the trustee, and to the vesting in the co-trustees alone of the trust property, the trustee desirous of being discharged shall be deemed to have retired from the trust, and shall, by the deed, be discharged therefrom under this Act, without any new trustee being appointed in his place.

(2)   Any assurance or thing requisite for vesting the trust property in the continuing trustees alone shall be executed or done.

10.3.1.3   Retirement under s. 19 Trusts of Land and Appointment of Trustees Act 1996

See **10.1.2**.

10.3.2   LIABILITY AFTER RETIREMENT

HEAD v GOULD [1898] 2 Ch 250, ChD

FACTS: This case concerned the trusts of the marriage settlement of Mr and Mrs Head, the settlement being held for them for their successive lives with powers of appointment in favour of any children they might have, which powers were never exercised. In default of appointment the fund would pass to any children they might have in equal shares upon their achieving the age of 21 or earlier marriage. A post-nuptial settlement was also made, by Mr Head, in similar terms. Mr Head died leaving his widow and three children. One of the trustees of the marriage settlement retired and Mrs Head appointed one Mr Clapp in his place, together with the continuing trustee, Mr Houlditch. Some years later the retiring trustee of the post-nuptial settlement appointed Messrs Houlditch and Clapp as trustees of that trust also. Mrs Head got into financial difficulties and at her request the trustees discharged certain of her debts out of the trust funds by a large cash advance. The trustees took certain securities for the advance, but these securities amounted to unauthorised investments. Such cash advances continued with some regularity. Ultimately there came a time when the trustees had advanced to Mrs Head her full entitlement. The trustees then wished to be discharged from their trust, but replacement trustees were hard to find. In the event the trustees handed over the trusteeship to Mrs Head's daughter and to a solicitor and family friend Mr Gould. After their appointment further breaches of trust ensued and the interest of an infant beneficiary was lost.
HELD: The retired trustees would not be held liable for the breaches of their successors. Liability will arise in such a case only if the retired trustees are proved to have actually contemplated the breaches which occurred. It is not sufficient to show merely that the retirement facilitated the breach.

KEKEWICH J: . . . It is the duty of trustees to protect the funds intrusted to their care, and to distribute those funds themselves or hand them over to their successors intact, that is, properly invested and without diminution, according to the terms of the mandate contained in the instrument of trust. This duty is imposed on them as long as they remain trustees and must be their guide in every act done by them as trustees. On retiring from the trust and passing on the trust estate to their successors—and this whether they appoint those successors or merely assign the property to the nominees of those who have the power of appointment—they are acting as trustees, and it is equally incumbent on them in this ultimate act of office to fulfil the duty imposed on them as at any other time. If therefore they neglect that duty and part with the property without due regard to it, they remain liable and will be held by the Court responsible for the consequences properly traceable to that neglect. This explanation will, I think, be found consistent with all judicial utterances on the subject, and haply aid to make them consistent with themselves. . . .

Messrs Houlditch and Clapp were anxious to be relieved of the trust. That can surprise no one who has studied even slightly the facts of this case, and no possible objection could be taken to their retirement if it was properly effected. I do not see what they could do towards that end but appoint, or concur in the appointment of, new trustees in their place. There was nothing on which they could properly apply to the Court, and at that time the appointment of a judicial trustee was unknown. There was of course great difficulty in finding new trustees, and this is a cogent factor in the solution of the question whether the appointment of G. D. Gould and Miss Head was justifiable. They ought to have avoided the appointment of Miss Head if possible, not merely because she was a beneficiary, but because she was known to be under the influence of her mother, and mainly perhaps, and to some extent certainly, by reason of that influence she had taken an active part in the importunities which had already led to a breach of trust, and in that breach of trust itself. But was it possible? They succeeded in finding, or rather Mrs Head found, a gentleman who was a solicitor ready to undertake the trust out of kindness to the family to which he seems to have owed a debt of gratitude, and although their inquiries respecting him were perhaps somewhat slight having regard to the serious position of the trust, I cannot say that they were not reasonably justified in approving him. It is urged that they could not completely discharge themselves without appointing two competent trustees. That may be admitted, but I cannot hold Miss Head to have been an incompetent trustee when linked with another whose professional position was of itself a security that the trust funds would be properly administered. I cannot blame Messrs Houlditch and Clapp for the appointment which they made, nor do I think that they had any reasonable ground for believing, or that they believed, that the trust would be otherwise than secure in the hands of their successors.

10.4   Removal of Trustees

LETTERSTEDT v *BROERS* (1884) 9 App Cas 371, PC

FACTS: The plaintiff sought the removal of a corporate trustee on the basis of various acts of 'misconduct and malversation' entered into on the basis of a corrupt motive by the members of the corporation. The members were said to have, *inter alia*, invested in a particular business with a view to profiting from commissions which they received from the business; and which commissions were, in addition, said to be wrongly inflated.
HELD: To warrant the removal of trustees their acts or omissions must endanger the proper exercise of the trust. Courts should exercise their jurisdiction according to the facts of each case with a view to meeting the beneficiaries' best interests. In this case the trustee was removed from office.

LORD BLACKBURN: . . . the whole case has been argued here, and, as far as their Lordships can perceive, in the Court below, as depending on the principles which should guide an English Court of Equity when called upon to remove old trustees and substitute new ones. It is not disputed that there is a jurisdiction 'in cases requiring such a remedy,' as is said in *Story's Equity Jurisprudence*, s. 1287, but there is very little to be found to guide us in saying what are the cases requiring such a remedy; so little that their Lordships are compelled to have recourse to general principles.

Story says, s. 1289,

But in cases of positive misconduct, Courts of Equity have no difficulty in interposing to remove trustees who have abused their trust; it is not indeed every mistake or neglect of duty, or inaccuracy of conduct of trustees, which will induce Courts of Equity to adopt such a course. But the acts or omissions must be such as to endanger the trust property or to shew a want of honesty, or a want of proper capacity to execute the duties, or a want of reasonable fidelity.

It seems to their Lordships that the jurisdiction which a Court of Equity has no difficulty in exercising under the circumstances indicated by Story is merely ancillary to its principal duty, to see that the trusts are properly executed. This duty is constantly being performed by the substitution of new trustees in the place of original trustees for a variety of reasons in non-contentious cases. And therefore, though it should appear that the charges of misconduct were either not made out, or were greatly exaggerated, so that the trustee was justified in resisting them, and the Court might consider that in awarding costs, yet if satisfied that the continuance of the trustee would prevent the trusts being properly executed, the trustee might be removed. It must always be borne in mind that trustees exist for the benefit of those to whom the creator of the trust has given the trust estate.

The reason why there is so little to be found in the books on this subject is probably that suggested by Mr Davey in his argument. As soon as all questions of character are as far settled as the nature of the case admits, if it appears clear that the continuance of the trustee would be detrimental to the execution of the trusts, even if for no other reason than that human infirmity would prevent those beneficially interested, or those who act for them, from working in harmony with the trustee, and if there is no reason to the contrary from the intentions of the framer of the trust to give this trustee a benefit or otherwise, the trustee is always advised by his own counsel to resign, and if, without any reasonable ground, he refused to do so, it seems to their Lordships that the Court might think it proper to remove him; but cases involving the necessity of deciding this, if they ever arise, do so without getting reported. It is to be lamented that the case was not considered in this light by the parties in the Court below, for, as far as their Lordships can see, the Board would have little or no profit from continuing to be trustees, and as such coming into continual conflict with the appellant and her legal advisers, and would probably have been glad to resign, and get out of an onerous and disagreeable position. But the case was not so treated.

In exercising so delicate a jurisdiction as that of removing trustees, their Lordships do not venture to lay down any general rule beyond the very broad principle above enunciated, that their main guide must be the welfare of the beneficiaries. Probably it is not possible to lay down any more definite rule in a matter so essentially dependent on details often of great nicety. . . .

It is quite true that friction or hostility between trustees and the immediate possessor of the trust estate is not of itself a reason for the removal of the trustees. But where the hostility is grounded on the mode in which the trust has been administered, where it has been caused wholly or partially by substantial overcharges against the trust estate, it is certainly not to be disregarded.

Looking therefore at the whole circumstances of this very peculiar case, the complete change of position, the unfortunate hostility that has arisen, and the difficult and delicate duties that may yet have to be performed, their Lordships can come to no other conclusion than that it is necessary, for the welfare of the beneficiaries, that the Board should no longer be trustees.

Probably if it had been put in this way below they would have consented. But for the benefit of the trust they should cease to be trustees, whether they consent or not.

IN RE HENDERSON [1940] 1 Ch 764, ChD

FACTS: The testator's widow and his niece were the sole beneficiaries of his estate; they were also the only trustees. Due to differences arising between them the widow stated her intention to retire from the trust, provided that the Public Trustee was appointed in her place. The niece concurred in this course of action. Later the widow added further conditions to her retirement, namely that the work of the trust be carried out in the Public Trustee's office and that independent solicitors be appointed. The niece took out a summons requesting that the widow be replaced by the Public Trustee, under the Court's power contained in s. 41 of the Trustee Act 1925.

HELD: As there was no dispute of fact in this case the court had jurisdiction to remove a trustee against her will and appoint a replacement. The Public Trustee was appointed trustee.

BENNETT J: . . . The language of s. 41, sub-s. 1, of the Trustee Act 1925, on which Mr Turnbull, for the niece, relies, is as follows: [see **10.1** for the text of s. 41].

. . . I do not think that it is open to doubt that on the language of the sub-section the Court has jurisdiction to displace a trustee against his will and to appoint a new trustee in substitution for him. Take the case of a trustee who is a convicted felon or a bankrupt whom the beneficiaries desire to have replaced by a new trustee. On the language of the sub-section, in my judgment, the Court has a discretion, which it can exercise, if it regards it as expedient so to do, by appointing a new trustee in place of the trustee who has been convicted of felony, or who is a bankrupt. That part of the sub-section which in terms refers to 'a trustee who is convicted of felony, or is a lunatic or a defective, or is a bankrupt' is expressly stated to be 'without prejudice to the generality of the foregoing provision.' I do not doubt that the section gives the Court jurisdiction in a proper case to appoint a new trustee in place of and against the will of an existing trustee. Before exercising that jurisdiction the Court must be satisfied that it is expedient to make such an appointment and that is the real question which I have to consider in the present case.

I must not lose sight of what was said by Cotton LJ, in the case of *In re Combs* 51 LT 45. Whenever there is a dispute as to some fact, as in that case, it may be that the Court should not exercise the jurisdiction under s. 41 against the will of a trustee who wants to continue to act as such. But here there is no dispute of fact and the Court is entitled to consider whether it is expedient to make the order asked for. The only question is whether on undisputed facts a case has arisen in which it is expedient to make an appointment. Having regard to the order for which the present respondent asked in the summons which she took out on December 16, 1938, having regard to the terms of her affidavit in support of that summons, and having regard to the agreement by the present applicant to concur with the present respondent in appointing the Public Trustee to be a trustee of the will, and to the form of the order made by Simonds J. I have come to the conclusion on the undisputed facts that it is expedient to exercise the jurisdiction.

The grounds on which the respondent has changed her mind are without real substance. Clearly the ground upon which she relies to explain why she has done so is that she says that there will not be independent administration of the trust by the Public Trustee unless some undertaking is given as to the solicitors to be employed in connection with it. There is no reason to suppose that if the Public Trustee be appointed there will not be independent administration of the trust.

I have come to the conclusion that it is expedient to appoint a new trustee, that it is impracticable to do so without the assistance of the Court and that there must be a substitution of the Public Trustee for the respondent.

10.5 End of Chapter Assessment Question

In 1997 Sarah settled an *inter vivos* trust. The deed appointed Tom, Tracy, Tim, Terry and Tarquin to be trustees and Albert who was then 17, to be the person able to appoint new trustees. The trust property consisted of two freehold houses, directed to be held upon trust for certain infant beneficiaries as joint tenants in equity. Immediately upon hearing of the trust the named trustees executed a 'Deed of Disclaimer'. Albert told a friend, Tabitha, that she could be a trustee and sometime afterwards he appointed himself as a trustee. A short while later Tabitha expressed a desire to be discharged from the trust. Albert agreed to release her.

Who are the current trustees, if any, of the trust?

10.6 End of Chapter Assessment Outline Answer

The original nominee trustees have executed a deed disclaiming the trust. The deed would be ineffective if they had already acted upon the trust, but the facts make it clear that they disclaimed the trust at the first opportunity. The disclaimer can, therefore, be assumed to have been valid. Does this mean, then, that the trust has failed? The rule is that a trust will not fail for want of a trustee—in other words, a trust without trustees is still valid. However, it has been argued that an *inter vivos* trust can be rendered void if it is disclaimed before it has been properly constituted. (P. Matthews [1981] Conv 141). If this argument is correct it does not offend against the rule that a trust does not fail for want of a trustee. On the contrary, where a trust is disclaimed before constitution, the trust would have failed *ab initio*. In other words, no trust would ever have come into existence. However, attractive though this argument is, the orthodox view remains that trusts have a notional validity until they are disclaimed (*Mallott v Wilson* [1903] 2 Ch 494).

The disclaimer has left the trust without trustees, and so a number of questions arise: can new trustees be appointed? Who may appoint them? Who may be appointed? How should the appointments be made? According to s. 36(1), appointments should be made by the person nominated in the trust instrument to appoint new trustees. (The Trusts of Land and Appointment of Trustees Act 1996 does not alter this). Albert answers this description, although the particular wording of his power must be scrutinised. If, for instance, he is empowered to appoint new trustees only when the current trustees 'die', he will not be able to appoint new trustees when the current trustees 'disclaim' (*Re Wheeler* [1896] 1 Ch 315 and *Re Sichel* [1916] 1 Ch 358). There is nothing in the facts of the present scenario to suggest that his power is limited in any way. However, because he is a minor (only 17 years old) any imprudent appointment he makes will be liable to be set aside. The fact that Tabitha is his friend might suggest that her appointment was not in the best interest of the trust—the court would set aside her appointment if this proved to be the case. This all assumes, of course, that her appointment was technically valid in the first place. There is a hint that it may not have been. New trustees must be appointed 'in writing'. Tabitha will not be a trustee if she has merely been 'told' of her 'appointment', as it appears on the facts.

Next, Albert decided to appoint himself as a trustee. This appointment will only be valid if Albert is now eighteen years old (trustees must be adults). There is nothing wrong, in principle, with Albert appointing himself as he is filling a genuine vacancy in the trust.

Finally, Tabitha claimed to have retired from the trust. We have already noted doubts about the correctness of her appointment, but, assuming that she has been validly appointed, the next question is whether she has validly retired. If she has not, she will not have been discharged from her obligations under the trust, and will continue to be liable, with Albert, to the beneficiaries (*Head v Gould* [1898] 2 Ch 250). She cannot have retired under s. 36 of the Trustee Act 1925 because no new trustee has been appointed in her place. This leaves retirement under s. 39. To retire under this section she must retire by deed, Albert's consent to her retirement must also be given by deed, and at least two trustees or a trust corporation must remain after her retirement. It is clear, therefore, that Tabitha has not been validly discharged from the trust. In conclusion, the current trustees are Albert and Tabitha, on the assumption that the appointments of Albert and Tabitha were valid.

CHAPTER ELEVEN

THE NATURE OF TRUSTEESHIP

11.1 Fiduciary Office

The trustee/beneficiary relationship is the fiduciary relationship *par excellence* and transactions carried out by the trustee will be scrutinised. In fact, the law will not permit trustees to put themselves in a position where there might be a conflict between their duty to the trust and their self-interest or a conflict between their duty to the trust and their duty to others.

BRISTOL AND WEST BUILDING SOCIETY v MOTHEW [1998] Ch 1, CA

FACTS: In 1988 the defendant solicitor acted for a husband and wife in the purchase of a house for £73,000 and also for the plaintiff to whom the purchasers had applied for a loan of £59,000 to finance the purchase. The plaintiff offered to advance the money on the express condition that the balance of the purchase price was provided by the purchasers without resort to further borrowing, and it instructed the solicitor to report, prior to completion, any proposal that the purchasers might create a second mortgage or otherwise borrow in order to finance part of the purchase price. The solicitor knew that the purchasers were arranging for an existing bank debt of £3,350 to be secured by a second charge on the new property but, due to an oversight, he stated in his report to the plaintiff that the balance of the purchase price was being provided by the purchasers without resort to further borrowing. The plaintiff advanced the loan and the purchase was completed. When the purchasers defaulted on their mortgage repayments the plaintiff enforced its security and the house was sold at a loss. The plaintiff sought to recover the whole of its loss on the transaction from the solicitor, alleging breach of contract, negligence and breach of trust.

HELD (*inter alia*): That the solicitor's conduct in providing the plaintiff with the wrong information, although a breach of duty, was neither dishonest nor intentional but due to an oversight and was unconnected to the fact that he was also acting for the purchasers; that, accordingly, his conduct and subsequent application of the money advanced by the plaintiff to complete the purchase was not a breach of trust or fiduciary duty; and that the order for damages for breach of trust would therefore be set aside. Appeal allowed on other grounds.

MILLETT LJ: . . . A fiduciary is someone who has undertaken to act for or on behalf of another in a particular matter in circumstances which give rise to a relationship of trust and confidence. The distinguishing obligation of a fiduciary is the obligation of loyalty. The principal is entitled to the single-minded loyalty of his fiduciary. This core liability has several facets. A fiduciary must act in good faith; he must not make a profit out of his trust; he must not place himself in a position where his duty and his interest may conflict; he may not act for his own benefit or the benefit of a third person without the informed consent of his principal. This is not intended to be an exhaustive list, but it is sufficient to indicate the nature of fiduciary obligations. They are the defining characteristics of the fiduciary. As Dr Finn pointed out in his classic work *Fiduciary Obligations*

(1977) p. 2, he is not subject to fiduciary obligations because he is a fiduciary; it is because he is subject to them that he is a fiduciary.

(In this survey I have left out of account the situation where the fiduciary deals with his principal. In such a case he must prove affirmatively that the transaction is fair and that in the course of the negotiations he made full disclosure of all facts material to the transaction. Even inadvertent failure to disclose will entitle the principal to rescind the transaction. The rule is the same whether the fiduciary is acting on his own behalf or on behalf of another. The principle need not be further considered because it does arise in the present case. The mortgage advance was negotiated directly between the society and the purchasers. The defendant had nothing to do with the negotiations. He was instructed by the society to carry out on its behalf a transaction which had already been agreed.)

The nature of the obligation determines the nature of the breach. The various obligations of a fiduciary merely reflect different aspects of his core duties of loyalty and fidelity. Breach of fiduciary obligation, therefore, connotes disloyalty or infidelity. Mere incompetence is not enough. A servant who loyally does his incompetent best for his master is not unfaithful and is not guilty of a breach of fiduciary duty.

In the present case it is clear that, if the defendant had been acting for the society alone, his admitted negligence would not have exposed him to a charge of breach of fiduciary duty. Before us counsel for the society accepted as much, but insisted that the fact that he also acted for the purchasers made all the difference. So it is necessary to ask: why did the fact that the defendant was acting for the purchasers as well as for the society convert the defendant's admitted breach of his duty of skill and care into a breach of fiduciary duty? To answer this question it is necessary to identify the fiduciary obligation of which he is alleged to have been in breach.

It is at this point, in my judgment, that the society's argument runs into difficulty. A fiduciary who acts for two principals with potentially conflicting interests without the informed consent of both is in breach of the obligation of undivided loyalty; he puts himself in a position where his duty to one principal may conflict with his duty to the other: see *Clark Boyce* v *Mouat* [1993] 4 All 268 and the cases there cited. This is sometimes described as 'the double employment rule'. Breach of the rule automatically constitutes a breach of fiduciary duty. But this is not something of which the society can complain. It knew that the defendant was acting for the purchasers when it instructed him. Indeed, that was the very reason why it chose the defendant to act for it. The potential was of the society's own making (see Finn p. 254 and *Kelly* v *Cooper* [1993] AC 205). . . .

That, of course, is not the end of the matter. Even if a fiduciary is properly acting for two principals with potentially conflicting interests he must act in good faith in the interests of each and must not act with the intention of furthering the interests of one principal to the prejudice of those of the other (see Finn p. 48). I shall call this 'the duty of good faith'. But it goes further than this. He must not allow the performance of his obligations to one principal to be influenced by his relationship with the other. He must serve each as faithfully and loyally as if he were his only principal. Conduct which is in breach of this duty need not be dishonest but it must be intentional. An unconscious omission which happens to benefit one principal at the expense of the other does not constitute a breach of fiduciary duty, though it may constitute a breach of the duty of skill and care. This is because the principle which is in play is that the fiduciary must not be inhibited by the existence of his other employment from serving the interests of his principal as faithfully and effectively as if he were the only employer. I shall call this 'the no inhibition principle'. Unless the fiduciary is inhibited or believes (whether rightly or wrongly) that he is inhibited in the performance of his duties to one principal by reason of his employment by the other, his failure to act is not attributable to the double employment.

Finally, the fiduciary must take care not to find himself in a position where there is an *actual* conflict of duty so that he cannot fulfil his obligations to one principal without failing in his obligations to the other: see *Moody* v *Cox* [1917] 2 Ch 71 and *Commonwealth Bank of Australia* v *Smith* (1991) 102 ALR 453. If he does, he may have no alternative but to cease to act for at least one and preferably both. The fact that he cannot fulfil his obligations to one principal without being in breach of his obligations to the other will not absolve him from liability. I shall call this 'the actual conflict rule'. . . .

In my judgment, the defendant was never in breach of the actual conflict rule. It is not alleged that he acted in bad faith or deliberately withheld information because he wrongly believed that his duty to the purchasers required him to do so. He was not guilty of a breach of fiduciary duty. . . .

Breach of trust

It is not disputed that from the time of its receipt by the defendant the mortgage money was trust money. It was client's money which belonged to the society and was properly paid into a client account. The defendant never claimed any beneficial interest in the money which remained throughout the property of the society in equity. The defendant held it in trust for the society but with the society's authority (and instructions) to apply it in the completion of the transaction of purchase and mortgage of the property. Those instructions were revocable but, unless previously revoked, the defendant was entitled and bound to act in accordance with them.

The society's instructions were not revoked before the defendant acted on them, and in my judgment there was no ground upon which the judge could properly conclude that his authority to apply the money in completing the transaction had determined.

If his judgment in the present case is considered without the benefit of his later explanation in *Bristol and West Building Society* v *May May & Merrimans* [1996] 2 All ER 801, it would appear that the judge was of opinion that the defendant's authority to deal with the money was automatically vitiated by the fact that it (and the cheque itself) was obtained by misrepresentation. But that is contrary to principle. Misrepresentation makes a transaction voidable not void. It gives the representee the right to elect whether to rescind or affirm the transaction. The representor cannot anticipate his decision. Unless and until the representee elects to rescind the representor remains fully bound. The defendant's misrepresentations merely gave the society the right to elect to withdraw from the transaction on discovering the truth. Since its instructions to the defendant were revocable in any case, this did not materially alter the position so far as he was concerned, though it may have strengthened the society's position in relation to the purchasers.

The right to rescind for misrepresentation is an equity. Until it is exercised the beneficial interest in any property transferred in reliance on the representation remains vested in the transferee. In *El Ajou* v *Dollar Land Holdings Plc* [1993] 3 All ER 717, 734 I suggested that on rescission the equitable title might revest in the representee retrospectively at least to the extent necessary to support an equitable tracing claim. I was concerned to circumvent the supposed rule that there must be a fiduciary relationship or retained beneficial interest before resort may be had to the equitable tracing rules. The rule would have been productive of the most extraordinary anomalies in that case, and its existence continually threatens to frustrate attempts to develop a coherent law of restitution. Until the equitable tracing rules are made available in support of the ordinary common law claim for money had and received some problems will remain incapable of sensible resolution.

But all that is by the way. Whether or not there is a retrospective vesting for tracing purposes it is clear that on rescission the equitable title does not revest retrospectively *so as to cause an application of trust money which was properly authorised when made to be afterwards treated as a breach of trust*. In *Lipkin Gorman* v *Karpnale Ltd* [1991] 2 AC 548 Lord Goff of Chieveley said, at p. 573:

> Of course, 'tracing' or 'following' property into its product involves a decision by the owner of the original property to assert his title to the product in place of his original property. This is sometimes referred to as ratification. I myself would not so describe it, but it has, in my opinion, at least one feature in common with ratification, that it cannot be relied upon so as to render an innocent recipient a wrongdoer (cf. *Bolton Partners* v *Lambert* (1889) 41 ChD 295, 307, *per* Cotton LJ.: 'an act lawful at the time of its performance [cannot] be rendered unlawful, by the application of the doctrine of ratification.')

In *Westdeutsche Landesbank Girozentrale* v *Islington London Borough Council* [1996] AC 669 Lord Browne-Wilkinson expressly rejected the possibility that a recipient of trust money could be personally liable, regardless of fault, for any subsequent payment away of the moneys to third parties even though, at the date of such payment, he was ignorant of the existence of any trust. He said, at p. 705:

> Since the equitable jurisdiction to enforce trusts depends upon the conscience of the holder of the legal interest being affected, he cannot be a trustee of the property if and so long as he is ignorant of the facts alleged to affect his conscience, i.e. until he is aware that he is intended to hold the property for the benefit of others in the case of an express or implied trust, or, in the case of a constructive trust, of the factors which are alleged to affect his conscience.

Mutatis mutandis that passage is directly applicable in the present case. The defendant knew that he was a trustee of the money for the society; but he did not realise that he had misled the society and could not know that his authority to complete had determined (if indeed it had). He could not be bound to repay the money to the society so long as he was ignorant of the facts which had brought his authority to an end, for those are the facts which are alleged to affect his conscience and subject him to an obligation to return the money to the society.

Before us the society put forward a more sophisticated argument. The defendant's instructions, it pointed out, expressly required him to report the arrangements in question 'to the society prior to completion.' This, it was submitted, made it a condition of the defendant's authority to complete that he had complied with his obligation. Whether he knew it or not, he had no authority to complete. It was not necessary for the society to revoke his authority or withdraw from the transaction. I do not accept this. The society's standing instructions did not clearly make the defendant's authority to complete conditional on having complied with his instructions. Whether they did so or not is, course, a question of construction, and it is possible that the society could adopt instructions which would have this effect. But it would in my judgment require very clear wording to produce so inconvenient and impractical a result. No solicitor could safely accept such instructions, he could never be certain that he was entitled to complete.

In my judgment the defendant's authority to apply the mortgage money in the completion of the purchase was not conditional on his having first complied with his contractual obligations to the society, was not vitiated by the misrepresentations for which he was responsible but of which he was unaware, had not been revoked, and was effective to prevent his payment being a breach of trust. Given his state of knowledge (and, more importantly, that his authority had not been revoked), he had no choice but to complete.

Conclusion

In my judgment the defendant was not guilty of breach of trust or fiduciary duty. This makes it unnecessary to consider what the consequences of such a breach would have been. I would allow the appeal and set aside the money judgment. I would leave undisturbed the judgments for damages to be assessed for breach of contract and negligence, but make it clear that it does not follow that the society will establish any recoverable loss.

11.1.1 CONFLICT OF INTEREST AND DUTY

SARGEANT AND ANOTHER v NATIONAL WESTMINSTER BANK PLC AND ANOTHER (1990) 61 P & CR 518, CA

FACTS: A testator let a number of farms to his children which they worked as a partnership. He then appointed his children to be executors and trustees under his will. When one of the children (Charles) died the surviving children exercised an option to purchase the deceased child's share of the partnership. Later they revealed plans to purchase the freehold of one of the farms of which they were tenants, and to sell the other freeholds. The administrators of the estate of the deceased child objected to these plans and argued that the surviving children would be in breach of their trust were they to sell, to themselves, the trust-owned freeholds of which they were trustees and under which they were tenants. The trustees sought a declaration that they would be entitled to sell the freeholds. This declaration was granted. The administrators appealed.

HELD: The trustees were in a position where their interest as tenants might conflict with their duties as trustees, but they had not put themselves in that position. The trustees' rights as tenants pre-dated their duties as trustees and they would therefore be permitted to assert those rights. They must nevertheless endeavour to obtain the best price for the freeholds in order to fulfil their obligations to the trust.

NOURSE LJ: The rule that a trustee must not profit from his trust holds that prevention is better than cure. While it invariably requires that a profit shall be yielded up, it prefers to intervene beforehand by dissolving the connection out of which the profit may be made. At that stage the rule is expressed by saying that a trustee must not put himself in a position where his interest and duty conflict. But to express it in that way is to acknowledge that if he is put there, not by himself, but by the testator or settlor under whose dispositions his trust arises, the rule does not apply. . . .

In this case two of the testator's children, as the trustees of his will, are the legal owners and trustees for sale of his three freehold farms. Under the terms of the will, each of them is absolutely entitled to one third of the net proceeds of sale and the net rents and profits until sale. They are also the tenants of the farms under tenancies which the testator originally granted to them and a deceased child during his life-time. The owners of the remaining third of the beneficial interest, subject to the tenancies, are the personal representatives of the deceased child. . . .

I now come to the first and second arguments which were advanced by Mr Romer on behalf of the administrators. Although he sought to keep them separate, they were both founded on the rule that a trustee must not put himself in a position where his interest and duty conflict. Mr Romer relied on the following passage in the judgment of Lord Herschell in *Bray* v *Ford* [1896] AC 44 which was described by Lord Upjohn in *Boardman* v *Phipps* [1967] 2 AC 46 as the best statement of the rule:

> It is an inflexible rule of a Court of Equity that a person in a fiduciary position . . . is not, unless otherwise expressly provided, entitled to make a profit, he is not allowed to put himself in a position where his interest and duty conflict. It does not appear to me that this rule is, as has been said, founded upon principles of morality. I regard it rather as based on the consideration that, human nature being what it is, there is a danger, in such circumstances, of the person holding a fiduciary position being swayed by interest rather than by duty, and thus prejudicing those whom he was bound to protect. It has, therefore, been deemed expedient to lay down this positive rule.

Mr Romer submitted that the trustees' duty is to obtain the best price for the freeholds of the farms, which admittedly can only be obtained by a sale with vacant possession, whereas their interest is to preserve their tenancies and to sell subject to them, in which event the best price will not be obtained. Mr Romer therefore submitted that if the trustees go ahead and sell subject to the tenancies, either to themselves or to a third party, they will be putting themselves in a position where their interest and duty conflict. . . .

What then happened on the death of Charles? He necessarily ceased to be a trustee of the will. His estate retained his beneficial interest in the farms, subject to the tenancies. The arrangements between the children might have been such that his estate retained his interest in the tenancies as well. No doubt for a short period it did. But under the provisions of the partnership deed, to which Charles himself had been a party, the trustees acquired his share in the partnership, including his share in the tenancies. Thenceforth each of the trustees continued to have the rights of a tenant and a beneficiary. But Charles' estate only had the rights of a beneficiary.

It cannot be doubted that the trustees have ever since been in a position where their interests as tenants *may* conflict with their duties as trustees to the estate of Charles. But the conclusive objection to the application of the absolute rule on which Mr Romer relies is that it is not they who have put themselves in that position. They have been put there mainly by the testator's grant of the tenancies and by the provisions of his will and partly by contractual arrangements to which Charles himself was a party and of which his representatives cannot complain. The administrators cannot therefore complain of the trustees' continued assertion of their rights as tenants.

Since the absolute rule on which Mr Romer relies does not apply, there is no absolute requirement that the trustees should appoint a new trustee before making any sale subject to the tenancies. Nor is there any absolute bar to their selling to themselves so long as the tenancies subsist. On the other hand, they must continue to discharge their fiduciary duties to Charles' estate in regard to the freeholds, in particular by obtaining the best price for them subject to the tenancies. In the end, the basis for Mr Romer's arguments was seen to be a fear or a suspicion that the trustees will not properly discharge that duty. But there is no evidence either that they have failed to discharge their duties in the past or that they will fail to do so in the future. Without such evidence, it is wholly inappropriate for the court to interfere. . . .

RE MULHOLLAND'S WT [1949] 1 All ER 460, ChD

FACTS: A testator leased land to a bank together with an option to purchase the freehold. The testator later appointed the bank and his widow to be the executors and trustees of his estate. Some time after the testator's death the bank exercised its option to purchase the freehold by giving notice to that effect. The beneficiaries brought an action seeking to have the conveyance set aside on the ground that it had been made in breach of the bank's fiduciary duties.
HELD: The notice exercising the option to purchase the freehold did not create a new contractual relationship between bank and trust. The bank's contract to purchase had in essence arisen before the bank had been placed in the position of trustee. The bank would therefore be permitted to exercise the option.

WYNN-PARRY J: . . . It was contended that the plaintiffs, as beneficiaries under the will, were entitled to have the conveyance set aside because at the date when the bank exercised the option they were trustees of the property the subject-matter of the option; that, as trustees, they were not entitled to place themselves in a position where their duty and their interests conflicted; and, therefore, having accepted the executorship and trusteeship, they had effectively precluded themselves from exercising the option.

But the principle . . . that the existence of the fiduciary relationship creates an inability in the trustee to contract in regard to the trust property . . . does not touch the position arising where the contract in question has been brought into existence before the fiduciary relationship.

11.1.1.1 The self-dealing rule and the fair dealing rule

RE THOMPSON'S SETTLEMENT [1986] 1 Ch 99, ChD

FACTS: The settlor, T, declared trusts of the sale proceeds of certain freehold properties which had been conveyed to trustees. At the date of the settlement the properties were let to a farming corporation of which T was the managing director. Other directors included T's sons, W and J, who were also trustees of the settlement. After T's death a meeting was held between W, J, their solicitor and the auditors of the farming corporation. At that meeting it was agreed that the corporation's tenancies of the various properties should be assigned to the businesses of W and J respectively, one business being a company, the other a partnership. The corporation was wound up without ever having formally consented to the assignments of the leases, and without having made any formal assignment of them. Some time later the family adopted a plan to distribute the properties amongst all the family members. In order to do this fairly it was necessary to make an accurate valuation of each of the properties. The valuations would be dramatically affected by W and J's leases if they were valid, the unencumbered freehold of the farm being more valuable than a freehold subject to a lease. W and J took out a summons to determine whether the tenancies would be voidable at the instance of a beneficiary even if the assignments had been fair.
HELD: according to the 'self-dealing rule' a trustee's purchase of trust property from the trust is voidable *ex debito justitiae* (out of a debt to justice). Accordingly such a purchase

would be set aside if any beneficiary wished it to be so set aside. It would be no defence to such an action for the trustee to show that the purchase had been fair or even generous to the beneficiaries. Nor would it be a defence, on the facts of the present case, to argue that the leases had never in fact been trust property (but had been property of the corporation). Nor could it be argued that the leases had not been taken by W and J personally, but had been taken by the businesses controlled by them. (In spite of the fact that one of those, being a company, was an independent legal person). The 'self-dealing' rule should not be narrowly construed, it is an application of the wider principle that trustees must not put themselves into a position where their duties and self interests may be in conflict, or where their duties to one may conflict with their duties to another. The principle is applied strictly where a trustee concurs in a transaction which cannot be carried into effect without his concurrence and who has a personal interest in or owes a fiduciary duty to another in relation to the same transaction.

VINELOTT J: . . . It is clear that the self-dealing rule is an application of the wider principle that a man must not put himself in a position where duty and interest conflict *or* where his duty to one conflicts with his duty to another: see in particular the opinion of Lord Dunedin in *Wright* v *Morgan* [1926] AC 788 which I have cited. The principle is applied stringently in cases where a trustee concurs in a transaction which cannot be carried into effect without his concurrence and who also has an interest in or owes a fiduciary duty to another in relation to the same transaction. The transaction cannot stand if challenged by a beneficiary because in the absence of an express provision in the trust instrument the beneficiaries are entitled to require that the trustees act unanimously and that each brings to bear a mind unclouded by any contrary interest or duty in deciding whether it is in the interest of the beneficiaries that the trustees concur in it.

The same principle also applies, but less stringently, in a case within the fair-dealing rule, such as the purchase by a trustee of a beneficiary's beneficial interest. There, there are genuinely two parties to the transaction and it will be allowed to stand if freely entered into and if the trustee took no advantage from his position or from any knowledge acquired from it.

In the instant case the concurrence of the trustees of the grandchildren's settlement was required if the leases were to be assigned to or new tenancies created in favour of the new company and the partnership. The beneficiaries were entitled to ask that the trustees should give unprejudiced consideration to the question whether they should refuse to concur in the assignments in the expectation that a surrender of the leases might be negotiated from the old company and the estates sold or let on the open market. . . .

11.1.1.2   The effect of retirement

RE BOLES AND BRITISH LAND COMPANY'S CONTRACT [1902] 1 Ch 244, ChD

FACTS: One of the trustees (and executor) of a will trust retired from office by deed and with the consent of the continuing trustees. Twelve years later the continuing trustees sold land owned by the trust to the trustee who had retired. The question arose whether the sale was valid or should be set aside.
HELD: The sale was valid.

BUCKLEY J: . . . Apart from any circumstances of doubt or suspicion, is there any rule of this Court that a person, who has ceased for twelve years to be a trustee of an instrument which contains a trust for sale, is precluded from becoming a purchaser of property subject to the trust? I think there is not. The principle that lies at the root of this matter is that a trustee for sale owes a duty to his *cestuis que trust* to do everything in his power for their benefit, and is therefore absolutely precluded from buying the trust property, irrespective of questions of undervalue or otherwise, because he may be thus induced to neglect his duty. Beyond that, if he retires with a view to becoming a purchaser so as to put himself in a position to do what would otherwise be a breach of trust, that will not do. But if he has retired and there is nothing to shew that at the time of the retirement there was any idea of a sale, and in fact there is no sale for twelve years after his retirement, is there anything to prevent him from becoming a purchaser? I think not. . . .

11.2 Trustees' Standard of Care

11.2.1 THE GENERAL OBJECTIVE STANDARD

SPEIGHT v *GAUNT* (1883) 22 ChD 727, CA

FACTS: The testator, Speight, had been a 'stuff manufacturer' in Bradford. In his will he bequeathed his estate to Messrs Gaunt and Wilkinson upon certain trusts for the benefit of Mrs Speight and her children. The trustees employed a stockbroker, Cooke, to sell some securities forming part of the estate and to reinvest the proceeds in new securities. Cooke was a broker of high repute. Having placed with the agent the securities to be sold, Gaunt made enquiries of Cooke on many occasions as to when the new securities would be handed over to the trust. Cooke gave excuses on these occasions. Eventually Cooke declared his firm insolvent and was declared personally bankrupt. £15,275 of trust monies were lost. Mrs Speight brought an action seeking a declaration that Mr Gaunt had breached his trust and seeking an order requiring him to account for the loss, together with interest at 4 per cent.
HELD: The Vice-Chancellor gave judgment for the beneficiaries at first instance. This was overturned by the Court of Appeal.

JESSEL MR: . . . It seems to me that on general principles a trustee ought to conduct the business of the trust in the same manner that an ordinary prudent man of business would conduct his own, and that beyond that there is no liability or obligation on the trustee. In other words, a trustee is not bound because he is a trustee to conduct business in other than the ordinary and usual way in which similar business is conducted by mankind in transactions of their own. It never could be reasonable to make a trustee adopt further and better precautions than an ordinary prudent man of business would adopt, or to conduct the business in any other way. If it were otherwise, no one would be a trustee at all. He is not paid for it. He says, 'I take all reasonable precautions and all the precautions which are deemed reasonable by prudent men of business, and beyond that I am not required to go.' Now what are the usual precautions taken by men of business when they make an investment? If the investment is an investment made on the Stock Exchange through a stockbroker, the ordinary course of business is for the investor to select a stockbroker in good credit and in a good position, having regard to the sum to be invested, and to direct him to make the investment. . . .
. . . You are to endeavour as far as possible, having regard to the whole transaction, to avoid making an honest man who is not paid for the performance of an unthankful office liable for the failure of other people from whom he receives no benefit. I think that is the view which has been taken by modern Judges, and some of the older cases in which a different view has been taken would now be repudiated with indignation. . . .

BUTTLE v *SAUNDERS* [1950] 2 All ER 193, ChD

FACTS: Trustees for sale of certain land had reached an advanced stage of negotiations for the sale of the land to Party A when Party B ('Canon Buttle') made a higher offer. The trustees refused the higher offer, believing themselves to be bound by commercial morality to complete with Party A.
HELD: The trustees had wrongly assumed that they could act like an ordinary beneficial owner of property. The trustees had breached their duty to obtain the best price for the beneficiaries.

WYNN-PARRY J: . . . It has been argued on behalf of the trustees that they were justified in the circumstances in not pursuing the offer made by Canon Buttle and in deciding to go forward with the transaction with Mrs Simpson. It is true that persons who are not in the position of trustees are entitled, if they so desire, to accept a lesser price than that which they might obtain on the sale of property, and not infrequently a vendor, who has gone some lengths in negotiating with a prospective purchaser, decides to close the deal with that purchaser, notwithstanding that he is presented with a higher offer. It redounds to the credit of a man who acts like that in such circumstances. Trustees, however, are not vested with such complete freedom. They have an overriding duty to obtain the best price which they can for their beneficiaries. It would, however, be an unfortunate simplification of the problem if one were to take the view that the mere production of an increased offer at any stage, however late in the negotiations, should throw on the trustees a duty to accept the higher offer and resile from the existing offer. For myself, I think that trustees have such a discretion in the matter as will allow them to act with proper prudence. I can see no reason why trustees should not pray in aid the common-sense rule underlying the old proverb: 'A bird in the hand is worth two in the bush.' I can imagine cases where trustees could properly refuse a higher offer and proceed with a lower offer. Each case must, of necessity, depend on its own facts. In regard to the case now before me, my view is that the trustees and their solicitors acted on an incorrect principle. The only consideration which was present to their minds was that they had gone so far in the negotiations with Mrs Simpson that they could not properly, from the point of view of commercial morality, resile from those negotiations. That being so, they did not, to any extent, probe Canon Buttle's offer as, in my view, they should have done. . . .

11.2.2 THE HIGHER OBJECTIVE STANDARD

BARTLETT AND OTHERS v BARCLAYS BANK TRUST CO. LTD
[1980] 1 All ER 139, ChD

FACTS: The settlor had settled 99·8 per cent of the shares in a private company ('BTL') on trust for his wife and issue. The trustee of the settlement was a Barclays Bank trust corporation. By 1960 the settlor and his wife had both died and no member of the settlor's family remained on the board of BTL. Neither did any members of the board regard themselves as representatives of the trust corporation. At various meetings the chairman of BTL put forward specific property development projects for the board's consideration, and without consulting the bank invested heavily in two of the projects. One of these projects (at Guildford) made a substantial profit, but the other (at the Old Bailey, London) made a significant loss. The market value of shares in BTL fell causing a great loss to the trust. The beneficiaries brought an action against the trustees to make good the losses.
HELD: The bank had failed to act as an ordinary prudent person of business would have acted in relation to his own affairs. Moreover, a professional, corporate trustee such as the bank owed an even higher standard of care than that and would be liable to the extent that it failed to exercise such higher standard of care.

BRIGHTMAN J: . . . What, then, was the duty of the bank and did the bank fail in its duty? It does not follow that because a trustee could have prevented a loss it is therefore liable for the loss. The questions which I must ask myself are: (1) what was the duty of the bank as the holder of 99·8 per cent of the shares in BTL and BTH ?(2) was the bank in breach of duty in any and if so what respect? (3) if so, did that breach of duty cause the loss which was suffered by the trust estate? (4) if so, to what extent is the bank liable to make good that loss? In approaching these questions, I bear in mind that the attack on the bank is based, not on wrongful acts, but on wrongful omissions, that is to say, non-feasance not misfeasance.

The cases established that it is the duty of a trustee to conduct the business of the trust with the same care as an ordinary prudent man of business would extend towards his own affairs;: see *Re Speight, Speight* v *Gaunt* (1883) 22 ChD 727 *per* Jessel MR and Bowen LJ (affirmed on appeal and see Lord Blackburn). In applying this principle, Lindley LJ (who was the third member of the court in *Re Speight*) added in *Re Whiteley* (1886) 33 ChD 347:

. . . care must be taken not to lose sight of the fact that the business of the trustee, and the business which the ordinary prudent man is supposed to be conducting for himself, is the business of investing money for the benefit of persons who are to enjoy it at some future time, and not for the sole benefit of the person entitled to the present income. The duty of a trustee is not to take such care only as a prudent man would take if he had only himself to consider; the duty rather is to take such care as an ordinary prudent man would take if he were minded to make an investment for the benefit of other people for whom he felt morally bound to provide. That is the kind of business the ordinary prudent man is supposed to be engaged in; and unless this is borne in mind the standard of a trustee's duty will be fixed too low: lower than it has ever yet been fixed, and lower certainly than the House of Lords or this Court endeavoured to fix it in *Speight* v *Gaunt*.

On appeal Lord Watson added:

> Business men of ordinary prudence may, and frequently do, select investments which are more or less of a speculative character; but it is the duty of a trustee to confine himself to the class of investments which are permitted by the trust, and likewise to avoid all investments of that class which are attended with hazard.

That does not mean that the trustee is bound to avoid all risk and in effect act as an insurer of the trust fund: in *Re Godfrey* (1883) 23 ChD 483 Bacon V-C said:

> No doubt it is the duty of a trustee, in administering the trusts of a will, to deal with property intrusted into his care exactly as any prudent man would deal with his own property. But the words in which the rule is expressed must not be strained beyond their meaning. Prudent businessmen in their dealings incur risk. That may and must happen in almost all human affairs.

The distinction is between a prudent degree of risk on the one hand, and hazard on the other. Nor must the court be astute to fix liability on a trustee who has committed no more than an error of judgment, from which no business man, however prudent, can expect to be immune: in *Re Chapman* [1896] 2 Ch 763 Lopes LJ said:

> A trustee who is honest and reasonably competent is not to be held responsible for a mere error in judgment when the question which he has to consider is whether a security of a class authorised, but depreciated in value, should be retained or realised, provided he acts with reasonable care, prudence, and circumspection.

If the trust had existed without the incorporation of BTL, so that the bank held the freehold and leasehold properties and other assets of BTL directly on the trusts of the settlement, it would in my opinion have been a clear breach of trust for the bank to have hazarded trust money in the Old Bailey development project in partnership with Stock Conversion. The Old Bailey project was a gamble, because it involved buying into the site at prices in excess of the investment values of the properties, with no certainty or probability, with no more than a chance, that planning permission could be obtained for a financially viable redevelopment, that the numerous proprietors would agree to sell out or join in the scheme, that finance would be available on acceptable terms, and that the development would be completed, or at least become a marketable asset, before the time came to start winding up the trust. However one looks at it, the project was a hazardous speculation on which no trustee could properly have ventured without explicit authority in the trust instrument. I therefore hold that the entire expenditure in the Old Bailey project would have been incurred in breach of trust, had the money been spent by the bank itself. The fact that it was a risk acceptable to the board of a wealthy company like Stock Conversion has little relevance.

I turn to the question, what was the duty of the bank as the holder of shares in BTL and BTH? I will first answer this question without regard to the position of the bank as a specialist trustee, to which I will advert later. The bank, as trustee, was bound to act in relation to the shares and to the controlling position which they conferred, in the same manner as a prudent man of business. The prudent man of business will act in such manner as is necessary to safeguard his investment. He will do this in two ways. If facts come to his knowledge which tell him that the company's affairs are not being conducted as they should be, or which put him on enquiry, he will take appropriate action. Appropriate action will no doubt consist in the first instance of enquiry of and consultation with the directors, and in the last but most unlikely resort, the convening of a general meeting to replace one or more directors. What the prudent man of business will *not* do is to content himself with the receipt of such information on the affairs of the company as a shareholder ordinarily receives at annual general meetings. Since he has the power to do so, he will go further and see that he has sufficient information to enable him to make a responsible decision from time to time either to let matters proceed as they are proceeding, or to intervene if he is dissatisfied. This topic was considered by Cross J in *Re Lucking's Will Trusts* [1968] 1 WLR 866. In that case nearly 70 per cent of the shares in the company were held by two trustees, L and B, as part of the estate of the deceased; about 29 per cent belonged to L in his own right, and 1 per cent belonged to L's wife. The directors in 1954 were Mr and Mrs L and D, who was the manager of the business. In 1956 B was appointed trustee to act jointly with L. The company was engaged in the manufacture and sale of shoe accessories. It had a small factory employing about 20 people, and one or two travellers. It also had an agency in France. D wrongfully drew some £15,000 from the company's bank account in excess of his remuneration, and later became bankrupt. The money was lost. Cross J said this:

> The conduct of the defendant trustees is, I think, to be judged by the standard applied in *Re Speight, Speight* v *Gaunt* (1883) 22 ChD 727, namely, that a trustee is only bound to conduct the business of the trust in such a way as an ordinary prudent man would conduct a business of his own. Now, what steps, if any, does a reasonably prudent man who finds himself a majority shareholder in a private company take with regard to the management of the company's affairs? He does not, I think, content himself with such information as to the management of the company's affairs as he is entitled to as shareholder, but ensures that he is represented on the board. He may be prepared to run the business himself as managing director or, at least, to become a non-executive director while having the business managed by someone else. Alternatively, he may find someone who will act as his nominee on the board and report to him from time to time as to the company's affairs. In the same way, as it seems to me, trustees holding a controlling interest ought to ensure so far as they can that they have such information as to the progress of the company's affairs as directors would have. If they sit back and allow the company to be run by the minority shareholder and receive no more information than shareholders are entitled to, they do so at their risk if things go wrong.

I do not understand Cross J to have been saying that in every case where trustees have a controlling interest in a company it is their duty to ensure that one of their number is a director or that they have a nominee on the board who will report from time to time on the affairs of the company. He was merely outlining convenient methods by which a prudent man of business (as also a trustee) with a controlling interest in a private company, can place himself in a position to make an informed decision whether any action is appropriate to be taken for the protection of his asset. Other methods may be equally satisfactory and convenient, depending on the circumstances of the individual case. Alternatives which spring to mind are the receipt of the copies of the agenda and minutes of board meetings if regularly held, the receipt of monthly management accounts in the case of a trading concern, or quarterly reports. Every case will depend on its own facts. The possibilities are endless. It would be useless, indeed misleading, to seek to lay down a general rule. The purpose to be achieved is not that of monitoring every move of the directors, but of making it reasonably probable, so far as circumstances permit, that the trustee or (as in *Re Lucking's Will Trusts* [1968] 1 WLR 866) one of them will receive an adequate flow of information in time to enable the trustees to make use of their controlling interest should this be necessary for the protection of their trust asset, namely the shareholding. The obtaining of information is not an end in itself, but merely a means of enabling the trustees to safeguard the interests of their beneficiaries. . . .

So far, I have applied the test of the ordinary prudent man of business. Although I am not aware that the point has previously been considered, except briefly in *Re Waterman's*

Will Trusts [1952] 2 All ER 1054, I am of opinion that a higher duty of care is plainly due from someone like a trust corporation which carries on a specialised business of trust management. A trust corporation holds itself out in its advertising literature as being above ordinary mortals. With a specialist staff of trained trust officers and managers, with ready access to financial information and professional advice, dealing with and solving trust problems day after day, the trust corporation holds itself out, and rightly, as capable of providing an expertise which it would be unrealistic to expect and unjust to demand from the ordinary prudent man or woman who accepts, probably unpaid and sometimes reluctantly from a sense of family duty, the burdens of a trusteeship. Just as, under the law of contract, a professional person possessed of a particular skill is liable for breach of contract if he neglects to use the skill and experience which he professes, so I think that a professional corporate trustee is liable for breach of trust if loss is caused to the trust fund because it neglects to exercise the special care and skill which it professes to have. The advertising literature of the bank was not in evidence (other than the scale of fees) but counsel for the bank did not dispute that trust corporations, including the bank, hold themselves out as possessing a superior ability for the conduct of trust business, and in any event I would take judicial notice of that fact. Having expressed my view of the higher duty required from a trust corporation, I should add that the bank's counsel did not dispute the proposition.

In my judgment the bank wrongfully and in breach of trust neglected to ensure that it received an adequate flow of information concerning the intentions and activities of the boards of BTL and BTH. It was not proper for the bank to confine itself to the receipt of the annual balance sheet and profit and loss account, detailed annual financial statements and the chairman's report and statement, and to attendance at the annual general meetings and the luncheons that followed, which were the limits of the bank's regular sources of information. Had the bank been in receipt of more frequent information it would have been able to step in and stop, and ought to have stopped, Mr Roberts and the board embarking on the Old Bailey project. That project was imprudent and hazardous and wholly unsuitable for a trust whether undertaken by the bank direct or through the medium of its wholly owned company. Even without the regular flow of information which the bank ought to have had, it knew enough to put it on enquiry. There were enough obvious points at which the bank should have intervened and asked questions. Assuming, as I do, that the questions would have been answered truthfully, the bank would have discovered the gamble on which Mr Roberts and his board were about to embark in relation to the Old Bailey site, and it could have, and should have, stopped the initial move towards disaster, and later on arrested further progress towards disaster. I have indicated in the course of this judgment a number of obvious points at which the bank should have intervened, and it would be repetitive to summarise them.

I hold that the bank failed in its duty whether it is judged by the standard of the prudent man of business or of the skilled trust corporation. The bank's breach of duty caused the loss which was suffered by the trust estate. If the bank had intervened as it could and should have, that loss would not have been incurred. By 'loss', I mean the depreciation which took place in the market value of the BTL and BTH shares, by comparison with the value the shares would have commanded if the loss on the Old Bailey project had not been incurred, and reduction of dividends through loss of income. The bank is liable for the loss so suffered by the trust estate, except to the extent that I shall hereafter indicate.

The bank also relies on cll 18 and 26 of the settlement. Clause 18 entitled the bank to—

act in relation to [BTL] or any other company and the shares securities and properties thereof in such way as it shall think best calculated to benefit the trust premises and as if it was the absolute owner of such shares securities and property.

In my judgment this is a clause which confers on the bank power to engage in a transaction which might otherwise be outside the scope of its authority; it is not an indemnity protecting the bank against liability for a transaction which is a breach of trust because it is one that a prudent man of business would have eschewed. . . .

Two particular defences remain. The Limitation Act 1939 is pleaded. It is relied on in relation to any income lost by Sir Basil on money spent in breach of trust prior to 19th

August 1971, six years before the writ was issued. The defence is sound unless it can be said that the right of action in relation to the lost income was 'concealed by the fraud' of the bank within the meaning of s. 26(b) of the 1939 Act. The purpose of the 1939 Act is to protect a defendant against stale claims, particularly where evidence for the defence may have been obscured or lost by the passage of time. Nothing like that has happened here. The beneficiaries never received the annual accounts or reports of BTL and BTH, or copies of board minutes or the chairman's statements. Sir Basil could not be expected by the bank to know of the various wrongful purchases into the Old Bailey site at inflated prices, or the diminished income resulting therefrom. Nor is it usual, in my experience, for life tenants to be sent annual trust accounts. 'Fraud', in the context of s. 26(b), does not mean common law fraud or deceit. But it does seem to envisage conduct which, if not fraudulent in the more usual sense, is unconscionable having regard to the relationship between the parties: see *Kitchen* v *Royal Air Forces Association* [1958] 2 All ER 241. 'Fraud' is used in the equitable sense to denote conduct by the defendant or his agent such that it would be against conscience for him to avail himself of the lapse of time. As Lord Denning MR said in *Applegate* v *Moss* [1971] 1 All ER 747:

> The section applies whenever the conduct of the defendant or his agent has been such as to hide from the plaintiff the existence of his right of action, in such circumstances that it would be inequitable to allow the defendant to rely on the lapse of time as a bar to the claim.

and in *King* v *Victor Parsons & Co.* [1972] 2 All ER 625:

> If the defendant was, however, quite unaware that he was committing a wrong or a breach of contract, it would be different.

In the instant case there was no cover-up by the bank. The bank had no inkling that it was acting in breach of trust. The defence is, in my judgment, available to the bank if its conscience permits it to rely on it having regard to the fact that the passage of time caused no prejudice whatever to the bank.

It follows that Sir Basil is not entitled to claim against the bank a share in any increased dividends which ought to have been declared by BTL over the six years prior to the issue of the writ.

Section 61 of the Trustee Act 1925 is pleaded. There is no doubt that the bank acted honestly. I do not think it acted reasonably. Nor do I think it would be fair to excuse the bank at the expense of the beneficiaries.

There remains this defence, which I take from para. 26 of the amended pleading:

> In about 1963 the Old Company purchased a site at Woodbridge Road, Guildford, pursuant to the policy pleaded in paragraph 19 hereof, for the sum of £79,000, and re-sold the same for £350,000 to MEPC Ltd. in 1973. The net profit resulting from such sale was £271,000. If, which is denied, the Defendant is liable for breach of trust, whether as alleged in the amended Statement of Claim or otherwise, the Defendant claims credit for such sum of £271,000 or other sum found to be gained in taking any accounts or inquiries.

The general rule as stated in all the textbooks, with some reservations, is that where a trustee is liable in respect of distinct breaches of trust, one of which has resulted in a loss and the other in a gain, he is not entitled to set off the gain against the loss, unless they arise in the same transaction: see *Halsbury's Laws of England, Snell's Equity, Lewin on Trusts, Underhill's Law of Trusts and Trustees*. The relevant cases are, however, not altogether easy to reconcile. All are centenarians and none is quite like the present. The Guildford development stemmed from exactly the same policy and (to a lesser degree because it proceeded less far) exemplified the same folly as the Old Bailey project. Part of the profit was in fact used to finance the Old Bailey disaster. By sheer luck the gamble paid off handsomely, on capital account. I think it would be unjust to deprive the bank of this element of salvage in the course of assessing the cost of the shipwreck. My order will therefore reflect the bank's right to an appropriate set-off.

11.2.3   A SUBJECTIVE STANDARD OF CARE?

Dennis R. Paling, 'The Trustee's Duty of Skill and Care' [1973] 37 Conv 48

. . .

2.   THE PRESENT STANDARD IS TOO ONEROUS AND TOO INFLEXIBLE FOR THE ROLE WHICH THE TRUST NOW PLAYS

There are several aspects of the standard at present applied which deserve comment. The standard is that of an ordinary prudent man, who is for these purposes a man of business. And it is the standard which such a man would exercise if he was regardful of the pecuniary interests in the future of those having claims upon him, which includes those having moral as well as legal claims. And this standard applies to the exercise of the trustees' discretionary powers generally and not merely to the trustees' powers of selecting investments.

However, the most remarkable feature of the trustees' duty of skill and care is its extremely onerous nature. In the words of Lord Hardwicke LC in *Knight* v *Earl of Plymouth* (1747) 1 Dick 120 when to the onerous nature of the duty of skill and care is added the fact that a trustee is also under a duty to act gratuitously, it would appear that the office of trustee is such that 'It is an act of great kindness in anyone to accept it.' This would have been particularly true in the eighteenth century, when the typical trustee would have been a private individual chosen because he was a friend of the settlor: and, even in the present century, when the trustee is often a banker or solicitor, the duty of skill and care remains extremely onerous. . . .

4.   PAID AND UNPAID TRUSTEES

The traditional view stated by Underhill and by the editors of subsequent editions of his textbook up to and including the tenth edition was that the same standard should be demanded of a trustee whether he acts gratuitously or receives payment. Romer J in *Jobson* v *Palmer* [1893] 1 Ch 71 expressed the same view. He thus held that a paid trustee, who had selected a servant with the same degree of prudence as an ordinary man of business would exercise in his own affairs, was not liable when the servant stole trust property.

But it is preferable to distinguish between the standards imposed upon paid and unpaid trustees, because the status of paid and unpaid trustees is different. The paid trustee is frequently a banker or actuary who advertises for business and has no personal relationship with the settlor. The unpaid trustee is frequently a personal friend of the settlor . . . if the standard of skill and care expected of an unpaid trustee is that of an ordinary prudent man in the conduct of his own affairs, the higher standard to be imposed upon a paid trustee must be oppressively high. This may make the trustee excessively cautious, and because he chooses the safest investments the income produced will often be relatively less. Moreover, unless the court is prepared to examine the adequacy of the payment, it may enable the settlor to impose the higher standard of liability by making a token payment.

The distinction between paid and unpaid trustees could however be retained and these unfortunate consequences could be avoided if the standard of skill and care demanded of an unpaid trustee were to be that which he is accustomed to exercise with regard to his own private affairs, whilst the standard of skill and care demanded of a paid trustee was henceforth that which the ordinary prudent man would exercise in the management of his own affairs if he were regardful of the pecuniary interests in the future of those having claims upon him. . . .

RE VICKERY, VICKERY v *STEPHENS* [1931] 1 Ch 572, ChD

FACTS: The trustee, a missionary 'ignorant of business affairs,' unwittingly employed a rogue solicitor to wind up a testatrix's estate. The beneficiaries requested the appointment of another solicitor but the defendant refused, believing that the rogue solicitor was about to settle the matter. In the event the rogue solicitor, after repeated requests, made off with a large sum of money belonging to the trust.
HELD: The trustee was not liable for a breach of trust.

MAUGHAM J: . . . In considering this question the Court has to bear in mind in particular two sections of the Trustee Act 1925. Section 23, sub-s. 1, is as follows: [His Lordship read the sub-section, and continued:] This sub-section is new and, in my opinion, authorised the defendant in signing the authorities to Jennens & Jennens to collect the two sums in question; for I do not think it can be doubted that the defendant acted in good faith in employing Jennens for the purpose. It will be observed that the sub-section has no proviso or qualification to it such as we find in relation to s. 23, sub-s. 3. It is hardly too much to say that it revolutionises the position of a trustee or an executor so far as regards the employment of agents. He is no longer required to do any actual work himself, but he may employ a solicitor or other agent to do it, whether there is any real necessity for the employment or not. No doubt he should use his discretion in selecting an agent, and should employ him only to do acts within the scope of the usual business of the agent; but, as will be seen, a question arises whether even in these respects he is personally liable for a loss due to the employment of the agent unless he has been guilty of wilful default. . . .

I have now to consider s. 30, sub-s. 1, of the Trustee Act 1925, a section which replaces s. 24 of the Trustee Act 1893, which in its turn re-enacted Lord Cranworth's Act, s. 31. It is in the following terms: [His Lordship read the sub-section, and continued;] Reliance has been placed on the words concluding the sub-section 'nor for any other loss, unless the same happens through his own wilful default.' To avoid misconception I wish to say that, having regard to the numerous decisions since the enactment of Lord Cranworth's Act in relation to the liability of trustees for innocent breaches of trust, it is impossible now to hold that the words 'for any other loss' are quite general, with the result that no trustee is ever liable for breach of trust unless the breach is occasioned by his own wilful default. In my opinion the words are confined to losses for which it is sought to make the trustee liable occasioned by his signing receipts for the sake of conformity or by reason of the wrongful acts or defaults of another trustee or of an agent with whom trust money or securities have been deposited, or for the insufficiency or deficiency of securities or some other analogous loss. It may be noted that if the phrase is not so limited it is difficult to see how there could have been any need for s. 3 of the Judicial Trustee Act 1896, now re-enacted as s. 61 of the Trustee Act 1925, or for s. 29 of that Act; nor would it be possible to explain the numerous cases before 1896 where trustees were made liable for honest mistakes either of construction or fact: see, for example, *Learoyd* v *Whiteley* see [*Re Whiteley* (1886) 33 ChD 347]; *National Trustees Co. of Australasia* v *General Finance Co. of Australasia* [1905] AC 373, and cases there cited.

On the other hand, since s. 30, sub-s. 1, expressly refers to the defaults of bankers, brokers, or other persons with whom any trust money or other securities may be deposited, I am unable—dealing here with the more limited case—to escape the conclusion that the trustee cannot be made liable for the default of such a person unless the loss happens through the 'wilful default' of the trustee. . . .

Now the meaning of the phrase 'wilful default' has been expounded by the Court of Appeal in the case of *In re Trusts of Leeds City Brewery, Ltd's, Deed* [1925] Ch 532n, and in the case of *In re City Equitable Fire Insurance Co.* [1925] Ch 407. It should be noted that in both those cases the indemnity, given to the trustees in the first case and to the directors and officers of the company in the second case, was worded in a general form so that it could not be contended that they were liable for any matter or thing done or omitted unless it could be shown that the loss so occasioned arose from their own wilful default. This, as I have said, is not true of an ordinary executor or trustee; but the exposition of the phrase 'wilful default' is not the less valuable. The Court of Appeal held, following in the case of *In re City Equitable Fire Insurance Co.* the decision of Romer J, that a person is not guilty of wilful neglect or default unless he is conscious that, in doing the act which is complained of or in omitting to do the act which it is said he ought to have done, he is committing a breach of his duty, or is recklessly careless whether it is a breach of his duty or not. I accept with respect what Warrington LJ said—namely, that in the case of trustees there are definite and precise rules of law as to what a trustee may or may not do in the execution of his trust, and that a trustee in general is not excused in relation to a loss occasioned by a breach of trust merely because he honestly believed that he was justified in doing the act in question. But for the reasons which I have given I think that, where an executor employs a solicitor or other agent to receive money belonging to the estate in reliance on s. 23, sub-s. 1, of the Trustee Act 1925, he will not be liable for a loss of the money occasioned by the misconduct of the agent unless the loss happens through the wilful default of the executor, using those words as implying, as the Court of Appeal have decided, either a consciousness of negligence or breach of duty, or a recklessness in the performance of a duty. . . .

. . . It is essential in this case to guard oneself against judging the conduct of the defendant in the light of subsequent events. To have employed a new solicitor as soon as the defendant became aware that H. H. Jennens [the rogue solicitor] was a person with a tarnished reputation for honesty would certainly have meant further costs. It might have proved quite unnecessary even on the supposition that Jennens was a rogue. Even a man of the world might have thought that the sum involved—the sum of 300*l.* or thereabouts—was far too small to make it probable that the solicitor would be likely—unless, indeed, in the case of stern necessity—for such a sum to expose himself to the orders of the Court and to the action of the Law Society. Nor must it be forgotten that upon the facts as I find them it was not till the month of September, 1927, that the defendant had any real reason for suspecting that Jennens was unworthy of confidence; and it seems that after that date he kept on pressing for an immediate settlement and kept on being assured that a settlement would immediately take place. On the whole I have come to the conclusion that the defendant was on any view of the facts guilty only of an error of judgment, and this, in the case of a loss occasioned by the defalcations of a solicitor, does not amount to wilful default on the part of the executor. The action accordingly in my judgment fails and must be dismissed.

For a critique of this case—see G. H. Jones, *'Delegation by Trustees? A Reappraisal'*.

11.2.4   EXEMPTION CLAUSES

ARMITAGE v *NURSE* [1997] 3 WLR 1046, CA

FACTS: By a settlement made on 11 October 1984 the plaintiff, who was then aged 17, became entitled in remainder to settled agricultural land of which her mother was tenant for life. Her portion was to be held on certain trusts until she reached the age of 40. Clause 15 of the settlement provided that no trustee should be liable for any loss or damage to the plaintiff's fund or the income thereof at any time or from any case unless it was caused by his own actual fraud. On appeal by the plaintiff from the judge's decision that the trustees were absolved by clause 15.
HELD: (dismissing the appeal): That, since it was open to contracting parties to exclude liability for ordinary or even gross negligence, such an exclusion was also open to the parties to a settlement; that, by referring to 'actual' fraud, clause 15 of the settlement excluded constructive fraud or equitable fraud and was apt to exclude liability for breach of trust in the absence of a dishonest intention; that, although trustees might deliberately commit a breach of trust by consciously acting beyond their powers, their conduct was not fraudulent if they did so in good faith and in the honest belief that they were acting in the interest of the beneficiaries; that a clause excluding the liability of a trustee for equitable fraud or unconscionable behaviour was not so repugnant to the trust or contrary to public policy as to be liable to be set aside at the suit of a beneficiary; and that, accordingly, since without amendment the pleadings could not support a plea of fraud, clause 15 of the settlement operated to absolve the trustees from liability for the alleged breaches so long as they had not acted dishonestly; but that the plaintiff would be allowed to examine the trust documents and investigate the trustees' management in order to re-amend her statement of claim.
Per curiam. The view is widely held that trustee exemption clauses have gone too far, and that trustees who charge for their services and who, as professional men, would not dream of excluding liability for ordinary professional negligence should not be able to rely on an exemption clause excluding liability for gross negligence. If such clauses are to be denied effect, however, it should be done by Parliament.

MILLETT LJ: . . . In my judgment clause 15 exempts the trustee from liability for loss or damage to the trust property no matter how indolent, imprudent, lacking in diligence, negligent or wilful he may have been, so long as he has not acted dishonestly.

The permitted scope of trustee exemption clauses
It is submitted on behalf of [the plaintiff] that a trustee exemption clause which purports to exclude all liability except for actual fraud is void, either for repugnancy or as contrary to public policy. There is some academic support for the submission (notably an article by Professor Matthews, 'The Efficacy of Trustee Exemption Clauses in English Law' [1989] Conv. 42 and *Hanbury & Martin's Modern Equity*, 14th ed. (1993), pp. 473–474) that liability for gross negligence cannot be excluded, but this is not the view taken in *Underhill and Hayton's Law of Trusts and Trustees*, 15th ed. (1995), pp. 560–561 (where it appears to be taken only because the editor confusingly uses the term 'gross negligence' to mean reckless indifference to the interests of the beneficiaries). In its consultation paper Fiduciary Duties and Regulatory Rules, A Summary (1992) (Law Com. No. 124), para. 3.3.41 the Law Commission states:

> Beyond this, trustees and fiduciaries cannot exempt themselves from liability for fraud, bad faith and wilful default. It is not, however, clear whether the prohibition on exclusion of liability for 'fraud' in this context only prohibits the exclusion of common law fraud or extends to the much broader doctrine of equitable fraud. It is also not altogether clear whether the prohibition on the exclusion of liability for 'wilful default' also prohibits exclusion of liability for gross negligence although we incline to the view that it does.

. . . the expression 'wilful default' is used in the cases in two senses. A trustee is said to be accountable on the footing of wilful default when he is accountable not only for money which he has in fact received but also for money which he could with reasonable diligence have received. It is sufficient that the trustee has been guilty of a want of ordinary prudence: see e.g. *In re Chapman; Cocks v Chapman* [1896] 2 Ch 763. In the context of a trustee exclusion clause, however, such as s. 30 of the Trustee Act 1925, it means a deliberate breach of trust: *In re Vickery: Vickery v Stephens* [1931] 1 Ch 572. The decision has been criticised, but it is in line with earlier authority: see *Lewis v Great Western Railway Co.* (1877) 3 QBD 195; *In re Trusts of Leeds City Brewery Ltd.'s Debenture Stock Trust Deed, Leeds City Brewery Ltd v Platts (Note)* [1925] Ch 532 and *In re City Equitable Fire Insurance Co. Ltd* [1925] Ch 407. Nothing less than conscious, and wilful misconduct is sufficient. The trustee must be

> conscious that, in doing the act which is complained of or in omitting to do the act which it said he ought to have done, he is committing a breach of his duty, or is recklessly careless whether it is a breach of his duty or not: see *In re Vickery* [1931] 1 Ch 572, 583, *per* Maugham J.

A trustee who is guilty of such conduct either consciously takes a risk that loss will result, or is recklessly indifferent whether it will or not. If the risk eventuates he is personally liable. But if he consciously takes the risk in good faith and with the best intentions, honestly believing that the risk is one which ought to be taken in the interests of the beneficiaries, there is no reason why he should not be protected by an exemption clause which excludes liability for wilful default. . . .

There can be no question of the clause being repugnant to the trust. In *Wilkins v Hogg* (1861) 31 LJ Ch 41, 42 Lord Westbury LC challenged counsel to cite a case where an indemnity clause protecting the trustee from his ordinary duty had been held so repugnant as to be rejected. Counsel was unable to do so. No such case has occurred in England or Scotland since.

I accept the submission made on behalf of [the plaintiff] that there is an irreducible core of obligations owed by the trustees to the beneficiaries and enforceable by them which is fundamental to the concept of a trust. If the beneficiaries have no rights enforceable against the trustees there are no trusts. But I do not accept the further submission that these core obligations include the duties of skill and care, prudence and diligence. The duty of the trustees to perform the trusts honestly and in good faith for the benefit of the beneficiaries is the minimum necessary to give substance to the trusts, but in my opinion it is sufficient. As Mr Hill pertinently pointed out in his able argument, a trustee who relied on the presence of a trustee exemption clause to justify what he proposed to do would thereby lose its protection: he would be acting recklessly in the proper sense of the term. . . .

The submission that it is contrary to public policy to exclude the liability of a trustee for gross negligence is not supported by any English or Scottish authority. . . .

At the same time, it must be acknowledged that the view is widely held that these clauses have gone too far, and that trustees who charge for their services and who, as professional men, would not dream of excluding liability for ordinary professional negligence should not be able to rely on a trustee exemption clause excluding liability for gross negligence. Jersey introduced a law in 1989 which denies effect to a trustee exemption clause which purports to absolve a trustee from liability for his own 'fraud, wilful misconduct or gross negligence.' The subject is presently under consideration in this country by the Trust Law Committee under the chairmanship of Sir John Vinelott. If clauses such as clause 15 of the settlement are to be denied effect, then in my opinion this should be done by Parliament, which will have the advantage of wide consultation with interested bodies and the advice of the Trust Law Committee. . . .

11.3 Trustee Decision-making

11.3.1 THE EXERCISE OF DISCRETION

GISBORNE v GISBORNE (1877) 2 App Cas 300, HL

FACTS: Trustees held a fund upon trust for the maintenance of the testator's mentally infirm wife. The terms of the trust granted the trustees 'uncontrollable authority' as to how the fund should be applied. The care of 'lunatics' (the unfortunate label then applied to the mentally ill) normally lay within the powers of the court, and so a decree of the Court of Chancery had recorded the court's approval of the trustees' chosen course of action.
HELD: That part of the decree should be struck out. The court had no jurisdiction to 'approve' that which was in the 'uncontrollable' discretion of trustees.

LORD CAIRNS LC: . . . My Lords, larger words than those, it appears to me, it would be impossible to introduce into a will. The trustees are not merely to have discretion, but they are to have 'uncontrollable,' that is, uncontrolled, 'authority.' Their discretion and authority, always supposing that there is no *mala fides* with regard to its exercise, is to be without any check or control from any superior tribunal. What is the subject-matter with regard to which they are to exercise this discretion and this authority? The subject-matter is the payment, or the application, not merely of the whole of the income of his real and personal estate, but of such portion only as they deem it proper to expend. It is for them to say whether they will apply the whole, or only a part, and if so what part. And how are they to decide, if they do not apply the whole; what is the part which they are to apply? They are to decide upon this principle, that it is to be such part as they shall think expedient, not such part as shall be sufficient, not such part as shall be demanded by or for the person to be benefited, but such part as they shall think expedient; and upon the question of what is expedient it is their discretion which is to decide, and that discretion according to which they are to decide is to be uncontrolled. . . .

. . . My Lords, in a case like this, where the Court of Chancery recognises that the trustees and not the Court, are to be the judges of the *quantum* to be allowed, where the trustees are willing to exercise the discretion which they claim to exercise, and where the Court allows and declares their right to exercise that discretion, I do not understand it to be the habit of the Court to go on and express any opinion as to whether the exercise of the discretion by the trustees is a wise or an unwise exercise of that discretion. . . .

RE LOCKER'S SETTLEMENT [1977] 1 WLR 1323, ChD

FACTS: The trustees of the settlement were empowered to distribute the income of the fund amongst a number of persons, and charitable (and other) institutions. Their discretion in this regard was stated to be 'absolute and uncontrolled'. Having accumulated all the income which had accrued since the inception of the trust (and having done so in breach of trust, but in accordance with the settlor's wishes) the trustees took out a summons for directions as to how the income ought to be distributed.

HELD: The trustees would be permitted to remedy their breach by making a 'tardy' distribution of the trust fund. The court was able to exercise its discretion in this way despite the provision in the settlement granting the trustees an 'absolute and unfettered' discretion as to the distribution of the income.

GOULDING J: . . . A court of equity, where trustees have failed to discharge their duty of prompt discretionary distribution of income, is concerned to make them as owners of the trust assets at law dispose of them in accordance with the requirements of conscience; that is, to give benefits to the cestuis que trust in accordance with the confidence that the settlor reposed in them, the trustees. In a case such as the present, where the trustees desire to repair their breach of duty, and to make restitution by doing late what they ought to have done early, and where they are in no way disabled from doing so, the court should, in my judgment, permit and encourage them to take that course. A tardy distribution at the discretion of the trustees is, after all, nearer to prompt distribution at the discretion of the trustees, which is what the settlor intended, than tardy distribution by the trustees at the discretion of someone else . . . That being my view of the matter on first impression and first principle, I turn to the arguments against it. . . .

Mr Blackburne framed an argument which can be summarised as follows: clause 3 of the settlement, he says, establishes a paramount duty of prompt distribution of income. The shares to be taken by different objects on any given distribution are within the discretion of the trustees. The discretion of the trustees is absolute and uncontrolled. Therefore, the court cannot assume the exercise of the discretion itself. It follows, says Mr Blackburne, that if the trustees do not exercise their discretion within a reasonable time, say a year after the income in question has been received, and the court, for reasons already given, cannot exercise it, then the court can only give effect, and must give effect, to the trust by equal distribution among eligible objects.

I do not find that reasoning compelling. I think it is fallacious in asserting that because the discretion is absolute and uncontrolled, the court cannot assume the exercise of discretion itself. It appears to me that Mr Blackburne (if his argument is closely examined) must find himself in a dilemma. If the discretion given to the trustees by the settlor is not automatically extinguished for all purposes through their failure to exercise it within a reasonable time, their claim to exercise it at a later date is all the stronger if the discretion is expressed to be absolute and uncontrolled. If, on the other hand, Mr Blackburne is right and the discretion is automatically extinguished on the lapse of a reasonable time, then it goes with all its attributes, and the court, in deciding how to execute the trust when the discretion is wholly extinct, is not concerned with such attributes at all. The court can then do the same as with any other trust where the trustees have failed to do their duty.

11.3.1.1 The rule in Hastings-Bass

METTOY PENSION TRUSTEES LTD v EVANS AND OTHERS [1990] 1 WLR 1587, ChD

FACTS: Mettoy, one of whose subsidiaries manufactured the miniature toy cars known as 'Dinky Toys', had fallen victim to the recession. The company went into liquidation. The pension funds of Mettoy employees were held by a trust corporation subject to rules governing the distribution of any surplus in the event of the company being wound up. The trust corporation was appointed by the previous trustees and it was those trustees who had laid down the rules governing the distribution of surplus pension funds. In the event the company was wound up with a surplus in the pension fund. The question arose whether the power to distribute the surplus pension funds was part of the company's assets and could be exercised by the receivers.

The rule governing the distribution of the surplus pension fund granted the trust corporation an 'absolute discretion' as to the mode of distribution. Accordingly, this rule granted the trust corporation a 'fiduciary power'. Such a power could not be released by the trust corporation: it could not therefore be treated as an asset of the insolvent company. As a result, the receivers had no authority to exercise the fiduciary power, and the court would have to decide the manner of its exercise.

The question arose, had the trustees understood the effect of the rules governing the distribution of the surplus, would they have appointed the trust corporation subject to those rules? In other words, in appointing the trust corporation, subject to the rules, had the trustees exercised a sound discretion? If they had not, the appointment of the trust corporation would be set aside.

HELD: There was no evidence to show that the trustees did not understand the effect of the rules, nor to show that they would have acted any differently had they been informed that the rules for distribution had conferred a 'fiduciary power' on the trust corporation. The appointment of the trust corporation would stand.

WARNER J: . . . I have come to the conclusion that there is a principle which may be labelled 'the rule in *Hastings-Bass*.' I do not think that the application of that principle is confined, as Mr Nugee suggested, to cases where an exercise by trustees of a discretion vested in them is partially ineffective because of some rule of law or because of some limit on their discretion which they overlooked. If, as I believe, the reason for the application of the principle is the failure by the trustees to take into account consider-ations that they ought to have taken into account, it cannot matter whether that failure is due to their having overlooked (or to their legal advisers having overlooked) some relevant rule of law or limit on their discretion, or is due to some other cause.

For the principle to apply however, it is not enough that it should be shown that the trustees did not have a proper understanding of the effect of their act. It must also be clear that, had they had a proper understanding of it, they would not have acted as they did. That is apparent from *In re Hastings-Bass* [1975] Ch 25 itself, . . .

. . . There may well be cases where the court, giving effect to the rule in *Hastings-Bass*, comes to the conclusion that, had the trustees not failed to take into account consider-ations which they ought to have taken into account, they would not have acted as they did at all, but would either have done nothing or done something quite different. In such a case the court must declare void the whole of the purported exercise of the trustees' discretion. There may however be cases where the court is satisfied that the trustees would have acted in the same way but with, for instance, the omission of a particular provision in a deed. I do not see why, in such a case, the court should not declare only that provision void. It seems to me, that the remedy to be adopted by the court must depend on the circumstances of each case.

In a case such as this, where it is claimed that the rule in *Hastings-Bass* applies, three questions arise: (1) What were the trustees under a duty to consider? (2) Did they fail to consider it? (3) If so, what would they have done if they had considered it? . . .

I now come to the all important *third* question: what would the trustees have done if they had considered the matters that they failed to consider? In dealing with that question, two important points must be borne in mind. First, as I have said, for the rule in *Hastings-Bass* to apply it must be clear that the trustees would not have done what in fact they did. The decision in *In re Hastings-Bass* itself [1975] Ch 25 shows how stringent a requirement that is. It is not enough to show that the trustees would have realised that what they were doing was to some extent unsatisfactory. Secondly, it is implicit I think in *In re Baron Vestey's Settlement* [1951] Ch 209 and in *In re Hastings-Bass* [1975] Ch 25 that the trustees would have been correctly advised as to the effect in law of what they were doing. It cannot be right to consider what they would have done if they had been wrongly or inadequately advised. . . .

11.3.2 REASONS FOR DECISIONS

WILSON v *LAW DEBENTURE TRUST CORP PLC* [1995] 2 All ER 337

FACTS: The plaintiffs were both formerly employees of a division of a company and had been members of and contributed to the company's pension scheme of which the defendant was the trustee.

The scheme's trust deed provided in cl 22(b) that the trustee was to appropriate and transfer to the CMP scheme such part of the assets of the scheme 'as the trustee determines to be appropriate having taken actuarial advice in all the circumstances'. Notwithstanding the fact that in the years preceding the transfer the employers had as a result of the fund being in surplus enjoyed a 'contributions holiday', the trustee determined to transfer to the CMP scheme an amount equal only to the past service reserve of the transferring employees, leaving the whole of the surplus in the scheme. The plaintiffs asked the trustee to disclose all the trust documents in its possession which indicated or might indicate the reasons for the trustee's determination. The trustee refused and the plaintiffs issued a summons seeking disclosure.

HELD: Where a discretion was entrusted to a trustee by the relevant trust instrument, the trustee was not required to give reasons for the exercise of that discretion and, in the absence of evidence apart from such disclosure that the trustee had acted improperly, whether from an improper motive or by taking account of factors which the trustee should not have taken into account or not taking into account factors which the trustee should have taken into account, the court would not interfere with the exercise of the trustee's discretion since, in general, the principles applicable to private trusts as a matter of trust law applied equally to pension schemes.

RATTEE J: . In *Re Londonderry's Settlement* [1964] 3 All ER 855 the relevant trust instrument with which the Court of Appeal was there concerned contained common form discretionary powers for the trustees to appoint capital and income in favour of a defined class of beneficiaries. On an application by the trustees of that settlement for directions it was held by the Court of Appeal that the trustees were not bound to disclose to their beneficiaries documents containing the reasons for the trustees exercising their discretionary powers in the way in which they had done, notwithstanding that the documents concerned might be documents to which the beneficiaries were prima facie entitled as being trust documents in which the *cestuis que trust* had a proprietary interest. The leading judgment in the case was given by Harman LJ, who said ([1964] 3 All ER 855 at 857):

> The court is really required here to resolve two principles that come into conflict, or at least apparent conflict. The first is that, as the defendant beneficiary admits, trustees exercising a discretionary power are not bound to disclose to their beneficiaries the reasons actuating them in coming to a decision. This is a long standing principle and rests largely, I think, on the view that nobody could be called on to accept a trusteeship involving the exercise of a discretion unless, in the absence of bad faith, he were not liable to have his motives or his reasons called in question either by the beneficiaries or by the court. To this there is added a rider, namely that if trustees do give reasons, their soundness can be considered by the court. Compare the observations of James LJ, in *Re Gresham Life Assurance Society, Ex p. Penney* (1872) 8 Ch App 446 at 449–450, on the analogous position of directors.

Later in his judgment Harman LJ said ([1964] 3 All ER 855 at 860):

> I would hold that, even if documents of this type ought properly to be described as trust documents, they are protected for the special reason which protects the trustees' deliberations on a discretionary matter from disclosure. If necessary, I hold that this principle overrides the ordinary rule. This is my judgment no less in the true interest of the beneficiary than of the trustees. Again, if one of the trustees commits to paper his suggestions and circulates them among his co-trustee, or if inquiries are made in writing as to the circumstances of a member of the class, I decline to hold that such documents are trust documents the property of the beneficiaries. In my opinion such documents are not trust documents in the proper sense at all.

Danckwerts LJ said ([1964] 3 All ER 855 at 861–862):

> It seems to me that, where trustees are given discretionary trusts which involve a decision on matters between beneficiaries, viewing the merits and other rights to

benefit under such trust, the trustees are given a confidential role and they cannot properly exercise that confidential role if at any moment there is likely to be an investigation for the purpose of seeing whether they have exercised their discretion in the best possible manner. Of course, if a case is made of lack of bona fides, that is an entirely different matter. In that case I agree it becomes necessary to examine exactly what has happened because that is in an action and not in a theoretical application for directions, as the present case appears to me to be. It appears to me that the documents are confidential, that trustees' duty would become impossible and that the execution of the trust would become impossible if the trustees were bound to disclose to any beneficiary any information or other matters in regard to beneficiaries that they had received.

Salmon LJ said ([1964] 3 All ER 855 at 862):

The settlement gave the absolute discretion to appoint to the trustees and not the courts. So long as the trustees exercise this power with the consent of persons called appointors under the settlement, and exercise it bona fide with no improper motive, their exercise of the power cannot be challenged in the courts—and their reasons for acting as they did are accordingly immaterial. This is one of the grounds for the rule that trustees are not obliged to disclose to beneficiaries their reasons for exercising a discretionary power. Another ground for this rule is that it would not be for the good of the beneficiaries as a whole, and yet another that it might make the lives of trustees intolerable should such an obligation rest on them: *Re Beloved Wilkes' Charity* (1851) 3 Mac & G 440, *Re Gresham Life Assurance Society, ex parte Penney* (1872) 8 Ch App 466. Nothing would be more likely to embitter family feelings and the relationship between the trustees and members of the family than that the trustees should be obliged to state their reasons for the exercise of the powers entrusted to them. It might indeed well be difficult to persuade any persons to act as trustees were a duty to disclose their reasons, with all the embarrassment, arguments and quarrels that might ensue, added to their present not inconsiderable burdens.

The defendant trustee by counsel says that those dicta of their Lordships and the decision in the case itself in *Re Londonderry's Settlement* recognised the well-established rule that where a discretion is entrusted to a trustee by the relevant trust instrument the trustee is not required to give reasons for the exercise of that discretion and that, in the absence of evidence apart from such disclosure that the trustee has acted improperly, whether from an improper motive or by taking account of factors which the trustee should not have taken into account or not taking into account factors which the trustee should have taken into account, the court will not interfere with the exercise of the trustee's discretion. . . .

In my judgment cl. 22(b) of the trust deed in the present case does confer a clear discretion on the trustee of the pension scheme to which the well-established principles of trust law to which I have referred apply, to the effect that the trustee is not bound to give reasons for the manner in which it exercised that discretion.

11.4   End of Chapter Assessment Question

Albert settled a trust on Beryl and Charlie as trustees for certain beneficiaries. The fund consisted of cash and freehold properties of which Beryl and Charlie were tenants. The trust instrument granted the trustees the power to invest in such investments as they in their absolute discretion and uncontrolled authority should think fit. The trust instrument also included a charging clause which permitted the trustees to be handsomely remunerated out of the fund. In the event, the trustees invested trust monies in shares in Y Co., a company with which they had no connection. Some time later the trustees purchased the freehold properties at market value by exercising options to purchase which they had been granted at the commencement of their leases. They also bought the shares in Y Co. off the trust for what was a very fair and even generous price, believing that the price of those shares was about to rise. In the event those shares did increase in value, but only very slightly. The trustees made fresh investments of the trust fund in Z Co., whose trading record they had taken no steps to investigate. The value of the shares in that company have now plummeted dramatically.

Advise the trustees, who are concerned that the beneficiaries might have grounds to take action against them for breach of their trust.

11.5   End of Chapter Assessment Outline Answer

The way to approach this question is to identify possible breaches of trust and then to advise the trustees as to whether or not a breach has actually occurred. Although the question raises technical issues relating to trustee investments you will not be expected to discuss those at this stage.

The first potential breach is the purchase by the trustees of the freehold titles to the properties of which they were tenants. The freeholds were trust property and the normal rule would be that the purchase must be set aside for breach of the rule against self-dealing. At the very least one might expect the trustees to be in breach of trust for putting themselves in a position where their self-interest might conflict with their duty to the trust. As for the rule against self-dealing, guidance is given by Wynn-Parry J in *Re Mulholland WT* (see **11.1.1**), where he stated that 'the existence of the fiduciary relationship creates an inability in the trustee to contract in regard to the trust property [but] does not touch the position arising where the contract in question has been brought into existence before the fiduciary relationship'. This dictum clearly applies to the present case. The trustees have exercised an option which was a contractual right they had held before they became trustees—accordingly there will be no breach of trust if the option was exercised according to its terms. If however, the trustees contrived to use their position to gain an extra advantage (perhaps by varying the terms of the option or by reducing the purchase price) this would be in breach of their trust. As for the possibility that the trustees have breached their trust by putting themselves in a position where their self-interest might conflict with their duty to the trust, guidance is given by the Court of Appeal in *Sargeant v National Westminster Bank Plc* (see **11.1.1**). The facts of that case are similar to those of the present. A testator let certain farms to his children, and when he died appointed them as trustees of the freeholds of those farms. The children were now both landlord and tenant, a clear position of conflict. The court held that they had not breached their trust because they had not **put themselves** in the position of conflict, the testator had done so. Therefore, it would not be a breach of trust for the children to sell the freeholds to themselves, which is what they did. Similarly, in our case, Beryl and Charlie will not have breached their trust, because Albert was responsible for putting them in the position of conflict. However, there will be a breach if Beryl and Charlie do not pay a fair price for the freehold.

The second potential breach is the purchase, from the trust, of the shares in Y Co. This is a clear case of self-dealing and the purchase must be set aside if any of the beneficiaries so requests. The fact that the trustees paid a generous price for the shares is no defence.

Justice, it is said, demands that the purchase be set aside (*Re Thompson's Settlement*, see **11.1.1.1**).

The third potential breach is the investment in Z Co. Here things look ominous for the trustees. The trust instrument grants them unlimited discretion to invest as they think fit. However, this does not mean that they can invest with a careless disregard for the well-being of the fund. Their administrative discretion to invest is subject to the proviso that they must invest within the limits of the duty, imposed upon them by the general law, to act prudently (*Bishop* v *Bonham*). The duty to act with prudence was described in *Speight* v *Gaunt* in terms that 'a trustee ought to conduct the business of the trust in the same manner that an ordinary prudent man of business would conduct his own'. In *Re Whiteley* Lindley LJ added that 'the duty rather is to take such care as a prudent man would take if he were minded to make an investment for other people for whom he felt morally bound to provide'. Beryl and Charlie have clearly breached this duty by investing in a company without first checking its viability.

The fact that the trustees have been handsomely paid for their services is unlikely, in itself, to subject them to an even higher standard of care, but it is probable that the court will be more reluctant to relieve the trustees from the consequences of liability for their breach (Brightman J in *Bartlett* v *Barclays Bank Trust Co. Ltd*).

CHAPTER TWELVE

TRUSTEES' DUTIES

12.1 Trustee Profits

TRUSTEE ACT 1925

30. Implied indemnity of trustees

(2) A trustee may reimburse himself or pay or discharge out of the trust premises all expenses incurred in or about the execution of the trusts or powers.

BRAY v *FORD* [1896] AC 44, HL

FACTS: The case involved an action in libel and the appeal was based on the fact that the judge had misdirected the jury in some material aspect of the case. The case is referred to because of an important *obiter* statement made by Lord Herschell in the course of his speech.

LORD HERSCHELL: . . . It is an inflexible rule of a Court of Equity that a person in a fiduciary position, such as the respondent's, is not, unless otherwise expressly provided, entitled to make a profit; he is not allowed to put himself in a position where his interest and duty conflict. It does not appear to me that this rule is, as has been said, founded upon principles of morality. I regard it rather as based on the consideration that, human nature being what it is, there is danger, in such circumstances, of the person holding a fiduciary position being swayed by interest rather than by duty, and thus prejudicing those whom he was bound to protect. It has, therefore, been deemed expedient to lay down this positive rule. But I am satisfied that it might be departed from in many cases, without any breach of morality, without any wrong being inflicted, and without any consciousness of wrong-doing. Indeed, it is obvious that it might sometimes be to the advantage of the beneficiaries that their trustee should act for them professionally rather than a stranger, even though the trustee were paid for his services. . . .

12.1.1 THE DUTY TO ACT GRATUITOUSLY

WILLIAMS v *BARTON* [1927] 2 Ch 9, ChD

FACTS: The defendant was a trustee who worked for a firm of stockbrokers. He received commission for any work introduced by him. He therefore recommended his firm to act for the trust of which he was a trustee. In due course the firm was appointed and the defendant received his commission. The plaintiff, the defendant's co-trustee, claimed that the defendant should account to the trust for the payment he had received.
HELD: The defendant had received his commission by virtue of his trusteeship. He would therefore be required to account to the trust.

RUSSELL J: . . . It is a well established and salutary rule of equity that a trustee may not make a profit out of his trust. A person who has the management of property as a trustee is not permitted to gain any profit by availing himself of his position, and will be a constructive trustee of any such profit for the benefit of the persons equitably entitled to the property. On the same principle a trustee has no right to charge for his time and trouble. The rule is thus stated by Lord Herschell in *Bray v Ford* [1896] AC 44: 'It is an inflexible rule of a Court of Equity that a person in a fiduciary position . . . . is not, unless otherwise expressly provided, entitled to make a profit; he is not allowed to put himself in a position where his interest and duty conflict.' It was argued on behalf of the defendant that the case was altogether outside that rule of equity, because the sums received by the defendant were merely parts of his salary paid to him by his employers under the contract of service and were not of a character for which he was liable to account.

The point is not an easy one and there is little, if any, authority to assist in its determination. The situation is an unusual one and the contract of service presents the following peculiar features. The remuneration has no relation to the services, which the defendant has to render to his employers. The defendant, while bound to render the services, might get no remuneration at all if he introduced no work, or introduced none which was acceptable to his employers. The amount of his remuneration depends (subject to his employers' acceptance of orders) upon his own efforts, but upon efforts not in relation to the work which he is engaged to do. Any increase of his remuneration rests with him.

From this it seems to me evident that the case falls within the mischief which is sought to be prevented by the rule. The case is clearly one where his duty as trustee and his interest in an increased remuneration are in direct conflict. As a trustee it is his duty to give the estate the benefit of his unfettered advice in choosing the stockbrokers to act for the estate; as the recipient of half the fees to be earned by George Burnand & Co. on work introduced by him his obvious interest is to choose or recommend them for the job.

12.1.1.1 The trust instrument

RE LLEWELLIN'S WT [1949] 1 Ch 225, ChD

FACTS: A testator by his will empowered his trustees to appoint themselves as directors of a trust-owned company. Two of them did so and took out a summons to establish whether or not they were accountable to the trust for remuneration received by them in their roles as directors.
HELD: On the proper construction of the terms of the will trust the trustees would be entitled to retain remuneration received in their capacity as directors of the trust-owned company. This was so notwithstanding the rule that trustees must not profit from their trust, for that rule is subject to the expressed wishes of the testator to allow remuneration.

JENKINS J: . . . The question which I now have to decide is whether the trustees of the testator's will are accountable to the estate for remuneration received by them as managing director and director of a company called Llewellin's Machine Company Ld., the bulk of the shares in which form part of the testator's estate.

The general principle of equity is plain. It is, that a trustee may not profit from his trust. Thus, if a trustee of shares in a company, by virtue of the control over the company which those shares give him, gets himself appointed to the post of director or managing director, then, although his remuneration is not paid to him in respect of the trust holding but in respect of the work he does as director or managing director, yet, because he gains that emolument by virtue of the trust holding he is not entitled to retain the remuneration for his own benefit. That principle is well-settled, and I have been referred to two recent cases in which it has been discussed, namely, *In re Macadam* [1946] Ch 73 and *In re Gee* [1948] Ch 284.

Now far be it from me to say anything purporting to trench upon that well-established and on the whole salutary rule. For the purpose of this judgment I wholly accept the position that, unless there is anything in the testator's will entitling the trustees to retain any remuneration which they may receive as director or managing director of this company, the rule must apply; but there is no rule of equity which says that a testator, if so minded, may not provide that his trustees can hold salaried offices in companies which the testator's estate controls and receive the emoluments attached to those offices without liability to account. A testator is perfectly at liberty to include such a provision in his will if he thinks fit, and, indeed, as a matter of business it is often a very sensible provision to make. . . .

RE CHALINDER & HERRINGTON [1907] 1 ChD 58, ChD

FACTS: By the terms of a will trust one of the trustees, a solicitor, was permitted to charge for 'all professional and other charges for his time and trouble'.
HELD: The clause would not permit the solicitor-trustee to charge for work which was not 'professional', even though it was work for which a solicitor could have charged a normal client.

WARRINGTON J: . . . The question turns upon the construction of the clause in the testator's will which allows this particular solicitor to make charges. . . .
   Now the clause starts with a direction that Mr Chalinder 'shall be the solicitor to my trust property.' I think that is the governing consideration in approaching the construction of the clause. That by itself would not be enough, because, notwithstanding that the testator might direct that one of his trustees should be employed by the others as solicitor to the trust property, it would not follow that that solicitor would be entitled to charge if he was a trustee. The testator then goes on: 'And shall be allowed all professional and other charges for his time and trouble notwithstanding his being such executor and trustee.' In my opinion that last clause is nothing more than this, that the testator adds to the direction that Mr Chalinder shall be the solicitor a direction that he shall be allowed his professional and other charges for his time and trouble as solicitor. I do not think that, to use the expression used by Lindley LJ in the case *In re Fish* [1893] 2 Ch 413, under this clause Mr Chalinder is entitled to charge not only for his professional services but for his trouble as a trustee. It is said that I cannot arrive at that conclusion without rejecting the words 'and other charges for his time and trouble.' I do not think I am driven to that alternative at all. It may well be that there may be charges for time and trouble as solicitor which may not be strictly professional charges; that is to say, there may be charges for business done, and properly done, by the person employed as solicitor to the trust estate which may yet not come strictly under the head of professional charges, such as advising, or drawing drafts, or things which a solicitor does in his strictly professional capacity. That seems to me to be the construction of the clause without reference to authority. Is there any authority which would justify me in interpreting this clause as meaning something more than which, in the absence of authority, I should take it to mean? I do not think there is. . . .

Law Commission Consultation Paper 146, 'The Powers and Duties of Trustees', 1997

PART X   PROFESSIONAL CHARGING CLAUSES

   10.26   We provisionally recommend that there should be an implied statutory charging clause and that it should apply—
   (1)   in relation to all trusts (other than charitable trusts and pension trusts) and to the unadministered estates of all deceased persons except—
      (a)   where there is a direction to the contrary in the will or trust instrument (but not merely some limitation on remuneration); or
      (b)   where some other benefit or remuneration is provided in the will or trust instrument;
   (2)   whether the trust arose or the deceased person died before or after any legislation was brought into force; and
   (3)   notwithstanding, but subject to, any previous order by a court . . . which has authorised the trustees or personal representatives to be remunerated for any work.
   10.27   We provisionally recommend that—
   (1)   the charging clause should permit any trustee or personal representative who is also engaged in a profession or business to charge and be paid out of the trust property for any business or act done, advice given, or time expended in connection with the trust;

(2) the power to charge in (1) should apply whether or not the matter was one which a trustee not being a professional could have undertaken; and

(3) those charges should be reasonable and should not exceed the amount which the trustee would charge for such work in the ordinary course of his or her business or profession.

We ask whether readers agree with our proposals for a default power in principle.

. . .

10.32 Finally, we consider that the rules by which express charging clauses are strictly construed against the professional trustee and confined to activities which require a profession unless the contrary is clearly expressed . . . should be abrogated. This is consistent with the widespread use of such clauses and with our proposal that there should be a statutory charging clause. We provisionally recommend that—

(1) a professional charging clause should be taken to permit a trustee to charge for work and services properly rendered for the trust, whether or not that work or those services could have been provided by a lay trustee, unless the trust instrument provides to the contrary; and

(2) this provision should apply to all professional charging clauses in wills and trusts, whenever made. . . .

RE DUKE OF NORFOLK'S SETTLEMENT TRUSTS [1981] 3 All ER 220, CA

FACTS: A trust corporation ('SETCO') and an individual trustee—the continuing trustees of a settlement set up in 1958—had, throughout the history of the trust, been called upon to devote increasing efforts to its good administration. The increased demands made upon them by the trust had arisen in large part due to the settlement of additional property upon the trust and changes in the tax laws. Accordingly, in 1977 the trustees applied to court for an order under its inherent jurisdiction authorising the trust corporation to claim remuneration at a level higher than that authorised by the trust instrument.

HELD: The court had inherent jurisdiction to authorise such increased remuneration if to do so would be in the interests of the good administration of the trust. It was nevertheless acknowledged that this involved balancing the proper administration of the trust against the fact that the trustee's office is essentially a gratuitous one. Having so declared, the matter was remitted to the Chancery Division to decide whether the jurisdiction should be exercised in the present case.

FOX LJ: . . . The evidence is that the general level of SETCO's fees is low compared with that of similar institutions and that the new scale proposed would still be below that charged by such institutions, especially the Public Trustee. There is also evidence that the amount of work transacted by SETCO as a trustee of the settlement is such that SETCO is incurring a substantial and continuing financial loss in consequence of its trusteeship. That, it is said, is because the amount of work now involved in administering the trust is so greatly in excess of anything contemplated when the trust was established.

The judge came to the conclusion that he had jurisdiction to authorise the payment of additional remuneration, both to Lord Perth and to SETCO, in respect of work which they had done in the past which was outside the scope of any duties which could reasonably have been expected to be rendered by them as trustees. He made certain orders authorising payments accordingly. Those orders are not appealed from and I need not refer to them further.

The judge also decided, however, that he had no inherent jurisdiction to authorise for the future any general increase in SETCO's remuneration as provided by cl 12 of the settlement. It is against that decision that this appeal is brought. . . .

. . . In my opinion the judge took too narrow a view of the inherent jurisdiction. There is, in my judgment, no doubt that the court has an inherent jurisdiction to authorise payment of remuneration to trustees. Danckwerts J in *Re Masters* [1953] 1 All ER 19 and Upjohn J in *Re Worthington* (*deceased*) [1954] 1 All ER 677, accepted that. The older authorities lead me to the same conclusion. In *Marshall* v *Holloway* Lord Eldon LC himself authorised remuneration for both past and future services. The existence of the jurisdiction is also supported by *Morison* v *Morison* (1838) 4 My & Cr 215,

Bainbrigge v *Blair* (1845) 8 Beav 588, *Forster* v *Ridley* (1864) 4 De GJ & Sm 452 and *Re Freeman's Settlement Trusts* (1887) 37 ChD 148.

The question is the extent of that jurisdiction. There can, in my view, be no doubt that there is an inherent jurisdiction on the appointment of a trustee to direct that he be remunerated; that was accepted by Leach V-C in *Brocksopp* v *Barnes* (1820) 5 Madd 90 and must be inherent in what was said in *Re Masters* and *Re Worthington* (*deceased*). Indeed, it is not really in dispute at all. In the present case, however, what is sought is the increase of remuneration authorised by the trust instrument. The judge said that there had never been a case in which that was done, unless it was *Re Codd* (*deceased*) [1975] 2 All ER 1051n, where the matter was not argued. I feel much doubt whether that proposition is in fact correct. Most cases relating to trustees' remuneration are dealt with in chambers and are not reported. My own impression, and, I understand, that of Brightman LJ also, is that since the early 1950s orders have been made in chambers, under the inherent jurisdiction, authorising increases in remuneration given by the trust instrument. But I do not rely on that. I will approach the matter as one of principle and on the reported cases. If it be the law, as I think it clearly is, that the court has inherent jurisdiction on the appointment of a trustee to authorise payment of remuneration to him, is there any reason why the court should not have jurisdiction to increase the remuneration already allowed by the trust instrument?

Two reasons are suggested. First, it is said that a trustee's right to remuneration under an express provision of the settlement is based on a contract between the settlor and the trustee which the trustee is not entitled to avoid; the benefit of that contract is to be regarded as settled by the trust instrument for the benefit of the beneficiaries. I find that analysis artificial. It may have some appearance of reality in relation to a trustee who, at the request of the settlor, agrees to act before the settlement is executed and approves the terms of the settlement. But very frequently executors and trustees of wills know nothing of the terms of the will until the testator is dead; sometimes in the case of corporate trustees such as banks, they have not even been asked by the testator whether they will act. It is difficult to see with whom, in such cases, the trustees are to be taken as contracting. The appointment of a trustee by the court also gives rise to problems as to the identity of the contracting party.

The position, it seems to me, is this. Trust property is held by the trustees on the trusts and subject to the powers conferred by the trust instrument and by law. One of those powers is the power to the trustee to charge remuneration. That gives the trustee certain rights which equity will enforce in administering the trust. How far those rights can properly be regarded as beneficial interests I will consider later. But it seems to me to be quite unreal to regard them as contractual. So far as they derive from any order of the court they simply arise from the court's jurisdiction and so far as they derive from the trust instrument itself they derive from the settlor's power to direct how this property should be dealt with. . . .

I come to the second objection. It is said that the right to remuneration is a beneficial interest in the trust property and can only be varied by an order under the Variation of Trusts Act 1958 or (in accordance with the principles established in *Chapman* v *Chapman* [1954] 1 All ER 798) under a compromise of a dispute as to beneficial interests or by way of salvage.

I do not doubt that, to some extent, the right of a trustee to remuneration is to be regarded as a beneficial interest . . . But, accepting that a trustee's right to remuneration may for certain purposes be treated as a beneficial interest in the trust property, I do not think that it comes within the principle laid down in *Chapman* v *Chapman* as to the general inability of the court under its inherent jurisdiction to vary beneficial interests.

Chapman v *Chapman*, it seems to me, was concerned with the power of the court to authorise variations in beneficial interests as such. The present problem is different. It is concerned not with beneficial interests as such, but with the administration of the trust fund. When the court authorises payment of remuneration to a trustee under its inherent jurisdiction it is, I think, exercising its ancient jurisdiction to secure the competent administration of the trust property just as it has done when it appoints or removes a trustee under its inherent jurisdiction. The result, in my view, is that there is nothing in the principles stated in *Chapman* v *Chapman* which is inconsistent with the existence of an inherent jurisdiction in the court to increase the remuneration payable to trustees under the trust instrument. In my view, therefore, neither of the two objections which have been raised as to existence of such a jurisdiction is well founded.

There remains the question whether, on principle and authority, we can properly infer that the jurisdiction does exist. As to principle, it seems to me that, if the court has jurisdiction, as it has, on the appointment of a trustee to authorise remuneration though no such power exists in the trust instrument, there is no legal reason why the court should not have power to increase the remuneration given by the instrument. In many cases the latter may involve a smaller interference with the provisions of the trust instrument than the former. Further, the law has not stopped short at authorising remuneration to a trustee only if he seeks the authority at the time when he accepts the trusts. That, in my view, appears from the observations of Lord Langdale MR in *Bainbrigge* v *Blair* (1845) 8 Beav 588 and from *Re Masters* [1953] 1 All ER 19. . . .

I appreciate that the ambit of the court's inherent jurisdiction in any sphere may, for historical reasons, be irrational and that logical extensions are not necessarily permissible. But I think that it is the basis of the jurisdiction that one has to consider. The basis, in my view, in relation to a trustee's remuneration is the good administration of trusts. The fact that in earlier times, with more stable currencies and with a plenitude of persons with the leisure and resources to take on unremunerated trusteeships, the particular problem of increasing remuneration may not have arisen does not, in my view, prevent us from concluding that a logical extension of admitted law which is wholly consistent with the apparent purpose of the jurisdiction is permissible. If the increase of remuneration be beneficial to the trust administration, I do not see any objection to that in principle.

As to authority, I do not find in the English authorities any decision which positively excludes any inherent jurisdiction to increase remuneration, unless it be *Robinson* v *Pett* (1734) 3 P Wms 249. But that was a case of a renouncing executor who was expressly given a legacy for his trouble if he did renounce. Lord Talbot LC said that he was unable to give him any more. I do not think *Robinson* v *Pett* really touches the present case. On the other hand, Lord Eldon LC's order in *Marshall* v *Holloway* (1820) 2 Swan 432, seems to have increased the benefit given by the will, and in *Re Barbour's Settlement* [1974] 1 All ER 1188 Megarry J did not really doubt that, on an application in proper form and supported by appropriate evidence, the court would have had jurisdiction to increase the remuneration of the corporate trustee.

I conclude that the court has an inherent jurisdiction to authorise the payment of remuneration of trustees and that that jurisdiction extends to increasing the remuneration authorised by the trust instrument. In exercising that jurisdiction the court has to balance two influences which are to some extent in conflict. The first is that the office of trustee is, as such, gratuitous; the court will accordingly be careful to protect the interests of the beneficiaries against claims by the trustees. The second is that it is of great importance to the beneficiaries that the trust should be well administered. If therefore the court concludes, having regard to the nature of the trust, to the experience and skill of a particular trustee and to the amounts which he seeks to charge when compared with what other trustees might require to be paid for their services and to all the other circumstances of the case, that it would be in the interests of the beneficiaries to increase the remuneration, then the court may properly do so.

Having regard to the view which I take as to the inherent jurisdiction, it is not necessary to consider the extent of the court's jurisdiction under s. 57 of the Trustee Act 1925 or otherwise.

I would allow the appeal, and make the declaration sought by the amended summons so far as it relates to the inherent jurisdiction. The matter should, I think, be remitted to the Chancery Division to enable the trustees to make such application and on such further evidence as they think fit. . . .

BRIGHTMAN LJ: . . . The contractual conception suffers from the difficulties explained in the judgment of Fox LJ. It also seems to me, in the context of the present debate, to give little weight to the fact that a trustee, whether paid or unpaid, is under no obligation, contractual or otherwise, to provide future services to the trust. He can at any time express his desire to be discharged from the trust and in that case a new trustee will in due course be appointed under s. 36 or s. 41 of the 1925 Act. The practical effect therefore of increasing the remuneration of the trustee (if the contractual conception is correct) will merely be to amend for the future, in favour of a trustee, the terms of a contract which the trustee has a unilateral right to determine. The interference of the court in such circumstances can hardly be said, in any real sense, to derogate from the contractual rights of the settlor or the beneficiaries if he or they are to be regarded as entitled to the benefit of the contract. . . .

12.1.1.2   *Quantum meruit*

See *Boardman* v *Phipps* [1967] 2 AC 46, HL (**16.3.1.1**).

O'SULLIVAN AND ANOTHER v MANAGEMENT AGENCY AND MUSIC LTD AND OTHERS [1985] 3 All ER 351, CA

FACTS: When still an unknown artist, Gilbert O'Sullivan, a composer and performer of pop music, signed management agreements with companies controlled by Mr Mills, a music agent. The terms of the agreements were not as favourable to O'Sullivan as they would have been had he had independent legal advice. O'Sullivan had trusted Mills and had not negotiated the agreements in the usual 'arm's-length' way. Nevertheless, the management and marketing prowess of Mills's companies brought O'Sullivan great success and the wealth that accompanies such success. In due course, however, their working relationship deteriorated and ultimately O'Sullivan brought an action against Mills and his companies, seeking to have his management contracts declared void on the basis that they had been obtained by undue influence. The trial judge set the contracts aside and ordered that Mills and his companies should account for profits made on O'Sullivan's music, together with compound interest on those profits. The defendants conceded that there had been undue influence on the part of Mills, but appealed against the companies' liability and against the remedies awarded aginst the companies and against Mills.

HELD: The companies were subject to the same liability as Mills as they were under the *de facto* control of Mills. It had therefore been proper to set aside all the contracts. However, in determining the appropriate remedy for the plaintiff it was necessary to make allowance for the work done by the companies on behalf of O'Sullivan. This would include allowing the companies to retain a reasonable profit even though they were in a fiduciary position in relation to O'Sullivan. Further, the defendants would not be required to pay compound interest on their account of profits because some of the monies made by the companies had been used for the benefit of the plaintiff.

DUNN LJ: Raymond O'Sullivan (professionally known as Gilbert O'Sullivan), to whom I shall refer as 'O'Sullivan', is a well known composer and performer of popular music. The retail sales of records of his music between 1970 and 1978 realised a gross figure of some £14·5m. In addition he has achieved worldwide fame as an artiste playing to packed houses in this country and the United States of America. He has won many awards. In 1970 he was 23 years old, and although he had a publishing agreement with April Music Ltd, and a recording agreement with CBS Inc, all his compositions and recordings had been failures. But he was convinced of his own talent and determined to attain success in the music world both as a composer and as a performer.

In 1969 he approached the third defendant, to whom I shall refer as 'Mills', known internationally as a manager, producer and performer, who managed amongst others Tom Jones and Engelbert Humperdinck. . . .

On 25 February 1970 O'Sullivan signed a management agreement with Mills, and a sole agency agreement with the first defendant. . . .

By 1972 O'Sullivan had achieved enormous success. 6·5 m of his records were sold and were at or near the top of the charts in this country and the USA. He was voted the biggest selling solo artiste in the world by the Music Business Association. In that year he moved out of the cottage and bought his own house for £95,000 with the assistance of a loan of £60,000. His success continued in 1973 with more records and a new album. He was composing at a prolific rate and travelling all over the world promoting his records. He was blissfully happy, having achieved his ambition. . . .

Counsel for Mr O'Sullivan submitted that the defendants had gained the following advantages: (1) profits from the agreements and (2) the copyrights in the songs and master tapes for the life of O'Sullivan and 50 years thereafter. He pointed out that none of the agreements obliged the defendants to do any work on behalf of O'Sullivan whether by promoting or exploiting him or his works or at all, although he conceded that the defendants had in fact done such work gratuitously. He accepted that the defendants in accounting for their profits were entitled to credit in respect of their proper and reasonable expenses for the work done, including work done gratuitously, but that they were not entitled to credit for any profit element in such work. He submitted that the exception made in *Boardman* v *Phipps* [1967] 2 AC 46, where the trustees were morally blameless, should not become the rule.

I do not think that equity requires such a narrow approach.

. . . It is true that in this case moral blame does lie on the defendants, as the judge's findings of fact show. On the other hand it is significant that until O'Sullivan met Mills he had achieved no success, and that after he effectively parted company with Mills in 1976 he achieved no success either. During the years that he was working with Mills his success was phenomenal. Although equity looks at the advantage gained by the wrongdoer rather than the loss to the victim, the cases show that in assessing the advantage gained the court will look at the whole situation in the round. And it is relevant that if the approach of counsel for O'Sullivan is applied O'Sullivan would be much better off than if he had received separate legal advice and signed agreements negotiated at arm's length on reasonable terms current in the trade at the time. This point was made forcibly by counsel for the first five defendants at the conclusion of his address in reply, when he relied on the maxim 'He who seeks equity must do equity' and submitted that equity required that the position of O'Sullivan was relevant in considering the appropriate remedy.

In my judgment the judge was right to set the agreements aside and to order an account of the profits and payment of the sums found due on the taking of the account. But in taking the account the defendants are entitled to an allowance as proposed by Fox LJ, whose judgment I have read in draft, for reasonable remuneration, including a profit element, for all work done in promoting and exploiting O'Sullivan and his compositions, whether such work was done pursuant to a contractual obligation or gratuitously. What constitutes 'reasonable remuneration' will depend on evidence on the taking of the account, but not the evidence of Mr Levison (an expert witness) who approached the question on a different basis. . . .

. . . Looking at the position in equity, that the defendants are bound to account for their actual profits, with the credits to which I have referred, their actual profits do not include tax paid and irrecoverable. In my opinion therefore it is right that, in computing the sums payable to O'Sullivan for the years during which tax was actually paid and is not reclaimable, credit should be given to the defendants for all sums paid to any tax authority or which would have been paid but for the utilisation of tax losses or group relief or advanced corporation tax surrendered. Sums payable to O'Sullivan in subsequent years should be paid without regard to tax.

Finally the question of interest. This is a financially significant matter since we were told that on the basis of the judge's order it is estimated that the amount of principal payable by the defendants is some £2·6m and the amount of interest £4·37m. The judge awarded compound interest in reliance on *Wallersteiner* v *Moir* (*No. 2*) [1975] 1 All ER 849. He held that since the defendants were fiduciaries who had used the money for the purposes of their business and had made a profit out of it he was justified on the authority of *Wallersteiner* v *Moir* (*No. 2*) in ordering compound interest.

. . . It is only in cases of breaches of fiduciary duty that compound interest can be awarded, since at common law the position is governed by s. 3(1) of the Law Reform (Miscellaneous Provisions) Act 1934, which provides that interest cannot be charged on interest. But in equity compound interest can be charged where the profits made in breach of a fiduciary duty have been used in trade. It is noteworthy that in none of the cases cited in this judgment, some of which involve breaches of fiduciary duty, was compound interest ordered, although in some of them at least it seems likely that the money must have been used in trade. In *Wallersteiner* v *Moir* (*No. 2*) the evidence was that Wallersteiner was a financier operating through a complex structure of companies, and that he used the moneys which he obtained or its capital equivalent in his operations. In those circumstances it was presumed that the money was worth to him the equivalent of compound interest at commercial rates with yearly rests at least. In the present case, accepting that the money was used by the defendants for their business purposes, part of it must have been used for the benefit of O'Sullivan himself.

If the various cases involving breach of fiduciary duty in which simple interest has been awarded in the past had been cited to the judge, and if the distinction between this case and *Wallersteiner* v *Moir* (*No. 2*) had been pointed out to him, I doubt if he would have awarded compound interest throughout. As they were not I am satisfied that he fell into error. I would vary the order as to interest by deleting the provision for annual yearly rests and awarding simple interest at 1% above bank rate or minimum lending rate in operation from time to time save for the calculation of profits from foreign sales under the publishing agreement. Sums payable in respect of those profits should carry compound interest with the rests and at the rates ordered by the judge.

In computing the amount of simple interest payable the same formula with regard to tax should be applied to that which I have proposed for the computation of the sums due by way of principal. The tax position with regard to compound interest is more complicated.

The purpose of the exercise is to remove from the defendants the profits to which they are not entitled. In calculating compound interest on such sums as are found due on the taking of the account, it will be necessary therefore to deduct in each and every year the amount of corporation tax paid or payable by the defendants, since it is only the net amount after payment of tax which would be available to them for investment in the succeeding year. The interest should accordingly be compounded year by year at the rate ordered by the judge, less tax at the appropriate rate which would have been paid by the defendants.

I would accordingly allow the appeal and vary the order of the judge in the following respects: (1) that, on taking the account of the sums payable to the plaintiff, the defendants are entitled to an allowance for reasonable remuneration for work done in promoting and exploiting the compositions and performances and managing the business affairs of O'Sullivan, including a profit element; (2) that, in computing the sums payable under (1) above, credit should be given to the defendants in respect of the years during which tax was paid and is not reclaimable for all the sums paid to any tax authority or which would have been paid but for utilisation of tax losses or group relief or advance corporation tax surrendered; (3) that the order for delivery up of the master tapes be varied so as to exclude all those tapes which have been delivered to EMI or the sixth defendant, and that the appeal of the sixth defendant be allowed; (4) that the order for interest be varied so as to provide that simple interest be paid on all sums found due on the taking of the account at 1% above bank rate, save for sums found due in respect of foreign sales under the publishing agreement, which will carry interest with yearly rests at the rates ordered by the judge; (5) that in computing simple interest credit should be given for tax paid or payable as in (2) above; (6) that compound interest where appropriate should be compounded year by year at the rate ordered by the judge, less tax which would have been paid by the defendants.

I would like to hear counsel as to the form of the order.

FOX LJ: . . . Once it is accepted that the court can make an appropriate allowance to a fiduciary for his skill and labour I do not see why, in principle, it should not be able to give him some part of the profit of the venture if it was thought that justice as between the parties demanded that. To give the fiduciary any allowance for his skill and labour involves some reduction of the profits otherwise payable to the beneficiary. And the business reality may be that the profits could never have been earned at all, as between fully independent persons, except on a profit-sharing basis. But, be that as it may, it would be one thing to permit a substantial sharing of profits in a case such as *Boardman* v *Phipps* where the conduct of the fiduciaries could not be criticised and quite another to permit it in a case such as the present where, though fraud was not alleged, there was an abuse of personal trust and confidence. I am not satisfied that it would be proper to exclude Mills and the MAM companies from all reward for their efforts. I find it impossible to believe that they did not make a significant contribution to O'Sullivan's success. It would be unjust to deny them a recompense for that. I would, therefore, be prepared, as was done in *Boardman v Phipps*, to authorise the payment (over and above out-of-pocket expenses) of an allowance for the skill and labour of the first five defendants in promoting the compositions and performances and managing the business affairs of O'Sullivan and that an inquiry (the terms of which would need to be considered with counsel) should be ordered for that purpose. Such an allowance could include a profit element in the way that solicitors' costs do.

In my view this would achieve substantial justice between the parties . . .

FOSTER AND OTHERS v SPENCER [1996] 2 All ER 672, ChD

FACTS: The trustees of a cricket club applied to court for an award of remuneration for services rendered to the club in the past. They also applied for approval for an award of future remuneration. In addition they sought reimbursement of past expenses and interest thereon.
HELD: They were entitled to remuneration for past services, but not to future remuneration. They were also entitled to past expenses, but not to any interest thereon.

PAUL BAKER QC: I now come to the application for remuneration. This falls into two parts. First, an application by Mr Sealey and Mr Foster for their services in bringing about the successful sale. Secondly, an application by all three for remuneration for the tasks which they have yet to perform.

It is trite law that a trustee is entitled to no allowance for his time and trouble unless it is authorised by the trust instrument. However, the court has power under its inherent jurisdiction to allow a trustee to retain remuneration. It also has statutory powers in relation to particular types of trustees. For example, under s. 42 of the 1925 Act, the court has power on appointing a corporation as trustee to authorise 'the corporation to charge such remuneration for its services as trustee as the court may think fit'.

The claim here is made under the inherent jusidiction. 'The leading case is now *Re Duke of Norfolk's Settlement Trusts* [1981] 3 All ER 220, decided at first instance by Walton J and by the Court of Appeal. In view of the arguments addressed to me, I should look at the judgments in both courts. . . .

[The judge then considered the judgment of Walton J at first instance, and the leading judgment of Fox LJ in the Court of Appeal (see **12.1.1.1**).]

Mr Henderson for the beneficiaries submitted that the trustees here were not entitled to remuneration either for the past or for the future. He drew from the judgment of Fox LJ the proposition that before one could award remuneration one had to find that the interests of the beneficiaries required the services of particular trustees who would not act unless remunerated. The alternative basis of an implied contract relied on by Walton J had been expressly disapproved of by the Court of Appeal. In the present case, he said, the trustees had completed the task for which their skill and time were required. For the remaining tasks there is no need to obtain the services of any particular trustee. Hence they are not entitled to be paid remuneration for their past services as the only basis on which it could be justified has been disapproved.

I regard this as too narrow a reading of the decision of the Court of Appeal. It fails to take account of the passages of the judgment of Fox LJ where he expressly indorses earlier cases allowing remuneration for past services (see [1981] 3 All ER 220 at 230. Where, as in this case, there were no funds out of which to pay remuneration at the time of their appointment, nor was a true appreciation of the extent of the task possible, a prospective application would be impracticable, if not impossible. The refusal of remuneration on the grounds suggested by Mr Henderson would result in the beneficiaries being unjustly enriched at the expense of the trustees. The right of the trustee to remuneration for past services cannot depend upon the circumstance that at the time he seeks it, his services are further required so that he is in a position to demand remuneration for the past as a condition of continuing in office.

The services rendered by the trustees were wholly outside their contemplation when appointed. They were appointed as trustees of a cricket club which had its own ground. They found themselves obliged by unforeseen circumstances to dispose of the ground. This proved far more difficult than would normally be expected and made great demands on the expertise of Mr Sealy and of Mr Foster, and on the time of all of them. I have no doubt that if they had realised what they were in for, they would have declined to act unless remunerated in some way. . . .

Finally I come to the application for future remuneration, which is sought on behalf of all the three trustees. The suggestion here is that I should make an order in the form of the normal wide professional charging clause.

I am unable to do that. The present position is that owing to the efforts of the trustees, the trust assets are now in the form of cash and deposits. The tasks remaining are quite different from those leading to the disposal of the ground. They consist of restoring the originating summons to determine the beneficial interests. I do not see that that calls for any special expertise on the part of the trustees. They have said that they are not willing to continue if not allowed to charge. It was submitted in reply that the experience of the trustees is very important and difficult to replace with anybody who would not charge. I am not persuaded of this. It may be that the knowledge of the trustees is important for the purpose of placing evidence before the court in determining the beneficial interest, but the duties of the trustees at this stage would not appear to be onerous. The burden will fall on solicitors who will be paid. There may be other beneficiaries who could be persuaded to take over if the plaintiffs insist on resigning. I do not say that if the burden proves too onerous than at present seems likely, a further application would be excluded. But as things stand, I cannot say that the continued services of these trustees is necessary for the good administration of the trusts, whether these take the form of a distribution among the contributors or the refounding of the cricket club elsewhere.

RE BERKELEY APPLEGATE (INVESTMENT CONSULTANTS) LTD [1989] Ch 32, ChD

FACTS: Berkeley Applegate Ltd had gone into liquidation and its free assets were not sufficient to cover the expenses and remuneration of the liquidator. Accordingly, the liquidator applied to the court for a determination of the question whether his expenses and remuneration might be met out of assets held by the company on trust for its clients. HELD: Although the company, and not the liquidator, was trustee of the assets, the client-beneficiaries of the trust were reliant upon the discretion of the court to enforce their equitable interests in the assets legally owned by the company. Accordingly the liquidator was granted remuneration and expenses out of the trust property because those who seek the assistance of equity must themselves act equitably. If the liquidator had not administered the liquidation the task would have fallen to a receiver appointed by the court and such a person would have been entitled to claim his fees out of the trust assets.

EDWARD NUGEE QC: . . . The allowance of fair compensation to the liquidator is in my judgment a proper application of the rule that he who seeks equity must do equity.

> That . . . is a rule of unquestionable justice, but which decides nothing in itself; for you must first inquire what are the equities which the defendant must do, and what the plaintiff ought to have: *Neesom* v *Clarkson* (1845) 4 Hare 97, 101 *per* Wigram V-C.
>
> The rule means that a man who comes to seek the aid of a court of equity to enforce a claim must be prepared to submit in such proceedings to any directions which the known principles of a court of equity may make it proper to give; he must do justice as to the matters in respect of which the assistance of equity is asked: *Halsbury's Laws of England*, 4th ed., vol. 16 (1976), p. 874, para. 1303, which in my judgment correctly states the law.

The authorities establish, in my judgment, a general principle that where a person seeks to enforce a claim to an equitable interest in property, the court has a discretion to require as a condition of giving effect to that equitable interest that an allowance be made for costs incurred and for skill and labour expended in connection with the administration of the property. It is a discretion which will be sparingly exercised; but factors which will operate in favour of its being exercised include the fact that, if the work had not been done by the person to whom the allowance is sought to be made, it would have had to be done either by the person entitled to the equitable interest (as in *In re Marine*

Mansions Co. LR 4 Eq 601 and similar cases) or by a receiver appointed by the court whose fees would have been borne by the trust property (as in *Scott v Nesbitt*, 14 Ves Jun 438); and the fact that the work has been of substantial benefit to the trust property and to the persons interested in it in equity (as in *Phipps v Boardman* [1964] 1 WLR 993). In my judgment this is a case in which the jurisdiction can properly be exercised.

It seems to me that this principle is entirely consistent with the basis upon which the Court of Appeal acted in *In re Duke of Norfolk's Settlement Trusts* [1982] Ch 61. What the Court of Appeal held in that case was that, if the increase of the trustees' remuneration was beneficial to the trust administration, there was an inherent jurisdiction to require the beneficiaries to accept, as a condition of effect being given to their equitable interests, that such an increase in remuneration should be authorised. The court there was concerned with the good administration of a settlement of a conventional kind; but the jurisdiction which was held to be exercisable in that case is in my judgment equally exercisable in other cases in which a person seeks to enforce an interest in property to which he is entitled in equity. The principles on which a court of equity acts are not divided into watertight compartments but form a seamless whole, however necessary it may be for the purposes of exposition to attempt to set them out under distinct headings . . .

Accordingly I propose to declare that the liquidator is entitled to be paid his proper expenses and remuneration out of the trust assets if the assets of the company are insufficient. . . .

12.1.1.3   The exception in *Cradock* v *Piper* (1850)

RE CORSELLIS (1887) 34 ChD 675, CA

FACTS: A next friend of an infant beneficiary made an application for maintenance of the infant. The two trustees of the trust were respondents to the application. One of the trustees, a solicitor's firm, sought to claim remuneration for acting in the application.

HELD: Although a trustee is not permitted to profit from the trust, there has existed for a long time an exception to that rule. The exception had been laid down in the case of *Cradock v Piper* (1850) 1 Mac & G 664 and permits a solicitor-trustee to be remunerated out of the trust fund for work done in litigation on behalf of himself and a co-trustee if the same costs would have been incurred through acting for the co-trustee alone. In the present case the litigation was not hostile, but a 'friendly' application in chambers on behalf of an infant beneficiary; nevertheless it was quite proper for the exception in *Cradock v Piper* to apply in such a case.

COTTON LJ: . . . Now, it is a well-established rule, and one founded on sound principles, that a trustee who is a solicitor cannot as a rule make any profits as a solicitor on business which is done by himself or by the firm of which he is a member in matters relating to the estate. There is one very obvious principle which applies, namely, that the trustee must discharge his duty without making any profit out of it. If there is business which a layman cannot properly perform he may employ a solicitor to do that legal business. If it is business which a trustee in his position cannot be expected to discharge, such as receiving rents from a number of small properties, he may employ an agent to collect those rents, but if he chooses to do work, he cannot make a charge against the estate; that is the rule as regards work done out of Court by a trustee, whether acting for himself or for the other trustee as well. . . .

From the rule I have stated one exception was established by *Cradock v Piper*:—that is to say, where there is work done in a suit not on behalf of the trustee, who is a solicitor, alone, but on behalf of himself and a co-trustee, the rule will not prevent the solicitor or his firm from receiving the usual costs, if the costs of appearing for and acting for the two have not increased the expense; that is to say, if the trustee himself has not added to the expense which would have been incurred if he or his firm had appeared only for his co-trustee. For that there is an obvious reason—that it is not the business of a trustee, although he is a solicitor, to act as solicitor for his co-trustee. But the exception in *Cradock v Piper* is limited expressly to the costs incurred in respect of business done in an action or a suit, and it may be an anomaly that that exception should apply to such a case, and should not apply to business done out of Court by the solicitor for himself as trustee and his co-trustee. But there may be this reason for it, that in an action, although costs are not always hostilely taxed, yet there may be a taxation where parties other than the trustee-solicitor may appear and test the propriety of the costs, and the Court can disallow altogether the costs of any proceedings which may appear to be vexatious or improperly undertaken. But whatever may be the principle, the question is whether that is not an established rule. In my opinion, as it is a rule laid down by Lord Cottenham so long ago as 1850, it would be wrong of this Court, even if they would not originally have arrived at the same conclusion as Lord Cottenham did in that case, to disturb the rule and reverse the decision. . . .

Then what is said to be the special difference in this case? It is said that the exception would not apply to costs in a hostile action, and that this was not an action at all, but only a summons, and that therefore the exception ought not to apply. Undoubtedly the proceeding was not in any hostile action, but was commenced, as I understand, by a summons; but, in my opinion, it would be frittering away the decision, which we ought not to overrule, by saying that it only applies to a hostile action, no such limitation being laid down by Lord Cottenham. . . .

12.2   The Duty of Personal Service

12.2.1   AUTHORITY TO DELEGATE

TRUSTEE ACT 1925

23.   Power to employ agents

(1)   Trustees or personal representatives may, instead of acting personally, employ and pay an agent, whether a solicitor, banker, stockbroker, or other person, to transact any business or do any act required to be transacted or done in the execution of the trust, or the administration of the testator's or intestate's estate, including the receipt and payment of money, and shall be entitled to be allowed and paid all charges and expenses so incurred, and shall not be responsible for the default of any such agent if employed in good faith.

(2)   Trustees or personal representatives may appoint any person to act as their agent or attorney for the purpose of selling, converting, collecting, getting in, and executing and perfecting insurances of, or managing or cultivating, or otherwise administering any property, real or personal, moveable or immoveable, subject to the trust or forming part of the testator's or intestate's estate, in any place outside the United Kingdom or executing or exercising any discretion or trust or power vested in them in relation to any such property, with such ancillary powers, and with and subject to such provisions and restrictions as they may think fit, including a power to appoint substitutes, and shall not, by reason only of their having made such appointment, be responsible for any loss arising thereby.

(3)   Without prejudice to such general power of appointing agents as aforesaid—

   (a)   A trustee may appoint a solicitor to be his agent to receive and give a discharge for any money or valuable consideration or property receivable by the trustee under the trust, by permitting the solicitor to have the custody of, and to produce, a deed having in the body thereof or endorsed thereon a receipt for such money or valuable consideration or property, the deed being executed, or the endorsed receipt being signed, by the person entitled to give a receipt for that consideration.

   (b)   A trustee shall not be chargeable with breach of trust by reason only of his having made or concurred in making any such appointment; and the production of any such deed by the solicitor shall have the same statutory validity and effect as if the person appointing the solicitor had not been a trustee;

A trustee may appoint a banker or solicitor to be his agent to receive and give a discharge for any money payable to the trustee under or by virtue of a policy of insurance, by permitting the banker or solicitor to have the custody of and to produce the policy of insurance with a receipt signed by the trustee, and a trustee shall not be chargeable with a breach of trust by reason only of his having made or concurred in making any such appointment:

Provided that nothing in this subsection shall exempt a trustee from any liability which he would have incurred if this Act and any enactment replaced by this Act had not been passed, in case he permits any such money, valuable consideration, or property to remain in the hands or under the control of the banker or solicitor for a period longer than is reasonably necessary to enable the banker or solicitor, as the case may be, to pay or transfer the same to the trustee.

This subsection applies whether the money or valuable consideration or property was or is received before or after the commencement of this Act.

25. Power to delegate trusts during absence abroad

[(1) Notwithstanding any rule of law or equity to the contrary, a trustee may, by power of attorney, delegate for a period not exceeding twelve months the execution or exercise of all or any of the trusts, powers and discretions vested in him as trustee either alone or jointly with any other person or persons.

(2) The persons who may be donees of a power of attorney under this section include a trust corporation but not (unless a trust corporation) the only other co-trustee of the donor of the power.

(3) An instrument creating a power of attorney under this section shall be attested by at least one witness.

(4) Before or within seven days after giving a power of attorney under this section the donor shall give written notice thereof (specifying the date on which the power comes into operation and its duration, the donee of the power, the reason why the power is given and, where some are delegated, the trusts, powers and discretions delegated) to—

(a) each person (other than himself), if any, who under any instrument creating the trust has power (whether alone or jointly) to appoint a new trustee; and

(b) each of the other trustees, if any; but failure to comply with this subsection shall not, in favour of a person dealing with the donee of the power, invalidate any act done or instrument executed by the donee.

(5) The donor of a power of attorney given under this section shall be liable for the acts or defaults of the donee in the same manner as if they were the acts or defaults of the donor.]

[(6) For the purpose of executing or exercising the trusts or powers delegated to him, the donee may exercise any of the powers conferred on the donor as trustee by statute or by the instrument creating the trust, including power, for the purpose of the transfer of any inscribed stock, himself to delegate to an attorney power to transfer but not including the power of delegation conferred by this section.]

[(7) The fact that it appears from any power of attorney given under this section, or from any evidence required for the purposes of any such power of attorney or otherwise, that in dealing with any stock the donee of the power is acting in the execution of a trust shall not be deemed for any purpose to effect any person in whose books the stock is inscribed or registered with any notice of the trust.]

[(8) This section applies to a personal representative, tenant for life and statutory owner as it applies to a trustee except that subsection (4) shall apply as if it required the notice there mentioned to be given—

(a) in the case of a personal representative, to each of the other personal representatives, if any, except any executor who has renounced probate;

(b) in the case of a tenant for life, to the trustees of the settlement and to each person, if any, who together with the person giving the notice constitutes the tenant for life;

(c) in the case of a statutory owner, to each of the persons if any, who together with the person giving the notice constitute the statutory owner and, in the case of a statutory owner by virtue of section 23(1)(a) of the Settled Land Act 1925, to the trustees of the settlement.]

30. Implied indemnity of trustees

(1) A trustee shall be chargeable only for money and securities actually received by him notwithstanding his signing any receipt for the sake of conformity, and shall be

answerable and accountable only for his own acts, receipts, neglects, or defaults, and nor for those of any other trustee, nor for any banker, broker, or other person with whom any trust money or securities may be deposited, nor for the insufficiency or deficiency of any securities, nor for any other loss, unless the same happens through his own wilful default. . . .

See *Re Vickery* [1931] 1 Ch 572 (**11.2.3**).

Jones, Gareth H., 'Delegation by Trustees: A Reappraisal' (1959) 22 MLR 381

. . . Re Vickery—a criticism
It is the present writer's submission that, although in the result *Re Vickery* might be correctly decided, the reasons given by Maugham J for the decision cannot be supported, and that it is consequently not safe or desirable for a trustee to rely on this decision as authority for the proposition that, 'I am safe if I act honestly but foolishly in appointing my agents.'

His Lordship in *Re Vickery* did not directly address his mind to the problem of reconciling s. 30(1) of the Trustee Act 1925, with s. 23(1). Maugham J limited s. 30(1) to 'bankers and brokers' and the words 'any other loss' to cases where the loss had arisen through the signing of receipts for the sake of conformity, or where the wrongful acts of another trustee or the agent with whom the trust money had been deposited had resulted in the loss, or where the loss is due to the deficiency or insufficiency of securities or other analogous loss. This limitation does not solve, unfortunately, the conundrum of how a trustee can be free of liability if he appoints in good faith and yet later be liable for the acts or defaults of these particular agents if he, the trustee, has been guilty of a wilful default. Further, the learned judge's definition of 'wilful default' as a conscious or reckless breach of duty on the part of the trustee cannot be supported; the words should have been construed, in their pre-1926 sense, so as to include want of reasonable care. His Lordship purported to follow the judgment of Romer J in the *Re City Equitable* [1925] Ch 407 case. . . .

It is submitted, with respect, that the translation of the definition of 'wilful default' in *Re City Equitable* to s. 30(1) of the Trustee Act 1925, was completely unjustified. Romer J was construing a particular set of articles of association and the decision on the facts of *Re City Equitable* was to have no application to the case of trustees, *strictu sensu*. This, indeed, was the view of Warrington LJ, in the Court of Appeal, in that case, and his approval of Romer J's definition, quoted by Astbury J in the above passage, was a strictly limited approval. The following extract from the learned Lord Justice's judgment is relevant.

> With all respect to counsel who cited those trustee cases to us, I think there is great danger of being misled if we attempt to apply decisions as to the duties of trustees to a case as to the conduct of persons in the position of auditors in this case. In the case of trustees there are certain definite and precise rules of law as to what a trustee may or may not do in the execution of his trust, and it is no answer for a trustee to say, if, for example, he invests the trust property in his hands in a security which the law regards as an unauthorised security: 'I honestly believed that I was justified in doing that.' No honest belief will justify him in committing that which is a breach of such a rule of law, and therefore the question which we have to determine in expressing a view on the construction of such words in a contract like the present is not solved by seeing how the question has been determined in a case relating to the duties of a trustee.

In effect, neither Romer J nor the Court of Appeal in *Re City Equitable* intended to derogate from the pre-1926 decisions, which, impliedly if not expressly, interpreted the words 'wilful default,' within s. 24 of the 1893 Act, so as to include lack of reasonable care. Section 30(1) is a mere re-enactment of s. 24 of the Trustee Act 1893, and like that section should, it is submitted, render the trustee liable if he failed to act with reasonable care. . . .

In conclusion, it is to be noted that s. 23(1) speaks simply of the liability of the trustee for the acts of his *agent*, and the section concludes that the trustee shall 'not be responsible for the default of any such agent if employed in good faith.' The section does not deal with the responsibility, which the *trustee* himself assumed when he undertook the trust. Thus, in *Re Vickery* Maugham J was concerned with the liability of the trustee for the act of the solicitor, and not with the question whether the trustee was in breach of his own *primary* duty as trustee to supervise the trust, and, in particular, his agents. What norm is to determine if the trustee has properly supervised the acts of his agent? The reasonable business man of *Speight* v *Gaunt*? If this be the standard, and it is suggested that it is, then the decision in *Re Vickery* is effectively circumscribed. The judgment of the trustee must be constantly exercised. To exercise this judgment, as a reasonable trustee should, will demand that the trustee appoints an agent to do work which he is qualified to do, to appoint a solicitor as a solicitor, a broker as a broker; and, after the appointment of such agents, to supervise their acts. A trustee cannot give an agent a carte blanche. This 'primary' liability of the trustee is independent of his vicarious liability for the acts or defaults of his agent, and it is with this latter head of liability that s. 23(1) is concerned. It is suggested, therefore, that it is open for the courts to hold that the trustee has a primary duty, imposed on him by equity, to supervise at all times the trust and the trust funds; and it is further submitted that the norm of the reasonable man of business will determine whether in fact he has discharged that duty.

RE LUCKING'S WT [1968] 3 All ER 726, ChD

FACTS: The plaintiff was a beneficiary entitled to a one-eighth share under a will trust. Lucking, the son of the testatrix, was the sole trustee of that trust and a beneficiary under it. Part of the trust property was a majority holding in a private company. In order to secure the profitable running of the company, Lucking appointed a Mr Dewar to be a director of the company. Over time a practice was established whereby Dewar sent blank cheques to Lucking to be signed (two signatures were needed to authorise drawings on the company's account) to cover Dewar's expenses. It became apparent to Lucking that Dewar was making withdrawals for his own ends, but Lucking took no action to prevent this; on the contrary, Lucking continued to sign Dewar's blank cheques. The company's gross profits had increased under Dewar's management, but so had its overdraft. Dewar's personal indebtedness to the company eventually reached such a level that he was dismissed from his executorship. He was declared bankrupt while still owing £15,890 to the company.

HELD: Lucking had failed adequately to supervise Dewar's financial activities. He should have exercised the care of an ordinary prudent person of business. Having failed to do so he was liable to the other beneficiaries for the devaluation in the shares owned by the trust.

CROSS J: . . . In support of the proposition that a trustee who is carrying on an unincorporated business is only liable for negligence in his supervision of a manager employed by him if the negligence amounts to 'wilful default', counsel relied on the decision of Maugham J, in *Re Vickery, Vickery* v *Stephens* [1931] 1 Ch 572. In that case an executor employed a solicitor to obtain payment of sums of money due to the estate and furnished him with documents of title for the purpose. The solicitor made away with the money and it was said that having regard to what the executor had learnt of the reputation of the solicitor in question he ought to have cancelled the authority given him before the money got into his hands. Maugham J held that s. 23 of the Trustee Act 1925, empowered the executor to employ the solicitor for the purpose in question in the first instance; and he held further that as s. 30 of the Act provided, inter alia, that a trustee should not be liable for the defaults of any person with whom any trust money or securities might be deposited unless the resulting loss happens through his own wilful default, the executor in the case before him would only be liable if he were guilty of wilful default. I see no reason whatever to think that Maugham J would have considered that a person employed by a trustee to manage a business owned by the trust was a person with whom trust money or securities were deposited within the meaning of s. 30. In support of the proposition that directors are only liable for 'wilful default' counsel referred to the *City Equitable* [1925] Ch 407 case; but there one of the company's articles provided that directors should only be liable for 'wilful default'. Romer J made it clear in his judgment that, but for that article, he would have held some of the directors liable in some matters for negligence falling short of 'wilful default'. In my view , 'wilful default' does not enter into the picture in this case at all. The conduct of the defendant trustees is, I think, to be judged by the standard applied in *Re Speight, Speight v Gaunt* (1883) 22 ChD 727, namely, that a trustee is only bound to conduct the business of the trust is such a way as an ordinary prudent man would conduct a business of his own.

Now what steps, if any, does a reasonably prudent man who finds himself a majority shareholder in a private company take with regard to the management of the company's affairs? He does not, I think, content himself with such information as to the management of the company's affairs as he is entitled to as shareholder, but ensures that he is represented on the board. . . .

12.2.2 CHOICE OF AGENT

FRY v TAPSON (1884) 28 ChD 268, ChD

FACTS: The trustees in this case had decided to invest in a mortgage of freehold land, such an investment being authorised under the terms of their trust. However, the trustees appointed a London-based valuer to value land in Liverpool and, what is more, the valuer was an agent of the proposed mortgagor and thus had a financial interest in inflating the value of the security. The valuer had been recommended by the trustees' solicitors. In the event the valuation turned out to have been inflated and proved to be inadequate security when the mortgagor became bankrupt in due course.

HELD: The trustees did not exercise sufficient care in their choice of agent. An agent should always be chosen to act within the agent's proper sphere of expertise; a London-based solicitor should not have been chosen to value a property in Liverpool. Further, the trustees had failed to consider the accuracy of the agent's valuation, but accepted it at face value. Although it was not doubted that the trustees had acted honestly, they had failed to act as ordinary prudent persons of business would have acted in business of their own and they would accordingly be liable to account to the beneficiaries for the losses caused through their lack of prudence.

KAY J: . . . *Speight* v *Gaunt* did not lay down any new rule, but only illustrated a very old one, viz., that trustees acting according to the ordinary course of business, and employing agents as a prudent man of business would do on his own behalf, are not liable for the default of an agent so employed. But an obvious limitation of that rule is that the agent must not be employed out of the ordinary scope of his business. If a trustee employs an agent to do that which is not the ordinary business of such an agent, and he performs that unusual duty improperly, and loss is thereby occasioned, the trustee would not be exonerated.

Suppose, for example, that in selling trust property, or changing an investment, trustees were to allow the trust fund to pass into the hands of their solicitors, and that it was lost in consequence, they would be liable. I take that illustration because I am afraid it not unfrequently happens that trustees do allow trust funds to be in their solicitors' hands without sufficient reason. It would be no excuse to say, as one of the witnesses said in this case, 'Solicitors often do so.' The question is not what they often do, but what is properly within the scope of their employment as solicitors. . . .

Suppose in *Speight* v *Gaunt* the trustee had exercised no discretion as to the choice of a broker, but had left that to his solicitors, who had employed a man known to them to be untrustworthy, would the trustee have been exonerated? In my opinion clearly not, because he would have delegated to his solicitors that which was not properly the business of the solicitors, but a matter as to which his own judgment should have been exercised. . . .

I am most reluctant to visit trustees acting *bona fide* with the consequences of a want of due caution, but I cannot avoid the conclusion that the trust fund has been diminished, if not lost, by their fault. They neglected the rule of not lending more than half on house property. They most incautiously employed the mortgagors' agent, who had been puffing the proposed security and was interested in obtaining the loan, to value on their behalf, and they accepted his valuation without attempting to check it, and this although he was a *London* surveyor, and it was most important to obtain the opinion of some experienced local surveyor as to property of this kind.

12.3   Proposals for Reform

**Law Commission Consultation Paper No. 146,
'The Powers and Duties of Transfer' 1998**

PART VI TRUSTEES' POWERS OF DELEGATION

Options for Reform

6.26   Our provisional view is that, subject to any expression of contrary intention in the trust instrument, trustees—

should have authority to delegate to agents their powers to administer the trust, including their powers of investment and management; but
should have no authority to delegate their powers to distribute the income or capital of the trust for the benefit of its objects, except in relation to trust property abroad.

The power to delegate under (1) could either be in relation to a specific act or acts, or by way of a general retainer. It should remain the case that the matters delegated were ones that were required to be done in the execution of the trust or the administration of a deceased's estate. There should be no requirement that the delegation should be made by power of attorney.

6.27   These recommendations would be without prejudice to—

the power of an individual trustee to delegate all or any of his or her trusts, powers and discretions under s. 25 of the Trustee Act 1925; or
the need to comply with any conditions laid down by law or by the instrument creating the trust in relation to the exercise of any power of investment or management.

6.31   Our provisional view is that—

trustees should review any delegation of their functions at regular intervals; and
trustees who wished to delegate the powers of management specified in the following paragraph should be required to—
consider the appropriateness of any such delegation before making it;
draw up and review at reasonable intervals a written statement of their policy in relation to the exercise of the powers delegated which reflected their fiduciary obligations to ensure that the trust was administered in the best interests of the objects of that trust;
inform the agent of that policy; and
take reasonable steps to ensure that he or she both complied with it and reported back to the trustees at regular intervals as to its execution.

6.32   The requirement in paragraph 6.31 would apply to the following powers—

to select investments;
to sell, lease, or charge trust property;
to grant options or rights of pre-emption over trust property; or
to acquire property for the benefit of the trust.

6.33   We do not wish to impose unnecessary burdens on trustees. It would (for example) be absurd to require them to have a written policy relating to the kinds of ministerial acts that they already have power to delegate under s. 23(1) of the Trustee Act 1925. We have therefore confined the written policy requirement to cases where they propose to delegate their fiduciary discretions. It may be that readers will consider that our proposals are either too restrictive or not restrictive enough. We therefore ask readers whether they agree with our proposals and, in particular, whether they consider that—

any powers should either be added to or removed from the list in the preceding paragraph; or

any other restrictions or conditions should be imposed.

6.34   We also propose that the existing statutory provisions that confer powers on trustees to pay agents and to be reimbursed for their own expenses incurred in the execution of their duties should be replaced by a provision that would make it clear that trustees were authorised to pay only the *reasonable* fees of their agents and to be reimbursed only for expenditure *reasonably* incurred by themselves. We ask whether readers agree with us.

6.37   We ask whether readers agree with our provisional view that trustees should have power—

to authorise their agents to employ sub-agents; and

to employ agents on terms which limit their liability;

provided that it was reasonably necessary for the trustees to do so. For these purposes, an act would be reasonably necessary if an ordinary prudent person would have done it.

12.4 End of Chapter Assessment Question

Trudy has been appointed trustee of a trust which contains the following clause:

> The trustees shall be entitled to all professional charges incurred in the execution of the trust and shall be entitled to delegate all or any of their duties in accordance with the general law.

Trudy has accepted the trust even though she is a total amateur and rather ignorant of business affairs. She purchases a large quantity of office equipment and stationery to facilitate the smooth running of her tasks but still finds that the job is too complicated. After putting in several months of work in service of the trust she eventually enlists the assistance of a friend who, having run his own betting office for many years, is more at ease with commercial matters. She transfers the trust fund into the friend's bank account with the instruction that he should invest it wisely for the benefit of the trust. In fact the friend 'invests' the money on *Lucky Laddie*, the favourite to win a greyhound race. Lucky Laddie loses the race and the trust fund is lost.

Is Trudy liable for breach of her trust, and, if so, why? If she is liable, will she be required to reinstate the full value of the fund, or can she claim remuneration and/or expenses?

12.5 End of Chapter Assessment Outline Answer

This question examines the trustee's duty to provide personal service to the trust and the trustee's duty to act gratuitously. The first issue is whether Trudy has breached her trust by breaching the duty to provide personal service, otherwise known as the rule against delegation. The rule was clarified by Viscount Radcliffe in the House of Lords in *Pilkington* v *IRC* [1964] AC 612 in the following terms: 'The law is not that a trustee cannot delegate: it is that trustees cannot delegate unless they have authority to do so'. In the present case a clause of Trudy's trust clearly authorises her to delegate in accordance with the general law. We must turn therefore to the provisions of the Trustee Act 1925 and to the case law.

Section 23(1) of the Trustee Act 1925 permits trustees to appoint an agent 'to transact any business or do any act required to be transacted or done in the execution of the trust'. And in such a case the trustee will not be liable for losses caused by the agent, so long as the agent was appointed in good faith. It is generally accepted that s. 23(1) permits trustees to delegate executive functions and ministerial acts, but not fundamental decision-making. Accordingly, Trudy would be entitled to appoint an agent to consider possible investments, but the agent would be acting outside his authority if he were to alter fundamentally the type of investments being made. On the facts of the present case Trudy's friend has clearly acted outside his authority and thus s. 23(1) will afford Trudy no defence to losses caused by the failed 'investment'. There is, in any event, another reason why s. 23(1) would probably have no application in the present case. The case of *Fry* v *Tapson* (see **12.2.2**) established that it will be a breach of the trustees' general duty of care to appoint an agent to perform acts outside their sphere of expertise. There can be no doubt that Trudy's friend, the bookmaker, has been appointed to perform a task he is not qualified to perform. Accordingly, he has not been 'employed' in the proper sense of that word and so s. 23 which applies only to the 'employment' of trustees will probably not protect Trudy.

Does s. 30(1) of the Trustee Act 1925 offer Trudy any comfort? This provides that a trustee will not be liable for losses arising from the acts of any co-trustee, agent or other person 'with whom trust money or securities may be deposited', unless the losses are caused through the trustee's 'own wilful default'. In the case of *Re Vickery* (see **11.2.3**) Maugham J defined wilful default as 'either a consciousness of negligence or breach of duty, or a recklessness in the performance of the duty'. In that case the trustee was a missionary, said to have been 'ignorant of business', who had deposited trust monies with a dishonest solicitor who absconded with the monies. The trustee was relieved from liability by s. 30(1). He would probably have been liable under the usual *Speight* v *Gaunt* standard of care (see **Chapter 11**), but he could not be said to have been in 'wilful default' for the purposes of s. 30(1). Trudy has also been described as an amateur and 'rather ignorant of business affairs', and there is no suggestion of dishonesty or bad faith on her part. Probably there has been no 'consciousness of negligence'. However, she was surely 'reckless . . in the performance of her duty' and will be unable to rely upon the immunity afforded by s. 30. *Re Vickery* has been restrictively applied since 1930 (see *Re Lucking's WT* **12.2.1**) and has been the subject of much academic criticism (see G H Jones at **12.2.1**). It will not be extended to protect a trustee, no matter how honest, who has deposited trust monies with a bookmaker.

The question remains whether Trudy can recover remuneration and expenses. The general rule, laid down in *Bray* v *Ford* (see **12.1.2**), is that a trustee will not be entitled to profit from their trust in the absence of express provision to the contrary. The trust instrument provides that Trudy is entitled to all 'professional charges'. Unfortunately for Trudy remuneration clauses are construed strictly against the trustee. It follows that, because Trudy is an 'amateur', she will be unable to claim remuneration under the trust instrument (see *Chalinder* v *Herrington* (**12.1.3.1**)). She will be able to apply to the court for an award (under its inherent jurisdiction to ensure the good administration of the trust) for remuneration for her past services to the trust (*Foster* v *Spencer* (**12.1.3.2**)) but such an application is likely to fail in view of her poor service. She will, however, be able to deduct reasonable expenses from the monies she must repay to the trust. The purchase of office equipment and stationery will be recoverable if they were expenses reasonably incurred (see s. 30(2) Trustee Act 1925 at **12.1.1**).

CHAPTER THIRTEEN

MAINTENANCE AND ADVANCEMENT

13.1 Maintenance

TRUSTEE ACT 1925

31. Power to apply income for maintenance and to accumulate surplus income during a minority

(1) Where any property is held by trustees in trust for any person for any interest whatsoever, whether vested or contingent, then, subject to any prior interests or charges affecting that property—

(i) during the infancy of any such person, if his interest so long continues, the trustees may, at their sole discretion, pay to his parent or guardian, if any, or otherwise apply for or towards his maintenance, education, or benefit, the whole or such part, if any, of the income of that property as may, in all the circumstances, be reasonable, whether or not there is—

(a) any other fund applicable to the same purpose; or

(b) any person bound by law to provide for his maintenance or education; and

(ii) if such person on attaining the age of [eighteen years] has not a vested interest in such income, the trustees shall thenceforth pay the income of that property and of any accretion thereto under subsection (2) of this section to him, until he either attains a vested interest therein or dies, or until failure of his interest:

Provided that, in deciding whether the whole or any part of the income of the property is during a minority to be paid or applied for the purposes aforesaid, the trustees shall have regard to the age of the infant and his requirements and generally to the circumstances of the case, and in particular to what other income, if any, is applicable for the same purposes; and where trustees have notice that the income of more than one fund is applicable for those purposes, then, so far as practicable, unless the entire income of the funds is paid or applied as aforesaid or the court otherwise directs, a proportionate part only of the income of each fund shall be so paid or applied.

(2) During the infancy of any such person, if his interest so long continues, the trustees shall accumulate all the residue of that income in the way of compound interest by investing the same and the resulting income thereof from time to time in authorised investments, and shall hold those accumulations as follows:—

(i) If any such person—

(a) attains the age of [eighteen years], or marries under that age, and his interest in such income during his infancy or until his marriage is a vested interest; or

(b) on attaining the age of [eighteen years] or on marriage under that age becomes entitled to the property from which such income arose in fee simple, absolute or determinable, or absolutely, or for an entailed interest;

the trustees shall hold the accumulations in trust for such person absolutely, but without prejudice to any provision with respect thereto contained in any settlement by him made under any statutory power during his infancy, and so that the receipt of such person after marriage, and though still an infant, shall be a good discharge; and

(ii) In any other case the trustees shall, notwithstanding that such person had a vested interest in such income, hold the accumulations as an accretion to the capital of the property from which such accumulations arose, and as one fund with such capital for all purposes, and so that, if such property is settled land, such accumulations shall be held upon the same trusts as if the same were capital money arising therefrom;

but the trustees may, at any time during the infancy of such person if his interest so long continues, apply those accumulations, or any part thereof, as if they were income arising in the then current year.

(3) This section applies in the case of a contingent interest only if the limitation or trust carries the intermediate income of the property, but it applies to a future or contingent legacy by the parent of, or a person standing in *loco parentis* to, the legatee, if and for such period as, under the general law, the legacy carries interest for the maintenance of the legatee, and in any such case as last aforesaid the rate of interest shall (if the income available is sufficient, and subject to any rules of court to the contrary) be five pounds per centum per annum.

(4) This section applies to a vested annuity in like manner as if the annuity were the income of property held by trustees in trust to pay the income thereof to the annuitant for the same period for which the annuity is payable, save that in any case accumulations made during the infancy of the annuitant shall be held in trust for the annuitant or his personal representatives absolutely.

(5) This section does not apply where the instrument, if any, under which the interest arises came into operation before the commencement of this Act.

13.1.1   GIFTS CARRYING INTERMEDIATE INCOME

LAW OF PROPERTY ACT 1925

175. Contingent and future testamentary gifts to carry the intermediate income
(1) A contingent or future specific devise or bequest of property, whether real or personal, and a contingent residuary devise of freehold land, and a specific or residuary devise of freehold land to trustees upon trust for persons whose interests are contingent or executory shall, subject to the statutory provisions relating to accumulations, carry the intermediate income of that property from the death of the testator, except so far as such income, or any part thereof, may be otherwise expressly disposed of.

(2) This section applies only to wills coming into operation after the commencement of this Act.

RE McGEORGE, DECD [1963] 1 Ch 544, ChD

FACTS: the case revolved around the construction of the following clause in a will trust:

> Clause 4: (a) I devise . . . to my daughter . . . certain agricultural land. . . . (b) I give my said son a pecuniary legacy equal in value . . . to the aforesaid agricultural land hereinbefore devised to my said daughter. (c) I declare: (i) that the aforesaid devise and pecuniary legacy shall not take effect until after the death of my said wife should she survive me. (ii) Should my said daughter die in the lifetime of the survivor of myself and my said wife leaving issue living at the death of such survivor such issue . . . shall take by substitution . . . the aforesaid devise in favour of my said daughter. (iii) If for any reason whatsoever the aforesaid devise shall fail then the aforesaid pecuniary legacy shall not take effect.

A summons was taken out to determine whether the gifts made by clause 4 carried the intermediate income.
HELD: The gift in 4(a) was vested, but was subject to possible defeasance during the mother's life; therefore, even if that gift carried the intermediate income, the income should be accumulated for the benefit of persons who might become entitled upon a defeasance. Accordingly, the daughter should not be maintained out of that income. The gift in 4(b) was also vested, but the words of 4(c)—'shall not take effect until after the

death of my said wife'—meant that the gift had been deferred and therefore would not carry the intermediate income.

CROSS J: It remains to consider whether as a matter of law the gifts as I have construed them do in fact carry any income or interest before the death of the widow. No doubt arises with regard to the legacy. A deferred legacy, such as I have construed the legacy to the son to be, does not carry interest until the date fixed for payment. Before 1926 I do not think that there would have been any doubt with regard to the devise either. A future specific devise would not have carried the rents accruing before it vested in possession. I must, however, consider whether the law in this respect has been altered by section 175 of the Law of Property Act 1925, which is in the following terms: (see **13.1.1.1**).

The devise in clause 4(a) is, it is said, a future specific devise within the meaning of the section; the testator has not made any express disposition of the income accruing from it between his death and the death of his widow, therefore that income is carried by the gift. At first sight it is hard to see how Parliament could have enacted a section which produces such a result. If a testator gives property to A after the death of B, then whether or not he disposes of the income accruing during B's life he is at all events showing clearly that A is not to have it. Yet if the future gift to A is absolute and the intermediate income is carried with it by force of this section, A can claim to have the property transferred to him at once, since no one else can be interested in it. The section, that is to say, will have converted a gift in remainder into a gift in possession in defiance of the testator's wishes. The explanation for the section taking the form it does is, I think, probably as follows. It has long been established that a gift of residuary personalty to a legatee in being on a contingency or to an unborn person at birth, carries the intermediate income so far as the law will allow it to be accumulated, but that rule had been held for reasons depending on the old land law not to apply to gifts of real property, and it was apparently never applied to specific dispositions of personalty. Section 175 of the Law of Property Act was plainly intended to extend the rule to residuary devises and to specific gifts whether of realty or of personalty. It is now, however, established at all events in courts of first instance that the old rule does not apply to residuary bequests whether vested or contingent which are expressly deferred to a future date which must come sooner or later. (See *In re Oliver* [1947] 2 All ER 162, *In re Gillett's Will Trusts* [1949] 2 All ER 893 and *In re Geering decd.* [1962] 3 All ER 1043.) There is a good reason for this distinction. If a testator gives property to X contingently on his attaining the age of 30 it is reasonable to assume, in the absence of a direction to the contrary, that he would wish X if he attains 30 to have the income produced by the property between his death and the happening of the contingency. If, on the other hand, he gives property to X for any sort of interest after the death of A, it is reasonable to assume that he does not wish X to have the income accruing during A's lifetime unless he directs that he is to have it. But this distinction betweeen an immediate gift on a contingency and a gift which is expressly deferred was not drawn until after the Law of Property Act 1925 was passed. There were statements in textbooks and even in judgments to the effect that the rule applied to deferred as well as to contingent gifts of residuary personalty. (See Jarman, 7th ed. (1930), p. 1006).

The legislature, when it extended this rule to residuary devises and specific gifts, must, I think, have adopted this erroneous view of the law. I would have liked, if I could, to construe the reference to 'future specific devises' and 'executory interest' in the section in such a way as to make it consistent with the recent cases on the scope of the old rule applicable to residuary bequests. But to do that would be to rectify the Act, not to construe it, and I see no escape from the conclusion that whereas before 1926 a specific gift or a residuary devise which was not vested in possession did not prima facie carry intermediate income at all, now such a gift may carry intermediate income in circumstances in which a residuary bequest would not carry it.

It was argued in this case that the fact that the will contained a residuary gift constituted an express disposition of the income of the land in question which prevented the section from applying. I am afraid that I cannot accept this submission. I have little doubt that the testator expected the income of the land to form part of the income of residue during his widow's lifetime, but he has made no express disposition of it. I agree with what was said in this connection by Eve J in *In re Raine* [1929] 1 Ch 716.

As the devise is not vested indefeasibly in the daughter but is subject to defeasance during the mother's lifetime the intermediate income which the gift carries by virtue of s. 175 ought prima facie to be accumulated to see who eventually becomes entitled to it. It was, however, submitted by counsel for the daughter that she could claim payment of it under s. 31(1) of the Trustee Act 1925. So far as material, that subsection provides that where any property is held by trustees in trust for any person for any interest whatsoever, whether vested or contingent, then, subject to any prior interests or charges affecting that property, if such person on attaining the age of 21 years has not a vested interest in such income, the trustees shall thenceforth pay the income of that property and of any accretion of such income made during his infancy to him until he either attains a vested interest therein or dies or until failure of his interest. There are, as I see it, two answers to the daughter's claim. The first—and narrower—answer is that her interest in the income of the devised land is in a vested interest. It is a future interest liable to be divested but it is not contingent. Therefore, s. 31(1)(ii) does not apply to it. The second—and wider—answer is that the whole framework of s. 31 shows that it is inapplicable to a future gift of this sort and that a will containing such a gift expresses a contrary intention within s. 69(2) which prevents the section from applying. By deferring the enjoyment of the devise until after the widow's death the testator has expressed the intention that the daughter shall not have the immediate income. It is true that as he has not expressly disposed of it in any other way, s. 175 of the Law of Property Act 1925 defeats that intention to the extent of making the future devise carry the income so that the daughter will get it eventually if she survives her mother or dies before her leaving no children to take by substitution. But even if the words of s. 31 fitted the case, there would be no warrant for defeating the testator's intention still further by reading it into the will and thus giving the daughter an interest in possession in the income during her mother's lifetime. In the result, in my judgment the income of the fund must be accumulated for 21 years if the widow so long lives.

Ker, B. S., 'Trustees' Powers of Maintenance' (1953) 17 Conv 273

WHEN A GIFT CARRIES THE INTERMEDIATE INCOME

The question now arises as to when a 'limitation or trust' carries the intermediate income of the property. The rules are as follows:—

1.   A contingent gift by will of *residuary* personalty carries with it all the income it earns from the testator's death, for the simple reason that there is no one besides the residuary legatee to whom it could go. North J said in *Re Adams* [1893] 1 Ch 829, at p. 884 'Here no child has [a vested interest in the residue]. How does the matter stand as to the income? It is said that they take an interest in the income, *qua* income of the capital they take an interest in. *But it is undisposed-of income, and as such becomes part of the residue*; but, being part of the residue, the income belongs contingently to the children, in the same way as the capital belongs contingently to them.' If this income is accumulated until the contingency vesting the money in the beneficiaries happens the rules in sections 164–166 of the Law of Property Act 1925, must be observed. (See *Bective* v *Hodgson* (1864) 10 HL Cas 656.)

2.   The rule as to the contingent *specific* gifts of personalty and contingent specific or residuary gifts of realty is contained in section 175 of the Law of Property Act 1925: 'A contingent or future specific devise or bequest of property, whether real or personal, and a contingent residuary devise of freehold land, and a specific or residuary devise of freehold land to trustees upon trust for persons whose interests are contingent or executory shall, subject to the statutory provisions relating to accumulations, carry the intermediate income of that property from the death of the testator, except so far as such income, or any part thereof, may be otherwise expressly disposed of.' This section applies only to *wills* coming into operation after 1925, but it has been held in *Re Raine* [1929] 1 Ch 716, not to apply to a pecuniary legacy. Further, it draws a distinction between 'land' and 'freehold land.' This is because leaseholds rank as personal property and therefore the ordinary rules (*supra* and *infra*) as to the income of contingent gifts of personalty apply: see *Guthrie* v *Walrond* (1883) 22 ChD 573, and *Re Woodin* [1895] 2 Ch 309, *per* Lindley LJ and Kay LJ.

Pecuniary Legacies

3.   In view of the decision in *Re Raine (supra)* the rules of the general law as to when contingent pecuniary legacies bear interest require examination. The broad rule is that no interest is payable on a contingent pecuniary legacy from the testator's death while the gift is in suspense (see *per* Kay LJ in *Re George* (1877) 5 ChD 837). There are, however, the following exceptions in which the legacy, subject to any contrary intention in the will, carries interest from the testator's death:

(a)   *Where the testator was the father of, or in loco parentis to, the infant legatee.* The idea is simple; a father is under an obligation to maintain his child and is therefore presumed to intend the income of the gift to be paid for his child's maintenance until the contingency happens. Although it is strictly an exception, we will refer to this rule hereafter for brevity's sake as 'the golden rule.' There are two exceptions to it.

First, it does not apply if the contingency is the attaining of some greater age than 21. In *Re Abrahams* [1911] 1 Ch 108, the testator gave a legacy to X contingently on his attaining 25. The judge reasoned that the legacy had clearly not been deferred simply on account of infancy, or the age specified would have been 21. All idea of X's infancy was thus ousted and hence no intention to maintain could be presumed; hence no interest was payable towards X's maintenance.

The second exception is where the testator has provided another fund out of which the infant is to be maintained: *Re West* [1913] 2 Ch 345. This is a clear intention which ousts the presumed intention underlying the rule.

Section 31(1)(i)(a), however might be thought to have altered the rule. We are considering the question 'Has the golden rule been ousted?' The old law said, 'Yes, if another fund has been provided for maintenance' But this part of section 31 says that maintenance can be paid 'whether or not there is another fund applicable to the same purpose.' However, no part of the section applies to a contingent gift at all unless the requirements of subsection (3) are satisfied. Section 31(1)(i)(a) therefore cannot come into play to oust the rule illustrated by *Re West (supra)*. Thus, where a father gives a contingent legacy to his infant child and also provides another fund for his maintenance the legacy does not carry interest and therefore section 31 does not apply to it.

(b)   *A contingent legacy to an infant carries interest from the date of death where the testator without being a parent of, or in loco parentis to the infant legatee, nevertheless shows an intention that the infant is to be maintained.* In *Re Churchill* [1909] 2 Ch 431 a testatrix gave a legacy to a grandnephew and directed the trustees at their discretion to pay any part, etc., of it, 'towards the advancement in life *or otherwise for the benefit*' of the legatee. It was held that the legacy carried interest from the date of death at 4 per cent .

(c)   *Where the testator segregates a fund for a legatee but makes the gift contingent.* The idea here is that if the testator says 'X is to have an ear-marked sum of £10,000 when he is 21' and nothing more, he must obviously have intended him to have the accretions earned meanwhile. But there must be a segregation of the legacy required inherently in the nature of the legacy itself. . . .

. . . in *Re Medlock* (1886) 55 LJ Ch 738 . . . the testator bequeathed £750 to trustees upon trust to pay and divide the same among three people contingently on their surviving him and attaining 21. If none got a vested interest the fund was to fall into residue. It was held that here a definite fund had been segregated by the will itself from the rest of the estate. . . .

13.1.2   Summary

Does the gift carry the 'Intermediate Income'?

		Testamentary Contingent ('might happen')					Testamentary Deferred ('will happen')	

Vested Absolutely or inter vivos contingent

Specific P/R	Residuary Pers	Residuary Realty	Pecuniary Legacy	Residuary Personalty	Specific P/R	Residue	Pecuniary Legacy
YES (unless contrary intention)	YES (s. 175)	YES (Re Adams)	YES (s. 175)	NO? (Re Raine)	NO (Re Geering) Residuary Realty NO (by extension of Re Geering)	YES (s. 175)	NO Personalty (Re Oliver) Realty (Re McGeorge)	NO? (Re Raine)

Key   P = Personalty
       R = Realty

NOTE   All 'yes' answers are subject to express contrary intention apparent from the terms of the trust (s. 69(2), LPA 1925).

13.2   Advancement

TRUSTEE ACT 1925

32.   Power of advancement

(1)   Trustees may at any time or times pay or apply any capital money subject to a trust, for the advancement or benefit, in such manner as they may, in their absolute discretion, think fit, of any person entitled to the capital of the trust property or of any share thereof, whether absolutely or contingently on his attaining any specified age or on the occurrence of any other event, or subject to a gift over on his death under any specified age or on the occurrence of any other event, and whether in possession or in remainder or reversion, and such payment or application may be made notwithstanding that the interest of such person is liable to be defeated by the exercise of a power of appointment or revocation, or to be diminished by the increase of the class to which he belongs:

Provided that—

(a)   the money so paid or applied for the advancement or benefit of any person shall not exceed altogether in amount one-half of the presumptive or vested share or interest of that person in the trust property; and

(b)   if that person is or becomes absolutely and indefeasibly entitled to a share in the trust property the money so paid or applied shall be brought into account as part of such share; and

(c)   no such payment or application shall be made so as to prejudice any person entitled to any prior life or other interest, whether vested or contingent, in the money paid or applied unless such person is in existence and of full age and consents in writing to such payment or application.

(2)   This section applies only where the trust property consists of money or securities or of property held upon trust for sale calling in and conversion, and such money or securities, or the proceeds of such sale calling in and conversion are not by statute or in equity considered as land, or applicable as capital money for the purposes of the Settled Land Act 1925.

(3)   This section does not apply to trusts constituted or created before the commencement of this Act.

13.2.1   CAPITAL MONEY

RE COLLARD'S WT [1961] 1 All ER 821, ChD

FACTS: Clause 7 of a will trust provided a power of advancement in the following terms: 'I declare that the statutory power of advancement of capital given to my trustees by s. 32 of the Trustee Act 1925, shall apply to the trusts hereof as if incorporated herein save that no such advancement shall be made to or on behalf of any beneficiary for the purpose of acquiring a share or interest . . . in any business'. The question arose whether the trustees could exercise the power of advancement by conveying a trust-owned farm to a beneficiary. The beneficiary was at that time working the farm. The plan was to avoid estate duty which would have been payable had the farm passed to the beneficiary on the death of his mother, another beneficiary.
HELD: The trustees would be permitted to convey the farm to the son by way of exercise of the power of advancement. There were two arguments supporting this conclusion. First, the trustees could have advanced the beneficiary by paying capital monies to him; the beneficiary could then have bought the farm with the capital monies. To avoid this circuitous result the farm would be conveyed to the beneficiary direct. Second, clause 7 of the will did not prevent such an advancement, because the purpose of the advancement was the avoidance of tax, it was not to further the beneficiary's business interests.

BUCKLEY J: . . . The first thing to notice is that what s. 32(1) authorises is that trustees may make payments or apply capital moneys in certain ways, and primarily the power is a power to deal with cash. But it is said that a court of equity will never insist on circuity of action, and if the trustees could properly make an advancement of cash, and having done so could properly sell some part of the trust property to the beneficiary for that sum of cash, so also they can exercise the power of advancement by merely transferring property to the beneficiary without going through the process of making the cash advancement and a sale. There is no doubt that the statutory power of advancement is constantly exercised by trustees transferring to beneficiaries Stock Exchange investments by way of advancement. Is there any distinction to be drawn in this respect between land and Stock Exchange investments? It is true that Stock Exchange investments are a form of property of which it is much easier to ascertain the value with accuracy than land. On the other hand, it may equally be said that Stock Exchange investments by and large are much more likely to fluctuate in value than is land. Those are considerations, however, which do not really go to principle. The principle is that the court will not insist on circuity of action if the same result as can legitimately be achieved by circuitous action can be achieved by direct action. . . .

13.2.2   THE MEANING OF ADVANCEMENT

PILKINGTON v IRC [1964] AC 612, HL

FACTS: A will trust directed trustees to hold the income on the testator's residuary estate upon protective trusts for his nephews and nieces. Should a nephew or niece die, their share was to be held on trust for such of their relations as the trustees might appoint. In default of appointment the income was to be held for their children at 21. In due course the trustees wished to exercise the power of advancement for the benefit of the child of one of the nephews, so as to avoid estate duties. They proposed to make the advancement by settling the child's share in a new settlement under which the child could be maintained out of income until the age of 21; therefore she would be absolutely entitled to the income until the age of 30, whereupon she would be entitled absolutely. If the child should die before the age of 30 her share was to be held on trust for her children at 21, and in default of that it would pass to the nephew's other children. The question before the court was whether the trustees could exercise their power of advancement in the proposed manner.
HELD: The advancement would have been permitted, even though the terms of the new settlement carried the possibility that some other person might benefit under the new settlement who would not have benefited under the terms of the old settlement. The prime consideration was that the advancement must be for the benefit of the primary

beneficiary. However, on the particular facts of the present case the advancement could not be permitted as the resettlement would infringe the rule against perpetuities.

VISCOUNT RADCLIFFE: . . . The word 'advancement' itself meant in this context the establishment in life of the beneficiary who was the object of the power or at any rate some step that would contribute to the furtherance of his establishment. Thus it was found in such phrases as 'preferment or advancement' (*Lowther* v *Bentinck* (1874) LR 19 Eq 166), 'business, profession, or employment or . . . advancement or 'preferment in the world' (*Roper-Curzon* v *Roper-Curzon* (1871) LR 11 Eq 452) and 'placing out or advancement in life' (*In re Breeds' Will* (1875) 1 ChD 226). Typical instances of expenditure for such purposes under the social conditions of the nineteenth century were an apprenticeship or the purchase of a commission in the army or of an interest in business. In the case of a girl there could be advancement on marriage (*Lloyd* v *Cocker* (1860) 27 Beav. 645). Advancement had, however, to some extent a limited range of meaning, since it was thought to convey the idea of some step in life of permanent significance, and accordingly, to prevent uncertainties about the permitted range of objects for which moneys could be raised and made available, such words as 'or otherwise for his or her benefit' were often added to the word 'advancement.' It was always recognised that these added words were 'large words' (see Jessel MR in *In re Breeds' Will*) and indeed in another case (*Lowther* v *Bentinck*) the same judge spoke of preferment and advancement as being 'both large words' but of 'benefit' as being the 'largest of all'. So, too, Kay J in *In re Brittlebank* (1881) 30 WR 99. Recent judges have spoken in the same terms—see Farwell J in *In re Halsted's Will Trusts* [1937] 2 All ER 570 and Danckwerts J in *In re Moxon's Will Trusts* [1958] 1 WLR 165. This wide construction of the range of the power, which evidently did not stand upon niceties of distinction provided that the proposed application could fairly be regarded as for the benefit of the beneficiary who was the object of the power, must have been carried into the statutory power created by s. 32, since it adopts without qualification the accustomed wording 'for the advancement or benefit in such manner as they may in their absolute discretion think fit.'

So much for 'advancement' which I now use for brevity to cover the combined phrase 'advancement or benefit.' It means any use of the money which will improve the material situation of the beneficiary. It is important, however, not to confuse the idea of 'advancement' with the idea of advancing the money out of the beneficiary's expectant interest. The two things have only a casual connection with each other. . . .

The commissioner's objections seem to be concentrated upon such propositions as that the proposed transaction is 'nothing less than a resettlement' and that a power of advancement cannot be used so as to alter or vary the trusts created by the settlement from which it is derived. Such a transaction, they say, amounts to using the power of advancement as a way of appointing or declaring new trusts different from those of the settlement. The reason why I do not find that these propositions have any compulsive effect upon my mind is that they seem to me merely vivid ways of describing the substantial effect of that which is proposed to be done and they do not in themselves amount to convincing arguments against doing it. Of course, whenever money is raised for advancement on terms that it is to be settled on the beneficiary, the money only passes from one settlement to be caught up in the other. It is therefore the same thing as a resettlement. But, unless one is to say that such moneys can never be applied by way of settlement, an argument which, as I have shown, has few supporters and is contrary to authority, it merely describes the inevitable effect of such an advancement to say that it is nothing less than a resettlement. Similarly, if it is part of the trusts and powers created by one settlement that the trustees of it should have power to raise money and make it available for a beneficiary upon new trusts approved by them, then they are in substance given power to free the money from one trust and to subject it to another. So be it: but, unless they cannot require a settlement of it at all, the transaction they carry out is the same thing in effect as an appointment of new trusts.

In the same way I am unconvinced by the argument that the trustees would be improperly delegating their trust by allowing the money raised to pass over to new trustees under a settlement conferring new powers on the latter. In fact I think that the whole issue of delegation is here beside the mark. The law is not that trustees cannot delegate: it is that trustees cannot delegate unless they have authority to do so. If the power of advancement which they possess is so read as to allow them to raise money for the purpose of having it settled, then they do have the necessary authority to let the money pass out of the old settlement into the new trusts. No question of delegation of their powers or trusts arises. . . .

To conclude, therefore, on this issue, I am of opinion that there is no maintainable reason for introducing into the statutory power of advancement a qualification that would exclude the exercise in the case now before us. . . .

The other issue on which this case depends, that relating to the application of the rule against perpetuities, does not seem to me to present much difficulty. It is not in dispute that, if the limitations of the proposed settlement are to be treated as if they had been made by the testator's will and as coming into operation at the date of his death, there are trusts in it which would be void *ab initio* as violating the perpetuity rule. They postpone final vesting by too long a date. It is also a familiar rule of law in this field that, whereas appointments made under a general power of appointment conferred by will or deed are read as taking effect from the date of the exercise of the power, trusts declared by a special power of appointment, the distinguishing feature of which is that it can allocate property among a limited class of persons only, are treated as coming into operation at the date of the instrument that creates the power. The question therefore resolves itself into asking whether the exercise of a power of advancement which takes the form of a settlement should be looked upon as more closely analogous to a general or to a special power of appointment.

On this issue I am in full agreement with the views of Upjohn LJ in the Court of Appeal. Indeed, much of the reasoning that has led me to my conclusion on the first issue that I have been considering leads me to think that for this purpose there is an effective analogy between powers of advancement and special powers of appointment. When one asks what person can be regarded as the settlor of Miss Penelope's proposed settlement, I do not see how it is possible to say that she is herself or that the trustees are. She is the passive recipient of the benefit extracted for her from the original trusts; the trustees are merely exercising a fiduciary power in arranging for the desired limitations. It is not their property that constitutes the funds of Miss Penelope's settlement; it is the property subjected to trusts by the will of the testator and passed over into the new settlement through the instrumentality of a power which by statute is made appendant to those trusts. I do not think, therefore, that it is important to this issue that money raised under a power of advancement passes entirely out of reach of the existing trusts and makes, as it were, a new start under fresh limitations, the kind of thing that happened under the old form of family resettlement when the tenant in tail in remainder barred the entail with the consent of the protector of the settlement. I think that the important point for the purpose of the rule against perpetuities is that the new settlement is only effected by the operation of a fiduciary power which itself 'belongs' to the old settlement.

In the conclusion, therefore, there are legal objections to the proposed settlement which the trustees have placed before the court. Again I agree with Upjohn LJ that these objections go to the root of what is proposed and I do not think that it would be satisfactory that the court should try to frame a qualified answer to the question that they have propounded, which would express the general view that the power to advance by way of a settlement of this sort does exist and the special view that the power to make this particular settlement does not. Nor, I think, is such a course desired either by the appellants or the trustees. They will, I hope, know where they stand for the future, and so will the commissioners, and that is enough.

13.2.3 THE MEANING OF BENEFIT

RE CLORE'S SETTLEMENT TRUSTS [1966] 1 WLR 955, ChD

FACTS: The beneficiary's father had established a charitable foundation to which the beneficiary felt morally obliged to contribute. It was more tax-efficient for the donation to be made out of the beneficiary's private funds. The trustees sought the court's approval of such a course.

HELD: The advancement was proper. The beneficiary was morally bound to make the donation. He would benefit financially from making the donation out of the trust fund as opposed to his private monies.

PENNYCUICK J: . . . Mr Brightman, who appears for the trustees, formulated his argument on clause 8 in the form of five propositions. The first is that payment or application for the advancement or benefit of a person means 'any use of the money which will improve the material situation of the beneficiary,' That expression is taken from the speech of Lord Radcliffe in *In re Pilkington's Will Trusts* [1964] AC 612. The proposition is well established and requires no further elaboration.

The second proposition is that the improvement of the material situation of a beneficiary is not confined to his direct financial advantage. That may be amplified, I think, by saying that it includes the discharge, at any rate, of certain moral or social obligations on the part of the beneficiary, for example towards dependants. In support of that, Mr Brightman cites a series of cases in which the court has held that trustees can properly exercise such a power by paying money to the trustees of a settlement for the benefit of the beneficiary and the members of his family. There is no doubt that that is so. *In re Pilkington's Will Trusts* is an example and there have been many others. In such a case the interest which the beneficiary would take on attaining the age at which the interest would vest absolutely is reduced from an absolute interest to a more limited interest, normally a life interest, but nonetheless the court treats the settlement as being for his benefit, that is, as improving his material situation.

The third proposition is the crux of the present application: it is that the court has always recognised that a weathly person has a moral obligation to make appropriate charitable donations. The court has certainly recognised this in several cases, although, generally, it has been concerned with relatively small sums of income: see, in particular, *In re Walker* [1901] 1 Ch 879. It seems to me that a beneficiary under a settlement may indeed in many cases be reasonably entitled to regard himself as under a moral obligation to make donations towards charity. The nature and amount of those donations must depend upon all the circumstances, including the position in life of the beneficiary, the amount of the fund and the amount of his other resources. Once that proposition is accepted, it seems to me that it must lie within the scope of a power such as that contained in clause 8 of this settlement for the trustees to raise capital for the purpose of relieving the beneficiary of his moral obligation towards whatever charity he may have in mind. If the obligation is not to be met out of the capital of the trust fund, he would have to meet it out of his own pocket, if at all. Accordingly, the discharge of the obligation out of the capital of the trust fund does improve his material situation. . . .

Mr Brightman added in his formulation two further propositions: fourthly, that a wealthy person can discharge his moral obligation at less cost to himself if he makes a charitable settlement and, fifthly, it follows that any advance of an appropriate sum under the settlement is capable of improving his material situation by enabling him to discharge his moral obligation without undue burden upon himself. It is certainly true that by making a capital settlement Alan Clore can confer the same benefit upon the charity at much less expense to himself than if he were to make a corresponding payment to the charity personally out of income, which at the present rate of income tax it would be impossible for him to do. This last consideration emphasises the desirability of making the proposed advance, but I do not think it is essential to the power of the trustees to make the advance. . . .

To avoid misunderstanding, it seems to me that in the case of a transaction of this kind, i.e., an advance of capital in discharge of a moral obligation towards charity, it is essential to a valid exercise of the power that the beneficiary himself should recognise the moral obligation. It is not open to the trustees to pay away the beneficiary's prospective capital over his head or against his will in discharge of what they consider to be his moral obligations.

13.2.4   THE PROVISOS TO SECTION 32

RE MARQUESS OF ABERGAVENNY'S ESTATE ACT TRUSTS [1981] 2 All ER 643, ChD

FACTS: Trustees exercised a discretionary power of advancement in full, paying over to the beneficiary one half of his share. The remainder was invested and greatly increased in value. At a later date the beneficiary took out a summons seeking the court's directions as to whether the trustees could make further advancements, which, combined with payments already made, would total one half of the present value of the fund.

HELD: The power had been totally exhausted on its initial exercise. The fact that the value of the remainder of the fund had now increased could not justify a fresh exercise of the power.

GOULDING J: . . . I think myself that the reason why there is no direct authority on the question is because the answer has always seemed plain. Any layman, and any lawyer I think, without such special and persuasive advocacy as I have heard this morning, would feel that where there is a power to make successive payments to a person up to a limit of a certain fraction of a fund and at a certain date he, the beneficiary, has received assets then fully reaching the prescribed limit thereafter no further exercise of the power is possible. All that the settlor authorised has been done. It would be to my mind strange and unexpected if the object of the power as such retained an interest or possibility of interest in the fund still in settlement, so that he could require accounts from the trustees and demand reconsideration of his position whenever there should be an appreciation of assets. It is perfectly true that even in the partial appropriation cases the beneficiary who has received something early may do very well because he may keep what has been given to him in some asset that appreciates while he only has to bring a cash sum, fixed once and for all, into account; it may of course go the other way. But some such possibility of good or ill fortune is inherent in the very nature of payments made under a duty or a power on successive occasions up to an aggregate limit. There is no reason that I can see why such inequality, or exposure to fortune, should be continued to the possible disadvantage of other beneficiaries after the limit has been reached. . . .

HENLEY v WARDELL, *The Times*, 29 January 1988, ChD

FACTS: According to s. 32(1)(c) of the Trustee Act 1925, before a payment is made to advance a beneficiary under a trust written consent must be obtained from any person with a prior entitlement under the trust. In the present case the testator had granted his trustees an 'absolute and uncontrolled discretion' to advance capital. The question was whether this removed the requirement that consent should be obtained from persons with prior interests.
HELD: The requirement for consent would still apply, despite the testator's attempt to enlarge the trustees' powers of advancement. The testator's desire to enlarge the trustees' powers was limited to their discretion as to the amount paid by way of advancement.

MR JOHN MOWBRAY QC: . . . It was true that a discretion which could only be exercised subject to a consent could not be said to be uncontrolled. Nevertheless his Lordship held that the single word 'uncontrolled' was not strong enough to bear the weight the trustees would put on it.

The flavour of clause 10 was to be distilled from the trustees' powers being 'enlarged' so as to permit the advancement of 'the whole' of a share. (It was common ground that proviso (a) to s. 32, limiting the statutory power of advancement to half the presumptive share of a beneficiary was excluded by the clause 10).

That showed that the only purpose of the enlargement of the powers was as to the size of the share that could be advanced and did not do away with the need for consents as provided for by s. 32(1)(c).

It was also unlikely that the testator had intended to put it in the power of a son and another executor to make advances to the son without the consent of the wife.

Therefore the requirement for consent in s. 32(1)(c) did apply and advances made without such consent were invalid.

13.2.5   EXERCISE OF DISCRETION

See **11.3**.

13.2.5.1   Trustees as incidental beneficiaries

See *Pilkington* v *IRC* [1964] at **13.2.2**.

MOLYNEUX v FLETCHER AND CLERK [1898] 1 QBD 648, QBD

FACTS: Trustees made a payment to a beneficiary out of her presumptive share in the capital of the trust fund, purporting to make the payment with a view to her 'advancement in life'. Payments of this sort had been authorised by the terms of the trust, but the particular payment had been made in the full knowledge that the sums paid to the beneficiary would be used to pay a debt owed by the beneficiary's husband to one of the trustees.

HELD: Although the trustees had a sole discretion as to how payments should be made for the advancement of the beneficiaries, the payment in the present case had been made in breach of trust.

KENNEDY J: . . . No doubt a large discretion is given to the trustees by the will, but I do not think that, large as that discretion is, it could be extended so as to cover these advances, The interests are given by the testator to his daughters for their respective lives for their separate use and free from anticipation, and I should doubt whether in the case of either daughter an advance to pay the debts of the husband of one of them could by any possibility be considered as an advance for her advancement in life. . . .

13.2.5.2   The fiduciary aspect

RE PAULING'S SETTLEMENT TRUSTS [1963] 3 All ER 1, CA

FACTS: A marriage settlement was made in 1910 to provide an income for a wealthy lady who had married a husband of moderate means. Subject to the provision of this income, the fund was to be held for the children of the family or remoter issue. Many years later the husband wished to purchase a house on the Isle of Man, but the family was not as wealthy as it had been. Counsel advised that the purchase monies could be obtained by advancing the children of the family out of the trust fund, the children could then resettle the funds on their mother for life and for themselves thereafter. The children were over 21 by this time. In due course, the trustee (Coutts & Co., a bank) paid over the price of the house to the adult children by way of advancement. However, rather than resettling the property in accordance with counsel's advice, the purchase monies were used to purchase the house direct, and it was conveyed to the father and mother. The bank knew what was going on. The adult children had not consented and had not had separate legal advice. In future years and months a number of other payments were made by the bank by way of advancement, and on many of these occasions the monies were used by the parents for their own purposes. The present action was brought by the four children against the trustee bank, seeking an account of the monies which had been paid over to them, supposedly for their advancement. In its defence the bank sought to rely upon the consent of the beneficiaries, the Limitation Act, *laches*, acquiescence and relief under s. 61 of the Trustee Act (see **Chapter 15**).

HELD: Advancements could be made only to benefit the advancees. This placed a duty on the bank to refuse to exercise their power of advancement if they had notice that, after previous payments by way of advancement, the monies had not been used for their intended purpose. The beneficiaries' apparent consent would be no defence to the bank if the bank ought reasonably to have known that the beneficiaries were acting under the undue influence of another. The presumption of undue influence of a parent over a child can continue for a short time beyond the child's majority. On this basis the bank was held liable to account to the beneficiaries. However, relief was granted under s. 61 for some of the advancements, though not others. The Limitation Act would not apply because the beneficiaries had future interests which could not be said to have vested in possession on the payment over, in breach of trust, of certain monies by way of 'advancement'. The doctrine of *laches* could not apply because the Limitation Act, though not applicable in the instant case, applied generally to actions of this sort. Acquiescence was not established.

WILLMER LJ: it is clear that the power under the first limb may be exercised, if the circumstances warrant it, either by making an out and out payment to the person to be advanced, or for a particular purpose specified by the trustees. Thus in argument an example was given that, when George was called to the Bar, the trustees might have quite properly advanced to him a sum of capital quite generally for his living expenses to support him while starting to practise, provided they thought that this was a reasonable thing to do, and that he was a type of person who could reasonably be trusted to make proper use of the money. On the other hand, if the trustees make the advance for a particular purpose which they state, they can quite properly pay it over to the advancee if they reasonably think they can trust him or her to carry out the prescribed purpose. What they cannot do is to prescribe a particular purpose, and then raise and pay the money over to the advancee leaving him or her entirely free, legally and morally, to apply it for that purpose or to spend it in any way he or she chooses, without any responsibility upon the trustees even to inquire as to its application.

Failure to appreciate this was one of the root causes of the trouble, for in the first opinion of counsel in 1948 (to which we shall refer later) he advised that the trustees could make an advancement out and out for the purpose of a purchase of a house in the Isle of Man, but he said this purchase

> depends on a voluntary act by the children and they should I think be seperately advised on this point. So far as the trustees are concerned they will be paying the money to the children for their own absolute use.

This, we think, was the wrong appoach. At that time both Francis and George were studying at university, and it was not suggested that they required any sum for their maintenance there; the only possible justification for advancing the very substantial sum of £5,000 to each of the two boys, one of them twenty-seven and the other just twenty-two, who had no other possible proper use for this money, was to invest it in a house in the Isle of Man as the settlement powers were insufficient, and the advancement could be justified only for that purpose. This error was perpetuated later by the children's solicitor, who got into the habit of advising them that, although purported advancements were, e.g., for the repair of a house or for the purchase of furniture, they were sums which the children could 'blue', e.g., on a horse.

This was wrong and misleading advice. If money was advanced for an express purpose by the bank, the advanced person was under a duty to carry that purpose out, and he could not properly apply it to another. We are not concerned with the question whether in such circumstances the bank could recover money so misapplied, but this much is plain, that, if such misapplication came to the bank's notice, they could not safely make further advances for particular purposes without making sure that the money was in fact applied to that purpose, since the advancee would have shown himself or herself quite irresponsible. It would be the bank's duty to proceed on future occasions on behalf of the particular child under the second limb of the power.

The first question, therefore, that arises in relation to each of the advances, which we shall consider seriatim, is whether there was a proper exercise of the power under either limb. No question arises as to the consent of the mother, for that was given in every case. If the advance were proper in any particular case, the question of the children's consent, although adult, would not arise; for, as has been made quite clear in *Pilkington* v *Inland Revenue Comrs.* [1964] AC 612, as there is no express provision in cl.11 requiring the adult beneficiary's consent to the advance being made for his or her benefit, it would not be necessary to obtain that consent, though no doubt any trustee intending to advance an adult beneficiary would normally do so only with his consent, and probably only at his request. But, if any advance were an improper exercise of the power in cl. 11 (and they all were in the judge's view) what is the position? *Prima facie*, having improperly exercised the power, the bank would be guilty of a breach of trust and must replace the money misapplied. . . .

The doctrine of undue influence . . . arises out of the fact that, while equity approves of gifts by a father to a child, and therefore invented the doctrine of presumption of advancement, so on the other hand it dislikes and distrusts gifts by a child to a parent, and therefore invented the presumption of undue influence. . . .

Without expressing a final opinion, we think that the true view may be that a trustee carrying out a transaction in breach of trust may be liable if he knew, or ought to have known, that the beneficiary was acting under the undue influence of another, or may be presumed to have done so, but will not be liable if it cannot be established that he so knew, or ought to have known.

That is sufficient for the purposes of the present case, for, of course, the bank knew very exactly the ages of each of the children, and knew further that, as each child attained twenty-one, that child received advances from the bank which went straight into the banking account of the mother. Indeed, in Ann's case plans were made to effect this unhappy result even before the child attained twenty-one. Accordingly, it seems to us clear that, if it can be established that the presumption exists in any given case, the bank are fixed with notice of it and cannot rely on any consents given under such influence.

The bank also rely for relief from the consequences of any breach of trust on s. 61 of the Trustee Act, 1925. At this stage all we propose to say is that it would be a misconstruction of the section to say that it does not apply to professional trustees, but, as was pointed out in the Judicial Committee of the Privy Council in *National Trustees Co. of Australasia, Ltd* v *General Finance Co. of Australasia Ltd* [1905] AC 373:

> Without saying that the remedial provisions of the section should never be applied to a trustee in the position of the appellants, their lordships think it is a circumstance to be taken into account.

Where a banker undertakes to acts as a paid trustee of a settlement created by a customer, and so deliberately places itself in a position where its duty as trustee conflicts with its interest as a banker, we think that the court should be very slow to relieve such a trustee under the provisions of the section.

We propose to deal with the bank's plea of the Limitation Act 1939, and the pleas of laches, acquiescence and delay when we have considered the detailed transaction. It only remains to state that the question of law on which this case was reported in the court below has not been argued before us, and many of the cases there cited have not been cited to us. Counsel for the plaintiffs, however, accepts as accurate the proposition which is contained in the report. We express no opinion on it. . . .

13.3   Contrary Intention

IRC v *BERNSTEIN* [1961] 1 CH 399, CA

FACTS: A settlor had directed that the income on his settlement should be accumulated during his lifetime, thereafter to pass, with the capital fund, to his wife and children. The Inland Revenue brought this action to recover tax which they claimed was chargeable on income which the wife could receive on capital paid to her under a power of advancement.

HELD: By directing that income should be accumulated the settlor has made clear his intention that a capital sum was to be built up for the future benefit of his wife and children. This intention to provide a capital sum in the future was incompatible with a power of advancement out of capital, therefore the power of advancement must be treated as having been excluded from the settlement in accordance with s. 69(2) of the Trustee Act 1925. In the absence of a power of advancement, the Inland Revenue's claim to tax income on advanced capital must fail.

LORD EVERSHED MR: . . . Section 69(2), which I have read, uses the language 'so far only as a contrary intention is not expressed in the instrument . . . creating the trust,' though those words are followed by this later phrase 'and have effect subject to the terms of that instrument.' At a first reading of the subsection it might seem that in order to exclude the power of advancement there would have to be an express exclusion or something equivalent thereto. But Mr Bathurst for the Crown has not here contended that the section requires anything so positive in expression. He has conceded (and for reasons which will in a moment appear, I think, if I may say so, rightly conceded) that it suffices to make the statutory power of s. 32 inapplicable if, on a fair reading of the instrument in question, one can say that such application would be inconsistent with the purport of the instrument. . . .

It is . . . a question in every case of examining the instrument and seeing what really was its effect or purpose. In this case it is quite apparent that the whole object of the instrument was to build up a capital sum which would be paid out to the beneficiary or her children, if any, upon the settlor's death. The trust for accumulation has, therefore, in this case a special importance and emphasis. Moreover, that circumstance is, I think, emphasised by the language of the clause to which Mr Bathurst referred us in Key and Elphinstone (15th ed. (1953), vol. 2, p. 635); for from that precedent this clause does in a material respect slightly differ. I refer to that part of it which states that the resulting investments of income are to go in augmentation of the capital of the trust fund and for the benefit of the person or persons who shall become entitled thereto (that is, to the trust fund); and by definition, taking the two clauses together, it is clear that the trust fund is meant to comprehend whatever from time to time shall be capital in the hands of the trustees. As I have said, there are no other purposes in this instrument save to provide for the event on the settlor's death of distributing a sum of capital to the persons who then became entitled to it. . . .

13.4   End of Chapter Assessment Question

Wilhelm, who died in 1986, left the residue of his estate in trust for his grandchildren, Betty and Andrew, at the age of 25, in equal shares absolutely. The trustees have invested the fund and accumulated all the income on it. The capital value of the fund is now £20,000.

Betty is 19 years old; Andrew is 12.

The trustees have received the following requests:

First, they have been asked to transfer £4,000 into a trust fund set up by the children's uncle in 1985 under which the fund trustees may, in their sole discretion, pay income or capital to any of his nephews or nieces who are students at university, and any capital remaining after a period of 21 years will be divided equally between all his nephews and nieces. At present the fund is valued at £6,000 and Betty is the only eligible beneficiary.

Secondly, Andrew's parents have asked the trustees to pay all the income of the fund to them for 10 years to enable them to meet the initial running costs of a riding school which they propose to establish at their home. Andrew is interested in riding and supports the proposal.

Advise whether the trustees may comply with these requests.

13.5   End of Chapter Assessment Outline Answer

The trustees have been asked to exercise their powers of advancement and maintenance.
   In the first place, they have been asked to resettle £4,000 out of capital into a trust set up by the children's uncle. The lump sum may be paid out under Trustee Act 1925, s. 32 which empowers trustees to apply capital money for the 'advancement or benefit, in such manner as they may, in their absolute discretion, think fit, of any person entitled to the capital of the trust'. This section is clearly wide enough to permit capital to be resettled on new trusts, but only if such a resettlement would genuinely be for the advancement or benefit of the persons entitled to the capital under the original trusts. Betty is currently 19 years old and attending university and therefore if the £4,000 is resettled on the terms of the uncle's trust she will have the opportunity to receive it for her use today, instead of having to wait until she reaches 25. This could be a real benefit to her. It is less likely that the resettlement would be of benefit to Andrew, who is now only twelve. The £4,000 could, if necessary, be paid entirely out of Betty's share (according to s. 32(1)(a) up to one-half of Betty's presumptive share may be advanced, her presumptive share being £10,000). The main problem with the proposed settlement is that the uncle's trust confers on the trustees of that trust an unfettered discretion as to whether or not to make payments out of it. This could mean that other 'nieces and nephews' will benefit, in the future, from the £4,000 of Wilhelm's Will Trust which would otherwise have been Betty's alone. That in itself is not fatal to the proposal, as Viscount Radcliffe has stated: 'it is no objection to the exercise of the power that other persons benefit incidentally from the exercise of the power' (*Pilkington* v *IRC* [1964] AC 612), but the fundamental difficulty with the proposed resettlement on the terms of the uncle's trust is that there is no guarantee that Betty will get anything at all from the fund! The risk that Betty will receive no benefit from the advancement, or that her cousins will be the principle beneficiaries, flows directly from the extensive discretion given to the trustees of the uncle's trusts. And, as Upjohn J has stated, 'unless upon its proper construction the power of advancement permits delegation of powers and discretion, a settlement created in exercise of the power of advancement cannot in general delegate any powers or discretion, at any rate in relation to beneficial interests' (per Upjohn J, *Re Wills* [1959] Ch 1). The power of advancement applicable in the present case is the basic statutory power

of advancement, there is nothing in that power to authorise the delegation of dispositive discretions and so the trustees in the present case should be advised to turn down the first request.

The second request comes from Andrew's parents. They have asked the trustees to pay all the income to them for 10 years to assist in setting up a riding school. The payment of income is authorised by the Trustee Act 1925, s. 31 but only where the payment is made for the maintenance of an infant beneficiary. There are a number of problems, therefore, with the parents' request. First, Andrew will only be an infant for the next six years, after which the trustees will not be able to pay over income for his maintenance. Secondly, Betty is an adult and income arising on her share of the fund must be accumulated and added to her share of the capital until she reaches 25, this income will not be available to Andrew. Thirdly, the power to maintain infant beneficiaries is discretionary and trustees must not fetter unduly the future exercise of this discretion. They cannot commit themselves to a 10-year scheme of payments.

There are other potential difficulties with the parents' request. First, the power of maintenance under s. 31 can only be used where the infant is the beneficiary of a gift which carries the intermediate income. Andrew's gift is a testamentary (by will) contingent gift of residue valued at £20,000. Such gifts will carry the intermediate income, and so Andrew will be able to be maintained out of that income unless there is an expressed contrary intention in the trust instrument (Trustee Act 1925, s. 69(2)). There being no evidence that Wilhelm did not wish Andrew to be maintained out of the fund, the trustees may maintain him if they so decide. In reaching their decision the trustees must be satisfied that the payment of income would genuinely be for the infant's 'maintenance, education or benefit' and the trustees in so deciding, 'shall have regarded to the age of the infant and his requirements and generally to the circumstances of the case, and in particular to what other income, if any, is applicable for the same purposes'. Perhaps the most crucial of the circumstances of the present case is the fact that Andrew is still under parental influence. It follows that the trustees should be very wary of paying over monies directly to the parents, even if Andrew 'consents'. If the trustees genuinely believe that the payments should be made, they should make the payments to the contractors, horse breeders and so on, whose activities make up the 'initial running costs' of the riding school, and not to the parents direct. If the trustees do pay the income to the parents direct they will be under a duty to make inquiries to establish that the monies have indeed been applied in keeping with the terms of the maintenance payment. The final problem with the request is the suggestion that the trustees should pay all Andrew's income entitlement in any given year. The risk is that a fundamental need will arise, such as money for a school uniform, and that there will be no income left to meet it.

In conclusion, on the facts as we have them, the trustees should be advised not to commit themselves to make payments for more than, say, two years, not to pay out Andrew's full income entitlement for the purpose of establishing the riding school, and not to pay any income if it is not genuinely for his maintenance, education or benefit. Additionally, if there are other funds available to establish the riding school the trustees should expect those funds to meet a reasonable amount of the expenditure.

CHAPTER FOURTEEN

INVESTMENT

14.1   The Meaning of Investment

14.1.1   THE NEED FOR DIRECT FINANCIAL BENEFITS

RE PECZENIK'S SETTLEMENT TRUSTS [1964] 1 WLR 720, ChD

FACTS: The terms of a settlement authorised the trustees to invest the trust funds 'in any shares stocks property or property holding company as the trustees in their discretion shall consider to be in the best interests of [the beneficiary]'. The question arose on the construction of this clause, whether the trustees were permitted to invest as they thought fit.

HELD: On the natural construction of the clause the trustees would be permitted to invest in any 'property' capable of being treated as an investment. They would not, however, be permitted to 'invest' on mere 'personal' security.

BUCKLEY J: I have been referred to the decision of Jenkins J in *In re Harari's Settlement Trusts* [1949] 1 All ER 430, and I recognise that there is a general rule that clauses in trust settlements which enlarge the power of trustees to invest beyond the class of investment which is authorised by the general law ought to be construed strictly. Nevertheless, I have to apply my mind to what is the proper construction to be placed upon the particular settlement before me, and that rule is not one which in any way imposes upon me the duty of putting any unduly restrictive construction upon the language which I have to consider. That was the view which Jenkins J took. He had to consider a settlement in which the trustees were authorised to invest 'in or upon such investments as to them may seem fit'. He came to the conclusion that those words conferred upon the trustees a general wide discretion, and that, on the plain meaning of those words, they could invest in any investments which they honestly thought desirable whether or not authorised by the general law for the investment of trust funds.

I have, therefore, to consider, what is the meaning of the language used in this particular document which is before me. I agree with the suggestion which was made that the term 'property holding company,' which is not any kind of term of art, is one to which, in this context, I really can give no precise meaning, and I think I should ignore the reference to 'property holding company,' for I cannot see how those words, whatever meaning is given to them, could really extend what is already covered by the words 'shares stocks property' in clause (1). Any investment in a company, whether a property holding company or a company of any other kind, must, it seems to me, be either a share, or stock, or some other form of property. I do not take the view, which was also urged before me, that 'property' here should be confined to real property. I see no reason for putting such a confined interpretation upon the words. Taking clause (1) by itself, it appears to me that the clause authorises the trustees to invest in any shares, any stock, or any property. It must, of course, be property of a kind capable of being treated as an investment, not property which is acquired merely for use and enjoyment. But, apart from that, it seems to me that clause (1) places no restriction upon the discretion of the trustees beyond saying that the investments must be investments in stocks or shares or something which can properly be described as property. The clause would not, I think, authorise investments merely upon personal security. . . .

RE POWER [1947] Ch 572, ChD

(Note: This case no longer applies to trusts of land: Trusts of Land etc. Act 1996, s. 12.)

FACTS: A will trust empowered the trustee (the Public Trustee in this case) to invest the trust fund 'in any manner in which he may in his absolute discretion think fit in all respects as if he were sole beneficial owner of such monies including the purchase of freehold property in England and Wales'. The testator's widow requested the trustees to purchase a freehold property as a residence for her and her children. The widow and children were the only beneficiaries under the will trust.
HELD: The terms of the will trust permitted freehold land to be purchased as an investment. But an 'investment' must, by definition, produce income, therefore the purchase of land for the beneficiaries to live in could not qualify as an investment.

JENKINS J: . . . there is a distinction between purchasing freehold property for the sake of the income one is going to get from it and purchasing freehold property for the sake of occupying it or permitting somebody else to occupy it. In the former case, the purchase is, in common parlance, and I think also in legal parlance, accurately described as an investment. In the latter case, it is not necessarily an investment, for it is a purchase for some other purpose than the receipt of income. It may be a purchase which would not be, from the financial point of view, attractive or indeed at all beneficial, because part of the price might be attributable to the special benefit represented by the acquisition of a suitable place in which to live. It follows, if I am right on the construction of the clause, that it does not authorise the purchase of a freehold house with vacant possession as a home for the tenant for life and the testator's children, because such purchase would not be a purchase by way of investment, or, perhaps, more accurately, might not be a purchase by way of investment, inasmuch as part of the money would or might be paid for the advantage of vacant possession and the benefit which the family would get by living in the house. . . .

14.1.1.1 Investment policy

COWAN AND OTHERS v SCARGILL AND OTHERS [1985] 1 Ch 270, ChD

FACTS: One half of the management committee of the National Coal Board's pension fund trusts brought an action against the members of the other half; the former having being appointed by the National Coal Board, the latter by the National Union of Mineworkers (NUM). The committee members appointed by the NUM included Mr Arthur Scargill, president of the union. The committee members were the trustees of pension funds worth approximately £3,000 million, with a responsibility to invest £200 million on an annual basis. Because the planned investment scheme included investments in overseas industries and in oil and gas, the union trustees refused to adopt the scheme. The union trustrees justified their actions as being in the beneficiaries' best interests, although they admitted that they had also been motivated by union policy. The National Coal Board trustees brought proceedings to determine whether the refusal of the union trustees had been in breach of trust.
HELD: The purpose of the trust was the provision of financial benefits, and it was therefore the duty of the trustees to invest with a view to securing those benefits. The trustees must set their personal views to one side, although the could in rare cases take into account personal views unanimously held by the beneficiaries. In the present case the union trustees had put their political views before the best financial interests of the beneficiaries. Further, they had been motivated not by the interests of the beneficiaries (retired miners), but by the contributors to the pension funds (working miners). They were, accordingly, in breach of trust for refusing to adopt the proposed investment scheme.

SIR ROBERT MEGARRY V-C: The starting point is the duty of trustees to exercise their powers in the best interests of the present and future beneficiaries of the trust, holding the scales impartially between different classes of beneficiaries. This duty of the trustees towards their beneficiaries is paramount. They must, of course, obey the law; but subject to that, they must put the interests of their beneficiaries first. When the purpose of the trust is to provide financial benefits for the beneficiaries, as is usually the case, the best interests of the beneficiaries are normally their best financial interests. In the case of a power of investment, as in the present case, the power must be exercised so as to yield the best return for the beneficiaries, judged in relation to the risks of the investments in question; and the prospects of the yield of income and capital appreciation both have to be considered in judging the return from the investment.

The legal memorandum that the union obtained from their solicitors is generally in accord with these views. In considering the possibility of investment for 'socially beneficial reasons which may result in lower returns to the fund,' the memorandum states that 'the trustees' only concern is to ensure that the return is the maximum possible consistent with security'; and the refers to the need for diversification. However, it continues by saying:

> Trustees cannot be criticised for failing to make a particular investment for social or political reasons, such as in South African stock for example, but may be held liable for investing in assets which yield a poor return or for disinvesting in stock at inappropriate times for non-financial criteria.

This last sentence must be considered in the light of subsequent passages in the memorandum which indicate that the sale of South African securities by trustees might be justified on the ground of doubts about political stability in South Africa and the long-term financial soundness of its economy, whereas trustees could not properly support motions at a company meeting dealing with pay levels in South Africa, work accidents, pollution control, employment conditions for minorities, military contracting and consumer protection. The assertion that trustees could not be criticised for failing to make a particular investment for social or political reasons is one that I would not accept in its full width. If the investment in fact made is equally beneficial to the beneficiaries, then criticism would be difficult to sustain in practice, whatever the position in theory. But if the investment in fact made is less beneficial, then both in theory and in practice the trustees would normally be open to criticism.

This leads me to the second point, which is a corollary of the first. In considering what investments to make trustees must put on one side their own personal views. Trustees may have strongly held social or political views. They may be firmly opposed to any investment in South Africa or other countries, or they may object to any form of investment in companies concerned with alcohol, tobacco, armaments or many other things. In the conduct of their own affairs, of course, they are free to abstain from making any such investments. Yet under a trust, if investments of this type would be more beneficial to the beneficiaries than other investments, the trustees must not refrain from making the investments by reason of the views that they hold.

Trustees may even have to act dishonourably (though not illegally) if the interests of their beneficiaries require it. Thus where trustees for sale had struck a bargain for the sale of trust property but had not bound themselves by a legally enforceable contract, they were held to be under a duty to consider and explore a better offer that they received, and not to carry through the bargain to which they felt in honour bound: *Buttle* v *Saunders* [1950] 2 All ER 193. In other words, the duty of trustees to their beneficiaries may include a duty to 'gazump,' however honourable the trustees. As Wynn-Parry J said at p. 195, trustees 'have an overriding duty to obtain the best price which they can for their beneficiaries.' In applying this to an official receiver in *In re Wyvern Developments Ltd* [1974] 1 WLR 1097, 1106, Templeman J said that he 'must do his best by his creditors and contributories. He is in a fiduciary capacity and cannot make moral gestures, nor can the court authorise him to do so.' In the words of Sir James Wigram V-C in *Balls* v *Strutt* (1841) 1 Hare 146, 149:

> It is a principle in this court, that a trustee shall not be permitted to use the powers which the trust may confer upon him at law, except for the legitimate purposes of his trust; ...

Powers must be exercised fairly and honestly for the purposes for which they are given and not so as to accomplish any ulterior purpose, whether for the benefit of the trustees or otherwise: see *Duke of Portland* v *Topham* (1864) 11 HL Cas. 32, a case on a power of appointment that must apply a fortiori to a power given to trustees as such.

Third, by way of caveat I should say that I am not asserting that the benefit of the beneficiaries which a trustee must make his paramount concern inevitably and solely means their financial benefit, even if the only object of the trust is to provide financial benefits. Thus if the only actual or potential beneficiaries of a trust are all adults with very strict views on moral and social matters, condemning all forms of alcohol, tobacco and popular entertainment, as well as armaments, I can well understand that it might not be for the 'benefit' of such beneficiaries to know that they are obtaining rather larger financial returns under the trust by reason of investments in those activities than they would have received if the trustees had invested the trust funds in other investments. The beneficiaries might well consider that it was far better to receive less than to receive more money from what they consider to be evil and tainted sources. 'Benefit' is a word with a very wide meaning, and there are circumstances in which arrangements which work to the financial disadvantage of a beneficiary may yet be for his benefit: see, for example, *In re T.'s Settlement Trusts* [1964] Ch 158 and *In re C.L.* [1969] 1 Ch 587. But I would emphasise that such cases are likely to be very rare, and in any case I think that under a trust for the provision of financial benefits the burden would rest, and rest heavy, on him who asserts that it is for the benefit of the beneficiaries as a whole to receive less by reason of the exclusion of some of the possibly more profitable forms of investment. Plainly the present case is not one of this rare type of case. Subject to such matters, under a trust for the provision of financial benefits, the paramount duty of the trustees is to provide the greatest financial benefits for the present and future beneficiaries.

Fourth, the standard required of a trustee in exercising his powers of investment is that he must 'take such care as an ordinary prudent man would take if he were minded to make an investment for the benefit of other people for whom he felt morally bound to provide': *per* Lindley LJ in *In re Whiteley* (1886) 33 ChD 347, 355; see also at pp. 350, 358; and see *Learoyd* v *Whiteley* (1887) 12 App Cas 727. That duty includes the duty to seek advice on matters which the trustee does not understand, such as the making of investments, and on receiving that advice to act with the same degree of prudence. This requirement is not discharged merely by showing that the trustee has acted in good faith and with sincerity. Honesty and sincerity are not the same as prudence and reasonableness. Some of the most sincere people are the most unreasonable; and Mr. Scargill told me that he had met quite a few of them. Accordingly, although a trustee who takes advice on investments is not bound to accept and act on that advice, he is not entitled to reject it merely because he sincerely disagrees with it, unless in addition to being sincere he is acting as an ordinary prudent man would act.

Fifth, trustees have a duty to consider the need for diversification of investments. By s. 6(1) of the Trustee Investments Act 1961:

> In the exercise of his powers of investment a trustee shall have regard—(a) to the need for diversification of investments of the trust, in so far as is appropriate to the circumstances of the trust; (b) to the suitability to the trust of investments of the description of investment proposed and of the investment proposed as an investment of that description.

The reference to the 'circumstances of the trust' plainly include matters such as the size of the trust funds: the degree of diversification that is practicable and desirable for a large fund may plainly be impracticable or undesirable (or both) in the case of a small fund.

In the case before me, it is not in issue that there ought to be diversification of the investments held by the fund. The contention of the defendants, put very shortly, is that there can be a sufficient degree of diversification without any investment overseas or in oil, and that in any case there is no need to increase the level of overseas investments beyond the existing level. Other pension funds got on well enough without overseas investments, it was said, and in particular the NUM's own scheme had, in 1982, produced better results than the scheme here in question. This was not so, said Mr

Jenkins, if you compared like with like, and excluded investments in property, which figure substantially in the mineworkers' scheme but not at all in the NUM scheme: and in any case the latter scheme was much smaller, being of the order of £7 million. . . .

14.1.1.2 Ethical considerations

HARRIES AND OTHERS v THE CHURCH COMMISSIONERS FOR ENGLAND AND ANOTHER [1992] 1 WLR 1241, ChD

FACTS: The Right Reverend Richard Harries, Bishop of Oxford, was one of the Church Commissioners. The Commissioners control and invest large sums of money on behalf of the Church of England, such funds being held under charitable trusts. The Bishop of Oxford, together with certain other Church of England clergy, brought proceedings against the other Commissioners, seeking declarations clarifying the Commissioners' obligation to invest in a manner compatible with Christian morality.
HELD: The declarations were refused. Charity trustees were required to invest with a view to securing the maximum financial return compatible with ordinary prudence. 'Christian morality' covered a range of divergent views which should not be accommodated if to do so would create significant financial prejudice to the funds. However, if some of those views could be accommodated without financial detriment, such an ethical investment policy would be proper.

SIR DONALD NICHOLLS V-C: The Church Commissioners for England administer vast estates and large funds. At the end of 1990 their holdings of land were valued at about £1.7bn, their mortgages and loans at about £165m, and their stock exchange investments at about £780m. In 1990 these items yielded altogether an investment income of £164m. The Commissioners' income included also some £66m derived principally from parish and diocesan contributions to clergy stipends. So the commissioners' total income last year was £230m. . . .
 . . . For some time there have been voices in the Church of England expressing disquiet at the investment policy of the commissioners. They do not question either the good faith or the investment expertise of the commissioners. Their concern is not that the commissioners have failed to get the best financial return from their property and investments. Their concern is that, in making investment decisions, the commissioners are guided too rigorously by purely financial considerations, and that the commissioners give insufficient weight to what are now called 'ethical' considerations.
 . . . In most cases the best interests of the charity require that the trustees' choice of investments should be made solely on the basis of well-established criteria, having taken expert advice where appropriate and having due regard to such matters as the need to diversify, the need to balance income against capital growth, and the need to balance risk against return.
 In a minority of cases the position will not be so straightforward. There will be some cases, I suspect comparatively rare, when the objects of the charity are such that investments of a particular type would conflict with the aims of the charity. Much-cited examples are those of cancer research companies and tobacco shares, trustees of temperance charities and brewery and distillery shares, and trustees of charities of the Society of Friends and shares in companies engaged in production of armaments. If, as would be likely in those examples, trustees were satisfied that investing in a company engaged in a particular type of business would conflict with the very objects their charity is seeking to achieve, they should not so invest. Carried to its logical conclusion the trustees should take this course even if it would be likely to result in significant financial detriment to the charity. The logical conclusion, whilst sound as a matter of legal analysis, is unlikely to arise in practice. It is not easy to think of an instance where in practice the exclusion for this reason of one or more companies or sectors from the whole range of investments open to trustees would be likely to leave them without an adequately wide range of investments from which to choose a properly diversified portfolio.
 There will also be some cases, again I suspect comparatively rare, when trustees' holdings of particular investments might hamper a charity's work either by making

potential recipients of aid unwilling to be helped because of the source of the charity's money, or by alienating some of those who support the charity financially. In these cases the trustees will need to balance the difficulties they would encounter, or likely financial loss they would sustain, if they were to hold the investments against the risk of financial detriment if those investments were excluded from their portfolio. The greater the risk of financial detriment, the more certain the trustees should be of countervailing disadvantages to the charity before they incur that risk. Another circumstance where trustees would be entitled, or even required, to take into account non-financial criteria would be where the trust deed so provides.

. . . The instances I have given are not comprehensive. But I must emphasise that of their very nature, and by definition, investments are held by trustees to aid the work of the charity in a particular way: by generating money. That is the purpose for which they are held. That is their raison d'être. Trustees cannot properly use assets held as an investment for other, viz., non-investment, purposes.

. . . Those who wish may do so with their own property, but that is not a proper function of trustees with trust assets held as an investment. . . .

Trustees may, if they wish, accommodate the views of those who consider that on moral grounds a particular investment would be in conflict with the objects of the charity, so long as the trustees are satisfied that course would not involve a risk of significant financial detriment. But when they are not so satisfied trustees should not make investment decisions on the basis of preferring one view of whether on moral grounds in investment conflicts with the objects of the charity over another. This is so even when one view is more widely supported than the other.

I have sought above to consider charity trustees' duties in relation to investment as a matter of basic principle. I was referred to no authority bearing directly on these matters. My attention was drawn to *Cowan* v *Scargill* [1985] Ch 270, a case concerning a pension fund. I believe the views I have set out accord with those expressed by Sir Robert Megarry V-C in that case, bearing in mind that he was considering trusts for the provision of financial benefits for individuals. In this case I am concerned with trusts of charities, whose purposes are multifarious.

The evidence does show that the commissioners have declined to adopt financially disadvantageous policies advocated by, among others, the Bishop of Oxford. In October 1989 his bishop's council passed a resolution urging his diocesan board of finance to adopt certain specific criteria in relation to South Africa. For example, investments should not be directly or indirectly in groups of companies (other than banks, for the time being) which derived more than £10m in annual profits from South Africa or more than three per cent of their worldwide profits from South African activities. As to that, the commissioners' ethical policy excludes about 13 per cent of listed United Kingdom companies (by value) from consideration. The companies in which the commissioners hold shares that would be excluded under the suggested criteria would comprise a further 24 per cent (by value) of listed United Kingdom companies, making a total exclusion of about 37 per cent. The part of the market excluded by the criteria would include some of the largest United Kingdom companies whose shares make up a very important part of the commissioners' total portfolio. The criteria would exclude two companies which make up 65 per cent of the oil sector, and a further two companies which make up 62 per cent of the chemical sector of the United Kindom equity market. Not surprisingly, the commissioners' view is that a portfolio thus restricted would be much less balanced and diversified, and they would not regard it as prudent or in the interests of those for whom they provide.

The investment issue raised by this resolution is another example of a moral question to which there can be no certain answer. The commissioners do not invest in a company where more than a small part of its business is in South Africa. The policy advocated by the Bishop of Oxford's council does not seek to exclude every company which has a South African business connection. The councils' policy embodies fixed, and to this extent, artificial limits on the degree of South African involvement which is acceptable. As between these two alternatives, there can be no right or wrong answer. This is a question of degree, and whether Christian ethics require a more restrictive policy than that adopted by the commissioners is a matter on which there can be literally endless argument and debate. The commissioners are therefore right not to prefer one view over the other beyond the point at which they would incur a risk of significant financial detriment.

Another example raised before me concerned land owned by the commissioners in a village where local young people are finding housing impossible to afford. Such land, it was suggested by the plaintiffs, could be made available for low-cost housing at a price below open-market value. Investing instead in a more expensive housing development with a higher rate of return would undermine the credibility of the Christian message by the affront such a policy would cause to the needs and consciences of local people. I do not think this example advances the plaintiffs' case. The commissioners are not a housing charity. There is force in the commissioners' contention that local housing needs are or should be reflected in local planning policies. When planning permission is available for a particular type of development, it is not a proper function for the commissioners to sell their land at an under-value in order to further a social objective on which the local planning authority has taken a different view. This, once more, is an illustration of a circumstance in which different minds within the Church of England, applying the highest moral standards, will reach different conclusions. If the commissioners' land is to be disposed of at an undervalue, they need an express power to do so. Such a disposition cannot properly be made in exercise of their power to make and change investments. . . .

Nobles, R., 'Charities and Ethical Investment' (1992) 56 Conv 115

Bishop of Oxford v The Church Commissioners

A world in which all individuals and institutions pursued maximum financial returns would be extremely unstable. There must be some spheres of activity, such as government and the family, in which individuals and institutions advance values other than profit or consumer satisfaction. The boundary between those areas of social life which can be left to market forces, and those which cannot, is a matter of controversy. But charity would, in most people's opinion, represent one area of social life in which the pursuit of values other than profit or consumer satisfaction must dominate.

Surprisingly, this is not the courts' view, or at least, not their view of how a charity should approach its investments. In *Bishop of Oxford* v *The Church Commissioners* [1992] 1 WLR 1241 Browne-Wilkinson V-C decided that the starting point for investment by charitable trustees must be the pursuit of maximum financial returns, and minimum financial risk. Where they felt such investment was contrary to the purposes of their charity they could relax their pursuit of financial aims, but only so long as this did not create a risk of significant financial detriment. Major financial risks could only be undertaken where the investment policy clearly undermined the charity's ability to carry out its work (the V-C gave the example of investments which outraged sponsors or caused the persons who were to be assisted to refuse its bounty), or where the conflict between the charity's purposes and its investment policy was apparent to all. The trustees could not incur the risk of significant financial detriment simply because they believed that the charity's purposes required this, or because a substantial majority of persons thought this was necessary, or where the investment could reasonably be seen to conflict with the charity's objects. If a minority of persons felt that the charity's objects could be pursued without undertaking an investment policy which carried major risks, then the trustees had to give effect to that minority's views.

This decision seems very peculiar. Charitable trustees can give money away in pursuit of their charity's purposes. In so doing, they are not required to limit their bounty to such as all persons would agree were within their objects. Charities can be somewhat more controversial and radical than this. . . .

The reasoning of the Vice Chancellor is persuasive, until one tries to apply it to the general work of the charity. Consider the following statement:

There will be instances today when those who support or benefit from a charity take a widely different view on a particular type of investment, some saying that on moral grounds it conflicts with the aims of the charity, others saying the opposite. . . . But frequently, when questions of the morality of conduct are being canvassed, there is no identifiable yardstick which can be applied to a set of facts so as to yield one answer which can be seen to be 'right' and another 'wrong'. If that situation confronts trustees of a charity, the law does not require them to find an answer to the unanswerable. Trustees may, if they wish, accommodate the views of those who consider that on moral grounds a particular investment would be in conflict with the objects of a charity, so long as the trustees are satisfied that course would not involve a risk of significant financial detriment. But when they are not so satisfied trustees should not make investment decisions on the basis of preferring one view of whether on moral grounds an investment conflicts with the objects of the charity over another. This is so even when one view is more widely supported than the other.

Apply this to the general work of charity, and you get some strange results. Because there are differences of opinion on what constitutes Christian ethics, the church may spend small amounts of money on projects that are only considered Christian by one group within the church. But they cannot spend large amounts of money unless all of the church agrees that the work accords with Christian doctrine.

There is no evidence that the V-C wished to restrict the general work of charities in this fashion and, once this is accepted, one struggles to find a reason why the investment powers of a charity should be subject to any greater restriction.

For example, the V-C ruled that the church commissioners could not sell land to a developer at under value, in order to provide low cost housing to needy families. Does this mean that the Church of England cannot sponsor low cost housing or hostels? If they can do the latter, then they presumably sell investments in order to raise the money. Why make them sell an investment when they could achieve the same purpose, probably at less cost, through the sale of land to a developer at below market value? What is the merit of saying that one can provide low cost housing through sponsorship provided that this comes within a reasonable interpretation of a charity's purposes, but one cannot provide low cost housing through investment unless all people agree that such a policy is necessary to the charity's purposes?

This decision is harder to justify than Megarry V-C's judgment in *Cowan* v *Scargill* [1985] 1 Ch 270, on pension scheme investment, or Wynn-Parry J's judgment in *Buttle* v *Saunders* [1950] 2 All ER 193, on investment within private family trusts. The ordinary business of a pension scheme is to provide financial benefits to individuals and, in the ordinary course of events, the best way to achieve this is to have the largest possible fund. The same logic applies to private family trusts. If the courts abandon the criteria of best financial interests they have no standard by which to control the trustees' investment policies other than the purely subjective one of whether they agree with the morals or politics of the trustees. But charitable trusts do provide criteria, other than financial interests, by which to assess their investment policies. They exist to further charitable purposes. The grant of bounty has to be assessed by reference to such purposes, and so should the investment policy. If trustees cannot make, or cannot be allowed to make, controversial moral judgments on the extent to which their investments give effect to their charity's purposes then they should not be able to make the same judgments when giving away its property. Conversely, if they can be trusted to make these judgments when giving away the charity's property, they can be trusted to make its investments on the same basis.

Lord Nicholls of Birkenhead, 'Trustees and their broader community: where duty, morality and ethics converge' (1995) 9(3) TLI 71

Preferring ethical ends to financial gain
Whether an expert or not, the ordinary prudent person is not to be regarded as wholly lacking in moral sensitivity. This person, the creation of equity, is surely as anxious as the next person to do all he can to promote good and to remedy injustices, whatever form they take. But this laudable characteristic is not easily translated into practice in the investment field. In the absence of a generally accepted attitude to the morality of investing in this or that investment, it cannot be right for moral considerations to displace beneficiaries' financial interests. Some people disapprove of investments in the armaments industry, others do not. Many people feel passionately about animal welfare, and

the fur trade and the conditions in which some animals are still reared, others less so. Increasing numbers of people are anxious about the environment and wish to support companies with an enlightened attitude on green issues, others' cares lie elsewhere. . . .

A further complication is that, increasingly, businesses are interdependent, so that clear-cut demarcation is often not possible. Instead there are questions of degree when considering investments, for example, in a food supermarket which sells cigarettes, or in a car manufacturer one of whose components is imported from a country with an oppressive regime.

In these circumstances equity's creature, the ordinary prudent person looking after another's financial affairs, would surely take the view that it is not for him to foist onto his beneficiaries his own particular views about ethical or green investments. He should not let his views, or the views of some of the fund members, despite being held very deeply, affect his investment policy decisions to the financial detriment of all the fund members. He should exercise a power of investment for the purpose for which it was created.

This is not a pusillanimous abdication of responsibilities in the modern world. Rather, it is a recognition that on moral issues on which there is no consensus, it is no part of the function of a trustee to reject one view and prefer another, whether his own or that of some of the beneficiaries, when to do so would be contrary to the financial interests of the beneficiaries. A pension fund trustee is not the guardian of the moral welfare of the fund members, and modern developments in social conditions do not compel the conclusion that he should assume this role. The fund exists to confer financial benefits on the members. The money in the fund represents part of the overall pay package of the members, in the form of deferred remuneration. It is not for the trustee to decide that, although it might mean a reduction in their income, the members ought to play their part in, say, encouraging investment in emerging markets or discouraging smoking, or that they should do so by the trustee seeking or shunning particular classes of investments. It is not for the trustee to decide that would be for the benefit of the beneficiaries. The trust fund was not set up for the purpose either of promoting or of discouraging these activities. If the trustee were to use his investment powers to one or other of these ends regardless of the financial consequences, he would be departing from the only purpose for which he holds the trust's funds. . . .

This analysis, however, by no means leads to the conclusion that trustees are precluded from having any regard to moral considerations. The range of sound investments available to trustees is so extensive that very frequently there is scope for trustees to give effect to moral considerations, either by positively preferring certain investments or negatively avoiding others, without thereby prejudicing beneficiaries' financial interests. In practice, the inclusion or exclusion of particular investments or types of investirnent will often be possible without incurring the risk of a lower rate of return or reducing the desirable spread of investments.

When this is so, there is no reason in principle why trustees should not have regard to moral and ethical considerations, vague and uncertain though these are. The trustees would not be departing from the purpose of the trust or hindering its fulfilment. The ordinary prudent person would surely feel no inhibitions in this situation, where the beneficiaries are not rquired to pay a financial price.

Take the simple example of dedicated employees who have worked for years seeking a cure for lung cancer. They would be horrified if their pension fund included shares in tobacco companies. Again, employees of a chain of hotels would be surprised were their pension fund trustee to invest in their keenest competitor. In practice, in these and most other cases where trustees or members of a pension fund have strong views about particular investments on non-financial grounds, it should be possible for trustees to exercise their investment powers in a manner avoiding embarrassment to all concemed without upsetting the balance of the portfolio.

In other words, in most cases trustees may adopt an ethical investment policy. This may not always be so rigorous as they or some beneficiaries might wish. However, the very lack of consensus on many of these issues should cause trustees to take care lest they become involved in controversies to which no certain outcome is possible. Here, as always, trustees should make use of two further attributes with which equity's ordinary prudent person is liberally endowed: tact and common sense. . . .

14.1.2 INVESTMENT IN LAND

14.1.2.1 Trusts of land

TRUSTS OF LAND AND APPOINTMENT OF TRUSTEES ACT 1996

6. General powers of trustees

(1) For the purpose of exercising their functions as trustees, the trustees of land have in relation to the land subject to the trust all the powers of an absolute owner.

(2) Where in the case of any land subject to a trust of land each of the beneficiaries interested in the land is a person of full age and capacity who is absolutely entitled to the land, the powers conferred on the trustees by subsection (1) include the power to convey the land to the beneficiaries even though they have not required the trustees to do so; and where land is conveyed by virtue of this subsection—

(a) the beneficiaries shall do whatever is necessary to secure that it vests in them, and

(b) if they fail to do so, the court may make an order requiring them to do so.

(3) The trustees of land have power to purchase a legal estate in any land in England or Wales.

(4) The power conferred by subsection (3) may be exercised by trustees to purchase land—

(a) by way of investment,

(b) for occupation by any beneficiary, or

(c) for any other reason.

(5) In exercising the powers conferred by this section trustees shall have regard to the rights of the beneficiaries.

(6) The powers conferred by this section shall not be exercised in contravention of, or of any order made in pursuance of, any other enactment or any rule of law or equity.

(7) The reference in subsection (6) to an order includes an order of any court or of the Charity Commissioners.

(8) Where any enactment other than this section confers on trustees authority to act subject to any restriction, limitation or condition, trustees of land may not exercise the powers conferred by this section to do any act which they are prevented from doing under the other enactment by reason of the restriction, limitation or condition.

12. The right to occupy

(1) A beneficiary who is beneficially entitled to an interest in possession in land subject to a trust of land is entitled by reason of his interest to occupy the land at any time if at that time—

(a) the purposes of the trust include making the land available for his occupation (or for the occupation of beneficiaries of a class of which he is a member or of beneficiaries in general), or

(b) the land is held by the trustees so as to be so available.

(2) Subsection (1) does not confer on a beneficiary a right to occupy land if it is either unavailable or unsuitable for occupation by him.

(3) . . .

14.1.2.2 Other trusts

The general law still provides that trustees may not invest in freehold land unless authorised to do so by the trust instrument. Investment in certain mortgages is, however, permitted (see para. 13 of Part II of the First Schedule to the Act).

14.2 Trustees Investments Act 1961

TRUSTEE INVESTMENTS ACT 1961

1. New powers of investment of trustees

(1) A trustee may invest any property in his hands, whether at the time in a state of investment or not, in any manner specified in Part I or II of the First Schedule to this Act

or, subject to the next following section, in any manner specified in Part III of that Schedule, and may also from time to time vary any such investments.

(2) The supplemental provisions contained in Part IV of that Schedule shall have effect for the interpretation and for restricting the operation of the said Parts I to III.

(3) No provision relating to the powers of the trustee contained in any instrument (not being an enactment or an instrument made under an enactment) made before the passing of this Act shall limit the powers conferred by this section, but those powers are exercisable only in so far as a contrary intention is not expressed in any Act or instrument made under an enactment, whenever passed or made, and so relating or in any other instrument so relating which is made after the passing of this Act.

For the purposes of this subsection any rule of the law of Scotland whereby a testamentary writing may be deemed to be made on a date other than that on which it was actually executed shall be disregarded.

(4) In the Act 'narrower-range investment' means an investment falling within Part I or II of the First Schedule to this Act and 'wider-range investment' means an investment falling within Part III of that Schedule.

2. Restrictions on wider-range investment

(1) A trustee shall not have power by virtue of the foregoing section to make or retain any wider-range investment unless the trust fund has been divided into two parts (hereinafter referred to as the narrower-range part and the wider-range part), the parts being, subject to the provisions of this Act, *equal in value at the time of the division* [the requirement of equal division has now been changed to a 3:1 division as to wider and narrower ranges respectively (Trustee Investments (Division of Trust Fund) Order 1996 (SI 1996 No. 845))]; and where such a division has been made no subsequent division of the same fund shall be made for the purposes of this section, and no property shall be transferred from one part of the fund to the other unless either—

(a)   the transfer is authorised or required by the following provisions of this Act, or

(b)   a compensating transfer is made at the same time.

In this section 'compensating transfer', in relation to any transferred property, means a transfer in the opposite direction of property of equal value.

(2) Property belonging to the narrower-range part of a trust fund shall not by virtue of the foregoing section be invested except in narrower-range investments, and any property invested in any other manner which is or becomes comprised in that part of the trust fund shall either be transferred to the wider-range part of the fund, with a compensating transfer, or be reinvested in narrower-range investments as soon as may be.

(3) Where any property accrues to a trust fund after the fund has been divided in pursuance of subsection (1) of this section, then—

(a)   if the property accrues to the trustee as owner or former owner of property comprised in either part of the fund, it shall be treated as belonging to that part of the fund;

(b)   in any other case, the trustee shall secure, by apportionment of the accruing property or the transfer of property from one part of the fund to the other, or both, that the value of each part of the fund is increased by the same amount.

Where a trustee acquires property in consideration of a money payment the acquisition of the property shall be treated for the purposes of this section as investment and not as the accrual of property to the trust fund, notwithstanding that the amount of the consideration is less than the value of the property acquired; and paragraph (a) of this subsection shall not include the case of a dividend or interest becoming part of a trust fund.

(4) Where in the exercise of any power or duty of a trustee property falls to be taken out of the trust fund, nothing in this section shall restrict his discretion as to the choice of property to be taken out.

3. Relationship between Act and other powers of investment

(1) The powers conferred by section one of this Act are in addition to and not in derogation from any power conferred otherwise than by this Act of investment or postponing conversion exercisable by a trustee (hereinafter referred to as a 'special power').

(2)   Any special power (however expressed) to invest property in any investment for the time being authorised by law for the investment of trust property, being a power conferred on a trustee before the passing of this Act or conferred on him under any enactment passed before the passing of this Act, shall have effect as a power to invest property in like manner and subject to the like provisions as under the foregoing provisions of this Act.

(3)   . . .

(4)   . . .

4. Interpretation of references to trust property and trust funds

(1)   In this Act 'property' includes real or personal property of any description, including money and things in action:

Provided that it does not include an interest in expectancy, but the falling into possession of such an interest, or the receipt of proceeds of the sale thereof, shall be treated for the purposes of this Act as an accrual of property to the trust fund.

(2)   So much of the property in the hands of a trustee shall for the purposes of this Act constitute one trust fund as is held on trusts which (as respects the beneficiaries or their respective interests or the purposes of the trust or as respects the powers of the trustee) are not identical with those on which any other property in his hands is held.

(3)   Where property is taken out of a trust fund by way of appropriation so as to form a separate fund, and at the time of the appropriation the trust fund had (as to the whole or part thereof) been divided in pursuance of subsection (1) of section two of this Act, or that subsection as modified by the Second Schedule to this Act, then if the separate fund is so divided the narrower-range and wider-range parts of the separate fund may be constituted so as either to be equal, or to bear to each other the same proportion as the two corresponding parts of the fund out of which it was so appropriated (the values of those parts of those funds being ascertained as at the time of appropriation), or some intermediate proportion.

(4)   . . .

5. Certain valuations to be conclusive for purposes of division of trust fund

(1)   If for the purposes of section two or four of this Act or the Second Schedule thereto a trustee obtains, from a person reasonably believed by the trustee to be qualified to make it, a valuation in writing of any property, the valuation shall be conclusive in determining whether the division of the trust fund in pursuance of subsection (1) of the said section two, or any transfer or appointment of property under that section or the said Second Schedule, has been duly made.

(2)   The foregoing subsection applies to any such valuation notwithstanding that it is made by a person in the course of his employment as an officer or servant.

6. Duty of trustees in choosing investments

(1)   In the exercise of his powers of investment a trustee shall have regard—

(a)   to the need for diversification of investments of the trust, in so far as is appropriate to the circumstances of the trust;

(b)   to the suitability to the trust of investments of the description of investment proposed and of the investment proposed as an investment of that description.

(2)   Before exercising any power conferred by section one of this Act to invest in a manner specified in Part II or III of the First Schedule to this Act, or before investing in any such manner in the exercise of a power falling within subsection (2) of section three of this Act, a trustee shall obtain and consider proper advice on the question whether the investment is satisfactory having regard to the matters mentioned in paragraphs (a) and (b) of the foregoing subsection.

(3)   A trustee retaining any investment made in the exercise of such a power and in such a manner as aforesaid shall determine at what intervals the circumstances, and in particular the nature of the investment, make it desirable to obtain such advice as aforesaid, and shall obtain and consider such advice accordingly.

(4)   For the purposes of the two foregoing subsections, proper advice is the advice of a person who is reasonably believed by the trustee to be qualified by his ability in and practical experience of financial matters; and such advice may be given by a person notwithstanding that he gives it in the course of his employment as an officer or servant.

(5)   A trustee shall not be treated as having complied with subsection (2) or (3) of this section unless the advice was given or has been subsequently confirmed in writing.

(6)   Subsections (2) and (3) of this section shall not apply to one of two or more trustees where he is the person giving the advice required by this section to his co-trustee or co-trustees, and shall not apply where powers of a trustee are lawfully exercised by an officer or servant competent under subsection (4) of this section to give proper advice.

(7)   Without prejudice to section eight of the Trustee Act 1925, or section thirty of the Trusts (Scotland) Act 1921 (which relate to valuation, and the proportion of the value to be lent, where a trustee lends on the security of property) the advice required by this section shall not include, in the case of a loan on the security of freehold or leasehold property in England and Wales or Northern Ireland or on heritable security in Scotland, advice on the suitability of the particular loan.

15.   Saving for powers of court
The enlargement of the investment powers of trustees by this Act shall not lessen any power of a court to confer wider powers of investment on trustees, or affect the extent to which any such power is to be exercised.

SCHEDULES

Section 1   FIRST SCHEDULE   MANNER OF INVESTMENT

PART I   NARROWER-RANGE INVESTMENTS NOT REQUIRING ADVICE
1.   In Defence Bonds, National Savings Certificates, Ulster Savings Certificates, Ulster Development Bonds, National Development Bonds, British Savings Bonds, National Savings Income Bonds, National Savings Deposit Bonds, National Savings Indexed-Income Bonds.

2.   In deposits in the National Savings Bank, . . . and deposits in a bank or department thereof certified under subsection (3) of section nine of the Finance Act 1956.

PART II   NARROWER-RANGE INVESTMENTS REQUIRING ADVICE
1.   In securities issued by Her Majesty's Government in the United Kingdom, the Government of Northern Ireland or the Government of the Isle of Man, not being securities falling within Part I of this Schedule and being fixed-interest securities registered in the United Kingdom or the Isle of Man, Treasury Bills or Tax Reserve Certificates or any variable interest securities issued by Her Majesty's Government in the United Kingdom and registered in the United Kingdom.

2.   In any securities the payment of interest on which is guaranteed by Her Majesty's Government in the United Kingdom or the Government of Northern Ireland.

3.   In fixed-interest securities issued in the United Kingdom by any public authority or nationalised industry or undertaking in the United Kingdom.

4.   In fixed-interest securities issued in the United Kingdom by the government of any overseas territory within the Commonwealth or by any public or local authority within such a territory, being securities registered in the United Kingdom.

References in this paragraph to an overseas territory or to the government of such a territory shall be construed as if they occurred in the Overseas Service Act 1958.

4A.   In securities issued in the United Kingdom by the government of an overseas territory within the Commonwealth or by any public or local authority within such a territory, being securities registered in the United Kingdom and in respect of which the rate of interest is variable by reference to one or more of the following:—

   (a)   the Bank of England's minimum lending rate;
   (b)   the average rate of discount on allotment on 91-day Treasury bills;
   (c)   a yield on 91-day Treasury bills;
   (d)   a London sterling inter-bank offered rate;
   (e)   a London sterling certificate of deposit rate.

References in this paragraph to an overseas territory or to the government of such a territory shall be construed as if they occurred in the Overseas Service Act 1958. . . .

10A.   In any units, or other shares of the investments subject to the trusts, of a unit trust scheme which, at the time of investment, is an authorised unit trust, within the meaning of section 358 of the Income and Corporation Taxes Act 1970, in relation to which, by virtue of section 60 of the Finance Act 1980, section 354 of the said Act of 1970 does not apply.

11. . . .

12. In deposits with a building society within the meaning of the Building Societies Act 1986.

13. In mortgages of freehold property in England and Wales or Northern Ireland and of leasehold property in those countries of which the unexpired term at the time of investment is not less than sixty years, and in loans on heritable security in Scotland.

14. In perpetual rent-charges charged on land in England and Wales or Northern Ireland and fee-farm rents (not being rent-charges) issuing out of such land, and in feu-duties or ground annuals in Scotland.

15. In Certificates of Tax Deposit.

16. In a fixed interest or variable interest securities issued by the government of a relevant state. . . .

PART III   WIDER-RANGE INVESTMENTS

1. In any securities issued in the United Kingdom by a company incorporated in the United Kingdom, being securities registered in the United Kingdom and not being securities falling within Part II of this Schedule.

2. In shares in a building society within the meaning of the Building Societies Act 1986.

3. In any units of an authorised unit trust scheme within the meaning of the Financial Securities Act 1986. . . .

PART IV   SUPPLEMENTAL

1. The securities mentioned in Parts I to III of this Schedule do not include any securities where the holder can be required to accept repayment of the principal, or the payment of any interest, otherwise than in sterling.

2. The securities mentioned in paragraph 1 to 8 of Part II, other than Treasury Bills or Tax Reserve Certificates, securities issued before the passing of the Act by the Government of the Isle of Man, securities falling within paragraph 4 of the said Part II issued before the passing of this Act or securities falling within paragraph 9 of that Part, and the securities mentioned in paragraph 1 of Part III of this Schedule, do not include—

(a)   securities the price of which is not quoted on *a recognised stock exchange within the meaning of the Prevention of Fraud (Investments) Act 1958, or the Belfast stock exchange;*

(b)   shares or debenture stock not fully paid up (except shares or debenture stock which by the terms of issue are required to be fully paid up within nine months of the date of issue).

3. The securities mentioned in paragraph 6 of Part II and paragraph 1 of Part III of this Schedule do not include—

(a)   shares or debentures of an incorporated company of which the total issued and paid up share capital is less than one million pounds;

(b)   shares or debentures of an incorporated company which has not in each of the five years immediately preceding the calendar year in which the investment is made paid a dividend on all the shares issued by the company, excluding any shares issued after the dividend was declared and any shares which by their terms of issue did not rank for the dividend for that year.

For the purposes of sub-paragraph (b) of this paragraph a company formed—

(i)   to take over the business of another company or other companies, or

(ii)   to acquire the securities of, or control of, another company or other companies, or for either of those purposes and for other purposes shall be deemed to have paid a dividend as mentioned in that sub-paragraph in any year in which such a dividend has been paid by the other company or all the other companies, as the case may be. . . .

Section 3   SECOND SCHEDULE MODIFICATION OF S. 2 IN
RELATION TO PROPERTY FALLING WITHIN S. 3(3)

1. In this Schedule 'special-range property' means property falling within subsection (3) of section three of this Act.

2.(1)   Where a trust fund includes special-range property, subsection (1) of section two of this Act shall have effect as if references to the trust fund were references to so much thereof as does not consist of special-range property, and the special-range property shall be carried to a separate part of the fund. . . .

TRUSTEE ACT 1925

8.   Loans and investments by trustees not chargeable as breaches of trust

(1)   A trustee lending money on the security of any property on which he can properly lend shall not be chargeable with breach of trust by reason only of the proportion borne by the amount of the loan to the value of the property at the time when the loan was made, if it appears to the court—

(a)   that in making the loan the trustee was acting upon a report as to the value of the property made by a person whom he reasonably believed to be an able practical surveyor or valuer instructed and employed independently of any owner of the property, whether such surveyor or valuer carried on business in the locality where the property is situate or elsewhere; and

(b)   that the amount of the loan does not exceed two third parts of the value of the property as stated in the report; and

(c)   that the loan was made under the advice of the surveyor or valuer expressed in the report.

(2)   A trustee lending money on the security of any leasehold property shall not be chargeable with breach of trust only upon the ground that in making such loan he dispensed either wholly or partly with the production or investigation of the lessor's title.

(3)   A trustee shall not be chargeable with breach of trust only upon the ground that in effecting the purchase, or in lending money upon the security, of any property he has accepted a shorter title than the title which a purchaser is, in the absence of a special contract, entitled to require, if in the opinion of the court the title accepted be such as a person acting with prudence and caution would have accepted.

(4)   This section applies to transfers of existing securities as well as to new securities and to investments made before as well as after the commencement of this Act.

9.   Liability for loss by reason of improper investment

(1)   Where a trustee improperly advances trust money on a mortgage security which would at the time of the investment be a proper investment in all respects for a smaller sum than is actually advanced thereon, the security shall be deemed an authorised investment for the smaller sum, and the trustee shall only be liable to make good the sum advanced in excess thereof with interest.

(2)   This section applies to investments made before as well as after the commencement of this Act.

PENSIONS ACT 1995

33.   Investment powers duty of care

(1)   Liability for breach of an obligation under any rule of law to take care or exercise skill in the performance of any investment functions, where the function is exercisable—

(a)   by a trustee of a trust scheme, or

(b)   by a person to whom the function has been delegated under section 34, cannot be excluded or restricted by any instrument or agreement.

34.   Power of investment and delegation

(1)   The trustees of a trust scheme have, subject to any restriction imposed by the scheme, the same power to make an investment of any kind as if they were absolutely entitled to the assets of the scheme.

35.   Investment principles

(1)   The trustees of a trust scheme must secure that there is prepared, maintained and from time to time revised a written statement of the principles governing decisions about investments for the purposes of the scheme.

(2)   The statement must cover, among other things—
  (a)   the trustees' policy for securing compliance with sections 36 and 56, and
  (b)   their policy about the following matters.
(3)   Those matters are—
  (a)   the kinds of investments to be held,
  (b)   the balance between different kinds of investments,
  (c)   risk,
  (d)   the expected return on investments,
  (e)   the realisation of investments, and
  (f)   such other matters as may be prescribed.
(4)   Neither the trust scheme nor the statement may impose restrictions (however expressed) on any power to make investments by reference to the consent of the employer.
(5)   The trustees of a trust scheme must, before a statement under this section is prepared or revised—
  (a)   obtain and consider the written advice of a person who is reasonably believed by the trustees to be qualified by his ability in and practical experience of financial matters and to have the appropriate knowledge and experience of the management of the investments of such schemes, and
  (b)   consult the employer.
(6)   If in the case of any trust scheme—
  (a)   a statement under this section has not been prepared or is not being maintained, or
  (b)   the trustees have not obtained and considered advice in accordance with subsection (5),
section 3 [Prohibition Orders] and 10 [Civil penalties] apply to any trustee who has failed to take all steps as are reasonable to secure compliance.

14.2.1   THE NEED FOR DIVERSITY

NESTLE v NATIONAL WESTMINSTER BANK PLC (1996) 10(4) TLI 11

Facts and the decision on appeal, see **14.3.3**.

HOFFMANN J: . . .
IV. The Investment Duties of Trustees

1.   The Law
There was no dispute over the general principles to be applied. First, there is the prudence principle. The classic statement is that of Lindley LJ:

> The duty of a trustee is not to take such care only as a prudent man would take if he had only himself to consider; the duty rather is to take such care as an ordinary prudent man would take if he were minded to make an investment for the benefit of other people for whom he felt morally bound to provide.

This is an extremely flexible standard capable of adaptation to current economic conditions and contemporary understanding of markets and investments. For example, investments which were imprudent in the days of the gold standard may be sound and sensible in times of high inflation. Modern trustees acting within their investment powers are entitled to be judged by the standards of current portfolio theory, which emphasises the risk level of the entire portfolio rather than the risk attaching to each investment taken in isolation. But in reviewing the conduct of trustees over a period of more than 60 years, one must be careful not to endow the prudent trustee with prophetic vision or expect him to have ignored the received wisdom of his time.

Mr Gerard Wright, who appeared for Miss Nestle, referred me to another passage in *Re Whiteley* (1887) 12 App Cas 727 in which Cotton LJ said:

> Trustees are bound to preserve the money for those entitled to the *corpus* in remainder, and they are bound to invest it in such a way as will produce a reasonable income for those enjoying the income for the present.

In 1886 what Cotton LJ had in mind was the safety of the capital in purely monetary terms. But Mr Wright submitted that in the conditions which prevail a century later, the trustees were under an overriding duty to preserve the *real* value of the capital. In my judgment this cannot be right. The preservation of the monetary value of the capital requires no skill or luck. The trustees can discharge their duties, as they often did until 1961, by investing the whole fund in gilt-edged securities. Preservation of real values can be no more than an aspiration which some trustees may have the good fortune to achieve. Plainly they must have regard to the interests of those entitled in the future to capital and such regard will require them to take into consideration the potential effects of inflation, but a rule that real capital values must be maintained would be unfair to both income beneficiaries and trustees.

This brings me to the second principle on which there was general agreement, namely that the trustee must act fairly in making investment decisions which may have different consequences for different classes of beneficiaries. There are two reasons why I prefer this formulation to the traditional image of holding the scales equally between tenant for life and remainderman. The first is that the image of the scales suggests a weighing of known quantities whereas investment decisions are concerned with predictions of the future. Investments will carry current expectations of their future income yield and capital appreciation and these expectations will be reflected in their current market price, but there is always a greater or lesser risk that the outcome will deviate from those expectations. A judgment on the fairness of the choices made by the trustees must have regard to these imponderables. The second reason is that the image of the scales suggests a more mechanistic process than I believe the law requires. The trustees have in my judgment a wide discretion. They are for example entitled to take into account the income needs of the tenant for life or the fact that the tenant for life was a person known to the settlor and a primary object of the trust whereas the remainderman is a remoter relative or a stranger. Of course these cannot be allowed to become the overriding considerations but the concept of fairness between classes of beneficiaries does not require them to be excluded. It would be an inhuman law which required trustees to adhere to some mechanical rule for preserving the real value of the capital when the tenant for life was the testator's widow who had fallen upon hard times and the remainderman was young and well off.

14.3   The Trust Instrument

14.3.1   CONSTRUCTION OF TRUST INSTRUMENTS

RE HARARI'S SETTLEMENT TRUSTS [1949] 1 All ER 430, ChD

FACTS: In this case the trustees took out an originating summons to determine the proper construction to be placed upon an investment clause contained in the settlement of which they were trustees. The clause was in the following terms:

> The trustees shall hold the said investments so transferred to them as aforesaid upon trust that they may either allow the same to remain in their present state of investment so long as the trustees may think fit or may at any time or times with the consent of the daughter realise the said investments or any of them or any part thereof respectively and shall with the like consent invest the moneys produced thereby and also all capital moneys which may be or become subject to the trusts of this settlement in the names or under the control of the trustees in or upon such investments as to them may seem fit. . . .

HELD: The clause should not be restrictively construed, it should be given its natural meaning. Giving the words 'in or upon such investment as to them may seem fit' their true construction, it was clear that the trustees had power to invest in any investments which they honestly believed to be suitable, even if their chosen investment was not an investment of a type authorised by the general law.

JENKINS J: I have to decide whether, on the true construction of the few words in the settlement referring to investment, the trustees have an unrestricted discretion to invest in such investments as they think fit, whether they are or are not of a kind authorised by law for the investment of trust funds, or whether such discretion as they have should be construed as limited in its operation to the trustee range of investments.

The question turns primarily on the meaning to be attached to the words 'in or upon such investments as to them may seem fit.' *Prima facie* those words mean what they say—that the trustees are not to be limited in any way by any statutory range of investments, but can invest in any investment which they may select as seeming to them a fit one for the moneys subject to the trusts of the settlement. There is, however, a good deal of authority, which must be borne in mind, to the effect that investment clauses should be strictly construed and should not be construed as authorising investments outside the trustee range unless they clearly and unambiguously indicate an intention to that effect . . . it seems to me that I am left free to construe this settlement according to what I consider to be the natural and proper meaning of the words used in their context, and, so construing the words 'in or upon such investments as to them may seem fit,' I see no justification for implying any restriction. I think the trustees have power, under the plain meaning of those words, to invest in any investments which, to adopt Kekewich J's observation, they 'honestly think' are desirable investments for the investment of moneys subject to the trusts of the settlement. To hold otherwise would really be to read words into the settlement which are not there. . . .

Latham, A., 'Powers of Investment—A Gap between the Law and Practice?'
[1994] Nott LJ 95

III. EXPRESS INVESTMENT POWERS

A. Interpretation
The response to the criticisms of the [1961] Act has been to abandon entirely the scheme of investment prescribed by it. Instead, a power is inserted to invest 'with as much freedom as an absolute beneficial owner' or 'in all respects as if they were absolutely entitled beneficially to the money liable to be invested'. Barlow, King and King in *Wills, Administration and Taxation* conclude 'Because [the Act] provides for only a limited range of investments and because the rules on division make administration of the trust rather complicated it is usual for wills to confer on trustees an unfettered discretion in their choice of investment giving them the power to invest as though they were absolute beneficial owners'. It is the writer's contention that wording of this type confers powers that are far too wide for funds of an average size and for smaller trust funds. For good reasons the pendulum has swung away from the earlier practice of granting narrow investment powers to trustees—but it has swung too far in the direction of giving them no guidance at all as to what they should do.

What does the phrase to invest '. . . with as much freedom as an absolute beneficial owner' mean? The writer has not been able to find much authority. It is quoted but not much analysed in the textbooks. Should it be seen as a special power to invest under s. 3 of the Act or as excluding the Act altogether? It is usually treated as meaning the latter.

It is usually assumed that this wording is apt to by-pass the First Schedule to the Act (dealing with permissible types of investment) and ss. 2 to 4, requiring division of the fund, so that these provisions do not apply. It is also usually assumed that this wording does not exclude s. 6(1), which requires the trustees to diversify investments. The general opinion seems to be that this wording excludes the rest of s. 6, which requires trustees to take advice, but that they should do this anyway! The whole approach seems to be an object lesson on how to treat a statute selectively. . . .

14.3.2 EXTENSION OF INVESTMENT POWERS

TRUSTEES OF THE BRITISH MUSEUM v *ATTORNEY-GENERAL*
[1984] 1 All ER 337, ChD

FACTS: The trustees of the British Museum, a charity, applied to court for an extension of their investment powers. The question therefore arose whether the investment scheme set out in the 1961 Act was *prima facie* sufficient, or whether changes in the commercial environment and investment market meant that the provisions of the 1961 Act were now out of date.

HELD: In a large, well-supervised, well-advised trust such as the present, approval would be given for an investment scheme which went beyond the provisions of the 1961 Act, especially in view of the fact that the trust needed to raise funds in order to compete in an inflationary market for the purchase of museum exhibits. The decision in *Re Kolb's WT* should be interpreted in its historical context, coming, as it did, soon after the 1961 Act. *Re Kolb's WT* should not be followed, with the result that it would no longer be necessary to show 'special circumstances' in order to avoid the restrictions of the 1961 Act. 'General' economic changes since the 1961 Act would justify an enlargement of the investment powers in a case such as the present.

SIR ROBERT MEGARRY V-C: . . . The Act was passed on 3 August 1961; and in October of that year the first three cases that I have cited, *Kolb, Cooper* and *Porritt*, all fell for decision. In each case an application had been made, doubtless before the Act was passed, for an extension of the powers of investment. Each case seems to have been decided without either of the others being cited; but in each the judge (Cross, Buckley and Pennycuick JJ respectively) reached the same conclusion. In the words of Cross J in *Re Kolb's Will Trusts* [1961] 3 All ER 811 at 815:

> . . . the powers given by the [1961] Act must, I think, be taken to be prima facie sufficient and ought only to be extended if, on the particular facts, a special case for extending them can be made out. . . .

That was in 1961; and no doubt for some time that doctrine remained soundly based. However, in recent years the court, usually in chambers, has become ready to authorise extensions of the power of investment, often by an increased willingness to accept circumstances as being 'special'. . . .

1. In my judgment, the principle laid down in the line of cases headed by *Re Kolb's Will Trusts* [1961] 3 All ER 811 is one that should no longer be followed, since conditions have changed so greatly in the last 20 years. Though authoritative, those cases were authorities only rebus sic stantibus; and in 1983 they bind no longer. However, if Parliament acts on the recommendation of the Law Reform Committee and replaces the 1961 Act with revised powers of investment, the *Kolb* principle may well become applicable once more. Until then, the court should be ready to grant suitable applications for the extension of trustees' powers of investment, judging each application on its merits, and without being constrained by the provisions of the 1961 Act.

2. In determining what extended powers of investment should be conferred, there are many matters which will have to be considered. I shall refer to five, without in any way suggesting that this list is exhaustive, or that anything I say is intended to fetter the discretion that the court has to exercise in each case.

(i) The court is likely to give great weight to the width and efficacy of any provisions for advice and control. The wider the powers, the more important these provisions will be. An existing system of proven efficacy, as here, is likely to be especially cogent.

(ii) Where the powers are of great width, as in the present case, there is much to be said for some scheme of fractional division, confining part of the fund to relatively safe investments, and allowing the other part to be used for investments in which the greater risks will be offset by substantial prospects of a greater return. On the other hand, when the powers are appreciably less wide than they are in the present case, I would in general respectfully concur with the views expressed by the Law Reform Committee that no division of the fund into fractions should be required, and that the only division should be into investments which require advice and those which do not. Nevertheless, although a division of the fund into fractions should not be essential, there may well be cases where such a division may be of assistance in obtaining the approval of the court.

(iii) The width of the powers in the present scheme seems to me to be at or near the extreme limit for charitable funds. Without the fractional division of the fund and the assurance of effective control and advice I very much doubt whether such a scheme could have been approved. What the court has to judge is the combined effect of width, division, advice and control, which all interact, together with the standing of the trustees.

(iv)   The size of the fund in question may be very material. A fund that is very large may well justify a latitude of investment that would be denied to a more modest fund; for the spread of investments possible for a larger fund may justify the greater risks that wider powers will permit to be taken.

(v)   The object of the trust may be very material. In the present case, the desirability of having an increase of capital value which will make possible the purchase of desirable acquisitions for the museum despite soaring prices does something to justify the greater risks whereby capital appreciation may be obtained.

Since writing this judgment I have been referred to the very recent decision in *Mason v Farbrother* [1983] 2 All ER 1078; and counsel on both sides sent me a helpful joint note on the subject. Much of the judgment is directed to questions of jurisdiction and the details of the revised investment clause there under consideration. Of these matters I need say nothing. However, in considering whether the jurisdiction to approve the revised clause ought to be exercised, his Honour Judge Blackett-Ord, Vice-Chancellor of Lancaster, appears to have treated the *Kolb* line of cases as still being binding authorities, saying (as indeed is the case) that the rule was not absolute but applied in the absence of special circumstances. He then said (at 1086–1087) that 'the special circumstances in the present case are manifest: in a word, inflation since 1961'. He added that the trust in question was unusual in that it was not a private or family trust but a trust of a pension fund with perhaps something of a public element in it.

For my part, I would hesitate to describe inflation since 1961 as amounting to 'special circumstances'; it is, unhappily, a very general circumstance. With all respect, I can see little virtue (judicial comity and humility apart) in seeking to preserve the rule and yet establishing universal special circumstances that will engulf the rule. I do not, of course, know what arguments on this point were addressed to the court, but for the reasons that I have given I would prefer to say that the rule has gone, and with it any question of what circumstances are special. However, the ultimate result is much the same, and although the reasoning in the two cases differs, I am happy to think that there is this support for my conclusion in the present case.

STEEL AND OTHERS v WELLCOME CUSTODIAN TRUSTEES AND ANOTHER
[1988] 1 WLR 167, ChD

FACTS: The trustees of a large charitable trust (the value of the fund was approximately £3,200 million) applied to the court for an extension of their investment powers. They wished to be permitted to invest as if they were beneficial owners of the property, although subject to the requirement that investments should be made upon expert advice and subject to certain guidelines as to suitable investments.
HELD: The extension of investment powers was approved as asked.

HOFFMAN J: . . . For some time after the Trustee Investments Act 1961 the courts were reluctant to exercise that jurisdiction to confer wider investment powers on the ground that the Act was a recent parliamentary statement of what the prudence principle required and that in the absence of special circumstances the statutory powers should therefore suffice. In *Trustees of the British Museum* v *Attorney-General* [1984] 1 WLR 418 Sir Robert Megarry V-C decided that the Act of 1961 was now sufficiently in the past to cease casting any shadow over the court's jurisdiction to mould investment clauses in accordance with what appeared to satisfy the prudence principle at the present time and in the particular circumstances of the case.

Sir Robert Megarry V-C, at pp. 422–423, drew attention to several features of the case which are also present in the application before me. First, there was general evidence of changes in investment practice over the previous 20 years. Inflation had caused a general movement away from long-term investment in fixed interest securities and into equities and property. The abandonment of exchange control and fixed parities had made it possible and desirable to invest in the securities of various foreign countries and to hedge against currency losses. Small companies with specialist markets had grown faster than old established giants in sunset industries. New financial investments such as Eurobonds had been created. Evidence to much the same effect, updated to 1987, was contained in the affidavits before me. Secondly, the Vice-Chancellor drew attention to the relatively large size of the fund, which had a value of between £5 million and £6 million. The fund with which I am concerned is about 600 times as big. Thirdly, he was impressed by the expert advice available to the trustees from Lazard Securities Ltd and two distinguished unpaid investment advisers, as well as the eminent character of the trustees themselves. In this case the trustees propose to engage four professional fund managers each to manage a part of the fund, as well as a specialist firm to monitor and report on their performance.

It seems to me clear that the powers conferred [on the trustees in the present case] are hopelessly out of date. The only reason why the present application was not forced on the trustees at a much earlier date is because, until the Wellcome Plc flotation, only a relatively tiny part of the value of the fund was subject to those investment powers,. The requirement that a third of the fund must be in fixed interest securities is unnecessarily restrictive and the provision for determining the proportions from time to time is both administratively cumbersome and a penalty on success. . . . The Attorney-General therefore accepts that the investment powers must be recast. . . .

There is also a particular feature of this case which makes it desirable to avoid any restriction upon the discretion of the trustees. As I have mentioned, about 90 per cent. of the fund is invested in Wellcome Plc and is likely to remain so invested for some time to come. The object of the sale and flotation of Wellcome stock was to enable the trustees to diversify some of their holding. It seems to me important that in dealing with the remaining 10 per cent., the trustees should have as much flexibility as possible. In respect of this part of the fund, the trustees should be left to apply the prudence principle at a fairly high level of abstraction, with the safeguards entrusted to the provisions for expert advice in accordance with the guidelines of the scheme rather than confining them to fixed categories of authorised investments.

Having regard therefore to the size of this fund, the eminence of the trustees, the provisions of the scheme for obtaining and acting on advice and the quality of advice available, as well as the special circumstances pertaining to the large holding in the shares of a single company, I am willing to approve the present scheme without any restriction on the kind of assets in which all or any of the fund may be invested. . . .

14.3.3   OVER-CAUTIOUS INVESTMENT?

NESTLE v NATIONAL WESTMINSTER BANK PLC [1993] 1 WLR 1260, CA

FACTS: A testator died in 1922 leaving a fund worth approximately £54,000 on trust for various descendants. The plaintiff, the testator's only granddaughter, became solely and absolutely entitled to the fund in 1986, at which time it was valued at approximately £270,000. She claimed that with proper investment the present value of the fund should have been more than 1m.
HELD: The bank had misinterpreted the powers of investment granted to it by the terms of the will trust and should have taken legal advice as to them. The bank should also have made regular reviews of the investments under its control. However, the plaintiff had failed to show that the bank's breaches of duty had resulted in a loss to the fund and on that basis the appeal was dismissed.

DILLON LJ: . . . It was the duty of the bank to acquaint itself with the scope of its powers under the will. . . . It is inexcusable that the bank took no step at any time to obtain legal advice as to the scope of its power to invest in ordinary shares. Instead the bank administered the trusts, until the enactment of the Trustee Investments Act 1961, on the basis that while it could continue to retain ordinary shares which had been held by the testator at the date of his death, the power it had to invest in further ordinary shares was limited to investment in further ordinary shares in the companies in which it still retained ordinary shares which had been held by the testator at the date of his death, or ordinary shares in 'similar companies' e.g. ordinary shares in a further insurance company at a time when the bank still retained insurance shares which the testator had held at his death.

After the enactment of the Trustee Investments Act 1961, the bank erroneously assumed that its powers of investment were wholly governed by that Act.

On 25 November 1959 an official of the bank told John Nestle, in a spuriously knowledgable way, that this seemed to the bank to be a case where the bank should apply to the court under the Variation of Trusts Act 1958 for a widening of its investment powers. But again nothing was ever done, and no advice as to the scope of the bank's investment powers was ever sought. . . .

The bank should, in my judgment, have appreciated the true scope of its powers of investment and should have reviewed the investments in the annuity fund regularly (if not necessarily strictly annually) with that in mind.

Mr Lyndon-Stanford submits that, if the bank had done that, the equities would have been diversified and the equities in the annuity fund in 1960 would have been substantially higher in value by 1960 than they actually were. . . .

The difficulty about that approach is however, as Hoffmann J pointed out, that the evidence showed that if the BZW Equity Index was applied over the period from July 1974 to December 1986 to 'growth' unit trusts (as opposed to 'income' unit trusts) it appeared that 12 of the 'growth' trusts had done better than the index, but 21 had done worse. It is impossible to say that those 21 unit trusts must have been managed with a degree of incompetence which, in a trustee like the bank, would have amounted to a breach of trust. . . .

Mr Nugee for the bank rightly stressed the duty of a trustee to act prudently.

. . . This principle remains applicable however wide, or even unlimited, the scope of the investment clause in a trust instrument may be. Trustees should not be reckless with trust money. But what the prudent man should do at any time depends on the economic and financial conditions of that time—not on what judges of the past, however eminent, have held to be the prudent course in the conditions of 50 or 100 years before. It has seemed to me that Mr Nugee's submissions placed far too much weight on the actual decisions of the courts in the last century, when investment conditions were very different. Indeed Mr Nugee's submissions accorded scant justice to such common sense and initiative as his client the bank actually displayed in the management of the Nestle trust funds.

If what had happened in the present case had been that the bank, through failure to inform itself as to the true scope of its investment powers, had invested the whole of the annuity fund in fixed interest securities, and no part in equities, for the whole period from 1922 to 1960, then, as on the evidence loss would clearly have been proved to have been suffered, the appropriate course would have been to require the bank to make good to the trust fair compensation—and not just the minimum that might have got by without challenge. . . .

The case for the plaintiff in the court below seems largely to have been founded on the BZW Equity Index and the opinions of her expert witnesses, as against the opinion of the bank's expert witnesses, on the desirability or prudence of investment in equities at various stages between 1922 and 1986. On that controversy the judge made his findings, and those findings have not really been challenged on this appeal. Mr Lyndon-Stanford has concentrated instead on the practicalities of what the bank was actually doing, or failing to do, with the trust funds, rather than on the expert evidence. Mr Lyndon-Stanford has put his case with very considerable skill, and there is at the end of the day not much for the bank to be proud of in its administration of the Nestle trusts . . . But I am unable to see that any breach of trust which has caused loss to the plaintiff has been proved. Accordingly this appeal must, in my judgment, be dismissed.

STAUGHTON LJ: . . . the misunderstanding of the investment clause and the failure to conduct periodic reviews do not by themselves, whether separately or together, afford the plaintiff a remedy. They were symptoms of incompetence or idleness—not on the part of National Westminster Bank but of their predecessors; they were not, without more, breaches of trust. The plaintiff must show that, through one or other or both of those causes, the trustees made decisions which they should not have made or failed to make decisions which they should have made. If that were proved, and if at first sight loss resulted, it would be appropriate to order an inquiry as to the loss suffered by the trust fund.

. . . I would dismiss the appeal. The judge took the view that 'the bank had acted conscientiously, fairly and carefully throughout the administration of [the] trust.' I cannot join in that accolade. But it is not shown that there was loss arising from a breach of trust for which the trustees ought to compensate the trust fund.

LEGGATT LJ: . . . A breach of duty will not be actionable, and therefore will be immaterial, if it does not cause loss. In this context I would endorse the concession of Mr Nugee for the bank that 'loss' will be incurred by a trust fund when it makes a gain less than would have been made by a prudent businessman. A claimant will therefore fail who cannot prove a loss in this sense caused by breach of duty. So here in order to make a case for an inquiry, the plaintiff must show that loss was caused by breach of duty on the part of the bank. . . . it does not follow from the fact that a wider power of investment was available to the bank than it realised either that it would have been exercised or that, if it had been, the exercise of it would have produced a result more beneficial to the bank than actually was produced. Loss cannot be presumed, if none would necessarily have resulted. Until it was proved that there was a loss, no attempt could be made to assess the amount of it. . . .

No testator, in the light of this example, would choose this bank for the effective management of his investment. But the bank's engagement was as a trustee; and as such, it is to be judged not so much by success as by absence of proven default. The importance of preservation of a trust fund will always outweigh success in its advancement. Inevitably, a trustee in the bank's position wears a complacent air, because the virtue of safety will in practice put a premium on inactivity. Until the 1950s active management of the portfolio might have been seen as speculative, and even in these days such dealing would have to be notably successful before the expense would be justified. The very process of attempting to achieve a balance, or (if that be old-fashioned) fairness, as between the interests of life-tenants and those of a remainderman inevitably means that each can complain of being less well served than he or she ought to have been. But by the undemanding standard of prudence the bank is not shown to have committed any breach of trust resulting in loss.

I am therefore constrained to agree that the appeal must be dismissed.

14.4 Proposals for Reform

Law Reform Committee 23rd Report 'The Powers and Duties of Trustees' (1982 Cmnd 8733) paras 9.1 II 6–10

(a) *Investment in Land*

6. Trustees' powers to purchase freehold and leasehold land should be widened as follows:—

    (i)   all trustees should have the power to buy freehold property as an investment, subject to their first obtaining favourable professional advice;

    (ii)   all trustees should be empowered to invest in leasehold land, provided that appropriate advice is taken;

    (iii) the absolute prohibition on the purchase of leaseholds with less than sixty years to run should be removed;

    (iv)   the decision in *Re Power* [1947] Ch 572, should be reversed and a new statutory power introduced enabling trustees to purchase a residence for occupation by the person entitled to the income on the moneys laid out in the purchase or eligible to have it applied for his benefit;

7. Trustees should be empowered to make purchases under recommendation 6(iv) above on mortgage.

8. Trustees' powers to invest in mortgages should be widened so as to permit them to invest in second mortgages.

9. The 10 year limit on the exercise of options should be abolished and trustees should be empowered to stipulate that the purchase price may be calculated by reference to the market value of the property at the time of the exercise of the option.

(b) *The Trustee Investments Act 1961*

10.   The statutory powers contained in the Trustee Investments Act 1961 are out of date and ought now to be revised. We recommend that the 1961 Act be repealed and the following new powers be conferred upon trustees:—

(i)   investments should be divided into those which can be made without advice and those which can be made only with advice;

(ii)   the former category should comprise those investments presently known as narrower-range securities and listed in Parts I and II of the 1961 Act and also unit trusts and investment trusts, as defined in section 359 of the Income and Corporation Taxes Act 1970;

(iii)   the latter category should comprise any other investment quoted on the English Stock Exchange;

(iv)   trustees should be free to invest in such proportions as they choose;

(v)   the provisions on advice presently contained in section 6 of the 1961 Act should be retained;

(vi)   express reference should be made in the new statutory provision to the duty of trustees to maintain a balance between income and capital so as to protect all those interested under the trust fund;

(vii)   the requirement in section 6(1)(a) of the 1961 Act which compels trustees to have regard to the need for diversification of investments in so far as is appropriate to the circumstances of the trust is sufficient and further restrictions on the trustees' discretion are not required;

(viii)   investments in foreign securities should not be made unless expressly authorised by the trust instrument;

(ix)   trustees should continue to be able to apply to the court under section 57 of the Trustee Act 1925 to make otherwise unauthorised investments;

(x)   additionally, since section 57 is concerned only with the authorisation of specific dealings trustees should be entitled to make an application under the Variation of Trusts Act 1958 to ask the court to widen their investment powers generally.

Law Commission Consultation Paper No. 146, Trustee Powers and Duties, 1997

. . .

2.4   In May 1996, HM Treasury issued a Consultation Document in which it was proposed to repeal the Trustee Investments Act 1961 under the provisions of the Deregulation and Contracting Out Act 1994 and to give trustees the same investment powers as beneficial owners. Instead of safeguarding beneficiaries by restricting the range of investments that trustees could make, their protection would lie in the duty of the trustees . . . to act in the best interests of the trust. An essential element in fulfilling that duty in relation to a trust of any size would in practice have been the obtaining of investment or management advice. Of the 146 respondents to the Consultation Document, all but two supported the essentials of the proposed scheme.

2.5   In February 1997, a draft Order under the Deregulation and Contracting Out Act 1994 was laid before Parliament. It transpired that it was not possible under the terms of that Act to implement all of the proposals contained in the Consultation Document. Instead of repealing the Trustee Investments Act 1961, the draft Order contained provisions for its amendment. In essence, the effect of the draft Order would have been—

(1)   to abolish the requirement that trustees should split the fund into two parts if they wished to invest in wider range investments, such as shares;

(2)   to make the obligations to take advice less onerous; and

(3)   to remove some of the restrictions which had the effect of excluding certain investments from the list of those which would otherwise have been authorised for trustees.

The draft Deregulation Order was to be supplemented by an Order made under section 12 of the Trustee Investment Act 1961, extending the range of authorised trustee investments.

2.6   As a result of the dissolution of Parliament for the General Election, the Deregulation Order did not complete its passage and was lost. However, the Deregulation Committee of the House of Commons urged HM Treasury 'to bring this measure forward as early as possible in the new Parliament'. . . .

2.7   The main impact of the changes proposed in the draft Deregulation Order, if they are implemented, will be felt primarily in relation to—

    (1)   trusts arising under home-drawn wills;
    (2)   cases of intestacy; and
    (3)   trusts that either pre-date the 1961 Act or were created shortly after its enactment.

As regards professionally drawn trust instruments and wills, it has been the normal practice for many years to include powers which enable trustees to invest as if they were beneficial owners. If the proposals contained in the draft Deregulation Order are eventually implemented, virtually all trustees would enjoy substantially wider investment powers either by express provision in the trust deed or by law. Given that the range and sophistication of investments is now such as to be beyond the knowledge and abilities of most non-professional trustees, it is of the greatest importance that trustees have the necessary powers to manage their portfolios effectively . . .

14.5   End of Chapter Assessment Question

Steve and Jane are trustees of a £300,000 cash fund for the benefit of their sister Joanne for her life, remainder to her sons Mark and Peter. Joanne is a widow and her only source of income is the trust.

The trust instrument states that the trustees may invest up to a quarter of the fund in any investments which they consider suitable.

Steve and Jane propose to purchase a freehold premise for Joanne to live in. The freehold is valued at £50,000. They also propose to put aside £10,000 for investment in Chelsea porcelain figurines, as Jane collects these, and £10,000 to put into the next government privatisation issue which one of Steve's friends says is going to be 'a winner'. The remainder is to be put in a bank account.

Advise Steve and Jane on the proposed investments.

14.6   End of Chapter Assessment Outline Answer

Steve and Jane have been authorised to invest up to a quarter of the £300,000 fund in any investments which they consider suitable. It follows that the restrictive provisions of the Trustee Investments Act 1961 have been excluded as regards £75,000 of the fund. The basic scheme of the Act requires that at least one quarter of the trust fund should be invested in narrow range investments (typically very safe), and up to three quarters of the fund may be invested in wider range investments (including shares in certain highly secure UK listed companies). In the present case the £75,000 which is authorised to be invested outside the general scheme of the Act is said to form the 'Special Range'. Special range property can be bought with monies taken from the narrow and/or the wider range.

Steve and Jane have invested £70,000 in specific investments and have deposited the remaining £230,000 in a bank account. Not one of the £70,000 worth of investments is authorised within the general scheme of the Act, and must be assumed to have been made with the £75,000 special range fund. However, 'special range' investments, although they stand outside the restrictions of the narrow range and the wider range, must nevertheless fall within the legal definition of an 'investment' and must be made according to the trustees' usual standard of care. With these requirements in mind we now turn to examine each of the investments in turn.

First, the investment in the freehold property for Joanne to live in. In *Re Power* Jenkins J pointed out that 'there is a distinction between purchasing freehold property for the income one is going to get from it and purchasing freehold property for the sake of occupying it'. He held that the latter would not be an 'investment' because it would not yield income. In a similar vein Buckley J has stated that 'property which is acquired merely for use and enjoyment is not an investment' (*Re Peczenik's Settlement*). Steve and Jane should be advised not to purchase a freehold for Joanne to live in. They could, however, invest in a freehold with a view to letting it out and paying the rent to Joanne in the form of income. The artificiality and circularity of this arrangement shows that the law is in need of reform. Indeed, the Law Reform Committee and the Law Commission have proposed that the rule in *Re Power* should be abolished.

The purchase of the Chelsea porcelain figurines also appears to fail the judicial definition of 'investment'. It might be different were they displayed to fee-paying visitors, or used to furnish a rented apartment, because in such a case they would be producing income. Jane might well be able to show that the trust would benefit from an appreciation in the capital value of the figurines, but capital appreciation does not yet qualify property as an 'investment' within the judicial definition. (Except, see Nicholls VC in *Harries* where he talks of the need for charity trustees to balance income against *capital* growth.)

The purchase of £10,000 worth of shares in the next government privatisation would not be authorised under the 1961 Act (the Act restricts investment to listed companies which have declared a dividend in each of the last five years), but the shares would be a valid investment within the 'special range'. Having said that, the trustees should be advised that they are still under a duty to 'obtain and consider' proper written advice as to the suitability of a particular investment (Trustee Investments Act 1961, s. 6). In *Cowan* v *Scargill* [1985] 1 Ch 270 Megarry VC stated that the duty to take advice was part of the trustees' general duty to act as an ordinary prudent person of business. Accordingly, Steve and Jane should not rely upon the casual advice of Steve's friend.

Finally, the deposit of the residue in a bank account. *Prima facie* there is nothing objectionable in such an investment, particularly as many types of bank account fall within the 'narrow range' of investments authorised by the Act. However, the Trustee Investment Act imposes upon the trustees a duty to diversify the investments (s. 6(1)). Again, this is part of the trustees' general duty to act with prudence. It might be argued that £230,000, representing the vast majority of the fund, should not be left in a single bank account. In recent years we have seen all too clearly that banks are not immune from financial collapse. Steve and Jane should be advised to divide the remainder into two unconnected banks. They should be wary, however, of over-diversification as this will lead to increased banking charges and administration expenses. It might be thought that the duty to act prudently would require the trustees to invest a large part of the £230,000 in wider range investments, as these have the potential to yield higher rates of income, but Steve and Jane should be advised that their first duty is caution. In *Nestle* v *National Westminster Bank plc* [1993] 1 WLR 1260, Leggatt LJ stated that a trustee is to be judged 'not so much by success as by absence of proven default' and that 'the importance of preservation of a trust fund will always outweigh success in its advancement'.

CHAPTER FIFTEEN

BREACH OF TRUST: DEFENCES AND RELIEF

15.1 Beneficiaries' Remedies

15.1.1 ELECTION BETWEEN INCONSISTENT REMEDIES

TANG MAN SIT (DECD) (PERSONAL REPRESENTATIVE) v *CAPACIOUS INVESTMENTS LTD* [1996] 1 All ER 193, PC

FACTS: Mr Tang, the owner of land, was party to a joint venture for the building of houses on the land. He agreed to assign some of the houses to the plaintiff after completion of the building works. No assignment was made. Instead, Mr Tang let out the houses as homes for the elderly without the plaintiff's knowledge or approval. The plaintiff's claim was, on the one hand, for damages for loss of use and occupation and diminution of the value of the property due to wrongful use and occupation, and on the other hand for an account of unauthorised profits and for compensation for breach of trust.

HELD: The two sides of the plaintiff's claim were mutually exclusive, and the plaintiff would have to elect between the two remedies.

LORD NICHOLLS OF BIRKENHEAD: . . . The law frequently affords an injured person more than one remedy for the wrong he has suffered. Sometimes the two remedies are alternative and inconsistent. The classic example, indeed, is (1) an account of the profits made by a defendant in breach of his fiduciary obligations and (2) damages for the loss suffered by the plaintiff by reason of the same breach. The former is measured by the wrongdoer's gain, the latter by the injured party's loss. . . .

Alternative remedies
Faced with alternative and inconsistent remedies a plaintiff must choose, or elect, between them. He cannot have both. The basic principle governing when a plaintiff must make his choice is simple and clear. He is required to choose when, but not before, judgment is given in his favour and the judge is asked to make orders against the defendant. A plaintiff is not required to make his choice when he launches his proceedings. He may claim one remedy initially, and then by amendment of his writ and his pleadings abandon that claim in favour of the other. He may claim both remedies, as alternatives. But he must make up his mind when judgment is being entered against the defendant. Court orders are intended to be obeyed. In the nature of things, therefore, the court should not make orders which would afford a plaintiff both of two alternative remedies.

In the ordinary course, by the time the trial is concluded a plaintiff will know which remedy is more advantageous to him. By then, if not before, he will know enough of the facts to assess where his best interests lie. There will be nothing unfair in requiring him to elect at that stage. Occasionally this may not be so. This is more likely to happen when the judgment is a default judgment or a summary judgment than at the conclusion of a trial. A plaintiff may not know how much money the defendant has made from the wrongful use of his property. It may be unreasonable to require the plaintiff to make his choice without further information. To meet this difficulty, the court may make discovery and other orders designed to give the plaintiff the information he needs, and which in fairness he ought to have, before deciding upon his remedy.

In the ordinary course the decision made when judgment is entered is made once and for all. That is the normal rule. The order is a final order, and the interests of the parties and the public interest alike dictate that there should be finality. The principle, however, is not rigid and unbending. Like all procedural principles, the established principles regarding election between alternative remedies are not fixed and unyielding rules. These principles are the means to an end, not the end in themselves. They are no more than particular applications of a general and overriding principle governing the conduct of legal proceedings, namely that proceedings should be conducted in a manner which strikes a fair and reasonable balance between the interests of the parties, having proper regard also to the wider public interest in the conduct of court proceedings. Thus in *Johnson* v *Agnew* [1979] 1 All ER 883 the House of Lords held that when specific performance fails to be realised, an order for specific performance may subsequently be discharged and an inquiry as to damages ordered. Lord Wilberforce observed ([1979] 1 All ER 883 at 894): 'Election, though the subject of much learning and refinement, is in the end a doctrine based on simple considerations of common sense and equity.' . . .

15.1.2 CAPITAL REPAYMENT

TARGET HOLDINGS LTD v *REDFERNS (A FIRM) AND ANOTHER* [1995] 3 All ER 785

FACTS: The defendants were a firm of solicitors acting on behalf of a mortagor (an established client) and a mortgagee on the creation of a mortgage. The defendants held the loan monies on trust for the mortgagee, but paid them over to the mortgagor before the mortgage had been completed. This was in breach of trust. The mortgagee sued the firm of solicitors. In their defence the solicitors argued that they had committed only a technical breach of trust and that the plaintiff had not suffered any loss because the solicitors had acquired the mortgages to which the plaintiffs were entitled.
HELD: The Court of Appeal had held that when the 'trustees' (solicitors) had paid away the 'trust' monies to the stranger (mortgagor) they came under a duty to reinstate the trust fund immediately. An inquiry into whether the breach of trust actually *caused* loss to the trust fund was unnecessary; the causal connection being obvious. The defendants appealed to the House of Lords. Appeal allowed.

LORD BROWNE-WILKINSON: My Lords, this appeal raises a novel point on the liability of a trustee who commits a breach of trust to compensate beneficiaries for such breach. Is the trustee liable to compensate the beneficiary not only for losses caused by the breach but also for losses which the beneficiary would, in any event, have suffered even if there had been no such breach? . . .
. . . the decision of the Court of Appeal in this case can only be maintained on the basis that, even if there is no causal link between the breach of trust and the actual loss eventually suffered by Target (i.e. the sum advanced less the sum recovered) the trustee in breach is liable to bear (at least in part) the loss suffered by Target.

The transaction in the present case is redolent of fraud and negligence. But, in considering the principles involved, suspicions of such wrongdoing must be put on one side. If the law as stated by the Court of Appeal is correct, it applies to cases where the breach of trust involves no suspicion of fraud or negligence. For example, say an advance is made by a lender to an honest borrower in reliance on an entirely honest and accurate valuation. The sum to be advanced is paid into the client account of the lender's solicitors. Due to an honest and non-negligent error (e.g. an unforeseeable failure in the solicitors' computer) the moneys in client account are transferred by the solicitors to the borrower one day before the mortgage is executed. That is a breach of trust. Then the property market collapses and when the lender realises his security by sale he recovers only half the sum advanced. As I understand the Court of Appeal decision, the solicitors would bear the loss flowing from the collapse in the market value: subject to the court's discretionary power to relieve a trustee from liability under s. 61 of the Trustee Act 1925, the solicitors would be bound to repay the total amount wrongly paid out of the client account in breach of trust receiving credit only for the sum received on the sale of the security.

To my mind in the case of an unimpeachable transaction this would be an unjust and surprising conclusion. At common law there are two principles fundamental to the award of damages. First, that the defendant's wrongful act must cause the damage complained of. Second, that the plaintiff is to be put 'in the same position as he would have been in if he had not sustained the wrong for which he is now getting his compensation or reparation' (see *Livingstone* v *Rawyards Coal Co.* (1880) 5 App Cas 25 at 39 *per* Lord Blackburn). Although, as will appear, in many ways equity approaches liability for making good a breach of trust from a different starting point, in my judgment those two principles are applicable as much in equity as at common law. Under both systems liability is fault based: the defendant is only liable for the consequences of the legal wrong he has done to the plaintiff and to make good the damage caused by such wrong. He is not responsible for damage not caused by his wrong or to pay by way of compensation more than the loss suffered from such wrong. The detailed rules of equity as to causation and the quantification of loss differ, at least ostensibly, from those applicable at common law. But the principles underlying both systems are the same. On the assumptions that had to be made in the present case until the factual issues are resolved (i.e. that the transaction would have gone through even if there had been no breach of trust), the result reached by the Court of Appeal does not accord with those principles. Redferns as trustees have been held liable to compensate Target for a loss caused otherwise than by the breach of trust. I approach the consideration of the relevant rules of equity with a strong predisposition against such a conclusion. . . .

. . . The basic right of a beneficiary is to have the trust duly administered in accordance with the provisions of the trust instrument, if any, and the general law. Thus, in relation to a traditional trust where the fund is held in trust for a number of beneficiaries having different, usually successive, equitable interests, (e.g. A for life with remainder to B), the right of each beneficiary is to have the whole fund vested in the trustees so as to be available to satisfy his equitable interest when, and if, it falls into possession. Accordingly, in the case of a breach of such a trust involving the wrongful paying away of trust assests, the liability of the trustee is to restore to the trust fund, often called 'the trust estate', what ought to have been there.

The equitable rules of compensation for breach of trust have been largely developed in relation to such traditional trusts, where the only way in which all the beneficiaries' rights can be protected is to restore to the trust fund what ought to be there. In such a case the basic rule is that a trustee in breach of trust must restore or pay to the trust estate either the assets which have been lost to the estate by reason of the breach or compensation for such loss. Courts of Equity did not award damages but, acting in personam, ordered the defaulting trustee to restore the trust estate (see *Nocton* v *Lord Ashburton* [1914] AC 932 at 952, 958, *per* Viscount Haldane LC). If specific restitution of the trust property is not possible, then the liability of the trustee is to pay sufficient compensation to the trust estate to put it back to what it would have been had the breach not been committed (see *Caffrey* v *Darby* (1801) 6 Ves 488 and *Clough* v *Bond* (1838) 3 My & Cr 490). Even if the immediate cause of the loss is the dishonesty or failure of a third party, the trustee is liable to make good that loss to the trust estate if, but for the breach, such loss would not have occurred (see Underhill and Hayton *Law of Trusts and Trustees* (14th edn, 1987) pp. 734–736, *Re Dawson (decd), Union Fidelity Trustee Co. Ltd* v *Perpetual Trustee Co. Ltd* [1966] 2 NSWR 211 and *Bartlett* v *Barclays Bank Trust Co. Ltd (No. 2)* [1980] 2 All ER 92). Thus the common law rules of remoteness of damage and causation do not apply. However, there does have to be some causal connection between the breach of trust and the loss to the trust estate for which compensation is recoverable, viz the fact that the loss would not have occurred but for the breach (see also *Re Miller's Deed Trusts* (1978) 75 LS Gaz 454 and *Nestle* v *National Westminster Bank plc* [1994] 1 All ER 118).

Hitherto I have been considering the rights of beneficiaries under traditional trusts where the trusts are still subsisting and therefore the right of each beneficiary, and his only right, is to have the trust fund reconstituted as it should be. But what if at the time of the action claiming compensation for breach of trust those trusts have come to an end? Take as an example again the trust for A for life with remainder to B. During A's lifetime B's only right is to have the trust duly administered and, in the event of a breach, to have the trust fund restored. AfterA's death, B becomes absolutely entitled. He of course has the right to have the trust assets retained by the trustees until they have fully accounted for them to him. But if the trustees commit a breach of trust, there is no reason for compensating the breach of trust by way of an order for restitution and compensation *to the trust fund* as opposed to the beneficiary himself. The beneficiary's right is no longer simply to have the trust duly administered: he is, in equity, the sole owner of the trust estate. Nor, for the same reason, is restitution to the trust fund necessary to protect other beneficiaries. Therefore, although I do not wholly rule out the possibility that even in those circumstances an order to reconstitute the fund may be appropriate, in the ordinary case where a beneficiary becomes absolutely entitled to the trust fund the court orders, not restitution to the trust estate, but the payment of compensation directly to the beneficiary. The measure of such compensation is the same, ie the difference between what the beneficiary has in fact received and the amount he would have received but for the breach of trust. . . .

For these reasons I reach the conclusion that, on the facts which must currently be assumed, Target has not demonstrated that it is entitled to any compensation for breach of trust. Assuming that moneys would have been forthcoming from some other source to complete the purchase from Mirage if the moneys had not been wrongly provided by Redferns in breach of trust, Target obtained exactly what it would have obtained had no breach occurred, i.e. a valid security for the sum advanced. Therefore, on the assumption made, Target has suffered no compensatable loss. Redferns are entitled to leave to defend the breach of trust claim. . . .

SWINDLE v HARRISON [1997] 4 All ER 705

FACTS: In June 1991, in order to finance the purchase of a hotel intended to be run as a family restaurant business, the second defendant, H, borrowed £80,000 from NHL on the security of a mortgage of her house. A further substantial sum was required to pay the balance of the purchase price and, on the basis that that could be raised by a loan from a brewery, H instructed her solicitor, S. to exchange contracts for the purchase of the hotel. In the event, the brewery loan was not received and in 1994 S's firm issued proceedings against the defendants claiming possession of the hotel. H counterclaimed for, inter alia, breach of fiduciary duty and sought to recover as damages or equitable compensation the value of the equity she had formerly held in her house.

HELD: In order to recover compensation for breach of fiduciary duty, a plaintiff had to show that the loss he had suffered had been caused by the defendant's breach of duty. Furthermore, (per Evans LJ) unless the breach could properly be regarded as the equivalent of fraud, he was not entitled to be placed financially in the same position as he was in before the breach occurred but only in the same position as he would have been in if the breach of duty had not occurred. In the instant case, there had been no allegation or finding that the breach of fiduciary duty was the equivalent of fraud. Moreover, the loss suffered by H did not flow from the plaintiffs' breach of fiduciary duty in relation to their loan, but from her own decision to take the risk involved in mortgaging her home, since she would have accepted the loan and completed the purchase of the hotel even if full disclosure had been made. It followed that she would have lost the value of the equity in her home in any event and therefore that that loss was not recoverable. Accordingly, the appeal would be dismissed.

EVANS LJ: When the breach of duty falls within the rather wider category of inequitable conduct which equity regards as fraud, then the defendant's liability in damages is measured in the same way as if fraud was proved at common law. He is liable to restore the plaintiff to the situation he was in when the defendant did him wrong. . . .

The authorities . . . show, in my judgment, that what I have called the stringent rule of causation or measure of damages does not apply as regards breaches of equitable duties unless the breach can properly be regarded as the equivalent of fraud. In other cases the plaintiff is entitled to be placed in the same position financially as he would have been in if the breach of duty had not occurred—not necessarily the same as he was in before it occurred.

These propositions seem to me to be established by *Bristol and West Building Society* v *Mothew (t/a Stapley & Co.)* [1996] 4 All ER 698. The defendant had not breached his duties of loyalty and fidelity to his principal and so he could not be held to be liable for losses suffered as the result of entering into the transaction, as distinct from the consequences of the particular breach. Those were likely to be minimal (because, in short, the principal would have made the mortgage loan in any event) and they did not include the intervening market loss. . . .

It is also consistent, in my judgment, with the House of Lords decision in *Target Holdings Ltd* v *Redferns (a firm)* [1995] 3 All ER 785. The defendants had committed a breach of trust, but the default was remedied and therefore they were not liable to 'reconstitute the fund'. They remained liable to pay compensation, but the amount had to be assessed at the date of judgment rather than the date of breach. The plaintiffs had obtained precisely what they would have acquired had no breach occurred, and therefore they appeared to have suffered no compensatable loss.

BRISTOL AND WEST BUILDING SOCIETY v MOTHEW [1998] 1 Ch 1

For the facts and decision, see **11.1**.

MILLETT LJ: . . . Although the remedy which equity makes available for breach of the equitable duty of skill and care is equitable compensation rather than damages, this is merely the product of history and in this context is in my opinion a distinction without a difference. Equitable compensation for breach of the duty of skill and care resembles common law damages in that it is awarded by way of compensation to the plaintiff for his loss. There is no reason in principle why the common law rules of causation, remoteness of damage and measure of damages should not be applied by analogy in such a case. It should not be confused with equitable compensation for breach of fiduciary duty, which may be awarded in lieu of rescission or specific restitution. . . .

15.1.3 INTEREST ON THE JUDGMENT

WESTDEUTSCHE LANDESBANK GIROZENTRALE v ISLINGTON LBC
[1996] 2 WLR 802, HL

For the facts and decision, see **16.1**.

LORD BROWNE-WILKINSON . . .

Compound interest in equity
It is common ground that in the absence of agreement or custom the court has no jurisdiction to award compound interest either at law or under s. 35A of the Supreme Court Act 1981. It is also common ground that in certain limited circumstances courts of equity can award compound interest. . . .

In the absence of fraud courts of equity have never awarded compound interest except against a trustee or other person owing fiduciary duties who is accountable for profits made from his position. Equity awarded simple interest at a time when courts of law had no right under common law or statute to award any interest. The award of compound interest was restricted to cases where the award was in lieu of an account of profits improperly made by the trustee. We were not referred to any case where, compound interest had been awarded in the absence of fiduciary accountability for a profit. The principle is clearly stated by Lord Hatherley LC in *Burdick* v *Garrick* LR 5 Ch App 233, 241:

the court does not proceed against an accounting party by way of punishing him for making use of the plaintiff's money by directing rests, or payment of compound interest, but proceeds upon this principle, either that he has made, or has put himself into such a position as that he is to be presumed to have made, 5 per cent., or compound interest, as the case may be.

The principle was more fully stated by Buckley LJ in *Wallersteiner v Moir (No. 2)* [1975] QB 373, 397:

> Where a trustee has retained trust money in his own hands, he will be accountable for the profit which he has made or which he is assumed to have made from the use of the money. In *Attorney-General v Alford* 4 De GM & G 843, 851 Lord Cranworth LC said: 'What the court ought to do, I think, is to charge him only with the interest which he has received, or which it is justly entitled to say he ought to have received, or which it is so fairly to be presumed that he did receive that he is estopped from saying that he did not receive it.' This is an application of the doctrine that the court will not allow a trustee to make any profit from his trust. The defaulting trustee is normally charged with simple interest only, but if it is established that he has used the money in trade he may be charged compound interest. . . . The justification for charging compound interest normally lies in the fact that profits earned in trade would be likely to be used as working capital for earning further profits. Precisely similar equitable principles apply to an agent who has retained moneys of his principal in his hands and used them for his own purposes: *Burdick v Garrick.*

See also *Bartlett* (**11.2.2**) and *O'Sullivan* (**12.1.1.2**).

15.1.4   IS LIABILITY NET OF TAX?

See *O'Sullivan* (**12.1.1.2**).

15.2   Defences

15.2.1   LIMITATION ACT 1980

LIMITATION ACT 1980

21.   Time limit for actions in respect of trust property
   (1)   No period of limitation prescribed by this Act shall apply to an action by a beneficiary under a trust, being an action—
   (a)   in respect of any fraud or fraudulent breach of trust to which the trustee was a party or privy; or
   (b)   to recover from the trustee property or the proceeds of trust property in the possession of the trustee, or previously received by the trustee and converted to his use.
   (2)   Where a trustee who is also a beneficiary under the trust receives or retains trust property or its proceeds as his share on a distribution of trust property under the trust, his liability in any action brought by virtue of subsection (1)(b) above to recover that property or its proceeds after the expiration of the period of limitation prescribed by this Act for bringing an action to recover trust property shall be limited to the excess over his proper share.
   This subsection only applies if the trustee acted honestly and reasonably in making the distribution.
   (3)   Subject to the preceding provisions of this section, an action by a beneficiary to recover trust property or in respect of any breach of trust, not being an action for which a period of limitation is prescribed by any other provision of this Act, shall not be brought after the expiration of six years from the date on which the right of action accrued.
   For the purposes of this subsection, the right of action shall not be treated as having accrued to any beneficiary entitled to a future interest in the trust property until the interest fell into possession.

(4)   No beneficiary as against whom there would be a good defence under this Act shall derive any greater or other benefit from a judgment or order obtained by any other beneficiary than he could have obtained if he had brought the action and this Act had been pleaded in defence.

23.   Time limit in respect of actions for an account
An action for an account shall not be brought after the expiration of any time limit under this Act which is applicable to the claim which is the basis of the duty to account.

24.   Time limit for actions to enforce judgments
(1)   An action shall not be brought upon any judgment after the expiration of six years from the date on which the judgment became enforceable.

(2)   No arrears of interest in respect of any judgment debt shall be recovered after the expiration of six years from the date on which the interest became due.

28.   Extension of limitation period in case of disability
(1)   Subject to the following provisions of this section, if on the date when any right of action accrued for which a period of limitation is prescribed by this Act, the person to whom it accrued was under a disability, the action may be brought at any time before the expiration of six years from the date on which he ceased to be under a disability or died (whichever first occurred) notwithstanding that the period of limitation has expired.

(2)   This section shall not affect any case where the right of action first accrued to some person (not under a disability) through whom the person under a disability claims.

(3)   When a right of action which has accrued to a person under a disability accrues, on the death of that person while still under a disability, to another person under a disability, no further extension of time shall be allowed by reason of the disability of the second person.

(4)   No action to recover land or money charged on land shall be brought by virtue of this section by any person after the expiration of thirty years from the date on which the right of action accrued to that person or some person through whom he claims.

(4A)   If the action is one to which section 4A of this Act applies subsection (1) above shall have effect as if for the words from 'at any time' to 'occurred)' there were substituted the words 'by him at any time before the expiration of three years from the date when he ceased to be under a disability'.

(5)   If the action is one to which section 10 of this Act applies, subsection (1) above shall have effect as if for the words 'six years' there were substituted the words 'two years'.

(6)   If the action is one to which section 11 or 12(2) of this Act applies, subsection (1) above shall have effect as if for the words 'six years' there were substituted the words 'three years'. . . .

32.   Postponement of limitation period in case of fraud, concealment or mistake
(1)   Subject to subsections (3) and (4A) below, where in the case of any action for which a period of limitation is prescribed by this Act, either—
    (a)   the action is based upon the fraud of the defendant; or
    (b)   any fact relevant to the plaintiff's right of action has been deliberately concealed from him by the defendant; or
    (c)   the action is for relief from the consequences of a mistake;
the period of limitation shall not begin to run until the plaintiff has discovered the fraud, concealment or mistake (as the case may be) or could with reasonable diligence have discovered it.

References in this subsection to the defendant include references to the defendant's agent and to any person through whom the defendant claims and his agent.

(2)   For the purposes of subsection (1) above, deliberate commission of a breach of duty in circumstances in which it is unlikely to be discovered for some time amounts to deliberate concealment of the facts involved in that breach of duty.

(3)   Nothing in this section shall enable any action—
    (a)   to recover, or recover the value of, any property; or
    (b)   to enforce any charge against, or set aside any transaction affecting, any property;

to be brought against the purchaser of the property or any person claiming through him in any case where the property has been purchased for valuable consideration by an innocent third party since the fraud or concealment or (as the case may be) the transaction in which the mistake was made took place.

(4)   A purchaser is an innocent third party for the purposes of this section—

(a)   in the case of fraud or concealment of any fact relevant to the plaintiff's right of action, if he was not a party to the fraud or (as the case may be) to the concealment of that fact and did not at the time of the purchase know or have reason to believe that the fraud or concealment had taken place; and

(b)   in the case of mistake, if he did not at the time of the purchase know or have reason to believe that the mistake had been made.

(4A)   Subsection (1) above shall not apply in relation to the time limit prescribed by section 11A(3) of this Act or in relation to that time limit as applied by virtue of section 2(1) of this Act.

(5)   Sections 14A and 14B of this Act shall not apply to any action to which subsection (1)(b) above applies (and accordingly the period of limitation referred to in that subsection, in any case to which either of those sections would otherwise apply, is the period applicable under section 2 of this Act).

36.   Equitable jurisdiction and remedies

(1)   The following time limits under this Act, that is to say—

(a)   the time limit under section 2 for actions founded on tort;

(aa)   the time limit under section 4A for actions for libel or slander;

(b)   the time limit under section 5 for actions founded on simple contract;

(c)   the time limit under section 7 for actions to enforce awards where the submission is not by an instrument under seal;

(d)   the time limit under section 8 for actions on a specialty;

(e)   the time limit under section 9 for action to recover a sum recoverable by virtue of any enactment; and

(f)   the time limit under section 24 for actions to enforce a judgment;

shall not apply to any claim for specific performance of a contract or for an injunction or for other equitable relief, except in so far as any such time limit may be applied by the court by analogy in like manner as the corresponding time limit under any enactment repealed by the Limitation Act 1939 was applied before 1st July 1940.

(2)   Nothing in this Act shall affect any equitable jurisdiction to refuse relief on the ground of acquiescence or otherwise.

15.2.2   SITUATIONS TO WHICH THE ACT DOES NOT APPLY

WASSELL v *LEGGATT* [1896] 1 Ch 554, ChD

FACTS: A husband forcibly deprived his wife of certain monies which he knew had been left to her personal use by the terms of a will. Only after her husband's death were proceedings commenced to recover the monies.

HELD: The husband had constituted himself a trustee of the monies and accordingly the Statute of Limitations could not be raised to bar proceedings by his wife against the executors of her husband's estate.

ROMER J: The plaintiff took the legacy before the coming into operation of the Married Woman's Property Act, 1882, and the husband, when he got hold of the money, became a trustee of it for his wife. That he became a trustee is clear upon consideration of what her remedies were. She was entitled to recover the money; but how could she then do so? She had no right to the money at common law. In equity he could be sued, but that must have been because he was a trustee for her, and she was beneficially entitled; for I do not know how her right in equity could have been described except as one arising from the position of trustee on his part and *cestui que trust* on hers. This being the position in equity, no Statute of Limitations ran against the wife. He was her trustee at first, and never ceased to be her trustee. No statute applies to the case, for the husband's executors cannot on his behalf avail themselves of s. 8 of the Trustee Act 1888, inasmuch as he retained the money and never accounted for or parted with the possession of it. The Statute of Limitations, therefore, cannot be relied on as a defence. . . .

RE HOWLETT [1949] 2 All ER 490, ChD

FACTS: A son was entitled, during his infancy, to the rents and profits arising out of premises which had devolved on him on his mother's intestacy. However, his father, the administrator of the estate, occupied the premises for his own purposes and had never paid any rent to the son. After his father's death the son brought an action against his estate for an account of the unpaid rents.

HELD: Many defences were considered. As to the defence that the son's claim was time-barred under the Limitation Act 1939, it was held that the father had continued in his breach of trust by his continuing to hold trust property and therefore he would not be entitled to raise the time-bar as a defence. An account was ordered out of the father's estate.

DANCKWERTS J: . . . I think, . . . that there is force in the contention which counsel for the plaintiff makes that a trustee who remains in occupation of trust property for his own purposes—and, undoubtedly, the husband did so remain in occupation in the present case—cannot be heard to say that he has not received any rents or profits in respect of the property. Having received, therefore, in theory rents and profits, because he is chargeable with an occupation rent, he cannot discharge himself unless he can show that he has paid moneys away, and, therefore, either discharge himself by proper payments, or, indeed, perhaps escape under the Limitation Act 1939, having made improper payments. But here the husband, it seems, did not make any payments of any kind. He merely used the property for his own purposes, and I think the submission of counsel for the plaintiff is justified, that, having received the occupation rent for which he is chargeable, he must be considered as still having it in his own pocket at the material date, and therefore, cannot escape under the provisions of the Limitation Act 1939.

NELSON v RYE [1996] 1 WLR 1378

FACTS: In August 1980 the plaintiff, a professional solo musician, orally appointed the defendant to manage his affairs and account to him annually in consideration of his expenses and 20 per cent commission on the plaintiff's gross income. In October 1990 the defendant, without having submitted any formal accounts, terminated their business relationship. On 23 December; 1991 the plaintiff issued a writ against the defendant claiming an account for the whole period of the relationship on the footing that the defendant had occupied a fiduciary position in regard to any balance of profits in his hands, that he should be treated as a constructive trustee of such balance and that, accordingly no limitation period applied to the claim for an account over the entire period. The defendant denied that there was any balance in the plaintiff's favour, counterclaimed for a balance of commission and expenses, and pleaded that in any event the plaintiff's claim relating to any period prior to 24 December 1985 was barred by section 5 of the Limitation Act 1980

On the question whether any limitation period applied to the plaintiff's claim:

HELD: Although the defendant was in breach of a fiduciary duty to account to the plaintiff annually, so that by virtue of s. 21(1)(b) no limitation period applied, in the circumstances, the plaintiff's delay in commencing the proceedings had caused the defendant substantial prejudice such that it would be unreasonable and unjust to allow the plaintiff to assert his right to an account for the period prior to 24 December 1985.

LADDIE J: . . . Outside the statutory provisions there are principles which provide that in some circumstances, normally associated with significant delay, it will be inequitable to allow a plaintiff to enforce his rights. The requirements and limitations of this equitable doctrine will be considered later. For present purposes it is sufficient to note that whether the plaintiff is barred from relief is determined on the particular facts of the case. Account is taken of the actions and behaviour of the plaintiff and defendant and sometimes the impact on third parties. It is a flexible defence.

This is to be compared with limitation periods provided by statute particularly the Limitation Act 1980 and its predecessors. The statutes have imposed essentially arbitrary time limits on certain defined causes of action. It does not matter in such cases whether the plaintiff is to blame for not keeping within the time limit nor is it relevant that in some cases it will be thought unfair that the defendant is allowed off the hook. The defendant is entitled to play possum in the hope that the plaintiff will make a mistake and fail to commence proceedings before the statutory time limit is breached. If the limitation period is exceeded then the defendant is entitled to call down the guillotine om the plaintiff's action unless a statutory exception exists, such as the extension of time provided by s. 32 of the Act of 1980 in cases where there is fraud or concealment.

Furthermore the arbitrary time limits imposed by statute vary from cause of action to cause of action. For example, an action for breach of contract must be commenced within six years, an action upon a specialty must be commenced within 12 years and an action in respect of personal injuries must be commenced in many cases within three years. What then if one set of facts gives rise to two or more potential causes of action with different limitation periods? For example, it may well be that the breakdown of a relationship which arises out of a contract gives rise to alternative causes of action for breach of contract, negligence and breach of trust. No doubt the injured party cannot use the alternatives so as to receive duplicate or triplicate relief (see *United Australia Ltd* v *Barclays Bank Ltd* [1941] AC 1; *Attorney-General for Hong Kong* v *Reid* [1994] 1 AC 324), but that does not mean that he cannot sue under all of the heads simultaneously. Each cause of action may have its own strengths and weaknesses, so that, say, the plaintiff may succeed in his cause of action-based in negligence but fail in his action for breach of contract or viceversa. In particular where a limitation period exists and can be invoked in relation to one cause of action, it is nihil ad rem that no, or a different, limitation period applies to an alternative cause of action which has been or could have been pleaded by the plaintiff.

Historically, actions by beneficiaries against trustees for misappropriation of trust property have been excluded from the imposition of such arbitrary time limits. The courts and the legislature have treated trustees as bearing a special responsibility to the trust property and the beneficiary's interest in it. The beneficiary's right to complain of breach of trust has been treated as persisting indefinitely unless, of course, in all the circumstances it would be inequitable to allow him to enforce his rights. There is nothing to which my attention has been drawn which suggests that the Act of 1980 effected a significant change in this area.

With those considerations in mind it is possible to address the arguments advanced by the parties to this action. . . .

In a case where, because of the existence of a fiduciary duty, a constructive trust comes into existence, breach of trust and breach of fiduciary duty are the same cause of action. Similarly, where an express trust has been created, breach of that trust and breach of fiduciary duty are also the same cause of action. It is therefore not possible to sidestep the limitation provisions of s. 21(3) by referring to the action as one for breach of fiduciary duty.

Since I accept Mr Oppenheim's argument that not all breaches of fiduciary duty give rise to constructive trusts, the following propositions appear to follow. (1) An action for breach of fiduciary duty simpliciter is outside the provisions of the Limitation Act 1980 and therefore is not subject to a period of limitation: see *Attorney-General* v *Cocke* [1988] Ch 414. (2) Where breach of fiduciary duty gives rise to a constructive trust, the provisions of s. 21 of the Act determine whether there is a limitation period and its duration. (3) An action for breach of an express trust is, in like manner, subject to the limitation provisions of s. 21. (4) In neither case (2) nor (3) is it possible to avoid any limitation period imposed by the Act by treating the case as one of breach of fiduciary duty.

There is no dispute between the parties that Mr Rye owed Mr Nelson a fiduciary duty. He was obliged to account to Mr Nelson annually. He did not. There has been a breach of that duty and, prima facie, no limitation period applies. Mr Oppenheim's arguments to the effect that the cause of action did not fall within the ambit of s. 21(1)(b) would only help Mr Rye if he had also succeeded in persuading me that the action should be treated as one for breach of contract rather than breach of fiduciary duty. Since he has failed to persuade me of that, no limitation period applies either because the cause of action is outwith the Act or because it falls within s. 21(1)(b) (it was not suggested that the action came within s. 21(3)). In the circumstances it is not necessary to determine under which head this action falls. Nevertheless, it is clear to me that this case does fall within s. 21(1)(b). Although not all fiduciary relationships give rise to constructive trusts, this one did. . . .

In this case Mr Nelson left all of his financial affairs to Mr Rye. All of his various sources of income were to be handled by his manager. Mr Rye accepted that he was not free to treat Mr Nelson's income as his own. He never did. The fact, as I find, that Mr Rye did not take out all the commission to which he was entitled and put his own funds in to keep Mr Nelson afloat does not alter the nature of his interest in Mr Nelson's income. If it were otherwise, any agent in a fiduciary relationship to his principal could prevent a constructive trust from arising by failing to take his permissible deductions from the trust fund or by putting his own money in, even if this was not sought by the beneficiary. Furthermore I reject Mr Oppenheim's argument that s. 21(1)(b) does not apply because the constructive trust contains no property in specie. The subsection requires that the action be one to recover from the trustee "trust property or the proceeds of trust property in the possession of the trustee.' Mr Rye received Mr Nelson's income. That was trust property. The balance left after all property deductions is also trust property. This is an action to recover that property.

It follows that no limitation period applies here. However, that does not dispose of this part of the case. Mr Rye argues that it would be inequitable by reason of laches, acquiescence and delay to allow Mr Nelson to maintain this action at least in respect of the period before 24 December 1985.

The equitable defence . . .
It can be misleading to approach the equitable defences of laches and acquiescence as if they consisted of a series of precisely defined hurdles over each of which a litigant must struggle before the defence is made out.

. . . these defences are not technical or arbitrary. The courts have indicated over the years some of the factors which must be taken into consideration in deciding whether the defence runs. Those factors include the period of the delay, the extent to which the defendant's position has been prejudiced by the delay and the extent to which that prejudice was caused by the actions of the plaintiff. I accept that mere delay alone will almost never suffice, but the court has to look at all the circumstances, including in particular those factors set out above, and then decide whether the balance of justice or injustice is in favour of granting the remedy or withholding it. If substantial prejudice will be suffered by the defendant, it is not necessary for the defendant to prove that it was caused by the delay. On the other hand the plaintiff's knowledge that the delay will cause such prejudice is a factor to be taken into account. . . .

ATTORNEY-GENERAL v *COCKE* [1988] 1 Ch 414, ChD

FACTS: The Attorney-General brought an action for an account against the trustees of a charitable trust. The defendant trustees sought to show that the Attorney-General was time-barred from bringing the action.
HELD: The Limitation Act 1980, s. 21(3) had no application to a case such as the present. First, because a charitable trust has no beneficiary, as such, capable of bringing an action which could be time-barred. Secondly, because the writ had not alleged a breach of trust, nor had it sought to recover property owing to the trust.

HARMAN J: . . . For the Attorney-General, Mr Crampin's first point is that the section has no application whatever to claims of this sort. This, he says, is an action by the Attorney-General. The Attorney-General plainly is not personally a beneficiary of this trust. Even taking a broader view, as Lord Cranworth LC did in *President and Scholars of the College of St. Mary Magdalen, Oxford* v *Attorney-General* (1857) 6 HL Cas 189, and looking through the person who sues (the Attorney) to the persons for whose benefit the action is brought, I look through the Attorney-General and ask: 'who here are the

318 BREACH OF TRUST: DEFENCES AND RELIEF

beneficiaries on whose behalf the Attorney acts?' Mr Crampin submits that the beneficiaries are non-existent; that there are no beneficiaries of a public charitable trust. . . . He asks rhetorically 'Who then are the beneficiaries of it?' The only answer can be 'the public at large'. In my judgment there can be no other answer, if the word 'beneficiaries' has any proper meaning. But that would mean that I, as a member of the public, am an interested beneficiary and plainly ought not to adjudicate upon the claim.

. . . It seems probable to me that in almost all charitable trusts there are no individual beneficiaries. As it seems to me, Mr Crampin is correct when he says that however Lord Cranworth LC regarded the poor of the parish of St. Olave, Southwark in the *St, Mary Magdalen College* case as being a class of the public within the Limitation Act then under consideration, that does not run to the words inserted by the Act of 1939, 'an action by a beneficiary,' and that there are, in cases where the Attorney is suing for the benefit of the public at large, truly no beneficiaries, and s. 21(3) of the Act of 1980 has no application at all.

He points further, in support of the probability that that is accurate, of the tail piece to s. 21(3) referring to the accrual to a beneficiary of the right of action which does not happen until the interest vests in possession. Plainly such a concept is only appropriate to persons who have property rights under a trust and in whom those property rights can vest at some date. No 'right' properly so-called ever vests in any member of the public individually under a charitable trust. Equally plainly, nobody has a property right under a public charitable trust and nothing can be said to vest in them at any date, present or future. . . . In the result, as it seems to me, s. 21(3) has no application whatever to claims by the Attorney to enforce public charitable trusts.

Mr Crampin went on to argue that in any event this claim was not a claim within s. 21(3) of the Limitation Act 1980, not only because it was not a beneficiary, as I have held is correct, but also because it was neither an action to recover trust property—there was no claim to recover anything—nor was it in respect of any breach of trust, there being no allegation of breach of trust at any time made. . . .

. . . it seems to me, Mr Crampin is also right on his second point and this is not 'an action . . . to recover trust property or [for] any breach of trust' within s. 21(3) of the Act of 1980. It follows that no limitation applies and s. 23 has nothing to do with the case because there is no basis of the duty which is otherwise dealt with in the Limitation Act 1980 itself. Thus, as it seems to me, on both grounds Mr Crampin is correct in his view of the law, and in my view the Limitation Act 1980 has nothing to do with the case.

15.2.3 LACHES

RE SHARPE [1892] 1 Ch 154, CA

FACTS: The liquidator of an insolvent company brought an action against one of the former directors of the company, seeking to recover monies which had been paid (in the form of interest payments) to the shareholders of the company in the years prior to its insolvency.
HELD: The directors were to be treated as being in the position of trustees, accordingly the defendant could not raise the Statute of Limitations as a bar to the action. Neither would the action be barred as a 'stale demand'.

LINDLEY LJ: . . . That staleness of demand as distinguished from the Statute of Limitations and analogy to it may furnish a defence in Equity to an equitable claim was settled at least as early as *Smith* v *Clay* 3 Bn CC 639n. The principles on which the doctrine is based will be found clearly set forth by the Privy Council in *Lindsay Petroleum Company* v *Hurd* Law Rep 5 PC 221, and in the judgment of Lord Blackburn in *Erlanger* v *New Sombrero Phosphate Company* (1878) 3 App Cas 1218. Whether these principles are applicable to the case of a company seeking relief in respect of a misapplication of its money which neither the directors nor the company could authorise or ratify has not, I believe, been decided, and need not be decided on the present occasion, for the circumstances of this case are insufficient to support a defence founded on the equitable doctrine in question. A defence based on staleness of demand renders it necessary to consider the time which has elapsed and the balance of justice or injustice in affording or refusing relief. I do not disregard, but I do not attach much importance to, the time which elapsed before Captain Bennett's death, nor, for reasons already given, to that which has elapsed between the winding up of the company and the commencement of the action. The remaining time is about two years and a quarter, which I do not consider long. . . .

(See, further, *Nelson* v *Rye* at **15.2.2**.)

15.2.4 BENEFICIARY'S INSTIGATION OF OR CONSENT TO THE BREACH

RE SOMERSET v *EARL POULETT* [1894] 1 ChD 231, CA

FACTS: Trustees of a settlement committed an innocent breach of trust when they invested in an under-secured mortgage. One of the beneficiaries had consented in writing to investing by way of mortgage, the question therefore arose whether the trustees should for that reason be indemnified by the beneficiaries for the consequences of their breach.

HELD: If the beneficiary has instigated, requested or consented to an investment which amounts to a breach of trust, the beneficiary will be liable to indemnify the trustee for any liability arising from that breach. If, however, the beneficiary has instigated, requested or consented to an investment which is not of itself a breach of trust, the beneficiary will not be liable if the trustee proceeds to make that investment with a lack of ordinary prudence. In the present case the beneficiary had consented to an investment within the terms of the trust and the trustees would therefore be liable in full. When considering whether a beneficiary had instigated, requested or consented to a breach of trust it was not necessary to show that the beneficiary knew the investment was, in law, a breach of trust.

LINDLEY LJ: . . . If a *cestui que trust* instigates, requests, or consents in writing to an investment not in terms authorised by the power of investment, he clearly falls within the section; and in such a case his ignorance or forgetfulness of the terms of the power would not, I think, protect him—at all events, not unless he could give some good reason why it should, e.g., that it was caused by the trustee. But if all that a *cestui que trust* does is to instigate, request, or consent in writing to an investment which is authorised by the terms of the power, the case is, I think, very different. He has a right to expect that the trustees will act with proper care in making the investment, and if they do not they cannot throw the consequences on him unless they can show that he instigated, requested, or consented in writing to their non-performance of their duty in this respect. . . .

15.3 Relief From Liability

15.3.1 SET-OFF

See *Bartlett* v *Barclays* (**11.2.2**).

15.3.2 CONTRIBUTION

BAHIN v *HUGHES* (1886) 31 ChD 390, CA

FACTS: There were two trustees and the management of the trust was left in the hands of one of them. Following a breach of trust resulting in a loss to the fund the two trustees were sued by the beneficiaries for an account. The 'passive trustee' claimed a right of indemnity against the 'active trustee'.

HELD: The trustees were equally liable to the beneficiaries. The trustee who did nothing had neglected his duty to supervise and participate in the activities of the active trustee.

COTTON LJ: . . . But then we come to another and more difficult question, namely, how far Mr Edwards can, as against Miss Hughes, have indemnity for the loss, on the ground that she was the acting trustee, that she and Mrs Burden took upon themselves to invest this money, and that although both she and Mr Edwards are liable to the beneficiaries, she is liable to Mr Edwards, who left the matter in her hands. On going into the authorities, there are very few cases in which one trustee, who has been guilty with a co-trustee of breach of trust and held answerable, has successfully sought indemnity as against his co-trustee. *Lockhart* v *Reilly* 25 LJ (Ch) 697 and *Thompson* v *Finch* 22 Beav 316 are the only cases which appear to be reported. Now in *Lockhart* v *Reilly*, it appears from the report of the case in the Law Journal that the trustee by whom the loss was sustained had been not only trustee, but had been and was a solicitor, and acting as solicitor for himself and his co-trustee, and it was on his advice that Lockhart had relied in making the investment which gave rise to the action of the *cestui que trust*. The Lord Chancellor (Lord Cranworth) refers to the fact that he was a solicitor, and makes the remark: 'The whole thing was trusted to him. He was the solicitor, and, independently of the consideration that one cannot help seeing it was done with a view of favouring his own family, yet, if that had not been so, the co-trustee leaves it with the solicitor-trustee, by whose negligence (I use no harsher word) all this evil, in a great degree, has arisen.' Therefore the Lord Chancellor, in giving his decision, relies upon the fact of the trustee being a solicitor. . . . Now I think it wrong to lay down any limitation of the circumstances under which one trustee would be held liable to the other for indemnity, both having been held liable to the *cestui que trust*; but so far as cases have gone at present, relief has only been granted against a trustee who has himself got the benefit of the breach of trust, or between whom and his co-trustees there has existed a relation, which will justify the Court in treating him as solely liable for the breach of trust. Here, when Miss Hughes got the money, she handed it over to the mortgagor—as I understand, she handed over to them the actual cheque received from the Mersey Docks Company. The Appellant, Mr Edwards, relies on the fact that she sent him a letter with the cheque for him and his wife to indorse, saying that nothing should be done with the money without consulting him; but I think Mr Edwards' own conduct shewed that that was not the view which he took. For she said in that letter that when a suitable mortgage was found and approved of, notice should be sent to the trustees; and undoubtedly on the 2nd of November, after the mortgage was completed, she wrote him with the information that the money had been invested upon leasehold houses. But nothing was done by him with reference to the matter till the 18th of May following, and I can hardly suppose that if he wished for information before the investment was taken that he would have made no inquiry as to what had been done with the money after he had notice that it had been invested. Miss Hughes was the active trustee and Mr Edwards did nothing, and in my opinion it would be laying down a wrong rule to hold that where one trustee acts honestly, though erroneously, the other trustee is to be held entitled to indemnity who by doing nothing neglects his duty more than the acting trustee. That Miss Hughes made an improper investment is true, but she acted honestly, and intended to do the best she could, and believed that the property was sufficient security for the money, although she made no inquiries about their being leasehold houses. In my opinion the money was lost just as much by the default of Mr Edwards as by the innocent though erroneous action of his co-trustee, Miss Hughes. All the trustees were in the wrong, and everyone is equally liable to indemnify the beneficiaries.

15.3.3　INDEMNITY

CHILLINGWORTH v *CHAMBERS* [1896] 1 Ch 685, CA

FACTS: The parties to this action were trustees of the same trust. The plaintiff was also entitled to a share under the trust. Together they made certain authorised investments which proved to have been inadequate, and they were declared jointly and severally liable to account for the resulting loss to the trust.

HELD: The whole of the loss must be satisfied out of the plaintiff's share as a beneficiary under the trust.

KAY LJ: . . . Here we have a plaintiff who was both trustee and also *cestui que trust* as to one-fifth of the property; and, if the cases I have referred to apply, it follows that he is not estopped by his concurrence in the breach of trust from claiming contribution. But as *cestui que trust* he is prevented from requiring trustees to make good any loss sustained by him in that character. The loss he seeks to make his co-trustee share is not the loss of his one-fifth share as *cestui que trust*, but the amount he has had to pay as trustee to recoup the deficiency of the trust estate. If he is primarily liable to the extent of his one-fifth share, this claim must fail. If liable only to the amount of the benefit received from the improper investment, the balance of the loss, after deducting that amount, should be shared by himself and his co-trustee.

On the whole, I think that the weight of authority is in favour of holding that a trustee who, being also *cestui que trust*, has received, as between himself and his co-trustee, an exclusive benefit by the breach of trust, must indemnify his co-trustee to the extent of his interest in the trust fund, and not merely to the extent of the benefit which he has received. I think that the plaintiff must be treated as having received such an exclusive benefit.

I am of opinion, for these reasons, that the plaintiff's action fails, and the appeal must be dismissed.

RE TOWNDROW [1911] 1 Ch 662, ChD

FACTS: A trustee who was entitled to a specific legacy under the trust of which he was trustee misappropriated part of the residue of the trust fund. The residuary beneficiaries brought an action seeking to make good their loss out of the trustee's legacy, which had been assigned to a third party.

HELD: The legacy and residue were held upon entirely separate trusts, therefore the residuary beneficiaries could not take advantage of the principle that a trustee who had caused a loss to his trust could not assert his entitlement to a share in the trust fund. The trustee's assignees took the legacy free from any equitable charge or lien in favour of the residuary beneficiaries.

PARKER J: . . . I think that the real principle is stated by Stirling J in *Doering* v *Doering* 42 ChD 203 where he says, 'The law has gone to this extent, that though the breach of trust is committed after the assignment, nevertheless, the rule applies, and the assignee or mortgagee is not entitled to any share in the estate until the default is made good. The theory on which that rule is based is that the Court treats the trustee as having received his share by anticipation, and the answer to any claim made by the trustee is this: "You have already received your share; you have it in your own hands."' Therefore you must, I take it, have a defaulting trustee claiming a share in the aggregate amount of a certain fund, and the answer to him is, 'You cannot have it; you have already had it.' But that cannot apply to a case like the present, where the only interest which the trustee has is in another fund in which the *cestuis que trust* whose property has been misappropriated have no interest at all; it cannot apply so as to give them a lien on that other fund. The trustee in this case is not claiming a share in the residue, and, therefore, his default has no effect on the distribution of that residue, and, in my opinion, his assigns under the settlement, there being no default at the date of the assignment, take clear of and are entitled to hold the settled fund free from any equity against them. . . .

15.3.4   SECTION 61, TRUSTEE ACT 1925

TRUSTEE ACT 1925

61.   Power to relieve trustee from personal liability
If it appears to the court that a trustee, whether appointed by the court or otherwise, is or may be personally liable for any breach of trust, whether the transaction alleged to be

a breach of trust occurred before or after the commencement of this Act, but has acted honestly and reasonably, and ought fairly to be excused for the breach of trust and for omitting to obtain the directions of the court in the matter in which he committed such breach, then the court may relieve him either wholly or partly from personal liability for the same.

See, also, *Re Pauling's ST* (**13.2.5.2**).

15.3.5   IMPOUNDING THE BENEFICIARY'S INTEREST

The court has the power to impound a beneficiary's interest under the trust in certain circumstances. That impounded interest can then be used, in whole or in part, to relieve a trustee from their liability to the other trustees.

15.3.5.1   Impounding under the court's inherent jurisdiction

Under its inherent jurisdiction the court can impound if the beneficiary:

■ **instigated** or **requested** the breach **with the intention of obtaining a personal benefit**; or

■ **consented** to the breach and **actually benefited** from it.

15.3.5.2   Impounding under s. 62 Trustee Act 1925

Under this section the court can impound if the beneficiary:

■ **instigated** or **requested** the breach; or

■ **consented in writing** to the breach.

15.3.6   TRUSTEE ACT 1925

TRUSTEE ACT 1925

62.   Power to make beneficiary indemnify for breach of trust
   (1)   Where a trustee commits a breach of trust at the instigation or request or with the consent in writing of a beneficiary, the court may, if it thinks fit [. . .] make such order as to the court seems just, for impounding all or any part of the interest of the beneficiary in the trust estate by way of indemnity to the trustee or persons claiming through him.
   (2)   This section applies to breaches of trust committed as well before as after the commencement of this Act.

15.4   Exemption from Liability

HAYIM AND ANOTHER v CITIBANK NA AND ANOTHER [1987] 1 AC 730, PC

FACTS: A testator made two wills, one dealing primarily with his American property, another with property outside of America (this latter was called the 'Hong Kong' will). The first defendant was executor and trustee of the American will, the second defendant was executor and trustee of the Hong Kong will. The plaintiffs directed the second defendant to sell a house in Hong Kong, where the testator's elderly brother and sister were living. The brother and sister were not entitled under either will to remain in the house and a sale of the house would have been for the benefit of the beneficiaries of the American will. Nevertheless, the first defendant directed the second defendant not to sell the house. When the house was eventually sold it had fallen in value, causing a loss to the beneficiaries of the American will.

HELD: On the question whether the second defendant was liable for delaying the sale of the house, there had been no breach of trust because the second defendant owed no duty to the beneficiaries of the American will. On a proper construction of the trust, the second defendant was actually obliged to act on the instructions of the first defendant. As regards the liability of the first defendant, clause 10 of the American will expressly relieved the first defendant of any 'responsibility or duty' to the 'American' beneficiaries with respect to the house.

LORD TEMPLEMAN: . . . a beneficiary has no cause of action against a third party save in special circumstances which embrace a failure, excusable or inexcusable, by the trustees in the performance of the duty owed by the trustees to the beneficiary to protect the trust estate or to protect the interests of the beneficiary in the trust estate. By the Hong Kong will the testator conferred on the first defendant the power to give instructions binding on the second defendant to sell or to retain the Hong Kong house. By clause 10 of the American will the testator relieved the first defendant from any responsibility to the beneficiaries interested in the American estate in respect of the Hong Kong house. As a result of clause 10 the first defendant did not therefore owe any duty to the beneficiaries. The first defendant lawfully instructed the second defendant to postpone sale and the second defendant lawfully complied with those instructions. Mr Nugee referred to principles which applied to trusts, bailments, contracts and torts respectively. In the view of their Lordships the principles relied upon are not inconsistent with the principles which their Lordships consider to be applicable to the present appeal. Their Lordships will humbly advise Her Majesty that this appeal should be dismissed with costs.

15.5   End of Chapter Assessment Question

Theresa died in 1986. By her will she settled a trust of £20,000 cash on trustees for the benefit of her nephew Bill and her niece Barbara, 'in equal shares upon their attaining the age of 21'. At the date of Theresa's death Bill was 14 and Barbara was 15. Theresa had also made a gift in her will of £10,000 to another nephew, Barry.

The trustees are Tricia, Tracy and Barry. Tricia is a solicitor.

In 1988 Tricia urged Tracy and Barry to join her in investing in a private limited company which, she said, promised to be a very profitable investment. She explained to the trustees that although the investment was 'technically unauthorised', it was very secure. In the event the trustees went ahead with the investment in the company, having first obtained the consent of Bill and Barbara, who had been told that the investment was a 'secure one'.

Shortly after making the investment the shares rose in value and yielded large dividends to the trust, but later they fell in value and today they are practically worthless.

It is now April 1996 and Bill and Barbara have issued proceedings against the trustees. Advise the trustees as to the possible extent of their liability to the trust and any defences which might be open to them.

15.6   End of Chapter Assessment Outline Answer

The remedy which the beneficiaries are most likely to seek against the trustees is compensation for loss caused to the trust fund. The liability of the trustees in such a case is, so far as possible, to put the fund in the position it would have been in had the breach of trust not occurred. It will first of all be necessary to consider the basic extent of the trustees' liability to compensate the fund, secondly to consider whether they might raise any defences to the beneficiaries' action and finally, to consider whether, if they cannot raise a defence, the court will relieve the trustees of the consequences of their breach.

First, how much compensation will the trustees be liable to pay? This breaks down into two important sub-questions. One, what will be the quantum of capital repayment? Two, is interest payable, and if so, how much?

Recently the Court of Appeal held that beneficiaries should be able to recover the lost value of the trust property calculated at the peak value of that property during the period of the continuing breach of trust (*Jaffray* v *Marshall* [1993] 1 WLR 1285). This case has, however, been overruled by the House of Lords in *Target Holdings* v *Redferns* [1995] 3 All ER 785. In that case their lordships held that the quantum of capital repayment in a successful action for compensation should be equivalent to the plaintiff's actual loss assessed at the date of the court hearing with the full benefit of hindsight. The trustees should only be liable to compensate to the extent that they, 'on a common sense view' caused the loss. However, in *Target* their Lordships were dealing with a bare trust in a commercial context. The instant case does not involve a bare trust in a commercial context, it is a traditional trust which has come to an end, the beneficiaries having both now reached the age of 21. Lord Browne Wilkinson stated that 'in the ordinary case where a beneficiary becomes absolutely entitled to the trust fund the court orders, not restitution to the trust estate, but the payment of compensation directly to the beneficiary. The measure of compensation is the same (as for a bare trust in a commercial context), i.e. the difference between what the beneficiary has in fact received and the amount he would have received but for the breach of trust'.

As regards interest on the compensatory award, the crucial question is whether interest will be simple or compound, the former being interest charged on capital alone, the latter being interest charged on capital plus interest. An award of compound interest is usually reserved for cases where the trustee has used misapplied trust funds for their own private purposes (*Wallersteiner* v *Moir* [1975] 1 QB 373). The award of compound interest is designed to ensure that the trustee does not retain any profit from their breach. Accordingly, an award of simple interest is probably appropriate in the present case, as there appears to be no possibility that the trustees could have profitted from their breach. Simple interest will be charged from the date of the misapplication of the trust funds through the unauthorised investment.

Next we turn to consider defences which might be available to the trustees. The trustees will be immune to the beneficiaries' claims if they can show that the claims are time-barred under the Limitation Act 1980 or estopped because of undue delay ('laches') in bringing the action. It will also be a defence to a claim to show that the beneficiary bringing the action had instigated, consented to, or acquiesced in, the breach of trust. However, this defence may not be raised against beneficiaries who were not party to such instigation, consent or acquiescence.

Claims are generally time-barred under the Limitation Act if they are brought more than six years after the breach of trust occurred. The breach in the present case occurred eight years ago, and so the trustees have a *prima facie* defence (assuming it is now April 1996). However, time does not begin to run against beneficiaries until their interests vest in possession. Bill's interest vested three years ago, and so his action is not time-barred. Barbara's interest vested 10 years ago, and so her claim will be time-barred, there being no suggestion that the trustees have acted fraudulently or have concealed their breach of trust. As Bill's claim is covered by the Limitation Act 'laches' is not relevant. Nor can Bill's consent to the unauthorised investment be raised as a defence, as he was an infant at the time he gave it.

So far it would appear that the trustees have no answer to Bill's claim. They may, however, be able to claim some degree of relief from the full extent of his claim. In particular, Tracy and Barry might seek to be indemnified by Tricia on the ground that she is a solicitor with a controlling influence over them (*Re Partington* (1887) 57 LT 654). It will not, however, be presumed that Tricia had a controlling influence, the issue will be decided in the light of the experience, expertise and personal fortitude of the other trustees. On the other hand, Tricia and Tracy might look to Barry to meet a large part of their liability. As well as being a trustee, Barry is a beneficiary under the trust and the usual rule in such a case is that the trustee-beneficiary will not be able to claim his beneficial entitlement until he has made good his default. The good news for Barry is, however, that his interest under Theresa's will arises from trusts which are quite distinct from those under which Bill and Barbara are entitled. It follows that the usual rule will not apply in the present case (*Re Towndrow* [1911] 1 Ch 662). At the final hearing of Bill's claim, the judge, if he concludes that the trustees are jointly and severally liable for the breach, will no doubt apportion liability between the trustees according to whatever is 'just and equitable' (Civil Liability (Contributions) Act 1978).

In conclusion, the trustees will be liable to compensate Bill for lost capital, plus simple interest thereon, and the court will apportion the judgment debt against the trustees in whatever proportions appear to be just and equitable. The trustees will not be able to set-off, against the lost value of the shares, the large dividends made thereon, because the profit and loss arose from a single breach of trust (*Bartlett* v *Barclay's Bank Trust Co. (No. 2)* [1980] 1 All ER 139 can be distinguished). Nor will the trustees be relieved of liability under the Trustee Act, s. 61. Relief will only be given under this section if the trustees have acted, *inter alia*, reasonably. Tricia, Tracy and Barry should be advised that they have not acted reasonably, and that their honesty and good intentions will not save them from what could amount to extensive liability to compensate Bill.

CHAPTER SIXTEEN

RESULTING AND CONSTRUCTIVE TRUSTS

16.1   Resulting Trusts

WESTDEUTSCHE LANDESBANK GIROZENTRALE v ISLINGTON LBC
[1996] 2 WLR 802, HL

FACTS: The parties entered into a 10-year interest rate swap agreement starting on 18 June 1987 based on a notional principal sum of £25m. Additionally, the plaintiff bank as the fixed rate payer paid the defendant council as the floating rate payer a lump sum of £2·5m. Pursuant to the agreement, the council made 'interest' payments in December 1987, June and December 1988 and June 1989 to the bank totalling £1,354,474·07. On 1 November 1989 the Divisional Court of the Queen's Bench Division held in an unrelated case that interest rate swap transactions by local authorities were ultra vires. Following that decision, the council made no more payments. The bank brought an action against the council claiming repayment of the balance of the £2·5m. amounting to £1,145,525·93 plus interest from 18 June 1987. The judge gave judgment for the bank for the principal sum plus compound interest from 1 April 1990. The Court of Appeal dismissed an appeal by the council and allowed a cross-appeal by the bank against the judge's rejection of 18 June 1987 as the date from which interest should run.

On appeal by the council against the award of compound interest:

HELD: (1) That in a common law action for money had and received the bank was entitled to recover only simple interest under s. 35A of the Supreme Court Act 1981; that in the absence of fraud equity had never awarded compound interest except against a trustee or other person in a fiduciary position in respect of profits improperly made; that the recipient of moneys under a contract subsequently held void for mistake or as being ultra vires did not hold those moneys on a resulting trust and it would be undesirable so to develop the law of resulting trusts since to do so would give the claimant a proprietary interest in the moneys and produce injustice to third parties and commercial uncertainty; and that the council was not otherwise in a fiduciary position vis-à-vis the bank.

(2) Allowing the appeal (Lord Goff of Chieveley and Lord Woolf dissenting), that a claim founded on an ultra vires contract for moneys had and received was not based on an implied contract or on an equitable proprietary claim but was a personal action based on total failure of consideration; that it would be undesirable for equity to award compound interest in aid of the bank's common law claim having regard, inter alia, to the fact that Parliament had twice since 1934 considered what interest should be awarded on claims at common law and had expressly not authorised the award of compound interest, and that accordingly, the bank should recover simple interest only as from 18 June 1987, the date of accrual of its cause of action.

NOTE: Under an interest rate swap transaction one party (the fixed rate payer) agrees to pay the other over a certain period interest at a fixed rate on a notional capital sum; and the other party (the floating rate payer) agrees to pay to the former over the same period interest on the same notional sum at a market rate.

LORD GOFF OF CHIEVELEY: . . . As my noble and learned friend, Lord Browne-Wilkinson, observes, it is plain that the present case falls within neither of the situations which are traditionally regarded as giving rise to a resulting trust, viz. (1) voluntary payments by A to B, or for the purchase of property in the name of B or in his and A's joint names, where there is no presumption of advancement or evidence of intention to make an out-and-out gift; or (2) property transferred to B on an express trust which does not exhaust the whole beneficial interest. The question therefore arises whether resulting trusts should be extended beyond such cases to apply in the present case, which I shall treat as a case where money has been paid for a consideration which fails.

In a most interesting and challenging paper, 'Restitution and Resulting Trusts,' published in *Equity: Contemporary Legal Developments* (1992) (ed. Goldstein), p. 335, Professor Birks has argued for a wider role for the resulting trust in the field of restitution, and specifically for its availability in cases of mistake and failure of consideration. His thesis is avowedly experimental, written to test the temperature of the water. I feel bound to respond that the temperature of the water must be regarded as decidedly cold: see, e.g., Professor Burrows, 'Swaps and the Friction between Common Law and Equity' [1995] RLR 15, and Mr W. J. Swadling, 'A new role for resulting trusts?' (1996) 16 Legal Studies 133.

In the first place, as Lord Browne-Wilkinson points out, to impose a resulting trust in such cases is inconsistent with the traditional principles of trust law. For on receipt of the money by the payee it is to be presumed that (as in the present case) the identity of the money is immediately lost by mixing with other assets of the payee, and at that time the payee has no knowledge of the facts giving rise to the failure of consideration. By the time that those facts come to light, and the conscience of the payee may thereby be affected, there will therefore be no identifiable fund to which a trust can attach. But there are other difficulties. First, there is no general rule that the property in money paid under a void contract does not pass to the payee; and it is difficult to escape the conclusion that, as a general rule, the beneficial interest to the money likewise passes to the payee. This must certainly be the case where the consideration for the payment fails after the payment is made, as in cases of frustration or breach of contract; and there appears to be no good reason why the same should not apply in cases where, as in the present case, the contract under which the payment is made is void ab initio and the consideration for the payment therefore fails at the time of payment. It is true that the doctrine of mistake might be invoked where the mistake is fundamental in the orthodox sense of that word. But that is not the position in the present case; moreover the mistake in the present case must be classified as a mistake of law which, as the law at present stands, creates its own special problems. No doubt that much criticised doctrine will fall to be reconsidered when an appropriate case occurs; but I cannot think that the present is such a case, since not only has the point not been argued but (as will appear) it is my opinion that there is in any event jurisdiction to award compound interest in the present case. For all of these reasons I conclude, in agreement with my noble and learned friend, that there is no basis for holding that a resulting trust arises in cases where money has been paid under a contract which is ultra vires and therefore void ab initio. This conclusion has the effect that all the practical problems which would flow from the imposition of a resulting trust in a case such as the present, in particular the imposition upon the recipient of the normal duties of trustee, do not arise. The dramatic consequences which would occur are detailed by Professor Burrows in his article on 'Swaps and the Friction between Common Law and Equity' [1995] RLR 15, 27: the duty to account for profits accruing from the trust property; the inability of the payee to rely upon the defence of change of position; the absence of any limitation period; and so on. Professor Burrows even goes so far as to conclude that the action for money had and received would be rendered otiose in such cases, and indeed in all cases where the payer seeks restitution of mistaken payments. However, if no resulting trust arises, it also follows that the payer in a case such as the present cannot achieve priority over the payee's general creditors in the event of his insolvency; a conclusion which appears to me to be just.

For all these reasons I conclude that there is no basis for imposing a resulting trust in the present case, and I therefore reject the bank's submission that it was here entitled to proceed by way of an equitable proprietary claim. I need only add that, in reaching that conclusion, I do not find it necessary to review the decisions of Goulding J in *Chase Manhatten Bank NA* v *Israel-British Bank (London) Ltd* [1981] Ch 105. . . .

LORD BROWNE-WILKINSON: . . . My Lords, wise judges have often warned against the wholesale importation into commercial law of equitable principles inconsistent with the certainty and speed which are essential requirements for the orderly conduct of business affairs: see *Barnes* v *Addy* (1874) LR 9 Ch App 244, 251 and 255; *Scandinavian Trading Tanker Co. A.B.* v *Flota Petrolera Ecuatoriana* [1983] 2 AC 694, 703–704. If the bank's arguments are correct, a businessman who has entered into transactions relating to or dependent upon property rights could find that assets which apparently belong to one person in fact belong to another; that there are 'off balance sheet' liabilities of which he cannot be aware; that these property rights and liabilities arise from circumstances unknown not only to himself but also to anyone else who has been involved in the transactions. A new area of unmanageable risk will be introduced into commercial dealings. If the due application of equitable principles forced a conclusion leading to these results, your Lordships would be presented with a formidable task in reconciling legal principle with commercial common sense. But in my judgment no such conflict occurs. The resulting trust for which the bank contends is inconsistent not only with the law as it stands but with principled development of it.

The relevant principles of trust law

(i)   Equity operates on the conscience of the owner of the legal interest. In the case of a trust, the conscience of the legal owner requires him to carry out the purposes for which the property was vested in him (express or implied trust) or which the law imposes on him by reason of his unconscionable conduct (constructive trust).

(ii)   Since the equitable jurisdiction to enforce trusts depends upon the conscience of the holder of the legal interest being affected, he cannot be a trustee of the property if and so long as he is ignorant of the facts alleged to affect his conscience, i.e. until he is aware that he is intended to hold the property for the benefit of others in the case of an express or implied trust, or, in the case of a constructive trust, of the factors which are alleged to affect his conscience.

(iii)   In order to establish a trust there must be identifiable trust property. The only apparent exception to this rule is a constructive trust imposed on a person who dishonestly assists in a breach of trust who may come under fiduciary duties even if he does not receive identifiable trust property.

(iv)   Once a trust is established, as from the date of its establishment the beneficiary has, in equity, a proprietary interest in the trust property, which proprietary interest will be enforceable in equity against any subsequent holder of the property (whether the original property or substituted property into which it can be traced) other than a purchaser for value of the legal interest without notice.

These propositions are fundamental to the law of trusts and I would have thought uncontroversial. However, proposition (ii) may call for some expansion. There are cases where property has been put into the name of X without X's knowledge but in circumstances where no gift to X was intended. It has been held that such property is recoverable under a resulting trust: *Birch* v *Blagrave* (1755) 1 Amb 264; *Childers* v *Childers* (1857) 1 De G & J 482; *In re Vinogradoff, Allen* v *Jackson* [1935] WN 68; *In re Muller, Cassin* v *Mutual Cash Order Co. Ltd* [1953] NZLR 879. These cases are explicable on the ground that, by the time action was brought, X or his successors in title have become aware of the facts which gave rise to a resulting trust; his conscience was affected as from the time of such discovery and thereafter he held on a resulting trust under which the property was recovered from him. There is, so far as I am aware, no authority which decides that X was a trustee, and therefore accountable for his deeds, at any time before he was aware of the circumstances which gave rise to a resulting trust.

Those basic principles are inconsistent with the case being advanced by the bank. The latest time at which there was any possibility of identifying the 'trust property' was the date on which the moneys in the mixed bank account of the local authority ceased to be traceable when the local authority's account went into overdraft in June 1987. At that date, the local authority had no knowledge of the invalidity of the contract but regarded the moneys as its own to spend as it thought fit. There was therefore never a time at which both (a) there was defined trust property and (b) the conscience of the local authority in relation to such defined trust property was affected. The basic requirements of a trust were never satisfied.

Resulting trust
This is not a case where the bank had any equitable interest which pre-dated receipt by the local authority of the upfront payment. Therefore, in order to show that the local authority became a trustee, the bank must demonstrate circumstances which raised a trust for the first time either at the date on which the local authority received the money or at the date on which payment into the mixed account was made. Counsel for the bank specifically disavowed any claim based on a constructive trust. This was plainly right because the local authority had no relevant knowledge sufficient to raise a constructive trust at any time before the moneys, upon the bank account going into overdraft, became untraceable. Once there ceased to be an identifiable trust fund, the local authority could not become a trustee: *In re Goldcorp Exchange Ltd* [1995] 1 AC 74. Therefore, as the argument for the bank recognised, the only possible trust which could be established was a resulting trust arising from the circumstances in which the local authority received the upfront payment.

Under existing law a resulting trust arises in two sets of circumstances: (A) where A makes a voluntary payment to B or pays (wholly or in part) for the purchase of property which is vested either in B alone or in the joint names of A and B, there is a presumption that A did not intend to make a gift to B: the money or property is held on trust for A (if he is the sole provider of the money) or in the case of a joint purchase by A and B in shares proportionate to their contributions. It is important to stress that this is only a *presumption*, which presumption is easily rebutted either by the counter-presumption of advancement or by direct evidence of A's intention to make an outright transfer: see *Underhill and Hayton, Law of Trusts and Trustees*, pp. 317 et seq. *Vandervell v Inland Revenue Commissioners* [1976] 2 AC 291, 312 et seq.; *In re Vandervell's Trusts (No. 2)* [1974] Ch 269, 288 et seq. (B) Where A transfers property to B *on express trusts*, but the trusts declared do not exhaust the whole beneficial interest: ibid. and *Quistclose Investment Ltd v Rolls Razor Ltd (In Liquidation)* [1970] AC 567. Both types of resulting trust are traditionally regarded as examples of trusts giving effect to the common intention of the parties. A resulting trust is not imposed by law against the intentions of the trustee (as is a constructive trust) but gives effect to his presumed intention. Megarry J in *In re Vandervell's Trusts (No. 2)* suggests that a resulting trust of type (B) does not depend on intention but operates automatically. I am not convinced that this is right. If the settlor has expressly, or by necessary implication, abandoned any beneficial interest in the trust property, there is in my view no resulting trust: the undisposed-of equitable interest vests in the Crown as bona vacantia: see *In re West Sussex Constabulary's Widows, Children and Benevolent (1930) Fund Trusts* [1971] Ch 1. . . .

16.1.1 PRESUMED RESULTING TRUSTS ON A VOLUNTARY CONVEYANCE OR PAYMENT

VANDERVELL v INLAND REVENUE COMMISSIONERS [1967] 1 All ER 1, HL

FACTS: In 1958 the taxpayer, who controlled a very successful private company, decided to give £150,000 to the Royal College of Surgeons to found a chair of pharmacology. The company's issued ordinary share capital was (i) five hundred thousand ordinary shares, substantially all of which were held by the taxpayer; (ii) one hundred thousand 'A' ordinary shares held by a bank as nominee for the taxpayer and (iii) 2,600,000 'B' ordinary shares, of which the taxpayer held 546,692 and the remaining 2,053,308 were held by VT Ltd as trustees of a family settlement. Only the first class of shares carried voting rights. In order to achieve his purpose the taxpayer, through R his financial adviser, suggested giving to the college the one hundred thousand 'A' ordinary shares, intending to pass to the college both the legal and beneficial interest in them. Subsequently, on the advice of R and by way of second thoughts in order to avoid any future difficulties if the company were to be converted into a public company, the taxpayer acceded to R's suggestion that the college should give an option to VT Ltd to purchase the shares for £5,000 within five years. In November 1958, R delivered to the college the transfer by the bank of the 'A' ordinary shares and an option deed. The college sealed these deeds and were registered as owners of the shares. Dividends on the 'A' shares, amounting to £145,000 less tax at the standard rate, were paid to the college. On 11 October 1961, VT Ltd exercised the option. The £5,000 was paid to the college. The taxpayer was assessed to surtax on the basis that the dividends in the years 1958–59 and 1959–60 which, with the £5,000 on the exercise of the option, made up the gift to the college, were his income or were required to be treated as his income under s. 415 of the Income Tax Act 1952. It was not disputed that there was a settlement within the meaning of s. 411(2) of that Act. The taxpayer contended that he had by the settlement within s. 411(2) divested himself absolutely of the property and thus came within the exception provided by s. 415(1)(d) and (2).

HELD: (i) (Lord Reid and Lord Donovan dissenting) the option to purchase the 'A' shares was vested in the trustee company in 1958, either (per Lord Upjohn and Lord Pearce) as a matter of inference from the primary facts on such trusts as might be declared subsequently, or (per Lord Wilberforce) as a matter of interpretation of the evidence on trusts which were undefined, and on either basis the consequence in law was that the option was held on a resulting trust for the taxpayer; accordingly the taxpayer had failed to divest himself absolutely of the property which was the source of the dividends paid to the college, and had not brought himself within the exempting provisions of s. 415(1)(d), (2) of the Income Tax Act 1952, with the consequence that the assessments should stand.

(ii) since a transfer of the 'A' shares had been executed by the bank, which was nominee for the taxpayer, and had been delivered on the taxpayer's behalf to the college, which became registered as owners of the shares, there had been no need for a separate transfer of the taxpayer's equitable interest in the 'A' shares and s. 53(1)(c) of the Law of Property Act 1925 had no application. . . .

LORD UPJOHN: . . . The question is whether, notwithstanding the plainly expressed intention of the taxpayer by himself or his agents, the absence of writing prevented any equitable or beneficial interest in the shares passing to the college so that contrary to his wishes and understanding they remained bare trustees for him. This depends entirely on the true construction of s. 53(1)(c) of the Law of Property Act 1925, which the Crown maintain makes writing necessary to pass the beneficial interest. . . .

. . . the object of the section, as was the object of the old Statute of Frauds, is to prevent hidden oral transactions in equitable interests in fraud of those truly entitled, and making it difficult, if not impossible, for the trustees to ascertain who are in truth his beneficiaries. When the beneficial owner, however, owns the whole beneficial estate and is in a position to give directions to his bare trustee with regard to the legal as well as the equitable estate there can be no possible ground for invoking the section where the beneficial owner wants to deal with the legal estate as well as the equitable estate.

I cannot agree with Diplock LJ that prima facie a transfer of the legal estate carries with it the absolute beneficial interest in the property transferred; this plainly is not so, e.g., the transfer may be on a change of trustee; it is a matter of intention in each case. If, however, the intention of the beneficial owner in directing the trustee to transfer the legal estate to X is that X should be the beneficial owner, I can see no reason for any further document or further words in the document assigning the legal estate also expressly transferring the beneficial interest; the greater includes the less. X may be wise to secure some evidence that the beneficial owner intended him to take the beneficial interest in case his beneficial title is challenged at a later date but it certainly cannot, in my opinion, be a statutory requirement that to effect its passing there must be some writing under s. 53(1)(c). . . .

LORD WILBERFORCE: . . . The Court of Appeal, starting from the fact that the trustee company took the option as a volunteer, thought that this was a case where the presumption of a resulting trust arose and was not displaced. For my part, I prefer a slightly different and simpler approach. The transaction has been investigated on the evidence of the settlor and his agent and the facts have been found. There is no need, or room, as I see it, to invoke a presumption. The conclusion, on the facts found, is simply that the option was vested in the trustee company as a trustee on trusts, not defined at the time, possibly to be defined later. But the equitable, or beneficial interest, cannot remain in the air: the consequence in law must be that it remains in the settlor. There is no need to consider some of the more refined intellectualities of the doctrine of resulting trust, nor to speculate whether, in possible circumstances, the shares might be applicable for Mr. Vandervell's benefit: he had, as the direct result of the option and of the failure to place the beneficial interest in it securely away from him, not divested himself absolutely of the shares which it controlled.

RE VANDERVELL'S TRUSTS (No. 2) [1974] 3 All ER 205

FACTS: . . . Although the trustee company did not hold the option beneficially, V did not specify on what trusts it was to be held. He had in mind that it would either be held on the trusts of the children's settlement or on trust for employees of the products company. Between 1958 and 1961 V saw to it that the products company declared dividends, amounting to £157,000 after tax, which were paid to the college. The Revenue took the view that V was liable to surtax on the dividends since he had not divested himself of the beneficial interest in the option which was held by the trustee company on a resulting trust. That view was ultimately confirmed by the House of Lords. Accordingly, in October 1961 the trustee company, with V's approval, exercised the option. It paid £5,000 out of the funds of the children's settlement and the college duly transferred the shares. On 2 November the trustee company's solicitors wrote to the Revenue authorities informing them that the option had been exercised and that 'consequently such shares will henceforth be held by [the trustee company] upon the trusts of the [children's] Settlement'. In the years 1962 to 1964 V procured the products company to declare substantial dividends on the shares. Those dividends were paid to the trustee company which, with V's approval, added them to the funds of the children's settlement. The Revenue, however, claimed that V had still failed to divest himself of his interest in the shares. Accordingly, on 19 January 1965 V executed a deed transferring to the trustee company all right, title or interest which he had in the option, the shares or the dividends and declaring that the trustee company was to hold them on the trusts of the children's settlement. V died in 1967. His executors brought proceedings against the trustee company claiming that the dividends declared on the shares in the period from October 1961 to January 1965 were held on a resulting trust for V. They contended that, at the time of the transfer of the shares by the college in 1961, V had not disposed of his equitable interest in the shares in writing as required by s. 53(1)(c) of the Law of Property Act 1925.

HELD: The executors' claim failed. During the period from 1961 to 1965 the shares were held by the trustee company on the trusts of the children's settlement for the following reasons—

(i) In view of the fact that the trustee company had, with V's approval, (a) used money from the children's settlement to acquire the shares, (b) expressly stated to the Revenue that the shares would be held on the trusts of that settlement, and (c) thereafter paid dividends on the shares into the settlement, there was ample evidence to show that, when the option was exercised and the shares transferred, the trustee company had made an effective declaration of trust whereby the shares were to be held on the trusts of the children's settlement. . . .

(ii) It was immaterial that V had not made any disposition in writing of his equitable interest in the option, for the exercise of the option and the transfer of the shares to the trustee company necessarily put an end to the resulting trust of the option. Neither the extinction of the resulting trust of the option resulting from its exercise nor the creation of a beneficial interest in the shares by the declaration of trust amounted to a disposition of an equitable interest or trust within s. 53(1)(c) of the 1925 Act. . . .

(iii) In any event (per Lord Denning MR and Lawton LJ) in view of the part that V had played in the transfer of the shares to the trustee company and in procuring the products company to declare dividends on those shares, he would have been estopped from alleging thereafter that he had any beneficial interest in the dividends and, accordingly, the executors could be in no better position in that respect. . . .

LORD DENNING MR: . . . Counsel for the executors admitted that the intention of Mr Vandervell and the trustee company was that the shares should be held on trust for the children's settlement. But he said that this intention was of no avail. He said that during the first period Mr Vandervell had an equitable interest in the property, namely, a resulting trust; that he never disposed of this equitable interest (because he never knew he had it); and that in any case it was the disposition of an equitable interest which, under s. 53 of the Law of Property Act 1925, had to be in writing, signed by him or his agent, lawfully authorised by him in writing (and there was no such writing produced). He cited *Grey* v *Inland Revenue Comrs* and *Oughtred* v *Inland Revenue Comrs*.

There is a complete fallacy in that argument. A resulting trust for the settlor is born and dies without any writing at all. It comes into existence wherever there is a gap in the beneficial ownership. It ceases to exist whenever that gap is filled by someone becoming beneficially entitled. As soon as the gap is filled by the creation or declaration of a valid trust, the resulting trust comes to an end. In this case, before the option was exercised, there was a gap in the beneficial ownership. So there was a resulting trust for Mr Vandervell. But, as soon as the option was exercised and the shares registered in the trustees' name, there was created a valid trust of the shares in favour of the children's settlement. Not being a trust of land, it could be created without any writing. A trust of personalty can be created without writing. Both Mr Vandervell and the trustee company had done everything which needed to be done to make the settlement of these shares binding on them. So there was a valid trust: see *Milroy* v *Lord* **[5.1.1]** . . .

So here Mr Vandervell made a perfect gift to the trustee company of the dividends on the shares, so far as they were handed over or treated by him as belonging to the trustee company for the benefit of the children. Alternatively, there was an equitable estoppel. His conduct was such that it would be quite inequitable for him to be allowed to enforce his strict rights (under a resulting trust) having regard to the dealings which had taken place between the parties: see *Hughes* v *Metropolitan Railway Co*. (1877) 2 App Cas 439.

RE VANDERVELL'S TRUSTS [1974] 1 All ER 47

HELD: (i) On the evidence it was V and not the college which had provided the option to the defendant company. It was immaterial that the option had been provided by V indirectly by procuring the college to grant the option and that V could not have compelled the college to grant it. The grant was part of the overall scheme devised by R on behalf of V whereby the shares of which V was the sole beneficial owner, were to be disposed of in such a way as to yield to the college sufficient dividends to provide the promised sum; apart from that scheme the college would not have had any motive or justification for granting the option to the defendant company. Accordingly the option had been provided by V and he was the true grantor of it.

(ii)   Rights under an option, like other rights, could be held on a resulting trust just as they could be held on other trusts. On the evidence the option had been granted to the defendant company on trust and not beneficially. However, since no effective trusts had ever been established by V, the result was that V had failed to dispose of his beneficial interest in the option and, in consequence, the option was held on an automatic resulting trust for V.

(iii)   The fact that, in exercising the option, the defendant company had used £5,000 of the moneys held by them on the trusts of the children's settlement did not, and could not, have the effect that the shares obtained by exercising the option were held on the trusts of the children's settlement rather than on the resulting trust. As a general rule a person who expended money on the property of another had no lien on it and, if there was not even a lien, a fortiori there was no ownership.

(iv)   V, and through him the plaintiffs, were not estopped from asserting any claim to the beneficial interest in the shares acquired by exercising the option by reason of the fact that the price had been paid out of the funds of the children's settlement. It could not be asserted that V had knowingly allowed the defendant company, as trustee of the children's settlement, to incur expenditure in enhancing the value of his own property, since at the relevant time V had no knowledge that he was the beneficial owner of the option. Furthermore the defendant company could not rely on promissory estoppel since, even if the defendant company had acted to its detriment in using the money from the children's settlement, there was nothing to prevent it from resuming its former position, since it was accepted that the shares were held subject to a lien in favour of the children's settlement for the sum expended and interest thereon.

(v)   No reliance could be placed on the fact that the dividends paid during the period had, to V's knowledge, been dealt with, and accounted for, by the defendant company as trustee of the children's settlement. The dividends had come from VP Ltd and not from V and therefore the presumption of advancement in favour of the children had no application, since VP Ltd was not their father and did not stand in loco parentis to them.

(vi)   The execution of the deed of release in 1965 did not have the effect of estopping V, or the plaintiffs, from asserting any claim to be beneficially entitled to the option or to the shares when the option had been exercised or from making any claim to the dividends. At the time when the deed was executed the strong probabilities were that, although the dividends might, or might not, be traceable into a credit in a bank account, or into investments, none of them still existed as a dividend. Accordingly the operative words, construed simpliciter, were ineffective to carry any of the disputed dividends and that construction was confirmed by the recitals and the surrounding circumstances. Accordingly the deed had no effect on any interest that V had in the dividends that had already been paid or the proceeds thereof.

(vii)   It followed therefore that, during the period, the defendant company had held the 'A' shares on a resulting trust for V absolutely, subject only to a lien in favour of the children's settlement for the sum of £5,000 and interest, and that the plaintiffs were therefore, subject to that lien, entitled to such sum as might be shown on taking accounts and enquiries to represent the dividends or the proceeds of the dividends declared on the 'A' shares during the period.

MEGARRY J: . . . At this stage I am concerned with the option. In form, the college was the grantor; but in substance and reality, as I have held, the grantor was Mr Vandervell. It was he who provided the benefits that produced the grant of the option to the defendant company. The essential question is whether the defendant company took the option beneficially or whether the defendant company held it on trust. In discussing this, it is difficult to do so in isolation, without considering to some extent the second main issue, namely, if the defendant company took the option on trust, what those trusts were: was the option held on a resulting or other trust for Mr Vandervell, or was it held on the trusts of the children's settlement, subject or not to a power to divert the beneficial interest to some other trust? . . . Indeed, I do not think that Mr Vandervell ever really concerned himself in any way about the option; he certainly showed no trace of intending that it should be held on the substitutional trusts. I think he was probably interested to the extent of wishing to be kept informed about what happened, but his main interest and concern was to get rid of the shares to the college and not to get them back. Yet I cannot see how an intention not to get the shares back can negative a resulting trust if in the event he made no effective disposition of his beneficial interest in them and the operation of equity brought them back to him in ways never considered by him. Whatever may be the position under a presumed resulting trust, I do not see how the donor's intention not to have the beneficial interest can prevail where the resulting trust is automatic. My conlusion is that there is nothing in the evidence before me that warrants any conclusion different from that reached in *Vandervell No. 1*, namely, that the option was granted to the defendant company on trust, but that no effective trusts were ever established and so the defendant company held the option on a resulting trust for Mr Vandervell. . . . First, this action is not an action on the deed. It is an action wholly outside the deed, and the deed comes into the picture only because the defendant company relies on it by way of defence. The recitals are thus not conclusive, though they can be relied on as evidence. But then when one turns to the recitals I cannot see that they provide any real evidence of the ownership of the disputed dividends. Indeed, as I pointed out, there is not one word in the recitals about the dividends. There are recitals about how the defendant company intended to hold the option, about Mr Vandervell's knowledge and consent to the payment of the £5,000 out of the funds of the children's trusts, about how the defendant company has in fact held the shares, and about what Mr Vandervell did not intend in relation to the shares and the option, and the existence of doubts, and so on; but there is not a word about the dividends. . . . as is shown by what I have said about *Vandervell No. 1*, there are branches of resulting trusts where the proof of an intention carries one a very little distance, and here the recitals are mainly recitals of intentions. . . .

Equally I cannot see how any effective case of an election to abandon any claim to the disputed dividends has been made out; and the same applies to the contention that Mr Vandervell has acquiesced in the dividends being treated as being subject to the trusts of the children's settlement, if by that it is meant that by any such acquiescence Mr Vandervell precluded himself in some way from claiming the dividends. I cannot see that it has been brought home to Mr Vandervell that he knew enough about what the deed was doing for it to bind him in this way, even if, contrary to my opinion, its terms would have sufficed to do this had he known enough about it.

16.1.1.1   Rebutting the presumption of a resulting trust

FOWKES v PASCOE (1875) 10 Ch App 343

FACTS: A testatrix, both before and after she made her will, purchased sums of stock in the names of herself and the son of her daughter-in-law. By her will she gave the residue of her estate to her daughter-in-law for life, and after her death to the son and the daughter of the daughter-in-law:—
HELD: Under the circumstances, the sums of stock so purchased were a gift to the son of the daughter-in-law. That in such a case the evidence of the son and his wife was admissible, and could not be disregarded as rebutting the presumption of a resulting trust; and that, coupled with the circumstances under which the stock was purchased, it was sufficient to rebut the presumption. On the facts, that the testatrix had not placed herself *in loco parentis* to the son of her daughter-in-law or to the other residuary legatee, and that both these facts would have to be proved to make the gift an ademption of the residuary bequest.

SIR W M JAMES LJ: I will assume, for the present purpose, that the origin and nature of the relations between the parties did not affect the legal presumption of resulting trust. I will assume, further, that the implication of a resulting trust does arise as much in the case of a transfer as in that of a purchase of stock, although that certainly is not the case with regard to a conveyance of land; and I will proceed to consider how the evidence stands on these assumptions. To my mind, differing in this respect altogether from the Master of the Rolls, the evidence in favour of gift and against trust is absolutely conclusive. There is, to begin with, in respect of the two first purchases, an inference from the facts themselves which is, to my mind, irresistible. Whatever may be the presumption as to one purchase or one transfer standing by itself, the fact of the contemporaneous purchases of small distinct sums in different names,—in the name of a *quasi* son or grandson, and of a companion, and the subsequent repetition of those purchases, is not to be got over. The lady had £500 to invest; she had already large sums of stock standing in her own name, besides other considerable property. Is it possible to reconcile with mental sanity the theory that she put £250 into the names of herself and her companion, and £250 into the names of herself and Defendant, as trustees upon trust for herself? What trust—what object is there conceivable in doing this? . . .

But the case is far from resting here. The defendant swears positively to their having been gifts, and although I concur in what the Master of the Rolls has said, and although this Court has more than once said that it is too dangerous to rely on the mere evidence of a party interested as to conversations with a deceased person, yet it is legally admissible evidence, and is not to be disregarded when adduced by a man in support of his claim to that which is indisputably his at law, and which an attempt is made to deprive him of. Where the Court of Chancery is asked, on an equitable assumption or presumption, to take away from a man that which by the common law of the land he is entitled to, he surely has a right to say: 'Listen to my story as to how I came to have it, and judge that story with reference to all the surrounding facts and circumstances.' The evidence is to be weighed, of course, with reference to that danger, but still is to be weighed like every other piece of evidence, together with every other fact and inference in the case.

16.1.1.2 Illegality and the presumption of a resulting trust

TINSLEY v *MILLIGAN* [1994] 1 AC 340, HL

FACTS: The plaintiff and the defendant, two single women, formed a joint business venture to run lodging houses. Using funds generated by the business they purchased a house in which they lived together and which was vested in the sole name of the plaintiff, but on the understanding that they were joint beneficial owners of the property. The purpose of that arrangement was to assist in the perpetration of frauds on the Department of Social Security ('DSS') and over a number of years the defendant, with the connivance of the plaintiff, made false benefit claims on the DSS. The plaintiff did likewise. The money thus obtained helped the parties meet their bills but did not represent a substantial part of their income and contributed only in a small way to their acquisition of the equity in the house. Subsequently the defendant repented of the frauds and disclosed them to the DSS. A quarrel between the parties led to the plaintiff moving out, leaving the defendant in occupation. Thereafter the plaintiff gave the defendant notice to quit and in due course brought proceedings against the defendant claiming possession and asserting sole ownership of the property. The defendant counterclaimed for an order for sale and for a declaration that the property was held by the plaintiff on trust for the parties in equal shares. The judge dismissed the plaintiff's claim and allowed the counterclaim. On appeal by the plaintiff, the Court of Appeal (by a majority) dismissed the appeal on the ground that in the circumstances the public conscience would not be affronted if the defendant's counterclaim were to succeed.

On appeal by the plaintiff:—

HELD: Dismissing the appeal (Lord Keith of Kinkel and Lord Goff of Chieveley dissenting), that a claimant to an interest in property, whether based on a legal or equitable title, was entitled to recover if he was not forced to plead or rely on an illegality, even although it transpired that the title on which he relied was acquired in the course of carrying through an illegal transaction; that, in the circumstances, by showing that she had contributed to the purchase price of the property and that there was a common understanding between the parties that they owned the property equally the defendant had established a resulting trust; that there was no necessity to prove the reason for the conveyance into the sole name of the plaintiff, which was irrelevant to the defendant's claim, and that since there was no evidence to rebut the presumption of a resulting trust the defendant was entitled to succeed on her counterclaim.

Per curiam. A public conscience test has no place in determining the extent to which rights created by illegal transactions should be recognised.

LORD BROWNE-WILKINSON: My Lords, I agree with the speech of my noble and learned friend, Lord Goff of Chieveley, that the consequences of being a party to an illegal transaction cannot depend, as the majority in the Court of Appeal held, on such an imponderable factor as the extent to which the public conscience would be affronted bv recognising rights created by illegal transactions. However, I have the misfortune to disagree with him as to the correct principle to be applied in a case where equitable property rights are acquired as a result of an illegal transaction. . . .

In the present case, Miss Milligan claims under a resulting or implied trust. The court below have found, and it is not now disputed, that apart from the question of illegality Miss Milligan would have been entitled in equity to a half share in the house in accordance with the principles exemplified in *Gissing* v *Gissing* [1971] AC 886; *Grant* v *Edwards* [1986] Ch 638 and *Lloyds Bank Plc* v *Rosset* [1991] 1 AC 107. The creation of such an equitable interest does not depend upon a contractual obligation but on a common intention acted upon by the parties to their detriment. It is a development of the old law of resulting trust under which, where two parties have provided the purchase money to buy a property which is conveyed into the name of one of them alone, the latter is presumed to hold the property on a resulting trust for both parties in shares proportionate to their contributions to the purchase price. In arguments, no distinction was drawn between strict resulting trusts and a *Gissing* v *Gissing* type of trust.

A presumption of resulting trust also arises in equity when A transfers personalty or money to B: see *Snell's Equity*, 29th ed. (1990), pp. 183–184; *Standing* v *Bowring* (1885) 31

ChD 282, 287, *per* Cotton LJ and *Dewar v Dewar* [1975] 1 WLR 1532, 1537. Before 1925, there was also a presumption of resulting trust when land was voluntarily transferred by A to B: it is arguable, however, that the position has been altered by the 1925 property legislation: see *Snell's Equity*, p. 182. The presumption of a resulting trust is, in my view, crucial in considering the authorities. On that presumption (and on the contrary presumption of advancement) hinges the answer to the crucial question 'does a plaintiff claiming under a resulting trust have to rely on the underlying illegality?' Where the presumption of resulting trust applies, the plaintiff does not have to rely on the illegality. If he proves that the property is vested in the defendant alone but that the plaintiff provided part of the purchase money, or voluntarily transferred the property to the defendant, the plaintiff establishes his claim under a resulting trust unless either the contrary presumption of advancement displaces the presumption of resulting trust or the defendant leads evidence to rebut the presumption of resulting trust. Therefore, in cases where the presumption of advancement does not apply, a plaintiff can establish his equitable interest in the property without relying in any way on the underlying illegal transaction. In this case Miss Milligan as defendant simply pleaded the common intention that the property should belong to both of them and that she contributed to the purchase price: she claimed that in consequence the property belonged to them equally. To the same effect was her evidence in chief. Therefore Miss Milligan was not forced to rely on the illegality to prove her equitable interest. Only in the reply and the course of Miss Milligan's cross-examination did such illegality emerge: it was Miss Tinsley who had to rely on that illegality.

Although the presumption of advancement does not directly arise for consideration in this case, it is important when considering the decided cases to understand its operation. On a transfer from a man to his wife, children or others to whom he stands in loco parentis, equity presumes an intention to make a gift. Therefore in such a case, unlike the case where the presumption of resulting trust applies, in order to establish any claim the plaintiff has himself to lead evidence sufficient to rebut the presumption of gift and in so doing will normally have to plead, and give evidence of, the underlying illegal purpose.

Against this background, I turn to consider the authorities dealing with the position in equity where A transferred property to B for an illegal purpose. . . .

. . . during the 19th century . . . there was originally a difference of view as to whether a transaction entered into for an illegal purpose would be enforced at law or in equity if the party had repented of his illegal purpose before it had been put into operation, i.e. the doctrine of locus poenitentiae. It was eventually recognised both at law and in equity that if the plaintiff had repented before the illegal purpose was carried through, he could recover his property: see *Taylor v Bowers*, 1 QBD 291; *Symes v Hughes* LR 9 Eq 475. The principle of locus poenitentiae is in my judgment irreconcilable with any rule that where property is transferred for an illegal purpose no equitable proprietary right exists. The equitable right, if any, must arise at the time at which the property was voluntarily transferred to the third party or purchased in the name of the third party. The existence of the equitable interest cannot depend upon events occurring after that date. Therefore if, under the principle of locus poenitentiae, the courts recognise that an equitable interest did arise out of the underlying transaction, the same must be true where the illegal purpose was carried through. The carrying out of the illegal purpose cannot, by itself, destroy the pre-existing equitable interest. The doctrine of locus poenitentiae therefore demonstrates that the effect of illegality is not to prevent a proprietary interest in equity from arising or to produce a forfeiture of such right: the effect is to render the equitable interest unenforceable in certain circumstances. The effect of illegality is not substantive but procedural. The question therefore is, 'In what circumstances will equity refuse to enforce equitable rights which undoubtedly exist.' . . .

Equally I cannnot see how any effective case of an election to abandon any claim to the disputed dividends has been made out; and the same applies to the contention that Mr Vandervell has acquiesced in the dividends being treated as being subject to the trusts of the children's settlement, if by that it is meant that by any such acquiescence Mr Vandervell precluded himself in some way from claiming the dividends. I cannot see that it has been brought home to Mr Vandervell that he knew enough about what the deed was doing for it to bind him in this way, even if, contrary to my opinion, its terms would have sufficed to do this had he known enough about it.

16.1.1.3 The presumption of advancement

PETTITT v PETTITT [1969] 2 All ER 385, HL

LORD DIPLOCK: the intention with which an act is done affects its legal consequences and the evidence here does not disclose what was the actual intention with which [Mr Pettit] did it. This situation commonly occurs when the actor is deceased. When the act is of a kind to which this technique has frequently to be applied by the courts the imputed intention may acquire the description of a 'presumption'—but presumptions of this type are not immutable. A presumption of fact is no more than a consensus of judicial opinion disclosed by reported cases as to the most likely inference of fact to be drawn in the absence of any evidence to the contrary—for example, presumptions of legitimacy, of death, of survival and the like. But the most likely inference as to a person's intention in the transactions of his everyday life depends on the social environment in which he lives and the common habits of thought of those who live in it. The consensus of judicial opinion which gave rise to the presumptions of 'advance-ment' and 'resulting trust' in transactions between husband and wife is to be found in cases relating to the propertied classes of the nineteenth century and the first quarter of the twentieth century among whom marriage settlements were common, and it was unusual for the wife to contribute by her earnings to the family income. It was not until after World War II that the courts were required to consider the proprietary rights in family assets of a different social class. The advent of legal aid, the wider employment of married women in industry, commerce and the professions and the emergence of a property-owning, particularly a real-property-mortgaged-to-a-building-society-owning, democracy has compelled the courts to direct their attention to this during the last 20 years. It would, in my view, be an abuse of the legal technique for ascertaining or imputing intention to apply to transactions between the post-war generation of married couples 'presumptions' which are based on inferences of fact which an earlier generation of judges drew as to the most likely intentions of earlier generations of spouses belonging to the propertied classes of a different social era.

TINKER v TINKER [1970] 1 All ER 540

FACTS: The husband acting honestly, on the advice of his solicitors, had conveyed into his wife's name a property which was intended for use as the matrimonial home in order to avoid it being claimed by creditors of the husband's business if the business failed. The contract to purchase was also in the wife's name. The purchase money was supplied by the husband. The marriage then broke up. On an application under s. 17 of the Married Women's Property Act 1882:
HELD: The presumption that the property was conveyed to the wife for her own use was not rebutted by the husband's evidence that it was conveyed to defeat his creditors, and accordingly the house belonged to the wife . . .

LORD DENNING MR: . . . So it is plain that the husband had the house put into his wife's name so as to avoid any risk of it being taken by his creditors in case his business was not a success. What is the result in law? In *Gascoigne v Gascoigne* [1918] 1 KB 223 it was held that, when a husband put a house in his wife's name so as to avoid it being taken by his creditors, the house belonged to his wife. The husband could not be heard to say that it belonged to him, because he could not be allowed to take advantage of his own dishonesty. That case was applied in *Re Emery's Investments Trusts, Emery v Emery* [1959] Ch 410, and also in *McEvoy v Belfast Banking Co. Ltd*. We were invited by counsel for the husband to overrule those decisions. But in my opinion they are good law.

Then counsel for the husband said that *Gascoigne v Gascoigne* is distinguishable, because there the husband was dishonest, whereas here the registrar has found that the husband was honest. Counsel relied in this regard on *Davies v Otty*. There a man's wife had left him ten years ago. He justifiably believed that she was dead and married another woman. Then he was told that his first wife was still alive. Being fearful that he might be charged with bigamy, he conveyed property to the defendant on the distinct understanding that it was 'to be done away with when the unpleasantness was over'. He was, of course, quite innocent of bigamy. The court ordered the defendant to reconvey the property to him. In that case it is obvious that the defendant was trustee for the plaintiff who throughout was acting quite honestly and quite consistently.

Accepting that in the present case the husband was honest—he acted, he said, on the advice of his solicitor—nevertheless I do not think that he can claim that the house belongs to him. The solicitor did not give evidence. But the only proper advice that he could give was: 'In order to avoid the house being taken by your creditors, you can put it into your wife's name; but remember that, if you do, it is your wife's and you cannot go back on it'.

But, whether the solicitor gave that advice or not, I am quite clear that the husband cannot have it both ways. So he is on the horns of a dilemma. He cannot say that the house is his own and, at one and the same time, say that it is his wife's. As against his wife, he wants her to say that it belongs to *him*. As against his creditors, that it belongs to *her*. That simply will not do. Either it was conveyed to her for her own use absolutely; or it was conveyed to her as trustee for her husband. It must be one or the other. The presumption is that it was conveyed to her for her own use; and he does not rebut that presumption by saying that he only did it to defeat his creditors. I think that it belongs to her.

16.2   Constructive Trusts

16.2.1   CONSTRUCTIVE TRUST: PROPERTY-BASED OR FREE-STANDING REMEDY?

RE SHARPE (A BANKRUPT) [1980] 1 WLR 219

FACTS: On April 27, 1978, a receiving order was made against a bankrupt. He and his wife and his aunt J, aged 82, were living together in a maisonette, which with a shop formed leasehold premises purchased by the bankrupt in 1975 for £17,000. J had provided £12,000 of the purchase price, the remainder having been raised on mortgage. In providing the money, J had been told, according to her affidavit evidence, that she would be able to stay in the premises for as long as she liked, and that she would be looked after by the bankrupt and his wife. J also paid some £2,271·16 for decorations and fittings for the property. She also paid some £9,000 in an attempt to stave off the bankrupt's bankruptcy. In September 1975 on the advice of her solicitor, J got from the bankrupt a promissory note for £15,700, the reason being that by her will she had left her estate to her three nephews equally, and she felt that it would be unfair if the bankrupt were to take one third of what remained without bringing into account what he had already received. The trustee in bankruptcy took steps to find out what rights, if any, J claimed arising out of the provision by her of £12,000 towards the purchase price but J did not reply to his letters. On April 30, 1979, the trustee in bankruptcy contracted to sell the premises to a purchaser for £17,000 with vacant possession, completion being fixed for May 29, 1979. After the date of the contract J for the first time put forward a claim to an interest in the premises.

On the trustee in bankruptcy's motion for an order that the bankrupt and J give vacant possession of the premises.
HELD: Dismissing the application, (1) that J had provided the £12,000 by way of loan and not as a gift and, accordingly, no interest in her favour was created under a resulting trust but since it was an essential feature of the loan that J was to make her home in the premises to be acquired with the money lent, she had, as against the bankrupt, the right to occupy the premises for as long as she liked while the loan remained unrepaid.

(2)   That J's right of occupation did confer some interest in the property under a constructive trust and that, since in the circumstances she was not barred from asserting her right by reason of any laches or acquiescence on her part, the trustee in bankruptcy took the property subject to her right and, accordingly, he was not entitled to an order for possession.

BROWNE-WILKINSON J: . . . Even if it be right to say that the courts can impose a constructive trust as a remedy in certain cases—which to my mind is a novel concept in English law—in order to provide a remedy the court must first find a right which has been infringed. So far as land is concerned an oral agreement to create any interest in it must be evidenced in writing: see s. 40 of the Law of Property Act 1925. Therefore if these irrevocable licences create an interest in land, the rights cannot rest simply on an oral contract. The introduction of an interest under a constructive trust is an essential ingredient if the plaintiff has any right at all. Therefore in cases such as this, it cannot be that the interest in property arises for the first time when the court declares it to exist. The right must have arisen at the time of the transaction in order for the plaintiff to have any right the breach of which can be remedied. Again, I think the *D. H. N. Food Distributors Ltd* case [1976] 1 WLR 852 shows that the equity pre-dates any order of the court. The right to compensation in that case depended on substantive rights at the date of compulsory acquisition, not on what remedy the court subsequently chose to grant in the subsequent litigation.

Accordingly, if I am right in holding that as between the debtor and Mrs Johnson she had an irrevocable licence to remain in the property, authority compels me to hold that that gave her an interest in the property before the bankruptcy and the trustee takes the property subject to that interest. In my judgment the mere intervention of the bankruptcy by itself cannot alter Mrs Johnson's property interest. If she is to be deprived of her interest as against the trustee in bankruptcy, it must be because of some conduct of hers which precludes her from enforcing her rights, that is to say, the ordinary principles of acquiescence and laches which apply to all beneficiaries seeking to enforce their rights apply to this case.

I am in no way criticising the trustee in bankruptcy's conduct; he tried to find out if she made any claim relating to the £12,000 before he contracted to sell the property. But I do not think that on ordinary equitable principles Mrs Johnson should be prevented from asserting her rights at this late stage. She is very old and in bad health. No one had ever advised her that she might have rights to live in the property. As soon as she appreciated that she was to be evicted she at once took legal advice and asserted her claim. This, in my judgment, is far removed from conduct which precludes enforcement by a beneficiary of his rights due to his acquiescence, the first requirement of acquiescence being that the beneficiary knows his or her rights and does not assert them.

Accordingly, I hold that Mrs Johnson is entitled as against the trustee in bankruptcy to remain in the property until she is repaid the sums she advanced. I reach this conclusion with some hesitation since I find the present state of the law very confused and difficult to fit in with established equitable principles. I express the hope that in the near future the whole question can receive full consideration in the Court of Appeal, so that, in order to do justice to the many thousands of people who never come into court at all but who wish to know with certainty what their proprietary rights are, the extent to which these irrevocable licences bind third parties may be defined with certainty. Doing justice to the litigant who actually appears in the court by the invention of new principles of law ought not to involve injustice to the other persons who are not litigants before the court but whose rights are fundamentally affected by the new principles. . . .

16.2.2   THE OBLIGATIONS OF A CONSTRUCTIVE TRUSTEE

LONRHO PLC v *FAYED (No. 2)* [1992] 1 WLR 1, ChD

FACTS: In 1991 the plaintiff, a large shareholder in another company, gave an undertaking to the Secretary of State for Trade and Industry that it would not acquire more than 30 per cent. of its share capital. In 1984 when it held 29.9 per cent., it sold all but 1,200 shares to the fourth defendant, a company owned by the first three defendants. It hoped thereby to secure a release from its undertaking to the Secretary of State, and therefore gain control of the company. In 1985, however, the fourth defendant made a public offer for the remaining shares in the company and acquired more than 50 per cent. of the shares, so that when the Secretary of State later released the plaintiff from its undertaking it was then too late to make a bid for the company. In 1990 the plaintiff sought a declaration that the fourth defendant held the entire issued share capital of the company in trust for the plaintiff on the ground that favourable responses by the company's board and the Secretary of State to the fourth defendant's bid had been procured by fraud, namely the giving of a false picture of the first three defendants' commercial standing, background and financial position; and that in consequence the bid had succeeded and the plaintiff had been deprived of any opportunity to make a bid.

HELD: That although equity would intervene by way of constructive trust where a party had acquired property and subsequently denied another's beneficial interest in it, the plaintiff had demonstrated no more than that the company might have been acquired by fraud, and had not shown that it was unconscionable to deny the plaintiff's beneficial interest: that a contract induced by fraudulent misrepresentation was voidable rather than void and could not retrospectively subject the defendants to a fiduciary obligation to act as a trustee and refrain from bidding for the company on their own account; that, in any event, given the plaintiff's failure, with full knowledge of the fraud, to object to the defendant's acquisition of the company it would have been unconscionable for the plaintiff to assert any beneficial interest; that, further, any order for divestment of the company, even if appropriate, could only be made at the suit of the Secretary of State, since he alone would have been the victim of the fraud; and that accordingly, the claim for a constructive trust or for divestment disclosed no cause of action.

MILLETT J: It is, as Lonrho submits, the independent jurisdiction of equity as a court of conscience to grant relief for every species of fraud and other unconscionable conduct. When appropriate, the court will grant a proprietary remedy to restore to the plaintiff property of which he has been wrongly deprived, or to prevent the defendant from retaining a benefit which he has obtained by his own wrong. It is not possible, and it would not be desirable, to attempt an exhaustive classification of the situations in which it will do so. Equity must retain what has been called its 'inherent flexibility and capacity to adjust to new situations by reference to mainsprings of the equitable jurisdiction:' *Meagher, Gummon & Lehane, Equity, Doctrines & Remedies*, 2nd ed. (1984), p. 327. All courts of justice proceed by analogy, but a court of equity must never be deterred by the absence of a precise analogy, provided that the principle invoked is sound. In *Taylor* v *Salmon* (1838) 4 My & Cr. 134, 141, Lord Cottenham LC remarked:

> I have before taken occasion to observe that I thought it the duty of this court to adapt its practice and course of proceedings as far as possible to the existing state of society, and to apply its jurisdiction to all those new cases which, . . . daily . . . in the affairs of men, must continually arise, and not, from too strict an adherence to forms and rules established under very different circumstances, decline to administer justice, and to enforce rights for which there is no other remedy.

The same attitude should still inform the approach of equity today. But its intervention must be based on principle; there must be some relationship between the relief granted and the circumstances which give rise to it.

The present claim is not concerned with an alleged misappropriation by the defendants of an asset previously belonging to Lonrho. In the restitutionary language of unjust enrichment, Lonrho's claim does not have a proprietary base. Most of the shares were acquired from third parties. The fact that some were acquired from Lonrho itself either forms the subject of the claim to rescission or is an embarrassment. To some extent, this is artfully obscured by the pleading, which alleges fraudulent deprivation of Lonrho's opportunity to bid. But Holdings did not exploit Lonrho's opportunity to bid but its own; if anything, it took advantage of Lonrho's inability to bid by reason of the undertaking which it had given to the Secretary of State. The alleged fraud may have enabled Holdings' bid to succeed; it did not deprive Lonrho of its own opportunity to bid.

The present claim, therefore, is concerned with a different class of case, in which the plaintiff's claim is to an asset acquired from other sources which should have been acquired for, the plaintiff. Equity will intervene by way of constructive trust, not only to compel a defendant to restore the plaintiff's property to him, but also to require a defendant to disgorge property which he should have acquired, if at all, for the plaintiff. In the latter category of case, the defendant's wrong lies not in the acquisition of the property, which may or may not have been lawful, but in his subsequent denial of the plaintiff's beneficial interest. For such to be the case, however, the defendant must either have acquired property which but for his wrongdoing would have belonged to the plaintiff, or he must have acquired property in circumstances in which he cannot conscientiously retain it as against the plaintiff.

. . . In *Reading* v *Attorney-General* [1951] AC 507 a former army sergeant was held accountable to the Crown for illicit profits he had obtained by exploiting his uniform and military status. In answer to the argument that by claiming the money the Crown would be affirming the criminal acts of its servant, Lord Porter, at p. 515, denied that this was the case; it would only be saying that as between it and its servant the servant could not set up his own wrong as a defence. But that was not the basis on which the Crown's claim succeeded; so far as it was based on any equitable principle, it was the principle referred to by Lord Oaksey, at p. 517:

> an agent is accountable for profits made in the course of his agency without the knowledge and consent of his principal, and no less accountable if the profits arise out of corrupt transactions; . . .

In so far as the claim succeeded in equity, the wrong which induced equity to intervene was not the unlawful means by which the profits were earned by the agent, but his subsequent refusal to account for them to his principal. Similarly in the present case, the fact that the defendants acquired the shares by means of a fraud practised on other parties would not afford them a defence to a claim by Lonrho if it had any basis for one, but it could not by itself found such a claim. . . .

The falsehoods allegedly told to third parties are plainly not enough to sustain Lonrho's claim. They may demonstrate that the Fayeds acquired House of Fraser by unlawful means, as the sergeant in *Reading* v *Attorney-General* [1951] AC 507 made his ill-gotten gains, but that is all. They do not demonstrate what needs to be established, namely that it would be unconscionable for the Fayeds to deny Lonrho's beneficial interest. Lonrho sought to demonstrate this by an argument which attempted to link its claim to relief to the fraud alleged to have been practised on it. The argument is to the following effect. The Fayeds obtained the shareholding from Lonrho by fraud, with the result that Lonrho is entitled to rescind the sale. Accordingly, so the argument runs, Holdings has held the shareholding in trust for Lonrho from the start; and as a constructive trustee it was subject to all the fiduciary obligations and disabilities of an express trustee. In particular, it was bound to abstain from placing itself in a position where its interest conflicted with its duty. Given that it held the shareholding in trust for Lonrho, it was bound to refrain from using the trust shareholding in order to mount a bid on its own account for the remaining shares, especially since it knew that Lonrho still wanted to bid for them itself.

In my judgment, the argument is misconceived. A contract obtained by fraudulent misrepresentation is voidable, not void, even in equity. The representee may elect to avoid it, but until he does so the representor is not a constructive trustee of the property transferred pursuant to the contract, and no fiduciary relationship exists between him and the representee: see *Daly* v *Sydney Stock Exchange Ltd* (1986) 160 CLR 371, 387–390), *per* Brennan J. It may well be that if the representee elects to avoid the contract and set aside a transfer of property made pursuant to it the beneficial interest in the property will be treated as having remained vested in him throughout, at least to the extent necessary to support any tracing claim. But the representee's election cannot retrospectively subject the representor to fiduciary obligations of the kind alleged. It is a mistake to suppose that in every situation in which a constructive trust arises the legal owner is necessarily subject to all the fiduciary obligations and disabilities of an express trustee. Even after the representee has elected to avoid the contract and reclaim the property, the obligations of the representor would in my judgment be analogous to those of a vendor of property contracted to be sold, and would not extend beyond the property actually obtained by the contract and liable to be returned.

But even if this were not the case, there is on the facts of this case a short and complete answer to Lonrho's claim. In March 1985 and with full knowledge of the fraud alleged to have been practised on it, Lonrho stood by without protest and allowed Holdings to bid

342 RESULTING AND CONSTRUCTIVE TRUSTS

for the outstanding shares in House of Fraser in the belief that it was acquiring them for its own benefit. As I have already observed, that puts rescission of the sale of the shareholding out of the question. But even if it did not, it would plainly be unconscionable for Lonrho afterwards to assert a beneficial interest in the remaining shares. To accede to such a claim would not be consonant with the fundamental principles on which a court of equity acts. It would convert the constructive trust into an instrument of fraud. . . .

16.3   Types of Constructive Trusts

16.3.1   CONSTRUCTIVE TRUSTEE OF UNAUTHORISED PROFITS

16.3.1.1   Claims against a fiduciary for an account of unauthorised profits

BOARDMAN v *PHIPPS* [1967] 2 AC 46, HL

FACTS: The defendants, a solicitor to the trustees and a beneficiary under the trust, attended the AGM of a company in which the trust had a substantial shareholding. Unhappy with the state of the company, the defendants decided to launch a take-over bid personally for those shares in the company which were not already trust-owned. The inside knowledge of the company which enabled the defendants to make a take-over bid was based on information received at the AGM while acting as proxies for the trustees. The solicitor (Boardman) wrote to the beneficiaries outlining his plans to take a personal interest in the company, thus giving them an opportunity to raise any objections they might have to his so doing. No objections having been made, the defendants proceeded with their take-over. In the event the take-over was very successful and the value of the shares in the company greatly increased in value. The trust profited and so did the defendants. The present action was brought by Phipps, a beneficiary under the trust, for an account of profits made by Boardman in his fiduciary capacity as solicitor to the trust. The trial judge, Wilberforce J, found as a fact that Phipps had not been fully informed by Boardman as to the precise nature of his plans.
HELD: (Viscount Dilhorne and Lord Upjohn dissenting.) The defendants had placed themselves in a fiduciary position in relation to the trust and would therefore be accountable for the profits they had made on information obtained by virtue of their fiduciary position. However, the defendants had acted honestly and openly throughout and their actions had yielded profits for the trust. They would accordingly be entitled to generous remuneration on account of their work and skill.

VISCOUNT DILHORNE: . . . Was the information they obtained the property of the trust? If so, then they made use of trust property in securing a profit for themselves and they would be accountable. While it may be that some information and knowledge can properly be regarded as property, I do not think that the information supplied by Lester & Harris and obtained by Mr Boardman as to the affairs of that company is to be regarded as property of the trust in the same way as shares held by the trust were its property. Nor do I think that saying that they represented the trust without authority amounted to use of the trust holding. . . .

LORD COHEN: In the case before your Lordships it seems to me clear that the appellants throughout were obtaining information from the company for the purpose stated by Wilberforce J but it does not necessarily follow that the appellants were thereby debarred from acquiring shares in the company for themselves. They were bound to give the information to the trustees but they could not exclude it from their own minds. As Wilberforce J said, the mere use of any knowledge or opportunity which comes to the trustee or agent in the course of his trusteeship or agency does not necessarily make him liable to account. In the present case had the company been a public company and had the appellants bought the shares on the market, they would not, I think, have been accountable. But the company is a private company and not only the information but the opportunity to purchase these shares came to them through the introduction which Mr Fox gave them to the board of the company and in the second phase when the discussions related to the proposed split-up of the company's undertaking it was solely on behalf of the trustees that Mr Boardman was purporting to negotiate with the board of the company. The question is this: when in the third phase the negotiations turned to the purchase of the shares at £4 10s. a share, were the appellants debarred by their fiduciary position from purchasing on their own behalf the 21,986 shares in the company without the informed consent of the trustees and the beneficiaries?. . . . the appellants obtained both the information which satisfied them that the purchase of the shares would be a good investment and the opportunity of acquiring them as a result of acting for certain purposes on behalf of the trustees. Information is, of course, not property in the strict sense of that word and, as I have already stated, it does not necessarily follow, that because an agent acquired information and opportunity while acting in a fiduciary capacity he is accountable to his principals for any profit that comes his way as the result of the use he makes of that information and opportunity. His liability to account must depend on the facts of the case. In the present case much of the information came the appellants' way when Mr Boardman was acting on behalf of the trustees on the instructions of Mr Fox and the opportunity of bidding for the shares came because he purported for all purposes except for making the bid to be acting on behalf of the owners of the 8,000 shares in the company. In these circumstances it seems to me that the principle of the *Regal* case applies and that the courts below came to the right conclusion. . . .

I desire to repeat that the integrity of the appellants is not in doubt. They acted with complete honesty throughout and the respondent is a fortunate man in that the rigour of equity enables him to participate in the profits which have accrued as the result of the action taken by the appellants in March 1959 in purchasing the shares at their own risk. As the last paragraph of his judgment clearly shows, the trial judge evidently shared this view. He directed an inquiry as to what sum is proper to be allowed to the appellants or either of them in respect of his work and skill in obtaining the said shares and the profits in respect thereof. The trial judge concluded by expressing the opinion that payment should be on a liberal scale. With that observation I respectfully agree.

In the result I agree in substance with the judgments of Wilberforce J and of Lord Denning MR and Pearson LJ in the Court of Appeal, and I would dismiss the appeal.

LORD HODSON: . . . The position of law involved in this case is that no person standing in a fiduciary position, when a demand is made upon him by the person to whom he stands in the fiduciary relationship to account for profits acquired by him by reason of his fiduciary position and by reason of the opportunity and the knowledge, or either, resulting from it, is entitled to defeat the claim upon any ground save that he made profits with the knowledge and assent of the other person. . . .

The persons concerned in this case, namely, Mr Thomas Boardman and Mr Tom Phipps, are not trustees in the strict sense but are said to be constructive trustees by reason of the fiduciary position in which they stood. As Lord Selborne pointed out in *Barnes* v *Addy*:

That responsibility (viz, that of trustees) may no doubt be extended in equity to others who are not properly trustees, if they are found either making themselves trustees de son tort, or actually participating in any fraudulent conduct of the trustee to the injury of the cestui que trust. But, on the other hand, strangers are not to be made constructive trustees merely because they act as the agents of trustees in transactions within their legal powers, transactions, perhaps, of which a court of equity may disapprove, unless those agents receive and become chargeable with some part of the trust property, or unless they assist with knowledge in a dishonest and fraudulent design on the part of the trustees.

There is no question of fraud in this case; it has never been suggested that the appellants acted in any other than an open and honourable manner.

If, however, they are in a fiduciary position they are as trustees bound by duty, succinctly stated by Lord Cranworth LC in *Aberdeen Railway Co.* v *Blaikie Brothers* (1854) 1 Macq 461:

And it is a rule of universal application, that no one, having such duties to discharge, shall be allowed to enter into engagements in which he has, or can have, a personal interest conflicting, or which possibly may conflict, with the interests of those whom he is bound to protect.

. . . it is said on behalf of the appellants that information as such is not necessarily property and it is only trust property which is relevant. I agree, but it is nothing to the point to say that in these times corporate trustees, e.g. the Public Trustee and others, necessarily acquire a mass of information in their capacity of trustees for a particular trust and cannot be held liable to account if knowledge so acquired enables them to operate to their own advantage, or to that of other trusts. Each case must depend on its own facts and I dissent from the view that information is of its nature something which is not properly to be described as property. We are aware that what is called 'know-how' in the commercial sense is property which may be very valuable as an asset. I agree with the learned judge and with the Court of Appeal that the confidential information acquired in this case which was capable of being and was turned to account can be properly regarded as the property of the trust. It was obtained by Mr Boardman by reason of the opportunity which he was given as solicitor acting for the trustees in the negotiations with the chairman of the company, as the correspondence demonstrates. The end result was that out of the special position in which they were standing in the course of the negotiations the appellants got the opportunity to make a profit and the knowledge that it was there to be made. . . .

I agree with the decision of the learned judge and with that of the Court of Appeal which, in my opinion, involves a finding that there was a potential conflict between Boardman's position as solicitor to the trustees and his own interest in applying for the shares. He was in a fiduciary position vis-à-vis the trustees and through them vis-à-vis the beneficiaries. For these reasons in my opinion the appeal should be dismissed; but I should add that I am in agreement with the learned judge that payment should be allowed on a liberal scale in respect of the work and skill employed in obtaining the shares and the profits therefrom. . . . base my opinion upon the broader ground which was epitomised by Mr Walton in his closing submission. Boardman and Tom Phipps, he said, placed themselves in a special position which was of a fiduciary character in relation to the negotiations with the directors of Lester & Harris relating to the trust shares. Out of such special position and in the course of such negotiations they obtained the opportunity to make a profit out of the shares and knowledge that the profit was there to be made. A profit was made and they are accountable accordingly.

I would dismiss the appeal.

LORD UPJOHN: . . . Rules of equity have to be applied to such a great diversity of circumstances that they can be stated only in the most general terms and applied with particular attention to the exact circumstances of each case. The relevant rule for the decision of this case is the fundamental rule of equity that a person in a fiduciary capacity must not make a profit out of his trust which is part of the wider rule that a trustee must not place himself in a position where his duty and his interest may conflict. . . .

It is perhaps stated most highly against trustees or directors in the celebrated speech of Lord Cranworth LC in *Aberdeen Railway* v *Blaikie*, where he said:

And it is a rule of universal application, that no one, having such duties to discharge, shall be allowed to enter into engagements in which he has, or can have, a personal interest conflicting, or which possibly may conflict, with the interests of those whom he is bound to protect.

The phrase 'possibly may conflict' requires consideration. In my view it means that the reasonable man looking at the relevant facts and circumstances of the particular case would think that there was a real sensible possibility of conflict; not that you could imagine some situation arising which might, in some conceivable possibility in events not contemplated as real sensible possibilities by any reasonable person, result in a conflict. . . .

In the long run the appellants have bought for themselves at entirely their own risk with their own money shares which the trustees never contemplated buying and they did so in circumstances fully known and approved of by the trustees.

To extend the doctrines of equity to make the appellants accountable in such circumstances is, in my judgment, to make unreasonable and unequitable applications of such doctrines.

I would allow the appeal and dismiss the action.

16.3.1.2 Can a distinction between the fiduciary account and the constructive trust be justified?

ATTORNEY GENERAL FOR HONG KONG v REID [1994] 1 All ER 1

FACTS: R was convicted of accepting bribes given to him in the course of his position as a public prosecutor in Hong Kong as an inducement to exploit his official position by obstructing the prosecution of certain criminals. He was sentenced to eight years' imprisonment and ordered to pay the Crown the sum of $HK12·4m, being the value of assets then controlled by him which could only have been derived from bribes. No payment to the Crown was made by R. The Attorney General for Kong Kong registered caveats on behalf of the Hong Kong government against the titles to three properties in New Zealand registered in the names of R and his wife or his solicitors which were alleged to have been bought with bribes received by R. In an application in the High Court of New Zealand to renew the caveats the Attorney General claimed that the three properties, the value of which had increased since their purchase, were held on a constructive trust in favour of the Crown. The respondents claimed that the Crown had no equitable interest in the properties. The judge held that the Crown as caveator could not as a matter of law establish an arguable case that it had a proprietary interest in the three properties. On appeal by the Attorney General the Court of Appeal of New Zealand, following a long-established English Court of Appeal authority, upheld the judge's decision on the grounds that as between principal and fiduciary the receipt of a bribe by the fiduciary only gave rise to the relationship of creditor and debtor and not trustee and cestui que trust as the principal had no proprietary interest in the bribe or moneys or investments representing it. The Attorney General appealed to the Privy Council.

HELD: When a fiduciary accepted a bribe as an inducement to betray his trust he held the bribe in trust for the person to whom he owed the duty as fiduciary; and, if property representing the bribe increased in value, the fiduciary was not entitled to retain any surplus in excess of the initial value of the bribe because he was not allowed by any means to make a profit out of a breach of duty. A bribe was a secret benefit which the fiduciary derived from trust property or obtained from knowledge which he acquired in the course of acting as a fiduciary and he was accountable under a constructive trust for that secret benefit to the person to whom the fiduciary duty was owed as soon as the bribe was received, whether in cash or in kind, under the equitable principle that equity considered as done that which ought to have been done. If property representing the bribe increased in value or if a cash bribe was invested advantageously the false fiduciary was accountable not only for the original amount or value of the bribe but also for the increased value of the property representing the bribe otherwise he would receive a benefit from his breach of duty. Accordingly, the three properties so far as they represented bribes accepted by R were held in trust for the Crown, which was entitled to have the caveats renewed. The appeal would therefore be allowed . . .

LORD TEMPLEMAN: . . . It has always been assumed and asserted that the law on the subject of bribes was definitively settled by the decision of the Court of Appeal in *Lister & Co. v Stubbs* (1890) ChD 1.

In that case the plaintiffs, Lister & Co, employed the defendant, Stubbs, as their servant to purchase goods for the firm. Stubbs, on behalf of the firm, bought goods from Varley & Co. and received from Varley & Co. bribes amounting to £5,541. The bribes were invested by Stubbs in freehold properties and investments. His masters, the firm Lister & Co., sought and failed to obtain an interlocutory injunction restraining Stubbs from disposing of these assets pending the trial of the action in which they sought, inter alia, £5,541 and damages. In the Court of Appeal.

. . . Lindley LJ said that the relationship between the plaintiffs, Lister & Co., as masters and the defendant, Stubbs, as servant who had betrayed his trust and received a bribe—

> . . . is that of debtor and creditor, it is not that of trustee and cestui que trust. We are asked to hold that it is—which would involve consequences which, I confess, startle me. One consequence, of course, would be that, if Stubbs were to become bankrupt, this property acquired by him with the money paid to him by Messrs Varley would be withdrawn from the mass of his creditors and be handed over bodily to Lister & Co. Can that be right? Another consequence would be that, if the Appellants are right, Lister & Co. could compel Stubbs to account to them, not only for the money with interest, but for all the profit which he might have made by embarking in trade with it. Can that be right?' (See 45 ChD 1 at 15.)

For the reasons which have already been advanced, their Lordships would respectfully answer both these questions in the affirmative. If a trustee mistakenly invests moneys which he ought to pay over to his cestui que trust and then becomes bankrupt, the moneys together with any profit which has accrued from the investment are withdrawn from the unsecured creditors as soon as the mistake is discovered. A fortiori, if a trustee commits a crime by accepting a bribe which he ought to pay over to his cestui que trust, the bribe and any profit made therefrom should be withdrawn from the unsecured creditors as soon as the crime is discovered.

The decision in *Lister & Co.* v *Stubbs* is not consistent with the principles that a fiduciary must not be allowed to benefit from his own breach of duty, that the fiduciary should account for the bribe as soon as he receives it and that equity regards as done that which ought to be done. From these principles it would appear to follow that the bribe and the property from time to time representing the bribe are held on a constructive trust for the person injured. A fiduciary remains personally liable for the amount of the bribe if, in the event, the value of the property then recovered by the injured person proved to be less than that amount. . . .

A bribe is a gift accepted by a fiduciary as an inducement to him to betray his trust. A secret benefit, which may or may not constitute a bribe, is a benefit which the fiduciary derives from trust property or obtains from knowledge which he acquires in the course of acting as a fiduciary. A fiduciary is not always accountable for a secret benefit but he is undoubtedly accountable for a secret benefit which consists of a bribe. In addition a person who provides the bribe and the fiduciary who accepts the bribe may each be guilty of a criminal offence. In the present case Mr Reid was clearly guilty of a criminal offence.

Bribery is an evil practice which threatens the foundations of any civilised society. In particular, bribery of policemen and prosecutors brings the administration of justice into disrepute. Where bribes are accepted by a trustee, servant, agent or other fiduciary, loss and damage are caused to the beneficiaries, master or principal whose interests have been betrayed. The amount of loss or damage resulting from the acceptance of a bribe may or may not be quantifiable. In the present case the amount of harm caused to the administration of justice in Hong Kong by Mr Reid in return for bribes cannot be quantified.

When a bribe is offered and accepted in money or in kind, the money or property constituting the bribe belongs in law to the recipient. Money paid to the false fiduciary belongs to him. The legal estate in freehold property conveyed to the false fiduciary by way of bribe vests in him. Equity however which acts in personam insists that it is unconscionable for a fiduciary to obtain and retain a benefit in breach of duty. The provider of a bribe cannot recover it because he committed a criminal offence when he paid the bribe. The false fiduciary who received the bribe in breach of duty must pay and account for the bribe to the person to whom that duty was owed. In the present case, as soon as Mr Reid received a bribe in breach of the duties he owed to the Government of Hong Kong, he became a debtor in equity to the Crown for the amount of that bribe. So much is admitted. But, if the bribe consists of property which increases in value or if a cash bribe is invested advantageously, the false fiduciary will receive a benefit from his breach of duty unless he is accountable not only for the original amount or value of the bribe but also for the increased value of the property representing the bribe. As soon as the bribe was received it should have been paid or transferred instanter to the person who suffered from the breach of duty. Equity considers as done that which ought to have been done. As soon as the bribe was received, whether in cash or in kind, the false fiduciary held the bribe on a constructive trust for the person injured. Two objections have been raised to this analysis. First it is said that, if the fiduciary is in equity a debtor to the person injured, he cannot also be a trustee of the bribe. But there is no reason why equity should not provide two remedies, so long as they do not result in double recovery. If the property representing the bribe exceeds the original bribe in value, the fiduciary cannot retain the benefit of the increase in value he obtained solely as a result of his breach of duty. Secondly, it is said that if the false fiduciary holds property representing the bribe in trust for the person injured, and if the false fiduciary is or becomes insolvent, the unsecured creditors of the false fiduciary will be deprived of their right to share in the proceeds of that property. But the unsecured creditors cannot be in a better position than their debtor. The authorities show that property acquired by a trustee innocently but in breach of trust and the property from time to time representing the same belong in equity to the cestui que trust and not to the trustee personally whether he is solvent or insolvent. Property acquired by a trustee as a result of a criminal breach of trust and the property from time to time representing the same must also belong in equity to his cestui que trust and not to the trustee whether he is solvent or insolvent.

When a bribe is accepted by a fiduciary in breach of his duty then he holds that bribe in trust for the person to whom the duty was owed. If the property representing the bribe decreases in value the fiduciary must pay the difference between that value and the initial amount of the bribe because he should not have accepted the bribe or incurred the risk of loss. If the property increases in value, the fiduciary is not entitled to any surplus in excess of the initial value of the bribe because he is not allowed by any means to make a profit out of a breach of duty.

16.4   End of Chapter Assessment Question

In his recent book, *Property and Justice* (Clarendon Press, Oxford, 1996), Professor J. W. Harris observed that the strict rule that a fiduciary must account for unauthorised profit 'confers the windfall constituted by the fiduciary's profit, not on the community, but on his principal', with the result that the principal is entitled to claim it in preference to the fiduciary's creditors. Professor Harris asks: 'Why should the principal take a windfall in priority to those to whom the fiduciary owes purchased obligations?'

Outline the reasons why English law takes this approach, and state why, in your opinion, this is (or is not) the correct approach for the law to take.

16.5   End of Chapter Assessment Outline Answer

In *AG for Hong Kong* v *Reid* [1994] 1 All ER 1, the Privy Council held that whenever a fiduciary receives property of his principal in breach of his fiduciary duty, he is a constructive trustee of it, and of any traceable profit from and proceeds of it. Mr Reid was acting Director of Public Prosecutions in Hong Kong. In breach of his fiduciary duty to the Crown he received substantial bribes in consideration of which he obstructed the prosecution of certain criminals. The Crown was able to trace the bribe monies through to three freehold properties in New Zealand, and to assert a restitutionary claim to them under a constructive trust. Lord Templeman held: 'Equity considers as done that which ought to be done. As soon as the bribe was received, whether in cash or in kind, the false fiduciary held the bribe on a constructive trust for the person injured.'

It is by means of a constructive trust that English law requires a 'false fiduciary' to disgorge unauthorised profits. Consequently, the unauthorised profits in the hands of the fiduciary are regarded as a trust fund. Every private trust must have a beneficiary (subject to those limited exceptions considered in the **Learning Text** at **7.2**). and English law has chosen to fasten on the fiduciary's principal as being the appropriate beneficiary. There are a number of reasons for this choice. One is the fact that English law does not recognise pure remedial constructive trusts, but only acknowledges constructive trusts where they vindicate pre-existing proprietary entitlements (*Re Sharpe (a bankrupt)* [1980] 1 All ER 198; *Chase Manhattan Bank NA* v *Israel-British Bank (London) Ltd* [1981] Ch 105). Thus the principal is in most cases automatically better placed to claim the benefit of the constructive trust than would be the fiduciary's creditors or society at large. A second reason is the principle of insolvency law that the creditors of the insolvent should not be placed in a position better than the insolvent himself could have occupied. If the insolvent (the false fiduciary) would not have been permitted to retain the profits as part of his estate, those profits cannot be permitted to form part of his estate for the purpose of meeting the claims of the insolvent's creditors.

The first of these reasons is, of course, rather circular, for its justification for the law's approach is the law's usual practice. It is therefore not surprising that it is a reason that does little to illuminate the actual judgments in a number of decided cases. The *Reid* case is itself a good example. In what sense did the constructive trust in that case operate to vindicate the Crown's pre-existing proprietary entitlement to the bribe? The Crown was surely no more entitled to the bribe prior to its receipt by Reid than was he himself.

Another interesting case is *Boardman* v *Phipps* [1967] 2 AC 46. There, Boardman (the solicitor to the trust) wrote to the beneficiaries outlining his plans to take a personal interest in the company, thus giving them an opportunity to raise any objections they might have to his so doing. No objectors having come forward, Boardman proceeded with the take-over. In the event the take-over was very successful and the value of all the shares in the company increased in value. The present action was brought by Phipps, a beneficiary under the trust, for an account of profits made by Boardman in his fiduciary capacity. The trial judge found as a fact that Phipps had not been fully informed by Boardman as to the precise nature of his plans. A bare majority of their Lordships

(Viscount Dilhorne and Lord Upjohn dissenting) held that Boardman had placed himself in a fiduciary position in relation to the trust and would therefore be accountable for the profits that he had made on information obtained in his fiduciary capacity. There was only a slight suggestion in their Lordships' speeches that the inside information had itself been property of the trust. In fact, Boardman was held to be a constructive trustee, not to vindicate the beneficiary's pre-existing rights in property held by Boardman (he had not held any such property), but 'by reason of the fiduciary *position* in which [he] stood' (emphasis added).

Professor Birks has suggested ((1988) LMCLQ 128) that the use of constructive trust language was inappropriate to the facts of this case. For Birks, *Boardman* v *Phipps* was a case which should have been disposed of as a straightforward personal claim against the principal, and that in essence, despite the occasional unconvincing reference to constructive trusteeship, this is how the case *was* disposed of. It is true that the House of Lords made no order requiring that the defendants should transfer the shares to the plaintiff. Against this Professor Andrew Burrows points out that a declaration that the defendant held the shares on constructive trust *was* made at first instance, and (that judgment having been upheld) 'it must follow that the plaintiffs would have been entitled to proprietary remedies, affording priority, had the defendants been insolvent' (*The Law of Restitution* (1993), p. 413).

The second reason for English law's preference for the fiduciary's principal ahead of his creditors, namely that the creditors of the insolvent fiduciary cannot be placed in a better position than the fiduciary himself, is surely open to attack. For the fiduciary's creditors do not claim any part of the unauthorised profits, but merely that their legitimate contractual claims will be satisfied out of the fiduciary's general estate. They might legitimately argue that equity, with its purported concern for justice, has no business awarding a windfall to the fiduciary's principal (especially where it cannot, without straining imagination, be said to vindicate a pre-existing proprietary entitlement) when that windfall must inevitably be taken from the total fund available to satisfy the creditors' various claims.

It is suggested that the right approach would be for the courts to find a constructive trust in favour of the principal where the unauthorised profits were made through the use of the principal's property in the hands of the fiduciary, but in other cases to allow the creditors to prove their claims ahead of any windfall to the principal in the guise of a constructive trust.

CHAPTER SEVENTEEN

INFORMAL TRUSTS OF LAND

17.1 Problems in Defining the Trust

DRAKE v *WHIPP* [1996] 1 FLR 826

FACTS: A barn was purchased for conversion in the man's sole name. The woman provided approximately 40% of the total purchase price and the man provided the remainder. No mention was made of a trust. Both parties contributed to the conversion work by way of direct labour and financially. The woman purchased food and met household expenses for them both. In 1991 the man formed a new relationship and the woman moved out. In 1993 the woman issued an application for a declaration that the man held the barn in trust for the woman and himself in equal shares or such shares as the court might think fit, an order for sale and division of the net proceeds, alternatively a payment by the man to the woman of a sum equal to her interest in the barn. The judge held that the woman's share of the total expenditure entitled her to 19.4% of the value of the barn by way of a resulting trust. The woman appealed.

HELD: Allowing the appeal.

(1) The case was one of constructive trust rather than resulting trust.

(2) All that was required to give rise to a constructive trust was that (a) there should be a common intention that the party who was not the legal owner should have a beneficial interest, and (b) that that party should act to his or her detriment in reliance thereon.

(3) It was impossible in the light of *Gissing* v *Gissing* and other authorities to argue that a common understanding or intention as to the respective shares to be taken was necessary to give rise to a constructive trust. In constructive trust cases the court could adopt a broad brush approach to determining the parties' respective shares.

(4) In the absence of any evidence that the woman intended her share to be limited to her direct contributions to the acquisition and conversion costs, the matter should be approached more broadly, looking at the parties' entire course of conduct together.

PETER GIBSON LJ: Yet again this court is asked to rule on a dispute between a man and a woman, who cohabited but were not married to each other, as to their respective beneficial interests in a property which they purchased to be their home but which was put into the man's name only. The usual lengthy litany of authorities as well as more recent additions have been recited to us and, as is notorious, it is not easy to reconcile every judicial utterance in this well-travelled area of the law. A potent source of confusion, to my mind, has been suggestions that it matters not whether the terminology used is that of the constructive trust, to which the intention, actual or imputed, of the parties is crucial, or that of the resulting trust which operates as a presumed intention of the contributing party in the absence of rebutting evidence of actual intention. I therefore, like Waite LJ in *Midland Bank* v *Cooke and Another* [1995] 2 FLR 915, 916, welcome the announcement earlier this year that the Law Commission is to examine the property rights of home-sharers (Item 8, Sixth Programme of Law Reform: Law Com Paper No. 234). . . .

[Counsel for Mrs Drake] submits that the judge wrongly conflated the separate doctrines of constructive trust and resulting trust, whereas he was only concerned with a resulting trust. That, he submitted, required attention to be paid only to the cost of acquisition of the property, the cost of its subsequent enhancement being irrelevant. When it was put to him that this was a case of a constructive trust by reason of common understanding or intention acted on by his client to her detriment, he submitted that there had to be a common understanding or intention as to the respective shares to be taken by the intended beneficial owners. That is an impossible argument in the light of the authorities (see, for example, the speech of Lord Diplock in *Gissing* v *Gissing* [1971] AC 886, 907–909). All that is required for the creation of a constructive trust is that there should be a common intention that the party who is not the legal owner should have a beneficial interest and that that party should act to his or her detriment in reliance thereon.

Given the clear view which I and, I understand, my Lords have formed that the present case is one of a constructive trust . . . it would in my judgment be artificial in the extreme to proceed to decide this appeal on the false footing that the parties' shares are to be determined in accordance with the law on resulting trusts. However, it would be wrong to proceed on the true basis if Mrs Drake were thereby put at a disadvantage which would not have happened but for the concession. As [her counsel] rightly pointed out, in constructive trust cases, the court can adopt a broad brush approach to determining the parties' respective shares. . . .

In the present case the judge has found what was the common intention of the parties as to their beneficial shares, but the only direct evidence in support of that finding was Mr Whipp's evidence as to his own intention. The judge appears to have imputed the like intention to Mrs Drake although there is nothing in her evidence to support it. Further, the judge refused to take into account the contributions of the parties by way of their labour, being unquantified in monetary terms, and similarly Mrs Drake's other contributions to the household were ignored. No doubt this was because he was not invited to consider the matter on the basis of a constructive trust.

In my judgment the judge's finding on common intention cannot stand in the absence of any evidence that Mrs Drake intended her share to be limited to her direct contributions to the acquisition and conversion costs. I would approach the matter more broadly, looking at the parties' entire course of conduct together. I would take into account not only those direct contributions but also the fact that Mr Whipp and Mrs Drake together purchased the property with the intention that it should be their home, that they both contributed their labour in 70/30% proportions, that they had a joint account out of which the costs of conversion were met, but that that account was largely fed by his earnings, and that she paid for the food and some other household expenses and took care of the housekeeping for them both. I note that whilst it was open to Mrs Drake to argue at the trial for a constructive trust and for a 50% share, she opted to rely solely on a resulting trust and a 40.1% share. In all the circumstances I would hold that her fair share should be one-third.

I would allow the appeal to this extent, and grant a declaration that Mr Whipp holds the property in trust for Mrs Drake and himself in the proportions one-third and two-thirds respectively and I would direct that unless Mr Whipp pays Mrs Drake £75,000, the property be sold. I would hear counsel on how much time Mr Whipp should be given to make that payment.

17.1.1 CONSTRUCTIVE TRUSTS

LLOYDS BANK PLC v *ROSSET* [1991] 1 AC 107, HL

FACTS: Mr Rosset had received a loan to buy a derelict house on the understanding that the house should be in his name alone. Mrs Rosset did a limited amount of work helping in the renovation of the house, in particular she helped with the interior decorations. However, the vast bulk of the work was carried out by contractors employed and paid for by the husband.

Following matrimonial problems the husband left home, leaving his wife and children in the premises. The loan which the husband had taken out was not, in the event, repaid. Consequently, the bank brought proceedings for possession. The husband raised no defence to that action, but the wife did resist. She claimed to have a beneficial interest in the house under a constructive trust. She also claimed to have been in actual occupation of the property at the time of the completion of the loan (mortgage) from the bank. Accordingly, she claimed to have an interest in the land which would override the bank's right to enforce its security. (Section 70(1)(g) of the Land Registration Act 1925 provides that the rights of any person in actual occupation of land shall be 'overriding'.) The judge at first instance held in favour of the bank, but the Court of Appeal allowed the wife's appeal. The bank appealed to the House of Lords.

HELD: The appeal was allowed.

LORD BRIDGE OF HARWICH: . . . the judge based his inference of a common intention that Mrs Rosset should have a beneficial interest in the property under a constructive trust essentially on what Mrs Rosset did in and about assisting in the renovation of the property between the beginning 'of November 1982 and the date of completion on 17 December 1982. Yet by itself this activity, it seems to me, could not possibly justify any such inference. It was common ground that Mrs Rosset was extremely anxious that the new matrimonial home should be ready for occupation before Christmas if possible. In these circumstances it would seem the most natural thing in the world for any wife, in the absence of her husband abroad, to spend all the time she could spare and to employ any skills she might have, such as the ability to decorate a room, in doing all she could to accelerate progress of the work quite irrespective of any expectation she might have of enjoying a beneficial interest in the property. The judge's view that some of this work was work 'upon which she could not reasonably have been expected to embark unless she was to have an interest in the house' seems to me, with respect, quite untenable. The impression that the judge may have thought that the share of the equity to which he held Mrs Rosset to be entitled had been 'earned' by her work in connection with the renovation is emphasised by his reference in the concluding sentence of his judgment to the extent to which her 'qualifying contribution' reduced the cost of the renovation.

On any view the monetary value of Mrs Rosset's work expressed as a contribution to a property acquired at a cost exceeding £70,000 must have been so trifling as to be almost *de minimis*. I should myself have had considerable doubt whether Mrs Rosset's contribution to the work of renovation was sufficient to support a claim to a constructive trust in the absence of writing to satisfy the requirements of s. 51 of the Law of Property Act 1925 even if her husband's intention to make a gift to her of half or any other share in the equity of the property had been clearly established or if he had clearly represented to her that that was what he intended. But here the conversations with her husband on which Mrs. Rosset relied, all of which took place before November 1982, were incapable of lending support to the conclusion of a constructive trust in the light of the judge's finding that by that date there had been no decision that she was to have any interest in the property. The finding that the discussion 'did not exclude the possibility' that she should have an interest does not seem to me to add anything of significance.

These considerations lead me to the conclusion that the judge's finding that Mr Rosset held the property as constructive trustee for himself and his wife cannot be supported and it is on this short ground that I would allow the appeal. . . .

The first and fundamental question which must always be resolved is whether, independently of any inference to be drawn from the conduct of the parties in the course of sharing the house as their home and managing their joint affairs, there has at any time prior to acquisition, or exceptionally at some later date, been any agreement, arrangement or understanding reached between them that the property is to be shared beneficially. The finding of an agreement or arrangement to share in this sense can only, I think, be based on evidence of express discussions between the partners, however imperfectly remembered and however imprecise their terms may have been. Once a finding to this effect is made it will only be necessary for the partner asserting a claim to a beneficial interest against the partner entitled to the legal estate to show that he or she acted to his or her detriment or significantly altered his or her position in reliance on the agreement in order to give rise to a constructive trust or a proprietary estoppel.

In sharp contrast with this situation is the very different one where there is no evidence to support a finding of an agreement or arrangement to share, however reasonable it might have been for the parties to reach such an arrangement if they had applied their minds to the question, and where the court must rely entirely on the conduct of the parties both as the basis from which to infer a common intention to share the property beneficially and as the conduct relied on to give rise to a constructive trust. In this situation direct contributions to the purchase price by the partner who is not the legal owner, whether initially or by payment of mortgage instalments, will readily justify the inference necessary to the creation of a constructive trust. But, as I read the authorities, it is at least extremely doubtful whether anything less will do.

The leading cases in your Lordships' House are *Pettitt v Pettitt* [1970] AC 777 and *Gissing v Gissing* [1971] AC 866. Both demonstrate situations in the second category to which I have referred and their Lordships discuss at great length the difficulties to which these situations give rise. The effect of these two decisions is very helpfully analysed in the judgment of Lord MacDermott LCJ in *McFarlane v McFarlane* [1972] NI 59.

Outstanding examples on the other hand of cases giving rise to situations in the first category are *Eves v Eves* [1975] 1 WLR 1338 and *Grant v Edwards* [1986] Ch 638. In both these cases, where the parties who had cohabited were unmarried, the female partner had been clearly led by the male partner to believe, when they set up home together, that the property would belong to them jointly. In *Eves v Eves* the male partner had told the female partner that the only reason why the property was to be acquired in his name alone was because she was under 21 and that, but for her age, he would have had the house put into their joint names. He admitted in evidence that this was simply an 'excuse.' Similarly in *Grant v Edwards* the female partner was told by the male partner that the only reason for not acquiring the property in joint names was because she was involved in divorce proceedings and that, if the property were acquired jointly, this might operate to her prejudice in those proceedings. As Nourse LJ put it, at p. 649:

> Just as in *Eves v Eves* [1975] 1 WLR 1338, these facts appear to me to raise a clear inference that there was an understanding between the plaintiff and the defendant, or a common intention, that the plaintiff was to have some sort of proprietary interest in the house; otherwise no excuse for not putting her name on to the title would have been needed.

The subsequent conduct of the female partner in each of these cases, which the court rightly held sufficient to give rise to a constructive trust or proprietary estoppel supporting her claim to an interest in the property, fell far short of such conduct as would by itself have supported the claim in the absence of an express representation by the male partner that she was to have such an interest. It is significant to note that the share to which the female partners in *Eves v Eves* and *Grant v Edwards* were held entitled were one quarter and one half respectively. In no sense could these shares have been regarded as proportionate to what the judge in the instant case described as a 'qualifying contribution' in terms of the indirect contributions to the acquisition or enhancement of the value of the houses made by the female partners.

I cannot help thinking that the judge in the instant case would not have fallen into error if he had kept clearly in mind the distinction between the effect of evidence on the one hand which was capable of establishing an express agreement or an express representation that Mrs Rosset was to have an interest in the property and evidence on the other hand of conduct alone as a basis for an inference of the necessary common intention. . . .

For the reasons I have indicated I would allow the appeal. . . .

17.1.2 EXPRESS AGREEMENT PLUS DETRIMENTAL RELIANCE

17.1.2.1 'Express'

GRANT v EDWARDS AND ANOTHER [1986] 2 All ER 426

FACTS: In 1969 the plaintiff gave birth to the defendant's son and the couple decided to live together. A house was purchased and transferred into the name of the defendant and his brother, who was a purely nominal party with no beneficial interest in the

property. The defendant told the plaintiff that her name would not go onto the title because it would cause some prejudice in the matrimonial proceedings pending between the plaintiff and her husband. Prior to 1969 the plaintiff worked but between 1969 and 1972 she was on supplementary benefit. However, she contributed £6 a week towards general expenses for a time after they moved into the house. In 1971 a second child was born. From August 1972 onwards the plaintiff made very substantial indirect contributions to the mortgage repayments by applying her earnings to the joint household expenses, and by housekeeping and bringing up the children. In February 1975, after a fire at the property, the family moved into council accommodation. The defendant received £4,000 from a fire insurance policy, the bulk of which was spent on making repairs to the property, which was then let, the rent being used to pay the instalments on the first mortgage. In September 1975 the sum of £1,037 left over from the moneys from the fire insurance policy was paid into a joint account at a building society which was shared equally between the plaintiff and the defendant. In 1980 the couple separated. There was then £3,800 outstanding on the first mortgage. The plaintiff claimed a share in the beneficial interest in the property on the grounds, inter alia, that she had contributed very substantially to the repayment of both mortgages by means of her contribution to the joint household expenses, and by housekeeping, feeding and bringing up the children.
HELD: Where an unmarried couple lived in a house which was registered or held in the name of only one of the parties, the other party could establish a beneficial interest in the property if he or she could establish a constructive trust by showing that it would be inequitable for the legal owner to claim sole beneficial ownership. That in turn had to be demonstrated by a common intention that they should both have a beneficial interest (which was required to be proved by direct evidence or inferred from their actions, including indirect contributions to the purchase such as mortgage payments, housekeeping expenses etc.) and also that the claimant had acted to his or her detriment on the basis of that common intention and in the belief that by so acting he or she would acquire a beneficial interest. Once it had been established that the claimant was entitled to a beneficial interest in the property the quantification of that right depended on the direct and indirect contributions made by the parties to the cost of acquiring the property. On the facts, the defendant's statement that the plaintiff's name would have been on the title deeds but for her matrimonial proceedings (per Sir Nicolas Browne-Wilkinson V-C and Nourse LJ) sufficed to show the necessary common intention or (per Mustill LJ) precluded the defendant from denying that the plaintiff had a proprietary interest in the house from the outset. Furthermore (per Sir Nicolas Browne-Wilkinson V-C and Nourse LJ) the plaintiff had acted to her detriment in reliance on that common intention by making the financial contributions without which the mortgage instalments could not have been paid by the defendant. Moreover, the act of the defendant in crediting the balance of the insurance moneys to a joint account, when viewed against the background of the initial common intention and the substantial indirect contributions made by the plaintiff to the mortgage payments from August 1972 onwards, was the best evidence of how the parties intended the property to be shared. Accordingly, the plaintiff was entitled to a half share in the house and a declaration would be made to that effect.

NOURSE LJ: . . . In most of these cases the fundamental, and invariably the most difficult, question is to decide whether there was the necessary common intention, being something which can only be inferred from the conduct of the parties, almost always from the expenditure incurred by them respectively. In this regard the court has to look for expenditure which is referable to the acquisition of the house: see *Burns* v *Burns* [1984] 1 All ER 244 at 252–253, *per* Fox LJ. If it is found to have been incurred, such expenditure will perform the twofold function of establishing the common intention and showing that the claimant has acted on it.

There is another and rarer class of case, of which the present may be one, where, although there has been no writing, the parties have orally declared themselves in such a way as to make their common intention plain. Here the court does not have to look for conduct from which the intention can be inferred, but only for conduct which amounts to an acting on it by the claimant. And, although that conduct can undoubtedly be the incurring of expenditure which is referable to the acquisition of the house, it need not necessarily be so.

The clearest example of this rarer class is *Eves* v *Eves* [1975] 3 All ER 768. That was a case of an unmarried couple where the conveyance of the house was taken in the name of the man alone. At the time of the purchase he told the woman that, if she had been 21 years of age, he would have put the house into their joint names, because it was to be their joint home. He admitted in evidence that that was an excuse for not putting the house into their joint names, and this court inferred that there was an understanding between them, or a common intention, that the woman was to have some sort of proprietary interest in it; otherwise no excuse would have been needed. After they had moved in, the woman did extensive decorative work to the downstairs rooms and generally cleaned the whole house. She painted the brickwork of the front of the house. She also broke up with a 14-lb sledge hammer the concrete surface which covered the whole of the front garden and disposed of the rubble into a skip, worked in the back garden and, together with the man, demolished a shed there and put up a new shed. She also prepared the front garden for turfing. Pennycuick V-C at first instance, being unable to find any link between the common intention and the woman's activities after the purchase, held that she had not acquired a beneficial interest in the house. On an appeal to this court the decision was unanimously reversed, by Lord Denning MR on a ground which I respectfully think was at variance with the principles stated in *Gissing* v *Gissing* and by Browne LJ and Brightman J on a ground which was stated by Brightman J as follows ([1975] 3 All ER 768 at 774):

> The defendant clearly led the plaintiff to believe that she was to have some undefined interest in the property, and that her name was only omitted from the conveyance because of her age. This, of course, is not enough by itself to create a beneficial interest in her favour; there would at best be a mere voluntary declaration of trust which would be unenforceable for want of writing: *Gissing* v *Gissing*. If however, it was part of the bargain between the parties, expressed or to be implied, that the plaintiff should contribute her labour towards the reparation of a house in which she was to have some beneficial interest, then I think that the arrangement becomes one to which the law can give effect. This seems to be consistent with the reasoning of the speeches in *Gissing* v *Gissing* [1970] 2 All ER 780 at 790 .

He added that he did not find much in inferring the link which Pennycuick V-C had been unable to find, observing in the process that he found it difficult to suppose that the woman would have been wielding the 14-lb sledge hammer and so forth except in pursuance of some expressed or implied arrangement and on the understanding that she was helping to improve a house in which she was to all practical intents and purposes promised that she had an interest. Browne LJ agreed with Brightman J about the basis for the court's decision in favour of the woman and was prepared to draw the inference that the link was there (see [1975] 3 All ER 768 at 772–773).

About that case the following observations may be made. First, as Brightman J himself observed, if the work had not been done the common intention would not have been enough. Second, if the common intention had not been orally made plain, the work would not have been conduct from which it could be inferred. That, I think, is the effect of the actual decision in *Pettitt* v *Pettitt*. Third, and on the other hand, the work was conduct which amounted to an acting on the common intention by the woman.

It seems therefore, on the authorities as they stand, that a distinction is to be made between conduct from which the common intention can be inferred on the one hand and conduct which amounts to an acting on it on the other. There remains this difficult question: what is the quality of conduct required for the latter purpose? The difficulty is caused, I think, because, although the common intention has been made plain, everything else remains a matter of inference. Let me illustrate it in this way. It would be possible to take the view that the mere moving into the house by the woman amounted to an acting on the common intention. But that was evidently not the view of the majority in *Eves* v *Eves*. And the reason for that may be that, in the absence of evidence, the law is not so cynical as to infer that a woman will only go to live with a man to whom she is not married if she understands that she is to have an interest in their home. So what sort of conduct is required? In my judgment it must be conduct on which the woman could not reasonably have been expected to embark unless she was to have an interest in the house. If she was not to have such an interest, she could reasonably be expected to go and live with her lover, but not, for example, to wield a 14-lb sledge hammer in the front garden. In adopting the latter kind of conduct she is seen to act to her detriment on the faith of the common intention. . . .

SIR NICOLAS BROWNE-WILKINSON V-C: I agree. In my judgment, there has been a tendency over the years to distort the principles as laid down in the speech of Lord Diplock in *Gissing* v *Gissing* [1970] 2 All ER 780, by concentrating on only part of his reasoning. For present purposes, his speech can be treated as falling into three sections: the first deals with the nature of the substantive right; the second with the proof of the existence of that right; the third with the quantification of that right.

(1)   *The nature of the substantive right* (see [1970] 2 All ER 780 at 790). If the legal estate in the joint home is vested in only one of the parties (the legal owner) the other party (the claimant), in order to establish a beneficial interest, has to establish a constructive trust by showing that it would be inequitable for the legal owner to claim sole beneficial ownership. This requires two matters to be demonstrated: (a) that there was a common intention that both should have a beneficial interest; *and* (b) that the claimant has acted to his or her detriment on the basis of that common intention.

(2)   *The proof of the common intention*

(a)   Direct evidence (see [1970] 2 All ER 780 at 790). It is clear that mere agreement between the parties that both are to have beneficial interests is sufficient to prove the necessary common intention. Other passages in the speech point to the admissibility and relevance of other possible forms of direct evidence of such intention (see [1970] 2 All ER 780 at 791–792).

(b)   Inferred common intention (see [1970] 2 All ER 780 at 790–792). Lord Diplock points out that, even where parties have not used express words to communicate their intention (and therefore there is no direct evidence), the court can infer from their actions an intention that they shall both have an interest in the house. This part of his speech concentrates on the types of evidence from which the courts are most often asked to infer such intention, viz contributions (direct and indirect) to the deposit, the mortgage instalments or general housekeeping expenses. In this section of the speech, he analyses what types of expenditure are capable of constituting evidence of such common intention; he does not say that if the intention is proved in some other way such contributions are essential to establish the trust.

(3)   *The quantification of the right* (see [1970] 2 All ER 780 at 792–793). Once it has been established that the parties had a common intention that both should have a beneficial interest and that the claimant has acted to his detriment, the question may still remain: what is the extent of the claimant's beneficial interest? This last section of Lord Diplock's speech shows that here again the direct and indirect contributions made by the parties to the cost of acquisition may be crucially important.

If this analysis is correct, contributions made by the claimant may be relevant for four different purposes, viz: (1) in the absence of direct evidence of intention, as evidence from which the parties' intentions can be inferred; (2) as corroboration of direct evidence of intention; (3) to show that the claimant has acted to his or her detriment in reliance on the common intention (Lord Diplock's speech does not deal directly with the nature of the detriment to be shown); (4) to quantify the extent of the beneficial interest. . . .

Applying those principles to the present case, the representation made by the defendant to the plaintiff that the house would have been in the joint names but for the plaintiff's matrimonial disputes is clear direct evidence of a common intention that she was to have an interest in the house: see *Eves* v *Eves*. Such evidence was in my judgment sufficient by itself to establish the common intention; but in any event it is wholly consistent with the contributions made by the plaintiff to the joint household expenses and the fact that the surplus fire insurance moneys were put into a joint account.

But as Lord Diplock's speech ([1970] 2 All ER 780 at 790) and the decision in *Midland Bank plc* v *Dobson and Dobson* [1986] 1 FLR 171 make clear, mere common intention by itself is not enough: the claimant has also to prove that she has acted to her detriment in the reasonable belief that by so acting she was acquiring a beneficial interest.

There is little guidance in the authorities on constructive trusts as to what is necessary to prove that the claimant so acted to her detriment. What 'link' has to be shown between the common intention and the actions relied on? Does there have to be positive evidence that the claimant did the acts in conscious reliance on the common intention? Does the court have to be satisfied that she would not have done the acts relied on but for the common intention, e.g. would not the claimant have contributed to household expenses out of affection for the legal owner and as part of their joint life together even if she had no interest in the house? Do the acts relied on as detriment have to be inherently referable to the house, e.g. contribution to the purchase or physical labour on the house?

I do not think it is necessary to express any concluded view on these questions in order to decide this case. *Eves v Eves* indicates that there has to be some 'link' between the common intention and the acts relied on as a detriment. In that case the acts relied on did inherently relate to the house (viz the work the claimant did to the house) and from this the Court of Appeal felt able to infer that the acts were done in reliance on the common intention. So, in this case, as the analysis of Nourse LJ makes clear, the plaintiff's contributions to the household expenses were essentially linked to the payment of the mortgage instalments by the defendant: without the plaintiff's contributions, the defendant's means were insufficient to keep up the mortgage payments. . . .

I suggest that, in other cases of this kind, useful guidance may in the future be obtained from the principles underlying the law of proprietary estoppel which in my judgment are closely akin to those laid down in *Gissing v Gissing*. In both, the claimant must to the knowledge of the legal owner have acted in the belief that the claimant has or will obtain an interest in the property. In both, the claimant must have acted to his or her detriment in reliance on such belief. In both, equity acts on the conscience of the legal owner to prevent him from acting in an unconscionable manner by defeating the common intention. The two principles have been developed separately without cross-fertilisation between them; but they rest on the same foundation and have on all other matters reached the same conclusions.

In many cases of the present sort, it is impossible to say whether or not the claimant would have done the acts relied on as a detriment even if she thought she had no interest in the house. Setting up house together, having a baby and making payments to general housekeeping expenses (not strictly necessary to enable the mortgage to be paid) may all be referable to the mutual love and affection of the parties and not specifically referable to the claimant's belief that she has an interest in the house. As at present advised, once it has been shown that there was a common intention that the claimant should have an interest in the house, any act done by her to her detriment relating to the joint lives of the parties is, in my judgment, sufficient detriment to qualify. The acts do not have to be inherently referable to the house: see *Jones v Jones* [1977] 2 All ER 231 and *Pascoe v Turner* [1979] 2 All ER 945. The holding out to the claimant that she had a beneficial interest in the house is an act of such a nature as to be part of the inducement to her to do the acts relied on. Accordingly, in the absence of evidence to the contrary, the right inference is that the claimant acted in reliance on such holding out and the burden lies on the legal owner to show that she did not do so: see *Greasley v Cooke* [1980] 3 All ER 710.

The possible analogy with proprietary estoppel was raised in argument. However, the point was not fully argued and, since the case can be decided without relying on such analogy, it is unsafe for me to rest my judgment on that point. I decide the case on the narrow ground already mentioned.

What then is the extent of the plaintiff's interest? It is clear from *Gissing v Gissing* that, once the common intention and the actions to the claimant's detriment have been proved from direct or other evidence, in fixing the quantum of the claimant's beneficial interest the court can take into account indirect contributions by the plaintiff such as the plaintiff's contributions to joint household expenses: see *Gissing v Gissing* [1970] 2 All ER 780 at 793. In my judgment, the passage in Lord Diplock's speech ([1970] 2 All ER 780 at 793) is dealing with a case where there is no evidence of the common intention other than contributions to joint expenditure; in such a case there is insufficient evidence to prove any beneficial interest and the question of the extent of that interest cannot arise.

Where, as in this case, the existence of some beneficial interest in the claimant has been shown, prima facie the interest of the claimant will be that which the parties intended: see *Gissing v Gissing* [1970] 2 All ER 780 at 792. In *Eves v Eves* [1975] 3 All ER 768 at 775 Brightman LJ plainly felt that a common intention that there should be a joint interest pointed to the beneficial interests being equal. However, he felt able to find a lesser beneficial interest in that case without explaining the legal basis on which he did so. With diffidence, I suggest that the law of proprietary estoppel may again provide useful guidance. If proprietary estoppel is established, the court gives effect to it by giving effect to the common intention so far as may fairly be done between the parties. For that purpose, equity is displayed at its most flexible: see *Crabb* v *Arun DC* [1975] 3 All ER 865. Identifiable contributions to the purchase of the house will of course be an important factor in many cases. But, in other cases, contributions by way of the labour or other unquantifiable actions of the claimant will also be relevant.

17.1.2.2 'Agreement'
GISSING v *GISSING* [1970] 2 All ER 780

FACTS: The parties were married in 1935. In 1951, the matrimonial home was purchased for £2,695 and conveyed into the sole name of the appellant. The purchase price was raised as to £2,150 on mortgage repayable by instalments, as to £500 by a loan to the appellant by his employers, and the balance of £45 and the legal charges were paid by the appellant from his own money. At no time was there any express agreement as to how the beneficial interest in the matrimonial home should be held. The respondent (who was earning £500 per annum) made no direct contribution to the initial deposit or legal charges, nor to the repayment of the loan of £500 nor to the mortgage instalments. The respondent provided some furniture and equipment for the house and for improving the lawn and in all spent £220 on this. The respondent also paid for her and her son's clothes and some extras. It was not suggested that either the respondent's efforts or earnings made it possible for the appellant to raise the £500 loan or the mortgage. Nor was it suggested that the purchase of the respondent's clothes, or her son's was undertaken to assist the appellant in meeting the repayment of the loan or the payment of the mortgage instalments which he undertook. The appellant also paid the outgoings on the house and gave to the respondent a housekeeping allowance, and he paid for the holidays. In 1961, the marriage broke down and, in 1966, the respondent obtained a decree absolute. On the question whether the respondent had any beneficial interest in the former matrimonial home.
HELD: On the facts it was not possible to draw an inference that there was any common intention that the respondent should have any beneficial interest in the matrimonial home.

LORD DIPLOCK: . . . In all the previous cases about the beneficial interests of spouses in the matrimonial home the arguments and judgments have been directed to the question whether or not an agreement between the parties as to their respective interests can be established on the available evidence. This appoach to the legal problem involved is in most cases adequate, but it passes over the first stage in the analysis of the problem, viz the role of the agreement itself in the creation of an equitable estate in real property. In the instant appeal, I think it is desirable to start at the first stage.

Any claim to a beneficial interest in land by a person, whether spouse or stranger, in whom the legal estate in the land is not vested must be based on the proposition that the person in whom the legal estate is vested holds it as trustee on trust to give effect to the beneficial interest of the claimant as cestui que trust. The legal principles applicable to the claim are those of the English law of trusts and in particular, in the kind of dispute between spouses that comes before the courts, the law relating to the creation and operation of 'resulting, implied or constructive trusts'. Where the trust is expressly declared in the instrument by which the legal estate is transferred to the trustee or by written declaration of trust by the trustee, the court must give effect to it. But to constitute a valid declaration of trust by way of gift of a beneficial interest in land to a cestui que trust the declaration is required by s. 53(1) of the Law of Property Act 1925, to be in writing. If it is not in writing it can only take effect as a resulting, implied or constructive trust to which that section has no application.

A resulting, implied or constructive trust—and it is unnecessary for present purposes to distinguish between these three classes of trust—is created by a transaction between the trustee and cestui que trust in connection with the acquisition by the trustee of a legal estate in land, whenever the trustee has so conducted himself that it would be inequitable to allow him to deny to the cestui que trust a beneficial interest in the land acquired. And he will be held so to have conducted himself if by his words or conduct he has induced the cestui que trust to act to his own detriment in the reasonable belief that by so acting he was acquiring a beneficial interest in the land.

This is why it has been repeatedly said in the context of disputes between spouses as to their respective beneficial interests in the matrimonial home, that if at the time of its acquisition and transfer of the legal estate into the name of one or other of them an express agreement has been made between them as to the way in which the beneficial interests shall be held, the court will give effect to it—notwithstanding the absence of any written declaration of trust. Strictly speaking this states the principle too widely, for if the agreement did not provide for anything to be done by the spouse in whom the legal estate was not vested, it would be a merely voluntary declaration of trust and unenforceable for want of writing. But in the express oral agreements contemplated by these dicta it has been assumed sub silentio that they provide for the spouse in whom the legal estate in the matrimonial home is not vested to do something to facilitate its acquisition, by contributing to the purchase price or to the deposit or the mortgage instalments when it is purchased on mortgage or to make some other material sacrifice by way of contribution to or economy in the general family expenditure. What the court gives effect to is the trust resulting or implied from the common intention expressed in the oral agreement between the spouses that if each acts in the manner provided for in the agreement the beneficial interests in the matrimonial home shall be held as they have agreed.

An express agreement between spouses as to their respective beneficial interests in land conveyed into the name of one of them obviates the need for showing that the conduct of the spouse into whose name the land was conveyed was intended to induce the other spouse to act to his or her detriment on the faith of the promise of a specified beneficial interest in the land and that the other spouse so acted with the intention of acquiring that beneficial interest. The agreement itself discloses the common intention required to create a resulting, implied or constructive trust. But parties to a transaction in connection with the acquisition of land may well have formed a common intention that the beneficial interest in the land shall be vested in them jointly without having used express words to communicate this intention to one another; or their recollections of the words used may be imperfect or conflicting by the time any dispute arises. In such a case—a common one where the parties are spouses whose marriage has broken down—it may be possible to infer their common intention from their conduct.

As in so many branches of English law in which legal rights and obligations depend on the intentions of the parties to a transaction, the relevant intention of each party is the intention which was reasonably understood by the other party to be manifested by that party's words or conduct notwithstanding that he did not consciously formulate that intention in his own mind or even acted with some different intention which he did not communicate to the other party. On the other hand, he is not bound by any inference which the other party draws as to his intention unless that inference is one which can reasonably be drawn from his words or conduct. It is in this sense that in the branch of English law relating to constructive, implied or resulting trusts effect is given to the inferences as to the intentions of parties to a transaction which a reasonable man would draw from their words or conduct and not to any subjective intention or absence of intention which was not made manifest at the time of the transaction itself. It is for the court to determine what those inferences are.

In drawing such an inference, what spouses said and did which led up to the acquisition of a matrimonial home and what they said and did while the acquisition was being carried through is on a different footing from what they said and did after the acquisition was completed. Unless it is alleged that there was some subsequent fresh agreement, acted on by the parties, to vary the original beneficial interests created when the matrimonial home was acquired, what they said and did after the acquisition was completed is relevant if it is explicable only on the basis of their having manifested to one another at the time of the acquisition some particular common intention as to how the beneficial interests should be held. But it would in my view be unreasonably legalistic to treat the relevant transaction involved in the acquisition of a matrimonial home as restricted to the actual conveyance of the fee simple into the name of one or other spouse. Their common intention is more likely to have been concerned with the economic realities of the transaction than with the unfamiliar technicalities of the English law of legal and equitable interests in land. The economic reality which lies behind the conveyance of the fee simple to a purchaser in return for a purchase price the greater part of which is advanced to the purchaser on a mortgage repayable by instalments over a number of years, is that the new freeholder is purchasing the matrimonial home on credit and that the purchase price is represented by the instalments by which the mortgage is repaid in addition to the initial payment in cash. The conduct of the spouses in relation to the payment of the mortgage instalments may be no less relevant to their common intention as to the beneficial interests in a matrimonial home acquired in this way than their conduct in relation to the payment of the cash deposit.

It is this feature of the transaction by means of which most matrimonial homes have been acquired in recent years that makes difficult the task of the court in inferring from the conduct of the spouses a common intention as to how the beneficial interest in it should be held. Each case must depend on its own facts but there are a number of factual situations which often recur in the cases. Where a matrimonial home has been purchased outright without the aid of an advance on mortgage it is not difficult to ascertain what part, if any, of the purchase price has been provided by each spouse. If the land is conveyed into the name of a spouse who has not provided the whole of the purchase price, the sum contributed by the other spouse may be explicable as having been intended by both of them either as a gift or as a loan of money to the spouse to whom the land is conveyed or as consideration for a share in the beneficial interest in the land. In a dispute between living spouses the evidence will probably point to one of these explanations as being more probable than the others, but if the rest of the evidence is neutral the prima facie inference is that their common intention was that the contributing spouse should acquire a share in the beneficial interest in the land in the same proportion as the sum contributed bears to the total purchase price. This prima facie inference is more easily rebutted in favour of a gift where the land is conveyed into the name of the wife; but as I understand the speeches in *Pettitt* v *Pettitt* four of the members of your Lordships' House who were parties to that decision took the view that even if the 'presumption of advancement' as between husband and wife still survived today, it could seldom have any decisive part to play in disputes between living spouses in which some evidence would be available in addition to the mere fact that the husband had provided part of the purchase price of property conveyed into the name of the wife.

Similarly when a matrimonial home is not purchased outright but partly out of moneys advanced on mortgage repayable by instalments, and the land is conveyed into the name of the husband alone, the fact that the wife made a cash contribution to the deposit and legal charges not borrowed on mortgage gives rise, in the absence of evidence which makes some other explanation more probable, to the inference that their common intention was that she should share in the beneficial interest in the land conveyed. But it would not be reasonable to infer a common intention as to what her share should be without taking account also of the sources from which the mortgage instalments were provided. If the wife also makes a substantial direct contribution to the mortgage instalments out of her own earnings or unearned income this would be prima facie inconsistent with a common intention that her share in the beneficial interest should be determined by the proportion which her original cash contribution bore either to the total amount of the deposit and legal charges or to the full purchase price. The more likely inference is that her contributions to the mortgage instalments were intended by the spouses to have some effect on her share.

Where there has been an initial contribution by the wife to the cash deposit and legal charges which points to a common intention at the time of the conveyance that she should have a beneficial interest in the land conveyed to her husband, it would however be unrealistic to attach significance to the wife's subsequent contributions to the mortgage instalments only where she pays them directly herself. It may be no more than a matter of convenience which spouse pays particular household accounts, particularly when both are earning, and if the wife goes out to work and devotes part of her earnings or uses her private income to meet joint expenses of the household which would otherwise be met by the husband, so as to enable him to pay the mortgage instalments out of his moneys, this would be consistent with and might be corroborative of an original common intention that she should share in the beneficial interest in the matrimonial home and that her payments of other household expenses were intended by both spouses to be treated as including a contribution by the wife to the purchase price of the matrimonial home.

Even where there has been no initial contribution by the wife to the cash deposit and legal charges but she makes a regular and substantial direct contribution to the mortgage instalments it may be reasonable to infer a common intention of the spouses from the outset that she should share in the beneficial interest or to infer a fresh agreement reached after the original conveyance that she should acquire a share. But it is unlikely that the mere fact that the wife made direct contributions to the mortgage instalments would be the only evidence available to assist the court in ascertaining the common intention of the spouses.

Where in any of the circumstances described above contributions, direct or indirect, have been made to the mortgage instalments by the spouse into whose name the matrimonial home has not been conveyed, and the court can infer from their conduct a common intention that the contributing spouse should be entitled to *some* beneficial interest in the matrimonial home, what effect is to be given to that intention if there is no evidence that they in fact reached any express agreement as to what the respective share of each spouse should be?

I take it to be clear that if the court is satisfied that it was the common intention of both spouses that the contributing wife should have a share in the beneficial interest and that her contributions were made on this understanding, the court in the exercise of its equitable jurisdiction would not permit the husband in whom the legal estate was vested and who had accepted the benefit of the contributions to take the whole beneficial interest merely because at the time the wife made her contributions there had been no express agreement as to how her share in it was to be quantified. In such a case the court must first do its best to discover from the conduct of the spouses whether any inference can reasonably be drawn as to the probable common understanding about the amount of the share of the contributing spouse on which each must have acted in doing what each did, even though that understanding was never expressly stated by one spouse to the other or even consciously formulated in words by either of them independently. It is only if no such inference can be drawn that the court is driven to apply as a rule of law, and not as an inference of fact, the maxim 'equality is equity', and to hold that the beneficial interest belongs to the spouses in equal shares.

The same result however may often be reached as an inference of fact. The instalments of a mortgage to a building society are generally repayable over a period of many years. During that period, as both must be aware, the ability of each spouse to contribute to the instalments out of their separate earnings is likely to alter, particularly in the case of the wife if any children are born of the marriage. If the contribution of the wife in the early part of the period of repayment is substantial but is not an identifiable and uniform proportion of each instalment, because her contributions are indirect or, if direct, are made irregularly, it may well be a reasonable inference that their common intention at the time of acquisition of the matrimonial home was that the beneficial interest should be held by them in equal shares and that each should contribute to the cost of its acquisition whatever amounts each could afford in the varying exigencies of family life to be expected during the period of repayment. In the social conditions of today this would be a natural enough common intention of a young couple who were both earning when the house was acquired but who contemplated having children whose birth and rearing in their infancy would necessarily affect the future earning capacity of the wife.

The relative size of their respective contributions to the instalments in the early part of the period of repayment, or later if a subsequent reduction in the wife's contribution is not to be accounted for by a reduction in her earnings due to motherhood or some other cause from which the husband benefits as well, may make it a more probable inference that the wife's share in the beneficial interest was intended to be in some proportion other than one-half. And there is nothing inherently improbable in their acting on the understanding that the wife should be entitled to a share which was not to be quantified immediately on the acquisition of the home but should be left to be determined when the mortgage was repaid or the property disposed of, on the basis of what would be fair having regard to the total contributions, direct or indirect, which each spouse had made by that date. Where this was the most likely inference from their conduct it would be for the court to give effect to that common intention of the parties by determining what in all circumstances was a fair share.

Difficult as they are to solve, however, these problems as to the amount of the share of a spouse in the beneficial interest in a matrimonial home where the legal estate is vested solely in the other spouse, only arise in cases where the court is satisfied by the words or conduct of the parties that it was their common intention that the beneficial interest was not to belong solely to the spouse in whom the legal estate was vested but was to be shared between them in some proportion or other.

Where the wife has made no initial contribution to the cash deposit and legal charges and no direct contribution to the mortgage instalments nor any adjustment to her contribution to other expenses of the household which it can be inferred was referable to the acquisition of the house, there is in the absence of evidence of an express agreement between the parties, no material to justify the court in inferring that it was the common intention of the parties that she should have any beneficial interest in a matrimonial home conveyed into the sole name of the husband, merely because she continued to contribute out of her own earnings or private income to other expenses of the household. For such conduct is no less consistent with a common intention to share the day-to-day expenses of the household, while each spouse retains a separate interest in capital assets acquired with their own money or obtained by inheritance or gift. There is nothing here to rebut the prima facie inference that a purchaser of land who pays the purchase price and takes a conveyance and grants a mortgage in his own name intends to acquire the sole beneficial interest as well as the legal estate; *and the difficult question of the quantum of the wife's share does not arise.*

17.1.2.3 'Detrimental reliance'

See *Grant* v *Edwards* [1986] Ch 638 at **17.1.2.1**.

17.1.3 INDIRECT FINANCIAL CONTRIBUTIONS

BURNS v *BURNS* [1984] 1 Ch 317, CA

FACTS: The plaintiff and the defendant set up home together in 1961 in rented accommodation where their first child was born. In 1963 when the plaintiff was expecting their second child, the defendant decided that it would be a better use of his money to buy a house. The house was purchased and conveyed in the sole name of the defendant who financed the purchase price out of his own money and by way of a mortgage. The plaintiff did not directly contribute to the purchase price or to the mortgage payments. She remained at home to look after the children and to perform domestic duties and was thus unable to earn until 1975 when she started working as a driving instructor. Although the defendant continued to give her a generous housekeeping allowance and did not ask her to contribute to the household expenses, she used her earnings to pay the rates and the telephone bills and to buy fixtures, fittings and certain domestic chattels for the house. She also redecorated the interior of the house. The plaintiff left the defendant in 1980 and brought proceedings against him claiming that she was entitled to a beneficial interest in the house by reason of her contributions to the household over the 17 years they had lived there. The judge dismissed the plaintiff's claim.
HELD: Dismissing the appeal, that since the plaintiff had not made a substantial financial contribution to the acquisition of the house the court could not impute a common intention that she should acquire a beneficial interest in it; that the plaintiff's contribution to the welfare of the family by performing the domestic duties of the household and bringing up the children were not factors which could be taken into account in determining whether or not she had acquired a beneficial interest in the house; and that, accordingly, the plaintiff had failed to demonstrate the existence of any trust in her favour.

FOX LJ: The house with which we are concerned in this case was purchased in the name of the defendant and the freehold was conveyed to him absolutely. That was in 1963. If, therefore, the plaintiff is to establish that she has a beneficial interest in the property she must establish that the defendant holds the legal estate upon trust to give effect to that interest. That follows from *Gissing* v *Gissing* [1971] AC 886. For present purposes I think that such a trust could only arise (a) by express declaration or agreement *or* (b) by way of a resulting trust where the claimant has directly provided part of the purchase price *or* (c) from the common intention of the parties.

In the present case (a) and (b) can be ruled out. There was no express trust of an interest in the property for the benefit of the plaintiff; and there was no express agreement to create such an interest. And the plaintiff made no direct contribution to the purchase price. Her case, therefore, must depend upon showing a common intention that she should have a beneficial interest in the property. Whether the trust which would arise in such circumstances is described as implied, constructive or resulting does not greatly matter. If the intention is inferred from the fact that some indirect contribution is made to the purchase price, the term 'resulting trust' is probably not inappropriate. Be that as it may, the basis of such a claim, in any case, is that it would be inequitable for the holder of the legal estate to deny the claimant's right to a beneficial interest.

In determining whether such common intention exists it is, normally, the intention of the parties when the property was purchased that is important. As to that I agree with the observations of Griffiths LJ in *Bernard* v *Josephs* [1982] Ch 391, 404. As I understand it, that does not mean that for the purpose of determining the ultimate shares in the property one looks simply at the factual position as it was at the date of acquisition. It is necessary for the court to consider all the evidence, including the contributions of the parties, down to the date of separation (which in the case of man and mistress will generally, though not always, be the relevant date). Thus the law proceeds on the basis that there is nothing inherently improbable in the parties acting on the understanding that the woman.

> should be entitled to a share which was not to be quantified immediately upon the acquisition of the home but should be left to be determined when the mortgage was repaid or the property disposed of, on the basis of what would be fair having regard to the total contributions, direct or indirect, which each spouse had made by that date: (see *Gissing* v *Gissing* [1971] AC 886, 909, *per* Lord Diplock.

That approach does not, however, in my view preclude the possibility that while, initially, there was no intention that the claimant should have any interest in the property, circumstances may subsequently arise from which the intention to confer an equitable interest upon the claimant may arise (e.g., the discharge of a mortgage or the effecting of capital improvements to the house at his or her expense). Further, subsequent events may throw light on the initial intention.

Looking at the position at the time of the acquisition of the house in 1963, I see nothing at all to indicate any intention by the parties that the plaintiff should have an interest in it. . . .

The judge's findings as to expenditure by the plaintiff were as follows. (i) She made gifts of clothing and other things to the defendant and the children. (ii) She paid for the housekeeping. The defendant allowed her, latterly, £60 per week for housekeeping. It seems to be accepted that the defendant was generous with money and the plaintiff was not kept short as regards housekeeping money. (iii) She paid the rates. The housekeeping payments made by the defendant were, however, fixed at an amount which took account of this. (iv) She paid the telephone bills. That was a matter of agreement between her and the defendant because she spent a lot of time on the telephone talking to her friends. (v) She bought a number of chattels for domestic use: a dishwasher, a washing machine, a tumble dryer and either a drawing room suite or three armchairs and a bed for her separate room. The bed, the dishwasher and the chairs she took with her when she left in 1980. (vi) She provided some doorknobs and door furnishings of no great value.

None of this expenditure, in my opinion, indicates the existence of the common intention which the plaintiff has to prove. What is needed, I think, is evidence of a payment or payments by the plaintiff which it can be inferred was referable to the acquisition of the house. Lord Denning MR in *Hazell* v *Hazell* [1972] 1 WLR 301, 304 thought that expression, which appears in the speech of Lord Diplock in *Gissing* v *Gissing*

[1971] AC 886 909 was being over-used. He said quoting from *Falconer* v *Falconer* [1970] 1 WLR 1333 1336, that if there was a substantial financial contribution towards the family expenses that would raise an inference of a trust. I do not think that formulation alters the essence of the matter for present purposes. If there is a substantial contribution by the woman to family expenses, and the house was purchased on a mortgage, her contribution is, indirectly, referable to the acquisition of the house since, in one way or another, it enables the family to pay the mortgage instalments. Thus, a payment could be said to be referable to the acquisition of the house if, for example, the payer either (a) pays part of the purchase price or (b) contributes regularly to the mortgage instalments or (c) pays off part of the mortgage or (d) makes a substantial financial contribution to the family expenses so as to enable the mortgage instalments to be paid.

But if a payment cannot be said to be, in a real sense, referable to the acquisition of the house it is difficult to see how, in such a case as the present, it can base a claim for an interest in the house. Looking at the items which I have listed above, and leaving aside, for the present, the housekeeping which I will deal with separately, none of the items can be said to be referable to the acquisition of the house. . . .

As regards work on the house, in 1971 a fairly substantial improvement was made to the house; the attic was converted into a bedroom with a bathroom en suite. That was paid for wholly by the defendant.

In 1977 or 1978 the plaintiff decorated the house throughout internally because she wished the house to be wallpapered and not painted. I do not think that carries her case any further. Thus in *Pettitt* v *Pettitt* [1970] AC 777, 826 Lord Diplock said:

> If the husband likes to occupy his leisure by laying a new lawn in the garden or building a fitted wardrobe in the bedroom while the wife does the shopping, cooks the family dinner and bathes the children, I, for my part, find it quite impossible to impute to them as reasonable husband and wife any common intention that these domestic activities or any of them are to have any effect upon the existing proprietary rights in the family home. . . .

Accordingly I think that the decoration undertaken by the plaintiff gives no indication of any such common intention as she must assert.

There remains the question of housekeeping and domestic duties. So far as housekeeping expenses are concerned, I do not doubt that (the house being bought in the man's name) if the woman goes out to work in order to provide money for the family expenses, as a result of which she spends her earnings on the housekeeping and the man is thus able to pay the mortgage instalments and other expenses out of his earnings, it can be inferred that there was a common intention that the woman should have an interest in the house—since she will have made an indirect financial contribution to the mortgage instalments. But that is not the case. . . .

For the reasons which I have given I think that the appeal must be dismissed. I only add this. The plaintiff entered upon her relationship with the defendant knowing that there was no prospect of him marrying her. And it is evident that in a number of respects he treated her very well. He was generous to her, in terms of money, while the relationship continued. And, what in the long term is probably more important he encouraged her to develop her abilities in a number of ways, with the result that she built up the successful driving instruction business. Nevertheless, she lived with him for 18 years as man and wife, and, at the end of it, has no rights against him. But the unfairness of that is not a matter which the courts can control. It is a matter for Parliament.

MAY LJ: . . . in some of the earlier decisions before *Pettitt* v *Pettitt* [1970] AC 777 and *Gissing* v *Gissing* [1971] AC 886 Lord Denning MR had held that the court did have a power 'to do what is fair and reasonable in all the circumstances.' In both *Pettitt's* case and *Gissing's* case the House of Lords made it quite clear, in my view, that no such general power exists. In all the decisions prior to *Hall's* case (1982) 3 FLR 379 in which the wife or woman was held to be entitled to a share in the family home, on the evidence she had made a 'real' or 'substantial' contribution either to the deposit paid for the acquisition of the family home or to the instalments of the mortgage with whose assistance it was bought. In *Pettitt's* case [1970] AC 777 Lord Diplock, whose speech was the most favourable to the applicant's case, said, at p. 826:

> It is common enough nowadays for husbands and wives to decorate and to make improvements in the family home themselves, with no other intention than to indulge in what is now a popular hobby, and to make the home pleasanter for their common use and enjoyment. If the husband likes to occupy his leisure by laying a new lawn in the garden or building a fitted wardrobe in the bedroom while the wife does the shopping, cooks the family dinner or bathes the children, I, for my part, find it quite impossible to impute to them as reasonable husband and wife any common intention that these domestic activities or any of them are to have any effect upon the existing proprietary rights in the family home on which they are undertaken. It is only in the bitterness engendered by the break-up of the marriage that so bizarre a notion would enter their heads.

In these circumstances, I respectfully think that the dictum of Lord Denning MR that the woman's contribution to the family well-being by keeping the house and looking after the children can be taken into account in assessing the extent to which a resulting trust has arisen in her favour was wrong.

On the other hand it would appear from a passage from the judgment of the judge in the county court quoted by Dunn LJ in the Court of Appeal in *Hall's* case, 3 FLR, 379, 384 that the woman had been working and had been applying substantially all her earnings towards the housekeeping. In these circumstances it may have been argued that the woman had made an actual financial contribution to the acquisition of the family home, in that her pooled earnings had at the least made it easier for the man to pay the mortgage instalments. . . .

In the light of all these cases, I think that the approach which the courts should follow, be the couples married or unmarried, is now clear. What is difficult, however, is to apply it to the facts and circumstances of any given case. Where the family home is taken in the joint names, then unless the facts are very unusual I think that both the man and the woman are entitled to a share in the beneficial interest. Where the house is bought outright and not on mortgage, then the extent of their respective shares will depend upon a more or less precise arithmetical calculation of the extent of their contributions to the purchase price. Where, on the other hand, and as is more usual nowadays, the house is bought with the aid of a mortgage, then the court has to assess each of the parties' respective contributions in a broad sense; nevertheless the court is only entitled to look at the financial contributions or their real or substantial equivalent, to the acquisition of the house; that the husband may spend his weekends redecorating or laying a patio is neither here nor there, nor is the fact the woman has spent so much of her time looking after the house, doing the cooking and bringing up the family.

The inquiry becomes even more difficult when the home is taken in only one of the two names. For present purposes I will assume that it is the man, although the same approach will be followed if it is taken in the name of the woman. Where a matrimonial or family home is bought in the man's name alone on mortgage by the mechanism of deposit and instalments, then if the woman pays or contributes to the initial deposit this points to a common intention that she should have *some* beneficial interest in the house. If thereafter she makes direct contributions to the instalments, then the case is a fortiori and her rightful share is likely to be greater. If the woman, having contributed to the deposit, but although not making direct contributions to the instalments, nevertheless uses her own money for other joint household expenses so as to enable the man the more easily to pay the mortgage instalments out of his money, then her position is the same. Where a woman has made no contribution to the initial deposit, but makes regular and substantial contributions to the mortgage instalments, it may still be reasonable to infer a common intention that she should share the beneficial interest from the outset or a fresh agreement after the original conveyance that she should acquire such a share. It is only when there is no evidence upon which a court can reasonably draw an inference about the extent of the share of the contributing woman, that it should fall back on the maxim 'equality is equity.' Finally, when the house is taken in the man's name alone, if the woman makes no 'real' or 'substantial' financial contribution towards either the purchase price, deposit or mortgage instalments by the means of which the family home was acquired, then she is not entitled to any share in the beneficial interest in that home even though over a very substantial number of years she may have worked just and hard as the man in maintaining the family in the sense of keeping the house, giving birth to and looking after and helping to bring up the children of the union.

17.2   Quantification of the Interest under the Trust

17.2.1   RESULTING TRUST

SPRINGETTE v DEFOE [1992] 2 FCR 561, CA

FACTS: The parties met in 1979. The appellant was the tenant of a council flat in the London Borough of Ealing. The respondent moved in and paid half the rent. They lived together as husband and wife. Early in 1982 they moved and became joint tenants of 49 St. Andrews Road, another council property. On June 30, 1982 the property was offered to them by the council at a price of £14,445. This gave a discount of 41% on the estimated market value because the appellant had been a tenant of the council for over 11 years. The parties arranged to buy the property jointly. At that stage they intended to marry.

The total purchase price was £14,706.35. £12,000 of that was raised by way of a mortgage to to the Nationwide Building Society in joint names. It was agreed that each would contribute half of the mortgage instalments. Of the balance, the respondent contributed £180 and the rest came out of the appellant's savings. The parties were registered as joint proprietors but the registered transfer was silent as to the beneficial interests.

The relationship broke down in 1985. Proceedings started in January 1987. It was common ground that the parties were each intended to have some beneficial interest in the property. The appellant claimed that she was entitled to a 75% share and the respondent to a 25% share on the basis that those were the proportions in which they provided the purchase money.

The recorder found that the parties never had any discussion at or before the time of the purchase about what their respective beneficial interests were to be. He concluded, however, that they were to share equally on the ground that each had in his or her own mind an uncommunicated belief or intention to that effect. He found that upon looking at the surrounding facts at the time of the acquisition there was sufficient evidence to infer a common intention that the property should be owned in equal shares.

The appellant appealed.

HELD: (allowing the appeal]. The principle of law invoked on behalf of the appellant was that if two or more persons purchased property in their joint names and there had been no declaration of the trusts upon which it was to be held, in the absence of evidence to the contrary they would hold that property on a resulting trust for the persons who provided the purchase money in the proportions in which they provided it: *Dyer* v *Dyer* (1788) 2 Cox Eq Cas 92; *Pettit* v *Pettit* [1970] AC 777 *per* Lord Upjohn at p. 814. The question was whether the recorder was right in concluding that an actual common intention to acquire the property in equal beneficial shares had been established on the evidence. It was established that there had been no discussion at all regarding the shares. It made no difference that both parties thought that they were acquiring equal shares if they did not say so to each other. The law had to concentrate on external signs of common intention rather than on what was privately thought or speculated. Inference of common intention might be drawn from circumstantial evidence. But those inferences would be drawn from the *words or conduct* of the parties. It was not capable of arising by virtue of any subjective intention or absence of intention which was not made manifest at the time of the transaction: *Gissing* v *Gissing* [1971] AC 886 at p. 906 B–D *per* Lord Diplock. It followed that it was not enough to establish common intention to found a trust of land that each party happened to be thinking the same thing at the same time while neither had any knowledge of the thinking of the other. No authority was put before the court to support a contrary proposition. Further, the evidence of surrounding facts before the recorder could not support the inference of common intention that he sought to draw. Accordingly, the appeal would be allowed and the recorder's decision varied to apportion the beneficial interest as 75% to the appellant and 25% to the respondent.

DILLON LJ: The common intention must be founded on evidence such as would support a finding that there is an implied or constructive trust for the parties in proportion to the purchase price. The court does not as yet sit, as under a palm tree, to exercise a general discretion to do what the man in the street, on a general overview of the case, might regard as fair.

But the common intention of the parties must, in my judgment, mean a shared intention communicated between them. It cannot mean an intention which each happened to have in his or her own mind but had never communicated to the other. I find some assistance in this respect in the observation of Lord Bridge of Harwich in *Lloyds Bank plc v Rosset* [1991] 107 where he said at p. 132F in relation to the question whether there had been any agreement, arrangement or understanding reached between the parties to the effect that a property was to be shared beneficially:

> This finding of an agreement or arrangement to share in this sense can only, I think, be based on evidence in express discussions between the partners, however imperfectly remembered and however imprecise their terms may have been.

It is not enough to establish a common intention which is sufficient to found an implied or constructive trust of land that each of them happened at the same time to have been thinking on the same lines in his or her uncommunicated thoughts, while neither had any knowledge of the thinking of the other.

Since, therefore, it is clear in the present case that there never was any discussion between the parties about what their respective beneficial interests were to be, they cannot, in my judgment, have had in any relevant sense any common intention as to the beneficial ownership of 49 St. Andrews Road. I cannot, therefore, support the conclusion of the recorder that the beneficial interest was held by Miss Springette and Mr Defoe in equal shares. The presumption of a resulting trust is not displaced. Accordingly, I would allow this appeal and would declare instead that they are beneficially entitled in the proportion of 75% to Miss Springette and 25% to Mr Defoe.

17.2.2 CONSTRUCTIVE TRUST

MIDLAND BANK PLC v COOKE AND ANOTHER [1995] 4 All ER 562, CA

FACTS: The husband and wife married in 1971 and moved into a house purchased for £8,500 in the husband's sole name. The purchase was financed by a mortgage of £6,450, with the balance provided from the husband's savings and a wedding gift of £1,100 from his parents. In 1978 the mortgage was replaced by a general mortgage in favour of the respondent bank granted to the husband to secure repayment of his company's business overdraft. In 1979, at the bank's request, the wife signed a form of consent to any present or future right or interest which she might have in the property being postponed to the bank's security under the mortgage. The property was subsequently transferred into the joint names of the husband and wife as tenants in common, following proceedings brought by the wife under the Married Women's Property Act 1964. In 1987 the bank commenced county court proceedings against the husband and wife, claiming payment of £52,491 as the sum due under the mortgage, and possession in default of payment. The wife filed a defence, asserting that her signature to the consent form had been procured to the knowledge of the bank by her husband's undue influence, and counterclaimed for declarations that she was the joint legal owner of the property and entitled to a beneficial half interest in the property overriding any interests of the bank under the mortgage. The judge held, on the undue influence issue, that the consent form was not binding on the wife and that her equitable interest took priority over the bank's claims. He further held that the wife's beneficial interest depended on her monetary contribution and that, since her maintenance contribution and improvement contribution did not amount to a contribution to the purchase price, she was entitled to a beneficial interest of 6·74% in the property, being the proportion represented by her half share of the wedding gift from the husband's parents (£550) to the total purchase price of the property (£8,500). The wife appealed, contending that the judge had adopted the wrong approach to the quantification of her beneficial interest. The bank cross-appealed.

HELD: (1) Where a partner in a matrimonial home without legal title had established an equitable interest through direct contribution, the court would assess (in the absence of express evidence of intention) the proportions the parties were to be assumed to have intended for their beneficial ownership by undertaking a survey of the whole course of dealing between the parties relevant to their ownership and occupation of the property and their sharing of its burdens and advantages and would take into consideration all conduct which threw light on the question what shares were intended. In particular, the court was not bound to deal with the matter on the strict basis of the trust resulting from the cash contribution to the purchase price, and was free to attribute to the parties an intention to share the beneficial interest in some different proportions; and the fact that the parties had neither discussed nor intended any agreement as to the proportions of their beneficial interest did not preclude the court from inferring one on general equitable principles.

(2) It followed that the judge had erred in treating the wife's cash contribution to the purchase price as wholly determinative of the issue of the current proportion of beneficial entitlement without regard to the other factors emerging from the whole course of dealing between the husband and wife. Applying the proper approach to the facts, it was clear that the couple's presumed intention was to share the beneficial interest in the property in equal shares and that intention was reinforced by the subsequent terms of their compromise of the Married Women's Property Act proceedings. The wife was therefore entitled to a beneficial half interest in the matrimonial home and a declaration would be granted to that effect. The appeal would therefore be allowed and the cross-appeal would be dismissed.

WAITE LJ: This appeal, concerning the disputed beneficial interests in a matrimonial home, was heard during the week in which the Law Commission published its *Sixth Programme of Law Reform* (Law Com No. 234). Item 8 of the programme recommends an examination of the property rights of home-sharers. The report comments (p. 34); 'The present legal rules are uncertain and difficult to apply and can lead to serious injustice'. Though that was a reference to the problems of unmarried home-owners, the rights of married occupiers can be equally problematic—as the present case shows—when the claims of third parties such as creditors or mortgagees become involved. The economic and social significance of home-ownership in modern society, and the frequency with which cases involving disputes as to the property rights of home-sharers (married or unmarried) are coming before the courts, suggest that the Law Commission's intervention is well-timed and has the potential to save a lot of human heartache as well as public expense. . . .

(A)   *Was there a gift by Mr Cooke's parents to both spouses?*
The judge was in my view (rejecting Mr Bergen's first submission) fully entitled, on the evidence which I have quoted, to hold that there was. In a case where the bride's parents were paying for the wedding and reception and the bridegroom's parents were providing a contribution to the purchase price of the matrimonial home, it would not only be sensible to draw the inference that the bridegroom's parents intended to make a present to them both of the moneys which were to be applied in the purchase, but highly artificial to draw any other inference.

(B)   *Is the proportion of Mrs Cooke's beneficial interest to be fixed solely by reference to the percentage of the purchase price which she contributed directly, so as to make all other conduct irrelevant?*
In contending that it is, Mr Bergin submits as follows.

(a)   It is now well settled that in determining (in the absence of evidence of express agreement) whether a party unnamed in the deeds has any beneficial interest in the property at all the test is the stringent one stated by Lord Bridge of Harwich in *Lloyds Bank plc v Rosset* [1990] 1 All ER 1111 at 1119:

In this situation direct contributions to the purchase price by the partner who is not the legal owner, whether initially or by payment of mortgage instalments, will readily justify the inference necessary to the creation of a constructive trust. But, as I read the authorities, it is at least extremely doubtful whether anything less will do.

(b)   By parity of reasoning, in cases where a direct contribution has been duly proved by the partner who is not the legal owner (thus establishing a resulting trust in his or her favour of *some* part of the beneficial interest) the proportion of that share will be fixed at the proportion it bears to the overall price of the property. Although the proportion may be enlarged by subsequent contribution to the purchase price, such contributions must be direct—i.e. further cash payments or contribution to the capital element in instalment repayments of any mortgage under which the unpaid proportion of the purchase remains secured. Nothing less will do. . . .

[His Lordship then referred to the judgment of Dillon LJ in *Springette* v *Defoe* [1992] 2 FCR 561 (see above).]

That decision has to be compared with *McHardy & Sons (a firm)* v *Warren* [1994] 2 FLR 338, a case in which (as here) it became necessary to quantify the interests of husband and wife on a strict equitable basis because of third party claims against the property. The purchase of the first matrimonial home was (again, as in this case) partly financed by a contribution from the husband's parents, but with the difference that in that instance the husband's parents paid the whole of the deposit (using that term in the sense of the net purchase price not covered by a mortgage) for the property, which was registered in the husband's sole name. The two subsequent homes successively purchased by the parties out of the net proceeds of sale of the former home were similarly taken in his name alone. The husband then executed a charge on the current home to secure his indebtedness to the plaintiffs, who were trade creditors. In proceedings by the plaintiffs against both husband and wife to enforce their charge, the plaintiffs asserted that the wife either had no beneficial interest or at most an interest equivalent to 8·97%, representing the proportion that half the initial deposit of £650 bore to the total purchase price of the first home. The judge rejected that claim, holding that the parties were beneficially entitled in equal shares. He was upheld on appeal. It does not appear from the law report that *Springette* v *Defoe* was cited, but the presiding Lord Justice was again Dillon LJ, who said (at 340):

> To my mind it is the irresistible conclusion that where a parent pays the deposit, either directly or to the solicitors or to the bride and groom, it matters not which, on the purchase of their first matrimonial home, it is the intention of all three of them that the bride and groom should have equal interests it the matrimonial home, not interests measured by reference to the percentage half the deposit [bears] to the full price . . .

I confess that I find the differences of approach in those two cases mystifying. In the one a strict resulting trust geared to mathematical calculation of the proportion of the purchase price provided by cash contribution is treated as virtually immutable in the absence of express agreement: in the other a displacement of the cash-related trust by inferred agreement is not only permitted but treated as obligatory. Guidance out of this difficulty is to be found, fortunately, in the passage in the speech of Lord Diplock in *Gissing* v *Gissing* [1970] 2 All ER 780 at 792–793 where he is dealing with the approach to be adopted by the court when evaluating the proportionate shares of the parties, once it has been duly established through the direct contributions of the party without legal title, that *some* beneficial interest was intended for both.

[His Lordship referred to the speech of Lord Diplock.]

The decision of this court in *Grant* v *Edwards* [1986] 2 All ER 426, [1986] Ch 638 also affords helpful guidance. The context was different, in that the court was there dealing with a legal owner who has made representation to the occupier on which the latter has relied to her detriment so as to introduce equities in the nature of estoppel. Once a beneficial interest had been established by that route, however, the court then proceeded—as I read the judgments—to fix the proportions of the beneficial interests on general grounds which were regarded as applying in all cases. . . .

The general principle to be derived from *Gissing* v *Gissing* and *Grant* v *Edwards* can in my judgment be summarised in this way. When the court is proceeding, in cases like the present where the partner without legal title has successfully asserted an equitable interest through direct contribution, to determine (in the absence of express evidence of intention) what proportions the parties must be assumed to have intended for their beneficial ownership, the duty of the judge is to undertake a survey of the whole course of dealing between the parties relevant to their ownership and occupation of the property and their sharing of its burdens and advantages. That scrutiny will not confine itself to the limited range of acts of direct contribution of the sort that are needed to found a beneficial interest in the first place. It will take into consideration all conduct which throws light on the question what shares were intended. Only if that search proves inconclusive does the court fall back on the maxim that 'equality is equity'.

My answer to question B would therefore be No. The court is not bound to deal with the matter on the strict basis of the trust resulting from the cash contribution to the purchase price, and is free to attribute to the parties an intention to share the beneficial interest in some different proportion.

Mr Bergin submits, however, that . . .

If the purchase parties themselves testify on oath that they made no agreement, there is no scope for equity to make one for them. . . .

[This] . . . I would reject instinctively on the ground that it runs counter to the very system of law—equity—on which it seeks to rely. Equity has traditionally been a system which matches established principle to the demands of social change. The mass diffusion of home ownership has been one of the most striking social changes of our own time. The present case is typical of hundreds, perhaps even thousands, of others. When people, especially young people, agree to share their lives in joint homes they do so on a basis of mutual trust and in the expectation that their relationship will endure. Despite the efforts that have ben made by many responsible bodies to counsel prospective co-habitants as to the risks of taking shared interests in property without legal advice, it is unrealistic to expect that advice to be followed on a universal scale. For a couple embarking on a serious relationship, discussion of the terms to apply at parting is almost a contradiction of the shared hopes that have brought them together. There will inevitably be numerous couples, married or unmarried, who have no discussion about ownership and who, perhaps advisedly, make no agreement about it. It would be anomalous, against that background, to create a range of home-buyers who were beyond the pale of equity's assistance in formulating a fair presumed basis for the sharing of beneficial title, simply because they had been honest enough to admit that they never gave ownership a thought or reached any agreement about it. . . .

17.3   Proprietary Estoppel

INWARDS v BAKER [1965] 2 QB 21, CA

FACTS: B junior was keen to build himself a bungalow, but could not afford to purchase a vacant plot. His father had some spare land. B senior said to his son, 'why not put the bungalow on my land and make the bungalow a little bigger?'. B junior did exactly that, and made the bungalow his permanent home.

B senior retained ownership of the fee simple to the land, and so the house also became *B senior's* property. All was well while both senior and junior were still alive, but when B senior died, his will left the land to Inwards. Inwards brought proceedings to recover possession of the bungalow.

HELD: The Court of Appeal found that where a landowner (L) encourages a third party (T) to expend money and/or effort on L's land, and T reasonably assumes that he will have some degree of permanence on the land, T acquires some sort of right with respect to the land. This right is (in principle) binding on third parties.

LORD DENNING MR: . . . We have had the advantage of cases which were not cited to the county court judge—cases in the last century, notably *Dillwyn* v *Llewelyn* (1862) 4 DeG F & J 517 and *Plimmer* v *Wellington Corporation* (1884) 9 App Cas 699, PC. This latter was a decision of the Privy Council which expressly affirmed and approved the statement of the law made by Lord Kingsdown in *Ramsden* v *Dyson* (1866) LR 1 HL 129. It is quite plain from those authorities that if the owner of land requests another, or indeed allows another, to expend money on the land under an expectation created or encouraged by the landlord that he will be able to remain there, that raises an equity in the licensee such as to entitle him to stay. He has a licence coupled with an equity. Mr Goodhart urged before us that the licensee could not stay indefinitely. The principle only applied, he said, when there was an expectation of some precise legal term. But it seems to me, from *Plimmer's* case in particular, that the equity arising from the expenditure on land need not fail 'merely on the ground that the interest to be secured has not been expressly indicated . . . the court must look at the circumstances in each case to decide in what way the equity can be satisfied.' . . .

Mr Goodhart put the case of a purchaser. He suggested that the father could sell the land to a purchaser who could get the son out. But I think that any purchaser who took with notice would clearly be bound by the equity. So here, too, the present plaintiffs, the successors in title of the father, are clearly themselves bound by this equity. It is an equity well recognised in law. It arises from the expenditure of money by a person in actual occupation of land when he is led to believe that, as the result of that expenditure, he will be allowed to remain there. It is for the court to say in what way the equity can be satisfied. I am quite clear in this case it can be satisfied by holding that the defendant can remain there as long as he desires to as his home.

I would allow the appeal accordingly and enter judgment for the defendant.

DANCKWERTS LJ: . . . It is not necessary, I think, to imply a promise. It seems to me that this is one of the cases of an equity created by estoppel, or equitable estoppel, as it is sometimes called, by which the person who has made the expenditure is induced by the expectation of obtaining protection, and equity protects him so that an injustice may not be perpetrated.

I am clearly of opinion that the appeal should be allowed and judgment should be entered for the defendant.

Hayton, D, 'Equitable Rights of Cohabitees' [1990] Conv 370

Recent English developments make it worthwhile to examine afresh the well-known problems that a female cohabitee, F, can face when title to the family home is in the sole name of the man, M, and the relationship has broken down. F then wants a share of the home or some compensation from M. If they are unmarried she cannot claim against M under divorce legislation. She will need to rely on alleging a contract or an equitable right under a resulting trust or a common intention constructive trust or an equitable estoppel claim. However, s. 2 of the Law of Property (Miscellaneous Provisions) Act 1989 abolishes the equitable doctrine of part performance, previously available to circumvent problems involving informal contracts, and requires all the terms of a contract relating to land actually to be in writing signed by both parties or the contract will be void. F will thus have to claim the informal arrangements between her and M led to a resulting or constructive trust enforceable even in the absence of the written evidence required by the Law of Property Act 1925, s. 53(l)(b), replacing the Statute of Frauds 1677, s. 7. If F directly or indirectly contributed a proportion of the purchase price of the home M will hold the legal title on resulting trust for M and F in proportion to their respective contributions. Thus, F obtains only what she paid for, though she will usually have contributed less than M because of lower earnings and the demands of childbirth and childcare. This limitation and the problems over what can amount to indirect financial contributions have led to F claiming, instead, on common intention constructive trust principles whereby F gets what was expressly or impliedly agreed with M, such as a half share.

Recently, problems over common intention constructive trust principles have led to the dilution of such principles by invocation of equitable proprietary estoppel principles so as to erode the distinction between the two sets of principles. Indeed, one is now led to wonder whether such distinction is really 'a distinction without a difference' in the immortal words of Sir George Jessel MR in another context.

Conventionally, the common intention constructive trust requires a bilateral under-standing or agreement that if F acts in a particular way then she will obtain an agreed share in the family house, usually a half share but sometimes a 'fair' share. If she so acts then she must obtain respectively the half share, leaving the court no discretion or a 'fair' share, leaving the court plenty of discretion. Equity acts 'in personam' to prevent M pleading the lack of formalities, so F gets what was agreed.

In contrast, for there to be a successful equitable proprietary estoppel claim by F there only needs to be unilateral conduct by M, leading F to believe that she has an interest in the family home so that she acts to her detriment, so that it then becomes unconscionable for M to insist on his formal 100 per cent. ownership of the home. The court, however, does not automatically perfect M's imperfect gift or promise and give the 'go-by' to the need to satisfy formal requirements or the contractual doctrine of consideration. The court intervenes only *pro tanto* to decide what is the 'minimum equity to do justice' to F so as to prevent M's unconscionable conduct affecting her detrimentally. Thus, though led to believe that the house is owned half-and-half, F may merely obtain an equitable life interest or a personal licence for life, perhaps determinable upon the man paying her £10,000, or upon the youngest child attaining 18 years, or upon her cohabiting with another man, or she may obtain only a personal right to be housed from time to time in some accommodation by M. Only in a most exceptional case will the court consider that the need to avoid the effects of M's unconscionable behaviour requires perfecting an imperfect gift. The concept of unconscionability underlying equitable estoppel claims is not, in the words of Professor Finn, 'a talisman for the idiosyncratic effectuation of promises and expectations'. . . .

CONCLUSION

It is time that the English courts accepted that the apparent distinction between common intention constructive trusts and equitable estoppel claims is illusory. In both cases the court is not perfecting imperfect gifts or bargains. Instead, it is analysing and assessing the conduct and relationship of M and F up to the date of the trial to ascertain whether the circumstances make it unconscionable for M to be allowed to assert his formal 100 per cent. ownership. The court, then intervenes to alter the formal position and prevent M's unconsciouable retention of full absolute ownership (i.e. prevent M's unjust enrichment) only to the extent necessary in all the circumstances to protect F's detrimental reliance. This allows plenty of flexibility for proprietary or personal prospective remedies. A third party need not worry about the uncertain flexibility of F's 'doubtful equity' before the court decree. He will only be bound if he agreed with F to recognise whatever right he agreed she had (or might turn out to have) or if he agreed with M positively to take subject to whatever right he agreed F had (or might turn out to have). Thus the courts should not be inhibited by worries about third parties in developing a flexible range of unjust enrichment remedies as between cohabitees.

Ferguson, P, 'Constructive Trusts – A Note of Caution' (1993) 109 LQR 114

In the last few years, academics and judges alike have advanced the view that the common intention constructive trust (hereinafter 'the constructive trust') and proprietary estoppel are, or have become, essentially indistinguishable, that one 'basic principle of unconscionability' underlies both concepts, and that it is this principle, rather than any apparent differences remaining between the two ideas, which should guide the courts in deciding cases.

Professor Hayton has put forward this argument in his discussion of the equitable rights of cohabitees—one of the most important areas of operation for both constructive trusts and estoppels, given the lack of statutory regulation of cohabitees' property relations and the unlikelihood of any express formal agreement being reached by the parties as to their respective rights. . . .

The object of this article is not to argue that Hayton's thesis is untenable; in fact, its plausibility in the light of recent case law is readily conceded. Rather, I intend to counsel caution, and to suggest that . . . line of argument overlooks both an important (arguably fundamental) distinction between the two concepts and the adverse consequences of the merging of the two sets of principles under discussion. . . .

Hayton's thesis, to recapitulate, is this: the distinction between the requirements of the two concepts is illusory. Both are based on the principle of unconscionability. There is thus no reason or justification for maintaining the distinction between the results of each concept. A constructive trust should no longer give rise to a proprietary right independent of and prior to the court's order.

I wish to make a contrary argument. The results of the two sets of principles are clearly different. This distinction is evidence of a conceptual difference. Estoppel is purely a *remedial* concept centred on the intervention of the court. The constructive trust is a *means of creating a proprietary right* which operates entirely independently of the court. This conceptual difference necessitates the recognition of and maintenance of the distinction between the evidentiary requirements of the constructive trust and proprietary estoppel. If (as argued by Hayton) recent cases have blurred that distinction, it is essential that it should be re-established. . . .

. . . The essential question—which Hayton nowhere addresses in terms—is whether the right generated by the operation of the constructive trust principle should be recognised as a pre-existing proprietary right. Hayton argues that because of the 'inchoate and uncertain nature of F's 'right,' 'third parties should not be bound merely by notice—which argument may be restated as the following proposition: so long as F's right is inchoate and uncertain (i.e. before any court hearing on the subject), that right should be personal only, and not proprietary. Only clear-cut rights—such as those generated by a resulting trust—should qualify as proprietary rights.

Against this, I would submit that the policy of the law is contrary to such an argument. Thus, for example, in Law Commission No. 158 (Land Registration), one of the arguments used to support the retention of s. 70(1)(g) within the category of overriding interests is that the rights of occupiers are often informal and arise without legal advice, and therefore it is not reasonable or sensible to expect or require registration to achieve a necessary protection against third parties. The system of land registration arguably places a much greater emphasis on the importance of certainty and clarity where third parties are involved than the general law. The fact that that system considers F's rights to be worthy of protection is therefore a strong argument against Hayton's postulated demotion of the constructive trust on the ground of the uncertain nature of those rights. . . .

. . . the consequence of his arguments would seem to be that F's lower earning capacity (this is, generally speaking, still true of most women), and thus her lower contribution capacity, is to prejudice F as regards her rights to the property of a relationship into which she has put as much effort as M. In the majority of cases F will only be able to obtain any proprietary interest by accepting this view of herself as a lesser partner in the relationship. It may be doubted whether the law should be actively seeking to perpetuate this type of implicit discrimination and gender stereotyping. If the law has learnt to quantify the value of a mother's or a housewife's services by reference to the wages charged by a nanny or a housekeeper insofar as the law of negligence is concerned, perhaps it is time that such techniques were considered in relation to the law of property. If Hayton's argument is accepted it may well be that cohabitees in future cases will seek to draw that analogy. . . .

CONCLUSION

I have attempted to show that the case law on the subject of constructive trusts and proprietary estoppel does not unambiguously correspond to Hayton's picture of an 'illusory distinction', particularly given the clear difference between the rights and remedies available once the relevant requirements of each concept have been satisfied. I have relied on this same clear difference to build up an argument that constructive trusts and proprietary estoppel should be distinguished:

a constructive trust automatically gives rise to a proprietary right independently of any court intervention, and this result justifies higher evidentiary requirements since it thus forms a means of creating interests in land without any prior regulation by the court; a proprietary estoppel gives rise only to a remedial jurisdiction in the court, and any proprietary right granted has effect only as a result of and subsequent to the court's order; this discretion justifies lower evidentiary requirements since the court is enabled to filter out only the deserving cases to receive proprietary interests. . . .

Hayton, D, 'Constructive Trusts of Homes — A Bold Approach' (1993) 109 LQR 485

Recently, Patricia Ferguson has sought to reject my view that the common intention constructive trust should be regarded as indistinguishable from equitable proprietary estoppel and to support the view that, while an estoppel only entitles the plaintiff to prospective rights originating in the order of the court, such a constructive trust automatically gives rise to an independent proprietary right in the plaintiff effective from the date of the plaintiff's detrimental conduct and retrospectively recognised by the order of the court. It follows that a plaintiff, F, in occupation of the quasi-matrimonial home held on such a constructive trust for her by the defendant, M, is fully protected against a third party, like a mortgagee, X, to whom M may have granted a proprietary interest after the date of her detrimental conduct. Her protection should not be weakened by subsuming common intention constructive trusts within proprietary estoppel principles. She should only be subordinated to X if she knew of and expressly or impliedly consented to M's transaction with X. Ferguson's illuminating article has stimulated me to develop further the question of priorities between F and X. . . .

Ferguson ripostes that the court's prospective remedy will not do F much good against the likes of X, so that F will instead need to rely on resulting trust principles, her equitable interest automatically arising thereunder as soon as she provides part of the purchase money. Because X in dealing with M will be bound by any equitable interest that F has under a resulting trust if F is in actual occupation X must ask her whether she claims any interest in the home. If she makes no claim to an interest under a purchase money resulting trust but claims that she has the foundation for a proprietary estoppel remedy to be declared by the court, whether a co-ownership share or a life interest or an equitable charge for a sum of money, the only sensible precaution for X, if he is to proceed, is to obtain F's written consent to his dealing with M.

If F is opposed to the grant of X's interest her only sensible precaution is to have M grant her a prior interest or to issue a writ (protected as a *lis pendens*) claiming a proprietary estoppel interest in the land against M and an injunction restraining him from proceeding with the proposed transaction with X. She will thus safeguard against X whatever interest the court eventually orders in her favour.

If X deliberately or recklessly failed to take the elementary conveyancing precaution of asking the occupier, F, whether she claims any interest in the home, so as to divest her of the opportunity she would otherwise have had to take the only sensible precautions set out in the last paragraph, is it not clearly unconscionable if X can then take advantage of his own wrong (such failure being inherently reckless) to have priority for his interest over whatever interest the court subsequently confers on F? Surely, a remedial constructive trust can be imposed upon X to accord priority to F's interest because X's conscience is affected, as recognised by the Court of Appeal in *Ashburn Anstalt v Arnold* [1989] Ch 1 where it was pointed out that a constructive trust could be imposed on a purchaser otherwise taking free of a contractual licence, as a personal and not a proprietary interest, if there were circumstances where it would be unconscionable if he were not bound by such licence. Thus, the court can make its normal prospective relief for F against M retrospective where the state of the defendant's conscience justifies this.

To help support a court decision in favour of F against X, it may also be possible to argue that M was in a fiduciary relationship with F, placed in a vulnerable position by M where he had led her to expect that he would at least act in their joint interest in respect of the legal estate to the exclusion of his own separate interest. In breach of M's fiduciary duty X received an interest in the fiduciary property with notice (if not also 'Nelsonian' or 'naughty' knowledge) of such breach and so took subject to F's rights as subsequently crystallised by the court.

Chancery judges can thus do more to safeguard the interests of women like F than Ferguson's narrow approach supposes. . . .

Hopefully, it should not be too long before we have a case with appropriate facts to justify a judgment clearly distinguishing between the exclusively proprietary institutional constructive trust, that arises and exists independently of the court order retrospectively recognising it, and the remedial constructive trust declaring at the time of the court order the extent of the proprietary or personal relief tailored to remedy the relevant unconscionable conduct. For ease of reference one should, perhaps, distinguish between 'automatic' and 'discretionary' constructive trusts, the former being an automatic incident of the institution of the express trust of property, and the latter involving discretionary relief of a proprietary or personal nature imposed on a defendant because of the poor state of his conscience.

CHAPTER EIGHTEEN

TRACING

18.1 Tracing at Common Law

AGIP (AFRICA) LTD v *JACKSON AND OTHERS* [1990] 1 Ch 265, ChD

FACTS: A senior officer of Agip (Africa) Ltd innocently signed a payment order which was then forged and used by a fraudulent accountant in their employ. The accountant took the order to a Tunisian bank, who in turn requested a payment from Lloyds Bank plc in accordance with the terms of the order. Lloyds Bank then made a payment over to the defendant's account, believing that it would be reimbursed by the recipient's New York bank. In doing so Lloyds took a delivery risk, as the New York bank had not yet opened for business. By the time the plaintiffs had discovered the fraud it was too late to stop the payment; neither could a refund be obtained from the defendants. The defendants claimed that they had acted innocently throughout and that the Tunisian bank, not the plaintiff, was entitled to bring the action.

HELD: The plaintiff was entitled to bring an action against the defendants, even though the bank had acted as their agent in the matter. Due to the fact that there had been no mixing of funds, the plaintiff would have been able to trace at common law had a physical asset changed hands between the various banks and companies; however, they would not be entitled to trace at common law where there had been a telegraphic transfer of monies. In such a case there was no physical asset which could be traced. Nevertheless, equitable tracing would still be available to the plaintiff, into any property still being held by the defendants. The fraudulent accountant had owed the plaintiff a fiduciary duty, thus a fundamental prerequisite to tracing in equity had been established. Further, the defendants would be personally liable to account as constructive trustees for monies which the plaintiffs had been unable to recover. This was because the defendants had knowingly assisted in a misapplication of the plaintiff's property.

MILLETT J: . . .The next question is whether the plaintiffs can follow the payment into the hands of Jackson & Co; for the fact that it was the plaintiffs' money which left the Banque du Sud does not mean that it was the plaintiff's money which reached Baker Oil or Jackson & Co. Tracing at common law, unlike its counterpart in equity, is neither a cause of action nor a remedy but serves an evidential purpose. The cause of action is for money had and received. Tracing at common law enables the defendant to be identified as the recipient of the plaintiff's money and the measure of his liability to be determined by the amount of the plaintiff's money he is shown to have received.

The common law has always been able to follow a physical asset from one recipient to another. Its ability to follow an asset in the same hands into a changed form was established in *Taylor* v *Plumer* 3 M & S 562. In following the plaintiff's money into an asset purchased exclusively with it, no distinction is drawn between a chose in action such as the debt of a bank to its customer and any other asset: *In re Diplock* [1948] Ch 465, 519. But it can only follow a physical asset, such as a cheque or its proceeds, from one person to another. It can follow money but not a chose in action. Money can be followed at common law into and out of a bank account and into the hands of a subsequent transferee, provided that it does not cease to be identifiable by being mixed with other money in the bank account derived from some other source. *Banque Belge pour l'Etranger v Hambrouck* [1921] 1 KB 321. Applying these principles, the plaintiffs claim to follow their money through Baker Oil's account where it was not mixed with any other money and into Jackson & Co.'s account at Lloyds Bank.

The defendants deny this. They contend that tracing is not possible at common law because the money was mixed, first when it was handled in New York, and secondly in Jackson & Co.'s own account at Lloyds Bank.

The latter objection is easily disposed of. The cause of action for money had and received is complete when the plaintiff's money is received by the defendant. It does not depend on the continued retention of the money by the defendant. Save in strictly limited circumstances it is no defence that he has parted with it. A fortiori it can be no defence for him to show that he has so mixed it with his own money that he cannot tell whether he still has it or not. Mixing by the defendant himself must, therefore, be distinguished from mixing by a prior recipient. The former is irrelevant, but the latter will destroy the claim, for it will prevent proof that the money received by the defendant was the money paid by the plaintiff.

In my judgment, however, the former objection is insuperable. The money cannot be followed by treating it as the proceeds of a cheque presented by the collecting bank in exchange for payment by the paying bank. The money was transmitted by telegraphic transfer. There was no cheque or any equivalent. The payment order was not a cheque or its equivalent. It remained throughout in the possession of the Banque du Sud. No copy was sent to Lloyds Bank or Baker Oil or presented to the Banque du Sud in exchange for the money. It was normally the plaintiffs' practice to forward a copy of the payment order to the supplier when paying an invoice but this was for information only. It did not authorise or enable the supplier to obtain payment. There is no evidence that this practice was followed in the case of forged payment orders and it is exceedingly unlikely that it was.

Nothing passed between Tunisia and London but a stream of electrons. It is not possible to treat the money received by Lloyds Bank in London or its correspondent bank in New York as representing the proceeds of the payment order or of any other physical asset previously in its hands and delivered by it in exchange for the money. The Banque du Sud merely telexed a request to Lloyds Bank to make a payment to Baker Oil against its own undertaking to reimburse Lloyds Bank in New York. Lloyds Bank complied with the request by paying Baker Oil with its own money. It thereby took a delivery risk. In due course it was no doubt reimbursed, but it is not possible to identify the source of the money with which it was reimbursed without attempting to follow the money through the New York clearing system. Unless Lloyds Bank's correspondent bank in New York was also Citibank, this involves tracing the money through the accounts of Citibank and Lloyds Bank's correspondent bank with the Federal Reserve Bank, where it must have been mixed with other money. The money with which Lloyds Bank was reimbursed cannot therefore, without recourse to equity, be identified as being that of the Banque du Sud. There is no evidence that Lloyds Bank's correspondent bank in New York was Citibank, and accordingly the plaintiff's attempt to trace the money at common law must fail. . . .

There is no difficulty in tracing the plaintiffs' property in equity, which can follow the money as it passed through the accounts of the correspondent banks in New York or, more realistically, follow the chose in action through its transmutation as a direct result of forged instructions from a debt owed by the Banque du Sud to the plaintiffs in Tunis into a debt owed by Lloyds Bank to Baker Oil in London.

The only restriction on the ability of equity to follow assets is the requirement that there must be some fiduciary relationship which permits the assistance of equity to be invoked. The requirement has been widely condemned and depends on authority rather than principle, but the law was settled by *In re Diplock* [1948] Ch 465. It may need to be reconsidered but not, I venture to think, at first instance. The requirement may be circumvented since it is not necessary that the fund to be traced should have been the subject of fiduciary obligations before it got into the wrong hands; it is sufficient that the payment to the defendant itself gives rise to a fiduciary relationship: *Chase Manhattan Bank NA v Israel-British Bank (London) Ltd* [1981] Ch 105. In that case, however, equity's assistance was not needed in order to trace the plaintiff's money into the hands of the defendant; it was needed in order to ascertain whether it had any of the plaintiff's money left. The case cannot, therefore, be used to circumvent the requirement that there should be an initial fiduciary relationship in order to start the tracing process in equity.

The requirement is, however, readily satisfied in most cases of commercial fraud, since the embezzlement of a company's funds almost inevitably involves a breach of fiduciary duty on the party of one of the company's employees or agents. That was so in present case. There was clearly a fiduciary relationship between Mr Zdiri and the plaintiffs. Mr Zdiri was not a director nor a signatory on the plaintiffs' bank account, but he was a senior and responsible officer. As such he was entrusted with possession of the signed payment orders to have them taken to the bank and implemented. He took advantage of his possession of them to divert the money and cause the separation between its legal ownership which passed to the payees and its beneficial ownership which remained in the plaintiffs. There is clear authority that there is a receipt of trust property when a company's funds are misapplied by a director and, in my judgment, this is equally the case when a company's funds are misapplied by any person whose fiduciary position gave him control of them or enabled him to misapply them. . . .

The tracing claim in equity gives rise to a proprietary remedy which depends on the continued existence of the trust property in the hands of the defendant. Unless he is a bona fide purchaser for value without notice, he must restore the trust property to its rightful owner if he still has it. But even a volunteer who has received trust property cannot be made subject to a personal liability to account for it as a constructive trustee if he has parted with it without having previously acquired some knowledge of the existence of the trust: *In re Montagu's Settlement Trusts* [1987] Ch 264. . . .

LIPKIN GORMAN (A FIRM) v KARPNALE LTD AND ANOTHER
[1992] 4 All ER 512, HL

FACTS: Cass, a partner in a firm of solicitors (the plaintiffs), had used monies from the firm's clients' account in order to gamble at the 'Playboy' casino (run by the first defendant, Karpnale Ltd). The firm brought an action in common law against the club for money had and received, and contended that the club was liable as a constructive trustee for knowing
receipt of trust property. There were other claims with which we are not here concerned.
HELD: The club was liable under the action for money had and received, and because it could not show that it had given consideration for the monies (gambling contracts being legally unenforceable) the club had been unjustly enriched and would have to account to the solicitors firm for trust monies received by it. However, the club did not have to pay back all the money which it had received; it was entitled to pay a sum net of winnings which it had paid out. This is because, by paying the winnings, the club had altered its position in good faith.

LORD TEMPLEMAN: . . . In the course of argument there was a good deal of discussion concerning tracing in law and in equity. In my opinion, in a claim for money had and received by a thief, the plaintiff victim must show that money belonging to him was paid by the thief to the defendant and that the defendant was unjustly enriched and remained unjustly enriched. An innocent recipient of stolen money may not be enriched at all; if Cass had paid £20,000 derived from the solicitors to a car dealer for a motor car priced at £20,000, the car dealer would not have been enriched. The car dealer would have received £20,000 for a car worth £20,000. But an innocent recipient of stolen money will be enriched if the recipient has not given full consideration. If Cass had given £20,000 of the solicitors' money to a friend as a gift, the friend would have been enriched and unjustly enriched because a donee of stolen money cannot in good conscience rely on the bounty of the thief to deny restitution to the victim of the theft. Complications arise if the donee innocently expends the stolen money in reliance on the validity of the gift before the donee receives notice of the victim's claim for restitution. Thus, if the donee spent £20,000 in the purchase of a motor car which he would not have purchased but for the gift, it seems to me that the donee has altered his position on the faith of the gift and has only been unjustly enriched to the extent of the secondhand value of the motor car at the date when the victim of the theft seeks restitution. If the donee spends the £20,000 in a trip round the world, which he would not have undertaken without the gift, it seems to me that the donee has altered his position on the faith of the gift and that he is not unjustly enriched when the victim of the theft seeks restitution. In the present case Cass stole and the club received £229,908·48 of the solicitors' money. If the club was in the same position as a donee, the club nevertheless in good faith allowed Cass to gamble with the solicitors' money and paid his winnings from time to time so that, when the solicitors sought restitution, the club only retained £154,695 derived from the solicitors. The question is whether the club which was enriched by £154,695 at the date when the solicitors sought restitution was unjustly enriched.

The club claims that it gave consideration for the sum of £154,695 by allowing Cass to gamble and agreeing to pay his winnings and therefore the club was not enriched or, alternatively, was not unjustly enriched. The solicitors claim that the club acquired £154,695 under void contracts and that, as between the club and the solicitors from whom the money was derived, the club is in no better position than an innocent donee from the thief, Cass. The resolution of this dispute depends on the true construction of s. 18 of the Gaming Act 1845, an analysis of the relationship between the club and Cass and a consideration of the authorities dealing with gaming and the authorities dealing with unjust enrichment.

Section 18 of the Gaming Act 1845, so far as material, provides:

> . . . all Contracts or Agreements, whether by Parole or in Writing, by way of gaming or wagering, shall be null and void; and . . . no Suit shall be brought or maintained in any Court of Law or Equity for recovering any Sum of Money or valuable Thing alleged to be won upon any Wager, or which shall have been deposited in the Hands of any Person to abide the Event on which any Wager shall have been made. . . .

The club contends that the club received money from Cass under a contract with him which was not a contract 'by way of gaming or wagering' and is not rendered null and void by s. 18 of the 1845 Act. Alternatively, even if the club received the money under a contract by way of gaming nevertheless, it is argued, the club was not unjustly enriched because, in the belief that the money tendered by Cass was his own personal money, the club accepted the money and altered the position of the club to the detriment of the club by allowing Cass to gamble and by paying his winnings when he won; the club, it is said, was enriched, but not unjustly enriched, and may retain the money which the club fairly and lawfully won. It is well settled that s. 18 of the 1845 Act does not enable a gambler to recover money which he has lost and paid. . . .

My Lords, when Cass paid money to the cashier, he was issued with a receipt in the form of a credit voucher and then in the form of a chip. The chip did not oblige Cass to avail himself of the facilities of the club and did not oblige the club to allow Cass to gamble or take advantage of any other facilities of the club. If a thief deposits stolen money in a building society, the victim is entitled to recover the money from the building society without producing the pass book issued to the thief. As against the victim, the building society cannot pretend that the building society have good consideration for the acceptance of the deposit. The building society has been unjustly enriched at the expense of the victim. Of course the building society has a defence if the building society innocently pays out the deposit before the building society realises that the deposit was stolen money. But in the present case the club retained some of the stolen money. The club cannot as against the solicitors retain the stolen money save by relying on the gaming contracts which, as between the club and Cass, entitled the club to retain the solicitors' money which Cass lost at the gaming table. Those gaming contracts were void. The club remains unjustly enriched to the extent of £154,695. . . .

In the result I would order judgment to be entered for the solicitors for the sum of £154,695. . . .

LORD GOFF OF CHIEVELEY: . . . I turn to the last point on which the respondents relied to defeat the solicitors' claim for the money. This was that the claim advanced by the solicitors was in the form of an action for money had and received, and that such a claim should only succeed where the defendant was unjustly enriched at the expense of the plaintiff. If it would be unjust or unfair to order restitution, the claim should fail. It was for the court to consider the question of injustice or unfairness, on broad grounds. If the court thought that it would be unjust or unfair to hold the respondents liable to the solicitors, it should deny the solicitors recovery. Mr Lightman, for the club, listed a number of reasons why, in his submission, it would be unfair to hold the respondents liable. These were (1) the club acted throughout in good faith, ignorant of the fact that the money had been stolen by Cass; (2) although the gaming contracts entered into by the club with Cass were all void, nevertheless the club honoured all those contracts; (3) Cass was allowed to keep his winnings (to the extent that he did not gamble them away); (4) the gaming contracts were merely void not illegal; and (5) the solicitors' claim was no different in principle from a claim to recover against an innocent third party to whom the money was given and who no longer retained it. . . .

It is therefore necessary to consider whether Mr Lightman's submission can be upheld on the basis of legal principle. In my opinion it is plain, from the nature of his submission, that he is in fact seeking to invoke a principle of change of position, asserting that recovery should be denied because of the change in position of the respondents, who acted in good faith throughout.

Whether change of position is, or should be, recognised as a defence to claims in restitution is a subject which has been much debated in the books. It is however a matter on which there is a remarkable unanimity of view, the consensus being to the effect that such a defence should be recognised in English law. I myself am under no doubt that this is right. . . .

In these circumstances it is right that we should ask ourselves: why do we feel that it would be unjust to allow restitution in cases such as these? The answer must be that, where an innocent defendant's position is so changed that he will suffer an injustice if called upon to repay or to repay in full, the injustice of requiring him so to repay outweighs the injustice of denying the plaintiff restitution. If the plaintiff pays money to the defendant under a mistake of fact, and the defendant then, acting in good faith, pays the money or part of it to charity, it is unjust to require the defendant to make restitution to the extent that he has so changed his position. Likewise, on facts such as those in the present case, if a thief steals my money and pays it to a third party who gives it away to charity, that third party should have a good defence to an action for money had and received. In other words, bona fide change of position should of itself be a good defence in such cases as these. The principle is widely recognised throughout the common law world. . . . The time for its recognition in this country is, in my opinion, long overdue.

. . . Let us suppose that only one bet was placed by a gambler at a casino with the plaintiff's money, and that he lost it. In that simple case, although it is true that the casino will have changed its position to the extent that it has incurred the risk, it will in the result have paid out nothing to the gambler, and so prima facie it would not be inequitable to require it to repay the amount of the bet to the plaintiff. The same would, of course, be equally true if the gambler placed a hundred bets with the plaintiff's money and lost them all; the plaintiff should be entitled to recover the amount of all the bets. This conclusion has the merit of consistency with the decision of the Court of King's Bench in *Clarke* v *Shee and Johnson* 1 Cowp 197. But then, let us suppose that the gambler has won one or more out of one hundred bets placed by him with the plaintiff's money at a casino over a certain period of time, and that the casino has paid him a substantial sum in winnings, equal, let us assume, to one half of the amount of all the bets. Given that it is not inequitable to require the casino to repay to the plaintiff the amount of the bets in full where no winnings have been paid, it would, in the circumstances I have just described, be inequitable, in my opinion, to require the casino to repay to the plaintiff more than one half of his money. The inequity, as I perceive it, arises from the nature of gambling itself. In gambling only an occasional bet is won, but when the gambler wins he will receive much more than the stake placed for his winning bet. True, there may be no immediate connection between the bets. They may be placed on different occasions, and each one is a separate gaming contract. But the point is that there has been a series of transactions under which all the bets have been placed by paying the plaintiff's money to the casino, and on each occasion the casino has incurred the risk that the gambler will win. It is the totality of the bets which yields, by the laws of chance, the occasional winning bet; and the occasional winning bet is therefore, in practical terms, the result of the casino changing its position by incurring the risk of losing on each occasion when a bet is placed with it by the gambler. So, when in such circumstances the plaintiff seeks to recover from the casino the amount of several bets placed with it by a gambler with his money, it would be inequitable to require the casino to repay in full without bringing into account winnings paid by it to the gambler on any one or more of the bets so placed with it. The result may not be entirely logical; but it is surely just. . . .

18.2 Equitable Tracing

RE HALLETT'S ESTATE (1880) 13 ChD 696, CA

FACTS: A solicitor mixed trust monies with monies in his personal bank account. When the solicitor died the beneficiaries under the trust sought to trace into the solicitor's estate.
HELD: The beneficiaries were successful with their equitable tracing claim even though the balance in the solicitor's personal account was not sufficient to satisfy the beneficiaries and other creditors.

JESSEL MR: . . . nothing can be better settled, either in our own law, or, I suppose, the law of all civilised countries, than this, that where a man does an act which may be rightfully performed, he cannot say that the act was intentionally and in fact done wrongly. A man who has a right of entry cannot say he committed a trespass in entering. A man who sells the goods of another as agent for the owner cannot prevent the owner adopting the sale, and deny that he acted as agent for the owner. It runs throughout our law, and we are familiar with numerous instances in the law of real property. A man who grants a lease believing he has sufficient estate to grant it, although it turns out that he has not, but has a power which enables him to grant it, is not allowed to say he did not grant it under the power. Whereever it can be done rightfully, he is not allowed to say, against the person entitled to the property or the right, that he has done it wrongfully. That is the universal law.

When we come to apply that principle to the case of a trustee who has blended trust moneys with his own, it seems to me perfectly plain that he cannot be heard to say that he took away the trust money when he had a right to take away his own money. The simplest case put is the mingling of trust moneys in a bag with money of the trustee's own. Suppose he has a hundred sovereigns in a bag, and he adds to them another hundred sovereigns of his own, that they are commingled in such a way that they cannot be distinguished, and the next day he draws out for his own purposes £100, is it tolerable for anybody to allege that what he drew out was the first £100, the trust money, and that he misappropriated it, and left his own £100 in the bag? It is obvious he must have taken away that which he had a right to take away, his own £100. What difference does it make if, instead of being in a bag, he deposits it with his banker, and then pays in other money of his own, and draws out some money for his own purposes? Could he say that he had actually drawn out anything but his own money? His money was there, and he had a right to draw it out, and why should the natural act of simply drawing out the money be attributed to anything except to his ownership of money which was at his bankers.

It is said, no doubt, that according to the modern theory of banking, the deposit banker is a debtor for the money. So he is, and not a trustee in the strict sense of the word. At the same time one must recollect that the position of a deposit banker is different from that of an ordinary debtor. Still he is for some purposes a debtor, and it is said if a debt of this kind is paid by a banker, although the total balance is the amount owing by the banker, yet considering the repayments and the sums paid in by the depositor, you attribute the first sum drawn out to the first sum paid in. That was a rule first established by Sir William Grant in *Clayton's Case* (1816) 1 Mer 572; a very convenient rule, and I have nothing to say against it unless there is evidence either of agreement to the contrary or of circumstances from which a contrary intention must be presumed, and then of course that which is a mere presumption of law gives way to those other considerations. Therefore, it does appear to me there is nothing in the world laid down by Sir William

Grant in *Clayton's Case*, or in the numerous cases which follow it, which in the slightest degree affects the principle, which I consider to be clearly established.

JAMES ROSCOE (BOLTON) LIMITED v WINDER [1915] 1 Ch 62, ChD

FACTS: A company sold its business to Winder, and one of the terms of the sale was that Winder would account to the company for certain sums received by him in satisfaction of the company's book debts. In fact, when Winder received payments in satisfaction of the company's debts, he paid them into his own private account. He then used the monies from the mixed account for his private ends, leaving a total balance, at its lowest, of only a few pounds. At a later date Winder paid several hundred pounds into his account; this was the state of his account when he went into bankruptcy. The company brought the present action against the trustee in bankruptcy to recover the monies representing their book debts.
HELD: The company could not trace into the final balance of the general account, but would be restricted to tracing into the balance of the account at its lowest level, when it stood at only a few pounds. The result would have been different had Winder's later payments into his account been 'ear-marked' for the benefit of the company.

SARGANT J: . . . after having heard *In re Hallett's Estate* stated over and over again, I should have thought that the general view of that decision was that it only applied to such an amount of the balance ultimately standing to the credit of the trustee as did not exceed the lowest balance of the account during the intervening period. That view has practically been taken, as far as I can make out, in the cases which have dealt with *In re Hallett's Estate*. *In re Oatway* [1903] 2 Ch 356, a decision of Joyce J, was cited to me in support of the plaintiffs' case, but I do not find anything in it to help them. All that Joyce J did in that case was to say that, if part of the mixed moneys can be traced into a definite security, that security will not become freed from the charge in favour of the trust, but will, together with any residue of the mixed moneys, remain subject to that charge. I am sure that nothing which he said was intended to mean that the trust was imposed upon any property into which the original fund could not be traced. The head-note to the decision of North J in *In re Stenning* [1895] 2 Ch 433 (which accurately represents the effect of the case) is stated in such terms as to indicate that the application of the doctrine in *In re Hallett's Estate* implied that there should be a continuous balance standing to the credit of the account equal to the balance against which the charge is sought to be enforced. And certainly in the recent case of *Sinclair v Brougham* [1914] AC 398 I can see nothing in any way to impeach the doctrine as to tracing laid down in *In re Hallett's Estate*.

   In my opinion, therefore, the only part of the balance of 358*l*. 5*s*. 5*d*. which can be made available by the plaintiffs is the sum of 25*l*. 18*s*., being the smallest amount to which the balance, to the credit of the account had fallen between May 19, 1913, and the death of the debtor.

RE DIPLOCK [1948] 1 Ch 465, ChD

FACTS: The executors of a will trust had distributed the residuary estate amongst a vast number of charities. However, the House of Lords later established that the original bequest had been invalid. The plaintiffs brought an action against the executors, which was compromised. They then brought the present actions against a number of the charitable institutions to which monies had been paid by mistake. The beneficiaries had two types of claim: first, claims *in personam*—the action which every under-paid legatee has against over-paid beneficiaries or strangers to the estate; secondly, claims *in rem*—that is, tracing claims in equity.
HELD: The claim *in personam* could succeed against a volunteer such as the charities in the present case; however, the beneficiaries must first bring an action (as they did) against the executors who were responsible for the mistaken payment to the charities. The sums recovered from the executors should be applied rateably to reduce the liability of the charities. The charities would not have to pay interest on the sums owed to the beneficiaries. The claims *in rem* (equitable tracing) also succeeded, even though the funds

into which tracing had been carried out had been mixed by innocent parties (the charities). However, equitable tracing would not be permitted if it would produce an inequitable result.

LORD GREENE MR: . . . In determining the difficult questions which the appeals have raised it is immaterial that the respondents are charitable institutions of the most deserving character. In considering the application of the principles of equity it does not seem to us that there is any different standard of conscientiousness for charitable or other corporations from that appropriate to an individual. . . .

We turn . . . first to the claims *'in personam'* . . . in approaching the question of the existence and characteristics of the direct equitable cause of action there is not, unless the authorities otherwise establish, any necessity in logic for regarding the claim as being clothed, as it were, with all the attributes or limitations appropriate to the common law action for money had and received. Nor, on similar grounds, does it appear that there is any conflict involved between law and equity. Equity here, as in other places, comes in, as Maitland has observed, 'not to destroy the common law but to fulfil it.' Since (for so runs the appellants' argument) the common law can only recognise the two parties to the transaction, payer and payee, or at most third parties asserting the rights of one or other of them, the common law does not, to borrow again from the language of Maitland 'comprehend the whole "truth"'. For the payers in the present case (namely the executors) were handling not their own money but the money of others who had a proprietary interest unknown to and unrecognised by the executors and who, from the moment when they became aware of their own rights and the transactions of the executors, immediately challenged and repudiated what the executors had done.

Nevertheless, if the claim in equity exists it must be shown to have an ancestry founded in history and in the practice and precedents of the courts administering equity jurisdiction. It is not sufficient that because we may think that the 'justice' of the present case requires it, we should invent such a jurisdiction for the first time. . . .

. . . the only claims which in our view can be supported on the basis of the so-called equitable doctrine of tracing are of a strictly limited character.

We shall endeavour to explain our views as to the basis on which the doctrine must now be taken to rest. In this connexion we regard the case of *Sinclair* v *Brougham* [1914] AC 398 as of fundamental importance. That decision, in our view, did not so much extend as explain the doctrine of *Hallett's* case (*In re Hallett's Estate* (1880) 13 ChD 696) which now must be regarded not so to speak, as a genus but as a species in a genus where equity works on the same basic principles but selects what on the particular case is the equitable method of applying them in practice. It will be found that our views as to the meaning and effect of the speeches in *Sinclair* v *Brougham* differ from those expressed by Wynn-Parry J. We should, however, be lacking in candour rather than showing respect if we refrained from saying that we find the opinions in *Sinclair* v *Brougham* in many respects not only difficult to follow but difficult to reconcile with one another.

Before passing to a consideration of the case of *Sinclair* v *Brougham* we may usefully make some observations of our own as to the distinction between the attitude of the common law and that of equity to these questions.

The common law approached them in a strictly materialistic way. It could only appreciate what might almost be called the 'physical' identity of one thing with another. It could treat a person's money as identifiable so long as it had not become mixed with other money. It could treat as identifiable with the money other kinds of property acquired by means of it, provided that there was no admixture of other money. It is noticeable that in this latter case the common law did not base itself on any known theory of tracing such as that adopted in equity. It proceeded on the basis that the unauthorised act of purchasing was one capable of ratification by the owner of the money (see *per* Lord Parker in *Sinclair* v *Brougham*.) Certain words of Lord Haldane in *Sinclair* v *Brougham* may appear to suggest a further limitation, i.e., that 'money' as we have used that word was not regarded at common law as identifiable once it had been paid into a banking account. We do not, however, think it necessary to discuss this point at length. We agree with the comments of Wynn-Parry J upon it and those of Atkin LJ (as he then was) in *Banque Belge* v *Hambrouck* [1921] 1 KB 321. If it is possible to identify a principal's money with an asset purchased exclusively by means of it we see no reason for drawing a distinction between a chose in action such as a banker's debt to his customer and any other asset. If the principal can ratify the acquisition of the one, we see no reason for supposing that he cannot ratify the acquisition of the other.

We may mention three several matters which we think are helpful in understanding the limitation of the common law doctrine and the reasons why equity was able to take a more liberal view. They are as follows:

(1) The common law did not recognise equitable claims to property, whether money or any other form of property. Sovereigns in A's pocket either belonged in law to A or they belonged in law to B. The idea that they could belong in law to A and that they should nevertheless be treated as belonging to B was entirely foreign to the common law. This is the reason why the common law doctrine finds its typical exemplification in cases of principal and agent. If B, a principal, hands cash to A, his agent, in order that it may be applied in a particular manner, the cash, in the eyes of the common law, remains the property of B. If, therefore, A, instead of applying it in the authorised manner, buries it in a sack in his garden or uses it for an unauthorised purchase, B can, in the former case, recover the cash as being still his own property and, in the latter case, affirm the purchase of something bought with his money by his agent. If, however, the relationship of A and B was not one which left the property in the cash in B but merely constituted a relationship of debtor and creditor between them, there could, of course, have been no remedy at law under this head, since the property in the cash would have passed out of B into A.

(2) The narrowness of the limits within which the common law operated may be linked with the limited nature of the remedies available to it. Specific relief as distinct from damages (the normal remedy at common law) was confined to a very limited range of claims as compared with the extensive uses of specific relief developed by equity. In particular, the device of a declaration of charge was unknown to the common law and it was the availability of that device which enabled equity to give effect to its wider conception of equitable rights.

(3) It was the materialistic approach of the common law coupled with and encouraged by the limited range of remedies available to it that prevented the common law from identifying money in a mixed fund. Once the money of B became mixed with the money of A its identification in a physical sense became impossible; owing to the fact of mixture there could be no question of ratification of an unauthorised act; and the only remedy of B, if any, lay in a claim for damages.

Equity adopted a more metaphysical approach. It found no difficulty in regarding a composite fund as an amalgam constituted by the mixture of two or more funds each of which could be regarded as having, for certain purposes, a continued separate existence. Putting it in another way, equity regarded the amalgam as capable, in proper circumstances, of being resolved into its component parts.

Adapting, for the sake of contrast, the phraseology which we have used in relation to the common law, it was the metaphysical approach of equity coupled with and encouraged by the far-reaching remedy of a declaration of charge that enabled enquity to identify money in a mixed fund. Equity, so to speak, is able to draw up a balance sheet on the righthand side of which appears the composite fund and on its lefthand side the two or more funds of which it is to be deemed to be made up.

Regarded as a pure piece of machinery for the purpose of tracing money into a mixed fund or into property acquired by means of a mixed fund, a declaration of charge might be thought to be a suitable means of dealing with any case where one person has, without legal title, acquired some benefit by the use of the money of another—in other words, any case of what is often called 'unjust enrichment.' The opinion of Lord Dunedin in *Sinclair* v *Brougham* appears to us to come very nearly to this, for he appears to treat the equitable remedy as applicable in any case where a superfluity, expressed or capable of being expressed in terms of money, is found to exist. Such a view would dispense with the necessity of establishing as a starting point the existence of a fiduciary or quasi-fiduciary relationship or of a continuing right of property recognised in equity. We may say at once that, apart from the possible case of Lord Dunedin's speech, we cannot find that any principle so wide in its operation is to be found enunciated in English law. The conditions which must exist before the equitable form of relief becomes available will be considered later in this judgment. But one truism may be stated here in order to get it out of the way. The equitable form of relief whether it takes the form of an order to restore an unmixed sum of money (or property acquired by means of such a sum) or a declaration of charge upon a mixed fund (or upon property acquired by means of such a fund) is, of course, personal in the sense that its efficacy is founded upon the jurisdiction of equity to enforce its rules by acting upon the individual. But it is not personal in the sense that the person against whom an order of this nature is sought can be made personally liable to repay the amount claimed to have belonged to the claimant. The equitable remedies pre-suppose the continued existence of the money either as a separate fund or as part of a mixed fund or as latent in property acquired by means of such a fund. If, on the facts of any individual case, such continued existence is not established, equity is as helpless as the common law itself. If the fund, mixed or unmixed, is spent upon a dinner, equity, which dealt only in specific relief and not in damages, could do nothing. If the case was one which at common law involved breach of contract the common law could, of course, award damages but specific relief would be out of the question. It is, therefore, a necessary matter for consideration in each case where it is sought to trace money in equity, whether it has such a continued existence, actual or notional, as will enable equity to grant specific relief. . . .

The first question which appears to us to fall for decision on this part of the present appeals may, we think, be thus formulated: Did the power of equity to treat Diplock 'money' as recoverable from the charity, which undoubtedly existed down to the moment when the cheque was paid by the bank on which it was drawn, cease the moment that the 'money' by the process of 'mixture' came to be represented by an accretion to or an enlargement of the chose in action consisting of a debt already owing to the charity by its own bankers? Wynn-Parry J, in effect, decided that it did. His reason for taking this view, shortly stated, was as follows: The principle applicable was to be extracted from the decision in *Hallett's* case and that principle was in no way extended by the decision in *Sinclair v Brougham*. The principle can operate only in cases where the mixing takes place in breach of a trust, actual or constructive, or in breach of some other fiduciary relationship and in proceedings against the trustee or fiduciary agent: here the mixing was not of this character, since it was effected by an innocent volunteer: there is no ground on which, according to principle, the conscience of such a volunteer can be held in equity to be precluded from setting up a title adverse to the claim: in every case, therefore, where a 'mixture' has been carried out by the charity, the claim, whether it be against a mixed monetary fund or against investments made by means of such a mixed fund, must fail in limine.

Now we may say at once that this view of the inability of equity to deal with the case of the volunteer appears to us, with all respect to Wynn-Parry J, to be in conflict with the principles expounded, particularly by Lord Parker, in *Sinclair v Brougham*. If Lord Parker means what we think he meant, and if what he said is to be accepted as a correct statement of the law, Mr Pennycuick, who argued this part of the case on behalf of the charities, admittedly felt great difficulty in supporting this part of the reasoning of the learned judge. We shall deal further with Lord Parker's observations on this topic when we come to them in our examination of *Sinclair v Brougham*. But here we may conveniently summarise what we consider to be the effect of them as follows: Where an innocent volunteer (as distinct from a purchaser for value without notice) mixes 'money' of his own with 'money' which in equity belongs to another person, or is found in possession of such a mixture, although that other person cannot claim a charge on the mass superior to the claim of the volunteer he is entitled, nevertheless, to a charge ranking pari passu with the claim of the volunteer. And Lord Parker's reasons for taking this view appear to have been on the following lines: Equity regards the rights of the equitable owner as being 'in effect rights of property' though not recognised as such by the common law. Just as a volunteer is not allowed by equity in the case, e.g., of a conveyance of the legal estate in land, to set up his legal title adversely to the claim of a person having an equitable interest in the land, so in the case of a mixed fund of money the volunteer must give such recognition as equity considers his in conscience (as a volunteer) bound to give to the interest of the equitable owner of the money which has been mixed with the volunteer's own. But this burden on the conscience of the volunteer is not such as to compel him to treat the claim of the equitable owner as paramount. That would be to treat the volunteer as strictly as if he himself stood in a fiduciary relationship to the equitable owner which ex hypothesi he does not. The volunteer is under no greater duty of conscience to recognise the interest of the equitable owner than that which lies upon a person having an equitable interest in one of two trust funds of 'money' which have become mixed towards the equitable owner of the other. Such a person is not in conscience bound to give precedence to the equitable owner of the other of the two funds . . . Equity will not restrain a defendant from asserting a claim save to the extent that it would be unconscionable for him to do so. If this limitation on the power of equity results in giving to a plaintiff less than what on some general ideal of fairness he might be considered entitled to, that cannot be helped. . . .

In the absence of authority to the contrary our conclusion is that as regards the Diplock money used in these cases it cannot be traced in any true sense; and, further, that even if this were not so, the only remedy available to equity, viz., that of a declaration of charge would not produce an equitable result and is inapplicable accordingly. . . .

We do not accept the view that the case ought to be treated as though we were subject to the rule in *Clayton's* case (1816) 1 Mer 572. We see no justification for extending that rule beyond the case of a banking account. . . .

CHASE MANHATTAN BANK NA v ISRAEL-BRITISH BANK (LONDON) LTD
[1981] 1 Ch 105, ChD

FACTS: The plaintiff bank paid £2 million to the defendant bank by mistake. When the defendant bank obtained a winding-up order, the plaintiff bank sought to trace in equity to recover the sums that had been paid by mistake.
HELD: The plaintiff had retained an equitable property right in the monies and would be able to trace in equity because that equitable right bound the conscience of the defendant bank.

GOULDING J: . . . the fund to be traced need not (as was the case in *In re Diplock* itself) have been the subject of fiduciary obligations before it got into the wrong hands. It is enough that, as in *Sinclair v Brougham* [1914] AC 398, the payment into wrong hands itself gave rise to a fiduciary relationship. The same point also throws considerable doubt on Mr Stubbs's submission that the necessary fiduciary relationship must originate in a consensual transaction. It was not the intention of the depositors or of the directors in *Sinclair v Brougham* to create any relationship at all between the depositors and the directors as principals. Their object, which unfortunately disregarded the statutory limitations of the building society's powers, was to establish contractual relationships between the depositors and the society. In the circumstances, however, the depositors retained an equitable property in the funds they parted with, and fiduciary relationships arose between them and the directors. In the same way, I would suppose, a person who pays money to another under a factual mistake retains an equitable property in it and the conscience of that other is subjected to a fiduciary duty to respect his proprietary right. . . .

SPACE INVESTMENTS LTD v CANADIAN IMPERIAL BANK OF COMMERCE TRUST CO. (BAHAMAS) LTD AND OTHERS [1986] 1 WLR 1072

FACTS: The defendant bank was trustee of various settlements and had deposited the funds in its own deposit account. The bank went into liquidation. The beneficiaries of the trusts attempted to trace into the bank's assets and recover ahead of the bank's unsecured creditors.
HELD: Although beneficiaries are prima facie entitled to trace into trust funds which have been misappropriated by a trustee for its own benefit, in the instant case the bank had been expressly authorised to deposit the funds in its own account, and accordingly the beneficiaries would have to rank with the bank's unsecured creditors.

LORD TEMPLEMAN: . . . A bank uses all deposit moneys for the general purposes of the bank. Whether a bank trustee lawfully receives deposits or wrongly treats trust money as on deposit from trusts, all the moneys are in fact dealt with and expended by the bank for the general purposes of the bank. In these circumstances it is impossible for the beneficiaries interested in trust money misappropriated from their trust to trace their money to any particular asset belonging to the trustee bank. But equity allows the beneficiaries, or a new trustee appointed in place of an insolvent bank trustee to protect the interests of the beneficiaries, to trace the trust money to all the assets of the bank and to recover the trust money by the exercise of an equitable charge over all the assets of the bank. Where an insolvent bank goes into liquidation that equitable charge secures for the beneficiaries and the trust priority over the claims of the customers in respect of their deposits and over the claims of all other unsecured creditors. This priority is conferred because the customers and other unsecured creditors voluntarily accept the risk that the trustee bank might become insolvent and unable to discharge its obligations in full. On the other hand, the settlor of the trust and the beneficiaries interested under the trust, never accept any risks involved in the possible insolvency of the trustee bank. On the contrary, the settlor could be certain that if the trusts were lawfully administered, the trustee bank could never make use of trust money for its own purposes and would always be obliged to segregate trust money and trust property in the manner authorised by law and by the trust instrument free from any risks involved in the possible insolvency of the trustee bank. It is therefore equitable that where the trustee bank unlawfully misappropriated trust money by treating the trust money as though it belonged to the bank beneficially, merely acknowledging and recording the amount in a trust deposit account with the bank, then the claims of the beneficiaries should be paid in full out of the assets of the trustee bank in priority to the claims of the customers and other unsecured creditors of the bank.

BARLOW CLOWES INTERNATIONAL LTD (IN LIQUIDATION) AND OTHERS v VAUGHAN AND OTHERS [1992] 4 All ER 22, CA

FACTS: An investment company went into liquidation leaving insufficient funds to satisfy the claims of all its investors. The judge at first instance held that investors should be able to trace into the funds on a 'first in, first out' basis, following the rule in *Clayton's Case*. HELD: On appeal. The 'first in, first out' rule was a rule of convenience only and should not be applied in the present case because it would result in injustice and there was a practical, alternative method of distribution, namely to allow the investors to claim shares of the fund *pari passu*, in proportion to the size of their original investment.

DILLON LJ: . . . *Clayton's Case* (1816) 1 Mer 572 was not a case of tracing at all, but a case as to the appropriation of payments. Clayton had been a customer of a banking partnership with an account in credit. One of the partners, Devaynes, had died in 1809 and the remaining partners became bankrupt at the end of July 1810. Clayton had had a running account with the bank before and after the death of Devaynes. The debits and credits made after the death of Devaynes were made without specific appropriation and the account had not been broken on the death of Devaynes. Clayton claimed after the bankruptcy to set his drawings on the account after the death of Devaynes against the credits to the account after the death of Devaynes; consequently he claimed to prove against the estate of Devaynes for the balance to his credit in the account at the death of Devaynes, on the footing that the balance had never been satisfied. Those claims were rejected by Grant MR, who said (1 Mer 572 at 608–609):

> But this is the case of a banking account, where all the sums paid in form one blended fund, the parts of which have no longer any distinct existence. Neither banker nor customer ever thinks of saying, this draft is to be placed to the account of the £500 paid in on *Monday*, and this other to the account of the £500 paid in on *Tuesday*. There is a fund of £1000 to draw upon, and that is enough. In such a case, there is no room for any other appropriation than that which arises from the order in which the receipts and payments take place, and are carried into the account. Presumably, it is the sum first paid in, that is first drawn out. It is the first item on the debit side of the account, that is discharged, or reduced, by the first item on the credit side. The appropriation is made by the very act of setting the two items against each other. Upon that principle, all accounts current are settled, and particularly cash accounts. . . .

That rule will apply to the appropriation of payments between any trader and customer where there is an account current or running account. But it will not apply unless there is a running account—see *per* Lord Halsbury LC in *Cory Bros & Co. Ltd* v *Turkish Steamship Mecca (owners), The Mecca* [1897] AC 286 at 290–291—and even in relation to the appropriation of payments it is not, as Lord Halsbury LC said, an invariable rule: '. . . the circumstances of a case may afford ground for inferring that transactions of the parties were not so intended as to come under this general rule. . . .

Mr Walker has accordingly submitted for the appellant in the present case, by what he called his narrower submission, that all investors who contributed to the two portfolios in question in the present case were contributing to common funds in which all investors were to participate and that, by analogy with *Re British Red Cross Balkan Fund* [1914] 2 Ch 419 and *Re Hobourn Aero Components Ltd's Air-Raid Distress Fund*, *Clayton's Case* should not be applied. . . .

I accordingly accept Mr Walker's narrower submission and would hold that *Clayton's Case* is not to be applied in the distribution of the available assets and moneys. . .

WOOLF LJ: . . . the approach, in summary, which I would adopt to resolving the issues raised by this appeal are as follows.

(1) While the rule in *Clayton's Case* is *prima facie* available to determine the interests of investors in a fund into which their investments have been paid, the use of the rule is a matter of convenience and if its application in particular circumstances would be impracticable or result in injustice between the investors it will not be applied if there is a preferable alternative.

(2) Here the rule will not be applied because this would be contrary to either the express or inferred or presumed intention of the investors. If the investments were required by the terms of the investment contract to be paid into a common pool this indicates that the investors did not intend to apply the rule. If the investments were intended to be separately invested, as a result of the investments being collectively misapplied by BCI a common pool of the investments was created. Because of their shared misfortune, the investors will be presumed to have intended the rule not to apply.

(3) As the rule is inapplicable the approach which should be adopted by the court depends on which of the possible alternative solutions is the most satisfactory in the circumstances. If the North American solution is practical this would probably have advantages over the pari passu solution. However, the complications of applying the North American solution in this case make the third solution the most satisfactory.

(4) It must however be remembered that any solution depends on the ability to trace and if the fund had been exhausted (ie the account became overdrawn) the investors whose moneys were in the fund prior to the fund being exhausted will not be able to claim against moneys which were subsequently paid into the fund.

Their claims will be limited to following, if this is possible, any of the moneys paid out of the fund into other assets before it was exhausted.

For these reasons I would allow the appeal and substitute the orders proposed by Dillon LJ.

P. Oliver, The Extent of Equitable Tracing (1995) 9(3) TLI 78

A possible way round *Roscoe* v *Winder* [1915] 1 Ch 62 was presented in *dicta* of Lord Templeman in *Space Investments Ltd* v *Canadian Imperial Bank of Commerce Trust Co. (Bahamas) Ltd* [1986] 3 All ER 75, PC. In that case the bank trustee had lawfully (according to the terms of the trust instrument) deposited trust money as a loan with itself and had subsequently gone into liquidation. Lord Templeman stated that the beneficiaries could do no more than claim as ordinary unsecured creditors. He then went on to consider what would have happened had the bank trustee *unlawfully* dissipated the trust money for its own purposes:

A bank in fact uses all deposit moneys for the general purposes of the bank. Whether a bank trustee lawfully receives deposits or wrongly treats trust money as on deposit from trusts, all the moneys are in fact dealt with and expended by the bank for the general purposes of the bank. In these circumstances, it is impossible for the beneficiaries interested in trust money misappropriated from their trust to trace their money to any particular asset belonging to the trustee bank. But equity allowes the beneficiaries . . . to trace the trust money to all the assets of the bank and to recover the trust money by the exercise of an equitable charge over all the assets of the bank.

Lord Templeman explained the favourable treatment of the beneficiaries at the expense of the unsecured creditors by stressing that those creditors 'voluntarily accept the risk that the trustee bank might become insolvent and unable to discharge its obligations in full', whereas the beneficiaries 'never accept any risks involved in the possible insolvency of the bank'. Both the primary analysis and the explanation were employed by Sir Robin Cooke of the New Zealand Court of Appeal (who was a member of the Board in the *Space Investments* case) in *Liggett* v *Kensington* [1993] NZLR 257; however, that decision was overturned on this and other grounds by the Judicial Committee in *Re Goldcorp*. The question now arises whether there is any life left in the *Space Investments* analysis; whether that appproach has any merit; and, assuming affirmative answers to both of those questions, whether and in what form this sort of analysis is most likely to reappear.
. . .

By citing *Roscoe* v *Winder* and *Re Diplock* with approval, the Judicial Committee in *Re Goldcorp* made clear that the more general proposition — that it is not possible to trace where the property or its proceeds cease to exist (as where an account balance dips below zero) — is still good law. This was the interpretation of *Re Goldcorp* taken by the Court of Appeal in *Bishosgate Investment Management* v *Homan* [1994] 3 WLR 1270 where Dillon LJ stated that Lord Templeman's observations in *Space Investments* were 'not concerned at all with the situation we have in the present case where trust moneys have been paid into an overdrawn bank account, or an account which has become overdrawn'. He reasserted the general rules as stated in *Re Diplock* and *Roscoe* v *Winder* as did Leggatt LJ.

Was there any justification for *Space Investments* understood in its broadest terms? It can be argued that when money is paid into a bank account, the recipient's assets as a whole are swollen, and that, accordingly, the true owner should be able to claim an equitable charge over those assets regardless of the continued identifiability of the original money or its proceeds, and regardless of the lowest balance reached in that bank account. Denial of the equitable owner's claim would result in the unjust enrichment of the recipient. Professor Goode has criticised this approach on the basis that a broad interpretation of *Space Investments* results in the unsecured creditors being subordinated to the proprietary claim of the equitable owner, despite the fact that they too have swollen the assets of the recipient. In support of this line of argument, it could also be observed that not all unsecured creditors can be said to have taken the risk of insolvency in the commercial sense of that phrase. For example, a successful plaintiff in an action for negligence against the (now bankrupt) recipient will also see her claim reduced by the equitable owner's dominant charge. . . .

BOSCAWEN v *BAJWA* [1995] 4 All ER 769, CA

FACTS: The registered proprietor of a property charged it to a building society and exchanged contracts for the sale of the property to purchasers who had obtained an offer of mortgage from a bank. The bank transferred cash to the purchasers' solicitors for the sole purpose of completing the purchase. The solicitors transferred the money to the vendor's solicitors who then paid it on to the building society in repayment of the vendor's mortgage arrears. The building society discharged the charge and forwarded the title deeds to the vendor's solicitors. However, the sale fell through. Later, the plaintiffs, who were judgment creditors of the vendor, obtained a charging order absolute on the property. The question was whether the plaintiffs had priority to the equitable claim of the bank.

HELD: Since the bank's money could be traced into the payment to the building society and was used towards the discharge of the latter's charge, the bank was entitled to a charge on the property by way of subrogation to the rights of the building society *to the extent that the money had been used to redeem the charge and in priority to any interest of the plaintiffs*.

MILLETT LJ . . . If the plaintiff succeeds in tracing his property, whether in its original or in some changed form, into the hands of the defendant and overcomes any defences which are put forward on the defendant's behalf, he is entitled to a remedy. The remedy will be fashioned to the circumstances. The plaintiff will generally be entitled to a personal remedy; if he seeks a proprietary remedy he must usually prove that the property to which he lays claim is still in the ownership of the defendant. If he succeeds in doing this, the court will treat the defendant as holding the property on a constructive trust for the plaintiff and will order the defendant to transfer it *in specie* to the plaintiff. But this is only one of the proprietary remedies which is available to a court of equity. If the plaintiff's money has been applied by the defendant, for example, not in the acquisition of a landed property but in its improvement, then the court may treat the land as charged with the payment to the plaintiff of a sum representing the amount by which the value of the defendant's land has been enhanced by the use of the plaintiff's money. And if the plaintiff's money has been used to discharge a mortgage on the defendant's land, then the court may achieve a similar result by treating the land as subject to a charge by way of subrogation in favour of the plaintiff.

Subrogation, therefore, is a remedy, not a cause of action (see Goff and Jones *Law of Restitution* (4th edn, 1993) pp 589 ff, *Orakpo v Manson Investments Ltd* [1977] 3 All ER 1 at 7, *per* Lord Diplock and *Re TH Knitwear (Wholesale) Ltd* [1988] 1 All ER 860 at 864, *per* Slade LJ). It is available in a wide variety of different factual situations in which it is required in order to reverse the defendant's unjust enrichment. Equity lawyers speak of a right of subrogation, or of an equity of subrogation, but this merely reflects the fact that it is not a remedy which the court has a general discretion to impose whenever it thinks it just to do so. The equity arises from the conduct of the parties on well-settled principles and in defined circumstances which make it unconscionable for the defendant to deny the proprietary interest claimed by the plaintiff. A constructive trust arises in the same way. Once the equity is established the court satisfies it by declaring that the property in question is subject to a charge by way of subrogation in the one case or a constructive trust in the other.

Accordingly, there was nothing illegitimate in the deputy judge's invocation of the two doctrines of tracing and subrogation in the same case. They arose at different stages of the proceedings. Tracing was the process by which the Abbey National sought to establish that its money was applied in the discharge of the Halifax's charge; subrogation was the remedy which it sought in order to deprive Mr Bajwa (through whom the appellants claim) of the unjust enrichment which he would thereby otherwise obtain at the Abbey National's expense.

Tracing

It is still a prerequisite of the right to trace in equity that there must be a fiduciary relationship which calls the equitable jurisdiction into being (see *Agip (Africa) Ltd* v *Jackson* [1992] 4 All ER 451 at 466, *per* Fox LJ). That requirement is satisfied in the present case by the fact that from the first moment of its receipt by Dave in its general client account the £140,000 was trust money held in trust for the Abbey National. . . .

. . . Equity's power to charge a mixed fund with the repayment of trust moneys enables the claimant to follow the money, not because it is his, but because it is derived from a fund which is treated as if it were subject to a charge in his favour (see *Re Hallett's Estate, Knatchbull* v *Hallett* (1880) 13 ChD 696, *Re Oatway, Hertslet* v *Oatway* [1903] 2 Ch 356 and *El Ajou* v *Dollar Land Holdings plc* [1993] 3 All ER 717).

The appellants accept this, but submit that for this purpose Mr Bajwa was not a wrongdoer. He was, as I have said, not guilty of any impropriety or want of probity. He relied on his solicitors, and they acted unwisely, perhaps negligently, and certainly precipitately, but not dishonestly. Mr Bajwa, it is submitted, was an innocent volunteer who mixed trust money with his own. As such, he was not bound to give priority to the Abbey National, but could claim parity with it. Accordingly, Mr Bajwa and the Abbey National must be treated as having contributed *pari passu* to the discharge of the Halifax's charge; and in the absence of the necessary evidence the amounts which were provided by Mr Bajwa and the Abbey National respectively cannot be ascertained. (In fact, on this footing the Abbey National would be entitled to succeed to the extent of one-half of its claim, but that is by the way.)

For this proposition the appellants rely on a passage in *Re Diplock's Estate*. . .

. . . But the present case is very different. Neither Mr Bajwa nor his solicitors acted dishonestly, but nor were they innocent volunteers. Hill Lawson knew that the money was trust money held to Dave's order pending completion and that it would become available for use on behalf of their client only on completion. They were manifestly fiduciaries. Mr Bajwa, who was plainly intending to redeem the Halifax's mortgage out of the proceeds of sale of the property, must be taken to have known that any money which his solicitors might receive from the purchasers or their mortgagees would represent the balance of the proceeds of sale due on completion and that, since he had made no arrangement with the purchasers to be advanced any part of that amount before completion, it would be available to him only on completion. He cannot possibly have thought that he could keep both the property and the proceeds of sale. Had he thought about the matter at all, he would have realised that the money was not his to mix with his own and dispose of as he saw fit. The only reason that he and his solicitors can be acquitted of dishonesty is that he relied on his solicitors and they acted in the mistaken belief that, save for the tidying up of some loose ends, they were on the point of completing.

It follows that Mr Bajwa cannot avail himself of the more favourable tracing rules which are available to the innocent volunteer who unconsciously mixes trust money with his own. . . .

RE TILLEY'S WT [1967] 1 Ch 1179, ChD

FACTS: The testator's widow and executor of his will trust mixed the trust monies with her own. After the death of one of the beneficiaries (the testator's daughter) her administrators brought the present action for an account against the estate of the widow who had also died in recent years. At her death the widow's account had been heavily overdrawn.

HOLD: Tracing could not succeed on the facts, because the widow had paid in the beneficiaries' monies in reduction of her overdraft.

UNGOED-THOMAS J: . . . The defendants relied on *In re Hallett's Estate, Knatchbull* v *Hallett* (1880) 13 ChD 696 with a view to establishing that the trustee must be presumed to have drawn out his own moneys from the bank account of mixed moneys in priority to trust moneys, with the result that property bought by such prior drawings must be the trustee's exclusive personal property. In that case the claim was against a bank balance of mixed fiduciary and personal funds, and it is in the context of such a claim that it was held that the person in a fiduciary character drawing out money from the bank account must be taken to have drawn out his own money in preference to the trust money, so that the claim of the beneficiaries prevailed against the balance of the account. *In re Oatway, Hertslet* v *Oatway* [1903] 2 Ch 356 was the converse of the decision in *In re Hallett's Estate*. In that case the claim was not against the balance left in the bank of such mixed moneys, but against the proceeds of sale of shares which the trustee had purchased with moneys which, as in *In re Hallett's Estate*, he had drawn from the bank account. But, unlike the situation in *In re Hallett's Estate*, his later drawings had exhausted the account, so that it was useless to proceed against the account. It was held that the beneficiary was entitled to the proceeds of sale of the shares, which were more than their purchase price but less than the trust moneys paid into the account. . . .

So, contrary to the defendants' contention, it is not a presumption that a trustee's drawings from the mixed fund must necessarily be treated as drawings of the trustee's own money where the beneficiary's claim is against the property bought by such drawings. . . .

It seems to me that if, having regard to all the circumstances of the case objectively considered, it appears that the trustee has in fact, whatever his intention, laid out trust moneys in or towards a purchase, then the beneficiaries are entitled to the property purchased and any profits which it produces to the extent to which it has been paid for out of the trust moneys. But, even by this objective test, it appears to me that the trust moneys were not in this case so laid out. It seems to me, on a proper appraisal of all the facts of this particular case, that Mrs Tilley's breach halted at the mixing of the funds in her bank account. Although properties bought out of those funds would, like the bank account itself, at any rate if the moneys in the bank account were inadequate, be charged with repayment of the trust moneys which then would stand in the same position as the bank account, yet the trust moneys were not invested in properties at all but merely went in reduction of Mrs Tilley's overdraft which was in reality the source of the purchase-moneys.

The plaintiff's claim therefore fails. . . .

JONES & SONS (A FIRM) v JONES [1996] 3 WLR 703, CA

FACTS: In 1984 a firm of potato growers got into financial difficulties and the partners committed an act of bankruptcy and were adjudicated bankrupt. After the act of bankruptcy but before the adjudication the defendant, the wife of one of the partners, opened an account with commodity brokers in order to deal in potato futures and paid in the proceeds of cheques totalling £11,700 drawn by her husband on a joint bank account in his name and that of one of the other partners. The defendant received £50,760 from her dealings which was paid into a deposit account with R. Plc. The Official Receiver informed R. Plc. of his claim to the money in the account and the defendant immediately demanded its release to her. R. Plc. interpleaded and the money was paid into court. The judge ordered the money to be paid out to the trustee.

On appeal by the defendant:

HELD: dismissing the appeal, that as from the date of the act of bankruptcy the money in the bankrupts' joint bank account belonged to the trustee in bankruptcy; that therefore the defendant's husband had no title to the £11,700 paid to the defendant either at law or in equity and could confer no title to it on her; that the trustee had to bring his claim at common law and trace his property into the proceeds of the defendant's dealings with the money, and the rules of equity had no role to play; that the chose in action constituted by the deposit of the trustee's money under the terms of the contract between the defendant and the commodity brokers belonged to the trustee, and was not a right to payment of the original amount deposited but a right to claim the balance standing to the defendant's account with R. Plc., whether greater or less than the amount of her original deposit; and that accordingly the trustee was entitled to both the £11,700 and the profits made by the defendant's use of that sum and the judge had been right to order that the money in court be paid out to him.

MILLET LJ: . . . the defendant was not a constructive trustee. She had no legal title to the money. She had no title to it at all. She was merely in possession; that is to say, in a position to deal with it even though it did not belong to her. . . .

The defendant had no title at all, at law or in equity. If she became bankrupt, the money would not vest in her trustee. But this would not be because it was trust property; it would be because it was not her property at all. If she made a profit, how could she have any claim to the profit made by the use of someone else's money? In my judgment she could not. If she were to retain the profit made by the use of the trustee's money, then, in the language of the modern law of restitution, she would be unjustly enriched at the expense of the trustee. If she were a constructive trustee of the money, a court of equity, as a court of conscience, would say that it was unconscionable for her to lay claim to the profit made by the use of her beneficiary's money. It would, however, be a mistake to suppose that the common law courts disregarded considerations of conscience. Lord Mansfield CJ, who did much to develop the early law of restitution at common law, founded it firmly on the basis of good conscience and unjust enrichment. It would, in my judgment, be absurd if a person with no title at all were in a stronger position to resist a proprietary claim by the true owner than one with a bare legal title. In the present case equity has no role to play. The trustee must bring his claim at common law. It follows that, if he has to trace his money, he must rely on common law tracing rules, and that he has no proprietary *remedy*. But it does not follow that he has no proprietary *claim*. His claim is exclusively proprietary. He claims the money because it belongs to him at law or represents profits made by the use of money which belonged to him at law.

The trustee submits that he has no need to trace, since the facts are clear and undisputed. The defendant did not mix the money with her own. The trustees money remained identifiable as such throughout. But of course, he does have to trace it in order to establish that the money which he claims represents his money. . . .

. . . In my judgment the concession that the trustee can trace the money at common law is rightly made. There are no factual difficulties of the kind which proved fatal in this court to the common law claim in *Agip (Africa) Ltd* v *Jackson* [1991] Ch 547. It is not necessary to trace the passage of the money through the clearing system or the London potato futures market. The money which the defendant paid into her account with the commodity brokers represented the proceeds of cheques which she received from her husband. Those cheques represented money in the bankrupts' joint account at Midland Bank which belonged to the trustee.

In *Lipkin Gorman* v *Karpnale Ltd* [1991] 2 AC 548, 573 Lord Goff of Chieveley held that the plaintiffs could trace or follow their 'property into its product' for this 'involves a decision by the owner of the original property to assert his title to the product in place of his original property.' In that case the original property was the plaintiffs' chose in action, a debt owed by the bank to the plaintiffs. Lord Goff held, at p. 574, that the plaintiffs could 'trace their property at common law in that chose in action, or in any part of it, into its product, i.e. cash drawn by Cass from their client account at the bank.'

Accordingly the trustee can follow the money in the joint account at Midland Bank, which had been vested by statute in him, into the proceeds of the three cheques which the defendant received from her husband. The trustee does not need to follow the money from one recipient to another or follow it through the clearing system; he can follow the cheques as they pass from hand to hand. It is sufficient for him to be able to trace the money into the cheques and the cheques into their proceeds. . . .

There is no merit in having distinct and differing tracing rules at law and in equity, given that tracing is neither a right nor a remedy but merely the process by which the plaintiff establishes what has happened to his property and makes good his claim that the assets which he claims can properly be regarded as representing his property. The fact that there are different tracing rules at law and in equity is unfortunate though probably inevitable, but unnecessary differences should not be created where they are not required by the different nature of legal and equitable doctrines and remedies. There is, in my view, even less merit in the present rule which precludes the invocation of the equitable tracing rules to support a common law claim; until that rule is swept away unnecessary obstacles to the development of a rational and coherent law of restitution will remain.

Given that the trustee can trace his money at Midland Bank into the money in the defendant's account with the commodity brokers, can he successfully assert a claim to that part of the money which represents the profit made by the use of his money? I have no doubt that, in the particular circumstances of this case, he can. There is no need to trace through the dealings of the London potato futures market. If the defendant, as the nominal account holder, had any entitlement to demand payment from the brokers, this was because of the terms of the contract which she made with them. Under the terms of that contract it is reasonable to infer that the brokers were authorised to deal in potato futures on her account, to debit her account with losses and to credit it with profits, and to pay her only the balance standing to her account. It is, in my opinion, impossible to separate the chose in action constituted by the deposit of the trustee's money on those terms from the terms upon which it was deposited. The chose in action, which was vested in the defendant's name but which in reality belonged to the trustee, was not a right to payment from the brokers of the original amount deposited but a right to claim the balance, whether greater or less than the amounted deposited; and it is to that chose in action that the trustee now lays claim.

Given, then, that the trustee has established his legal claim to the £11,700 and the profits earned by the use of his money, and has located the money, first, in the defendant's account with the commodity brokers and, later, in the defendant's account at Raphaels, I am satisfied that the common law has adequate remedies to enable him to recover his property. He did not need to sue the defendant; and he did not do so. He was entitled to bring an action for debt against Raphaels and obtain an order for payment. When he threatened to do so, Raphaels interpleaded, and the issue between the trustee and the defendant was which of them could give a good receipt to Raphaels. That depended upon which of them had the legal title to the chose in action. The money now being in court, the court can grant an appropriate declaration and make an order for payment. . . .

FOSKETT v *MCKEOWN* [1997] 3 All ER 392, CA

FACTS: Following the entry into contracts by a large number of purchasers for the purchase of plots of land on a site to be developed in the Algarve, M held the purchasers' money in respect of the purchase price on trust for them until the land was developed and then transferred. In the event, the land was never developed and M, in breach of trust, used the purchasers' money to pay several annual premiums of £10,220 payable under a life assurance policy.

M committed suicide and the sum of £1,000,589.04 was paid to certain of his relatives under the policy. The plaintiff, one of the prospective purchasers, issued proceedings against the defendants, purporting to sue on his own behalf and on behalf of all the other prospective purchasers, claiming the policy money paid to the defendants, contending that it was the purchasers' money which had kept the policy on foot and that they could trace their money into the proceeds of the policy.

HELD: Where a trustee of funds held on trust for prospective purchasers of land misapplied the funds and used them to pay premiums due on an existing policy of assurance on his own life for the benefit of others, the purchasers were entitled to a charge over the proceeds of the policy in order to recover such of their money as could be traced into the premiums together with interest thereon. They were not though (Morritt LJ dissenting), entitled to a pro rata share in the proceeds, since the beneficiaries under the policy were innocent of any part in the breach of trust, and the benefit which accrued to them from the use of the purchasers' money consisted merely of the keeping on foot of the policy of which they were already the beneficial owners. Moreover, payment of the premiums did not make the purchasers part-owners in equity of the policy. Accordingly, no question of any resulting or constructive trust arose.

SIR RICHARD SCOTT V-C: There are a number of well-established principles which bear upon the issue. Let me illustrate them by examples. First, if in breach of trust a trustee uses trust money to purchase some particular asset, the trust beneficiaries can, if the wish, claim the asset in specie. Alternatively, they can claim a charge over the asset to recover their money and interest and, after sale of the asset, recover any shortfall in an action for damages against the trustee (see *Snell's Equity* (29th edn, 1991 p. 303). This remedy of a charge over the asset is a restitutionary remedy. It is a consequence of the tracing of the beneficiaries' money into the asset. The beneficiaries' alternative right to claim the asset in specie can be explained as an example of a resulting trust. The beneficial interest in the purchased asset goes to the person or persons whose money has been used to pay the purchase price.

Second, if in purchasing the asset the trustee uses his own money as well as trust money, the beneficiaries can, as in the first example, claim the restitutionary remedy of a charge over the asset to recover their money and interest. Alternatively, the beneficiaries can claim a proportionate interest in the asset, the proportion being that which their money bears to the total purchase price. This alternative will, obviously, be preferred if the asset has increased in value since its purchase (see *Re Tilley's Will Trusts, Burgin* v *Croad* [1967] 2 All ER 303 at 310).

Third, if in purchasing the asset the trustee has used trust money from two different trust sources, neither set of beneficiaries can claim a first charge over the asset to recover its money. The equities as between the two sets of beneficiaries will be equal. Neither will be entitled to priority as against the other. It follows that they must share proportionately in the asset, bearing pro rata any shortfall and enjoying pro rata any increase in value (see the explanation of *Sinclair* v *Brougham* [1914] AC 398 given by Lord Greene MR in *Re Diplock's Estate, Diplock* v *Wintle* [1948] 2 All ER 318 at 353).

Each of these three examples involves the purchase of an asset. The situation is not necessarily the same in a case in which trust money is used not in purchasing an asset but in improving or maintaining an already acquired asset. In a case in which a trustee uses trust money in improving or maintaining a property which belongs to the trustee, the beneficiaries can claim the restitutionary remedy of a charge to recover their money with interest thereon. If the trust money has increased the value of the property they will be entitled in the alternative to a proportionate interest in the property, the proportion being that which their money bears to the value of the property before their money was expended on it. This alternative remedy is not attributable to a resulting trust, at least in the sense in which the term 'resulting trust' is normally used. It is a consequence of the principle that the trustee will be accountable to the beneficiaries for the benefit he has made out of the trust money. In order to render him accountable, equity will impose on the property a constructive trust under which the beneficiaries will be entitled to their proportionate share of its increased value.

But the position is otherwise if trust money has been spent by the trustee in improving or maintaining the property of someone else, some innocent third party. It may be that in some circumstances the restitutionary remedy of a charge over the property would be available to the beneficiaries. But even a restitutionary charge would not be available if to allow it would be unfair to the innocent third party. This is made clear in *Re Diplock's Estate*. Lord Greene MR, after considering a situation in which trust money had been applied in making alterations to the property of an innocent third party but had not added to the value of the property, said ([1948] 2 All ER 318 at 361):

> In the absence of authority to the contrary, our conclusion is that as regards the Diplock money used in these cases it cannot be traced in any true sense, and, further, that, even if this were not so, the only remedy available to equity, viz., that of a declaration of charge, would not produce an equitable result and is inapplicable accordingly.

Let me try and apply these principles to the facts of the present case. There are important uncertainties as to the provenance of the money that was used to pay the 1988 premium. Let me assume, first, that it was Mr Murphy's money that was used. On that footing the consequence of the payment by Mr Murphy of the first, second and third premiums, in 1986, 1987 and 1988, was that before any money of the purchasers had been applied in paying any premium the policy was held upon trust for a class of beneficiaries from which Mr Murphy was excluded. The purchasers' money was spent in 1989 and 1990 in maintaining a policy in which Mr Murphy had no beneficial interest and which already belonged to the beneficiaries.

In these circumstances, while I can see no inequity, and therefore no diffficulty, in a claim by the purchasers to the restitutionary remedy of a charge upon the proceeds of the policy to recover their money with interest, I can see great difficulty in their claim to a proportionate share in the proceeds. The case is not one in which any benefit accrued to Mr Murphy from his misuse of their money. The benefit from the use of the purchasers' money accrued to the beneficiaries who were innocent of any part in the breach of trust. The benefit to them consisted of the keeping on foot of the policy of which they were already the beneficial owners. Why should the use by Mr Murphy of the purchasers' money in paying premiums to keep the policy on foot have the effect of divesting the beneficiaries of a pro rata part of their beneficial ownership? . . .

18.3   End of Chapter Assessment Question

Trevor is a trustee of two trusts, Black's Settlement and White's Settlement, each comprising £50,000 in cash. The trust monies are kept in separate bank accounts. Trevor also has a private bank account in which he holds £100,000. Suppose that the following events take place, in the following order:

■ Trevor withdraws all the monies from the Black's Settlement account and places them in his own private account.

■ Trevor withdraws all the monies from the White's Settlement account and places them in his own private bank account.

■ Trevor withdraws £100,000 from his own account in order to purchase a piece of fine art.

■ Trevor withdraws £50,000 from his account and uses the monies to pay off the building society mortgage on his house.

■ Trevor withdraws the balance of his private account and spends the monies on a luxury world cruise.

■ Trevor finally pays £10,000 into his private account.

Trevor has just been declared bankrupt. His general creditors claim the work of fine art which is now worth £150,000, and the balance of monies in Trevor's private account. Advise the beneficiaries of the two trusts, who wish to recover the value of their misappropriated funds.

18.4   End of Chapter Assessment Outline Answer

The best way to approach a question on tracing is to arrange the facts of the question under headings representing the various bank accounts, funds and assets, as follows:

Trevor's a/c	Black S a/c	White S a/c	Fine Art	House
£100,000	£50,000	£50,000		
£150,000	nil	£50,000		
£200,000	nil	nil		
£100,000	nil	nil	£100,000	
£50,000	nil	nil	£100,000	£50,000
nil	nil	nil	£100,000	£50,000
(cruise)				
£10,000	nil	nil	£150,000	£50,000
			(appreciation)	

The beneficiaries of the Black Settlement and the Beneficiaries of the White Settlement are now seeking to trace their equitable interests through to the £10,000 cash, the £150,000 piece of fine art and Trevor's house.

The first point to make is that tracing at common law will not be possible because the trust monies have been mixed with Trevor's monies in his private account, subject to the possible application of the Rule in *Clayton's* case which is a rule of banking which has the effect of 'unmixing' mixed funds. The Rule in *Clayton's* case will be discussed below, but first we will consider the possibility of equitable tracing.

The great advantages of equitable tracing over common law tracing are, first, that tracing is possible through mixed funds, secondly, that trust beneficiaries can trace in equity and thirdly, that equitable tracing can lead to the assertion of a proprietary right against the defendant's property. In the present case such a right would rank ahead of the claims of Trevor's general creditors. The fact that successful tracing in equity leads to rights in a 'thing' means that the beneficiaries should, in principle, be able to claim some or all of any increase in value of the 'thing'. This will be of particular relevance when we consider the claim against the piece of fine art.

Unfortunately for the beneficiaries equitable tracing is also subject to certain limitations. The most significant of these for the purpose of the present case is that it is not possible to trace in equity into property which has been purchased in good faith and for value, by a person who had no notice (actual or constructive) of the beneficiaries' rights. This means that the beneficiaries will not be able to trace through to monies of the mortgagee, monies of the cruise organiser or monies of the person who sold the piece of fine art.

Before considering whether equitable tracing will be possible in the present case we will first dismiss the possibility that the rule in *Clayton's* case might be applicable. This rule is sometimes seen as part of the equitable tracing process, but it is more accurate to see it as a peculiar traditional rule of bank accounting which is effective to notionally 'unmix' monies in a mixed bank account. The rule is that where a number of payments are made into and out of a current bank account the first payment in is deemed to be paid out first. Applying the rule in the present case would have the result that Trevor's monies would be deemed to have been used to purchase the piece of fine art (a result which would also flow, incidentally, from the judgment in *Re Hallet's Estate* (1980) 13 ChD 696 which presumes that a trustee uses his own monies before using those of the trust when withdrawing monies from a mixed account to make an unauthorised investment), Black Settlement monies would have been used to reduce the mortgage, and White Settlement monies would have been dissipated on the cruise. The result of applying the rule in *Clayton's* case would, then, be manifestly unfair to the beneficiaries of the White Settlement. In such circumstances the application of the rule would not accord with the presumed intentions of the parties and will not, therefore, be applied (*Vaughan* v *Barlow Clowes* [1992] 4 All ER 717).

We must consider, next, whether equitable tracing will be possible into the piece of fine art, the house and the £10,000 balance in Trevor's a/c. A prerequisite of equitable tracing, that the property has, at some stage, been held in a fiduciary capacity, is clearly satisfied in the present case, by virtue of the fact that Trevor was a trustee. It follows that the beneficiaries should be entitled to a charge over the various exchange products of their trust monies (*Re Hallett's Estate*). But earlier we said that Trevor is deemed to have purchased the piece of art with his own monies, so how can the beneficiaries claim a charge over that? Further, the £10,000 was paid into an account with a nil balance, so how can those monies be said to represent the trust monies?

A solution to the problem of the piece of Art is to be found in the judgment in *Re Oatway* [1903] 2 Ch 356. There a trustee had bought shares out of a mixed account of his own monies and trust monies. At the time of the purchase of the shares enough money remained in the account to meet the claims of the trust beneficiaries, but later the balance in the account was dissipated. According to a basic reading of *Re Hallet's Estate* the trustee should be deemed to have withdrawn his own monies first, and therefore the shares would have been his. However, in *Re Oatway*, the court preferred a more sophisticated analysis and refused to allow the trustee in breach to set up a claim to the shares in priority to the claims of the beneficiaries. Similar reasoning would apply in the present case and the trustees should be entitled to a charge over the piece of fine art. If the piece of art is deemed to have been bought entirely with monies from the trusts the charge will be fixed over the whole asset, the beneficiaries will, therefore have an asset worth £150,000 even though their original funds amounted to only £100,000. If the court decides that some of Trevor's own monies are represented in the piece of art the court will probably divide the profit proportionally between Trevor and the trusts (*Re Tilley's WT* [1967] 1 Ch 1179), although it might be argued that the trustee should not be permitted to retain any profit from his breach!

One question which remains, then, is whether the beneficiaries will be able to assert a proprietary claim against the entirety of the piece of art, or whether some of their £100,000 is represented elsewhere. If *Re Oatway* is followed according to the letter, the problematic result might be that Trevor will be deemed to have used his own monies to purchase the art, to the extent only that such a presumption does not prejudice the claims of the beneficiaries. Strictly speaking, then, the court would grant each set of beneficiaries a £25,000 charge over Trevor's house and a floating charge over a quarter of the value of the piece of fine art. A more straightforward solution, which would also appear to accord with the spirit of common sense in *Re Oatway* would be to order a sale of the piece of art and to divide the sale proceeds equally between the beneficiaries. Equality between the beneficiaries of the two settlements is presumed throughout as they are all innocent volunteers and together victims of Trevor's accounting malpractice (*Re Diplock* [1948] 1 Ch 465).

CHAPTER NINETEEN

THE EQUITABLE LIABILITY OF STRANGERS TO THE TRUSTS

19.1 Knowing Receipt and Dishonest Assistance

SELANGOR UNITED RUBBER ESTATES LTD v CRADOCK AND OTHERS
[1968] 1 WLR 1555, ChD

FACTS: The plaintiff company was in liquidation and the present action was in fact brought by the Board of Trade on the company's behalf. Cradock had persuaded a bank to pay a banker's draft to him out of a company's account, supposedly to finance a take-over of that company from which Cradock would receive monies which would more than repay the draft. The take-over having been completed, the new board of directors issued a cheque in favour of a third party by way of a loan. This third party then endorsed the cheque over to Cradock who was accordingly able to repay the original draft at the bank. It was never suggested that the bank had acted dishonestly.
HELD: The bank was liable as a constructive trustee based on its knowing assistance in Cradock's fraudulent breach of his fiduciary duty.

UNGOED-THOMAS J: . . . I come now to the question how far a stranger to the trust can become liable as constructive trustee in respect of a breach of the trust.

It is essential at the outset to distinguish two very different kinds of so-called constructive trustees: (1) Those who, though not appointed trustees, take upon themselves to act as such and to possess and administer trust property for the beneficiaries, such as trustees de son tort. Distinguishing features for present purposes are (a) they do not claim to act in their own right but for the beneficiaries, and (b) their assumption to act is not of itself a ground of liability (save in the sense of course of liability to account and for any failure in the duty so assumed), and so their status as trustees precedes the occurrence which may be the subject of claim against them. (2) Those whom a court of equity will treat as trustees by reason of their action, of which complaint is made. Distinguishing features are (a) that such trustees claim to act in their own right and not for beneficiaries, and (b) no trusteeship arises before, but only by reason of, the action complained of.

Until the limitation provisions of the Trustee Act 1925, the first category of constructive trustees could not rely, in defence of claims against them, on statutory limitation or the analogous rules enforced by courts of equity. This was because they acted as trustees for others, and therefore held in right of those others and therefore time was held not to run in their favour against those others. But as the second category of trustees claimed in their own right, time ran in their favour from their obtaining possession. It is largely by reason of this distinction that the first category of constructive trustee is sometimes referred to or included in the authorities under the term 'express trustee': (see *Taylor* v *Davies* [1920] AC 636; *Soar* v *Ashwell* [1893] 2 QB 390, especially the judgments of Lord Esher MR and Bowen LJ.

It has long been well established that a bank is not a trustee for its customer of the amount to his credit in his bank account: (see, for example, *Foley* v *Hill* (1848) 2 HL Cas

28, *Burdick* v *Garrick* (1870) 5 Ch App 233, *per* Lord Hatherley LC). In view of this, and the circumstances in which the constructive trusteeship relied on by the plaintiff against the defendants is said to arise, the plaintiff does not rely at all in this case upon the establishment of the first category of constructive trusteeship, but exclusively on the second category. The first category is irrelevant to the plaintiff's case. *Soar* v *Ashwell* [1893] 2 QB 390, *Burdick* v *Garrick* (1870) 5 Ch App 233; *In re Barney, Barney* v *Barney*

[1892] 2 Ch 265, *Mara* v *Browne* [1896] 1 Ch 199; and *Williams-Ashman* v *Price and Williams* [1942] Ch 219 to which I was referred, fall within that first category.

Barnes v *Addy* (1874) 9 Ch App 244 contains a formulation of the second category of constructive trusteeship, upon which the plaintiff relies. In that case Barnes was husband of the life tenant of the trust, was appointed sole trustee by Addy, the sole surviving trustee, and subsequently he misappropriated the trust fund. The question before the Court of Appeal was whether the solicitors engaged in respect of the appointment were liable to make good the amount misappropriated. Lord Selborne LC referred to both categories of constructive trustees. He said:

> That responsibility—that is the responsibility of express trustees—may no doubt be extended in equity to others who are not properly trustees, if they are found either making themselves trustees de son tort, or actually participating in any fraudulent conduct of the trustee to the injury of the *cestui que trust*. But, on the other hand, strangers are not to be made constructive trustees merely because they act as the agents of trustees in transactions within their legal powers, transactions, perhaps of which a Court of Equity may disapprove, unless those agents receive and become chargeable with some part of the trust property, or unless they assist with knowledge in a dishonest and fraudulent design on the part of the trustees. . . .

It is this formulation in *Barnes* v *Addy* 'assist with knowledge in a dishonest and fraudulent design on the part of the trustee' that is the basis of the plaintiff's claim that the defendants are liable as constructive trustees. There are thus three elements: (1) assistance by the stranger, (2) with knowledge, (3) in a dishonest and fraudulent design on the part of the trustees. . . .

BADEN v *SOCIÉTÉ GÉNÉRALE POUR FAVORISER LE DÉVELOPPEMENT DU COMMERCE ET DE L'INDUSTRIE EN FRANCE* [1993] 1 WLR 509, ChD

FACTS: The plaintiffs (Baden and others) were liquidators of various investment funds. They brought this action to recover their clients' monies which the defendant bank had misapplied by transferring them electronically to a Panamanian bank. The monies had been dissipated after their arrival at the Panamanian bank.

HELD (in 1983): The defendant was not liable as a constructive trustee on the basis of 'knowing assistance' because it did not know *at the time* of the transfer to Panama that the former directors of the investment fund had been involved in a dishonest and fraudulent design.

PETER GIBSON J: . . . Mr Price accepts as pertinent the warning given by Lord Selborne LC in *Barnes* v *Addy* LR 9 Ch App 244, 251, and echoed frequently thereafter that the doctrine of constructive trusts must not be strained by unreasonable construction beyond its due and proper limits so as to render liable persons who may be practically innocent. In particular he accepts that the law should not be extended beyond the principle as formulated by Lord Selborne LC. However, he points out that Lord Selborne LC's statement of the principle should not be treated as though it were the words of a statute, and he submits that the remarks of Oliver J in *Taylors Fashions Ltd* v *Liverpool Victoria Trustees Co. Ltd (Note)* [1982] QB 133, 151, 152, albeit uttered in the context of equitable estoppel, are applicable to the present case, that is to say that, in considering whether or not to grant equitable relief, it is not enough merely to inquire whether the circumstances can be fitted within the confines of some preconceived formula serving as a universal yardstick for every form of unconscionable behaviour. Nevertheless Mr. Price accepts that there are four elements which must be established if a case is to be brought within the category of 'knowing assistance.' They are (1) the existence of a trust; (2) the existence of a dishonest and fraudulent design on the part of the trustee of the trust; (3) the assistance by the stranger in that design; and (4) the knowledge of the stranger. I would add that whilst it is of course helpful to isolate the relevant constituent elements of the 'knowing assistance' category in this way, it is important not to lose sight of the requirement that, taken together, those elements must leave the court satisfied that the alleged constructive trustee was a party or privy to dishonesty on the part of the trustee.

. . . As to the first element, the trust need not be a formal trust. It is sufficient that there should be a fiduciary relationship between the 'trustee' and the property of another person.

. . . In my judgment for the purpose of constructive trusteeship a person beneficially interested in trust property held by a corporate trustee can rely on the fiduciary relationship between the directors and the trustee company as well as on the trust affecting the trust property in the hands of the company. Accordingly if Mr Price can satisfy me that the moneys in the hands of BCB were trust moneys held for the Funds and that the directors of BCB were using their position as directors to cause the misappropriation of the trust moneys, I would regard the first element of the *Barnes* v *Addy* LR 9 Ch App 244, formulation as satisfied.

. . . As to the second element the relevant design in the part of the trustee must be dishonest and fraudulent. In the *Selangor case* [1968] 1 WLR 1555, 1582 and 1590, Ungoed-Thomas J held that this element must be understood in accordance with equitable principles for equitable relief and that conduct which is morally reprehensible can properly be said to be dishonest and fraudulent for the purposes of that element. But in *Belmont Finance Corporation Ltd* v *Williams Furniture Ltd* [1979] Ch 250 the Court of Appeal made clear that it is not sufficient that there should be misfeasance or a breach of trust falling short of dishonesty and fraud. For present purposes there is no distinction to be drawn between the two adjectives 'dishonest' and 'fraudulent:' see the *Belmont case* [1979] Ch 250, 267. It is common ground between the parties that I can take as a relevant description of fraud 'to take a risk to the prejudice of another's rights, which risk is known to be one which there is no right to take. . . .

It is also common ground that while the standard of proof of an allegation of fraud is no higher than a balance of probabilities, the more serious the allegation, the more cogent is the evidence required to overcome the unlikelihood of what is alleged and thus to prove it.

. . . As to the third element it seems to me to be a simple question of fact, whether or not there has been assistance. The payment by a bank on the instructions of fraudulent directors of a company of moneys of the company to another person may be such assistance as in the *Selangor case* [1968] 1 WLR 1555 and the *Karak case* [1972] 1 WLR 602. . . .

. . . It is in respect of the fourth element, knowledge, that there has been the greater part of the legal debate. . . .

. . . I start, first, by considering that it is that the alleged constructive trustee must know. I think it clear that he must know the three elements already mentioned. He must know that there was a trust though I do not think it necessary that he should know all the details of the trust: see for example *Foxton* v *Manchester and Liverpool District Banking Co.* [1881] 44 LT 406, 408. He must know of the dishonest and fraudulent design of the trustee. Again, however, I do not think it need be knowledge of the whole design: that would be an impossibly high requirement in most cases. What is crucial is that the alleged constructive trustee should know that a design having the character of being fraudulent and dishonest was being perpetrated. Further he must know that his act assisted in the implementation of such design. In circumstances such as the present the defendant must be shown to have known that the $4m was trust property, that the fraudulent and dishonest design extending to the $4m was being perpetrated by the directors of BCB and that by moving the $4m to Panama the defendant assisted in the implementation of this design.

. . . Further the relevant knowledge must be of facts and not of mere claims or allegations. This is established by the decision of the Court of Appeal in *Carl Zeiss Stiftung* v *Herbert Smith & Co.* (*No. 2*) [1969] 2 Ch 276. In that case the plaintiffs in an action in which they claimed that the property of the defendant belonged to them sought to make the solicitors to the defendant accountable for moneys received by the solicitors from the defendant for their fees and expenses. The basis of the claim against the solicitors was that they knew of all the matters averred by the plaintiffs in the action against the defendant and were therefore constructive trustees when they received moneys from the defendant for their fees. The Court of Appeal held that the solicitors had knowledge only of a disputed claim that the property of the defendant was held in trust for the plaintiffs and that they did not have knowledge that such property was in fact trust property; accordingly it was held that the solicitors having knowledge only of a doubtful equity lacked the requisite knowledge to be constructive trustees. Although the *Carl Zeiss* case was one relating to the 'knowing receipt or dealing' category of constructive trusteeship I can see no justification for treating the two categories of constructive trusteeship differently on this point. Each category requires knowledge of the trust. It seems to me also that for the 'knowing assistance' category a similar standard must apply to knowledge of the fraud and of the assistance. Again to differentiate between the different matters knowledge of which is requisite would not in my view be justified.

. . . What types of knowledge are relevant for the purposes of constructive trusteeship? Mr Price submits that knowledge can comprise any one of five different mental states which he described as follows: (i) actual knowledge; (ii) wilfully shutting one's eyes to the obvious; (iii) wilfully and recklessly failing to make such inquiries as an honest and reasonable man would make; (iv) knowledge of circumstances which would indicate the facts to an honest and reasonable man; (v) knowledge of circumstances which would put an honest and reasonable man on inquiry. More accurately, apart from actual knowledge they are formulations of the circumstances which may lead the court to impute knowledge of the facts to the alleged constructive trustee even though he lacked actual knowledge of those facts. Thus the court will treat a person as having constructive knowledge of the facts if he wilfully shuts his eyes to the relevant facts which would be obvious if he opened his eyes, such constructive knowledge being usually termed (though by a metaphor of historical inaccuracy) 'Nelsonian knowledge.' Similarly the court may treat a person as having constructive knowledge of the facts—'type (iv) knowledge'—if he has actual knowledge of circumstances which would indicate the facts to an honest and reasonable man. . . .

One logical basis for allowing, as relevant to constructive trusteeship types of constructive knowledge, would be to allow only those types arising from circumstances in which the conscience of the alleged constructive trustee was affected. This would accord with the equitable basis of constructive trusteeship. Thus if a person shuts his eyes to the obvious, or if he wilfully and recklessly fails to make obvious inquiries, that person is guilty of unconscionable behaviour such that a court of equity might wish to impute to him the knowledge that he would have gained by opening his eyes or making the obvious inquiries. . . .

. . . It is plainly right that a person with Nelsonian knowledge or type (iii) knowledge should be treated as having knowledge for the purpose of constructive trusteeship. It seems to me, as it did to Ungoed-Thomas J and Brightman J, that there is a sufficient line of authorities to justify treating a person with type (iv) or type (v) knowledge as having knowledge for that purpose. It is little short of common sense that a person who actually knows all the circumstances from which the honest and reasonable man would have knowledge of the relevant facts should also be treated as having knowledge of the facts. The dividing line between Nelsonian and type (iv) knowledge may often be difficult to discern. If an objective test is appropriate to let in type (iv) knowledge, it would be illogical not to apply a similar objective test in circumstances where the honest and reasonable man would be put on inquiry (type (v) knowledge).

. . . But in my judgment the court should not be astute to impute knowledge where no actual knowledge exists. In particular, it is only in exceptional circumstances that the court should impute type (v) knowledge to an agent like a bank acting honestly on the instructions of its principal but alleged to have provided knowing assistance in a dishonest and fraudulent design. It is not every inquiry that might be made that the court will treat the agent as having been under a duty to make inquiry even though the omitted inquiry would, if made, have led to the agent having knowledge of the facts. If an explanation is offered, the presumption of honesty is strong and the court will not require the agent to be hypercritical in examining that explanation. . . .

AGIP (AFRICA) LTD v JACKSON AND OTHERS [1989] 3 WLR 1367, ChD

FACTS: (These are set out at **18.1.**)
HELD: The defendants were not liable for 'knowing receipt of trust property in breach of trust' because some of the defendants had never received any of the property at all, and those that had received the property had not received it for their own benefit. However, they would be liable for 'knowing assistance in a dishonest and fraudulent design'; their indifference as to the true state of affairs was not honest behaviour.

MILLETT J: [affirmed by the Court of Appeal] . . . In *Baden, Delvaux and Lecuit* v *Société Générale pour Favoriser le Développement du Commerce et de l'Industrie en France SA* [1983] BCLC 325, 403, Peter Gibson J said:

> . . . why should a person who, having received trust property knowing it to be such but without notice of a breach of trust because there was none, subsequently deals with the property in a manner inconsistent with the trust not be a constructive trustee within the 'knowing receipt or dealing' category?

I respectfully agree. In my judgment, much confusion has been caused by treating this as a single category and by failing to differentiate between a number of different situations. Without attempting an exhaustive classification, it is necessary to distinguish between two main classes of case under this heading.

The first is concerned with the person who receives for his own benefit trust property transferred to him in breach of trust. He is liable as a constructive trustee if he received it with notice, actual or constructive, that it was trust property and that the transfer to him was a breach of trust; or if he received it without such notice but subsequently discovered the facts. In either case he is liable to account for the property, in the first case as from the time he received the property, and in the second as from the time he acquired notice.

The second and, in my judgment, distinct class of case is that of the person, usually an agent of the trustees, who receives the trust property lawfully and not for his own benefit but who then either misappropriates it or otherwise deals with it in a manner which is inconsistent with the trust. He is liable to account as a constructive trustee if he received the property knowing it to be such, though he will not necessarily be required in all circumstances to have known the exact terms of the trust. This class of case need not be considered further since the transfer to Baker Oil was not lawful.

In either class of case it is immaterial whether the breach of trust was fraudulent or not. The essential feature of the first class is that the recipient must have received the property for his own use and benefit. This is why neither the paying nor the collecting bank can normally be brought within it. In paying or collecting money for a customer the bank acts only as his agent. It is otherwise, however, if the collecting bank uses the money to reduce or discharge the customer's overdraft. In doing so it receives the money for its own benefit.

This is not a technical or fanciful requirement. It is essential if receipt-based liability is to be properly confined to those cases where the receipt is relevant to the loss. . .

A stranger to the trust will also be liable to account as a constructive trustee if he knowingly assists in the furtherance of a fraudulent and dishonest breach of trust. It is not necessary that the party sought to be made liable as a constructive trustee should have received any part of the trust property, but the breach of trust must have been fraudulent. The basis of the stranger's liability is not receipt of trust property but participation in a fraud.

. . . The various mental states which may be involved were analysed by Peter Gibson J in *Baden's case* [1983] BCLC 325 as comprising: (i) actual knowledge; (ii) wilfully shutting one's eyes to the obvious; (iii) wilfully and recklessly failing to make such inquiries as an honest and reasonable man would make; (iv) knowledge of circumstances which would indicate the facts to an honest and reasonable man; and (v) knowledge of circumstances which would put an honest and reasonable man on inquiry.

According to Peter Gibson J, a person in category (ii) or (iii) will be taken to have actual knowledge, while a person in categories (iv) or (v) has constructive notice only. I gratefully adopt the classification but would warn against over refinement or a too ready assumption that categories (iv) or (v) are necessarily cases of constructive notice only.

The true distinction is between honesty and dishonesty. It is essentially a jury question. If a man does not draw the obvious inferences or make the obvious inquiries, the question is: why not? If it is because, however foolishly, he did not suspect wrongdoing or, having suspected it, had his suspicions allayed, however unreasonably, that is one thing. But if he did suspect wrongdoing yet failed to make inquiries because 'he did not want to know ' (category (ii)) or because he regarded it as 'none of his business' (category (iii)), that is quite another. Such conduct is dishonest, and those who are guilty of it cannot complain if, for the purpose of civil liability, they are treated as if they had actual knowledge. . .

EAGLE TRUST PLC v SBC SECURITIES LTD [1992] 4 All ER 488, ChD

FACTS: The defendant company had underwritten the finance for a take-over bid being carried out by the plaintiff company. The chief executive of the defendant company had then arranged to sub-underwrite its liability. The present action was brought by the plaintiffs to recover monies which the chief executive had fraudulently used to clear personal, and other, debts arising out of the sub-underwriting arrangements. The plaintiff sought to fix the defendant with liability as a constructive trustee on the basis that it should have been aware that the executive would draw on the plaintiffs' monies in order to clear his debts, and that the defendant should at least have made enquiries as to how the executive had managed to pay off his debts.

HELD: In a commercial transaction where the defendant had received, but no longer held, misapplied funds it had to be shown that the defendant had known that the monies had been misapplied in order to fix them with liability as a constructive trustee on the basis of 'knowing receipt' of trust property. 'Knowledge' in this context meant actual knowledge or wilfully shutting one's eyes to the obvious, or wilfully and recklessly failing to make enquiries such as an honest and reasonable man would make. In short, not merely technical 'notice' had to be proven. On the facts, there were no grounds for making the defendant liable as a constructive trustee and the statement of claim was accordingly struck out. Further, it was stated that it would not be possible to fix liability for 'knowing assistance' in a fraudulent breach of trust unless dishonesty or 'want of probity' could be shown on the part of the defendant.

VINELOTT J: . . . 'notice' is often used in a sense or in contexts where the facts do not support the inference of knowledge. A man may have actual notice of a fact and yet not know it. He may have been supplied in the course of a conveyancing transaction with a document and so have actual notice of its content, but he may not in fact have read it; or he may have read it some time ago and have forgotten its content. Megarry V-C observed in *Re Montagu's Settlement Trusts* [1992] 4 All ER 308 at 329, 'I suppose that there may be some remarkable beings for whom once known is never forgotten; but apart from them, the generality of mankind probably forgets far more than is remembered.' So also by statute a man may be deemed to have actual notice of a fact which is clearly not within his knowledge. Constructive and imputed notice are most frequently, though not invariably, used in contrast to knowledge to describe a situation in which a man is treated for some purposes as if he had knowledge of facts which were clearly not known to him. . . .

It can . . . , in my judgment, now be taken as settled law that, notwithstanding the wider language in which the test of liability as constructive trustee in a 'knowing assistance' case is stated in *Selangor* and in *Karak* and, notwithstanding the concession made by counsel and accepted by Peter Gibson J in the *Baden* case, a stranger cannot be made liable for knowing assistance in a fraudulent breach of trust unless knowledge of the fraudulent design can be imputed to him on one of the grounds I have described. There must have been something amounting to want of probity on his part. Constructive notice is not enough, though, as I have said, knowledge may be inferred in the absence of evidence by the defendant if such knowledge would have been imputed to an honest and reasonable man. . . .

The doctrine of constructive notice was developed in the field of property transactions and at a time when full and careful investigation of title was called for before a purchaser could be satisfied that the vendor had legal title to the property sold and that there were no legal or equitable encumbrances on it. Judges have frequently warned of the danger of extending the doctrine beyond these bounds. Lindley LJ in an often-cited passage in *Manchester Trust* v *Furness* [1895] 2 QB 539 at 545 said:

> . . . as regards the extension of the equitable doctrines of constructive notice to commercial transactions, the Courts have always set their faces resolutely against it. The equitable doctrines of constructive notice are common enough in dealing with land and estates with which the Court is familiar; but there have been repeated protests against the introduction into commercial transactions of anything like an extension of those doctrines, and the protest is founded on perfect good sense. In dealing with estates and land title is everything, and it can be leisurely investigated; in commercial transactions possession is everything, and there is no time to investigate title; and if we were to extend the doctrine of constructive notice to commercial transactions we should be doing infinite mischief and paralysing the trade of the country. . . .

In my judgment, therefore, in a case of this kind, in order to make a defendant liable as a constructive trustee, it must be shown that he knew, in one of the senses set out in categories (i), (ii) or (iii) of Peter Gibson J's analysis in *Baden*, that the moneys were trust moneys misapplied; or the circumstances must be such that, in the absence of any evidence or explanation by the defendant, that knowledge can be inferred. And it may be inferred if the circumstances are such that an honest and reasonable man would have inferred that the moneys were probably trust moneys and were being misapplied, and would either not have accepted them or would have kept them separate until he had satisfied himself that the payer was entitled to use them in discharge of the liability. . . .

HILLSDOWN HOLDINGS PLC v PENSIONS OMBUDSMAN AND OTHERS
[1997] 1 All ER 862

FACTS: H plc was the parent company of a group which participated in a pension scheme (the FMC scheme). In 1989, following negotiations with H plc and on legal advice, the trustees of the scheme transferred the entire assets and liabilities of the fund to another pension scheme (the HF scheme). Prior to that transfer, the FMC scheme had a substantial actuarial surplus of funds in excess of permitted Revenue limits, but there was no provision under the scheme enabling the trustees to repay surplus funds to participating employers, save on a winding up, and the scheme could not be amended to confer such a power. Shortly after the transfer, an agreement previously negotiated between H plc and the FMC trustees to augment the benefits of FMC members and to pay the surplus funds to H plc was put into effect, and the rules of the HF scheme were changed to permit that payment to H plc, which was also made the administrator of the scheme. Thereafter H plc was paid sums in excess of £11m after tax. A pensioner, supported by 51 other complainants, complained to the Pensions Ombudsman that the transfer of the assets of the FMC scheme to the HF scheme and the amendment made to the HF scheme to enable the payment of surplus funds to be made to H plc were in breach of trust. The Ombudsman directed H plc to refund the surplus.
HELD: In the circumstances H plc could have been held liable by a court as a constructive trustee because, although it honestly believed itself to be entitled to do and receive what it did, it had taken an active part in persuading the trustees to agree the breach of trust, had used a threatening technique of persuasion to induce the breach of trust and was unjustly enriched. It followed that the ombudsman had jurisdiction to order H plc to refund the surplus and the appeal would therefore be dismissed.

KNOX J: The categories of constructive trust in this field are usually referred to as 'knowing assistance' and 'knowing receipt' cases of constructive trust. In either category some form of knowledge is required. The knowing assistance cases are not relevant here since Hillsdown did receive the sums paid out by the HF trustee which came from the FMC scheme and was not guilty of any such dishonest conduct as is requisite in knowing assistance constructive trusts.

The knowing receipt cases on the other hand are rather more complex. . . .

I would respectfully adopt what Megarry V-C said in *Re Montagu's Settlement Trusts* [1992] 4 All ER 308 at 330: 'In considering whether a constructive trust has arisen in a case of the knowing receipt of trust property, the basic question is whether the conscience of the recipient is sufficiently affected to justify the imposition of such a trust.' In my view, there has to be set in the scales over against the fact that Hillsdown honestly believed itself to be entitled to do and receive what it did and received the following factors. (a) Hillsdown took a very active part in persuading the FMC trustee to agree to what was a breach of trust. (b) Hillsdown's technique in that persuasion was to threaten to do something which Hillsdown was not entitled to do because: (i) it involved a combination of adhering additional employers and suspending employers' contributions in a manner which would have been a breach of implied good faith, as that expression is used by Browne-Wilkinson V-C in the *Imperial Group* case; (ii) it involved an interference with a discretion given exclusively to the FMC trustee under r. 23(a) in relation to the surplus as at 6 April 1988. (c) Hillsdown was unjustly enriched by the receipt of £18·4m less 40% tax and the FMC trust was the poorer by the same sum gross of that tax. There can be no doubt about the enrichment save possibly as regards quantum. As to its being unjust, in my view one only has to compare the position of Hillsdown who successfully wielded a big but misguided stick with that of the members of the FMC scheme who were never told anything of what was being done as regards the payment of surplus to Hillsdown to see which way the scales of justice fall.

Although it can be said in a sense that Hillsdown was an innocent instigator of a breach of trust in that it did not appreciate that a breach of trust was involved, it was also in a sense guilty because it played an active part in what was in my view an improper threat to interfere with that with which it had no right to interfere. That seems to me to constitute a quite different and lesser degree of innocence from that of the solicitors in the *Zeiss* case and the tenant for life in *Re Montagu's Settlement Trusts*.

For those reasons, I conclude that, subject to possible defences, Hillsdown could have been held liable by a court as a constructive trustee of the sums which it received from the HF trustee. . . .

If my conclusion on constructive trusteeship is wrong, there remain the alternative formulations of unjust enrichment, mistake and a tracing claim. As to unjust enrichment I doubt whether at this stage of the development of English law it is appropriate for a judge at first instance to give effect to a claim in restitution where a claim in constructive trust fails. The authority upon which reliance would be placed for such an attitude would doubtless be *Lipkin Gorman (a firm)* v *Karpnale Ltd* [1992] 4 All ER 512, where such a form of proceeding in the context of a common law claim for money had and received succeeded. I have already stated my opinion that there was unjust enrichment here and in the circumstances I think it will suffice if I express my view on the defences which Mr Oliver relied upon by way of change of position. The first was the consent by Hillsdown to pension increases in the HF scheme and the second was the payment of tax. I do not accept that either of them would constitute an adequate defence of change of position. The consent to pension increases was not in my view something which was, so far as the FMC trust was concerned in respect of which the unjust enrichment really occurred, within Hillsdown's gift. Hillsdown had no right of veto there, certainly so far as the surplus in the FMC scheme was concerned. It is in my view right to regard the unjust enrichment claim arising in the FMC scheme because the payments to the HF trustee and thence to Hillsdown were negotiated and caried through as a package deal. The HF trust was no more than a conduit pipe. On that basis Hillsdown did not do more than allow in part that which ought to have been done in the whole, ie apply the surplus as permitted by r. 23(a). That does not seem to me to constitute a defence by way of change of position. . . .

[His Lordship made no particular comment on the issues of mistake and tracing.]

POLLY PECK INTERNATIONAL PLC v *NADIR AND CENTRAL BANK OF NORTHERN CYPRUS AND OTHERS (No. 2)* [1992] 4 All 769, CA

FACTS: The administrators of PPI brought the present action against Nadir, the controlling shareholder of PPI, who, they claimed, had misapplied PPI funds. They also brought further action against the Central Bank of Northern Cyprus, through whose accounts the monies had passed. They sought to fix liability as a constructive trustee on the bank.

HELD: The fact that the Central Bank knew that PPI was exchanging large sums of money into foreign currencies was not enough to put the bank on enquiry as to whether there had been improprieties. The bank was not liable as a constructive trustee for 'knowing assistance'.

SCOTT LJ: . . . Millett J, in the judgment below, treated the present case as one of 'knowing assistance' rather than 'knowing receipt'. In respect of the nine sterling transfers I think that is right. The Central Bank received the funds transferred not in its own right but as a banker, and, as banker, credited the funds to IBK in Northern Cyprus. But in respect of the bulk of the transfers the case is, in my opinion, one of 'receipt' rather than 'assistance.' The Central Bank was exchanging Turkish lire for sterling and became entitled to the sterling not as banker for IBK but in its own right. IBK became entitled to the Turkish lire.

Liability as constructive trustee in a 'knowing receipt' case does not require that the misapplication of the trust funds should be fraudulent. It does require that the defendant should have knowledge that the funds were trust funds and that they were being misapplied. Actual knowledge obviously will suffice. Mr Potts has submitted that it will suffice if the defendant can be shown to have had knowledge of facts which would have put an honest and reasonable man on inquiry, or, at least, if the defendant can be shown to have wilfully and recklessly failed to make such inquiries as an honest and reasonable man would have made (see categoriess (iii) and (v) of the categories of mental state identified by Peter Gibson J in *Baden's* case [1992] 4 All ER 161 at 235). I do not think there is any doubt that, if the latter of the two criteria can be established against the Central Bank, that will suffice. I have some doubts about the sufficiency of the former criterion but do not think that the present appeal is the right occasion for settling the issue. The various categories of mental state identified in *Baden's* case are not rigid categories with clear and precise boundaries. One category may merge imperceptibly into another. . . .

I do not, for my part, find it difficult to accept that the Central Bank must have known that the funds IBK were transferring to the Central Bank's Midland Bank account were likely to be mainly funds belonging to PPI or to one or other of its group companies. The Central Bank knew IBK was owned and controlled by Mr Nadir. It knew that PPI was the flagship of the group. It knew that the scale of business transacted by PPI and its group companies was very substantial. Funds of the size of those being transferred could hardly have been other than, in the main, funds of the group. There is, however, no reason to infer that the Central Bank must have realised that the funds all belonged to PPI, as opposed to belonging to one or other of the group companies, or indeed, to Mr Nadir personally. There is evidence that PPI acted to some extent as banker for the group. It certainly made very large advances to corporate members of the group. So, although the Central Bank must have known that the £44m was group money or Nadir money, I do not see any basis on which it could be inferred that the Central Bank knew or ought to have known that the money was specifically PPI money.

The real question, however, is whether the circumstances in which the transfers were made should have made the Central Bank suspicious of the propriety of what was being done. . . .

ROYAL BRUNEI AIRLINES SDN BHD v PHILIP TAN KOK MING
[1995] 3 All ER 97, PC

FACTS: An insolvent travel agency owed money to the plaintiff airline. The present action was brought against the principal director and shareholder in the travel agency. The plaintiffs sought to fix the defendant with liability as a constructive trustee on the basis of the defendant's knowing assistance in a dishonest and fraudulent design. The 'design' was the use of the airline's monies by the travel agency for its own business purposes in breach of the trust under which those monies were held.

HELD: The defendant would be liable on the basis of his 'dishonest assistance in or procurement of the breach of trust'.

LORD NICHOLLS OF BIRKENHEAD: The proper role of equity in commercial transactions is a topical question. Increasingly plaintiffs have recourse to equity for an effective remedy when the person in default, typically a company, is insolvent. Plaintiffs seek to obtain relief from others who were involved in the transactions, such as directors of the company or its bankers or its legal or other advisers. They seek to fasten fiduciary obligations directly onto the company's officers or agents or advisers, or to have them held personally liable for assisting the company in breaches of trust or fiduciary obligations.

This is such a case. An insolvent travel agent company owed money to an airline. The airline seeks a remedy against the travel agent's principal director and shareholder. Its claim is based on the much-quoted dictum of Lord Selborne LC, sitting in the Court of Appeal in Chancery, in *Barnes* v *Addy* [1874] LR 9 Ch App 244 at 251–252:

> That responsibility [of a trustee] may no doubt be extended in equity to others who are not properly trustees, if they are found . . . actually participating in any fraudulent conduct of the trustee to the injury of the *cestui que trust*. But . . . strangers are not to be made constructive trustees merely because they act as the agents of trustees in transactions within their legal powers, transactions, perhaps of which a Court of Equity may disapprove, unless those agents receive and become chargeable with some part of the trust property, or unless they assist with knowledge in a dishonest and fraudulent design on the part of the trustees.

In the conventional shorthand the first of these two circumstances in which third parties (non-trustees) may become liable to account in equity is 'knowing receipt', as distinct from the second where liability arises from 'knowing receipt', as distinct from the second where liability arises from 'knowing assistance'. Stated even more shortly, the first limb of Lord Selborne LC's formulation is concerned with the liability of a person as a *recipient* of trust property or its traceable proceeds. The second limb is concerned with what, for want of a better compendious description, can be called the liability of an *accessory* to a trustee's breach of trust. Liability as an accessory is not dependent upon receipt of trust property. It arises even though no trust property has reached the hands of the accessory. It is a form of secondary liability in the sense that it only arises where there has been a breach of trust. In the present case the plaintiff relies on the accessory limb. The particular point in issue arises from the expression 'a dishonest and fraudulent design on the part of the trustees'. . . .

The honest trustee and the dishonest third party

It must be noted at once that there is a difficulty with the approach adopted on this point in the *Belmont* case. Take the simple example of an honest trustee and a dishonest third party. Take a case where a dishonest solicitor persuades a trustee to apply trust property in a way the trustee honestly believes is permissible but which the solicitor knows full well is a clear breach of trust. The solicitor deliberately conceals this from the trustee. In consequence, the beneficiaries suffer a substantial loss. It cannot be right that in such a case the accessory liability principle would be inapplicable because of the innocence of the trustee. In ordinary parlance, the beneficiaries have been defrauded by the solicitor. If there is to be an accessory liability principle at all, whereby in appropriate circumstances beneficiaries may have direct recourse against a third party, the principle must surely be applicable in such a case, just as much as in a case where both the trustee and the third party have been dishonest. Indeed, if anything, the case for liability of the dishonest third party seems stronger where the trustee is innocent, because in such a case the third party alone was dishonest and that was the cause of the subsequent misapplication of the trust property.

The position would be the same if, instead of *procuring* the breach the third party dishonestly *assisted* in the breach . . .

. . . what matters is the state of mind of the third party sought to be made liable, not the state of mind of the trustee . . . there has been a tendency to cite, interpret and apply Lord Selborne LC's formulation as though it were a statute. This has particularly been so with the accessory limb of Lord Selborne's apothegm. This approach has been inimical to analysis of the underlying concept. Working within this constraint, the courts have found themselves wrestling with the interpretation of the individual ingredients, es-pecially 'knowingly' but also 'dishonest and fraudulent design on the part of the trustees', without examining the underlying reason why a third party who has received no trust property is being made liable at all. One notable exception is the judgment of Thomas J in *Powell* v *Thompson* [1991] 1 NZLR 597 at 610–615. On this point he observed (at 613):

> Once a breach of trust has been committed, the commission of which has involved a third party, the question which arises is one as between the beneficiary and that third party. If the third party's conduct has been unconscionable, then irrespective of the degree of impropriety in the trustee's conduct, the third party is liable to be held accountable to the beneficiary as if he or she were a trustee.

To resolve this issue it is necessary to take an overall look at the accessory liability principle. A conclusion cannot be reached on the nature of the breach of trust which may trigger accessory liability without at the same time considering the other ingredients including, in particular, the state of mind of the third party. It is not necessary, however, to look even more widely and consider the essential ingredients of recipient liability. The issue on this appeal concerns only the accessory liability principle. Different consider-ations apply to the two heads of liability. Recipient liability is restitution-based, accessory liability is not.

No liability

The starting point for any analysis must be to consider the extreme possibility: that a third party who does not receive trust property ought never to be liable directly to the beneficiaries merely because he assisted the trustee to commit a breach of trust or procured him to do so. This possibility can be dismissed summarily. On this the position which the law has long adopted is clear and makes good sense. Stated in the simplest terms, a trust is a relationship which exists when one person holds property on behalf of another. If, for his own purposes, a third party deliberately interferes in that relationship by assisting the trustee in depriving the beneficiary of the property held for him by the trustee, the beneficiary should be able to look for recompense to the third party as well as the trustee. Affording the beneficiary a remedy against the third party serves the dual purpose of making good the beneficiary's loss should the trustee lack financial means and imposing a liability which will discourage others from behaving in a similar fashion. . . .

Strict liability

The other extreme possibility can also be rejected out of hand. This is the case where a third party deals with a trustee without knowing, or having any reason to suspect, that he is a trustee. Or the case where a third party is aware he is dealing with a trustee but has no reason to know or suspect that their transaction is inconsistent with the terms of the trust. The law has never gone so far as to give a beneficiary a remedy against a non-recipient third party in such circumstances. Within defined limits, proprietary rights, whether legal or equitable, endure against third parties who were unaware of their existence. But accessory liability is concerned with the liability of a person who has not received any property. His liability is not property-based. His only sin is that he interfered with the due performance by the trustee of the fiduciary obligations under-taken by the trustee. These are personal obligations. They are, in this respect, analogous to the personal obligations undertaken by the parties to a contract. But ordinary, everyday business would become impossible if third parties were to be held liable for *unknowingly* interfering in the due performance of such personal obligations. Benefici-aries could not reasonably expect that third parties should deal with trustees at their peril, to the extent that they should become liable to the beneficiaries even when they received no trust property and even when they were unaware and had no reason to suppose that they were dealing with trustees.

Fault-based liability

Given, then, that in some circumstances a third party may be liable direct to a beneficiary, but given also that the liability is not so strict that there would be liability even when the third party was wholly unaware of the existence of the trust, the next step is to seek to identify the touchstone of liability. By common accord dishonesty fulfils this role. . . .

Dishonesty
Before considering this issue further it will be helpful to define the terms being used by looking more closely at what dishonesty means in this context. Whatever may be the position in some criminal or other contexts (see, for instance, *R v Ghosh* [1982] 2 All ER 689,), in the context of the accessory liability principle acting dishonestly, or with a lack of probity, which is synonymous, means simply not acting as an honest person would in the circumstances. This is an objective standard. At first sight this may seem surprising. Honesty has a connotation of subjectivity, as distinct from the objectivity of negligence. Honesty, indeed, does have a strong subjective element in that it is a description of a type of conduct assessed in the light of what a person actually knew at the time, as distinct from what a reasonable person would have known or appreciated. Further, honesty and its counterpart dishonesty are mostly concerned with advertent conduct, not inadvertent conduct. Carelessness is not dishonesty. Thus for the most part dishonesty is to be equated with conscious impropriety. . . .

In most situations there is little difficulty in identifying how an honest person would behave. Honest people do not intentionally deceive others to their detriment. Honest people do not knowingly take others' property. Unless there is a very good and compelling reason, an honest person does not participate in a transaction if he knows it involves a misapplication of trust assets to the detriment of the beneficiaries. Nor does an honest person in such a case deliberately close his eyes and ears, or deliberately not ask questions, lest he learn something he would rather not know, and then proceed regardless.

Negligence
It is against this background that the question of negligence is to be addressed. This question, it should be remembered, is directed at whether an honest third party who receives no trust property should be liable if he procures or assists in a breach of trust of which he would have become aware had he exercised reasonable diligence. Should he be liable to the beneficiaries for the loss they suffer from the breach of trust?

The majority of persons falling into this category will be the hosts of people who act for trustees in various ways: as advisers, consultants, bankers and agents of many kinds. This category also includes officers and employees of companies in respect of the application of company funds. All these people will be accountable to the trustees for their conduct. For the most part they will owe to the trustees a duty to exercise reasonable skill and care. When that is so, the rights flowing from that duty form part of the trust property. As such they can be enforced by the beneficiaries in a suitable case if the trustees are unable or unwilling to do so. That being so, it is difficult to identify a compelling reason why, in addition to the duty of skill and care vis-à-vis the trustees which the third parties have accepted, or which the law has imposed upon them, third parties should also owe a duty of care directly to the beneficiaries. They have undertaken work for the trustees. They must carry out that work properly. If they fail to do so, they will be liable to make good the loss suffered by the trustees in consequence. This will include, where appropriate, the loss suffered by the trustees being exposed to claims for breach of trust.

Outside this category of persons who owe duties of skill and care to the trustees, there are others who will deal with trustees. If they have not accepted, and the law has not imposed upon them, any such duties in favour of the trustees, it is difficult to discern a good reason why they should nevertheless owe such duties to the beneficiaries. . . .

Unconscionable conduct
Mention, finally, must be made of the suggestion that the test for liability is that of unconscionable conduct. Unconscionable is a word of immediate appeal to an equity lawyer. Equity is rooted historically in the concept of the Lord Chancellor, as the keeper of the royal conscience, concerning himself with conduct which was contrary to good conscience. It must be recognised, however, that unconscionable is not a word in

everyday use by non-lawyers. If it is to be used in this context, and if it is to be the touchstone for liability as an accessory, it is essential to be clear on what, *in this context*, unconscionable *means*. If unconscionable means no more than dishonesty, then dishonesty is the preferable label. If unconscionable means something different, it must be said that it is not clear what that something different is. Either way, therefore, the term is better avoided in this context.

The accessory liability principle

Drawing the threads together, their Lordships' overall conclusion is that dishonesty is a necessary ingredient of accessory liability. It is also a sufficient ingredient. A liability in equity to make good resulting loss attaches to a person who dishonestly procures or assists in a breach of trust or fiduciary obligation. It is not necessary that, in addition, the trustee or fiduciary was acting dishonestly, although this will usually be so where the third party who is assisting him is acting dishonestly. 'Knowingly' is better avoided as a defining ingredient of the principle, and in the context of this principle the *Baden* scale of knowledge is best forgotten.

Conclusion

From this statement of the principle it follows that this appeal succeeds. The money paid to BLT on the sale of tickets for Royal Brunei Airlines was held by BLT upon trust for the airline. This trust, on its face, conferred no power on BLT to use the money in the conduct of its business. The trust gave no authority to BLT to relieve its cash flow problems by utilising for this purpose the rolling 30-day credit afforded by the airline. Thus BLT committed a breach of trust by using the money instead of simply deducting its commission and holding the money intact until it paid the airline, Mr Tan accepted that he knowingly assisted in that breach of trust. In other words, he caused or permitted his company to apply the money in a way he knew was not authorised by the trust of which the company was trustee. Set out in these bald terms, Mr Tan's conduct was dishonest. By the same token, and for good measure, BLT also acted dishonestly. Mr Tan was the company and his state of mind is to be imputed to the company. . . .

C. Harpum, 'Accessory Liability for Procuring or Assisting a Breach of Trust' (1995) 111 LQR 545

. . . Although *Royal Brunei Airlines Sdn Bhd* v *Tan* is a decision of the Privy Council, the English courts are entitled to (and no doubt will) follow it in preference to *Barnes* v *Addy* and *Belmont Finance Corporation Ltd* v *Williams Furniture Ltd* which it disapproves: see *Worcester Works Finance Ltd* v *Cooden Engineering Co. Ltd* [1972] 1 QB 210. Recognition of this broad principle of liability should render unnecessary further attempts to circumvent the strictures of 'knowing assistance' by having recourse to principles of 'knowing inducement', 'dealing inconsistently with trust property', or the development of a tort of procuring a breach of trust (as in *Crawley Borough Council* v *Ure* [1995] 3 WLR at p. 103) Although it will no doubt be necessary to continue to characterise accessory liability as a form of 'constructive trusteeship' for certain very limited purposes (such as service out of the jurisdiction under RSC, Ord. 11, r. 1(1)(t), it is noteworthy that the Privy Council nowhere described it as such. The use of the language of constructive trusteeship has done much to obscure and confuse the true nature of the liability which is as the equitable analogue of the economic torts. It should now be jettisoned.

The plaudits that the decision so richly merits should not blind us to certain problems that remain unresolved, of which two may be mentioned. First, although the substantive basis of accessory liability is now clear, claims may still be thwarted by the constraints of the adjectival law. One obvious difficulty is the rule against self-incrimination. In many cases of intermeddling in a trust, the defendant's conduct may be such as to expose him to prosecution for conspiracy to defraud and he may therefore decline to give evidence. The Lord Chancellor's Department has recommended that the rule against self-incrimination should be abolished in civil proceedings, subject to strict safeguards. So far this much-needed reform has not materialised. Secondly, it had always seemed likely that the reformulation of the principles of accessory liability would be achieved by judicial decision, because the issues lay within a manageable compass. The resolution of the problems of receipt-based liability, which is being considered by the Law Commission, is much harder to achieve. This is because of the complex interrelationship of the available remedies, some of them statutory. It will probably require legislation.

BRINKS LTD v *ABU-SALEH AND OTHERS (No. 3), The Times,* **23 October 1995, ChD**

FACTS: Brinks had suffered a bullion robbery in which gold and other valuables worth some £26 million were stolen from its warehouse at Heathrow on November 26, 1983. It brought civil proceedings against 57 defendants who had allegedly been involved in the robbery, and subsequent laundering operations, to recover the proceeds.

During the robbery, Anthony Black who was employed by Brinks as a security guard, had betrayed his employers by providing a key to and internal photographs of the warehouse and generally participated in the planning and execution of the robbery.

Brinks' case against Mrs Elcombe was that between August 1984 and February 1985 she assisted her husband, the twelfth defendant, in the part he played in laundering part of the proceeds of the stolen gold by carrying approximately £3 million in cash for Mr Parry, one of the convicted robbers, from England to Zurich by car. Mr Elcombe's reward for doing that was £30,000 plus expenses.

Brinks' claim against Mrs Elcombe was, inter alia, that as the gold was stolen from it with the assistance of a dishonest fiduciary, Mr Black, it had an equity to trace into the proceeds which were in the nature of trust moneys, and that in those circumstances she was liable to account to Brinks in equity because of a dishonest assistance in a breach of trust.

HELD: In order for a person to be liable in equity as an accessory to a breach of trust it was necessary for him to have given the relevant assistance in the knowledge of the existence of the trust or, at least, of the facts which gave rise to the trust.

RIMER J: His Lordship held that the only conclusion which he could properly draw from the evidence was that Mrs Elcombe went on the trips in the capacity of Mr Elcombe's wife. While not wishing to minimise the benefit to a husband of being able to enjoy the company of his wife, he did not regard her presence on such trips as constituting relevant 'assistance' in furtherance of the breach of trust.

Having come to that conclusion it was not strictly necessary to decide the issue as to whether or not it was sufficient to fix Mrs Elcombe with liability as an accessory to the breach of trust merely to prove that she had provided her assistance to the furtherance of a dishonest transaction, regardless of whether she knew that it involved a breach of trust or whether she also had to have had knowledge of the trust which was being breached.

His Lordship considered *Royal Brunei Airlines* . . . and said that he did not consider that the Privy Council intended to suggest that an accessory could be made accountable to the beneficiaries as a constructive trustee regardless of whether he had any knowledge of the existence of the trust.

In *Royal Brunei Airlines* the claim was one against the director of the trustee company which had committed the breach, and he had conceded that there had been a breach of trust in which he had assisted with actual knowledge. Thus that case was one where the accessory did have the relevant knowledge.

Further, in the analysis of the basis on which accessories had in the past been held liable for assisting in breaches of trust, the judgment made it clear that the law had never gone so far as to give a beneficiary a remedy against an accessory who dealt with a trustee in ignorance that he was a trustee, or who knew that he was a trustee but had no reason to know or suspect that the transaction in which he was assisting was a breach of trust. The judgment made no suggestion that in that respect the earlier authorities were wrong.

In his Lordship's view, the judgment proceeded on the basis that a claim based on accessory liability could only be brought against someone who knew of the existence of the trust, or at least of the facts giving rise to the trust; and all that the judgment was directed at clarifying was what further was also needed to be shown in order to make the accessory liable.

The only further ingredient was dishonesty on the part of the accessory, and that was a sufficient ingredient. It was unnecessary that there should also be any dishonesty on the part of the trustee.

But as his Lordship had already held that Mrs Elcombe's accompanying her husband was not sufficient to constitute assistance in the breach of trust, Brinks' claim against her would be dismissed.

S. Gardner, 'Knowing Assistance and Knowing Receipt? Taking Stock' (1996) 112 LQR 56

We are now in a position to give an account of the shape which the new decisions have given to knowing assistance and knowing receipt.

Knowing assistance

The new decisions seem generally agreed that notice will not suffice for knowing assistance. At first, the requirement was said to be one of knowledge, but the emphasis has more recently shifted to dishonesty. . . .

Most recently, the Privy Council in *Royal Brunei Airlines Sdn Bhd* v *Tan* has also stated that the requirement is one of dishonesty. But in a departure from the approach until now, the judgment, by Lord Nicholls of Birkenhead, goes on to point attention directly to the concept of dishonesty itself, adding that 'knowingly' is better avoided as a defining ingredient of the principle.' Accordingly, Lord Nicholls offers an analysis of the concept of dishonesty, something not to be found in the preceding authorities. . . .

As regards Lord Nicholls' statement that reference to knowledge should be avoided, however, there could be some difficulty. One can sympathise with his Lordship's desire to go straight to the core notion of (in his view) dishonesty, and not to be tripped up on the way by unnecessary mediating concepts. And it must be said that even the previous decisions which adverted to dishonesty appeared to use knowledge in such a mediating role. To that extent, the Privy Council's view seems commendable. But Lord Nicholls appears to go further, and say that there should be no further analysis of the concept of knowledge: 'in the context of this principle [of dishonesty] the *Baden* scale of knowledge is best forgotten. This cannot be right. Indeed, his Lordship himself states that an assessment of whether a certain action is dishonest requires reference to what the defendant knew as he performed it, both in the sense that his perfomance must have been advertent and (presumably) in the sense that he must have been alive to the potential effects. That seems correct, especially in view of the point elaborated in the previous paragraph. If a person's behaviour must be defined by a process which includes reference to the motives and attitudes with which he acted, reference must inevitably be made to that person's cognisance (to use a neutral term) of the potential harm in question. But one could not reasonably imagine that it should be self-evident what 'cognisance' means here, any more than it is in any other context. To be sure, the criminal law sometimes remits conundrums to the jury, rather than essaying an institutional position. But even that does not amount to an assertion that there is no difficulty of epistemology to be in fact grappled with.

It is doubtful, then, that the new law of direct reference to a concept of dishonesty obviates any need for an exegesis upon cognisance. It is nevertheless possible that for a while the difficulties will be ignored, and positions taken *sub silentio*. In that sense, the analysis of knowledge in the cases immediately preceding *Royal Brunei Airlines Sdn Bha* v *Tan* may indeed therefore drop out of the picture. But those difficulties will not have evaporated, and such jurists who do continue to ponder them will presumably wish to include the work done in those cases in their ruminations. . . .

Knowing receipt

The law on knowing receipt has in recent years veered markedly. In *Re Montagu's Settlement Trust*, Megarry V-C held that liability for knowing receipt could arise only if knowledge was present. To Megarry V-C, this apparently meant the kinds of cognisance identified in *Baden* categories (i)–(iii), though presumably they would be inferable in the manner more recently proposed by Vinelott J in *Eagle Trust Plc* v *SBC Securities Ltd*, discussed above. *Re Montagu's Settlement Trusts* was accepted as correct by Alliott J, in

Lipkin Gorman v *Karpnale Ltd* whose thinking was in turn accepted as correct by Steyn J in *Barclays Bank Plc* v *Quincecare Ltd*. But a quite different approach prevailed in the decision of Millet J in *Agip (Africa) Ltd* v *Jackson*, which in turn heralded a series of further analysis whose precise significance requires some thought.

In *Agip (Africa) Ltd* v *Jackson*, Millet J stated his view as follows:

> . . . the person who receives for his own benefit trust property transferred to him in breach of trust . . . is liable as a constructive trustee if he received it with notice, actual or constructive, that it was trust property and that the transfer to him was a breach of trust, or if he received it without such notice but subsequently discovered the facts. In either case he is liable to account for the property, in the first case as from the time he received the property and in the second as from the time he acquired notice.

So it seems clear enough that Millett J was accepting notice as sufficing for liability. It is true that in the variant where the defendant originally receives the property without notice, Millett J looks to his having subsequently 'discovered' the facts, but in the next sentence he refers to this event as the recipient having 'acquired notice,' which effects a reconciliation with his original mode of expression. The only other reason for uncertainty is that he later refers to Megarry V-C's 'doubt [in *Re Montagu's Settlement Trusts*] whether constructive notice is sufficient.' and continues: 'whether the doubt is well-founded or not . . . ' But taken with Millett J's other remarks, this passage seems a reflection rather of courtesy towards a brother judge than of uncertainty on Millett J's part over his own view.

Subsequent decisions have provided further discussion, principally by Vinelott J in *Eagle Trust Plc* v *SBC Securities Ltd* by Knox J in *Cowan de Groot Properties Ltd* v *Eagle Trust Plc*, and by Millett J again in *El Ajou* v *Dollar Land Holdings Plc*. None of these rejects Millett J's original ruling in *Agip (Africa) Ltd* v *Jackson* that a proper description of liability for knowing receipt will make reference to notice. But, as discussed above, they have demanded a more subtle understanding of what such a reference to notice entails. To recapitulate. All agree that 'constructive notice in the strict conveyancing sense' applies only to land transfer cases. So far as other types of case are concerned, there is a difference of approach. According to Vinelott and Knox JJ, the reference to notice should be read as requiring knowledge, though such knowledge is inferable, in the manner discussed earlier. According to Millet J on the other hand, the reference to notice remains an invocation of the standards of the reasonable person, but with the caveat that those standards vary according to the circumstances, and outside the context of land transfer are likely to be undemanding. In practice, however, the two approaches may largely coincide. . . .

The argument that knowledge alone should suffice is based on the idea that knowing receipt is about wrongfully causing loss to trusts, and the further idea that wrongfulness requires knowledge. This argument is not strong, however. It is incorrect to say that knowledge alone will show a defendant to have acted wrongfuly: he can in principle equally be said to act wrongfully if he is negligent, or has notice. Moreover, it is questionable whether knowing receipt is about wrongfully causing loss at all. There may be more than one other thing that it could be about, but most modern opinion takes it to be a restitutionary liability, based on the fact that the defendant has acquired the plaintiff's property.

It is the latter view that underlies the other dominant argument, that neither knowledge nor notice should be required for knowing receipt. The leading proponent of this view is Birks (see especially P.B.H. Birks [1989] LMCLQ 296, (1989) 105 LQR 352 and 528). Birks contends that the point of knowing receipt is to restore to the plaintiff the value of property lost by him to the defendant, and by which the defendant was unjustly enriched. And that can be the case, he says, even if the defendant had neither knowledge nor means of knowledge of the plaintiff's rights: it is enough that the defendant has indeed had the benefit of the plaintiff's property. Birks allows two palliatives against the strictness of this position, however. First, he recognises that a defence against liability may be available to a bona fide purchaser of the property for value without notice of the true position, and that reference to notice (though not to knowledge) may be condoned to that extent. (So he argues that the case supporting a requirement of notice may be acceptable as discussions of the defence of bona fide purchase for value without notice, the defendants in them happening to be purchasers for value.) Secondly, he argues that the defence of bona fide purchase should be either replaced or joined by a defence of change of position. Under this, a defendant who acts to his detriment on the faith of the acquisition, innocently of the plaintiff's right to reclaim it, is to that extent freed from liability. Although the defence of change of position has only recently been recognised in English law, and is as yet somewhat unchartered territory, it seems clear that the presence or absence of something in the way of notice or knowledge appears relevant to the issue of innocence. These two palliatives do not cover the whole ground, however, and so according to Birks at any rate some volunteer recipients would be liable even with no knowledge or notice.

This argument seems strong. At the very least, it can claim to handle cases of unjust enrichment at the expense of a trust in the same fashion as cases of unjust enrichment at the expense of a straightforward owner of property, which seems commendable. One can see the same point in another way. A general principle of restitution for unjust enrichment is now recognised to exist in English law, by virtue of the decision of the House of Lords in *Lipkin Gorman* v *Karpnale Ltd*. It is of strict liability, subject to defences such as bona fide purchase and change of position. There is no obvious reason why it should not apply to cases in which the loss is to a trust, as much as to any others. So if knowing receipt is *not* taken thus, it will be undercut and made irrelevant anyway. . . .

The present article . . . has reviewed the . . . different designs of these liabilities . . . and argued that a good case can be made for more than one of the possibilities. This should be quite unsurprising. Our society is a complex and compromised one on any front. When dealing with the protection of interests as sophisticated as those under trusts (as opposed, for example, to life and limb), we are least likely to find answers in the shape of transcedent verities: any position will be close to the line. And we are concerned here largely with financial dealings, a phenomenon as regards which orthodoxies are particularly short-lived. A pluralistic appreciation is therefore indispensable. . . .

19.2   End of Chapter Assessment Question

Mr Sleeson, a solicitor, is a sole practitioner with access to his clients' accounts. He withdraws money from 'the client account' and places it in his own private bank account which he holds with the Nelson Westminster bank. Later, he withdraws monies from his private account and plays it at a casino in the city. He places the winnings and the original withdrawals in his private account at the bank. This happens regularly and the bank manager suspects that something may be amiss, but turns a blind eye to Mr Sleeson's activities.

Eventually, Mr Sleeson 'went for the big gamble', lost all his money, and was declared bankrupt. The casino manager had accepted his bets because he 'knew that solicitors made a lot of money'.

Advise Mr Sleeson's clients who now seek to recover their lost funds.

19.3   End of Chapter Assessment Outline Answer

Mr Sleeson held his clients' monies on trust for his clients. It follows that he has breached this trust by placing those monies in his private bank account to be subsequently used to satisfy his gambling habit. The question for determination is whether the Nelson Westminster Bank, through the agency of Mr Sleeson's branch manager, could be held liable in equity to meet the claims of Mr Sleeson's defrauded clients.

The bank is a stranger to, and a commecial agent of, the trust. The courts have always been reluctant to visit such commercial agents with equitable liability based on trusts the existence of which was not reasonably apparent. The traditional reason for this reluctance is the fear that liability of this sort might discourage agents from offering their services, or else the fear that the free markets of the commercial world would become stultified by the need to make extensive and inappropriate enquiries of every party to every dealing. Nevertheless, a stranger to a trust might become liable to the beneficiaries of the trust in a number of ways. We shall consider some of these in turn.

First, trusteeship *de son tort*. This is a form of constructive trusteeship imposed upon a stranger, such as a bank, which deliberately takes it upon itself to intermeddle in the affairs of a trust in such a way that the stranger can be said to have interposed itself into the position of trustee (*Mara* v *Browne*). Such a scenario is a far cry from the present case.

Secondly, a stranger might be held liable as a constructive trustee for the knowing receipt of trust property. This complicated head of liability may apply in the present case. We will consider it in detail next. Related to it is liability for inconsistent dealing with trust property.

Thirdly, and finally, a stranger might be held liable in equity for dishonestly assisting in a breach of trust. We shall consider this head of liability last.

Knowing Receipt
For the bank to be liable under this head it must be shown that the bank has 'received' trust property, and it must be shown that the bank knew that the trust property it had received had come to it in breach of trust. According to Millet J in *Agip (Africa) Ltd* v *Jackson* [1989] 3 WLR 1367 'receipt' necessitates that 'the recipient must have received the property for his own use and benefit'. Accordingly, if a bank acts as a mere conduit for monies the appropriation of the monies by the bank will not be relevant to the loss to the beneficiaries and the bank will not be said to have 'received' trust monies. On the other hand, if the bank uses the monies for its own ends, perhaps by reducing the debit balance of an overdrawn account, the bank will be said to have 'received' the property for the purpose of liability for 'knowing receipt'. Applying this to the present case, it follows that the bank will probably not be liable for knowing receipt if Mr Sleeson's account has always been maintained with a healthy credit balance. Assuming, however, that the bank has, at some time, received the trust monies in reductioin of an overdraft, or in some other way for its own benefit, the next question is whether the bank can be

said to have 'known' that it was receiving trust monies in breach of the trust. Certainly the bank will not be taken to know something merely because it has heard rumours or disputed claims (Carl Zeiss Stiftung), but the bank will be liable if its agent, the bank manager, should have been suspicious. According to Peter Gibson J in *Baden v Société Générale* [1983] BCLC 325 knowledge for the purpose of knowing receipt could be of five types:

(1)   actual knowledge;
(2)   wilfully shutting ones eyes to the obvious;
(3)   wilfully and recklessly failing to make such enquiries as an honest and reasonable man would make;
(4)   knowledge of circumstances which would indicate the facts to an honest and reasonable man; and
(5)   knowledge of circumstances which would have put an honest and reaonable man on enquiry.

More recently, Megarry VC has stated that only types 1, 2 and 3 would suffice (*Re Montagu's ST*). He rejected types 4 and 5 because they did not evince 'want of probity' (dishonesty), which his lordship felt ought to be pre-requisite to the onerous nature of liability under this head. More recently still, Scott LJ in *Polly Peck International plc v Nadir (No. 2)* [1992] 4 All ER 769 stated that the Baden categories are not 'rigid categories with clear and precise boundaries. One category may merge imperceptibly with another'. For Scott LJ the real question which we ought to ask of the bank manager in the present case is whether he should have been suspicious. If he should have been, the bank will be liable, provided that 'receipt' is proven. Whether the bank manager should have been suspicious is a question that is difficult to answer on the bare facts as we have them. We are told that he suspects 'something' may be amiss, but the authorities are fairly clear in agreeing that liability will not arise unless the bank manager had suspected something in the nature of a breach of trust. For this it is not, of course, necessary to show that the bank manager knew the precise terms of the trust. Perhaps the bank manager genuinely believed that Mr Sleeson had only ever used his own monies, perhaps in suspecting that something might have been 'amiss' he meant only that he feared Mr Sleeson's gambling would lead to a crisis in Mr Sleeson's own financial circumstances, and not that of trust beneficiaries.

If the bank is guilty of 'knowing receipt' it will be held liable as a constructive trustee, which means, *inter alia*, that it will have a duty to account to the beneficiaries, from the moment it knew of the breach of trust, for the monies it had received, and may have to pay compound interest thereon (see **Chapter 15**). In the present case the breach of trust occurred before the monies reached the bank and therefore it would be otiose to consider the possibility of liability for inconsistent dealing.

Dishonest Assistance

We now move on to consider the possibility that the bank might be liable for dishonestly assisting in Mr Sleeson's breach of trust. In the usual case this head of liability will only be considered if knowing receipt cannot be proved. Liability for dishonest assistance is also said to be liability 'as a constructive trustee', but in the light of the fact that accessories (almost by definition) do not hold or control trust property it is arguable that dishonest assistance should, in the future, give rise to tortious liability, by analogy to the tort of procurement of a breach of contract.

This head of liability was previously labelled 'knowing assistance in a dishonest design', the dishonesty being that of the fiduciary. Since *Tan* (see below) the conscientious scrutiny has been shifted onto the accessory, (the bank, and possibly the bank manager, in our case) who will be liable only if he has 'dishonestly assisted in a breach of trust'.

The four ingredients of this head of liability are:

(1)   the existence of a trust;
(2)   breach of that trust;
(3)   assistance in the breach (a simple question of fact); and
(4)   dishonesty.

The first three being undoubtedly satisfied in the present case, the crucial question is whether the bank manager has been dishonest, if he has been his dishonesty will almost certainly be imputed to the bank.

In the leading case of *Royal Brunei Airlines Sdn Bhd* v *Philip Tan Kok Ming* [1995] 3 WLR 64, an opinion of the Judicial Committee of the Privy Council, Lord Nicholls purported to apply an 'objective standard' of honesty, with the result that an accessory will be unable to escape liability on the ground that he sees nothing wrong in his behaviour. However, Lord Nicholls went on to introduce personal considerations into the test. He said that, 'when called upon to decide whether a person was acting honestly, a court will look at all the circumstances known to the third party at the time. The court will have regard to personal attributes of the third party such as his experience and intelligence, and the reason why he acted as he did'. The bank manager in the present case has given a reason why he acted as he did, it would fall to the court which hears his case to decide whether his failure to act on his suspicions was dishonest or not, it is not a question to which a firm conclusion can be reached on the brief facts before us.